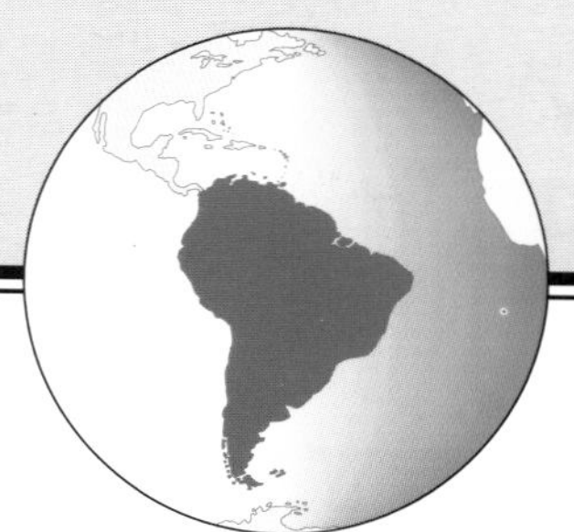

SOUTH AMERICA

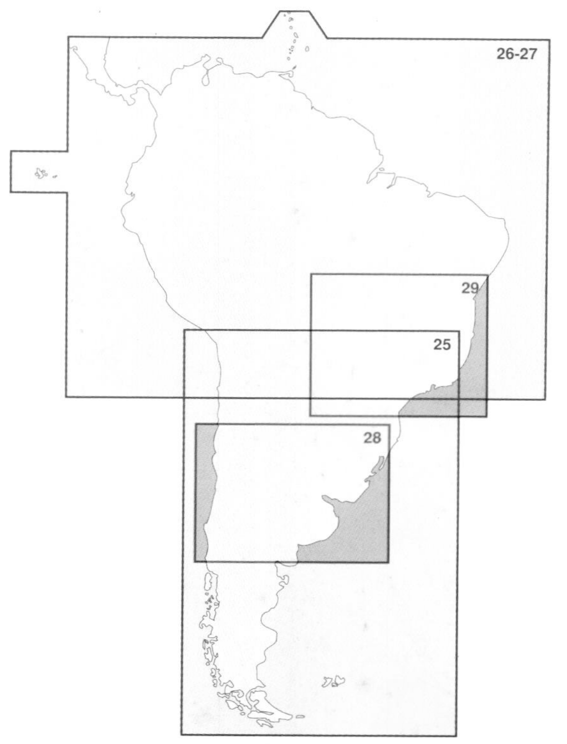

EUROPE

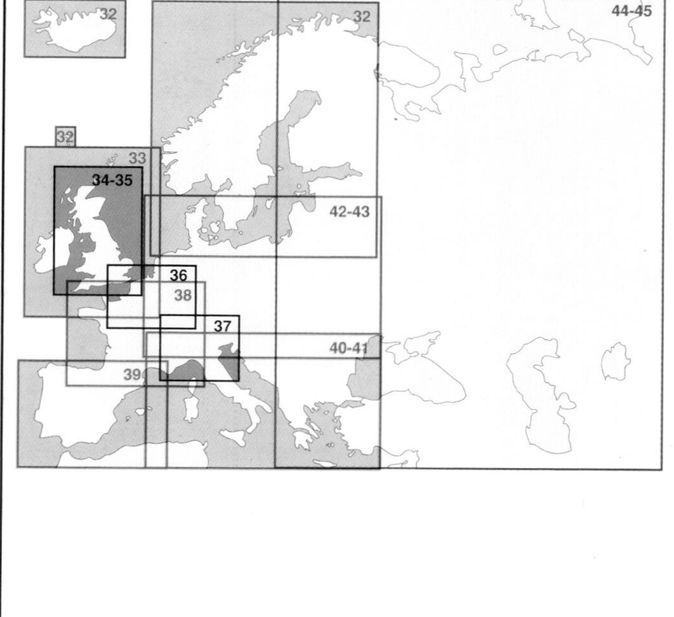

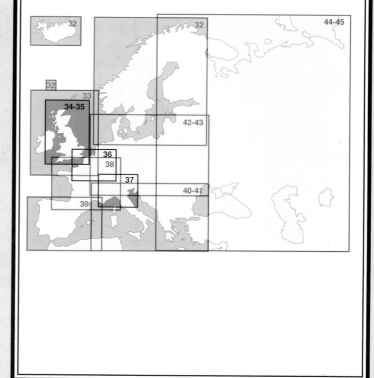

Bartholomew
A Division of HarperCollins Publishers
Duncan Street, Edinburgh EH9 1TA

First published by Bartholomew 1987
Revised edition 1992

© Bartholomew 1992

A CIP catalogue record for this book is available from the British Library

ISBN 0-7028-1341-9

Printed in Great Britain by HarperCollins Manufacturing, Glasgow

Details included in this atlas are subject to change without notice. Whilst every effort is made to keep
information up to date Bartholomew will not be responsible for any loss, damage or inconvenience caused
by inaccuracies in this atlas. The publishers are always pleased to acknowledge any corrections brought to
their notice, and record their appreciation of the valuable services rendered in the past by map users in
assisting to maintain the accuracy of their publications.

E/B4742

Acknowledgements

The Publishers acknowledge the assistance of the following in the preparation of material used in this
publication: Dr Walter Stephen, Senior Adviser, Curriculum, Dean Education Centre, Edinburgh; Alister
Hendrie, Assistant Headteacher, Portobello High School, Edinburgh; Andrew Grant, Principal Teacher,
Geography, Wester Hailes Education Centre, Edinburgh; Stephen Hamilton, Principal Teacher, Geography,
Broughton High School, Edinburgh.

The Publishers are grateful to the following for providing the photographs used in this atlas:
(picture number(s) shown in italics)
Travel Photo International: pages xxii-xxiii, savanna, rain forest, prairie, northern forest; page xxii, *7;* page
xviii, *2;* page xv , *11;* page xvi , *4, 5, 13, 14;* page xx , *7;* page xxi , *2;* page vi , *3, 4;* page viii,*3,4.*
Photographers' Library: page xxii-xxiii, scrub *Chris Knaggs photograph,* desert *Oliver Martel photograph;*
page x, *8 Clive Sawyer photograph;* page xiv, *8 Ian Wright photograph;* page xvii, *9 Tom Hustler
photograph;* page xx , *4 Robyn Beeche photograph. Biofotos:* page x , *5 Heather Angel photograph;* page
xx , *6 Andrew Henley photograph;* page xxi , *3 Soames Summerhays photograph. The Photo Source:*
page xii ,*10;* page xviii, *4;* page xiv, *7. Wade Cooper Associates,* Edinburgh: page xvi , *12;* page xvii, *10;*
page vi , *1. Pictor International:* page xiv, *6;* page vi , *2. B. and C. Alexander:* page xxii , tundra. *Bruce
Coleman Ltd:* page viii , *6 WWF/Eugen Schuhmacher. Mepha:* page xviii, *1 C. Osborne photograph. Michael
Scott:* page xxii , woodland and grass. *Yorkshire and Humberside Tourist Board:* page xi , *2. Spectrum
Colour Library:* page xiii, *12, 14.*

CONTENTS

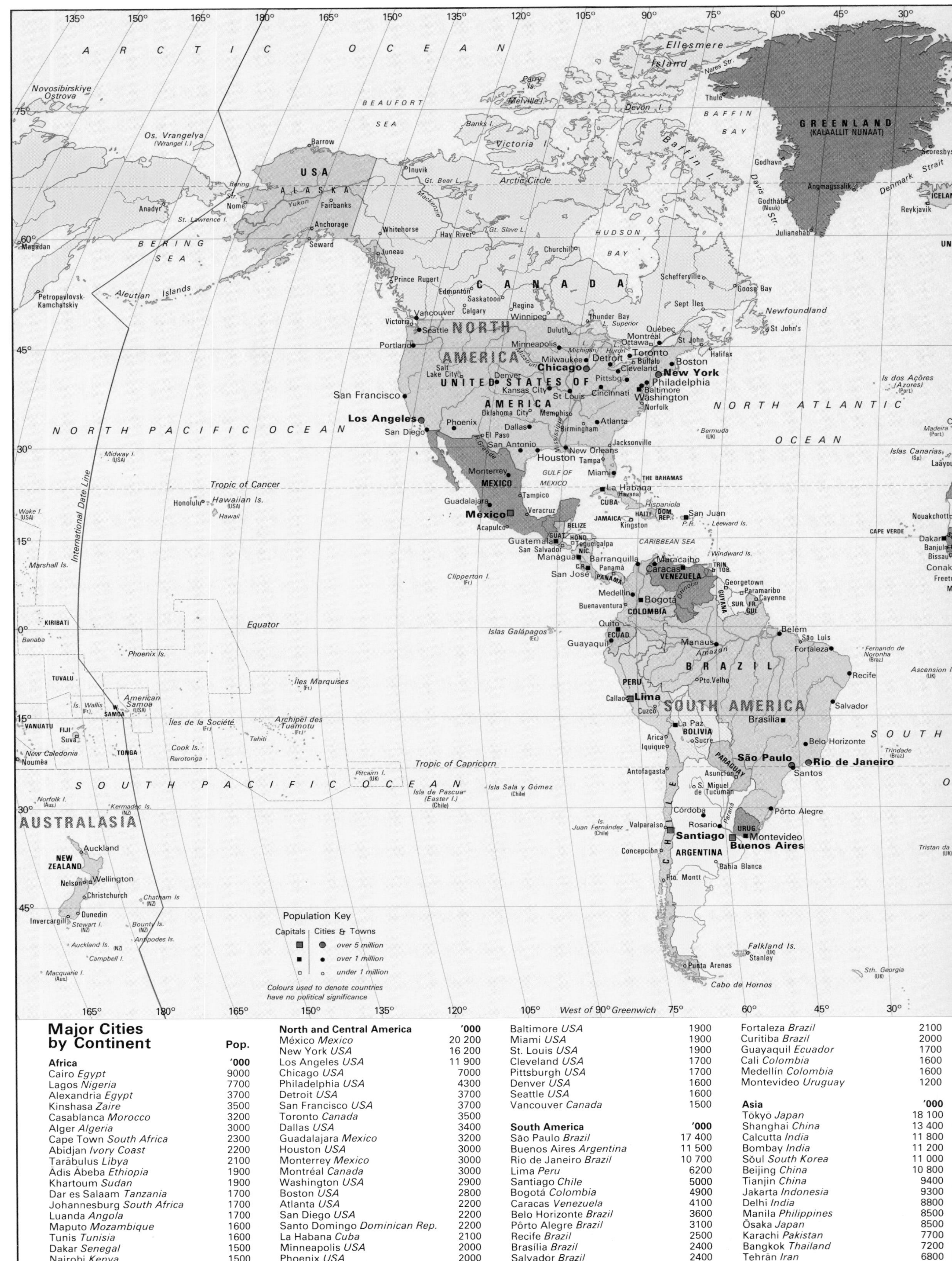

Major Cities by Continent

Africa	Pop. '000
Cairo *Egypt*	9000
Lagos *Nigeria*	7700
Alexandria *Egypt*	3700
Kinshasa *Zaire*	3500
Casablanca *Morocco*	3200
Alger *Algeria*	3000
Cape Town *South Africa*	2300
Abidjan *Ivory Coast*	2200
Tarábulus *Libya*	2100
Ádis Abeba *Ethiopia*	1900
Khartoum *Sudan*	1900
Dar es Salaam *Tanzania*	1700
Johannesburg *South Africa*	1700
Luanda *Angola*	1700
Maputo *Mozambique*	1600
Tunis *Tunisia*	1600
Dakar *Senegal*	1500
Nairobi *Kenya*	1500

North and Central America	'000
México *Mexico*	20 200
New York *USA*	16 200
Los Angeles *USA*	11 900
Chicago *USA*	7000
Philadelphia *USA*	4300
Detroit *USA*	3700
San Francisco *USA*	3700
Toronto *Canada*	3500
Dallas *USA*	3400
Guadalajara *Mexico*	3200
Houston *USA*	3000
Monterrey *Mexico*	3000
Montréal *Canada*	3000
Washington *USA*	2900
Boston *USA*	2800
Atlanta *USA*	2200
San Diego *USA*	2200
Santo Domingo *Dominican Rep.*	2200
La Habana *Cuba*	2100
Minneapolis *USA*	2000
Phoenix *USA*	2000
Baltimore *USA*	1900
Miami *USA*	1900
St. Louis *USA*	1900
Cleveland *USA*	1700
Pittsburgh *USA*	1700
Denver *USA*	1600
Seattle *USA*	1600
Vancouver *Canada*	1500

South America	'000
São Paulo *Brazil*	17 400
Buenos Aires *Argentina*	11 500
Rio de Janeiro *Brazil*	10 700
Lima *Peru*	6200
Santiago *Chile*	5000
Bogotá *Colombia*	4900
Caracas *Venezuela*	4100
Belo Horizonte *Brazil*	3600
Pôrto Alegre *Brazil*	3100
Recife *Brazil*	2500
Brasília *Brazil*	2400
Salvador *Brazil*	2400
Fortaleza *Brazil*	2100
Curitiba *Brazil*	2000
Guayaquil *Ecuador*	1700
Cali *Colombia*	1600
Medellín *Colombia*	1600
Montevideo *Uruguay*	1200

Asia	'000
Tōkyō *Japan*	18 100
Shanghai *China*	13 400
Calcutta *India*	11 800
Bombay *India*	11 200
Sŏul *South Korea*	11 000
Beijing *China*	10 800
Tianjin *China*	9400
Jakarta *Indonesia*	9300
Delhi *India*	8800
Manila *Philippines*	8500
Ōsaka *Japan*	8500
Karachi *Pakistan*	7700
Bangkok *Thailand*	7200
Tehrán *Iran*	6800

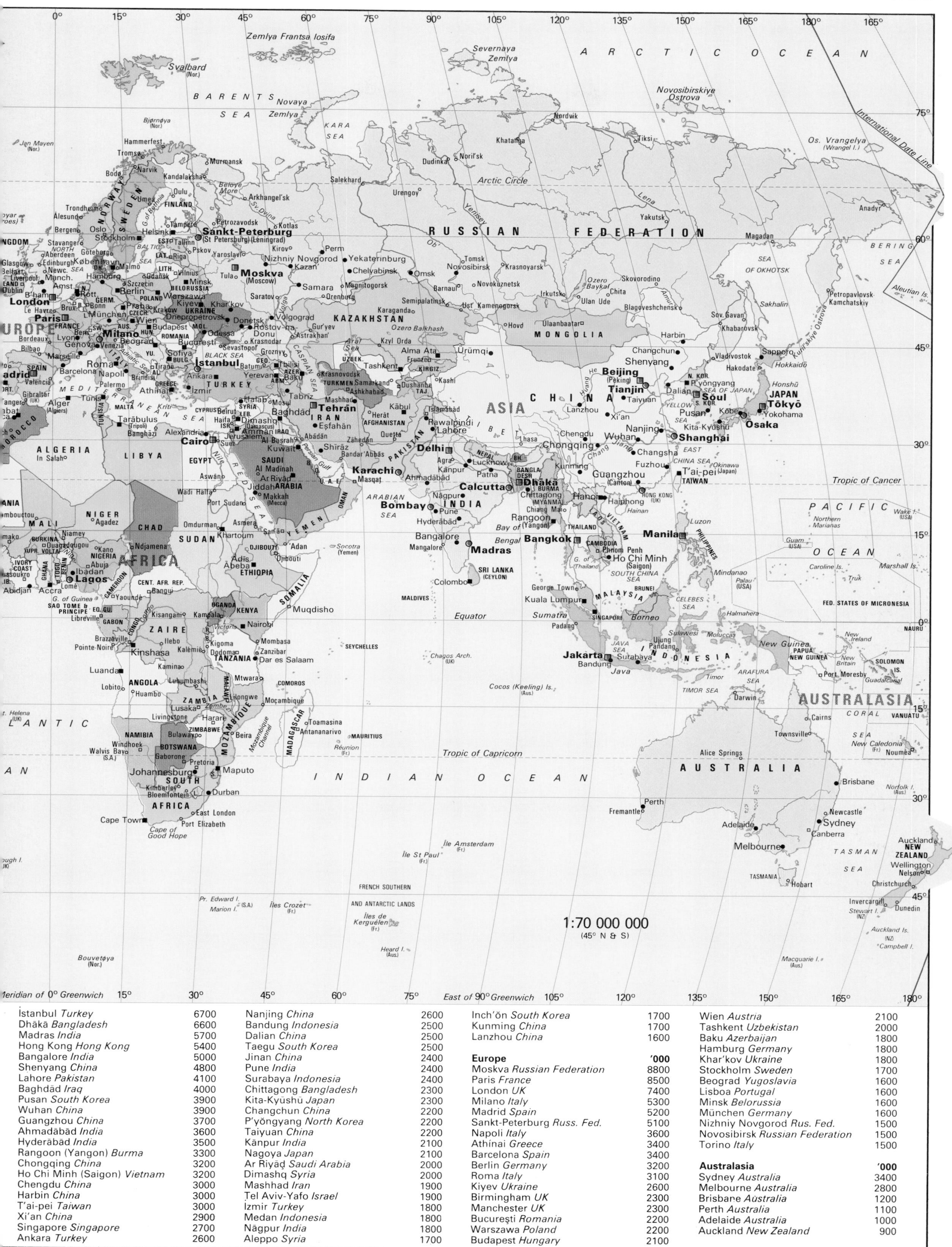

1:70 000 000
(45° N & S)

İstanbul *Turkey*	6700	Nanjing *China*	2600	Inch'ŏn *South Korea*	1700	Wien *Austria*	2100
Dhākā *Bangladesh*	6600	Bandung *Indonesia*	2500	Kunming *China*	1700	Tashkent *Uzbekistan*	2000
Madras *India*	5700	Dalian *China*	2500	Lanzhou *China*	1600	Baku *Azerbaijan*	1800
Hong Kong *Hong Kong*	5400	Taegu *South Korea*	2500			Hamburg *Germany*	1800
Bangalore *India*	5000	Jinan *China*	2400	**Europe**	**'000**	Khar'kov *Ukraine*	1800
Shenyang *China*	4800	Pune *India*	2400	Moskva *Russian Federation*	8800	Stockholm *Sweden*	1700
Lahore *Pakistan*	4100	Surabaya *Indonesia*	2400	Paris *France*	8500	Beograd *Yugoslavia*	1600
Baghdād *Iraq*	4000	Chittagong *Bangladesh*	2300	London *UK*	7400	Lisboa *Portugal*	1600
Pusan *South Korea*	3900	Kita-Kyūshū *Japan*	2300	Milano *Italy*	5300	Minsk *Belorussia*	1600
Wuhan *China*	3900	Changchun *China*	2200	Madrid *Spain*	5200	München *Germany*	1600
Guangzhou *China*	3700	P'yŏngyang *North Korea*	2200	Sankt-Peterburg *Russ. Fed.*	5100	Nizhniy Novgorod *Rus. Fed.*	1500
Ahmadābād *India*	3600	Taiyuan *China*	2200	Napoli *Italy*	3600	Novosibirsk *Russian Federation*	1500
Hyderābād *India*	3500	Kānpur *India*	2100	Athínai *Greece*	3400	Torino *Italy*	1500
Rangoon (Yangon) *Burma*	3300	Nagoya *Japan*	2100	Barcelona *Spain*	3400		
Chongqing *China*	3200	Ar Riyāḍ *Saudi Arabia*	2000	Berlin *Germany*	3200	**Australasia**	**'000**
Ho Chi Minh (Saigon) *Vietnam*	3200	Dimashq *Syria*	2000	Roma *Italy*	3100	Sydney *Australia*	3400
Chengdu *China*	3000	Mashhad *Iran*	1900	Kiyev *Ukraine*	2600	Melbourne *Australia*	2800
Harbin *China*	3000	Tel Aviv-Yafo *Israel*	1900	Birmingham *UK*	2300	Brisbane *Australia*	1200
T'ai-pei *Taiwan*	3000	İzmir *Turkey*	1800	Manchester *UK*	2300	Perth *Australia*	1100
Xi'an *China*	2900	Medan *Indonesia*	1800	Bucureşti *Romania*	2200	Adelaide *Australia*	1000
Singapore *Singapore*	2700	Nāgpur *India*	1800	Warszawa *Poland*	2200	Auckland *New Zealand*	900
Ankara *Turkey*	2600	Aleppo *Syria*	1700	Budapest *Hungary*	2100		

1:35M

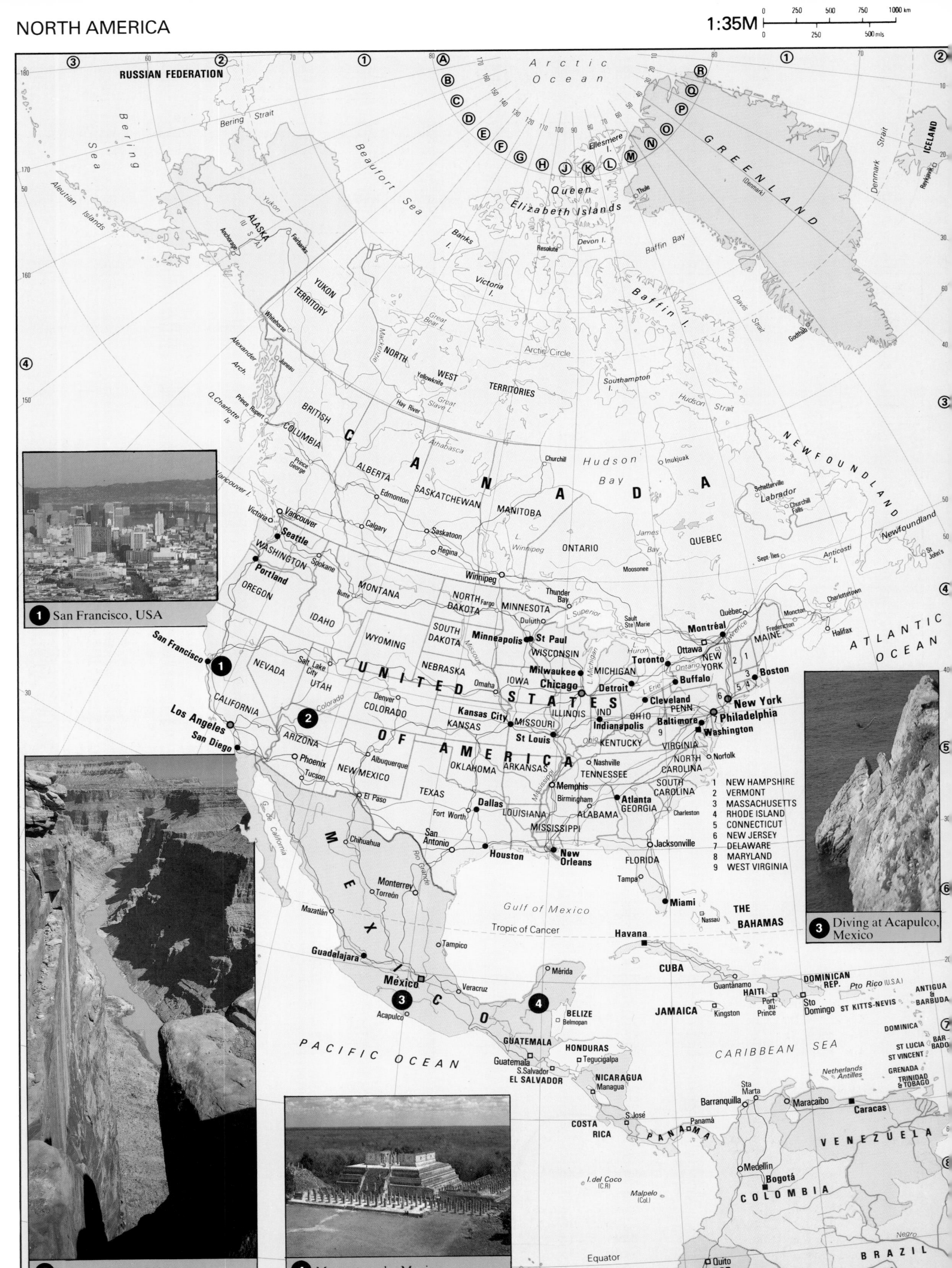

San Francisco, USA

Grand Canyon, USA

Mayan temple, Mexico

Diving at Acapulco, Mexico

1 NEW HAMPSHIRE
2 VERMONT
3 MASSACHUSETTS
4 RHODE ISLAND
5 CONNECTICUT
6 NEW JERSEY
7 DELAWARE
8 MARYLAND
9 WEST VIRGINIA

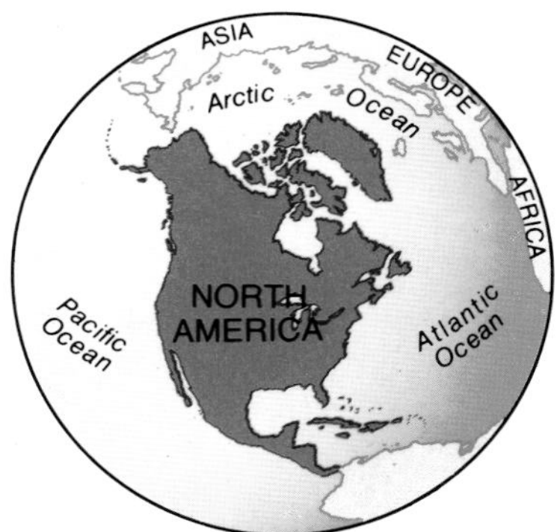

FACTS ABOUT NORTH AMERICA

1 The city of San Francisco was almost destroyed by an earthquake in 1906, and there could be another one soon. Right under the city runs the San Andreas fault, where two of the 'plates' which make up the earth's crust slide against one another. When they get jammed together at any point, pressure builds up, until finally they break apart. This causes an earthquake because of the sudden release of so much energy. The longer the plates stay jammed together, the greater the strength of the final earthquake: in 1906, the plates under San Francisco slid 6 m (20 feet) in a few minutes. Some parts of the fault have not moved for years – and scientists think there will be another big earthquake soon.

2 The huge Grand Canyon in Arizona, USA, was gouged out of the rock by the Colorado River. It is 1.6 km (1 mile) deep, a maximum of 29 km (18 miles) wide and no less than 446 km (227 miles) long! The Grand Canyon is still being carved deeper (though very slowly) by the river.

3 At La Questrada, Acapulco, Mexico, divers often swoop 36 m (118 feet) down into the sea. This is the highest dive which people do regularly.

4 The Maya were a tribe who lived in southern Mexico and Guatemala 1400 years ago. They built great cities with stone temples, public buildings and palaces. The picture shows one of their buildings which can be seen today. It was built without help from any modern machinery.

Cattle	Fruit	Wheat	6 Nickel	
Hogs	Sugar cane	Maize	7 Lead	
Bananas	Timber	Minerals	9 Silver	
Citrus fruit	Tobacco	1 Bauxite	11 Uranium	
Cotton	Coal	3 Copper	12 Zinc	
Fish	Oil	5 Iron		

NATURAL VEGETATION/PRODUCTS

Tundra/Mountain
Northern Forest
Woodland/Grass
Grassland
Scrub
Desert
Savanna
Rainforest

POPULATION

Vancouver, Winnipeg, Ottawa, Chicago, New York, San Francisco, Los Angeles, Houston, Havana, Mexico City

over 200 persons per km²
40 to 200 persons per km²
1 to 40 persons per km²
under 1 person per km²

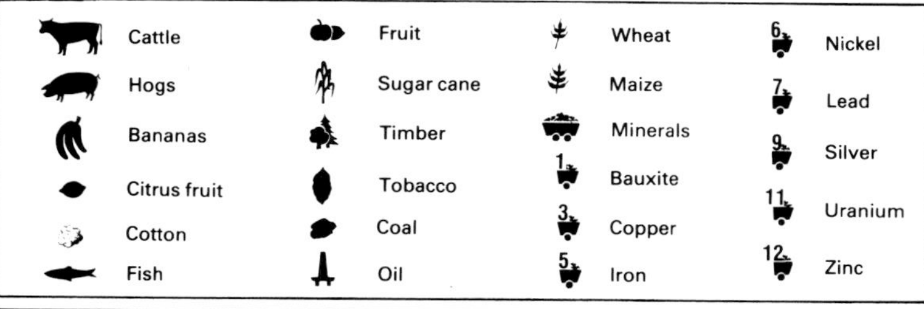

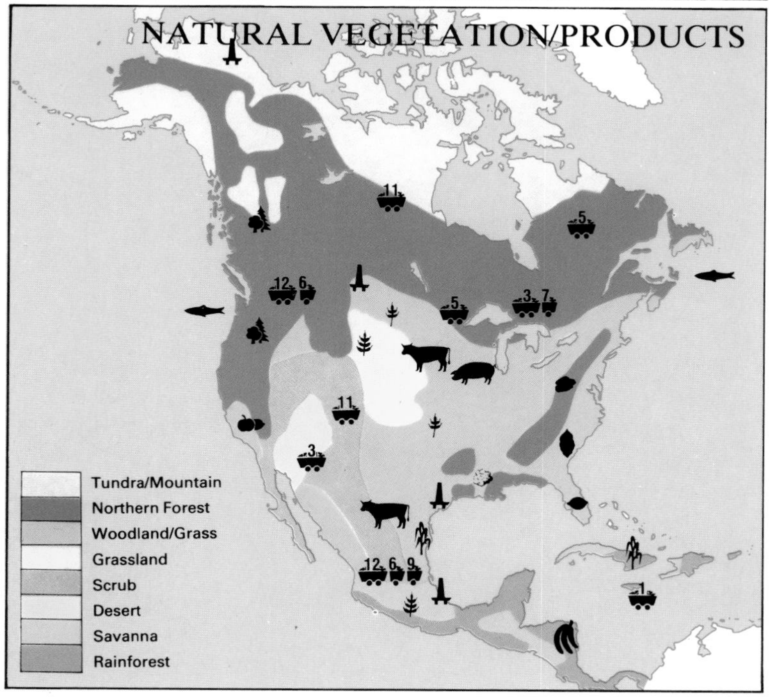

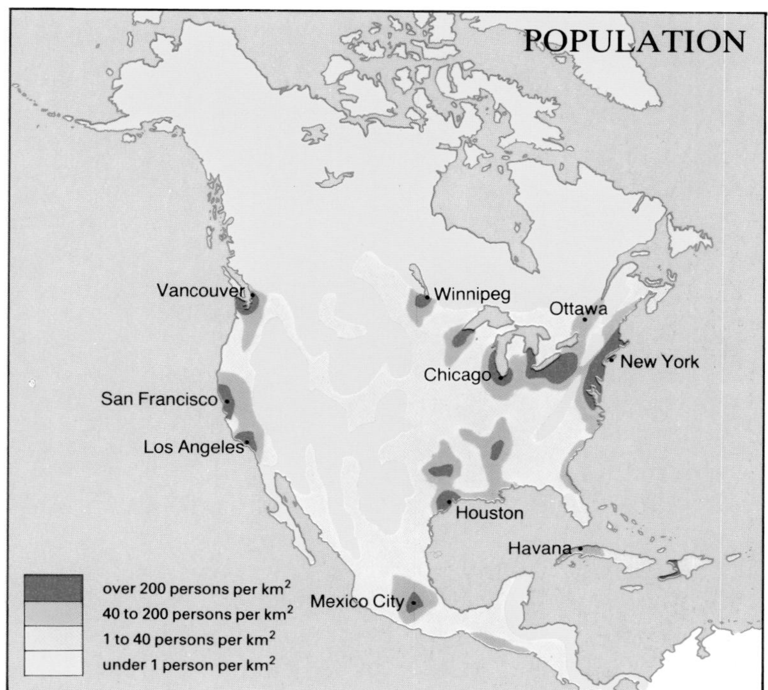

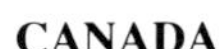

CANADA
Area: 9 976 147 sq km (3 851 790 sq miles)
Population: 26 500 000
Capital: Ottawa
Languages: English, French
Currency: Canadian Dollar

CUBA
Area: 114 524 sq km (44 218 sq miles)
Population: 10 600 000
Capital: Havana
Language: Spanish
Currency: Cuban Peso

EL SALVADOR
Area: 20 865 sq km (8056 sq miles)
Population: 5 300 000
Capital: San Salvador
Language: Spanish
Currency: Colon

GUATEMALA
Area: 108 888 sq km (42 042 sq miles)
Population: 9 200 000
Capital: Guatemala
Language: Spanish
Currency: Quetzal

JAMAICA
Area: 11 424 sq km (4411 sq miles)
Population: 2 500 000
Capital: Kingston
Language: English
Currency: Jamaican Dollar

MEXICO
Area: 1 967 180 sq km (759 528 sq miles)
Population: 88 600 000
Capital: Mexico City
Language: Spanish
Currency: Mexican Peso

NICARAGUA
Area: 139 000 sq km (53 668 sq miles)
Population: 3 900 000
Capital: Managua
Language: Spanish
Currency: Cordoba

UNITED STATES OF AMERICA
Area: 9 363 130 sq km (3 615 104 sq miles)
Population: 249 200 000
Capital: Washington
Language: English
Currency: U.S. Dollar

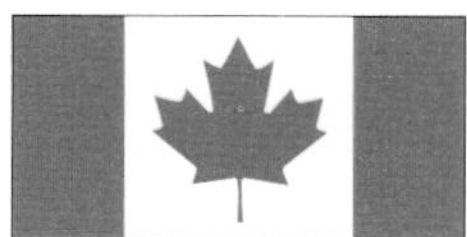

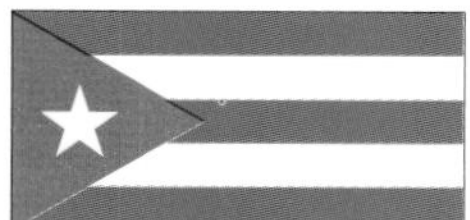

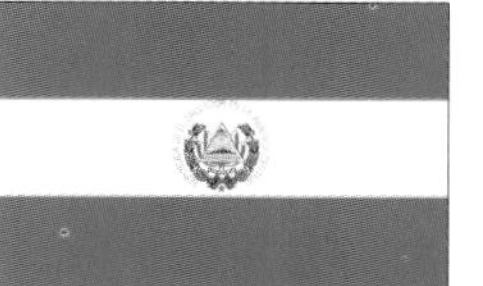

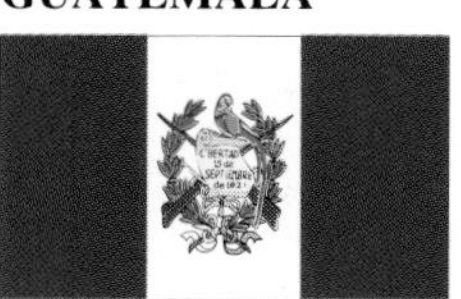

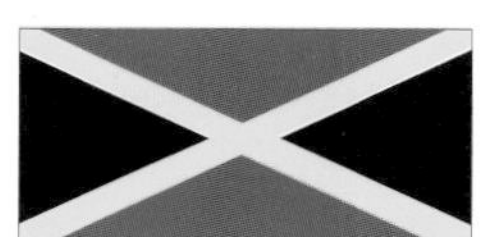

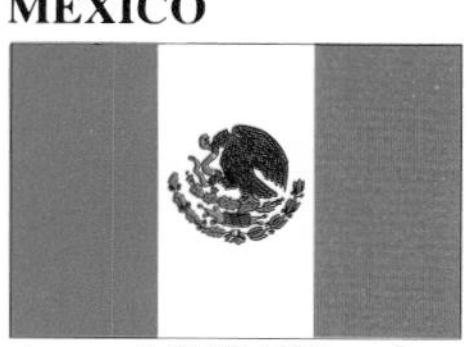

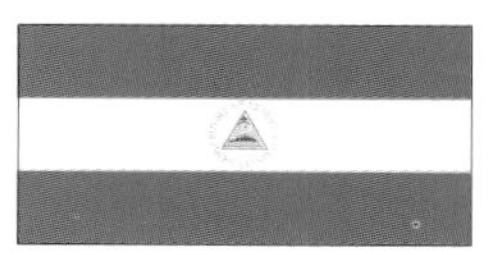

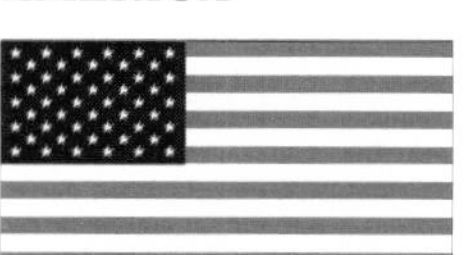

SOUTH AMERICA

1:35M

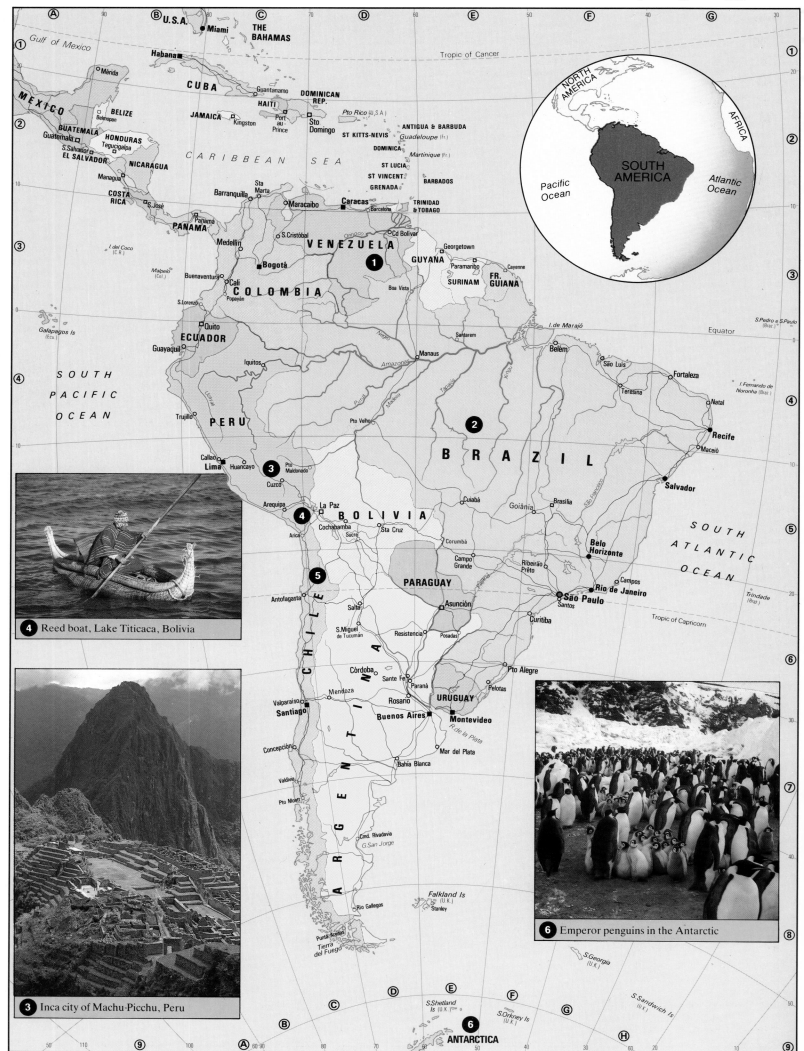

Gulf of Mexico

U.S.A.
Miami

THE BAHAMAS

Habana

Mérida

CUBA

MEXICO

BELIZE
Belmopan

GUATEMALA
Guatemala

HONDURAS
Tegucigalpa

S.Salvador
EL SALVADOR

NICARAGUA
Managua

COSTA RICA
S.José

PANAMA
Panamá

JAMAICA
Kingston

HAITI
Port au Prince

DOMINICAN REP.
Sto Domingo

Guantanamo

Pto Rico (U.S.A.)

ANTIGUA & BARBUDA
Guadeloupe (Fr.)

ST KITTS-NEVIS

DOMINICA

Martinique (Fr.)

ST LUCIA

ST VINCENT

BARBADOS

GRENADA

TRINIDAD & TOBAGO

CARIBBEAN SEA

Sta Marta
Barranquilla
Maracaibo
Caracas
Barcelona
Cd Bolivar

S.Cristóbal

VENEZUELA

Georgetown
GUYANA

Paramaribo
SURINAM

Cayenne
FR. GUIANA

Medellin
Bogotá
Buenaventura
Cali
Popayán

COLOMBIA

Boa Vista

S.Lorenzo

Quito
ECUADOR
Guayaquil

Galapagos Is (Ecu.)

I. del Coco (C.R.)

Malpelo (Col.)

Iquitos

Negro

Santarem

I. de Marajó

Belém

São Luis

Fortaleza

Teresina

Natal

Recife

Maceió

Salvador

S.Pedro e S.Paulo (Braz.)

I.Fernando de Noronha (Braz.)

Equator

Manaus

Amazonas

Purus

Madeira

Tapajós

Xingu

Tocantins

São Francisco

SOUTH PACIFIC OCEAN

Trujillo

PERU

Callao
Lima
Huancayo

Pto Maldonado

Cuzco

Arequipa

La Paz

Cochabamba
Sucre
Sta Cruz

BOLIVIA

Arica

Corumbá

Cuiabá

Goiânia

Brasília

BRAZIL

Belo Horizonte

Campos

Rio de Janeiro

São Paulo
Santos

Ribeirão Prêto

Campo Grande

PARAGUAY

Asunción

Paraná

Curitiba

Pto Alegre

Pelotas

SOUTH ATLANTIC OCEAN

Trindade (Braz.)

Tropic of Capricorn

Antofagasta

Salta

S.Miguel de Tucumán

Resistencia

Posadas

Córdoba

Sante Fe
Paraná
Rosario

Mendoza

Valparaiso
Santiago

Concepción

Valdivia

Pto Montt

CHILE

ARGENTINA

URUGUAY
Montevideo

Buenos Aires

R de la Plata

Mar del Plata

Bahía Blanca

Cmd. Rivadavia
G.San Jorge

Rio Gallegos

Falkland Is (U.K.)
Stanley

Punta Arenas
Tierra del Fuego

ANTARCTICA

S.Shetland Is (U.K.)

S.Orkney Is (U.K.)

S.Sandwich Is (U.K.)

S.Georgia (U.K.)

Tropic of Cancer

NORTH AMERICA

SOUTH AMERICA

AFRICA

Pacific Ocean

Atlantic Ocean

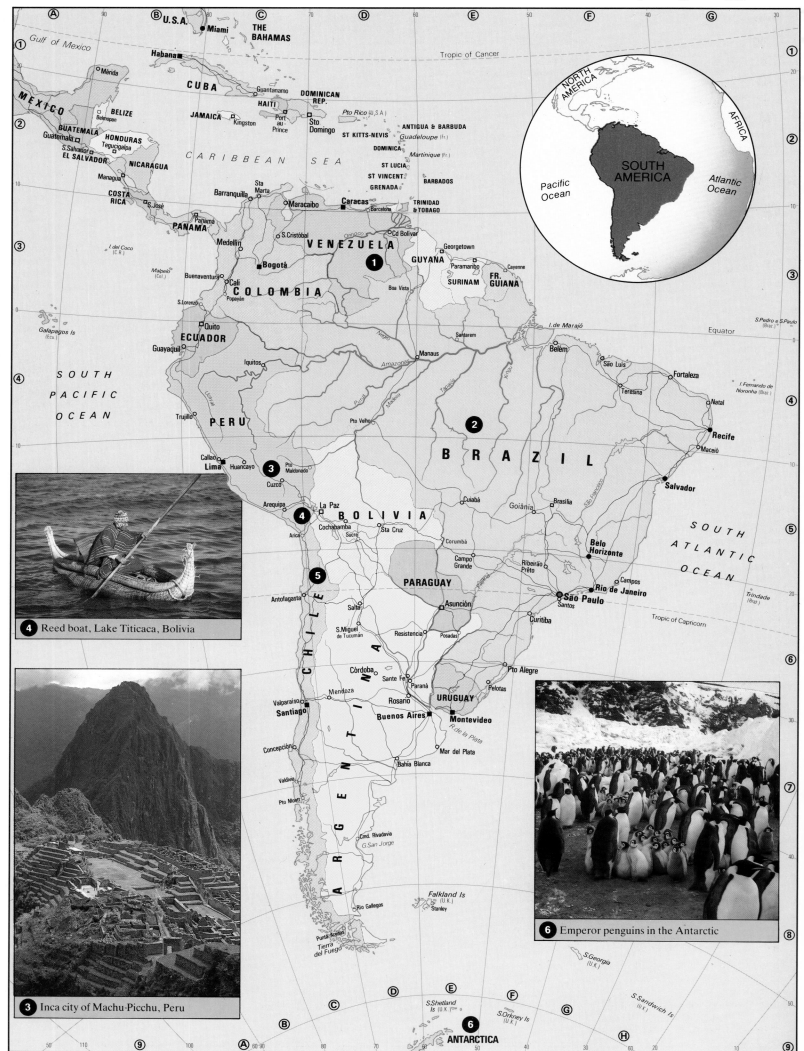

4 Reed boat, Lake Titicaca, Bolivia

3 Inca city of Machu-Picchu, Peru

6 Emperor penguins in the Antarctic

VIII

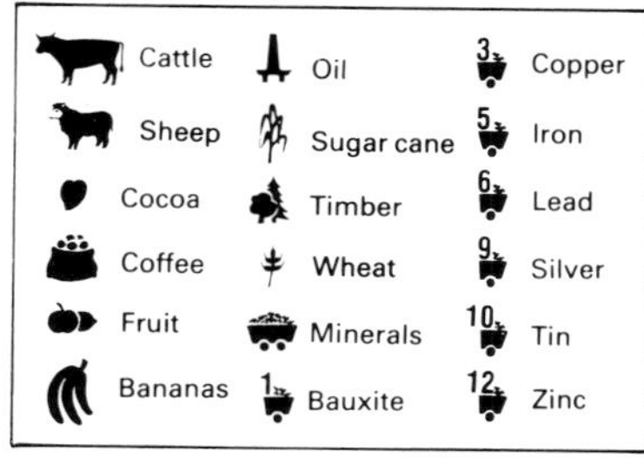

Cattle	Oil	3	Copper
Sheep	Sugar cane	5	Iron
Cocoa	Timber	6	Lead
Coffee	Wheat	9	Silver
Fruit	Minerals	10	Tin
Bananas	Bauxite	12	Zinc

FACTS ABOUT SOUTH AMERICA

1 The Angel Falls, Venezuela, are the highest waterfalls in the world, at 979 m (3212 feet).

2 Deforestation is a major problem in South America. About 1 per cent of the total area of forest is lost each year. Often trees are cut down to clear land for agriculture. On hillsides, the soil soon becomes too poor to grow crops and the land is abandoned. Trees cannot grow again, and so soil is eroded away by rain and wind. Trees are also lost when lakes are made for hydro-electric dams; when new towns are built; and as a result of the way people live – they take too much wood for fuel and timber, allow animals to graze on foliage, and light fires which get out of control.

3 In the Andes Mountains, in the north-west of South America, there are ruins of cities built by the Incas. They ruled the Indians in the area 500 years ago. The Incas had well-developed political and religious systems. They built their cities on terraces engineered from the mountain side. The Spanish, the first Europeans to discover these cities, killed the Incas to seize the gold and silver which they had mined, and their cities were abandoned.

4 The highest navigable lake in the world is Lake Titicaca, on the Peru/Bolivia border. It is no less than 3811 m (12 503 feet) above sea level. The local Indian people make boats from bundles of reeds tied together, to use for fishing. The reeds grow around the edge of the lake.

5 Although in the rain forests of the Amazon Basin it rains every day, in the Atacama Desert, Chile, hundreds of years can pass between one rain storm and the next. A storm in 1971 was the first for 400 years. The desert is the driest place in the world.

6 The Emperor Penguin, found in the Antarctic, does not make a nest. Instead, a single egg is carried on top of the male penguin's feet. It is kept warm by a fold of skin which hangs down and covers it. The penguin does not eat during the two months it takes for the egg to hatch out.

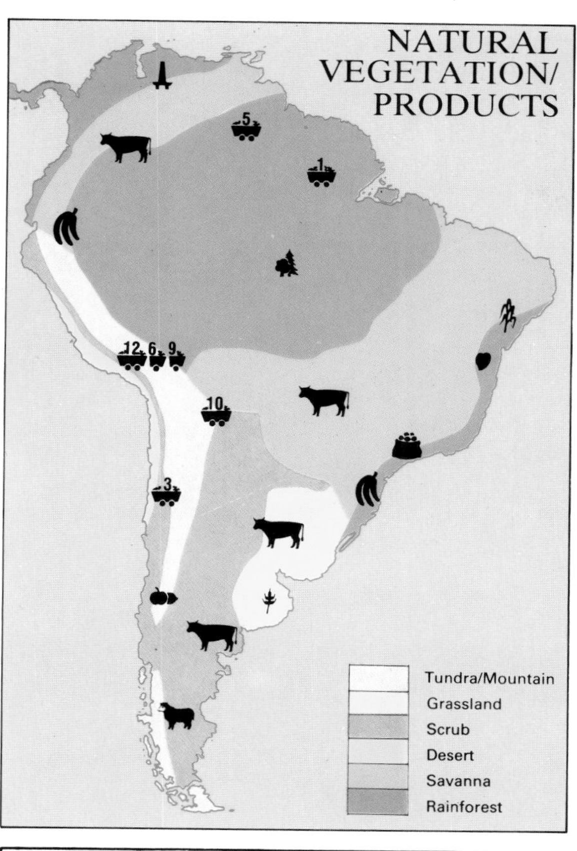

NATURAL VEGETATION/ PRODUCTS

Tundra/Mountain
Grassland
Scrub
Desert
Savanna
Rainforest

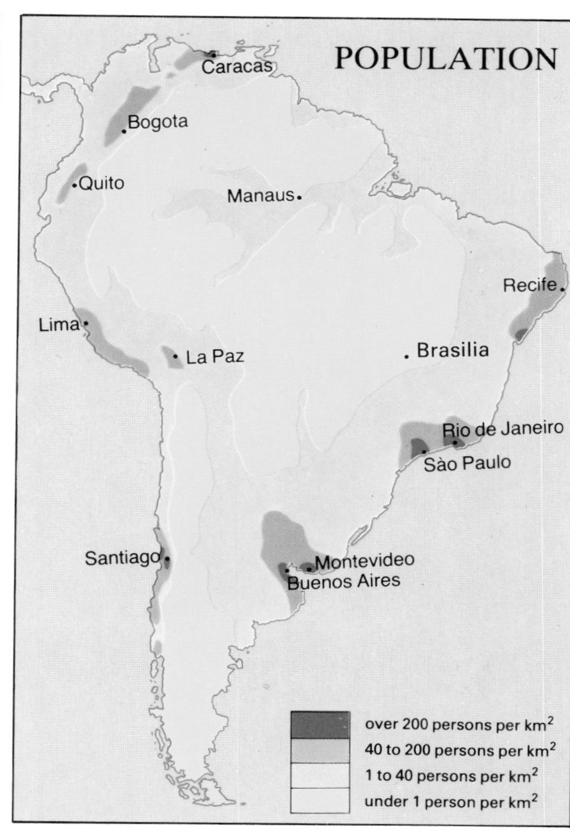

POPULATION

over 200 persons per km²
40 to 200 persons per km²
1 to 40 persons per km²
under 1 person per km²

ARGENTINA
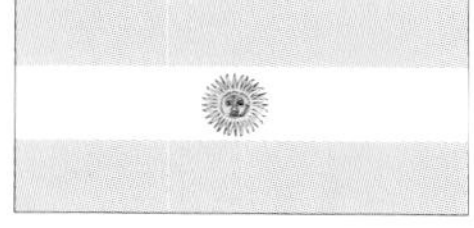

Area: 2 777 815 sq km (1 072 514 sq miles)
Population: 32 300 000
Capital: Buenos Aires
Language: Spanish
Currency: Argentine Peso

BOLIVIA
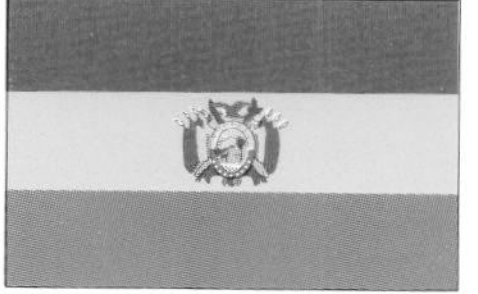

Area: 1 098 575 sq km (424 160 sq miles)
Population: 7 300 000
Capital: La Paz
Languages: Spanish, Aymara, Quechua
Currency: Bolivian Peso

BRAZIL
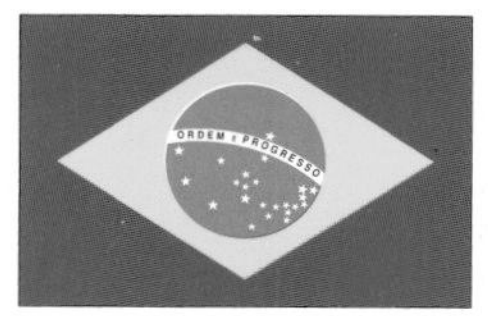

Area: 8 511 968 sq km (3 286 471 sq miles)
Population: 150 400 000
Capital: Brasilia
Language: Portuguese
Currency: Cruzeiro

CHILE
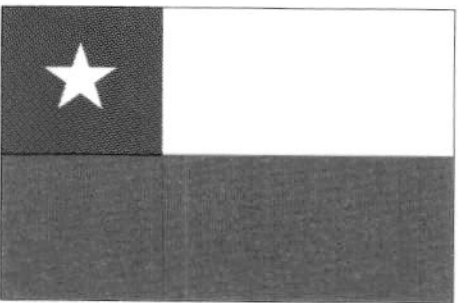

Area: 756 943 sq km (292 256 sq miles)
Population: 13 200 000
Capital: Santiago
Language: Spanish
Currency: Chilean Peso

COLOMBIA
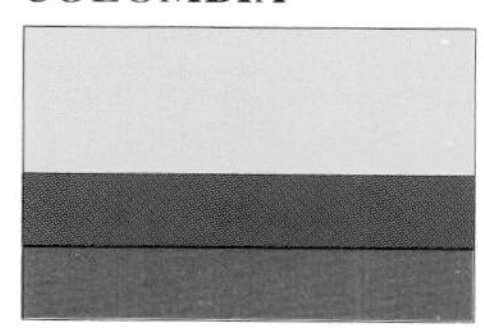

Area: 1 138 907 sq km (439 732 sq miles)
Population: 33 000 000
Capital: Bogota
Language: Spanish
Currency: Colombian Peso

ECUADOR
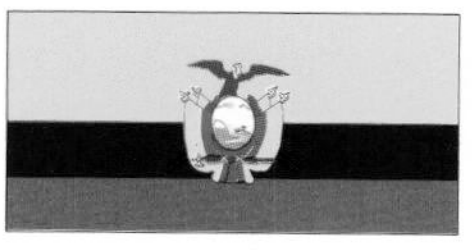

Area: 455 502 sq km (175 869 sq miles)
Population: 10 600 000
Capital: Quito
Language: Spanish
Currency: Sucre

GUYANA
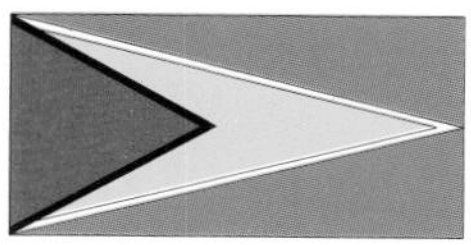

Area: 214 969 sq km (83 000 sq miles)
Population: 800 000
Capital: Georgetown
Language: English
Currency: Guyanese Dollar

PERU
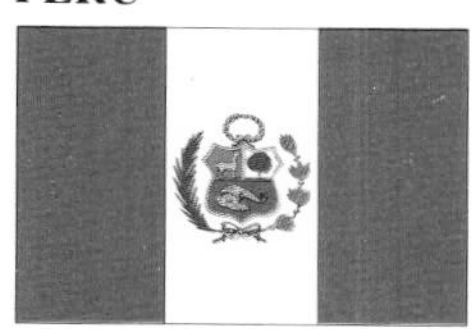

Area: 1 285 215 sq km (496 222 sq miles)
Population: 21 600 000
Capital: Lima
Languages: Spanish, Aymara, Quechua
Currency: Sol

VENEZUELA
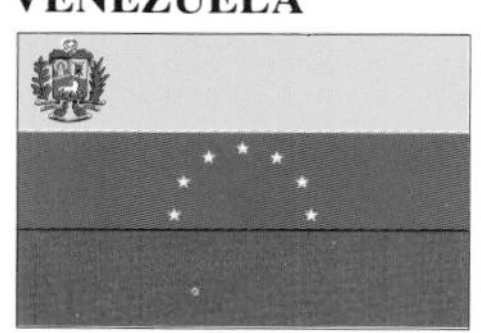

Area: 912 047 sq km (352 141 sq miles)
Population: 19 700 000
Capital: Caracas
Language: Spanish
Currency: Bolivar

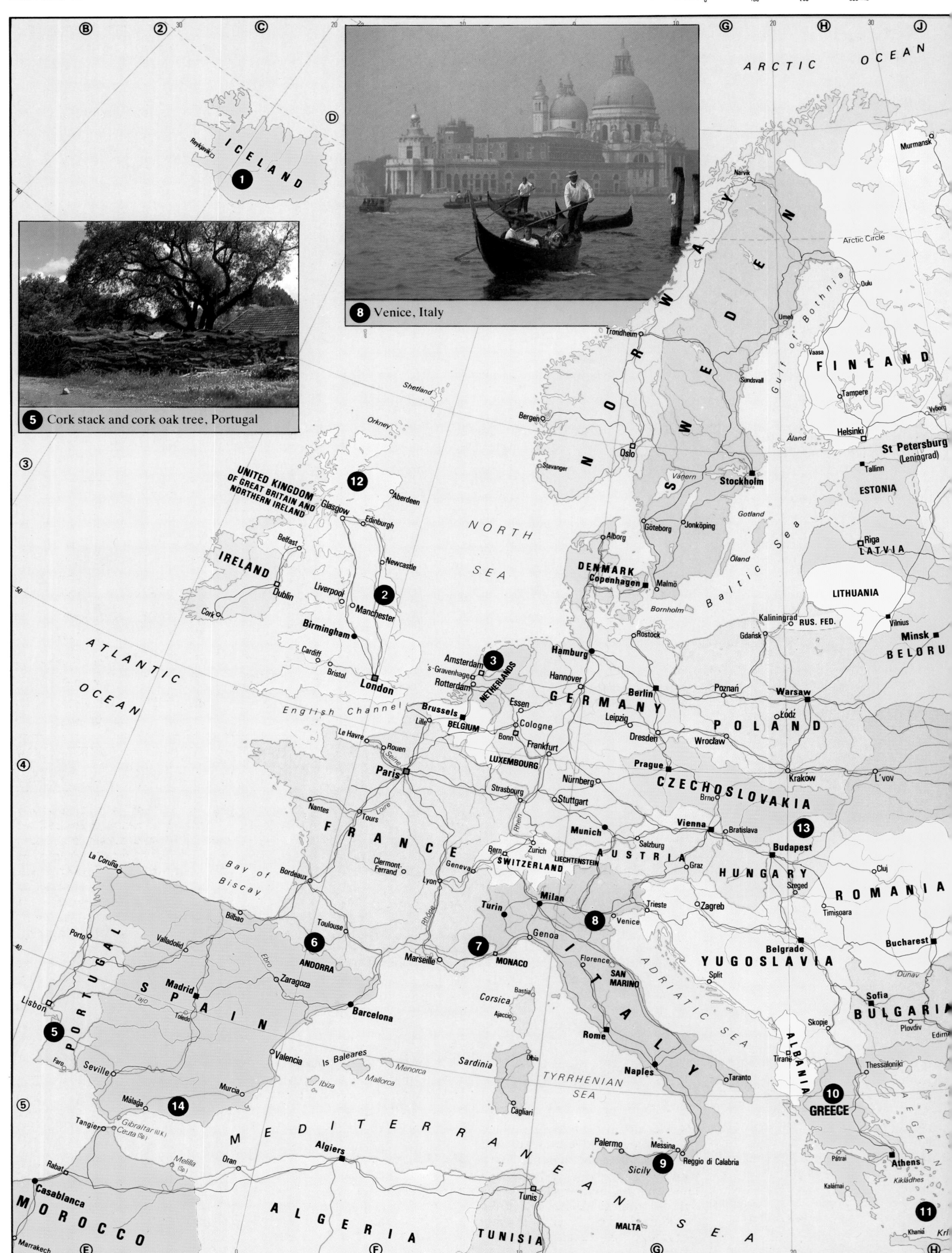

8 Venice, Italy

5 Cork stack and cork oak tree, Portugal

POPULATION

NATURAL VEGETATION/ PRODUCTS

	over 500 persons per km^2
	100-500 persons per km^2
	5-100 persons per km^2
	under 5 persons per km^2

	Tundra/Mountain
	Northern Forest
	Woodland/Grass
	Grassland
	Scrub

	Cattle		Oil
	Sheep		Coal
	Fish		Gas
	Fruit		Oats
	Citrus fruit		Wheat
	Grapes		Maize
	Yams		Rye
	Sugar beet		Barley
	Potatoes	5	Minerals
	Timber	6	Iron
	Cork	12	Lead
			Zinc

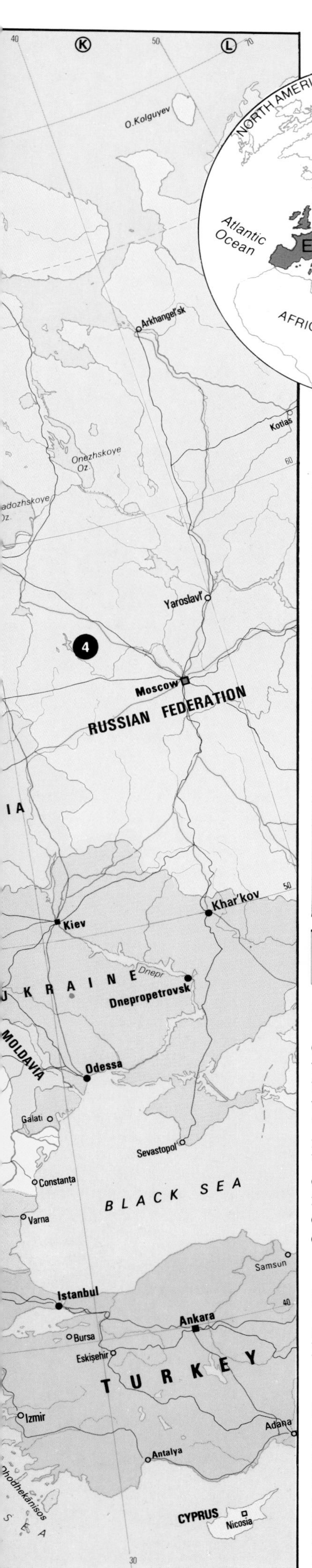

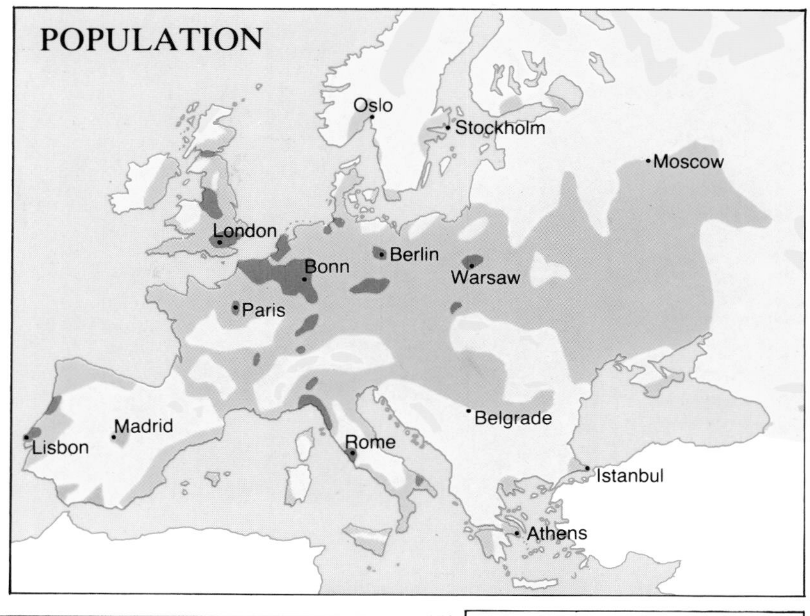

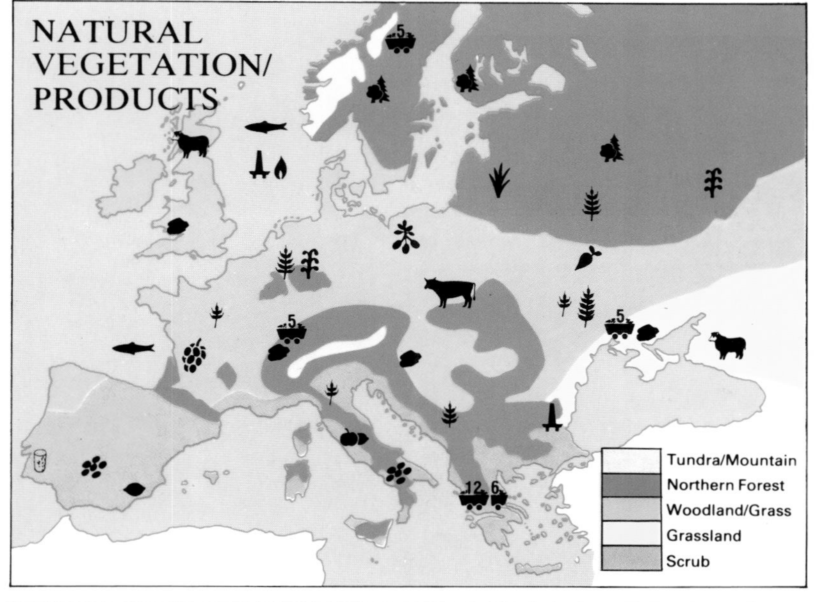

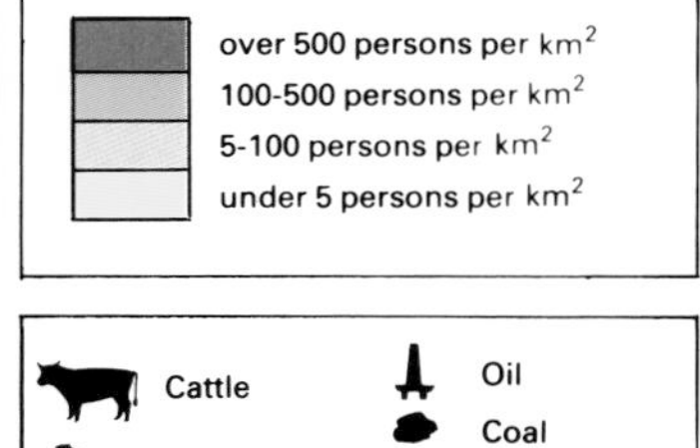

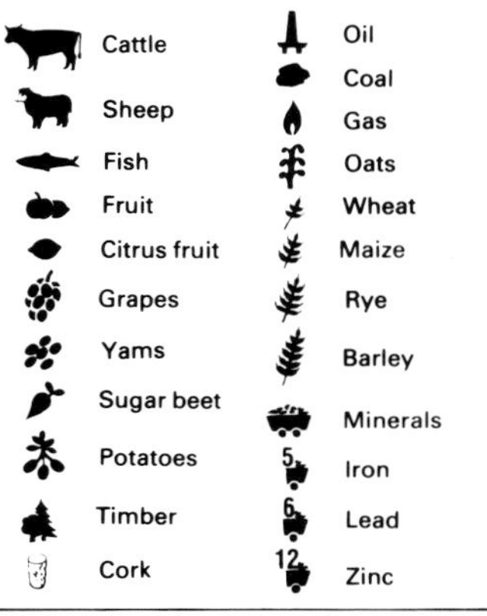

FACTS ABOUT EUROPE

1 In Iceland, ice and fire exist side by side. Many active volcanoes and geysers (hot springs which shoot a column of water into the air at intervals) can be seen, while glaciers (continually moving 'rivers' of ice) and ice sheets cover much of the land. One volcano – Vatnajokull – is particularly dangerous for an unusual reason: it is underneath a glacier and when it erupts, the ice melts very quickly, causing terrible floods.

2 The Humber Bridge, England, has one of the longest single spans of any bridge in the world. It stretches for 1410 m (4626 feet).

3 More than a third of the land area of the Netherlands has been reclaimed from the sea. These lands (the *polders*) are below sea level and the sea is kept out by dykes. Drainage ditches divide the fertile fields. The water from them is pumped into canals and rivers, then out to sea.

4 The longest river in Europe is the Volga, which runs for 3690 km (2292 miles) from the forests north west of Moscow all the way to the Caspian Sea.

5 Portugal is an important source of cork, which is actually the bark of a tree. The cork oak produces cork bark up to 15 cm (6 inches) thick and this is stripped off the trees every 10 to 15 years. Cork oaks grow throughout the western and central Mediterranean region.

6 The Pierre Saint Martin Cavern in the Pyrenees mountains, France, is the deepest cave system yet discovered in the world. It goes 1330 m (4364 feet) into the heart of the mountains.

7 The principality of Monaco is one of the most crowded countries in the world: 28 000 people live on 1.9 sq km (467 acres) of land! By contrast, most of Scandinavia has fewer than 40 people per square kilometre.

8 Venice, Italy, is built on no less than 118 islands. Instead of roads, there are canals, and boats are used for transport. Venice is sinking at a rate of 12 inches each century. Some of the reasons for this include water being extracted from wells, and the compression of the mud on the floor of the lagoon.

9 Mount Etna, Sicily, is the highest volcano in Europe (about 3323 m, 10 902 ft) and is still very active. Despite this, many people live on its lower slopes. This is because the soil there is very fertile and grows good produce.

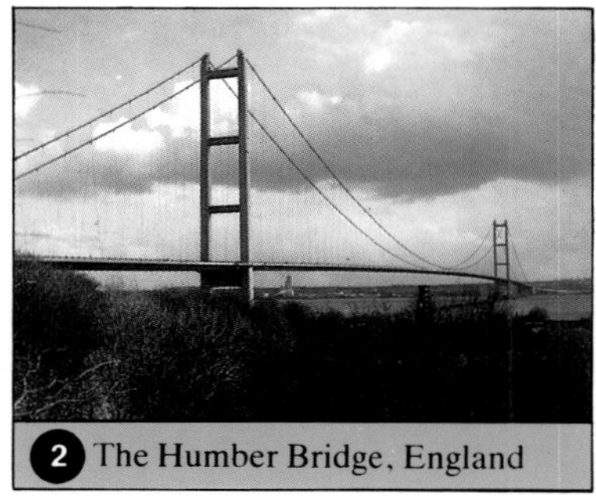

2 The Humber Bridge, England

ALBANIA

Area: 2 732 sq km
(1 055 sq miles)
Population: 3 200 000
Capital: Tirana
Languages: Albanian
(Tosk and Gheg)
Currency: Lek

ANDORRA

Area: 453 sq km
(175 sq miles)
Population: 47 000
Capital: Andorra-la-Vella
Language: Catalan
Currency: French Franc
and Spanish Peseta

AUSTRIA

Area: 83 848 sq km
(32 374 sq miles)
Population: 7 600 000
Capital: Vienna
Language: German
Currency: Schilling

BELGIUM

Area: 30 512 sq km
(11 781 sq miles)
Population: 9 900 000
Capital: Brussels
Languages: Flemish, French
Currency: Belgian Franc

BULGARIA

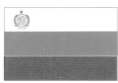

Area: 110 911 sq km
(42 822 sq miles)
Population: 9 000 000
Capital: Sofia
Language: Bulgarian
Currency: Lev

CZECHOSLOVAKIA

Area: 127 870 sq km
(49 370 sq miles)
Population: 15 700 000
Capital: Prague
Languages: Czech, Slovak
Currency: Koruna

DENMARK

Area: 43 030 sq km
(16 614 sq miles)
Population: 5 100 000
Capital: Copenhagen
Language: Danish
Currency: Krone

ESTONIA

Area: 45 100 sq km
(17 413 sq miles)
Population: 1 600 000
Capital: Tallinn
Language: Estonian
Currency: Ruble, Kroon
  proposed

FINLAND

Area: 337 032 sq km
(130 128 sq miles)
Population: 5 000 000
Capital: Helsinki
Languages: Finnish, Swedish
Currency: Mark

FRANCE

Area: 551 000 sq km
(212 741 sq miles)
Population: 56 100 000
Capital: Paris
Language: French
Currency: Franc

GERMANY

Area: 357 868 sq km
(138 173 sq miles)
Population: 79 000 000
Capital: Berlin, Bonn
Language: German
Currency: Deutschmark

GREECE

Area: 131 955 sq km
(50 948 sq miles)
Population: 10 000 000
Capital: Athens
Language: Greek
Currency: Drachma

HUNGARY

Area: 93 030 sq km
(35 919 sq miles)
Population: 10 600 000
Capital: Budapest
Language: Magyar
Currency: Forint

ICELAND

Area: 102 828 sq km
(41 131 sq miles)
Population: 250 000
Capital: Reykjavík
Language: Icelandic
Currency: Króna

IRELAND

Area: 70·282 sq km
(27 136 sq miles)
Population: 3 700 000
Capital: Dublin
Languages: Irish (Gaelic),
English
Currency: Irish Pound
(Punt)

10 Monasteries on rock pillars, Greece

10 Near Kalabaka, Greece, are a group of monasteries built for monks with no fear of heights! They are perched on top of pillars of rock, called meteora, 300 m (1 000 ft) high. The only way up was by ladders or baskets slung on the end of ropes. Now stairways have been constructed so that tourists can visit the buildings.

11 The island of Santorini (Thira) in Greece is the site of the world's largest natural disaster. About 1500 BC this volcanic island erupted leaving a *caldera* (hollow basin shape where the top of the volcano had been) about 13 km (8 miles) across. Many people believe that the destruction of this island is the origin of the story of Atlantis. The people of Atlantis are mentioned by the Greek writer Plato. Crime and corruption spread throughout their island as they became wealthier, until finally the Athenians conquered them. Later the island disappeared into the sea in a single day and night.

7 Monte Carlo, Monaco

12 Loch Ness, in the Highlands of Scotland, is one of the most famous freshwater expanses in the world. Its length and depth are so great that it could accommodate the population of the earth three times over. Its greatest mystery is the world-famous Loch Ness Monster which was first recorded in the 6th century by the Abbot of Iona. 'Nessie', as the monster is affectionately known, has been sighted by many people but evidence of the monster's existence is inconclusive. If it does exist, the most popular theory is that the monster is one of a small colony of unknown creatures which have descended from marine animals trapped in the loch at the end of the last Ice Age 12,000 years ago.

12 Loch Ness, Scotland

13 The stalactite caves of Aggtelek in Hungary form one of the largest cave systems in Europe. They are 23 km (14 miles) long and extend over the border into Czechoslovakia. The stalactites and stalagmites in the caves make a spectacular impact. Stalagmites on the floor of the Aggtelek caves bear a clear resemblance to the human form. Others resemble animals, temples, waterfalls, a 'Great Organ' and even a 'Butcher's Shop'.

14 The spectacularly beautiful Alhambra in Spain is situated on a hill overlooking Granada. From the outside, the fortress walls look plain but they belie the complex and colourful interior. Visitors find the intricate stonework, the sumptuous halls and the attractive gardens with their many fountains quite breathtaking. The Palace of the Alhambra was built as a home for the Moorish rulers in the 14th century and is a well-preserved example of the very best of Moorish art.

14 The Alhambra, Spain

ITALY

Area: 301 245 sq km (116 311 sq miles)
Population: 57 100 000
Capital: Rome
Language: Italian
Currency: Lira

LITHUANIA

Area: 65 200 sq km (25 170 sq miles)
Population: 3 700 000
Capital: Vilnius
Language: Lithuanian
Currency: Ruble, Litas proposed

NORWAY

Area: 324 218 sq km (125 180 sq miles)
Population: 4 200 000
Capital: Oslo
Language: Norwegian
Currency: Krone

ROMANIA

Area: 237 500 sq km (91 699 sq miles)
Population: 23 300 000
Capital: Bucharest
Language: Romanian
Currency: Leu

SWITZERLAND

Area: 41 287 sq km (15 941 sq miles)
Population: 6 600 000
Capital: Bern
Languages: German, French, Italian, Romansch
Currency: Franc

LATVIA

Area: 63 700 sq km (24 595 sq miles)
Population: 2 700 000
Capital: Riga
Language: Latvian
Currency: Ruble, Lat proposed

LUXEMBOURG

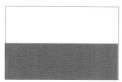

Area: 2 587 sq km (999 sq miles)
Population: 400 000
Capital: Luxembourg
Languages: Letzeburgish, French, German
Currency: Franc

POLAND

Area: 312 683 sq km (120 727 sq miles)
Population: 38 400 000
Capital: Warsaw
Language: Polish
Currency: Zloty

SPAIN

Area: 504 745 sq km (194 882 sq miles)
Population: 39 200 000
Capital: Madrid
Language: Spanish
Currency: Peseta

UNITED KINGDOM

Area: 244 104 sq km (94 249 sq miles)
Population: 57 200 000
Capital: London
Language: English
Currency: Pound Sterling

LIECHTENSTEIN

Area: 161 sq km (62 sq miles)
Population: 28 000
Capital: Vaduz
Language: German
Currency: Swiss Franc

NETHERLANDS

Area: 33 940 sq km (13 104 sq miles)
Population: 15 000 000
Capital: Amsterdam & The Hague
Language: Dutch
Currency: Guilder

PORTUGAL

Area: 91 671 sq km (35 394 sq miles)
Population: 10 300 000
Capital: Lisbon
Language: Portuguese
Currency: Escudo

SWEDEN

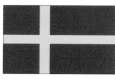

Area: 449 791 sq km (173 664 sq miles)
Population: 8 400 000
Capital: Stockholm
Language: Swedish
Currency: Krona

YUGOSLAVIA

Area: 255 803 sq km (98 766 sq miles)
Population: 23 800 000
Capital: Belgrade
Languages: Serbo-Croatian, Macedonian, Slovenian
Currency: Dinar

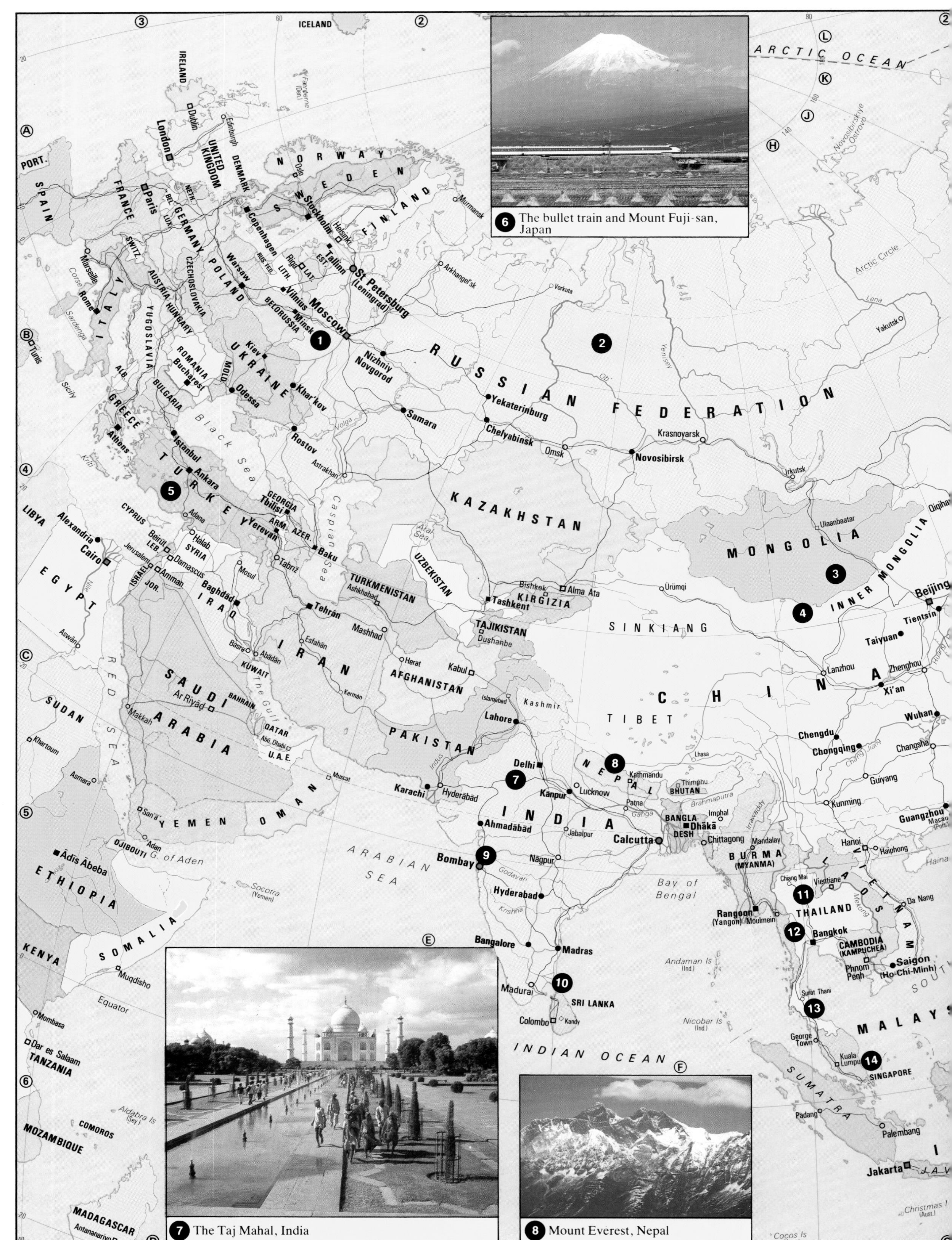

6 The bullet train and Mount Fuji-san, Japan

7 The Taj Mahal, India

8 Mount Everest, Nepal

ICELAND

IRELAND
Dublin
London
UNITED KINGDOM
Edinburgh
NORWAY
Oslo
DENMARK
Copenhagen
SWEDEN
Stockholm
Helsinki
FINLAND
Tallinn
EST.
Riga
LAT.
LITH.
Vilnius
Minsk
BELORUSSIA
St Petersburg (Leningrad)
Moscow
1
Murmansk
Arkhangel'sk
Vorkuta
ARCTIC OCEAN
Novosibirskye Ostrova
Arctic Circle
Lena
Yakutsk
Irkutsk
RUSSIAN FEDERATION
2
Ob'
Yenisey
Krasnoyarsk
Novosibirsk
Omsk
Chelyabinsk
Yekaterinburg
Samara
Nizhniy Novgorod
Khar'kov
Kiev
UKRAINE
Rostov
Odessa
Volga
Astrakhan
Black Sea
Istanbul
Ankara
TURKEY
5
GEORGIA
Tbilisi
ARM.
Yerevan
AZER.
Baku
Caspian Sea
Aral Sea
KAZAKHSTAN
Bishkek
Alma Ata
KIRGIZIA
Tashkent
UZBEKISTAN
TURKMENISTAN
Ashkhabad
TAJIKISTAN
Dushanbe
Mashhad
Tehrān
Esfahān
IRAN
Kermān
Herat
Kabul
AFGHANISTAN
Islamabad
Kashmir
Lahore
PAKISTAN
Karachi
Hyderābad
Indus
Delhi
7
Kanpur
Lucknow
NEPAL
8
Kathmandu
Thimphu
BHUTAN
Patna
Ganga
Brahmaputra
Imphal
BANGLA DESH
Dhāka
Calcutta
Chittagong
INDIA
Ahmadābād
Jabalpur
Nāgpur
Godavari
Bombay
9
Hyderabad
Krishna
Bangalore
Madras
Madurai
10
SRI LANKA
Colombo
Kandy
ÜRümqi
MONGOLIA
Ulaanbaatar
INNER MONGOLIA
SINKIANG
TIBET
Lhasa
CHINA
Lanzhou
Zhengzhou
Xi'an
Chengdu
Chongqing
Chang Jiang
Changsha
Guiyang
Kunming
Wuhan
Guangzhou
Macau
Beijing
Tientsin
Taiyuan
3
4
Qiqihar
Harbin
BURMA (MYANMA)
Mandalay
Rangoon (Yangon)
Moulmein
Chiang Mai
11
Vientiane
LAOS
THAILAND
Bangkok
12
13
CAMBODIA (KAMPUCHEA)
Phnom Penh
Saigon (Ho-Chi-Minh)
VIETNAM
Hanoi
Haiphong
Da Nang
Hainan
Surat Thani
George Town
Kuala Lumpur
14
SINGAPORE
SUMATRA
Padang
Palembang
Jakarta
JAVA
MALAYSIA

PORT.
SPAIN
Marseille
Corse
FRANCE
Paris
BEL.
LUX.
NETH.
GERMANY
SWITZ.
ITALY
Rome
Sardegna
Sicily
Tunis
ALB.
GREECE
Athens
Kriti
CYPRUS
Alexandria
Cairo
LIBYA
EGYPT
Nile
Aswān
SUDAN
Khartoum
Asmara
ETHIOPIA
Ādīs Ābeba
Adan
G. of Aden
Socotra (Yemen)
DJIBOUTI
Muqdisho
SOMALIA
KENYA
Mombasa
Equator
Dar es Salaam
TANZANIA
COMOROS
MOZAMBIQUE
MADAGASCAR
Antananarivo
Aldabra Is (Sey.)
POLAND
Warsaw
CZECHOSLOVAKIA
AUSTRIA
HUNGARY
YUGOSLAVIA
ROMANIA
Bucharest
BULGARIA
MOLD.
RUS. FED.
San'ā
YEMEN
OMAN
Muscat
U.A.E.
Abū Dhabi
QATAR
BAHRAIN
The Gulf
KUWAIT
SAUDI ARABIA
Ar Riyād
Makkah
RED SEA
ARABIAN SEA
Bay of Bengal
Andaman Is (Ind.)
Nicobar Is (Ind.)
Cocos Is (Aust.)
Christmas I. (Aust.)
INDIAN OCEAN
SOUTH
Mosul
Baghdād
Damascus
Amman
Jerusalem
Beirut
Halab
SYRIA
LEB.
ISRAEL
JOR.
IRAQ
Basra
Ābādān
Tabriz
Adana

A
B
C
D
E
F

2
3
4
5
6

L
K
J
H

POPULATION

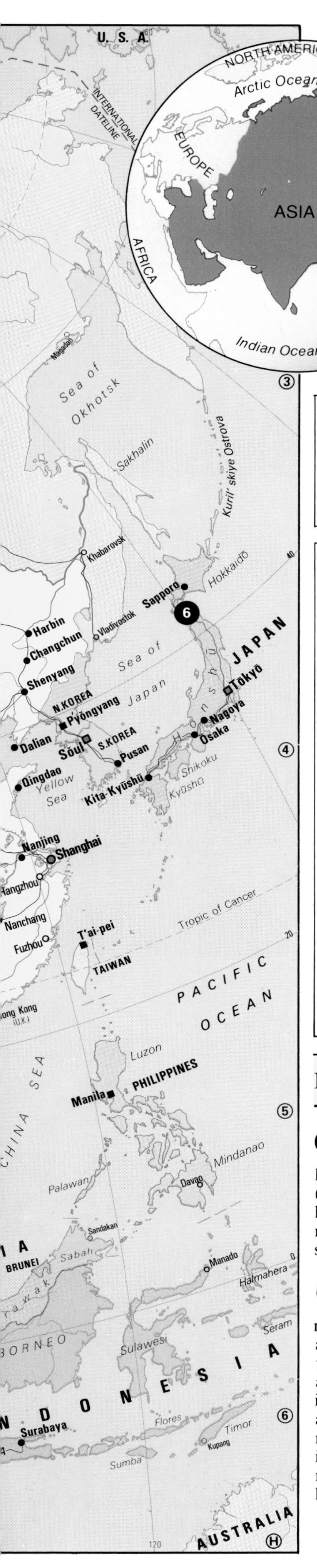

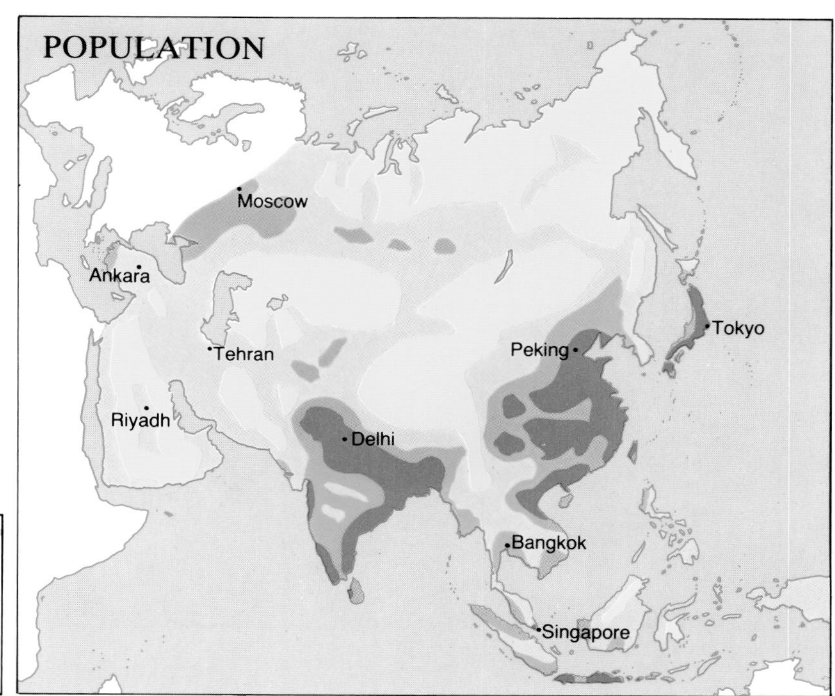

over 500 persons per km²
100-500 persons per km²
5-100 persons per km²
under 5 persons per km²

Symbol	Product	Symbol	Product
Cattle		Oil	
Citrus fruit		Barley	
Coconut		Wheat	
Cotton		Minerals	
Fish		3 Copper	
Rice		4 Gold	
Rubber		5 Iron	
Spices		6 Lead	
Tea		7 Nickel	
Timber		11 Uranium	
Coal		12 Zinc	

NATURAL VEGETATION/PRODUCTS

Tundra/Mountain
Northern Forest
Woodland/Grass
Grassland
Scrub
Desert
Rainforest

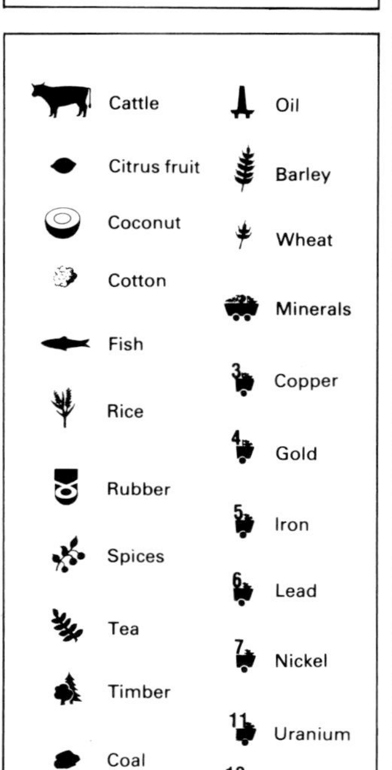

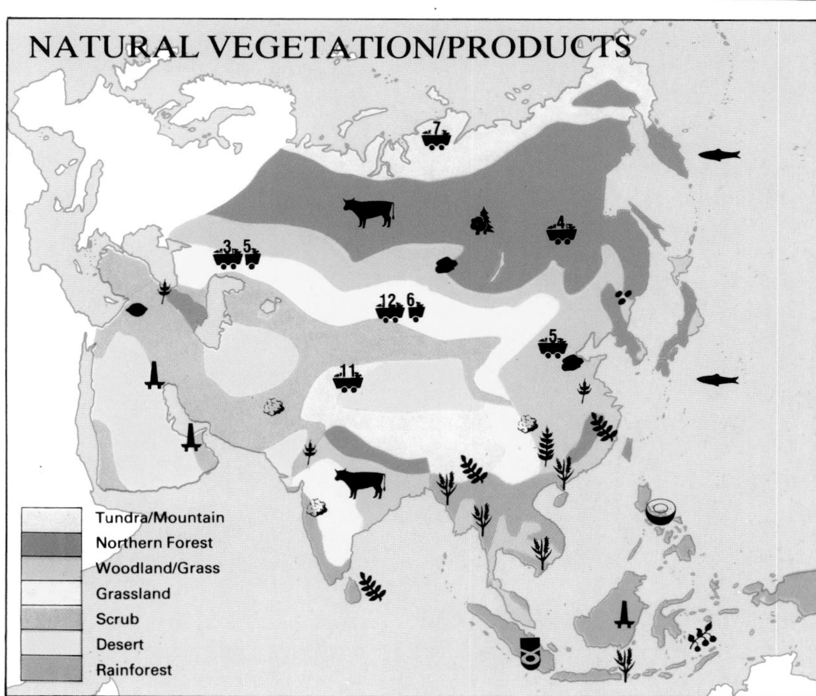

FACTS ABOUT ASIA

1 The world's heaviest bell is the *Czar Bell* in Moscow's Kremlin. It weighs a massive 196 tonnes (193 tons) and is 5.87 m (19 ft 3 in) high. The bell was cast in 1735. It is now cracked, and hasn't been rung since 1836.

2 In Siberia, there is a huge forest called the *taiga*, which makes up a quarter of the total area of forest in the world. The trees are mostly coniferous - pine and larch. Few people used to live in the taiga, as it is a very cold area, but because it is rich in minerals more people are moving into the forest. They live in industrial towns being built deep in its heart, to exploit the minerals.

3 The huge Gobi Desert covers much of Mongolia. The Gobi is a cold, barren region of rocky plains and hills. Water is very scarce and only a few nomads live here. They exist mainly by cattle raising and live in an unusual tent called a *yurt*, which is shaped like an upside-down bowl.

4 The Great Wall of China stretches for 3460 km (2150 miles), making it the longest in the world. It was built for defence in the 3rd century BC and kept in good repair until 400 years ago. Although part of the wall was blown up to make a dam in 1979, the many remaining sections of the wall are still impressive.

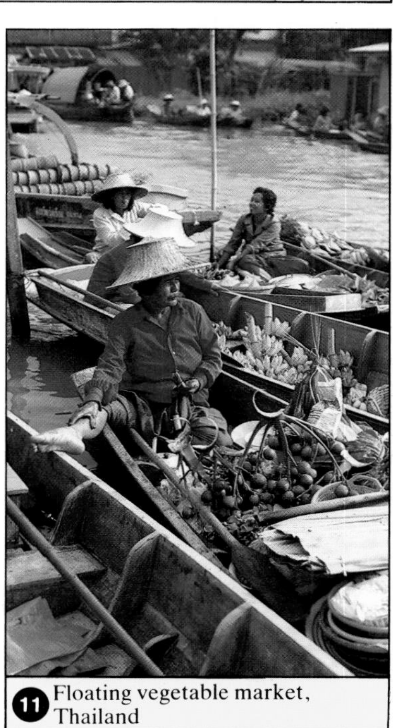

11 Floating vegetable market, Thailand

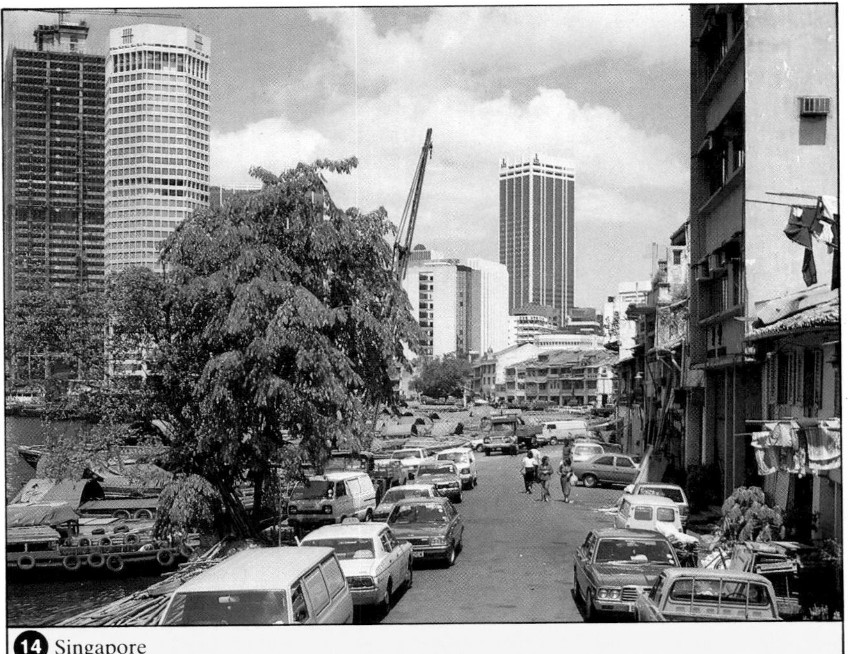

14 Singapore

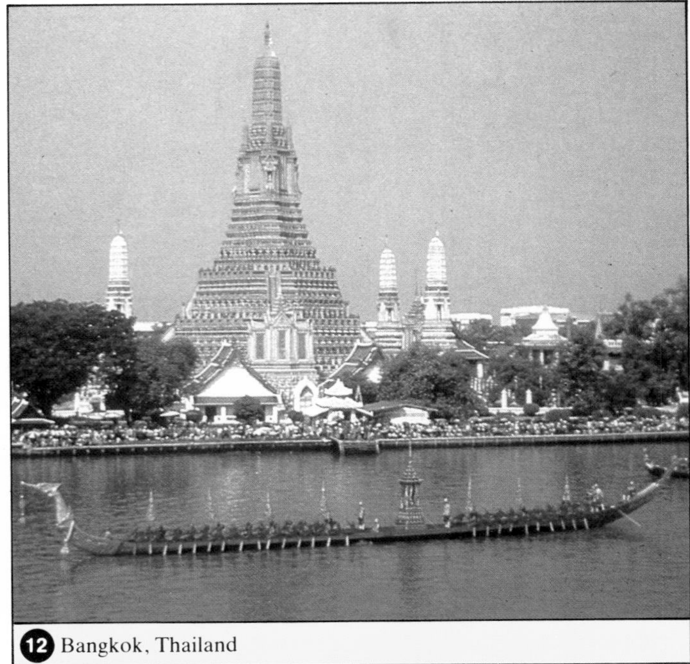

12 Bangkok, Thailand

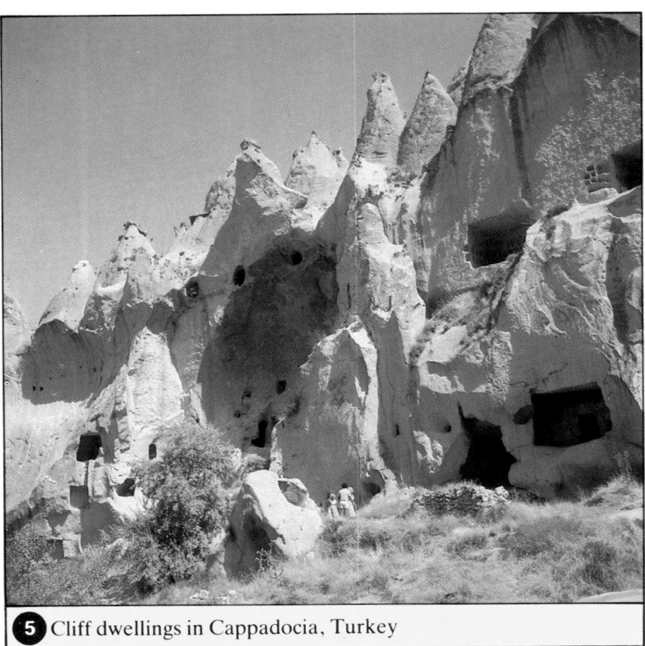

5 Cliff dwellings in Cappadocia, Turkey

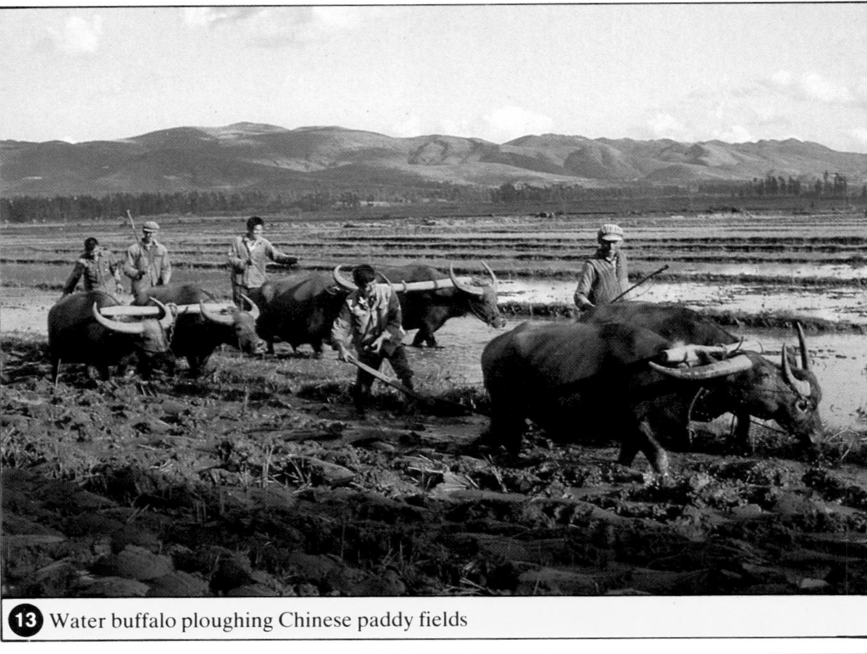

13 Water buffalo ploughing Chinese paddy fields

FACTS ABOUT ASIA

5 In central Turkey, near Urgup in the region called Cappadocia, an extraordinary landscape can be seen. There was once a plateau here, made up of layers of rock, some hard and some much softer. Over thousands of years the softer rocks have been eroded by the weather, by streams and even by men digging out caves to live in. The rocks are now shaped into strange cones, towers and 'mushrooms', with 'hats' of harder rock balancing on top. There are also complete 'villages' of caves connected to each other by passageways cut through the rock. Each cave has 'cupboards' and 'shelves' cut into its walls. Here many centuries ago people hid from religious persecution. Over 300 churches which they dug out of the rock have been found. Some people still live in caves in this region, today.

6 The Seikan Tunnel in Japan is the longest tunnel in the world. It is an underwater tunnel, stretching for 54 km (34 miles). It was built for Japan's famous *bullet train*, the first passenger train to travel at 200 kph.

7 There should have been two Taj Mahals in India – a black one and a white one. In 1648, Emperor Shah Jahan completed the present Taj Mahal. It was a tomb for his wife, and made of white marble. He then began building a tomb of black marble for himself. Before work had got very far, he was overthrown.

8 At 8848 m (29 028 ft) the peak of Mt Everest in the Himalayas is the Earth's highest point. In May 1953, New Zealander Sir Edmund Hillary was the first man to climb Everest. Twenty two years later, in 1975, the first woman to reach the summit was Junko Tabei of Japan.

9 In India cows are sacred animals and are allowed to wander freely, even in the centre of big cities! Drivers are used to going round cows lying peacefully in the middle of the road.

10 Banyan trees can be seen in India and Sri Lanka. They are very unusual to look at, because what seems to be several trees growing close together, is actually just one tree! Aerial roots grow down from the banyan's branches and root in the ground. They become extra 'trunks' and support a huge canopy of leaves, which gives a lot of shade, very useful in such a hot climate.

11 Throughout Asia there are areas where many people live on boats – because there is not enough room for them to live in houses on land (or they cannot afford to) or because they just prefer to live on water. In these places, even the shops are on boats.

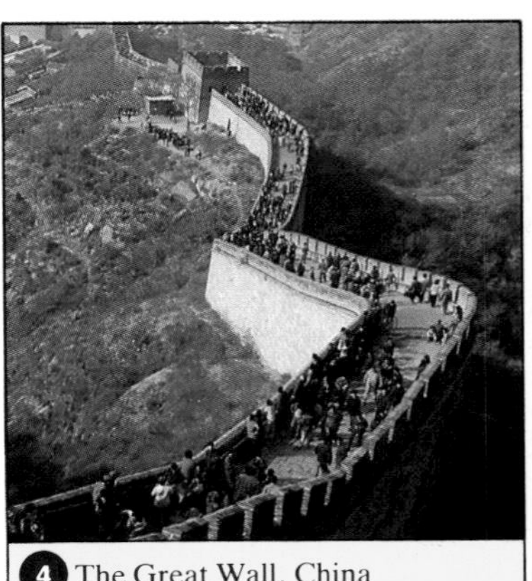

4 The Great Wall, China

10 Banyan tree, India

9 Street in India

12 Bangkok, Thailand, once had many canals, called *klongs*, instead of roads. (The city was called the 'Venice of the East' because the klongs reminded visitors of the canals in Venice, Italy.) They were used for transport and also helped to drain the land during the rainy season. After cars and lorries began to be used for transport, many of the klongs were filled in to make roads. Now Bangkok has problems with flooding when the monsoons come.

13 Paddy fields, the irrigated fields in which rice is grown, get their name from *padi*, the Malayan word for rice. Rice is grown throughout Asia in the fertile lowlands near the equator. Millions of people live in these areas, and rice is very important to them as it yields more food per acre than any other crop.

14 Over half the population of the world lives in Asia – that is 3 113 000 000 people. Some parts of Asia have many people living in a small area. One of the most densely populated countries is Singapore, which has an average of 4 420 people for each square kilometre of ground.

AFGHANISTAN

Area: 674 500 sq km (260 424 sq miles)
Population: 16 600 000
Capital: Kabul
Languages: Pashtu, Dari, Uzbek
Currency: Afghani

INDONESIA

Area: 1 919 263 sq km (741 027 miles)
Population: 185 000 000
Capital: Jakarta
Language: Bahasa (Indonesian)
Currency: Rupiah

ISRAEL

Area: 20 770 sq km (8019 sq miles)
Population: 4 600 000
Capital: Jerusalem
Languages: Hebrew, Arabic
Currency: Shekel

PAKISTAN

Area: 803 941 sq km (310 402 sq miles)
Population: 122 600 000
Capital: Islamabad
Language: Urdu
Currency: Pakistan Rupee

SINGAPORE

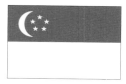

Area: 616 sq km (238 sq miles)
Population: 2 700 000
Capital: Singapore
Languages: Chinese, Malay, Tamil, English
Currency: Singapore Dollar

CHINA

Area: 9 561 000 sq km (3 691 502 sq miles)
Population: 1 118 800 000
Capital: Beijing
Language: Chinese (Mandarin)
Currency: Yuan

IRAN

Area: 1 648 184 sq km (636 364 sq miles)
Population: 54 600 000
Capital: Tehran
Language: Persian (Farsi)
Currency: Rial

JAPAN

Area: 371 000 sq km (143 243 sq miles)
Population: 123 500 000
Capital: Tokyo
Language: Japanese
Currency: Yen

PHILIPPINES

Area: 299 765 sq km (115 739 sq miles)
Population: 62 400 000
Capital: Manila
Language: Philipino
Currency: Philippine Peso

THAILAND

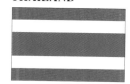

Area: 513 517 sq km (198 269 sq miles)
Population: 55 700 000
Capital: Bangkok
Languages: Thai, Chinese
Currency: Baht

INDIA

Area: 3 287 593 sq km (1 269 340 sq miles)
Population: 853 100 000
Capital: Delhi
Languages: Hindi, English
Currency: Indian Rupee

IRAQ

Area: 434 924 sq km (167 924 sq miles)
Population: 18 900 000
Capital: Baghdad
Language: Arabic
Currency: Iraqi Dinar

MALAYSIA

Area: 330 669 sq km (127 671 sq miles)
Population: 17 900 000
Capital: Kuala Lumpur
Language: Malay
Currency: Ringgit (Malaysian Dollar)

SAUDI ARABIA

Area: 2 400 930 sq km (927 000 sq miles)
Population: 14 100 000
Capital: Riyadh
Language: Arabic
Currency: Riyal

TURKEY

Area: 780 576 sq km (301 380 sq miles)
Population: 55 900 000
Capital: Ankara
Language: Turkish
Currency: Turkish Lira

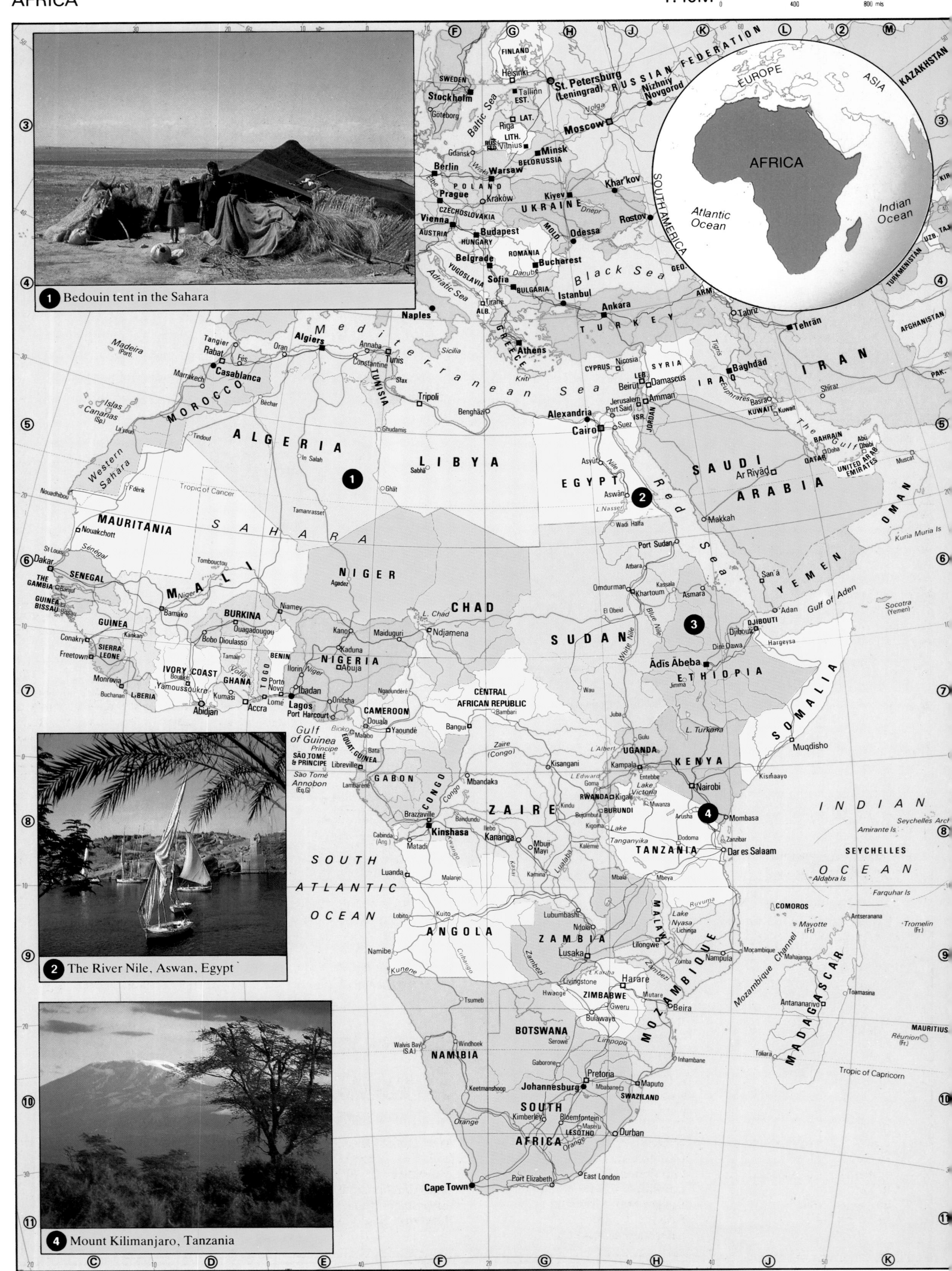

1:40M

400   800   1200   1600 km
400   800 mls

1 Bedouin tent in the Sahara

2 The River Nile, Aswan, Egypt

4 Mount Kilimanjaro, Tanzania

EUROPE   ASIA   KAZAKHSTAN

AFRICA

Atlantic
Ocean

Indian
Ocean

SOUTH AMERICA

FINLAND
Helsinki
SWEDEN
Stockholm   Tallinn   RUSSIAN FEDERATION
Göteborg   EST.   Nizhniy   Novgorod
St. Petersburg
(Leningrad)   Volga
Baltic Sea   Riga   LAT.
LITH.   Moscow
Gdansk   Vilnius
RUS.   Minsk
Berlin   FED.   Warsaw   BELORUSSIA
POLAND   Khar'kov
Prague   Kraków   Kiyev
CZECHOSLOVAKIA   UKRAINE   Dnepr
Vienna   MOLD.   Rostov
AUSTRIA   Budapest   Odessa
HUNGARY   ROMANIA
Belgrade   Bucharest
YUGOSLAVIA   Danube   Black Sea   GEO.
Sofia   Istanbul   Tabriz
BULGARIA
ALB.   Ankara   ARM.
Naples   Tirane   AZER.
GREECE   TURKEY   Tehrān
Athens
Kriti   CYPRUS   Nicosia   SYRIA   Baghdād   IRAN
Beirut   Damascus   IRAQ
LEB.   Euphrates   Shiraz   AFGHANISTAN
Jerusalem   Amman   Tigris   PAK.
Port Said   ISR.   JORDAN   KUWAIT   Kuwait
Alexandria   Suez   BAHRAIN   UZB.
Cairo   Abū   TURKMENISTAN
Asyūt   SAUDI   QATAR   Dhabi
EGYPT   Aswān   Ar Riyād   Doha   Muscat
L. Nasser   UNITED ARAB
EMIRATES
Wadi Halfa   Makkah   OMAN

Madeira
(Port.)
Tangier
Rabat   Algiers   Annaba   Mediterranean Sea
Fès   Oran   Tunis   Sicilia
Marrakech   Constantine   TUNISIA
Casablanca   Béchar
MOROCCO   Tripoli
Sfax
Islas   Benghāzi
Canarias   Ghudamis
(Sp.)   ALGERIA   LIBYA
La'youn   In Salah   Tropic of Cancer
Western   Tamanrasset
Sahara   F'dérik   Ghāt   Sabha
Nouadhibou   SAHARA
MAURITANIA
Nouakchott
St-Louis   Tombouctou   NIGER   Port Sudan
Dakar   Sénégal   Agadez   Omdurman   Atbara   YEMEN   Socotra
THE   Bamako   Niamey   Khartoum   Kassala   (Yemen)
GAMBIA   SENEGAL   MALI   CHAD   El Obeid   Asmara   San'ā   Gulf of Aden
Banjul   Bamako   N i g e r   L. Chad   SUDAN   Adan   Kuria Muria Is
GUINEA   BURKINA   Kano   Ndjamena   Blue Nile   DJIBOUTI
BISSAU   Ouagadougou   Maiduguri   Khartoum   Dire Dawa   Hargeysa
GUINEA   Bobo Dioulasso   Kaduna   Ādīs Ābeba   ETHIOPIA
Conakry   Kankan   BENIN   NIGERIA   Jimma
SIERRA   Tamale   Ilorin   Abuja   Wau   Juba
LEONE   Volta   TOGO   CENTRAL   SOMALIA
Freetown   IVORY COAST   GHANA   Niger   Ngaoundéré   AFRICAN REPUBLIC   L. Turkana
Monrovia   Bouaké   Porto   Ibadan   Bambari   Muqdisho
Buchanan   LIBERIA   Yamoussoukro   Novo   Onitsha   Gulu
Abidjan   Kumasi   Lagos   CAMEROON   UGANDA
Accra   Lomé   Port Harcourt   Douala   Yaoundé   Bangui   Kampala   KENYA   INDIAN
EQUAT. GUINEA   Bata   Zaire   L. Edward   Entebbe   Lake   Nairobi   OCEAN
Gulf of Guinea   Bioko   (Congo)   Kisangani   Goma   Victoria   Seychelles Arch
SÃO TOMÉ   Principe   GABON   Kindu   RWANDA   Kigali   Mombasa   Amirante Is
& PRINCIPE   São Tomé   Libreville   CONGO   Mbandaka   Bujumbura   Mwanza   Arusha   SEYCHELLES
Annobon   Lambaréné   Congo   BURUNDI   Dodoma   Dar es Salaam   OCEAN
(Eq. G)   ZAIRE   Kisangani   Kigoma   Lake
SOUTH   Brazzaville   Ilebo   Kananga   Lake   Tanganyika   TANZANIA   Aldabra Is
ATLANTIC   Kinshasa   Bandundu   Mbuji   Kalemie   Zanzibar   Farquhar Is
OCEAN   Cabinda   Matadi   Mayi   Kamina   Mbala   COMOROS
(Ang.)   Kwango   Luputa   Mbeya   Lake   Mayotte   Antseranana
Luanda   Malanje   Mweru   Nyasa   (Fr.)
Kuito   Lubumbashi   Lichinga   Nampula   Tromelin
ANGOLA   Ndola   MALAWI   Mozambique Channel   (Fr.)
Namibe   ZAMBIA   Lilongwe   Zumbo   Mahajanga
Lobito   Lusaka   L. Kariba   MADAGASCAR
Benguela   Cuito   Zambezi   Harare   MOZAMBIQUE   Antananarivo
Walvis Bay   Windhoek   Livingstone   Hwange   ZIMBABWE   Beira   Toamasina
(S.A.)   Tsumeb   Bulawayo   Mutare   MAURITIUS
NAMIBIA   BOTSWANA   Gweru   Réunion
Namib   Serowe   Limpopo   (Fr.)
Gaborone   Inhambane   Tropic of Capricorn
Keetmanshoop   Pretoria   Maputo   Toliara
Johannesburg   Mbabane   SWAZILAND
Kimberley   Bloemfontein   LESOTHO
SOUTH   Maseru
AFRICA   Orange   Durban
Orange   East London
Cape Town   Port Elizabeth

POPULATION

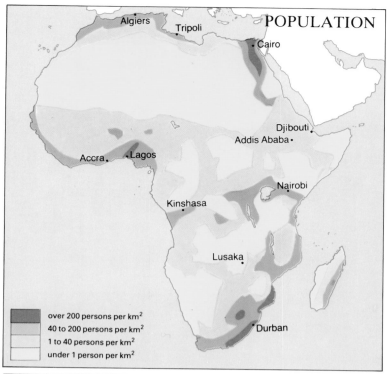

Algiers
Tripoli
Cairo
Djibouti
Addis Ababa
Accra • Lagos
Nairobi
Kinshasa
Lusaka
Durban

- over 200 persons per km²
- 40 to 200 persons per km²
- 1 to 40 persons per km²
- under 1 person per km²

NATURAL VEGETATION/ PRODUCTS

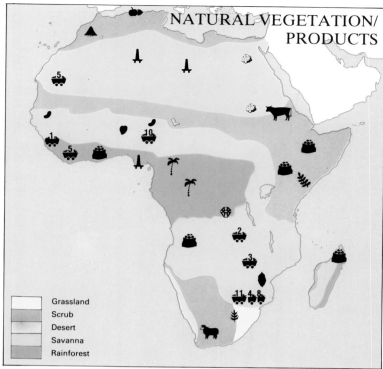

- Grassland
- Scrub
- Desert
- Savanna
- Rainforest

Cattle	Peanuts	Phosphates	4 Gold
Sheep	Palm oil	Maize	5 Iron
Cocoa	Tea	Minerals	8 Platinum
Coffee	Tobacco	1 Bauxite	10 Tin
Cotton	Diamonds	2 Cobalt	11 Uranium
Fruit	Oil	3 Copper	

FACTS ABOUT AFRICA

1 The largest desert in the world is the Sahara, but only about 30% of it is sand. The rest is rocky waste. People live mainly near oases, where the land is watered by springs rising to the surface and crops can be grown. The desert is very hot and dry, but there are a few plants and animals (like camels) specially adapted to these conditions.

2 The Nile is the longest river in the world and flows for 6650 km (4160 miles) through North Africa to the Mediterranean Sea.

The Nile used to flood its banks each year, but now the High Dam at Aswan controls the floods. When the dam was built, the temples of Abu Simbel (3000 years old) were moved to a higher site to stop them being flooded.

3 Some parts of Africa have had no rain, or very little, for several years. Food crops have failed and many people have died from malnutrition and starvation. A further problem has been wars, which have driven many people from their homes and fields. Even if part of a country can grow food, it is difficult to move that food into areas where none can be grown. There are few lorries and, where people are at war, transporting food may be dangerous. Although western countries have sent food supplies, there is still not enough to feed the hundreds of thousands of people who are starving. Governments are trying to find ways of growing more food and distributing it more quickly.

4 Kilimanjaro (now renamed Uhuru, meaning 'freedom') is the highest mountain in Africa (5895 m; 19 340 feet) and its peaks are always covered in snow.

EGYPT

Area: 1 000 250 sq km
(386 197 sq miles)
Population: 52 400 000
Capital: Cairo
Language: Arabic
Currency: Egyptian Pound

ETHIOPIA

Area: 1 221 918 sq km
(471 783 sq miles)
Population: 49 200 000
Capital: Addis Ababa
Language: Amharic
Currency: Birr

KENYA

Area: 582 644 sq km
(224 959 sq miles)
Population: 24 000 000
Capital: Nairobi
Languages: English, Swahili
Currency: Kenya Shilling

LIBYA

Area: 1 759 530 sq km
(679 355 sq miles)
Population: 4 500 000
Capital: Tripoli
Language: Arabic
Currency: Libyan Dinar

NIGERIA

Area: 923 769 sq km
(356 667 sq miles)
Population: 108 500 000
Capital: Lagos
Language: English
Currency: Naira

SOUTH AFRICA

Area: 1 221 038 sq km
(471 443 sq miles)
Population: 35 300 000
Capital: Pretoria
Languages: Afrikaans, English
Currency: Rand

SUDAN

Area: 2 505 792 sq km
(967 486 sq miles)
Population: 25 200 000
Capital: Khartoum
Language: Arabic
Currency: Sudanese Pound

ZAIRE

Area: 2 344 885 sq km
(905 360 sq miles)
Population: 35 600 000
Capital: Kinshasa
Language: French
Currency: Zaire

1:60M

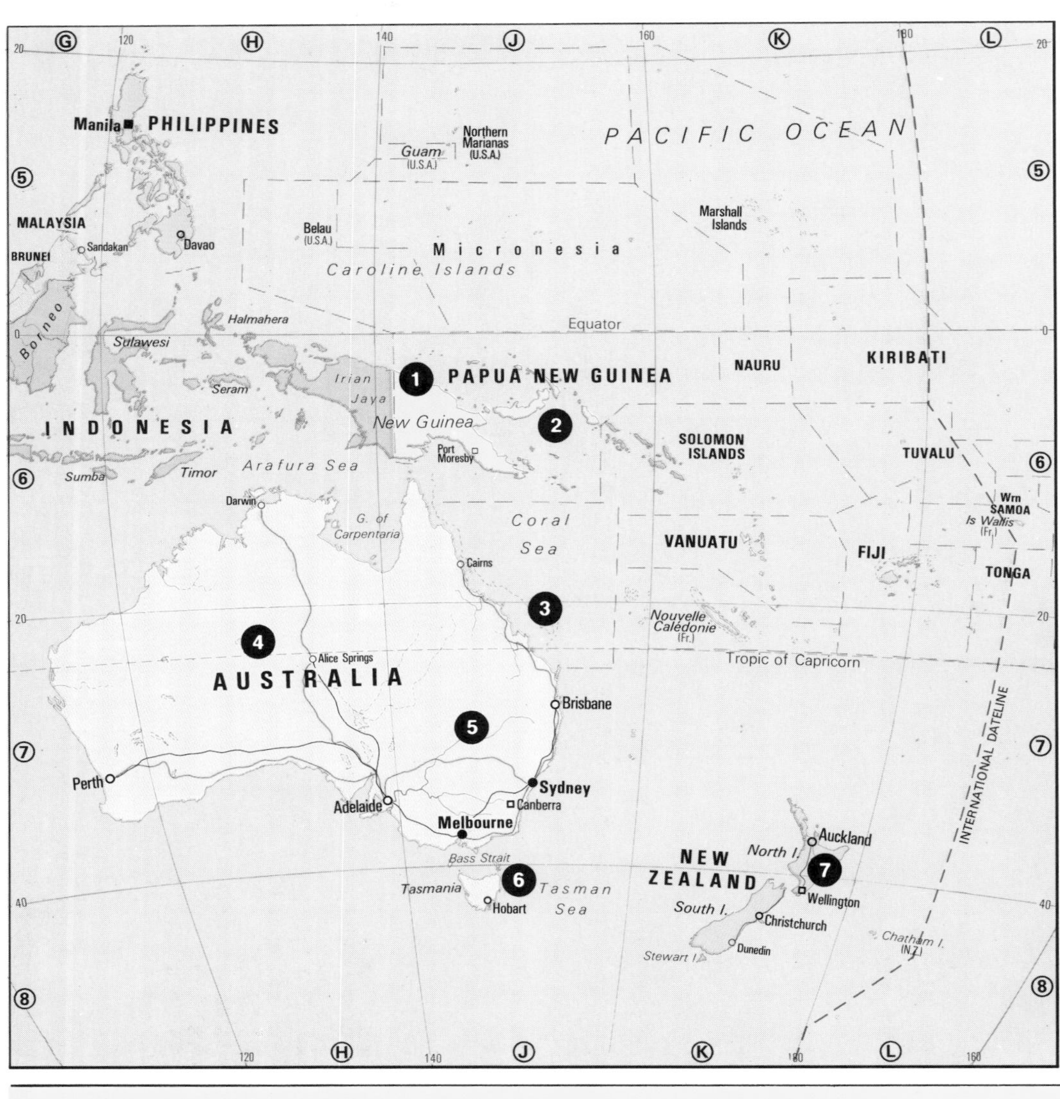

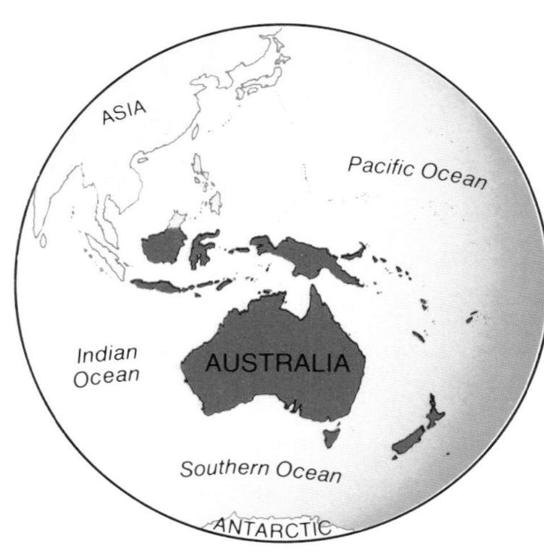

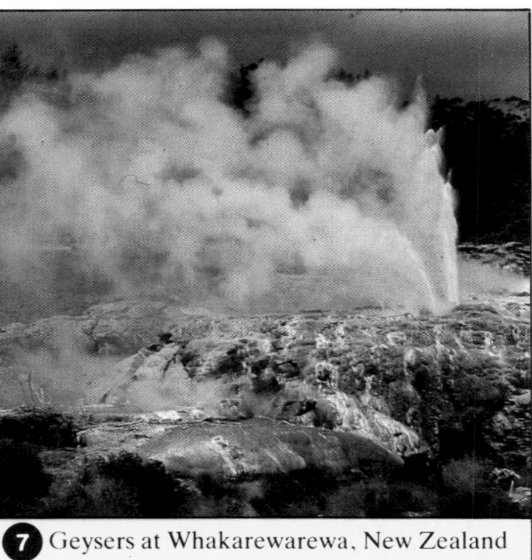

7 Geysers at Whakarewarewa, New Zealand

FACTS ABOUT AUSTRALASIA

1 Over 700 languages are spoken in Papua New Guinea. That is more than a quarter of all the languages spoken in the world. Papua New Guinea's mountains, thick forests and islands meant that different tribes did not mix, so they did not share a common language, but instead each developed its own. Today, Pidgin English and Police Motu have become the languages which the different tribes use to talk to each other.

2 No less than 38 different species of the beautiful Bird of Paradise are to be seen in Papua New Guinea. Another 5 species are found on neighbouring islands and in northern Australia. Their tail feathers are a traditional part of Papua New Guinea tribal costume, although the birds are now protected from hunting to a great extent.

3 Australia's Great Barrier Reef is formed from the shells of millions of tiny sea creatures. It is 2000 km (1250 miles) long and is the world's biggest coral reef. There are many thousands of coral islands or *atolls* in the Pacific region.

4 Ayers Rock is a huge sand-stone rock formation which rears up abruptly from the desert in central Australia. The rock is special because it changes colour with the light. Australia's native *aborigine* people believe there is something magical about the rock.

5 Australia is the driest of all the continents in the world. Rainfall is also very unevenly distributed: even though the tropical north has about 2000 mm (79 inches) a year, the central deserts have less than 150 mm (6 inches). Irrigation is important for agriculture, and rivers and artesian wells are used as a source of water. The Snowy Mountains reservoir and irrigation scheme has brought water from the mountains to irrigate farmland in the east of Australia.

6 A Tasmanian Devil is a little bear-like creature found only in Tasmania. It is just 60 cm (2 ft) long, with a big bushy tail. It has very sharp teeth and eats other

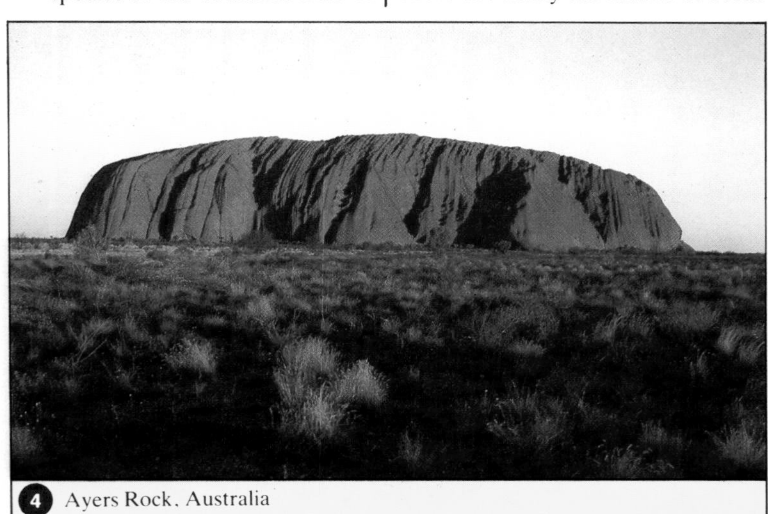

4 Ayers Rock, Australia

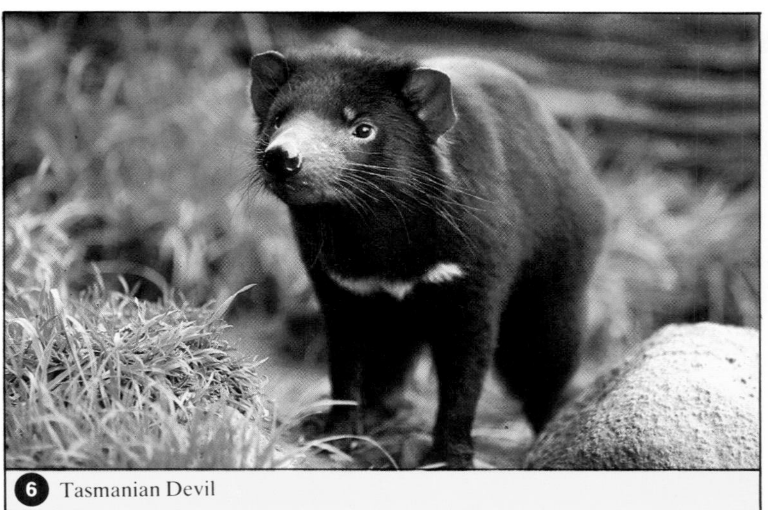

6 Tasmanian Devil

POPULATION

Darwin

Perth

Adelaide

Brisbane

Sydney

Canberra

Melbourne

Hobart

Wellington

over 500 persons per km²

100-500 persons per km²

5-100 persons per km²

under 5 persons per km²

NATURAL VEGETATION/PRODUCTS

Woodland/Grass

Scrub

Desert

Savanna

Rainforest

Sheep	Coffee	Coal	Minerals	6	Lead
Apples	Cocoa	Oil	1 Bauxite	9	Silver
Bananas	Rubber	Spices	3 Copper	11	Uranium
Grapes	Yams	Sugar cane	4 Gold	12	Zinc
Coconut	Rice	Wheat	5 Iron		

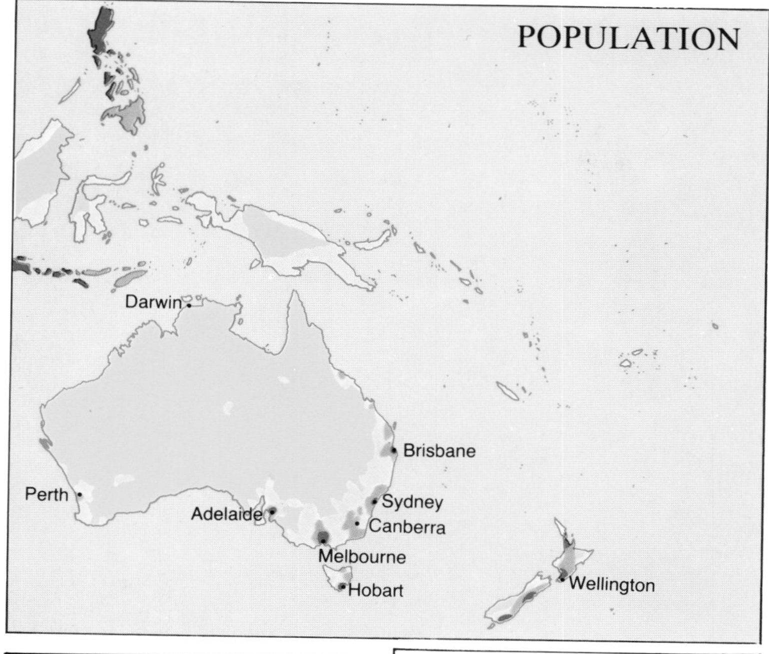

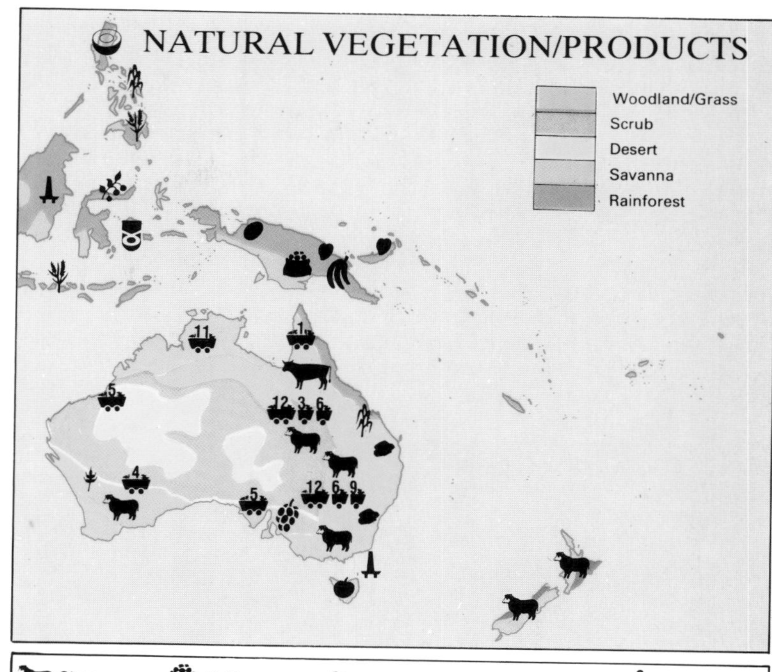

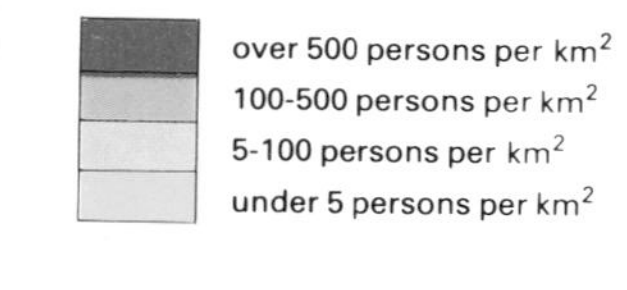

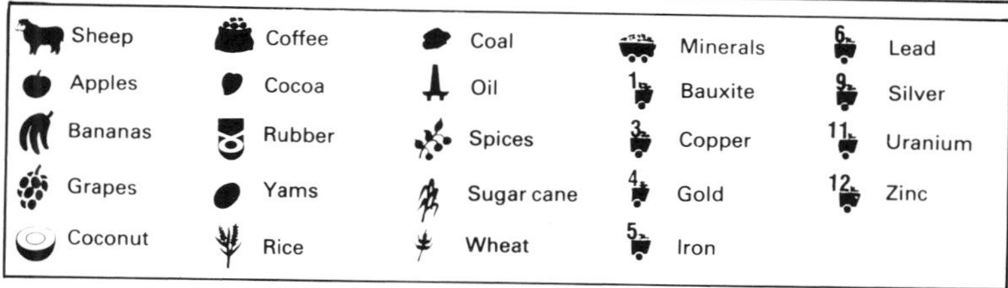

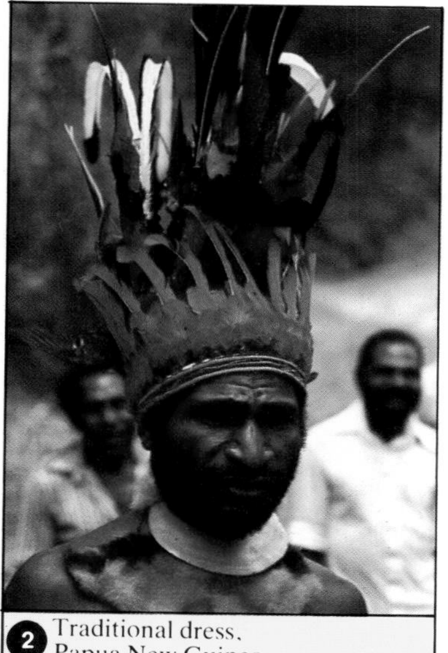

2 Traditional dress, Papua New Guinea

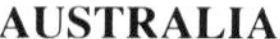

animals and small birds when it comes out at night. The Tasmanian Devil is a *marsupial*. This means it carries its young in a pouch.

7 The tallest geyser ever to have erupted was the Waimangu Geyser in New Zealand. In 1904 it rose to a height of 457 m (1500 ft). It last erupted in 1917, killing four people. Today, steam from New Zealand's hot springs and geysers is harnessed to generate electricity.

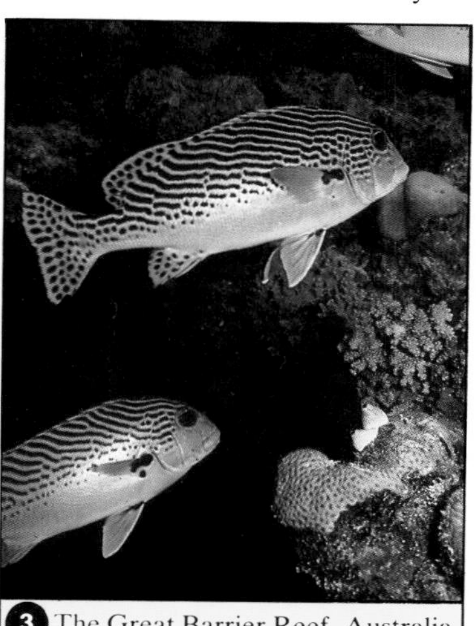

3 The Great Barrier Reef, Australia

AUSTRALIA

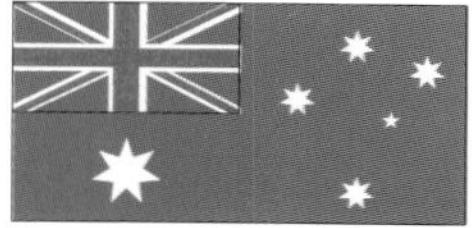

Area: 7 682 300 sq km (2 966 136 sq miles)
Population: 16 900 000
Capital: Canberra
Language: English
Currency: Australian Dollar

NEW ZEALAND

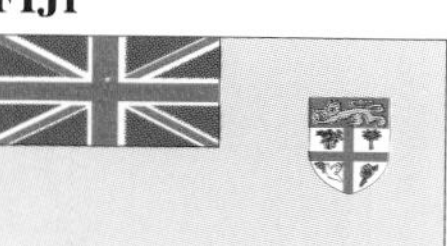

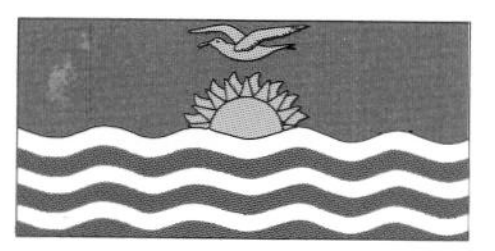

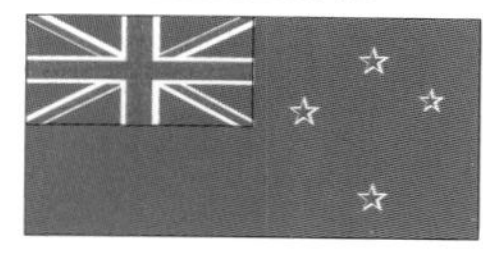

Area: 268 675 sq km (103 735 sq miles)
Population: 3 400 000
Capital: Wellington
Language: English
Currency: New Zealand Dollar

TONGA

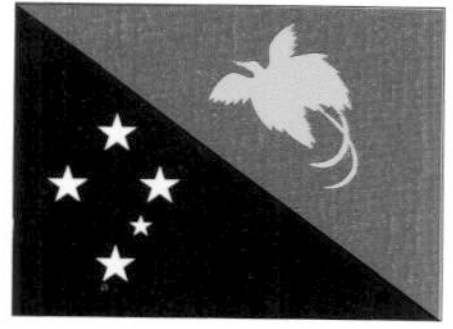

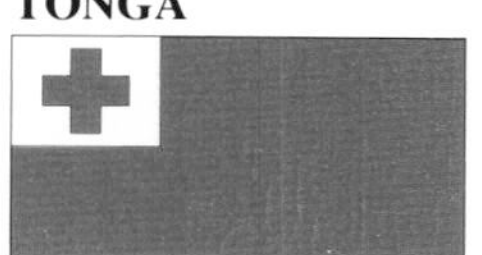

Area: 699 sq km (270 sq miles)
Population: 100 000
Capital: Nuku'alofa
Languages: English, Tongan
Currency: Pa'anga

FIJI

Area: 18 272 sq km (7055 sq miles)
Population: 800 000
Capital: Suva
Languages: English, Fijian
Currency: Fiji Dollar

PAPUA NEW GUINEA

Area: 461 692 sq km (178 259 sq miles)
Population: 3 900 000
Capital: Port Moresby
Languages: English, Melanesian Pidgin
Currency: Kina

VANUATU

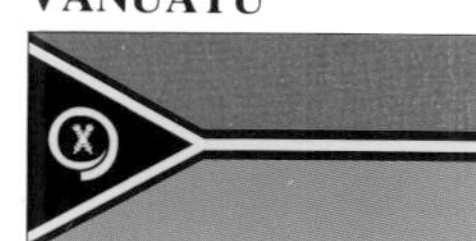

Area: 14 763 sq km (5700 sq miles)
Population: 160 000
Capital: Vila
Languages: Bislama, English, French
Currency: Australian Dollar, Vatu

KIRIBATI

Area: 800 sq km (309 sq miles)
Population: 66 000
Capital: Tarawa
Languages: English, I Kiribati
Currency: Australian Dollar

SOLOMON ISLANDS

Area: 29 785 sq km (11 500 sq miles)
Population: 320 000
Capital: Honiara
Languages: English, Pidgin
Currency: Solomon Islands Dollar

WESTERN SAMOA

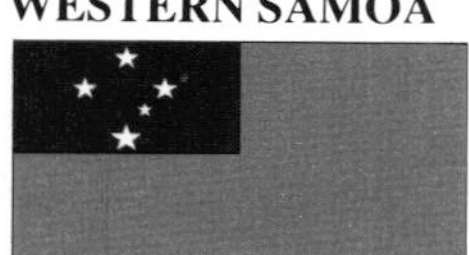

Area: 2831 sq km (1093 sq miles)
Population: 170 000
Capital: Apia
Languages: Samoan, English
Currency: Tala

WORLD ENVIRONMENT

The world can be divided into 8 broad 'climatic zones' (these are areas with a particular sort of weather). The natural types of plants and animals found in each zone are different and depend on the weather the zone has. This map shows which parts of the world are in each zone. The colour of the strip at the top of each zone description (for example, Desert, Rainforest) is the same as the colour used for the zone on the big map. The little map beside each zone description pinpoints where that type of habitat is found in the world. (For example, the Desert strip is orange/yellow. The little sketch map shows you where on the big map to look for this colour. You will find this colour in the north of Africa, the west of North America and in parts of Asia and Australia. All these places have deserts. The description tells you what the natural countryside looks like and what plants and animals live there.)

SCRUB OR MEDITERRANEAN

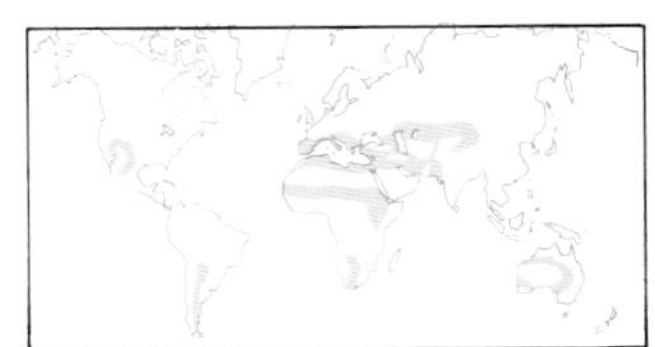 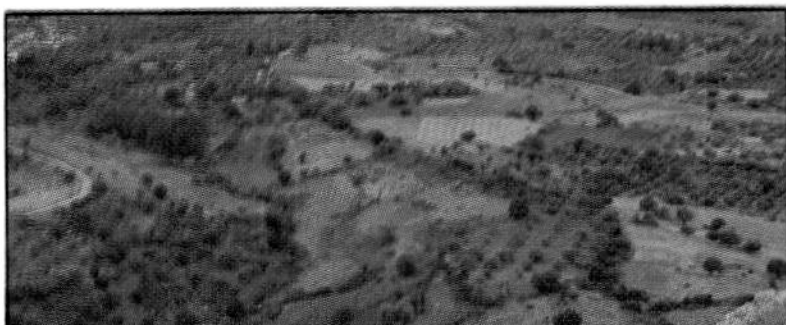

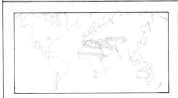

Areas of long, hot, dry summers and short, warm winters. The land used to be covered with trees, but man cleared it for crops and grazed his animals on it. Now there is evergreen scrub – vines and olive trees.

TUNDRA OR MOUNTAIN

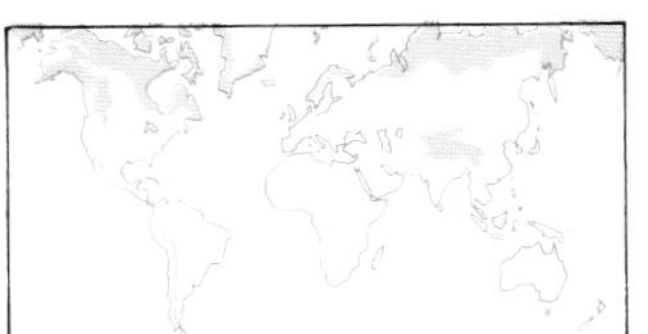 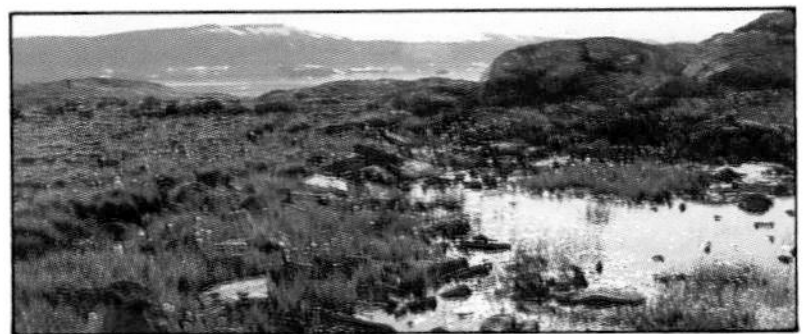

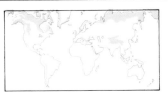

Polar areas which are usually frozen over. During the short summers the top layer of soil thaws, creating vast marshes. Compact, wind-resistant plants and lichens and mosses are found here. Animals include lemmings and reindeer.

NORTHERN FOREST (TAIGA)

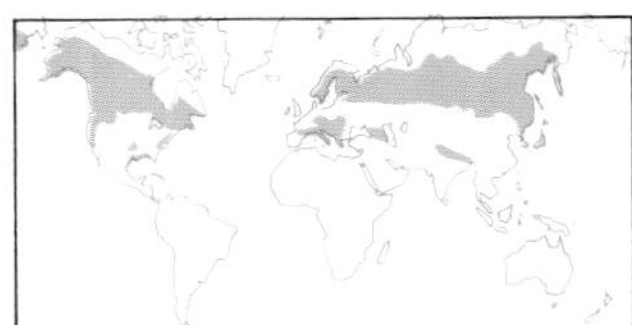 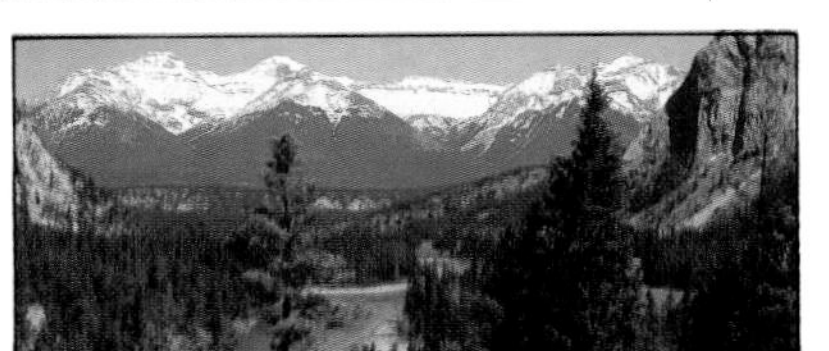

Forests of conifers growing over a large area. Winters are very cold and long. Summers are short. Trees include spruce and fir. Animals found here include beavers, squirrels and red deer.

WOODLAND AND GRASS

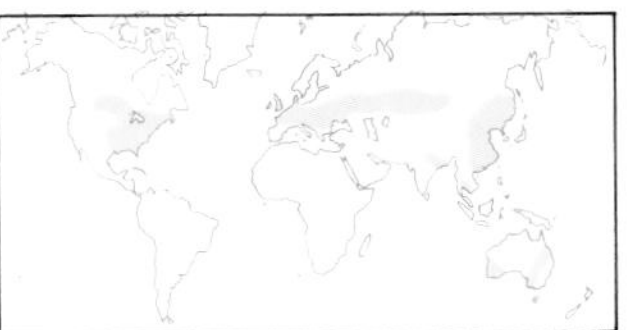 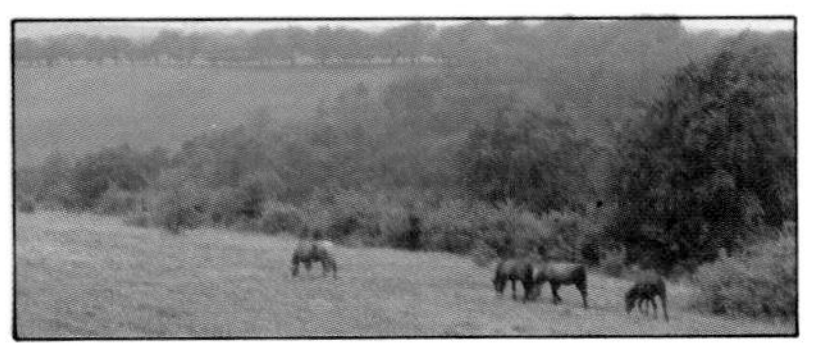

Temperate areas (where the weather is seldom very cold or very hot). Deciduous trees (which lose their leaves in winter) grow in the woodlands. They include oak, beech and maple. Man uses these areas most of all, for farming, building towns and villages, and industry.

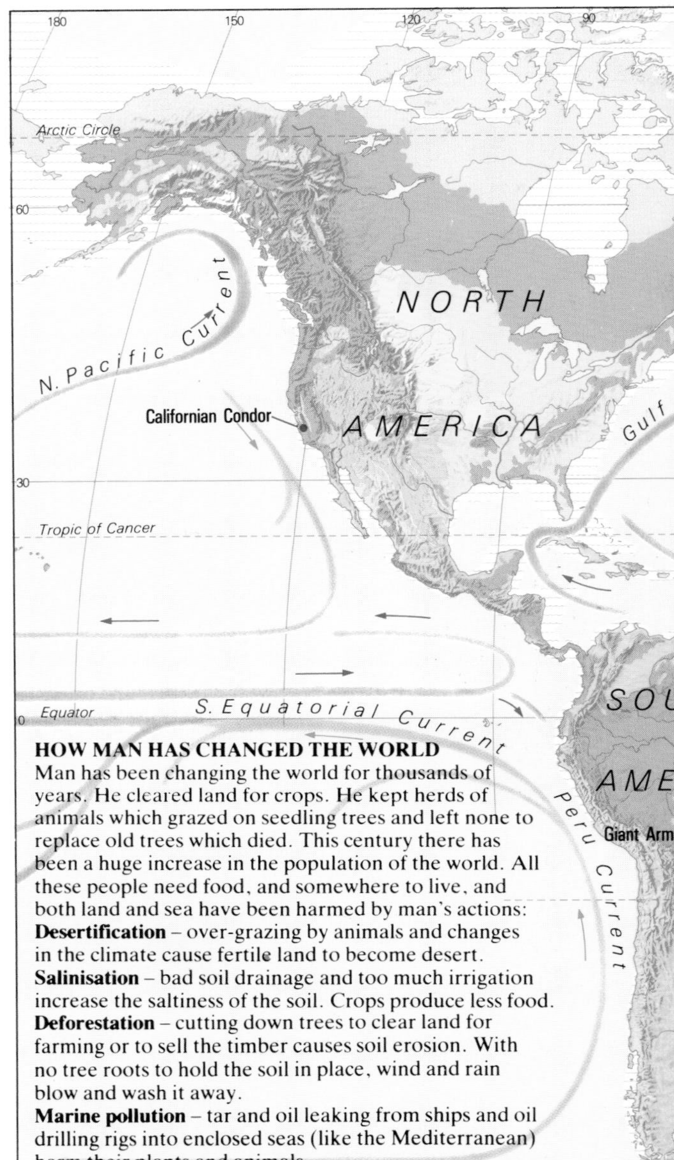

HOW MAN HAS CHANGED THE WORLD
Man has been changing the world for thousands of years. He cleared land for crops. He kept herds of animals which grazed on seedling trees and left none to replace old trees which died. This century there has been a huge increase in the population of the world. All these people need food, and somewhere to live, and both land and sea have been harmed by man's actions:
Desertification – over-grazing by animals and changes in the climate cause fertile land to become desert.
Salinisation – bad soil drainage and too much irrigation increase the saltiness of the soil. Crops produce less food.
Deforestation – cutting down trees to clear land for farming or to sell the timber causes soil erosion. With no tree roots to hold the soil in place, wind and rain blow and wash it away.
Marine pollution – tar and oil leaking from ships and oil drilling rigs into enclosed seas (like the Mediterranean) harm their plants and animals.

GRASSLAND

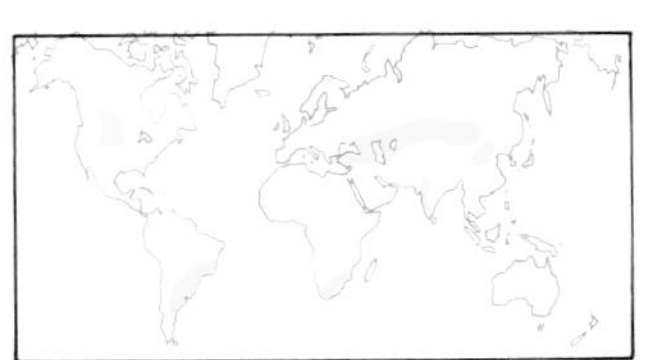 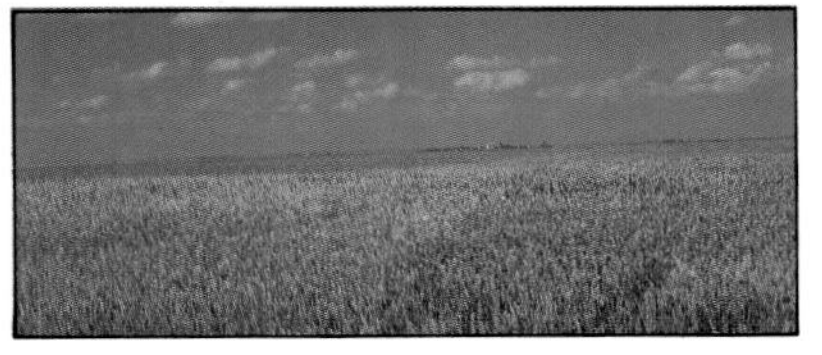

Hot summers, cold winters and moderate rainfall. Huge area of grassland and 'black' (very fertile) soils. Grain crops grow well, and so does rich pasture for beef cattle. Names for this kind of grassland include steppe, veld, pampas and prairie.

SAVANNA

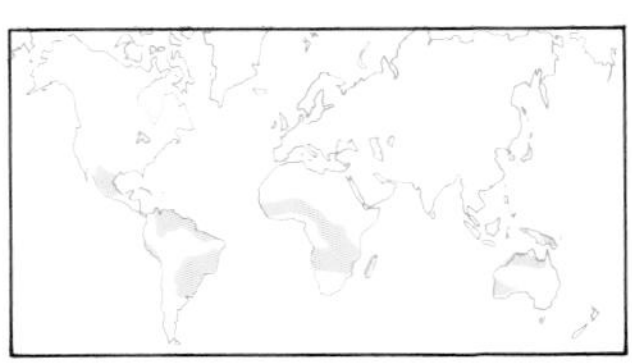 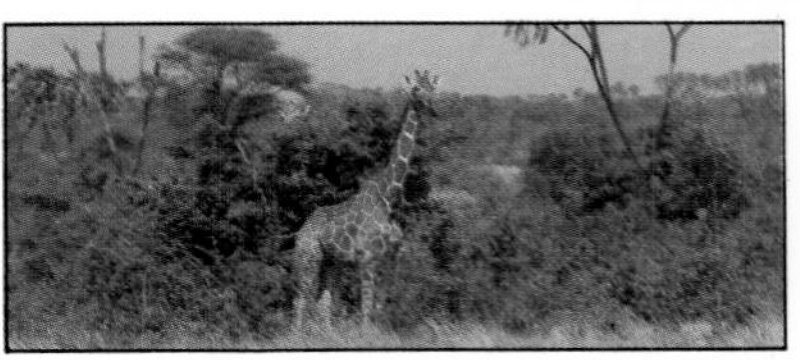

Tall grasses with thick stems, and flat-topped thorny trees grow here. Animals grazing here include giraffes and zebras. There is a short rainy season. Often it does not rain for a long time (a drought). Fires burn the dried out plants but they have adapted to survive this and grow again.

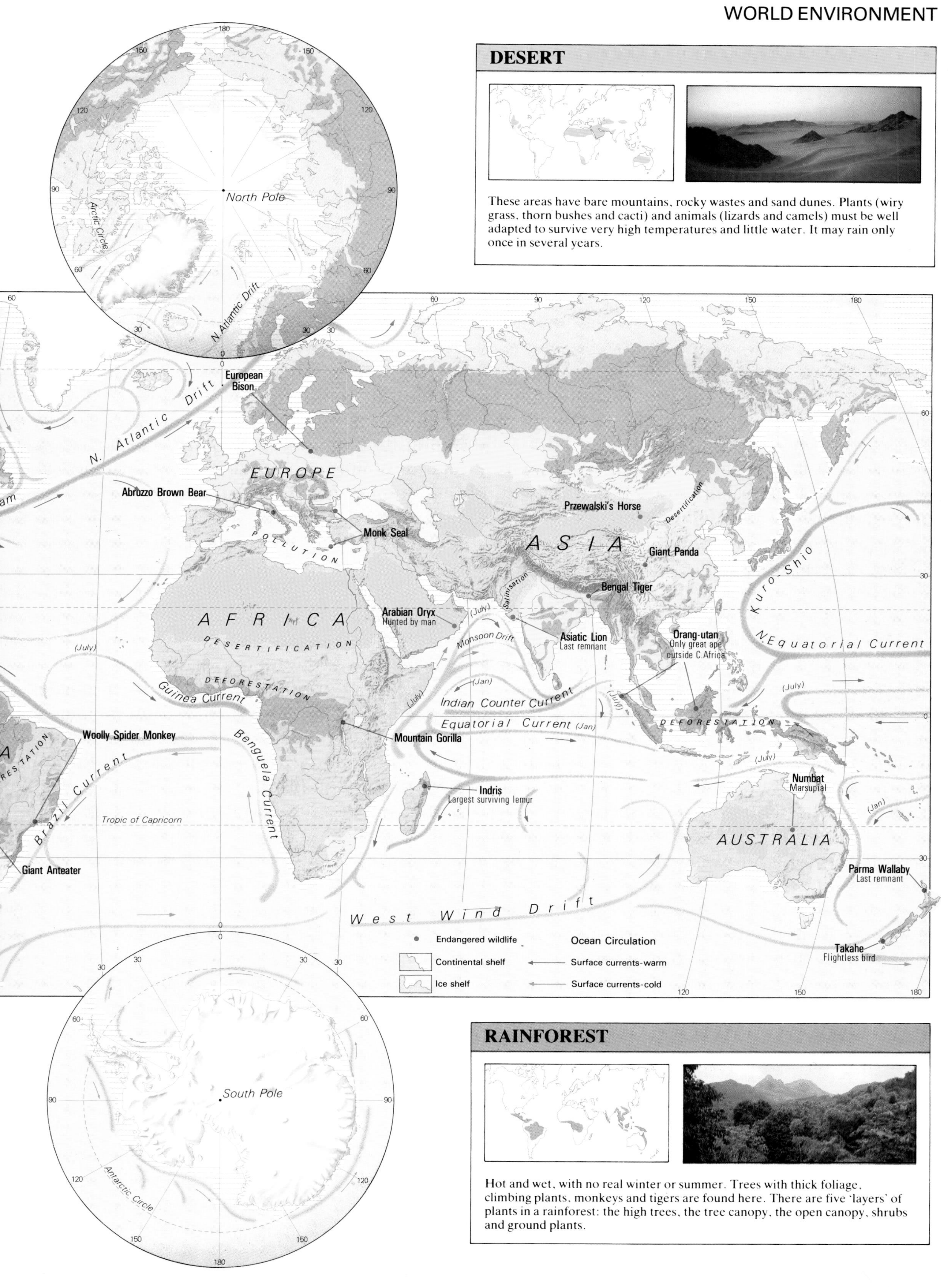

These areas have bare mountains, rocky wastes and sand dunes. Plants (wiry grass, thorn bushes and cacti) and animals (lizards and camels) must be well adapted to survive very high temperatures and little water. It may rain only once in several years.

North Pole

Arctic Circle

N Atlantic Drift

European Bison

N. Atlantic Drift

EUROPE

Abruzzo Brown Bear

Monk Seal

POLLUTION

Przewalski's Horse

Desertification

A S I A

Giant Panda

Bengal Tiger

Kuro-Shio

A F R I C A

DESERTIFICATION

DEFORESTATION

Arabian Oryx
Hunted by man

Salinisation

(July)

Asiatic Lion
Last remnant

Orang-utan
Only great ape outside C.Africa

N Equatorial Current

Guinea Current

Monsoon Drift

(Jan)

Indian Counter Current

Equatorial Current (Jan)

DEFORESTATION

(July)

Woolly Spider Monkey

Benguela Current

Mountain Gorilla

(July)

Numbat
Marsupial

Brazil Current

Indris
Largest surviving lemur

(Jan)

A

ORESTATION

Tropic of Capricorn

AUSTRALIA

Parma Wallaby
Last remnant

Giant Anteater

West Wind Drift

Takahe
Flightless bird

- Endangered wildlife

Ocean Circulation

Continental shelf — Surface currents-warm

Ice shelf — Surface currents-cold

South Pole

Antarctic Circle

Hot and wet, with no real winter or summer. Trees with thick foliage, climbing plants, monkeys and tigers are found here. There are five 'layers' of plants in a rainforest: the high trees, the tree canopy, the open canopy, shrubs and ground plants.

World climate has a profound influence upon mankind. Everything is affected by it, from our environment and ability to grow food to our mobility and health. The most important characteristics of climate are rainfall patterns and temperature variations. As the earth revolves around the sun the tilt of its axis causes each hemisphere in turn to be closer than the other to the sun for half a year. The hemisphere facing the overhead sun enjoys a warm summer season while the other experiences winter. Solar radiation, winds, ocean currents, latitude, altitude and land relief also determine types of climate, examples of which are illustrated by the graphs below.

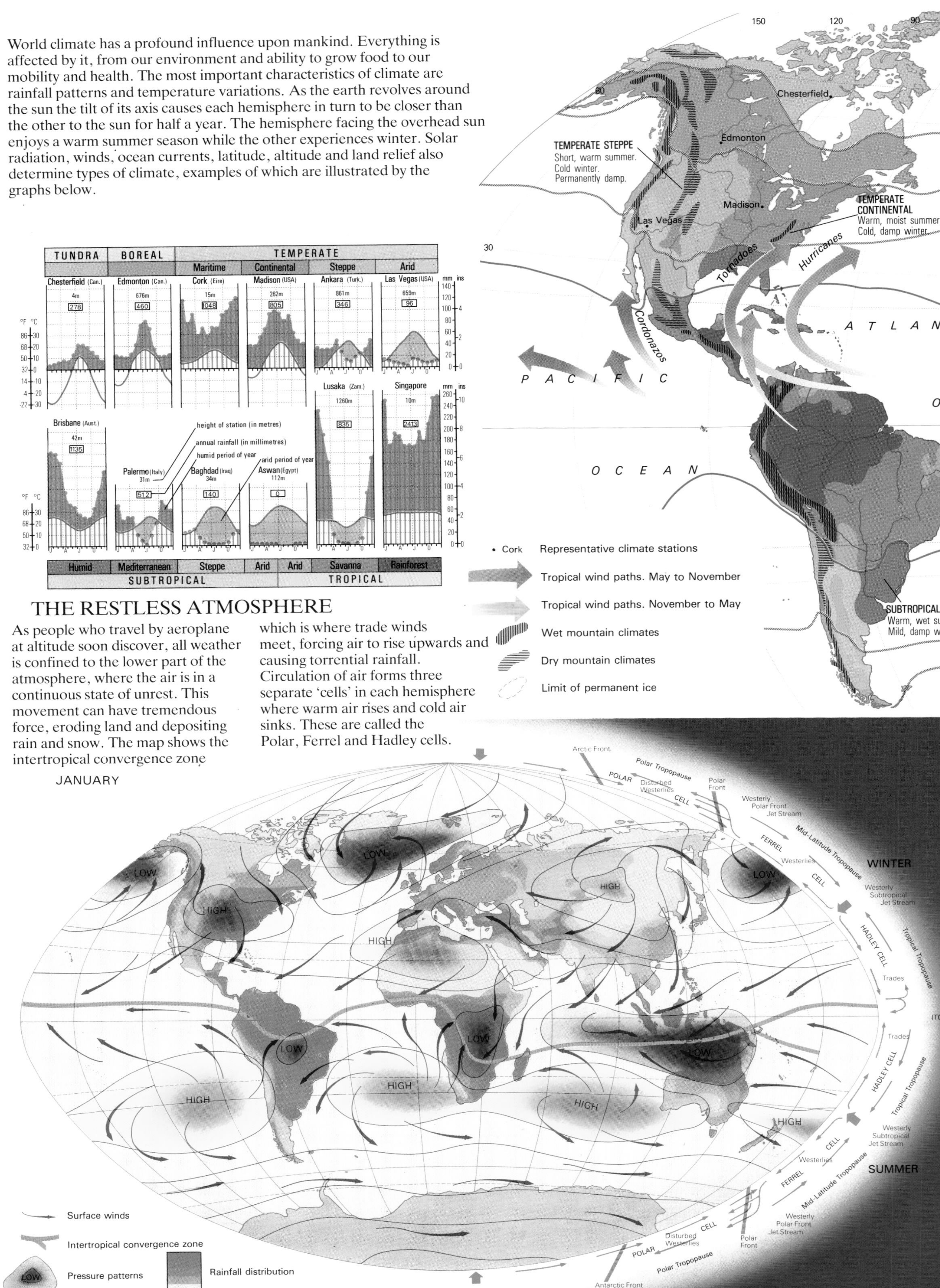

TEMPERATE STEPPE
Short, warm summer. Cold winter. Permanently damp.

TEMPERATE CONTINENTAL
Warm, moist summer. Cold, damp winter.

SUBTROPICAL HU...
Warm, wet summ...
Mild, damp wint...

- Cork — Representative climate stations
- Tropical wind paths. May to November
- Tropical wind paths. November to May
- Wet mountain climates
- Dry mountain climates
- Limit of permanent ice

THE RESTLESS ATMOSPHERE

As people who travel by aeroplane at altitude soon discover, all weather is confined to the lower part of the atmosphere, where the air is in a continuous state of unrest. This movement can have tremendous force, eroding land and depositing rain and snow. The map shows the intertropical convergence zone which is where trade winds meet, forcing air to rise upwards and causing torrential rainfall. Circulation of air forms three separate 'cells' in each hemisphere where warm air rises and cold air sinks. These are called the Polar, Ferrel and Hadley cells.

JANUARY

- Surface winds
- Intertropical convergence zone
- Pressure patterns
- Rainfall distribution

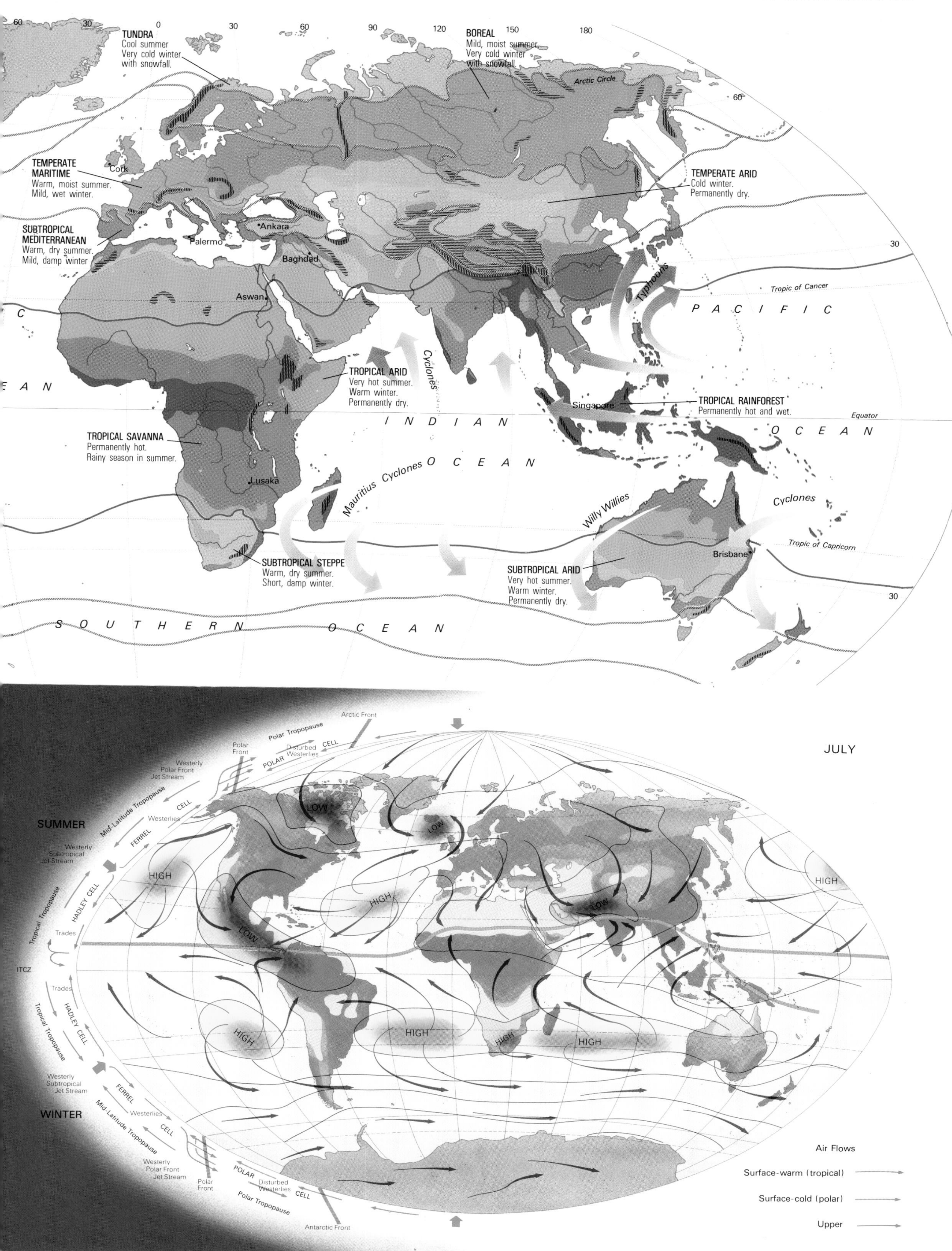

TUNDRA
Cool summer
Very cold winter
with snowfall.

BOREAL
Mild, moist summer
Very cold winter
with snowfall.

Arctic Circle

TEMPERATE MARITIME
Warm, moist summer.
Mild, wet winter.

Cork

TEMPERATE ARID
Cold winter.
Permanently dry.

SUBTROPICAL MEDITERRANEAN
Warm, dry summer.
Mild, damp winter.

•Ankara

Palermo

Baghdad

Aswan•

P A C I F I C

Tropic of Cancer

30

Typhoons

TROPICAL ARID
Very hot summer.
Warm winter.
Permanently dry.

Cyclones

TROPICAL RAINFOREST
Permanently hot and wet.

Singapore

Equator

I N D I A N

O C E A N

TROPICAL SAVANNA
Permanently hot.
Rainy season in summer.

Mauritius Cyclones O C E A N

•Lusaka

Cyclones

Willy Willies

Brisbane•

Tropic of Capricorn

SUBTROPICAL STEPPE
Warm, dry summer.
Short, damp winter.

SUBTROPICAL ARID
Very hot summer.
Warm winter.
Permanently dry.

30

S O U T H E R N   O C E A N

JULY

Arctic Front

Polar Tropopause

Polar Front

Disturbed Westerlies CELL

POLAR

Westerly Polar Front Jet Stream

Mid-Latitude Tropopause

Westerlies CELL

SUMMER

LOW

Westerly Subtropical Jet Stream

LOW

FERREL

HIGH

HADLEY CELL

Tropical Tropopause

HIGH

HIGH

LOW

HIGH

Trades

ITCZ

Trades

LOW

HADLEY CELL

Tropical Tropopause

HIGH

HIGH

HIGH

HIGH

Westerly Subtropical Jet Stream

FERREL

WINTER

Westerlies CELL

Mid-Latitude Tropopause

Westerly Polar Front Jet Stream

Polar Front

Disturbed Westerlies CELL

POLAR

Polar Tropopause

Antarctic Front

Air Flows

Surface-warm (tropical) →

Surface-cold (polar) →

Upper →

CLIMATE INDICATORS

Listed from north to south, is a selection of places from different climate zones of the world (see pp xxiv/xxv, indicating their mean monthly temperatures (in °C and °F) and rainfall (in mm and inches). Also shown are their average temperatures and total rainfall for the year.

REYKJAVIK Iceland 64·1°N 21·9°W *TUNDRA*

	J	F	M	A	M	J	J	A	S	O	N	D	Year
°C	-0·2	0·2	1·5	3·5	6·7	9·7	11·3	10·8	8·5	5·2	3·0	0·4	5·0
°F	32	32	35	38	44	49	52	51	47	41	37	33	41
mm	89	64	62	56	42	42	50	56	67	94	78	79	779
ins	3·5	2·5	2·4	2·2	1·6	1·6	2·0	2·2	2·6	3·7	3·1	3·1	30·7

ANCHORAGE U.S.A. 61·2°N 150·0°W *BOREAL*

	J	F	M	A	M	J	J	A	S	O	N	D	Year
°C	-10·4	-7·6	-4·8	2·0	7·7	12·2	14·1	13·1	8·7	1·8	-5·6	-10·2	1·7
°F	13	18	23	36	46	54	57	56	48	35	22	14	29
mm	20	18	13	11	13	25	47	65	63	47	26	24	372
ins	0·8	0·7	0·5	0·4	0·5	1·0	1·8	2·6	2·5	1·8	1·0	0·9	14·6

STOCKHOLM Sweden 59·3°N 18·1°E *TEMPERATE Continental*

	J	F	M	A	M	J	J	A	S	O	N	D	Year
°C	-3·0	-3·1	-0·5	4·6	10·2	15·0	18·5	16·6	12·3	7·1	2·7	0·0	6·6
°F	27	26	31	40	50	59	65	62	54	45	37	32	44
mm	43	30	25	31	34	45	61	76	60	48	53	48	554
ins	1·7	1·2	1·0	1·2	1·3	1·8	2·4	3·0	2·4	1·9	2·1	1·9	21·8

EDINBURGH U.K. 55·9°N 3·2°W *TEMPERATE Maritime*

	J	F	M	A	M	J	J	A	S	O	N	D	Year
°C	3·3	3·5	5·1	7·4	9·9	12·9	14·8	14·4	12·5	9·4	6·4	4·6	8·6
°F	38	38	41	45	50	55	59	58	54	49	43	40	47
mm	57	39	39	39	54	47	83	77	57	65	62	57	676
ins	2·2	1·5	1·5	1·5	2·1	1·8	3·3	3·0	2·2	2·6	2·4	2·2	26·6

MOSKVA Russian Federation 55·7°N 37·6°E *TEMPERATE Continental*

	J	F	M	A	M	J	J	A	S	O	N	D	Year
°C	-12·7	-9·6	-3·8	5·7	13·3	15·8	17·8	16·9	11·8	5·9	-0·9	-7·0	4·4
°F	9	15	25	42	56	60	64	62	53	43	30	19	40
mm	39	38	36	37	53	58	88	71	58	45	47	54	624
ins	1·5	1·5	1·4	1·5	2·1	2·3	3·5	2·8	2·3	1·8	1·8	2·1	24·6

VANCOUVER Canada 49·2°N 123·2°W *TEMPERATE Maritime*

	J	F	M	A	M	J	J	A	S	O	N	D	Year
°C	2·8	4·1	6·4	9·4	12·6	15·5	17·8	17·2	14·4	10·3	6·3	4·2	10·0
°F	37	39	43	49	55	60	64	63	58	50	43	40	50
mm	214	161	151	90	69	65	39	44	83	172	198	243	1529
ins	8·4	6·3	5·9	3·5	2·7	2·6	1·5	1·7	3·3	6·8	7·8	9·6	60·2

PARIS France 48·8°N 2·3°E *TEMPERATE Maritime*

	J	F	M	A	M	J	J	A	S	O	N	D	Year
°C	3·4	4·3	7·9	11·0	14·6	17·8	19·5	19·1	16·5	11·7	7·2	4·3	11·5
°F	38	40	46	52	58	64	67	66	62	53	45	40	53
mm	56	46	35	42	57	54	59	64	55	50	51	50	619
ins	2·2	1·8	1·4	1·6	2·2	2·1	2·3	2·5	2·2	2·0	2·0	2·0	24·3

BUCUREŞTI Romania 44·5°N 26·0°E *TEMPERATE Steppe*

	J	F	M	A	M	J	J	A	S	O	N	D	Year
°C	-4·2	-1·5	6·2	12·4	17·3	21·2	23·5	22·9	18·2	13·0	6·4	0·6	8·2
°F	24	29	43	54	63	70	74	73	65	55	43	33	47
mm	46	26	28	59	77	121	53	45	45	29	36	27	592
ins	1·8	1·0	1·1	2·3	3·0	4·8	2·1	1·8	1·8	1·1	1·4	1·1	23·4

NEW YORK U.S.A. 40·7°N 74·0°W *TEMPERATE Continental*

	J	F	M	A	M	J	J	A	S	O	N	D	Year
°C	0·7	0·8	4·7	10·5	16·3	21·2	24·1	23·3	19·8	14·3	8·1	2·2	12·2
°F	33	33	40	51	61	70	75	74	68	58	47	36	54
mm	89	74	104	89	91	86	102	119	89	84	89	84	1100
ins	3·5	2·9	4·1	3·5	3·6	3·4	4·0	4·7	3·5	3·3	3·5	3·3	43·3

TŌKYŌ Japan 35·7°N 139·8°E *TEMPERATE Continental*

	J	F	M	A	M	J	J	A	S	O	N	D	Year
°C	3·3	4·2	7·2	12·5	16·9	20·8	24·7	26·1	22·5	16·7	10·8	5·8	14·4
°F	38	40	45	54	62	69	76	79	72	62	51	42	58
mm	48	74	107	135	147	165	142	152	234	208	96	56	1565
ins	1·9	2·9	4·2	5·3	5·8	6·5	5·6	6·0	9·2	8·2	3·8	2·2	61·6

TANGER Morocco 35·8°N 5·8°W *SUBTROPICAL Mediterranean*

	J	F	M	A	M	J	J	A	S	O	N	D	Year
°C	11·9	12·5	13·6	14·4	17·2	20·0	22·2	23·0	21·4	18·6	14·7	12·4	16·7
°F	53	54	56	58	63	68	72	73	70	65	58	54	62
mm	114	107	122	89	43	15	2	2	23	99	147	137	897
ins	4·5	4·2	4·8	3·5	1·7	0·6	0·1	0·1	0·9	3·9	5·8	5·4	35·3

JERUSALEM Israel 31·8°N 35·2°E *SUBTROPICAL Steppe*

	J	F	M	A	M	J	J	A	S	O	N	D	Year
°C	8·9	9·4	13·0	16·4	20·5	22·5	23·9	24·1	23·0	21·1	16·4	11·1	17·2
°F	48	49	55	61	69	72	75	75	73	70	61	52	63
mm	132	132	63	28	2	1	0	0	1	13	71	87	528
ins	5·2	5·2	2·5	1·1	0·1	0·1	0·0	0·0	0·1	0·5	2·8	3·4	20·8

NEW ORLEANS U.S.A. 30·0°N 90·2°W *SUBTROPICAL Humid*

	J	F	M	A	M	J	J	A	S	O	N	D	Year
°C	12·5	13·9	16·3	19·9	23·5	26·7	27·6	27·7	25·7	21·3	15·5	13·0	20·3
°F	54	57	61	68	74	80	82	82	78	70	60	55	68
mm	97	102	135	114	112	112	170	135	127	71	84	104	1363
ins	3·8	4·0	5·3	4·5	4·4	4·4	6·7	5·3	5·0	2·8	3·3	4·1	53·7

BAHRAIN 26·2°N 50·5°E *SUBTROPICAL Arid*

	J	F	M	A	M	J	J	A	S	O	N	D	Year
°C	16·9	18·0	20·5	25·0	29·4	31·7	33·3	33·6	31·4	28·0	24·2	18·6	25·8
°F	62	64	69	77	85	89	92	92	88	82	75	65	78
mm	8	18	13	8	1	0	0	0	0	0	18	18	79
ins	0·3	0·7	0·5	0·3	0·1	0·0	0·0	0·0	0·0	0·0	0·7	0·7	3·2

HONG KONG 22·3°N 114·2°E *SUBTROPICAL Humid*

	J	F	M	A	M	J	J	A	S	O	N	D	Year
°C	15·5	15·0	17·5	21·7	25·5	27·5	28·0	28·0	27·2	25·0	20·8	17·5	22·5
°F	60	59	63	71	78	81	82	82	81	77	69	63	72
mm	33	46	74	137	292	394	381	361	256	114	43	30	2161
ins	1·3	1·8	2·9	5·4	11·5	15·5	15·0	14·2	10·1	4·5	1·7	1·2	85·1

MIAMI U.S.A. 25·8°N 80·3°W *TROPICAL Savanna*

	J	F	M	A	M	J	J	A	S	O	N	D	Year
°C	19·3	19·9	21·4	23·4	25·3	27·1	27·6	27·9	27·4	25·4	22·4	20·1	23·9
°F	67	68	70	74	77	81	82	82	81	78	72	68	75
mm	51	48	58	99	163	188	170	178	241	208	71	43	1518
ins	2·0	1·9	2·3	3·9	6·4	7·4	6·7	7·0	9·5	8·2	2·8	1·7	59·8

BANGKOK Thailand 13·7°N 100·5°E *TROPICAL Savanna*

	J	F	M	A	M	J	J	A	S	O	N	D	Year
°C	25·8	27·5	28·9	30·0	29·4	28·6	28·3	28·3	28·0	27·5	26·4	25·3	27·7
°F	78	81	84	86	85	83	83	83	82	81	79	77	82
mm	8	20	36	58	198	160	160	175	305	206	66	5	1397
ins	0·3	0·8	1·4	2·3	7·8	6·3	6·3	6·9	12·0	8·1	2·6	0·2	55·0

COLOMBO Sri Lanka 6·9°N 79·9°E *TROPICAL Rainforest*

	J	F	M	A	M	J	J	A	S	O	N	D	Year
°C	26·1	26·4	27·2	27·7	28·0	27·2	27·2	27·2	27·2	26·6	26·1	25·8	26·9
°F	79	80	81	82	82	81	81	81	81	80	79	78	80
mm	89	69	147	231	371	223	135	109	160	348	315	147	2344
ins	3·5	2·7	5·8	9·1	14·6	8·8	5·3	4·3	6·3	13·7	12·4	5·8	92·3

NAIROBI Kenya 1·3°S 36·8°E *TROPICAL Savanna*

	J	F	M	A	M	J	J	A	S	O	N	D	Year
°C	18·6	19·4	19·4	19·2	17·7	16·4	15·5	16·1	17·5	18·6	18·3	18·0	18·0
°F	65	67	67	67	64	61	60	61	63	65	65	64	64
mm	38	63	124	211	157	46	15	23	30	53	109	86	958
ins	1·5	2·5	4·9	8·3	6·2	1·8	0·6	0·9	1·2	2·1	4·3	3·4	37·7

LIMA Peru 12·1°S 77·0°W *TROPICAL Arid*

	J	F	M	A	M	J	J	A	S	O	N	D	Year
°C	23·3	23·8	23·6	21·9	19·4	17·2	16·7	16·1	16·9	18·0	19·4	21·1	20·0
°F	74	75	74	71	67	63	62	61	62	64	67	70	68
mm	1	1	1	1	5	5	8	8	8	2	2	1	41
ins	0·1	0·1	0·1	0·1	0·2	0·2	0·3	0·3	0·3	0·1	0·1	0·1	1·6

RIO DE JANEIRO Brazil 22·9°S 43·2°W *TROPICAL Savanna*

	J	F	M	A	M	J	J	A	S	O	N	D	Year
°C	25·8	26·1	25·3	23·6	21·9	21·1	20·5	21·1	21·1	21·9	23·0	24·7	23·0
°F	78	79	77	74	71	70	69	70	70	71	73	76	73
mm	124	122	130	107	79	53	41	43	66	79	104	137	1085
ins	4·9	4·8	5·1	4·2	3·1	2·1	1·6	1·7	2·6	3·1	4·1	5·4	42·6

JOHANNESBURG S. Africa 26·2°S 28·1°E *SUBTROPICAL Steppe*

	J	F	M	A	M	J	J	A	S	O	N	D	Year
°C	20·0	19·7	18·3	16·1	12·5	10·3	10·5	13·0	15·8	18·3	18·9	19·7	16·1
°F	68	67	65	61	54	50	51	55	60	65	66	67	61
mm	114	109	89	38	25	8	8	8	23	56	107	124	709
ins	4·5	4·3	3·5	1·5	1·0	0·3	0·3	0·3	0·9	2·2	4·2	4·9	27·9

PERTH Australia 31·9°S 115·8°E *SUBTROPICAL Mediterranean*

	J	F	M	A	M	J	J	A	S	O	N	D	Year
°C	23·3	23·3	21·7	19·2	16·1	13·9	13·0	13·3	14·7	16·4	19·2	21·7	17·8
°F	74	74	71	66	61	57	55	56	58	61	66	71	64
mm	8	10	20	43	130	180	170	145	86	56	20	13	881
ins	0·3	0·4	0·8	1·7	5·1	7·1	6·7	5·7	3·4	2·2	0·8	0·5	34·7

WELLINGTON New Zealand 41·3°S 174·8°E *TEMPERATE Maritime*

	J	F	M	A	M	J	J	A	S	O	N	D	Year
°C	16·9	16·9	15·8	13·9	11·4	9·7	8·6	9·2	10·8	12·2	13·6	15·8	12·8
°F	62	62	60	57	52	49	47	48	51	54	56	60	55
mm	81	81	81	97	117	117	137	117	97	102	89	89	1205
ins	3·2	3·2	3·2	3·8	4·6	4·6	5·4	4·6	3·8	4·0	3·5	3·5	47·4

Civilisation depends on trade for growth and travel makes this possible. Shipping is the most important method of world transport but economic progress and moblity are constantly being improved by the development of new routes and new modes of transport.

ROAD AND RAIL

Integrated road and rail networks are the basis of industrial society. Extended highway systems and improved containerisation techniques have made the whole road and rail system much more flexible.

Roads – comparative lengths (Log scale)

68 / 277	(24) USA 6366
49 / 23	(1) India 1604
16 / 115	(7) Brazil 1399
296 / 95	(34) Japan 1118
9 / 9	(1) China 890
9 / 367	(14) Canada 884
11 / 552	(9) Australia 817
146 / 149	(27) France 803
28 / 24	(11) Russian Federation 620
172 / 78	(54) Germany 613
154 / 63	(49) UK 353
96 / 83	(10) Poland 299
98 / 51	(64) Italy 294
7 / 74	(20) Argentina 208 —(000's km)

Network Densities

( ) Vehicles/km of road

— Motorways (bar length = 1% of network)

High	Medium	Low

km/100km^2
100km/million popl.
km/100km^2

3 / 8	UK 18 —(000's km)
4 / 7	Italy 20
7 / 8	Poland 24
2 / 7	Japan 26
3 / 0·4	Brazil 31
6 / 6	France 34
12 / 2	Argentina 35
27 / 0·5	Australia 40
5 / 13	Germany 41
1 / 0·5	China 50
1 / 2	India 61
28 / 7	Canada 68
6 / 0·5	Russian Federation 86
14 / 3	USA 320

Railways – comparative lengths (Log scale)

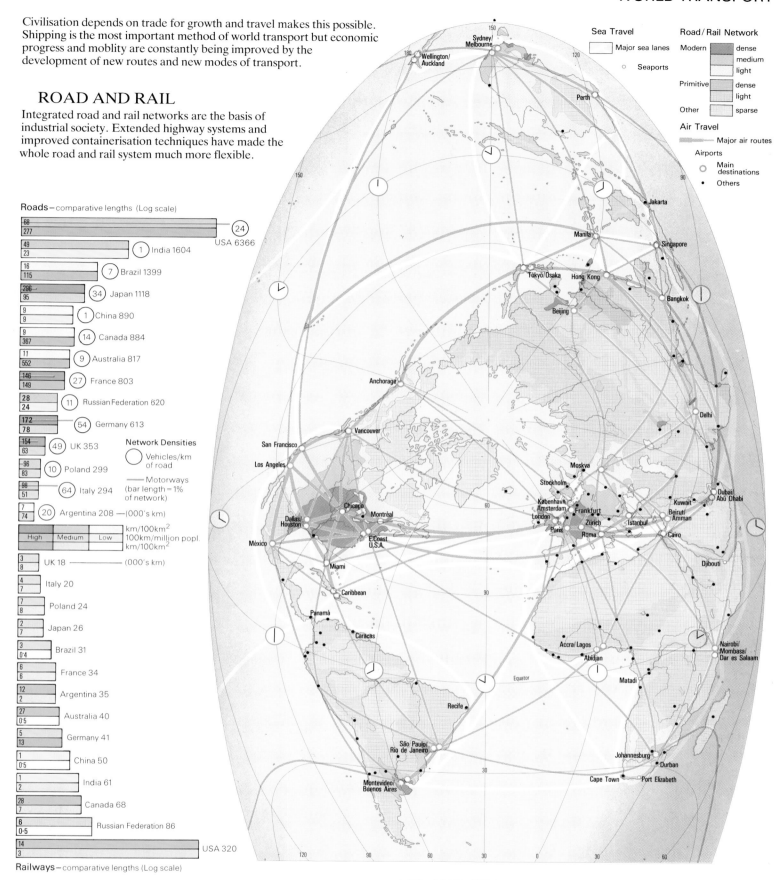

Sea Travel
□ Major sea lanes
○ Seaports

Road / Rail Network
Modern	dense
	medium
	light
Primitive	dense
	light
Other	sparse

Air Travel
— Major air routes

Airports
○ Main destinations
• Others

JOURNEY TIME

The Suez canal cuts 3600 miles off the London-Singapore route, while Concorde halves the London-New York journey time.

AIR AND SEA ROUTES

A complex network of primary air routes centred on the Northern Hemisphere provides rapid transit across the world for mass travel, mail and urgent freight. Ships also follow these principal routes, plying the oceans between major ports and transporting the commodities of world trade in bulk.

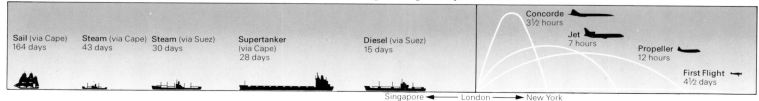

Sail (via Cape) 164 days
Steam (via Cape) 43 days
Steam (via Suez) 30 days
Supertanker (via Cape) 28 days
Diesel (via Suez) 15 days

Concorde 3½ hours
Jet 7 hours
Propeller 12 hours
First Flight 4½ days

Singapore ◄— London —► New York

1:60M

600   1200   1800   2400 km
600   1200 mils

Barents Sea

Norwegian Basin

Arctic Circle

ICELAND

North Sea

Sea of Okhotsk

Sakhalin

EUROPE

ASIA

Black Sea

Caspian Sea

Aral Sea

Sea of Japan

Vityaz Depth 10542

Kuril Trench

JAPAN

Mediterranean Sea

Red Sea

The Gulf

Chang Jiang

Huang He

S. Honshu Ridge

Japan Trench

Ganga

TAIWAN

Kyushu-Palau Ridge

Arabian Sea

Bay of Bengal

Hainan

Mariana Trench

Raas Caseyr

Arabian Basin

Andaman Is

SRI LANKA (CEYLON)

Mekong

South China Sea

PHILIPPINES

Mariana Is

Guam

MICRO

MADIVES

Nicobar Is

Philippine Trench

C. Johnson Depth 10497

11022 Challenger Depth

AFRICA

Carlsberg Ridge

Maldives Ridge

Belau

Caroline Is

Somali Basin

Celebes Sea

6920

MEL

SEYCHELLES

Mascarene Ridge

Chagos Arch.

Borneo

Celebes

INDONESIA

New Guinea

Planet Deep 9140

COMOROS

Mid Indian Basin

Ninety-East Ridge

Java

Java Trench

7450

Timor

Arafura Sea

INDIAN

MADAGASCAR

Mid-Indian Ridge

West Australian Basin

Cocos Is

Christmas I.

1737

Coral Sea Basin

Réunion

MAURITIUS

OCEAN

1924

Tropic of Capricorn

S. Madagascar Ridge

Madagascar Basin

AUSTRALIA

Natal Basin

2067

W. Australian Ridge

C. Agulhas

South West Indian Ridge

1198

7102

South Australia Basin

Tas

Agulhas Plateau

Crozet Basin

I. Amsterdam
I. St Paul

Indian-Antarctic Ridge

Tasmania

Agulhas Basin

Îs Crozet

Sea

Pr. Edward Is

Kerguelen Ridge

Îs Kerguelen

1922

Macquarie I.

Atlantic-Indian Ridge

Heard I.

Atlantic-Indian Antarctic Basin

Banzare Seamount 186

Indian-Antarctic Basin

ANTARCTICA

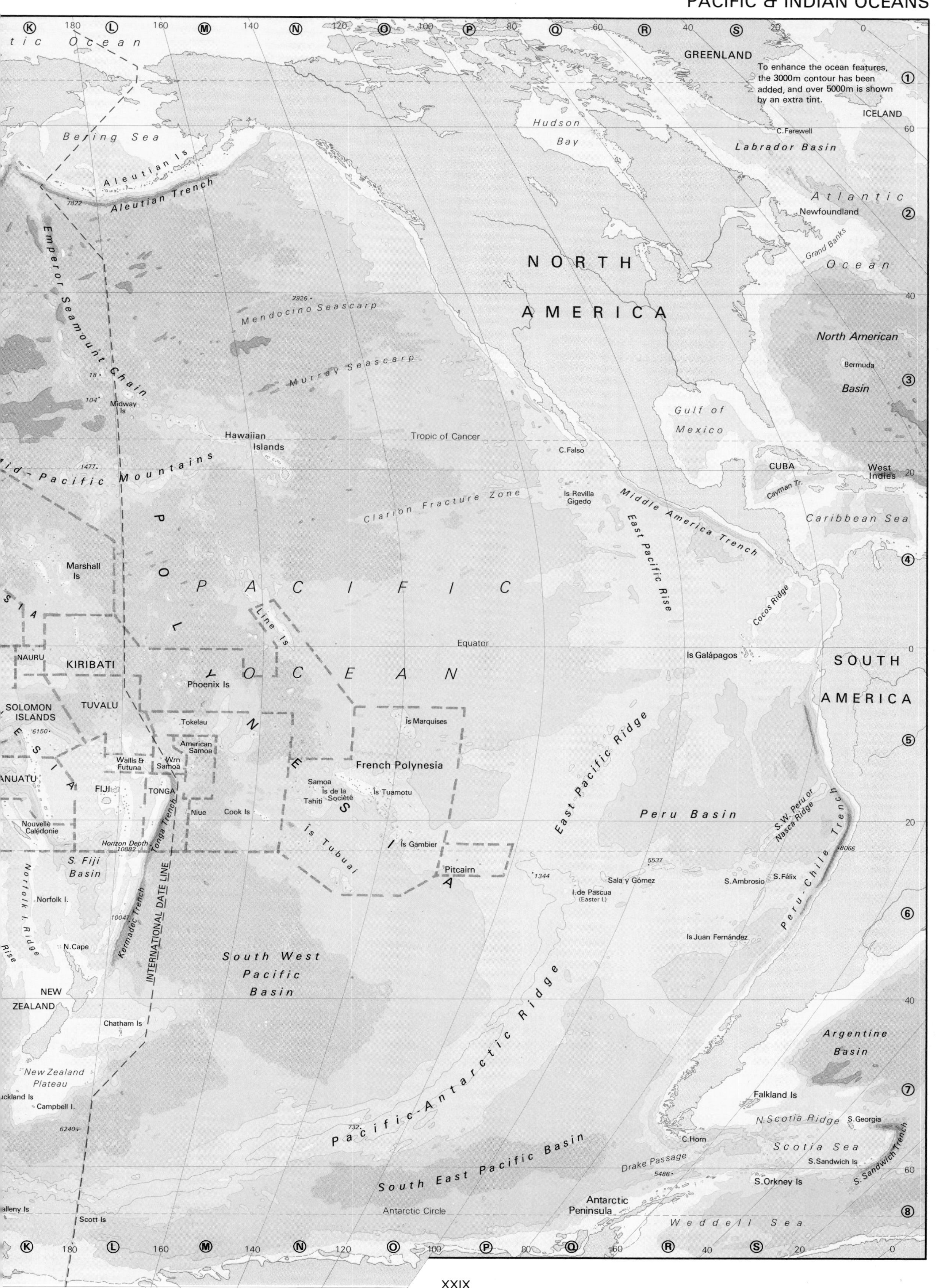

To enhance the ocean features, the 3000m contour has been added, and over 5000m is shown by an extra tint.

GREENLAND

ICELAND

C.Farewell   60

Hudson
Bay   Labrador Basin

Atlantic

Bering Sea   Newfoundland

Aleutian Is
Aleutian Trench   Grand Banks   Ocean

7822   NORTH   40

Emperor Seamount Chain   2926·   AMERICA   North American
                      Mendocino Seascarp
                                                                                Bermuda
18·   Murray Seascarp   Basin
104·   Midway
        Is   Gulf of
1477·   Hawaiian Islands   Tropic of Cancer   C.Falso   Mexico   West
Mid-Pacific Mountains   CUBA   Indies   20
                                      Clarion Fracture Zone   Is Revilla   Cayman Tr.
                                                             Gigedo   Middle America Trench Caribbean Sea

P   Marshall   East Pacific Rise   Cocos Ridge
O   Is
L   PACIFIC   Is Galápagos   0
NAURU Y   Equator   SOUTH
KIRIBATI N   AMERICA
        E OCEAN
Phoenix Is   Ìs Marquises
SOLOMON S   5
ISLANDS TUVALU   Tokelau
6150·   American   French Polynesia   East Pacific Ridge
     Wallis &   Samoa
ANUATU Futuna Wrn   Samoa   Peru Basin   S.W. Peru or
     FIJI   Samoa   Ìs de la Société   Ìs Tuamotu   Nasca Ridge   Peru-Chile Trench
            TONGA   Niue Cook Is Tahiti
Nouvelle   I Ìs Gambier   5537   20
Calédonie   Horizon Depth   Ìs Tubuai   1344   Sala y Gómez   S.Ambrosio S.Félix
Norfolk I.   10882   Pitcairn   I.de Pascua
Ridge S. Fiji   A   (Easter I.)
Basin Norfolk I.   Is Juan Fernández
Rise   10047   6
        N.Cape   Peru-Chile Trench   8066
NEW   South West
ZEALAND   Chatham Is   Pacific   40
                       Basin   Pacific-Antarctic Ridge   Argentine
New Zealand   Basin
Plateau
uckland Is   Falkland Is   7
Campbell I.   N.Scotia Ridge S.Georgia
6240·   732·   C.Horn   Scotia Sea
                         Pacific-Antarctic Ridge   S.Sandwich Is   S.Sandwich Trench
                                            South East Pacific Basin   Drake Passage   S.Orkney Is   60
alleny Is   5486·
Scott Is   Antarctic Circle   Antarctic   Weddell Sea   8
                                          Peninsula

INTERNATIONAL DATE LINE
Kermadec Trench
Tonga Trench
Line Is
POLYNESIA
MELANESIA

1:60M

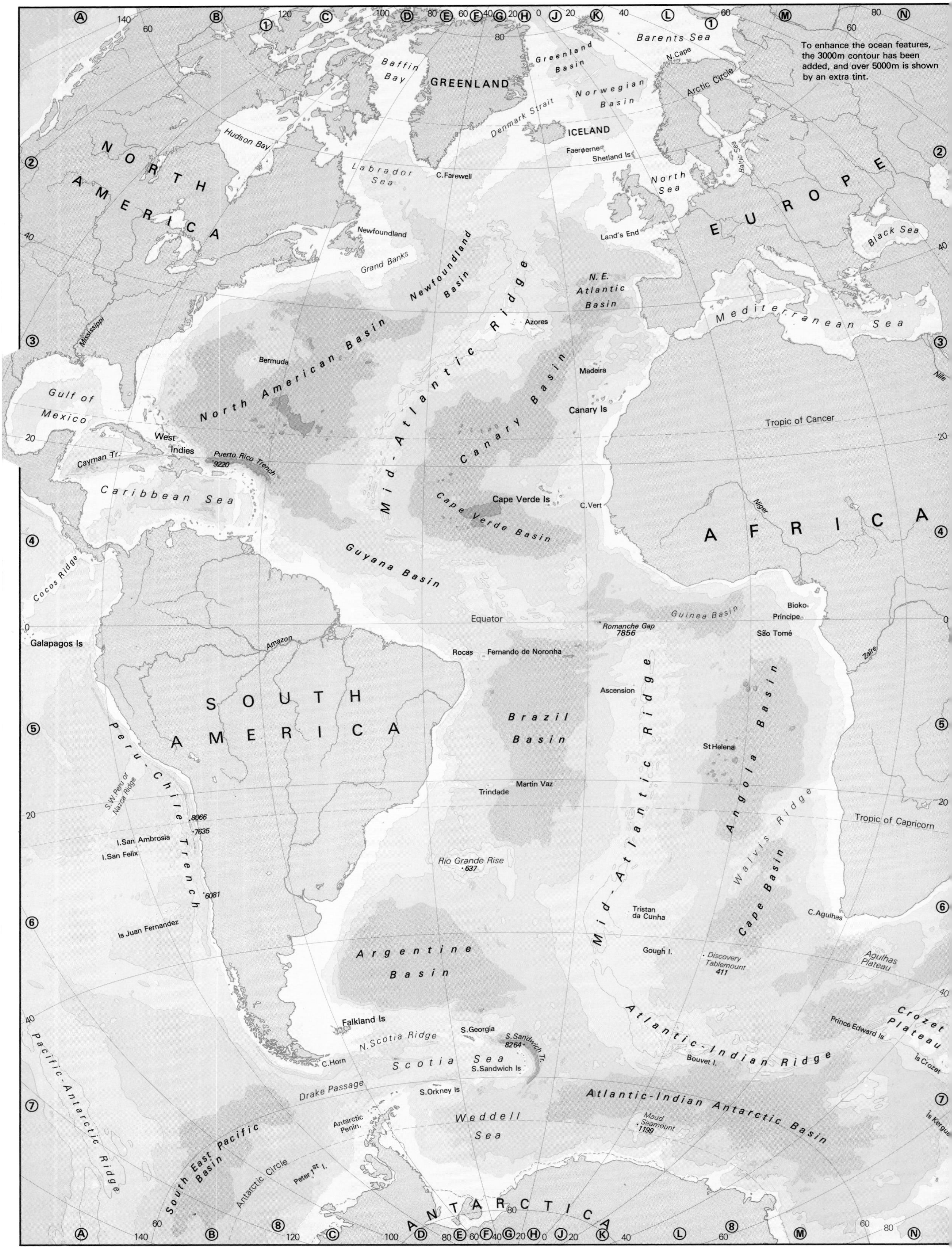

600   1200   1800   2400 km
600   1200 mls

To enhance the ocean features,
the 3000m contour has been
added, and over 5000m is shown
by an extra tint.

NORTH AMERICA

SOUTH AMERICA

EUROPE

AFRICA

ANTARCTICA

GREENLAND

ICELAND

Baffin Bay
Greenland Basin
Barents Sea
N. Cape
Arctic Circle
Norwegian Basin
Denmark Strait
Hudson Bay
Labrador Sea
C. Farewell
Faeroerne
Shetland Is
North Sea
Baltic Sea
Black Sea
Land's End
Newfoundland
Grand Banks
Newfoundland Basin
Mid-Atlantic Ridge
Azores
N.E. Atlantic Basin
Mediterranean Sea
Mississippi
North American Basin
Bermuda
Madeira
Tropic of Cancer
Gulf of Mexico
West Indies
Cayman Tr.
Puerto Rico Trench 9220
Canary Basin
Canary Is
C. Vert
Nile
Caribbean Sea
Cape Verde Basin
Cape Verde Is
Cocos Ridge
Guyana Basin
Niger
AFRICA
Galapagos Is
Equator
Amazon
Rocas
Fernando de Noronha
Romanche Gap 7856
Guinea Basin
Bioko
Príncipe
São Tomé
Zaïre
Ascension
Brazil Basin
Mid-Atlantic Ridge
Angola Basin
Peru-Chile Trench
S.W. Peru or Nazca Ridge
St Helena
8066
7635
I. San Ambrosia
I. San Felix
Martin Vaz
Trindade
Tropic of Capricorn
6081
Rio Grande Rise 637
Walvis Ridge
Cape Basin
C. Agulhas
Is Juan Fernandez
Tristan da Cunha
Gough I.
Discovery Tablemount 411
Agulhas Plateau
Argentine Basin
Crozet Plateau
Falkland Is
N. Scotia Ridge
S. Georgia
S. Sandwich Tr. 8264
Atlantic-Indian Ridge
Prince Edward Is
Is Crozet
C. Horn
Scotia Sea
S. Sandwich Is
Bouvet I.
Is Kergue
Drake Passage
S. Orkney Is
Atlantic-Indian Antarctic Basin
Pacific-Antarctic Ridge
Antarctic Penin.
Weddell Sea
Maud Seamount 1199
South East Pacific Basin
Antarctic Circle
Peter I st I.

MOUNTAIN HEIGHTS

Metres	Feet		Metres	Feet	
8848	29 028	Everest (Qomolangma Feng) *Nepal-Tibet*	6870	22 541	Bonete *Bolivia*
8611	28 250	K2 (Godwin Austen) *Kashmir-Sinkiang*	6800	22 310	Tupungato *Argentina-Chile*
8586	28 168	Kangchenjunga *Nepal-India*	6770	22 211	Mercedario *Argentina*
8475	27 805	Makalu *Tibet-Nepal*	6768	22 205	Huascarán *Peru*
8172	26 810	Dhaulagiri *Nepal*	6723	22 057	Llullaillaco *Argentina-Chile*
8126	26 660	Nanga Parbat *Kashmir*	6714	22 028	Kangrinboqê Feng (Kailas) *Tibet*
8078	26 504	Annapurna *Nepal*	6634	21 765	Yerupaja *Peru*
8068	26 470	Gasherbrum *Kashmir*	6542	21 463	Sajama *Bolivia*
8013	26 291	Xixabangma Feng (Gosainthan) *Tibet*	6485	21 276	Illampu *Bolivia*
7890	25 885	Distaghil Sar *Kashmir*	6425	21 079	Coropuna *Peru*
7820	25 656	Masherbrum *Kashmir*	6402	21 004	Illimani *Bolivia*
7817	25 645	Nanda Devi *India*	6388	20 958	Ancohuma *Bolivia*
7780	25 550	Rakaposhi *Kashmir*	6310	20 702	Chimborazo *Ecuador*
7756	25 447	Kamet *India-Tibet*	6194	20 320	McKinley *USA*
7756	25 447	Namcha Barwa *Tibet*	6050	19 850	Logan *Canada*
7728	25 355	Gurla Mandhata *Tibet*	5895	19 340	Kilimanjaro *Tanzania*
7723	25 338	Muztag (Ulugh Muztagh) *Sinkiang*	5700	18 700	Citlaltepetl *Mexico*
7719	25 325	Kongur Shan (Kungur) *Sinkiang*	5642	18 510	El'bruz *Russian Federation*
7690	25 230	Tirich Mir *Pakistan*	5452	17 887	Popocatepetl *Mexico*
7590	24 903	Gongga Shan (Minya Konka) *China*	5200	17 058	Kirinyaga (Kenya) *Kenya*
7546	24 757	Muztagata (Muztagh Ata) *Sinkiang*	5165	16 946	Ararat *Turkey*
7495	24 590	Pik Kommunizma *Tajikistan*	5140	16 864	Vinson Massif *Antarctica*
7439	24 407	Pik Pobedy (Tomur Feng) *Kirgizia-Sinkiang*	5110	16 763	Stanley *Zaire-Uganda*
7313	23 993	Chomo Lhari *Bhutan-Tibet*	5030	16 500	Jaya (Carstensz) *Indonesia*
7134	23 406	Pik Lenina *Kirgizia-Tajikistan*	4810	15 781	Mont Blanc *France*
6960	22 834	Aconcagua *Argentina*	4508	14 790	Wilhelm *Papua New Guinea*
6908	22 664	Ojos del Salado *Chile-Argentina*	4201	13 784	Mauna Kea *USA*

RIVER LENGTHS

Km	Miles		Km	Miles	
6695	4160	Nile *Africa*	2850	1770	Danube *Europe*
6570	4080	Amazon *South America*	2820	1750	Salween *Asia*
6380	3964	Yangtze *Asia*	2780	1730	São Francisco *South America*
6020	3740	Mississippi-Missouri *North America*	2655	1650	Zambezi *Africa*
5410	3360	Ob-Irtysh *Asia*	2570	1600	Nelson-Saskatchewan *North America*
4840	3010	Huang He (Yellow River) *Asia*	2510	1560	Ganges *Asia*
4630	2880	Zaïre (Congo) *Africa*	2430	1510	Euphrates *Asia*
4500	2796	Paraná *South America*	2330	1450	Arkansas *North America*
4440	2760	Irtysh *Asia*	2330	1450	Colorado *North America*
4416	2745	Amur *Asia*	2285	1420	Dnepr *Europe*
4400	2730	Lena *Asia*	2090	1300	Irrawaddy *Asia*
4240	2630	Mackenzie *North America*	2060	1280	Orinoco *South America*
4180	2600	Mekong *Asia*	2000	1240	Negro *South America*
4100	2550	Niger *Africa*	1870	1160	Don *Europe*
4090	2540	Yenisey *Asia*	1859	1155	Orange *Africa*
3969	2466	Missouri *North America*	1799	1118	Pechora *Europe*
3779	2348	Mississippi *North America*	1609	1000	Marañón *South America*
3750	2330	Murray-Darling *Australia*	1410	876	Dnestr *Europe*
3688	2292	Volga *Europe*	1320	820	Rhine *Europe*
3240	2013	Madeira *South America*	1183	735	Donets *Europe*
3058	1900	St. Lawrence *North America*	1159	720	Elbe *Europe*
3030	1880	Rio Grande *North America*	1094	680	Gambia *Africa*
3020	1870	Yukon *North America*	1080	671	Yellowstone *North America*
2960	1840	Brahmaputra *Asia*	1014	630	Vistula *Europe*
2896	1800	Indus *Asia*	1006	625	Tagus *Europe*

LAKE AND INLAND SEA AREAS

Areas are average and some are subject to seasonal variations.

Sq. Km	Sq. Miles		Sq. Km	Sq. Miles	
371 000	142 240	Caspian *Central Asia (salt)*	22 490	8680	Nyasa (Malawi) *Malawi-Mozambique*
82 900	32 010	Superior *USA-Canada*	19 400	7490	Ontario *USA-Canada*
68 800	26 560	Victoria *Kenya-Uganda-Tanzania*	18 390	7100	Ladoga *Russian Federation*
59 580	23 000	Huron *USA-Canada*	17 400	6700	Balkhash *Kazakhstan*
58 020	22 480	Michigan *USA*	10-26 000	4-10 000	Chad *Nigeria-Niger-Chad-Cameroon*
36 500	14 100	Aral *Central Asia (salt)*	9600	3710	Onega *Russian Federation*
32 900	12 700	Tanganyika *Tanzania-Zambia-Zaire-Burundi*	0-8900	0-3430	Eyre *Australia*
31 330	12 100	Great Bear *Canada*	8340	3220	Titicaca *Peru-Bolivia*
30 500	11 800	Baykal *Russian Federation*	8270	3190	Nicaragua *Nicaragua*
28 570	11 030	Great Slave *Canada*	6410	2470	Turkana (Rudolf) *Kenya-Ethiopia*
25 680	9910	Erie *USA-Canada*	5780	2230	Torrens *Australia (salt)*
24 390	9420	Winnipeg *Canada*	5580	2160	Vänern *Sweden*

GREATEST OCEAN DEPTHS

Metres	Feet	Location	Metres	Feet	Location
		PACIFIC OCEAN			**ATLANTIC OCEAN**
11 022	36 160	Marianas Trench	9220	30 249	Puerto Rico Trench
10 882	35 702	Tonga Trench	8264	27 113	South Sandwich Trench
10 542	34 586	Kuril Trench	7856	25 774	Romanche Gap
10 497	34 439	Philippine Trench	7500	24 600	Cayman Trench
10 047	32 962	Kermadec Trench			
9810	32 185	Izu-Bonin Trench			**INDIAN OCEAN**
9165	30 069	New Hebrides Trench	7450	24 442	Java Trench
9140	29 987	South Solomon Trench	7440	24 409	Weber Basin
8412	27 598	Japan Trench	7102	23 300	Diamantina Trench
8066	26 463	Peru-Chile Trench			
7822	25 662	Aleutian Trench			**ARCTIC OCEAN**
6662	21 857	Middle America	5570	18 274	Nansen Fracture Zone

STATES AND DEPENDENCIES

COUNTRY	Area (sq. km)	Population ('000)	Capital
North and Central America			
Anguilla (UK)	91	7	The Valley
Antigua and Barbuda	442	76	St. John's
The Bahamas	13 864	253	Nassau
Barbados	430	255	Bridgetown
Belize	22 965	187	Belmopan
Bermuda (UK)	53	58	Hamilton
Canada	9 976 147	26 521	Ottawa
Cayman Is. (UK)	259	25	George Town
Costa Rica	50 899	3 015	San José
Cuba	114 524	10 608	La Habana (Havana)
Dominica	751	82	Roseau
Dominican Republic	48 441	7 170	Santo Domingo
El Salvador	20 865	5 252	San Salvador
Grenada	344	85	St. George's
Guadeloupe (Fr.)	1 779	343	Basse Terre
Guatemala	108 888	9 197	Guatemala
Haiti	27 749	6 513	Port-au-Prince
Honduras	112 087	5 138	Tegucigalpa
Jamaica	11 425	2 456	Kingston
Martinique (Fr.)	1 101	341	Fort-de-France
Mexico	1 967 180	107 233	México
Montserrat (UK)	102	12	Plymouth
Netherlands Antilles (Neth.)	993	188	Willemstad
Nicaragua	139 000	3 871	Managua
Panama	75 648	2 418	Panamá
Puerto Rico (USA)	8 897	3 480	San Juan
St. Kitts-Nevis	260	44	Basseterre
St. Lucia	616	150	Castries
St. Vincent	389	116	Kingstown
Trinidad and Tobago	5 128	1 281	Port of Spain
United States of America	9 363 130	249 224	Washington
South America			
Argentina	2 777 815	32 322	Buenos Aires
Bolivia	1 098 575	7 314	La Paz
Brazil	8 511 968	150 368	Brasília
Chile	756 943	13 173	Santiago
Colombia	1 138 907	32 978	Bogotá
Ecuador	455 502	10 587	Quito
French Guiana (Fr.)	91 000	98	Cayenne
Guyana	214 969	796	George Town
Paraguay	406 750	4 277	Asunción
Peru	1 285 215	21 550	Lima
Surinam	163 820	422	Paramaribo
Uruguay	186 925	3 094	Montevideo
Venezuela	912 047	19 735	Caracas
Europe			
Albania	28 752	3 245	Tiranë (Tirana)
Andorra	453	47	Andorra-la-Vella
Armenia	29 800	3 283	Yerevan
Austria	83 848	7 583	Wien (Vienna)
Azerbaijan	86 600	7 029	Baku
Belgium	30 512	9 845	Bruxelles (Brussels)
Belorussia	207 600	10 200	Minsk
Bulgaria	110 911	9 010	Sofiya (Sofia)
Cyprus	9 251	701	Nicosia
Czechoslovakia	127 870	15 667	Praha (Prague)
Denmark	43 030	5 143	København (Copenhagen)
Estonia	45 100	1 573	Tallinn
Faroes (Den.)	1 399	47	Tórshavn
Finland	337 032	4 975	Helsinki
France	551 000	56 138	Paris
Georgia	69 700	5 449	Tbilisi
Germany	357 868	79 070	Berlin, Bonn
Gibraltar (UK)	6	30	Gibraltar
Great Britain and N. Ireland, see United Kingdom			
Greece	131 955	10 047	Athínai (Athens)
Greenland (Den.)	2 175 600	56	Godthåb
Hungary	93 030	10 552	Budapest
Iceland	102 828	253	Reykjavík
Ireland	70 282	3 720	Dublin
Italy	301 245	57 061	Roma (Rome)
Latvia	63 700	2 681	Riga
Liechtenstein	161	28	Vaduz
Lithuania	65 200	3 690	Vilnius
Luxembourg	2 587	373	Luxembourg
Malta	316	353	Valletta
Moldavia	33 700	4 341	Kishinev
Monaco	1.8	28	Monaco
Netherlands	33 940	14 951	Amsterdam/ 's-Gravenhage
Norway	324 218	4 212	Oslo
Poland	312 683	38 423	Warszawa (Warsaw)
Portugal	91 671	10 285	Lisboa (Lisbon)
Romania	237 500	23 272	Bucureşti (Bucharest)
Russian Federation	17 075 000	147 386	Moskva (Moscow)
San Marino	61	23	San Marino
Spain	504 745	39 187	Madrid
Sweden	449 791	8 444	Stockholm
Switzerland	41 287	6 609	Bern
Ukraine	603 700	51 704	Kiyev
United Kingdom	244 104	57 237	London
Vatican City	.4	1	Vatican City
Yugoslavia	255 803	23 807	Beograd (Belgrade)
Asia			
Afghanistan	674 500	16 557	Kābul
Bahrain	660	516	Al Manāmah
Bangladesh	144 020	115 593	Dhaka (Dacca)
Bhutan	46 620	1 516	Thimphu
Brunei	5 765	266	Bandar Seri Begawan
Burma (Myanma)	678 031	41 675	Rangoon (Yangon)
Cambodia	181 035	8 246	Phnom Penh
China	9 561 000	1 118 760	Beijing (Peking)
Hong Kong (UK)	1 062	5 851	
India	3 287 593	853 094	New Delhi
Indonesia	1 919 263	185 020	Jakarta
Iran	1 648 184	54 607	Tehrān
Iraq	434 924	18 920	Baghdād
Israel	20 770	4 600	Jerusalem
Japan	371 000	123 460	Tōkyō
Jordan	97 740	4 009	Amman
Kazakhstan	2 717 300	16 538	Alma Ata
Kirgizia	198 500	4 291	Bishkek (Frunze)
Korea, North	121 248	21 773	P'yŏngyang
Korea, South	98 447	42 793	Sŏul (Seoul)
Kuwait	24 300	2 039	Kuwait
Laos	236 798	4 139	Vientiane
Lebanon	10 399	2 701	Beirut
Macau (Port.)	16	479	Macao
Malaysia	330 669	17 891	Kuala Lumpur
Maldives	298	215	Malé
Mongolia	1 565 000	2 190	Ulaanbaatar (Ulan Bator)
Nepal	141 414	19 143	Kathmandu
Oman	212 379	1 502	Masqaṭ (Muscat)
Pakistan	803 941	122 626	Islamabad
Philippines	299 765	62 413	Manila
Qatar	11 437	368	Ad Dawḥah
Saudi Arabia	2 400 930	14 134	Ar Riyāḍ
Singapore	616	2 723	Singapore
Sri Lanka	65 610	17 217	Colombo
Syria	185 179	12 530	Dimashq (Damascus)
Taiwan	35 980	20 300	T'ai-pei
Tajikistan	143 100	5 112	Dushanbe
Thailand	513 517	55 702	Bangkok
Turkey	780 576	55 868	Ankara
Turkmenistan	488 100	3 534	Ashkhabad
United Arab Emirates	83 600	1 589	Abū Ẓabī
Uzbekistan	447 400	19 906	Tashkent
Vietnam	329 566	66 693	Hanoi
Yemen	528 038	11 687	Ṣan'ā'
Africa			
Algeria	2 381 731	24 960	Alger (El Djezair)
Angola	1 246 694	10 020	Luanda
Benin	112 622	4 630	Porto Novo
Botswana	582 000	1 304	Gaborone
Burkina	274 122	8 996	Ouagadougou
Burundi	27 834	5 472	Bujumbura
Cameroon	475 499	11 833	Yaoundé
Cape Verde	4 033	370	Praia
Central African Republic	622 996	3 039	Bangui
Chad	1 284 000	5 678	N'Djamena
Comoros	1 862	550	Moroni
Congo	342 000	2 271	Brazzaville
Djibouti	21 699	409	Djibouti
Egypt	1 000 250	52 426	Cairo
Equatorial Guinea	28 051	352	Malabo
Ethiopia	1 221 918	49 240	Ādīs Ābeba
Gabon	267 667	1 172	Libreville
The Gambia	10 688	861	Banjul
Ghana	238 538	15 028	Accra
Guinea	245 855	5 755	Conakry
Guinea-Bissau	36 125	964	Bissau
Ivory Coast	322 463	11 997	Yamoussoukro
Kenya	582 644	24 031	Nairobi
Lesotho	30 344	1 774	Maseru
Liberia	111 370	2 575	Monrovia
Libya	1 759 530	4 545	Tripoli
Madagascar	587 042	12 004	Antananarivo
Malawi	94 100	8 754	Lilongwe
Mali	1 240 142	9 214	Bamako
Mauritania	1 030 700	2 024	Nouakchott
Mauritius	1 865	1 082	Port Louis
Morocco	459 000	25 061	Rabat
Mozambique	784 961	15 656	Maputo
Namibia	824 293	1 781	Windhoek
Niger	1 267 000	7 731	Niamey
Nigeria	923 769	108 542	Abuja
Réunion (Fr.)	2 510	598	Saint-Denis
Rwanda	26 338	7 237	Kigali
São Tomé and Princípe	964	121	São Tomé
Senegal	196 722	7 327	Dakar
Seychelles	443	69	Victoria
Sierra Leone	71 740	4 151	Freetown
Somalia	637 539	7 497	Muqdisho (Mogadishu)
South Africa	1 221 038	35 282	Pretoria/ Cape Town
Sudan	2 505 792	25 203	Khartoum
Swaziland	17 366	788	Mbabane
Tanzania	942 000	27 318	Dodoma
Togo	56 785	3 531	Lomé
Tunisia	164 148	8 180	Tunis
Uganda	236 036	18 794	Kampala
Western Sahara	266 000	178	-
Zaire	2 344 885	35 568	Kinshasa
Zambia	752 617	8 452	Lusaka
Zimbabwe	390 308	9 709	Harare
Oceania			
American Samoa (USA)	197	38	Fagatogo
Australia	7 682 300	16 873	Canberra
Fiji	18 272	764	Suva
French Polynesia (Fr.)	4 198	206	Papeete
Guam (USA)	549	118	Agaña
Kiribati	800	66	Tarawa
Nauru	21	9	Yaren
New Caledonia (Fr.)	19 104	167	Nouméa
New Zealand	268 675	3 392	Wellington
Niue (NZ)	259	3	Alofi
Federated States of Micronesia	1 300	99	Kolonia
Papua New Guinea	461 692	3 874	Port Moresby
Solomon Islands	29 785	320	Honiara
Tonga	699	95	Nuku'alofa
Tuvalu	25	9	Funafuti
Vanuatu	14 763	158	Vila
Western Samoa	2 831	168	Apia

This page explains the main symbols, lettering style and height/depth colours used on the reference maps on pages 2 to 79. The scale of each map is indicated at the top of each page. Abbreviations used on the maps appear at the beginning of the index.

BOUNDARIES

————	International
– – – –	International under Dispute
· · · · · · · ·	Cease Fire Line
————	Autonomous or State
————	Administrative
– – – –	Maritime (National)
– – – –	International Date Line

COMMUNICATIONS

————	Motorway/Express Highway
=========	Under Construction
————	Major Highway
————	Other Roads
– – – –	Under Construction
- - - - -	Track
→—·—←	Road Tunnel
⇒=====⇐	
- - - - -	Car Ferry
————	Main Railway
————	Other Railway
– – – –	Under Construction
→—·—←	Rail Tunnel
- - - - -	Rail Ferry
┴—┴—┴	Canal
⊕	International Airport
✈	Other Airport

LAKE FEATURES

	Freshwater
	Saltwater
	Seasonal
	Salt Pan

LANDSCAPE FEATURES

	Glacier, Ice Cap
	Marsh, Swamp
	Sand Desert, Dunes

OTHER FEATURES

	River
	Seasonal River
≍	Pass, Gorge
	Dam, Barrage
	Waterfall, Rapid
	Aqueduct
	Reef
▲ 4231	Summit, Peak
. 217	Spot Height, Depth
⌄	Well
Δ	Oil Field
▲	Gas Field
Gas / Oil	Oil/Natural Gas Pipeline
Gemsbok Nat. Pk	National Park
∴UR	Historic Site

LETTERING STYLES

CANADA	Independent Nation
FLORIDA	State, Province or Autonomous Region
Gibraltar (U.K.)	Sovereignty of Dependent Territory
Lothian	Administrative Area
LANGUEDOC	Historic Region
Loire **Vosges**	Physical Feature or Physical Region

TOWNS AND CITIES

Square symbols denote capital cities. Each settlement is given a symbol according to its relative importance, with type size to match.

▣	◉	**New York**	Major City
■	●	**Montréal**	City
▢	○	Ottawa	Small City
■	●	**Québec**	Large Town
▫	○	St John's	Town
▫	○	Yorkton	Small Town
▫	○	Jasper	Village
			Built-up-area

Height

	6000m
	5000m
	4000m
	3000m
	2000m
	1000m
	500m
	200m
0	Sea Level

Depth

0	
200m	
2000m	
4000m	
6000m	
8000m	

1:35M

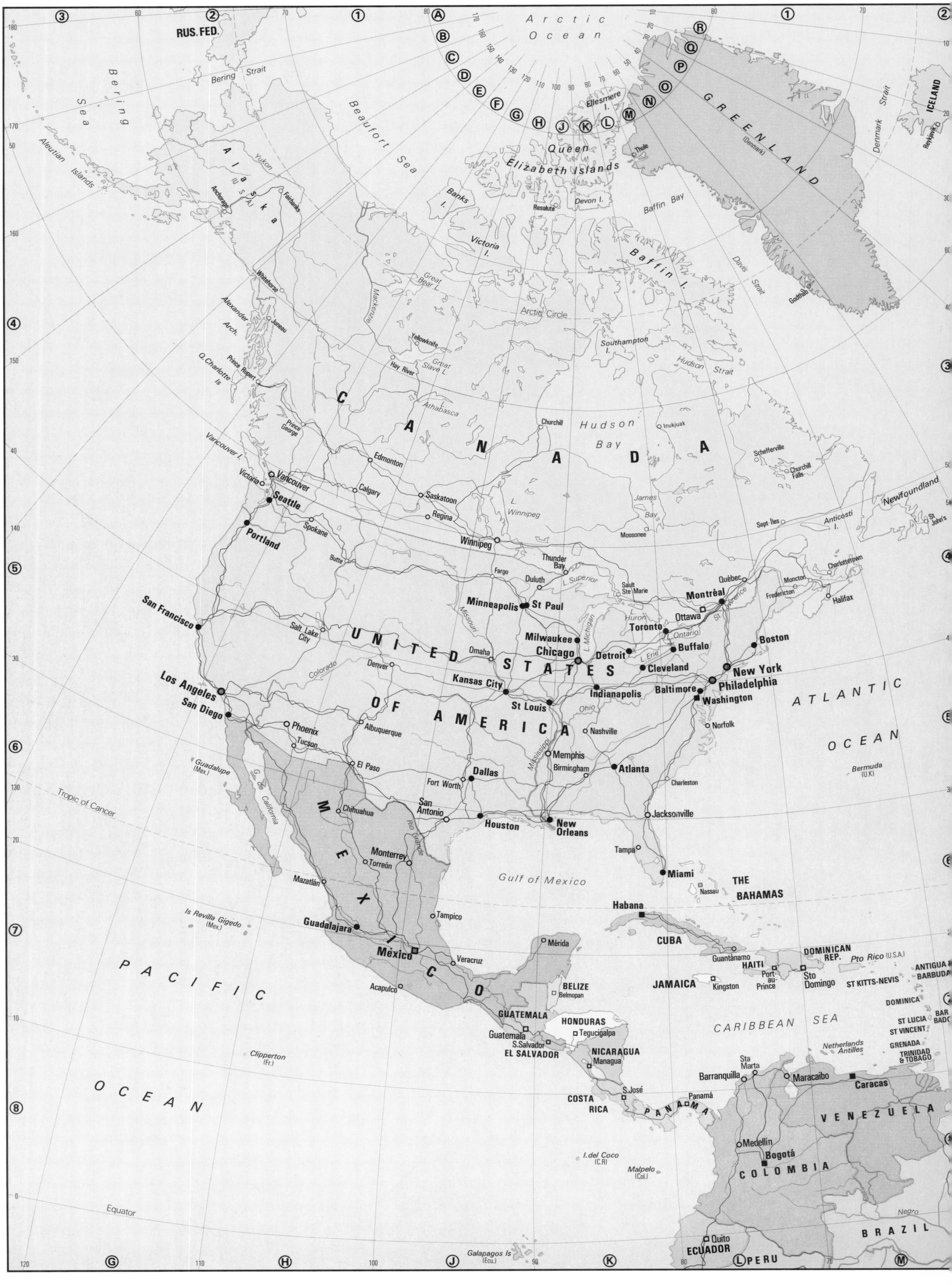

0 250 500 750 1000 1250 km
0 250 500 750 mls

Arctic Ocean

RUS. FED.

Ⓐ Ⓑ Ⓒ Ⓓ Ⓔ Ⓕ Ⓖ Ⓗ Ⓙ Ⓚ Ⓛ Ⓜ Ⓝ Ⓞ Ⓟ Ⓠ Ⓡ

Bering Strait

Bering Sea

GREENLAND (Denmark)

ICELAND
Reykjavik

Beaufort Sea

Denmark Strait

Ellesmere I.

Thule

Queen Elizabeth Islands

Banks I.

Devon I.

Resolute

Baffin Bay

Davis Strait

Goothåb

Aleutian Islands

A l a s k a

Yukon

Anchorage
Fairbanks

Whitehorse

Juneau

Alexander Arch.

Q. Charlotte Is

Prince Rupert

Mackenzie

Victoria I.

Great Bear L.

Yellowknife

Hay River

Great Slave L.

Athabasca

Arctic Circle

Hudson Bay

Churchill

Inukjuak

Southampton I.

Hudson Strait

Schefferville

Churchill Falls

C A N A D A

Vancouver I.

Prince George

Edmonton

Calgary

Saskatoon

Regina

L. Winnipeg

L. Athabasca

James Bay

Moosonee

Newfoundland

Anticosti I.

Sept-Îles

St John's

Charlottetwn

Victoria

Vancouver

Seattle

Portland

Spokane

Butte

Winnipeg

Thunder Bay

Fargo

Duluth

L. Superior

Sault Ste Marie

Québec

Moncton

Fredericton

Halifax

San Francisco

Salt Lake City

Minneapolis

St Paul

Milwaukee

L. Michigan

Chicago

Detroit

L. Huron

Toronto

Ottawa

L. Ontario

Montréal

St. Lawrence

Boston

Denver

Omaha

Kansas City

St Louis

Indianapolis

Cleveland

L. Erie

Buffalo

New York

Baltimore

Philadelphia

Washington

U N I T E D   S T A T E S

O F   A M E R I C A

Colorado

Los Angeles

San Diego

Phoenix

Tucson

Albuquerque

El Paso

Missouri

Ohio

Mississippi

Nashville

Norfolk

Memphis

Birmingham

Atlanta

Charleston

ATLANTIC OCEAN

Bermuda (U.K)

Dallas

Fort Worth

San Antonio

Houston

New Orleans

Jacksonville

Tampa

Miami

Guadalupe (Mex.)

Tropic of Cancer

Chihuahua

Rio Grande

M E X I C O

G. de California

Monterrey

Torreón

Mazatlán

Tampico

THE BAHAMAS

Nassau

Is Revilla Gigedo (Mex.)

Guadalajara

México

Veracruz

Mérida

Habana

CUBA

Guantánamo

HAITI

Port-au-Prince

DOMINICAN REP.

Sto Domingo

Pto Rico (U.S.A.)

ANTIGUA & BARBUDA

Acapulco

BELIZE

Belmopan

GUATEMALA

Guatemala

S.Salvador

EL SALVADOR

HONDURAS

Tegucigalpa

NICARAGUA

Managua

JAMAICA

Kingston

CARIBBEAN SEA

ST KITTS-NEVIS

DOMINICA

ST LUCIA

ST VINCENT

BARBADOS

GRENADA

Netherlands Antilles

TRINIDAD & TOBAGO

PACIFIC

OCEAN

Clipperton (Fr.)

COSTA RICA

S.José

Panamá

P A N A M A

Sta Marta

Barranquilla

Maracaibo

Caracas

VENEZUELA

I. del Coco (C.R)

Malpelo (Col.)

Medellín

Bogotá

COLOMBIA

Negro

Equator

B R A Z I L

Galapagos Is (Ecu.)

Quito

ECUADOR

PERU

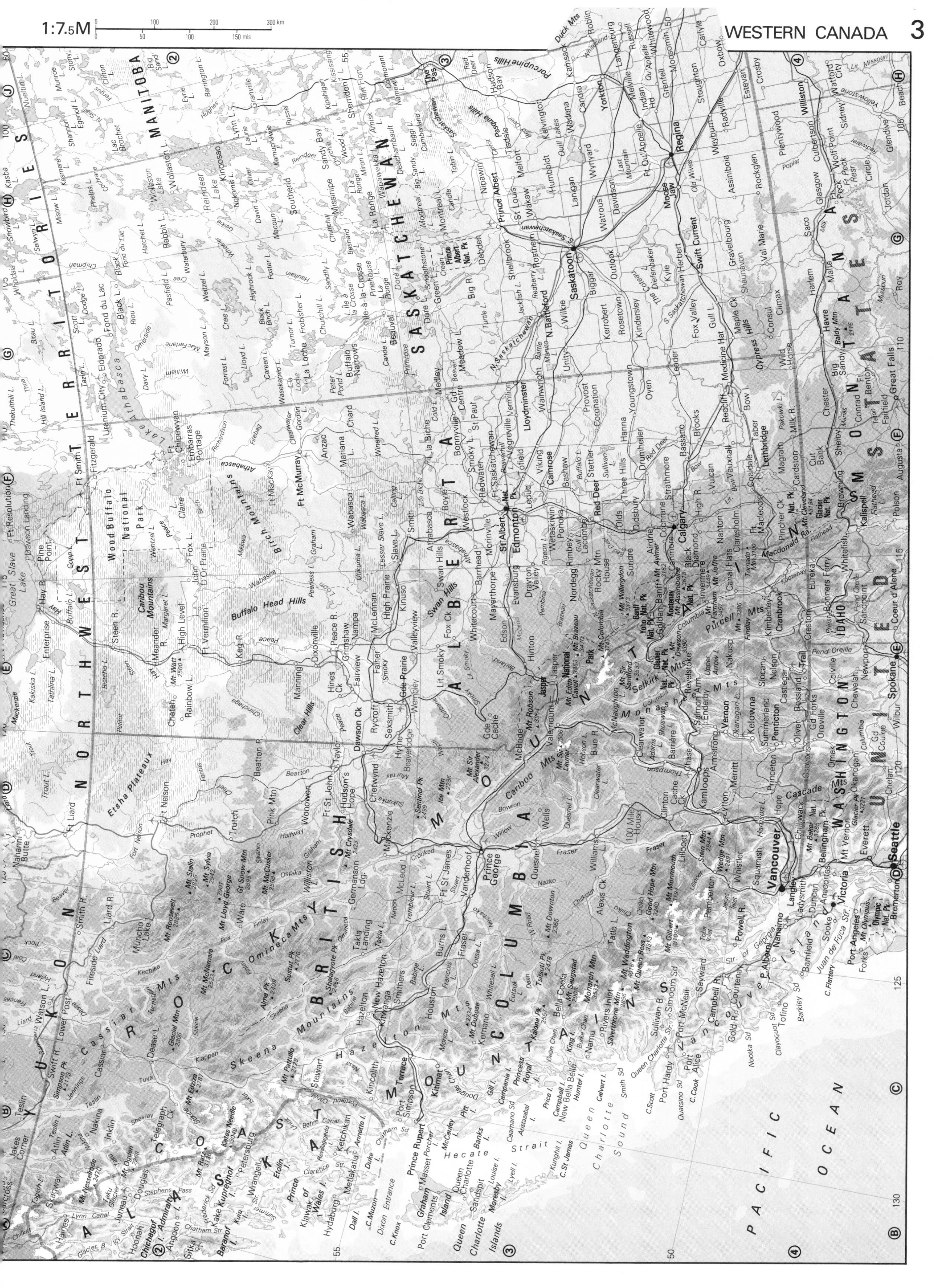
1:7.5M
0 100 200 300 km
0 50 100 150 mls
NORTHWEST TERRITORIES
MANITOBA
SASKATCHEWAN
ALBERTA
BRITISH COLUMBIA
YUKON
ALASKA
UNITED STATES
MONTANA
IDAHO
WASHINGTON
PACIFIC OCEAN
ROCKY MOUNTAINS
COAST MOUNTAINS

HUDSON

BAY

MANITOBA

ONTARIO

QUÉBEC

JAMES BAY

MINNESOTA

WISCONSIN

IOWA

ILLINOIS

MICHIGAN

UNITED STATES

NEW YORK

LAKE SUPERIOR

LAKE MICHIGAN

LAKE HURON

LAKE ERIE

LAKE ONTARIO

Georgian Bay

Belcher Islands

Nastapoka Islands

Sleeper Islands

King George Islands

Akimiski Island

Winnipeg **St. Paul** **Minneapolis** **Milwaukee** **Chicago** **Detroit** **Toronto** **Buffalo** **Cleveland** **Ottawa** Thunder Bay Duluth Sudbury North Bay

Lake Winnipeg Lake Winnipegosis Lake Manitoba Lake of the Woods Lake Nipigon

Churchill Thompson The Pas Flin Flon York Factory Port Nelson Fort Severn Winisk Attawapiskat Fort Albany Moosonee Radisson Chisasibi Eastmain Wemindji

Polar Bear Provincial Park Quetico Provincial Park Algonquin Prov. Park Pukaskwa Nat. Park Lake Superior Provincial Park La Vérendrye Prov. Park

Sault Ste. Marie Sault Ste. Marie Timmins Noranda Rouyn Val d'Or Kirkland Lake Cochrane Kapuskasing Hearst Geraldton Nipigon Schreiber Wawa Chapleau Gogama

Smith I. Akulivik Povungnituk Inukjuak Kuujjuarapik

Des Moines Rochester Madison Green Bay Grand Rapids Lansing Flint Windsor London Sarnia St. Catharines Niagara Falls Hamilton Kitchener Kingston Peterborough Belleville Syracuse Rochester

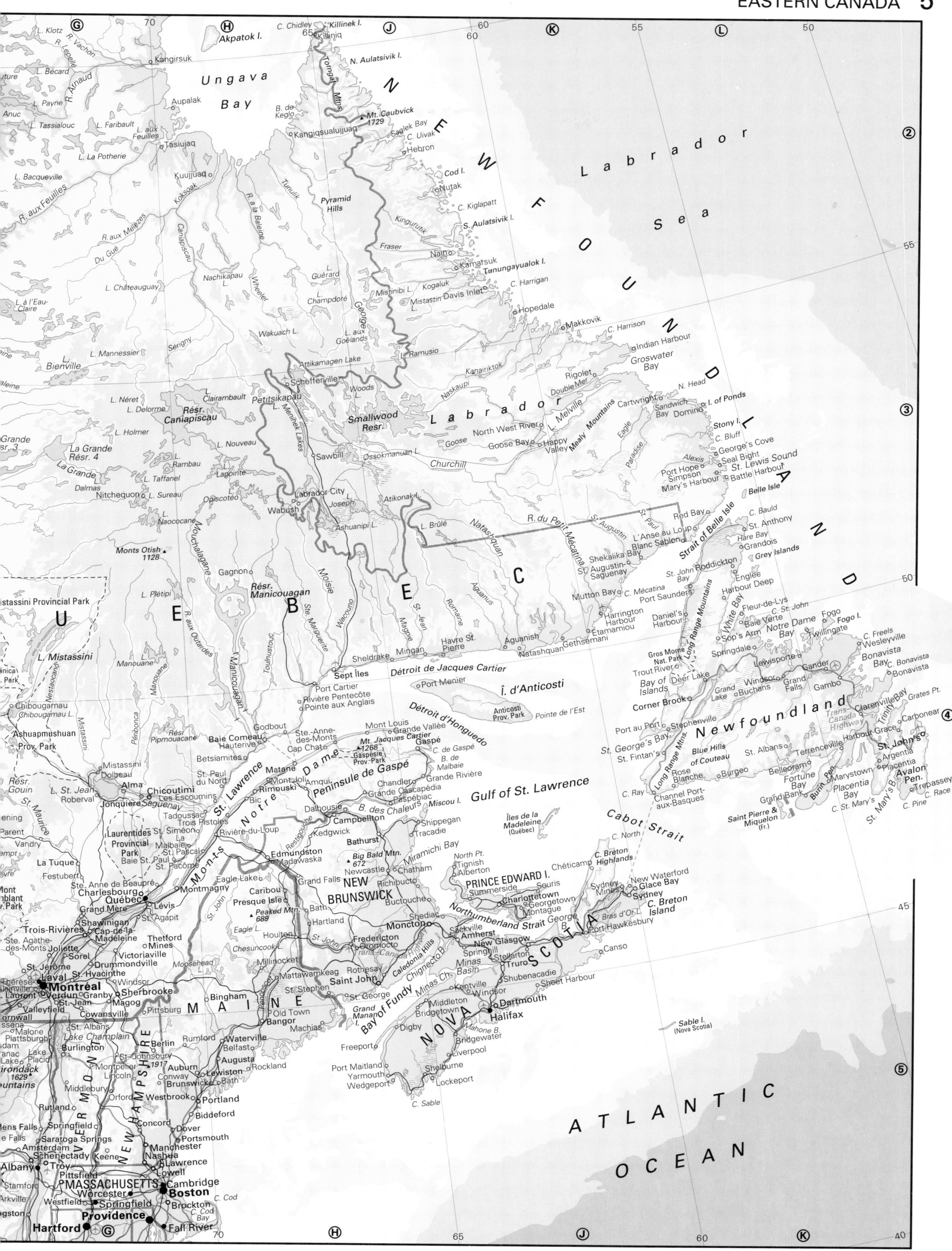

L. Klotz
R. Vachon
R. Lepelle
L. Bécard
L. Payne
ture
L. Tassiaⁱouc
Anuc
L. aux Feuilles
L. Faribault
L. La Potherie
R. aux Feuilles
L. Bacqueville
Bienville
aine
L. à l'Eau-Claire
Grande
sr. 3
Park
stassini Provincial Park
La Grande
Rés. 4
La Grande
Dalmas
U
Chibougamau
Chibougamau L.
Ashuapmushuan
Prov. Park
L. Mistassini
Park
Résr.
Gouin
ening
Parent
ant
Vandry
empt
La Tuque
Festubert
Mont
blant
Park
St. Jérome
St. Thérèse
Laurent
nville
onville
Laval
Verdun
Valleyfield
ornwall
ssena
Malone
Plattsburgh
dam
anac
Lake
Lake Placid
L. Placid
irondack
1629
untains
Saranac
ens Falls
Glens Falls
Saratoga Springs
Amsterdam
Schenectady
Albany
Troy
Pittsfield
Arkville
kgston

Kangirsuk
Aupalak
Kuujjuaq
Koksoak
Tasiujaq
R. à la Baleine
R. Caniapiscau
Nachikapau
Wheeler
L. Mannessier
Du Gué
L. Néret
L. Delorme
Résr.
Caniapiscau
L. Holmer
L. Nouveau
L. Rambau
L. Taffanel
Lapointe
Nitchequon
L. Sureau
Naococane
Opiscotéo
Monts Otish
1128
L. Plétipi
Gagnon
Résr.
Manicouagan
Peribonca
Manouane
Mistassini
Dolbeau
Alma
Chicoutimi
Roberval
L. St. Jean
Jonquière
Saguenay
Les Escoumins
St. Paul
du Nord
Tadoussac
Trois Pistoles
St. Siméon
La
Malbaie
Baie St. Paul
Ste. Anne de Beaupré
Charlesbourg
Grand Mère
Shawinigan
Cap-de-la-Madeleine
Trois-Rivières
Ste. Agathe-des-Monts
Joliette
Sorel
Drummondville
Victoriaville
Windsor
Granby
Sherbrooke
St-Hyacinthe
Cowansville
Magog
St. Albans
Burlington
Montpelier
Berlin
New Hampshire
Rumford
Waterville
Belfast
Augusta
Auburn
Lewiston
Brunswick
Rockland
Portland
Biddeford
Concord
Dover
Portsmouth
Manchester
Nashua
Lawrence
Lowell
Massachusetts
Worcester
Cambridge
Boston
Brockton
Cod Bay
Providence
Fall River
Springfield
Hartford
Westfield

C. Chidley
Killinek I.
Akpatok I.
65
Kangiqsualujjuaq
Kiⁱiniq
N. Aulatsivik I.
Torngat Mtns.
B. de Keglo
Mt. Caubvick
1729
Saglek Bay
C. Uivak
Cod I.
Nutak
Hebron
C. Kiglapatt
S. Aulatsivik I.
Pyramid
Hills
Kingurutik
Nain
Fraser
Kamatsuk
Tunungayualok I.
Mistinibi L.
Kogaluk
C. Harrigan
Champdoré
Mistastin
Davis Inlet
Hopedale
Wakuach L.
L. aux
Goélands
George
Ramusio
Makkovik
C. Harrison
Indian Harbour
Kanairiktok
Attikamagen Lake
Schefferville
Woods
L.
Naskaupi
North West River
Rigolet
Groswater
Bay
Menihek Lakes
Petitsikapau
Smallwood
Résr.
Labrador
Goose
Goose Bay
Double Mer
Melville
Cartwright
N. Head
Sawbill
Ossokmanuan L.
Churchill
Happy
Valley
Mealy Mountains
Eagle
Paradise
Sandwich
Bay
Domino
I. of Ponds
Labrador City
Joseph
Atikonak L.
L. Brûlé
R. du Petit Mécatina
Natashquan
Alexis
George's Cove
Seal Bight
St. Lewis Sound
Battle Harbour
Belle Isle
Wabush
Ashuanipi L.
St. Augustin
St. Paul
Red Bay
Strait of Belle Isle
C. Bauld
C. Bluff
Port Hope
Simpson
Mary's Harbour
L'Anse au Loup
Blanc Sablon
St. Augustin-Saguenay
C. Anthony
Hare Bay
Grandois
Grey Islands
Shekalika Bay
St. John
Roddickton
Bay
Englee
Ste. St. John
Harbour Deep
Fleur-de-Lys
Baie Verte
Long Range Mountains
Harrington
Harbour
Daniel's
Harbour
Mutton Bay
C. Mécatina
Port Saunders
Etamamiou
Aguanish
Natashquan
Gethsemani
White Bay
Sop's Arm
Notre Dame
Bay
Springdale
Twillingate
Fogo
Fogo I.
C. Freels
Wesleyville
Gros Morne
Nat. Park
Trout River
Deer Lake
Lewisporte
Gander
Bonavista
Bay
C. Bonavista
Bonavista
Bay of
Islands
Grand
Lake
Windsor
Buchans
Grand
Falls
Gambo
Corner Brook
Port au Port
Stephenville
Blue Hills
of Couteau
Newfoundland
St. Fintan's
Trans Canada Highway
Clarenville
Trinity Bay
Grates Pt.
St. George's Bay
Long Range Mtns.
St. Albans
Burgeo
Belleoram
Terrenceville
Harbour Grace
Carbonear
St. John's
C. Ray
Rose
Blanche
Fortune
Bay
Argentia
Placentia
Channel Port-aux-Basques
Grand
Bank
Burin
Pen.
Marystown
Placentia
Bay
Trepassey
Saint Pierre & Miquelon
(Fr.)
C. St. Mary's
Avalon
Pen.
C. Pine
C. Race

Labrador
Sea

Labrador

N
E
W
F
O
U
N
D
L
A
N
D

Ungava
Bay

QUEBEC

St. Lawrence
Notre Dame
Monts

Sept Îles
Port Cartier
Rivière Pentecôte
Pointe aux Anglais
Baie Comeau
Hauterive
Betsiamites
St. Jean
Matane
Mont Joli
Rimouski
Bic
Rivière-du-Loup
St. Pascal
St. Pacôme
Détroit de Jacques Cartier
Port Menier
Î. d'Anticosti
Anticosti
Prov. Park
Pointe de l'Est
Détroit d'Honguedo
Ste.-Anne-des-Monts
Cap Chat
Mont Louis
Grande Vallée
Mont Jacques Cartier
1268
Gaspésie
Prov. Park
Gaspé
C. de Gaspé
B. de
Malbaie
Péninsule de Gaspé
Grande Rivière
Grande Cascapédia
Paspébiac
B. des Chaleurs
Miscou I.
Gulf of St. Lawrence
Îles de la
Madeleine
(Québec)
Cabot Strait
C. North
C. Breton
Highlands
Chéticamp
C. Breton
Island
Amqui
Dalhousie
Campbellton
Restigouche
Kedgwick
Shippagan
Tracadie
Bathurst
North Pt.
Tignish
Alberton
Sydney
Mines
New Waterford
Glace Bay
Sydney
New Glasgow
Edmundston
Madawaska
Big Bald Mtn.
672
Newcastle
Chatham
Miramichi Bay
Summerside
Prince Edward I.
Georgetown
Montague
Souris
Charlottetown
Bras d'Or L.
Port Hawkesbury
Canso
Eagle Lake
Grand Falls
Richibucto
Buctouche
Northumberland Strait
George
Antigonish
Caribou
Presque Isle
Peaked Mtn.
689
New
Brunswick
Hartland
Fredericton
Oromocto
Moncton
Shediac
Sackville
Amherst
Springhill
Nova Scotia
Stellarton
Truro
Houlton
Chesuncook L.
St. John
Maine
Bath
Rothesay
Saint John
St. Stephen
St. George
Caledonia Hills
Chignecto
Minas
Basin
Minas Ch.
Kentville
Windsor
Shubenacadie
Sheet Harbour
Millinocket
Mattawamkeag
Bingham
Old Town
Bangor
Machias
Grand
Manan
I.
Bay of Fundy
Digby
Annapolis
Middleton
Bridgetown
Mahone B.
Dartmouth
Halifax
Sable I.
(Nova Scotia)
Freeport
Yarmouth
Wedgeport
Bridgewater
Liverpool
Port Maitland
Shelburne
Lockeport
C. Sable
Mooshead L.
L.

Trois-Rivières
Montmagny
Lévis
Québec
St. Agapit
Thetford
Mines
Eagle Lake
St. John
Eagle L.
Bangor

Atlantic
Ocean

200   400   600 km
100   200   300 mils

A R C T I C   O C E A N

BEAUFORT SEA

PACIFIC OCEAN

Gulf of Alaska

BERING SEA

Bering Str.

ALASKA (U.S.A.)

Alaska Range

Brooks Range

YUKON TERRITORY

NORTHWEST TERRITORIES

BRITISH COLUMBIA

ALBERTA

SASKATCHEWAN

MANIT...

Victoria Island

Banks Island

Kitikmeo...

Queen Charlotte Islands

Vancouver Island

Alexander Archipelago

Prince of Wales I.

Kodiak Island

Aleutian I.

Seward Peninsula

WASHINGTON

OREGON

MONTANA

IDAHO

WYOMING

NORTH DAKOTA

SOUTH DAKOTA

U.S.

Great Bear Lake

Great Slave Lake

Lake Athabasca

Reindeer Lake

Vancouver   Seattle   Tacoma   Olympia   Portland   Salem   Edmonton   Calgary   Saskatoon   Regina   Winnipeg

Names underlined indicate
Province/State capitals

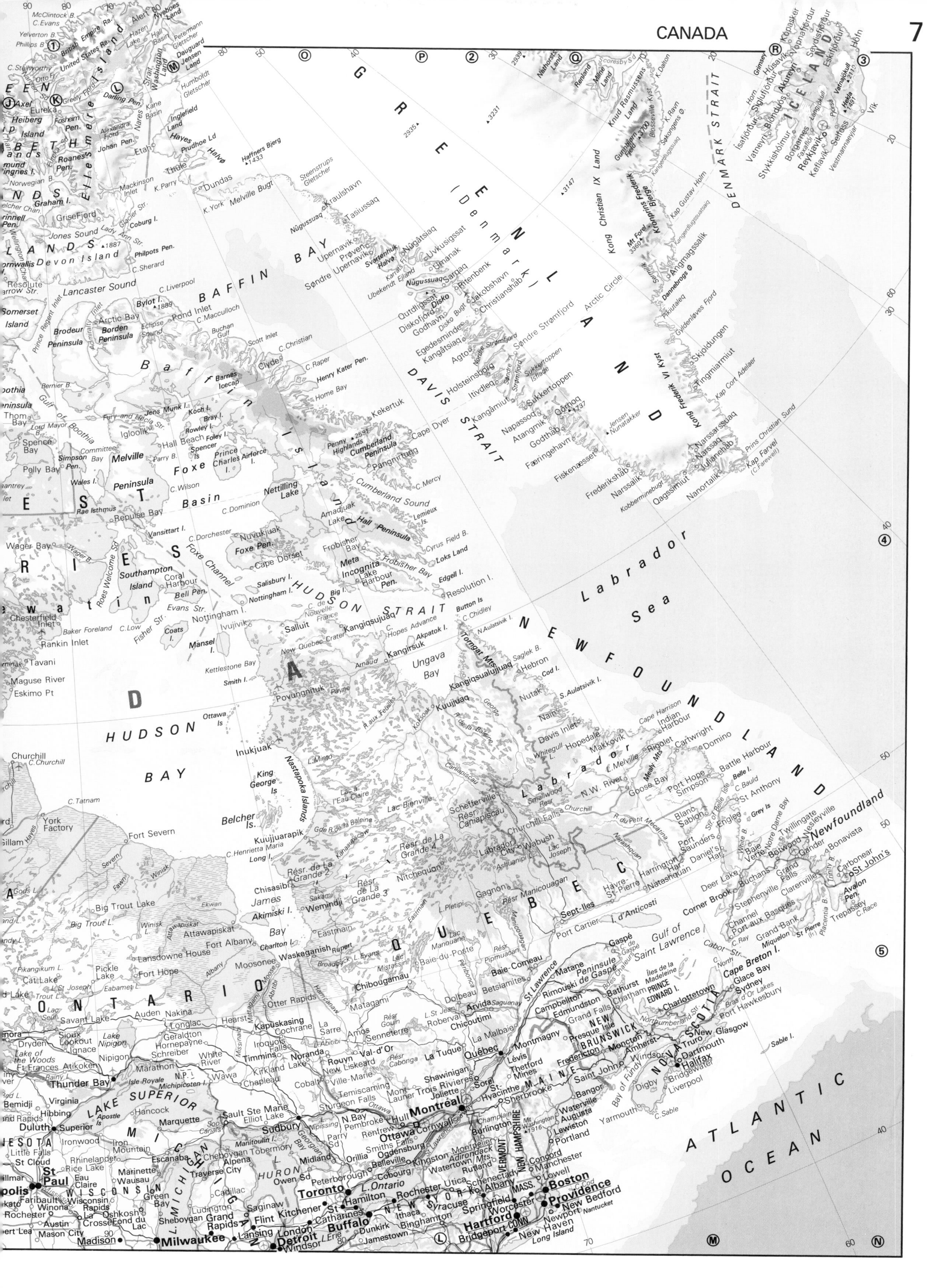
GREENLAND
(Denmark)
ICELAND
BAFFIN BAY
Baffin Island
DAVIS STRAIT
DENMARK STRAIT
Labrador Sea
HUDSON STRAIT
HUDSON BAY
Foxe Basin
Foxe Channel
Ungava Bay
James Bay
NEWFOUNDLAND
QUEBEC
ONTARIO
LAKE SUPERIOR
MICHIGAN
Gulf of Saint Lawrence
ATLANTIC OCEAN
Ellesmere Island
Devon Island
Lancaster Sound
Melville Peninsula
Southampton Island
Cumberland Sound
Labrador
Newfoundland
St John's
Gander
Corner Brook
Sept-Îles
Baie-Comeau
Chicoutimi
Québec
Montréal
Ottawa
Toronto
Hamilton
Buffalo
Rochester
Syracuse
Albany
Boston
Providence
Hartford
Springfield
Worcester
New Haven
New Bedford
Portland
Bangor
Fredericton
Saint John
Moncton
Halifax
Dartmouth
Truro
Sydney
Charlottetown
PRINCE EDWARD I.
NEW BRUNSWICK
NOVA SCOTIA
MAINE
VERMONT
NEW HAMPSHIRE
MASS.
CONN.
NEW YORK
Sudbury
Sault Ste Marie
Thunder Bay
Timmins
Kapuskasing
Chibougamau
Rouyn
Val-d'Or
Duluth
Superior
St Paul
Milwaukee
Madison
Detroit
Windsor
London
Kitchener
Lansing
Flint
Saginaw
Grand Rapids
Churchill
Fort Severn
Moosonee
Kuujjuaq
Kuujjuarapik
Inukjuak
Povungnituk
Nain
Hebron
Goose Bay
Schefferville
Labrador City
Wabush
Godthåb
Jakobshavn
Upernavik
Thule
Reykjavík
Akureyri
Baffin
Arctic Circle
Kong Christian IX Land
Kong Frederik VI Kyst
Cape Breton I.
Sable I.
Bay of Fundy
Long Island
L. Ontario
Anticosti

1:12.5M

100 200 300 400 500 km
100 200 300 mls

PACIFIC OCEAN

BRITISH COLUMBIA
ALBERTA
SASKATCHEWAN
MANITOBA

WASHINGTON
OREGON
IDAHO
MONTANA
NORTH DAKOTA
SOUTH DAKOTA
NEBRASKA
WYOMING
NEVADA
UTAH
COLORADO
KANSAS
CALIFORNIA
ARIZONA
NEW MEXICO
OKLAHOMA
TEXAS

UNITED STATES

ROCKY MOUNTAINS
CASCADE RANGE
SIERRA NEVADA
GREAT BASIN
COLORADO PLATEAU
SONORAN DESERT
MOJAVE Desert
Death Valley
Grand Canyon
PAINTED DESERT
LLANO ESTACADO
Edwards Plateau

MEXICO
BAJA CALIFORNIA
SIERRA MADRE OCCIDENTAL
SIERRA MADRE ORIENTAL

Vancouver Island
Vancouver
Victoria
Seattle
Tacoma
Olympia
Portland
Salem
Eugene
Spokane
Boise
Calgary
Edmonton
Regina
Saskatoon
Winnipeg
Helena
Great Falls
Billings
Bismarck
Pierre
Rapid City
Cheyenne
Denver
Colorado Springs
Pueblo
Salt Lake City
Ogden
Provo
Reno
Carson City
Sacramento
San Francisco
Oakland
San Jose
Fresno
Bakersfield
Los Angeles
Long Beach
San Diego
Phoenix
Tucson
Albuquerque
Santa Fe
El Paso
Amarillo
Lubbock
Midland
Odessa
San Angelo
Austin
San Antonio
Dallas
Fort Worth
Waco
Oklahoma City
Wichita
Tijuana
Mexicali
Ensenada
Hermosillo
Guaymas
Ciudad Obregón
Los Mochis
Culiacán
Mazatlán
Durango
Torreón
Monterrey
Chihuahua
Ciudad Juárez
Nuevo Laredo
Laredo
Brownsville
Matamoros
Corpus Christi

PACIFIC OCEAN

Tropic of Cancer

Guadalupe (Mex.)

50
130
40
30
120
110
100

Names underlined indicate Province/State capitals

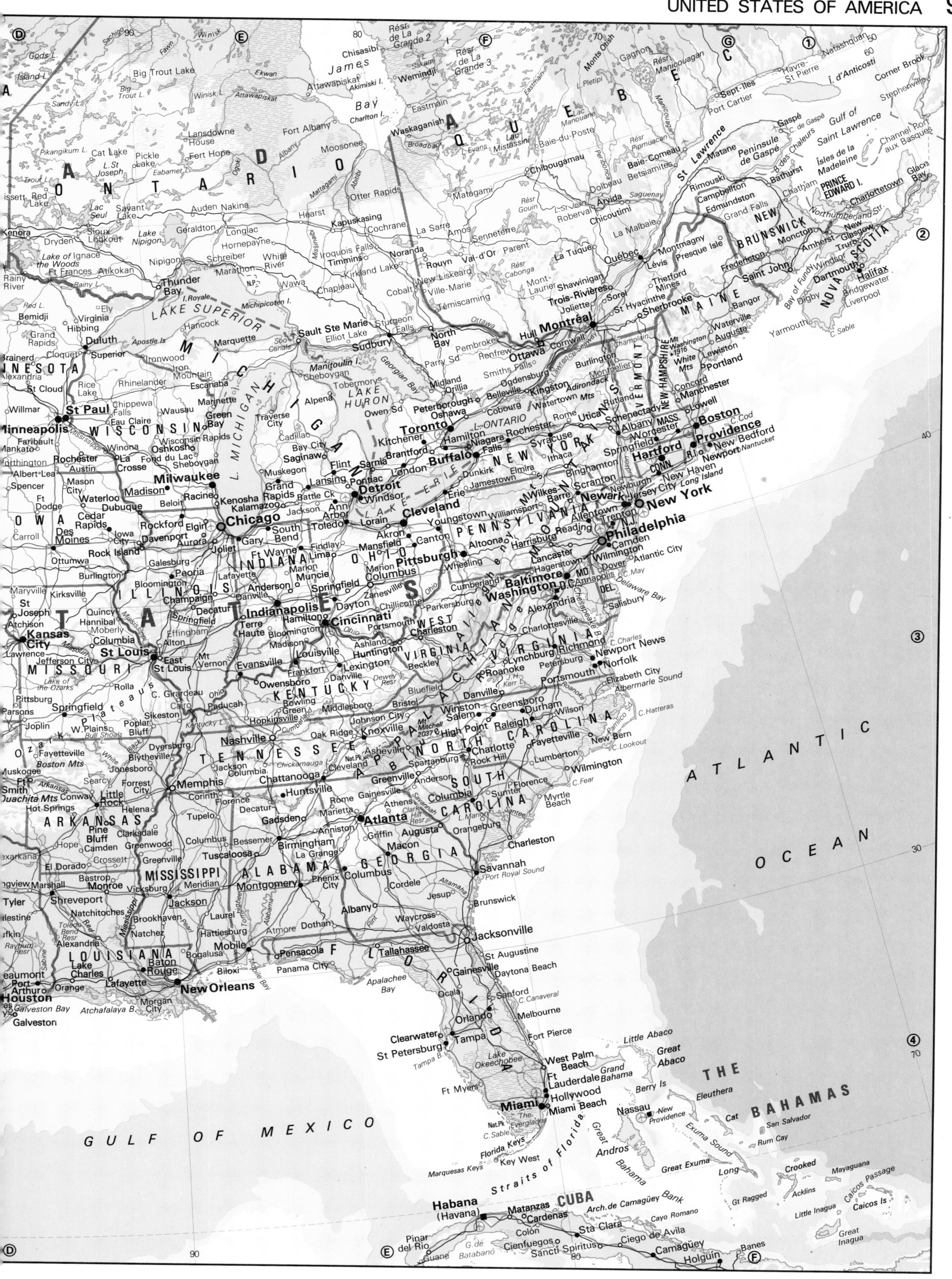
ONTARIO
QUEBEC
James Bay
LAKE SUPERIOR
LAKE HURON
LAKE ONTARIO
LAKE ERIE
L. MICHIGAN
MICHIGAN
WISCONSIN
MINNESOTA
IOWA
ILLINOIS
INDIANA
OHIO
PENNSYLVANIA
NEW YORK
VERMONT
NEW HAMPSHIRE
MAINE
MASS.
CONN.
R.I.
N.J.
MD
DEL.
WEST VIRGINIA
VIRGINIA
KENTUCKY
TENNESSEE
NORTH CAROLINA
SOUTH CAROLINA
GEORGIA
ALABAMA
MISSISSIPPI
LOUISIANA
ARKANSAS
MISSOURI
FLORIDA
NEW BRUNSWICK
NOVA SCOTIA
PRINCE EDWARD I.
APPALACHIAN MTS
Gulf of Saint Lawrence
ATLANTIC OCEAN
GULF OF MEXICO
THE BAHAMAS
CUBA
Straits of Florida
Habana (Havana)
Toronto
Montréal
Québec
Ottawa
Hamilton
Buffalo
Detroit
Cleveland
Chicago
Milwaukee
Minneapolis
St Paul
Kansas City
St Louis
Indianapolis
Cincinnati
Columbus
Pittsburgh
Philadelphia
New York
Newark
Boston
Providence
Hartford
Baltimore
Washington
Richmond
Norfolk
Newport News
Atlanta
Nashville
Memphis
Louisville
Birmingham
Charlotte
Jacksonville
Tampa
St Petersburg
Miami
Orlando
New Orleans
Baton Rouge
Houston
Galveston
Halifax
Saint John
Fredericton
Charlottetown
Sault Ste Marie
Sudbury
Thunder Bay
Duluth
Savannah
Charleston
Mobile
Tallahassee
Pensacola
Key West
Nassau

1:10M

0 100 200 300 400 km

0 100 200 mls

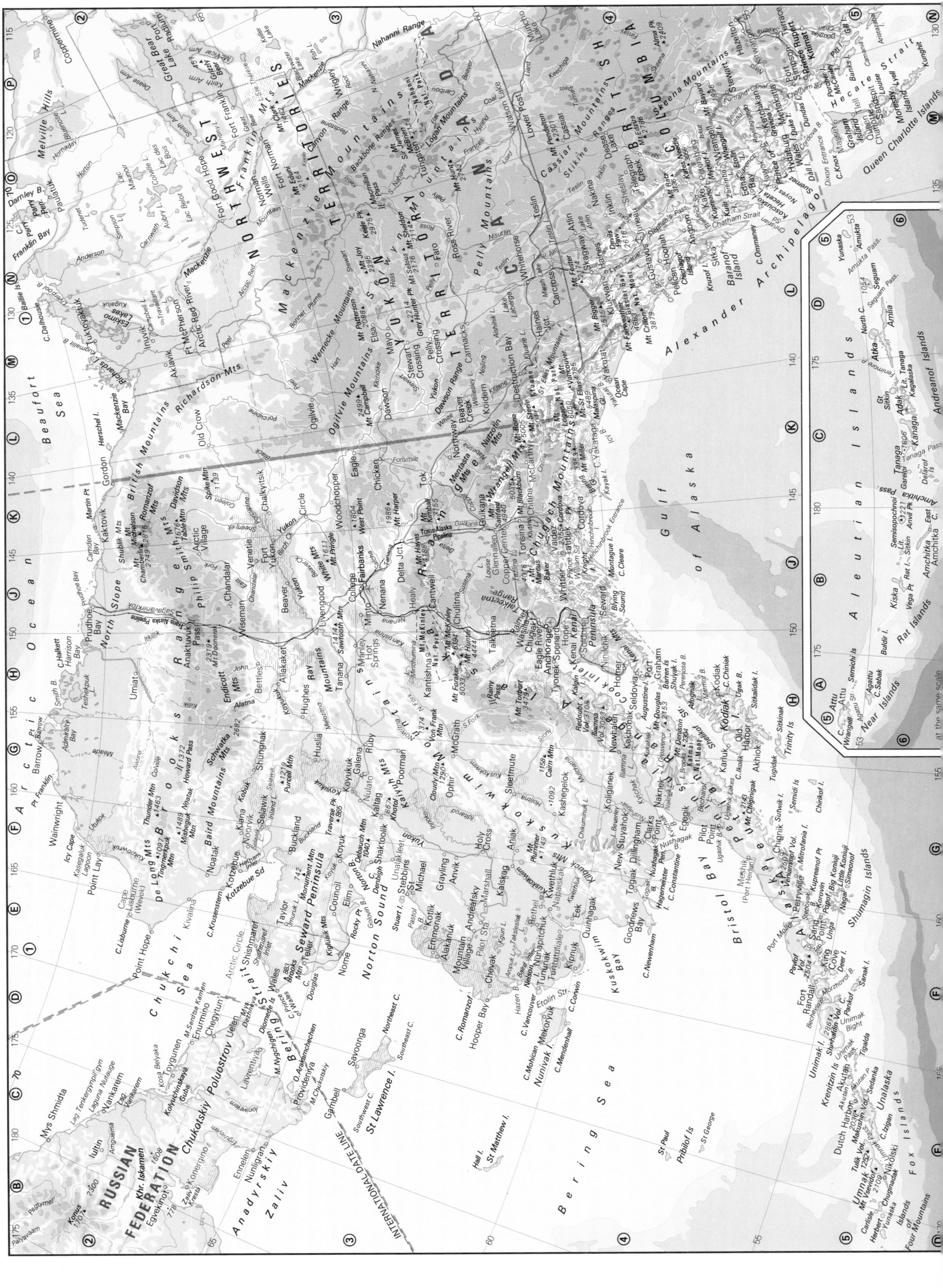

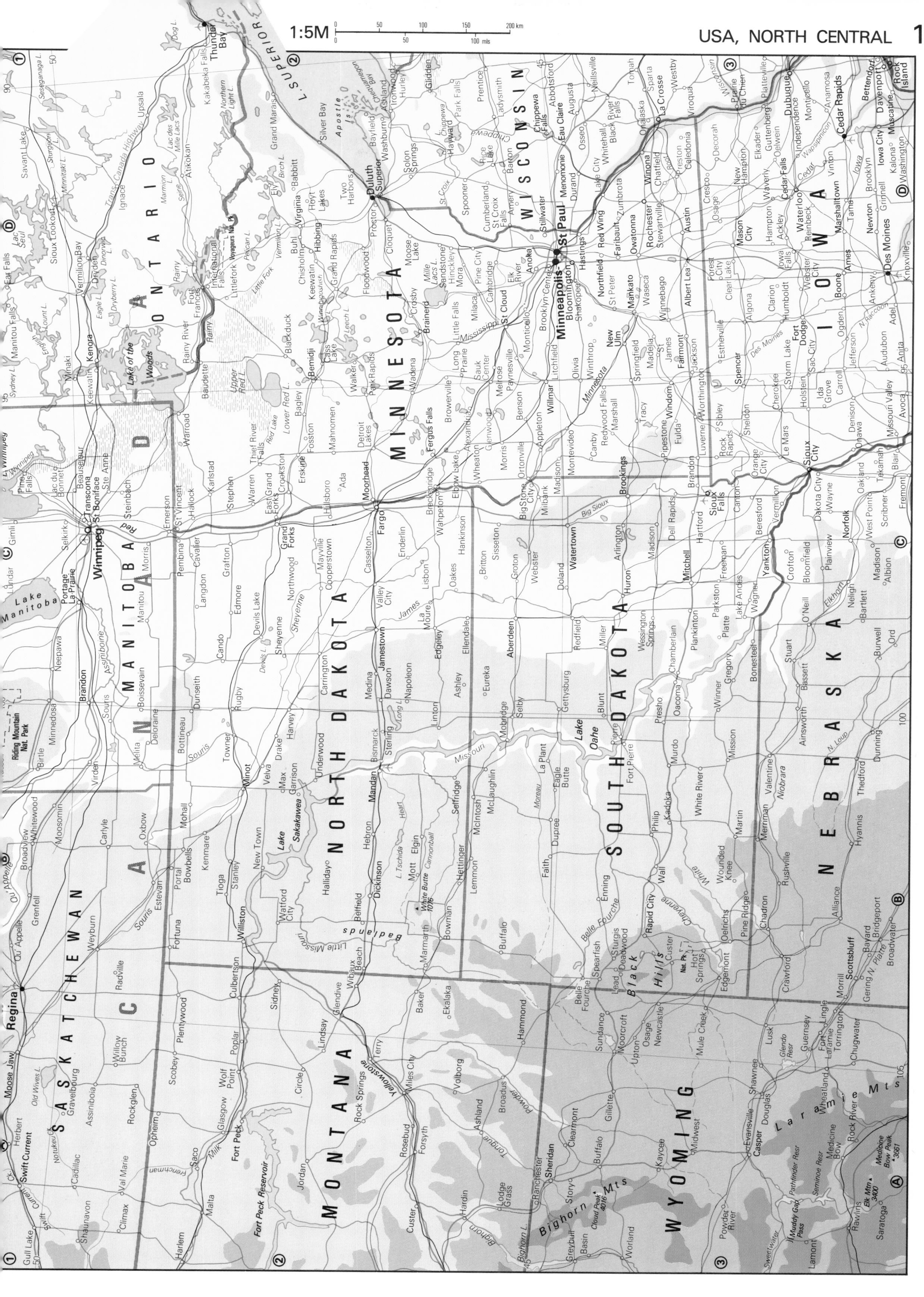

1:5M

50 100 150 200 km
50 100 mls

State / Province names:

ONTARIO

MANITOBA

SASKATCHEWAN

MINNESOTA

NORTH DAKOTA

SOUTH DAKOTA

WISCONSIN

IOWA

NEBRASKA

MONTANA

WYOMING

L. SUPERIOR

Lake of the Woods

Lake Winnipeg

Lake Manitoba

Lake Sakakawea

Lake Oahe

Fort Peck Reservoir

Black Hills

Bighorn Mts

Laramie Mts

Bighorn Mts

Badlands

Riding Mountain Nat. Park

Selected cities and towns:

Thunder Bay, Kakabeka Falls, Northern Light L., Dog L., Sesekanaga L., Savant Lake, Sioux Lookout, Eat Lake, Sturgeon, Minnitaki L., Lac des Mille Lacs, Ignace, Atikokan, Marmion, Seine, Fort Frances, International Falls, Kenora, Keewatin, Minaki, Dryden, Eagle L., Dinorwic, Vermilion Bay, Trans Canada Highway, Upsala, Lac Seul, Ear Falls, Manitou Falls, Sydney L., English River, Lundar, Gimli, Selkirk, Winnipeg, St Boniface, Transcona, Beausejour, Pine Falls, Lac du Bonnet, Ste Anne, Steinbach, St Vincent, Emerson, Morris, Portage La Prairie, Neepawa, Brandon, Minnedosa, Birtle, Souris, Boissevain, Deloraine, Melita, Virden, Carlyle, Moosomin, Whitewood, Broadview, Grenfell, Qu'Appelle, Regina, Moose Jaw, Gravelbourg, Assiniboia, Radville, Weyburn, Estevan, Oxbow, Carnduff, Willow Bunch, Gull Lake, Swift Current, Herbert, Cadillac, Val Marie, Shaunavon, Climax, Eastend, Maple Creek

Duluth, Superior, Two Harbors, Proctor, Cloquet, Virginia, Hibbing, Chisholm, Keewatin, Buhl, Grand Rapids, Floodwood, Moose Lake, Hinckley, Mora, Cambridge, Elk River, Anoka, Minneapolis, St Paul, Bloomington, Shakopee, Northfield, Faribault, Owatonna, Rochester, Red Wing, Hastings, Stillwater, Menomonie, Durand, Eau Claire, Chippewa Falls, Menomonie, Augusta, Osseo, Black River Falls, Sparta, La Crosse, Winona, Preston, Caledonia, Decorah, Cresco, New Hampton, Charles City, Mason City, Clear Lake, Forest City, Algona, Estherville, Spencer, Cherokee, Storm Lake, Sioux City, Le Mars, Rock Rapids, Sheldon, Sibley, Worthington, Jackson, Fairmont, Blue Earth, Albert Lea, Austin, Waseca, Mankato, New Ulm, Springfield, Redwood Falls, Marshall, Pipestone, Luverne, Brookings, Sioux Falls, Canton, Beresford, Vermillion, Yankton, Hartford, Madison, Mitchell, Huron, Watertown, Aberdeen, Redfield, Miller, Pierre, Fort Pierre, Chamberlain, Winner, Valentine, Gregory, Platte, Mission, Rapid City, Sturgis, Deadwood, Lead, Spearfish, Belle Fourche, Hot Springs, Custer, Chadron, Crawford, Alliance, Scottsbluff, Gering, Bridgeport, Bayard, Morrill, Chadron

Des Moines, Ames, Boone, Fort Dodge, Marshalltown, Newton, Grinnell, Iowa City, Cedar Rapids, Waterloo, Cedar Falls, Independence, Dubuque, Davenport, Muscatine, Rock Island, Washington, Knoxville, Ankeny, Adel

Bismarck, Mandan, Jamestown, Valley City, Fargo, Moorhead, Grand Forks, East Grand Forks, Crookston, Thief River Falls, Bemidji, Blackduck, Cass Lake, Walker, Park Rapids, Detroit Lakes, Fergus Falls, Wahpeton, Breckenridge, Ortonville, Morris, Montevideo, Willmar, Litchfield, St Cloud, Little Falls, Brainerd, Alexandria, Sauk Centre, Melrose, Appleton, Canby, Tracy, Windom, Fairmont, Minot, Velva, Rugby, Devils Lake, Langdon, Cando, Carrington, Harvey, Drake, Garrison, New Town, Williston, Watford City, Dickinson, Belfield, Beach, Bowman, Hettinger, Mott, Lemmon, McLaughlin, Mobridge, Selby, Gettysburg, Eagle Butte, Faith, Dupree, Philip, Wall, Kadoka, Martin, Pine Ridge, Wounded Knee, White River, Murdo, Presho

Glasgow, Wolf Point, Poplar, Culbertson, Sidney, Glendive, Wibaux, Baker, Ekalaka, Miles City, Terry, Forsyth, Rosebud, Hardin, Hysham, Jordan, Circle, Scobey, Plentywood, Malta, Saco, Harlem, Chinook, Havre, Fort Peck

Sheridan, Buffalo, Gillette, Newcastle, Lusk, Douglas, Casper, Glenrock, Medicine Bow, Rawlins, Saratoga, Encampment, Torrington, Lingle, Wheatland, Chugwater, Guernsey, Kaycee, Worland, Basin, Greybull, Lovell, Cody

50 100 150 200 km
50 100 mls

LAKE SUPERIOR

LAKE MICHIGAN

LAKE HURON

LAKE ERIE

Georgian Bay

MINNESOTA   WISCONSIN   MICHIGAN   ONTARIO   CANADA

IOWA   ILLINOIS   INDIANA   OHIO

MISSOURI   KENTUCKY   WEST VIRGINIA

TENNESSEE   NORTH

CENTRAL L... PLAIN

CUMBERLAND PLATEAU   ALLEGHENY

Ozark Plateau

Thunder Bay, Duluth, Superior, St Paul, Madison, Milwaukee, Chicago, Rockford, Peoria, Springfield, St Louis, Indianapolis, Cincinnati, Columbus, Dayton, Cleveland, Detroit, Toledo, Grand Rapids, Lansing, Flint, Akron, Youngstown, Canton, Fort Wayne, Evansville, Louisville, Lexington, Nashville, Cedar Rapids, Davenport, Rock Island, Dubuque, La Crosse, Eau Claire, Green Bay, Appleton, Oshkosh, Kenosha, Racine, Sault Ste Marie, Sudbury, Windsor, Sarnia, London, Kitchener, Guelph, Marquette, Escanaba, Marathon, Wawa, Chapleau, Timmins

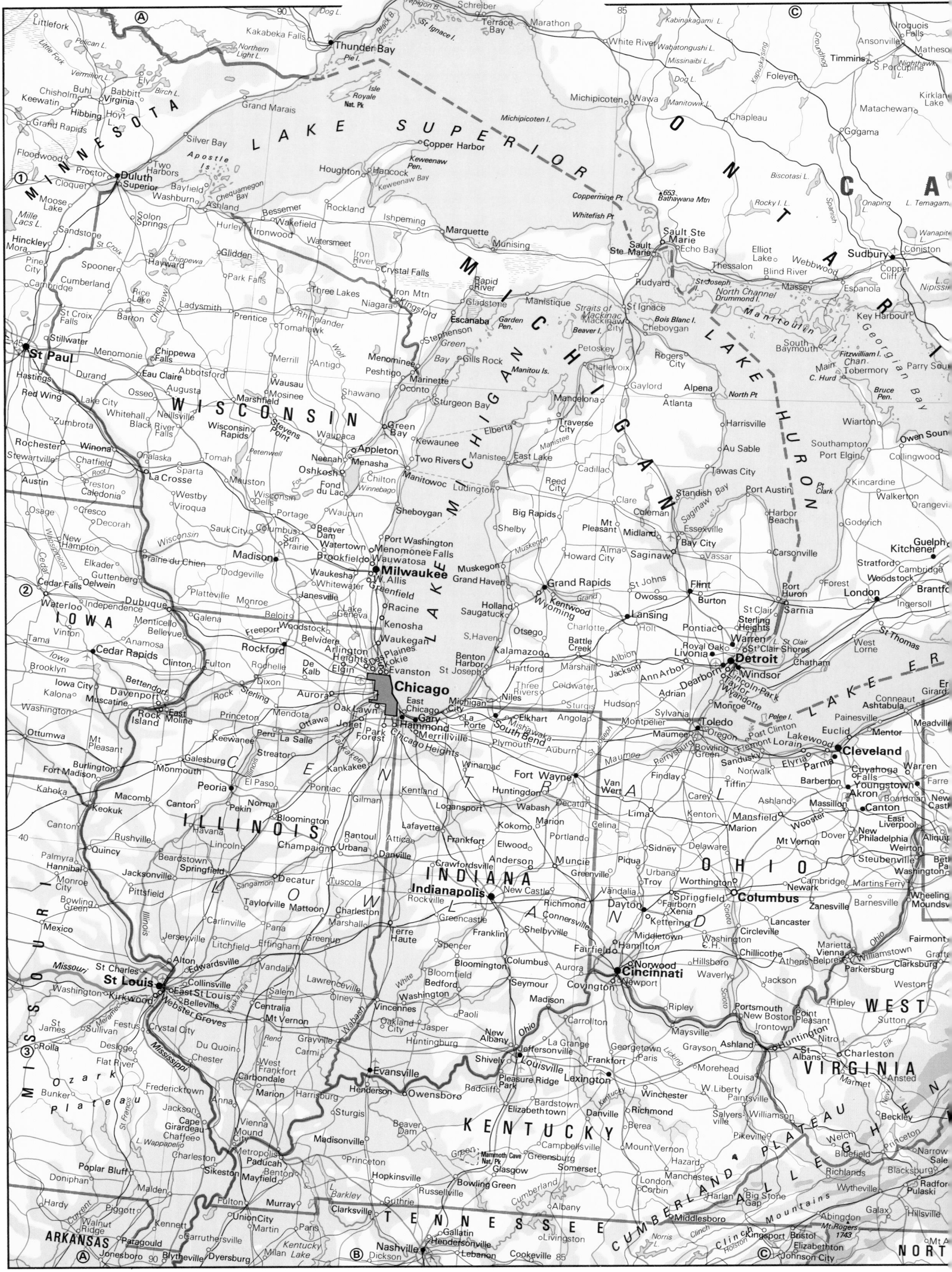

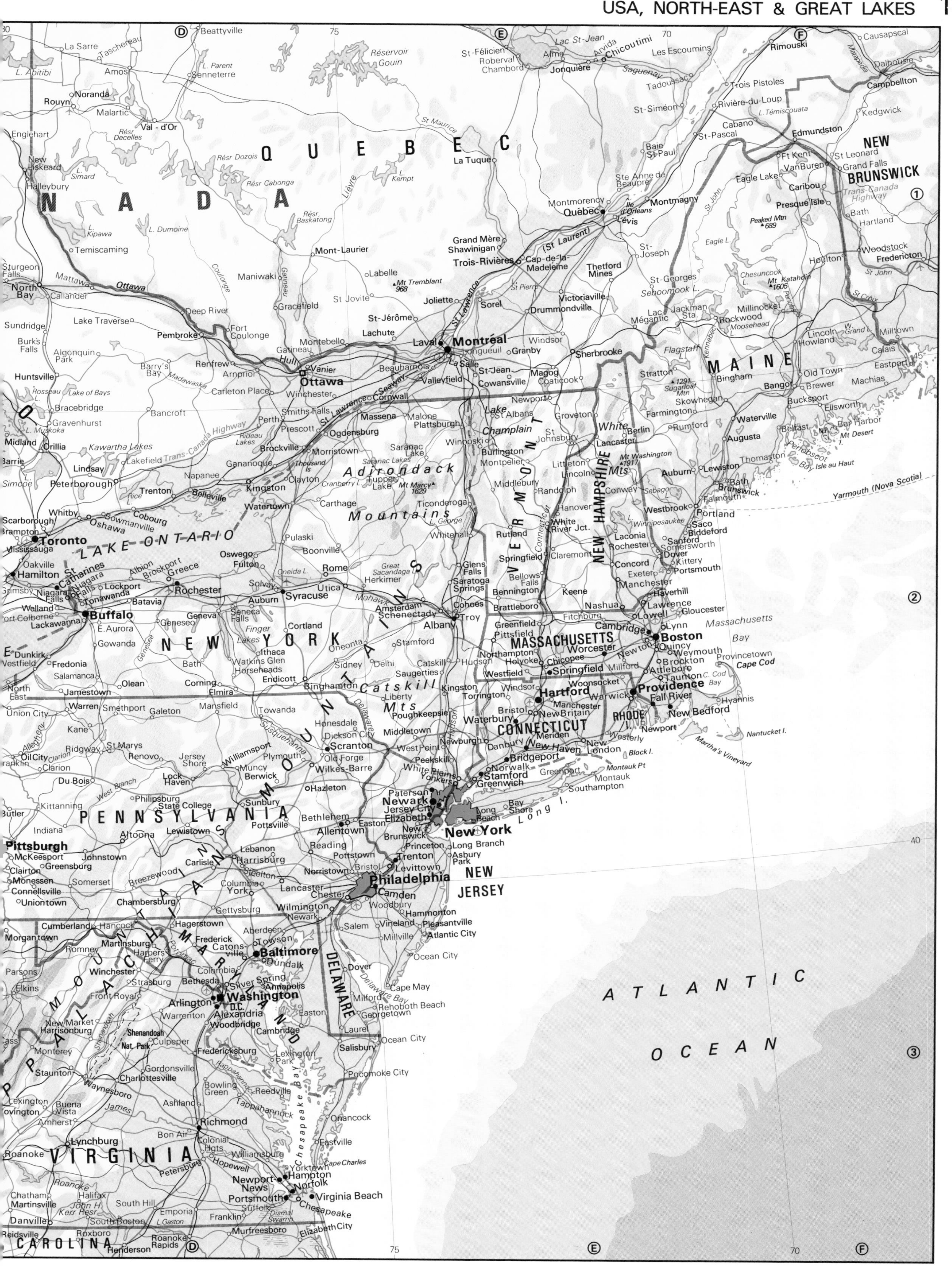

1:2.5M
0 25 50 75 100 km
0 25 50 mls

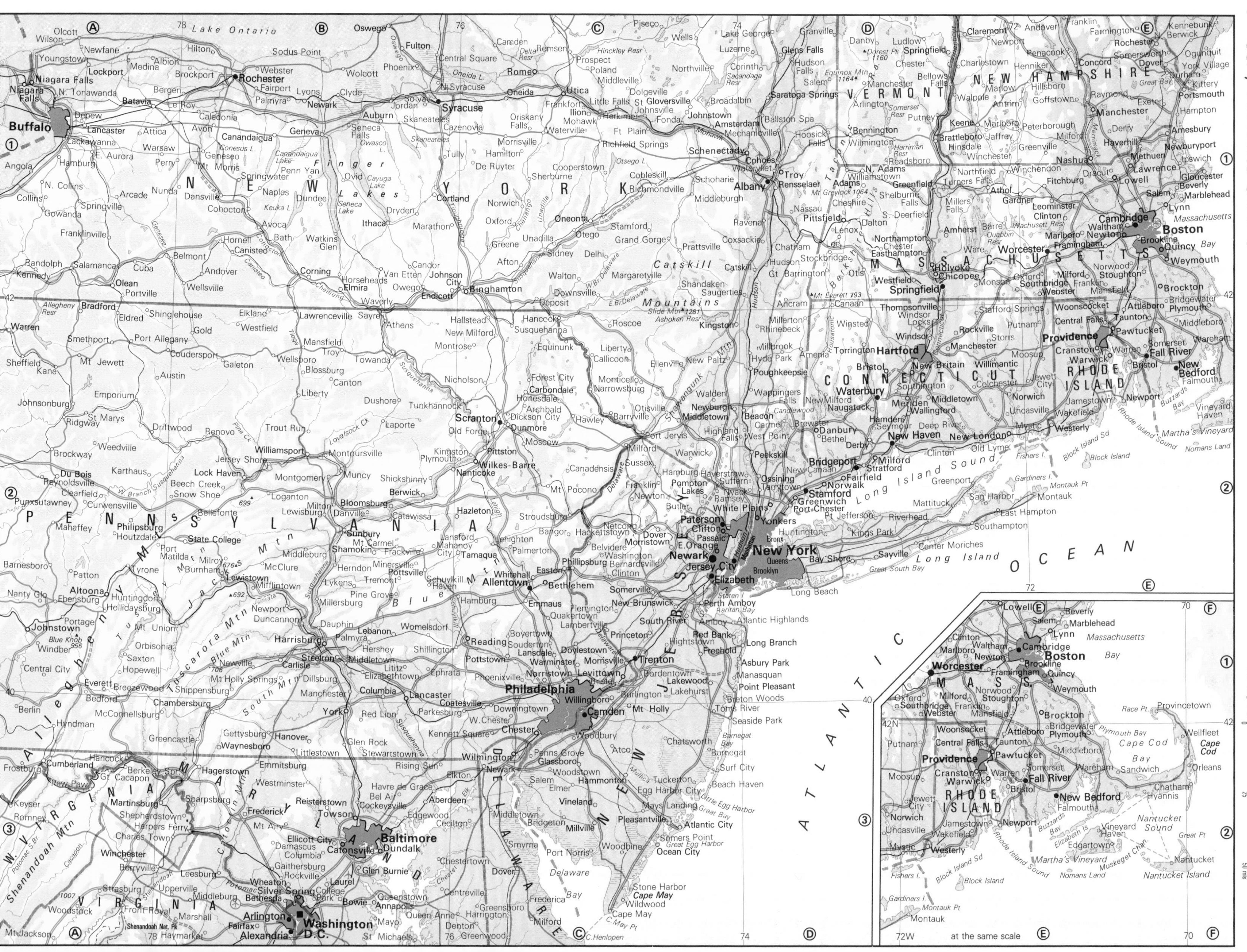
ATLANTIC OCEAN
NEW YORK
PENNSYLVANIA
NEW JERSEY
CONNECTICUT
MASSACHUSETTS
RHODE ISLAND
VERMONT
NEW HAMPSHIRE
MARYLAND
DELAWARE
VIRGINIA
W. VIRGINIA
New York
Philadelphia
Boston
Baltimore
Washington D.C.
Providence
Hartford
Albany
Buffalo
Rochester
Syracuse
Lake Ontario
Long Island
Long Island Sound
at the same scale

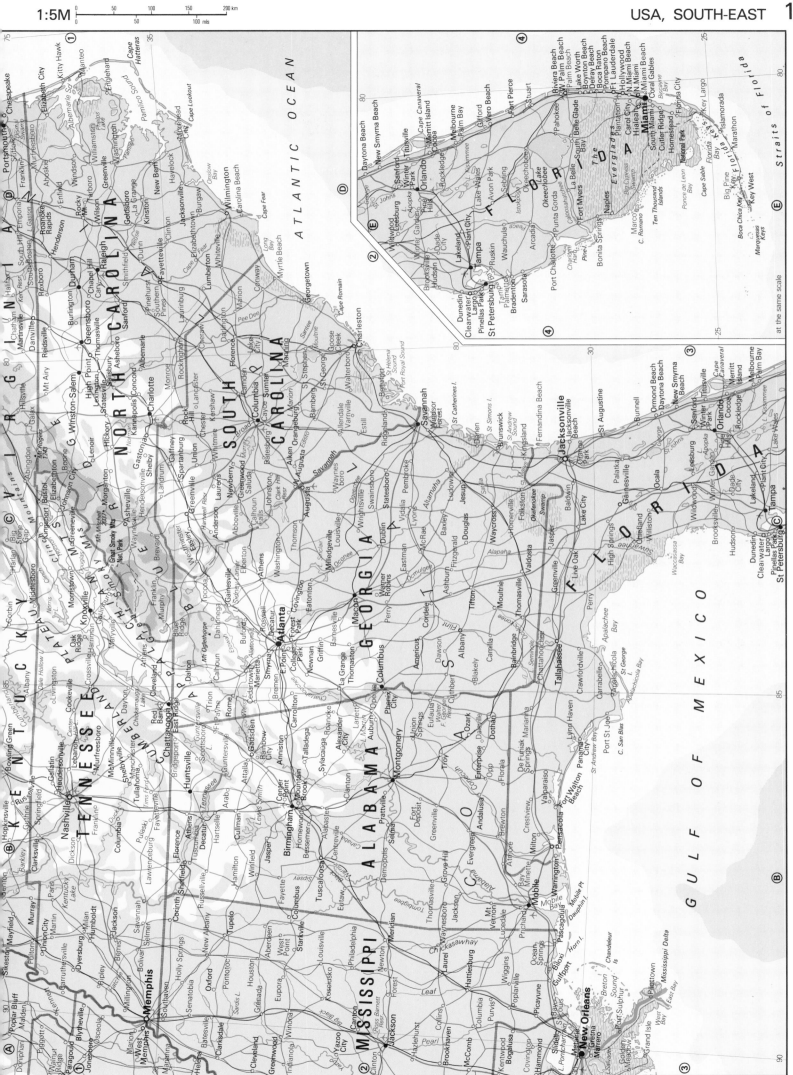

1:5M

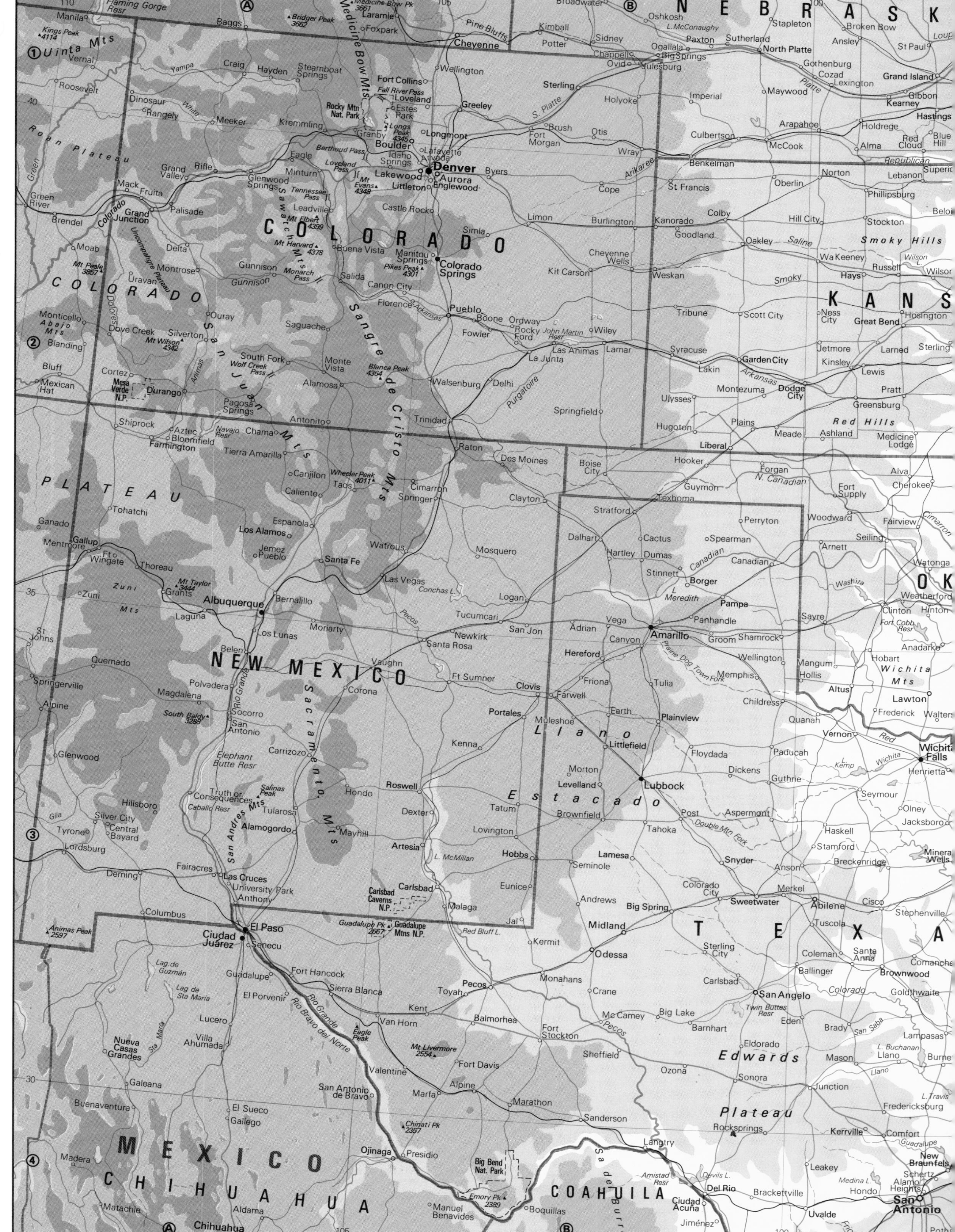

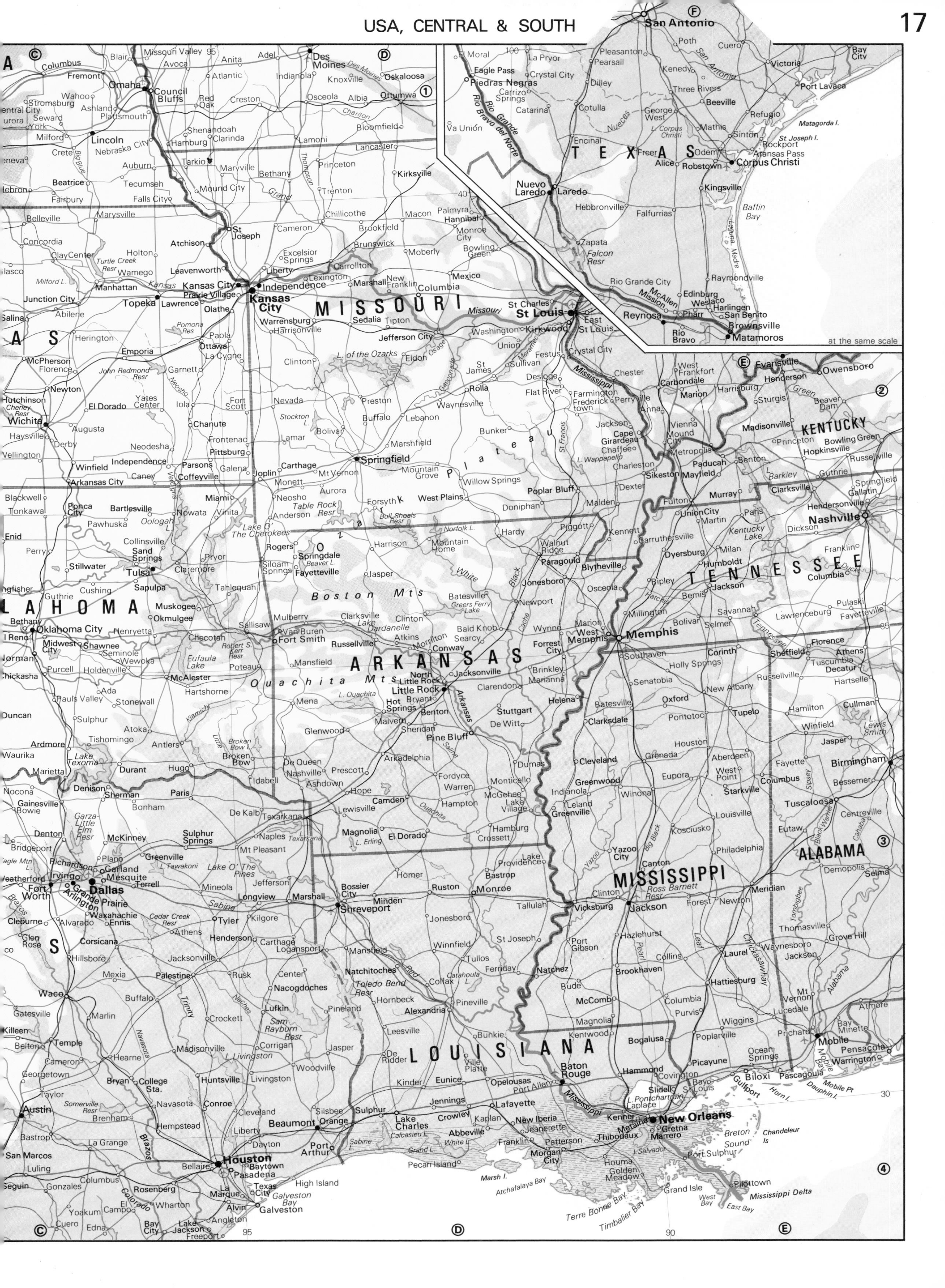

States: TEXAS, OKLAHOMA, MISSOURI, ARKANSAS, KANSAS, KENTUCKY, TENNESSEE, MISSISSIPPI, ALABAMA, LOUISIANA

at the same scale

Nebraska, Missouri, Ozark Plateau, Boston Mts, Ouachita Mts, Mississippi

Major cities: Omaha, Council Bluffs, Lincoln, Des Moines, Kansas City, Topeka, Wichita, St Louis, St Joseph, Springfield, Tulsa, Oklahoma City, Little Rock, North Little Rock, Hot Springs, Fort Smith, Memphis, Nashville, Jackson, Vicksburg, Shreveport, Dallas, Fort Worth, Arlington, Houston, Baton Rouge, New Orleans, Birmingham, Mobile, Corpus Christi, San Antonio, Austin, Brownsville, Matamoros, Nuevo Laredo, Laredo

1:5M 0 50 100 150 200 km; 0 50 100 mls

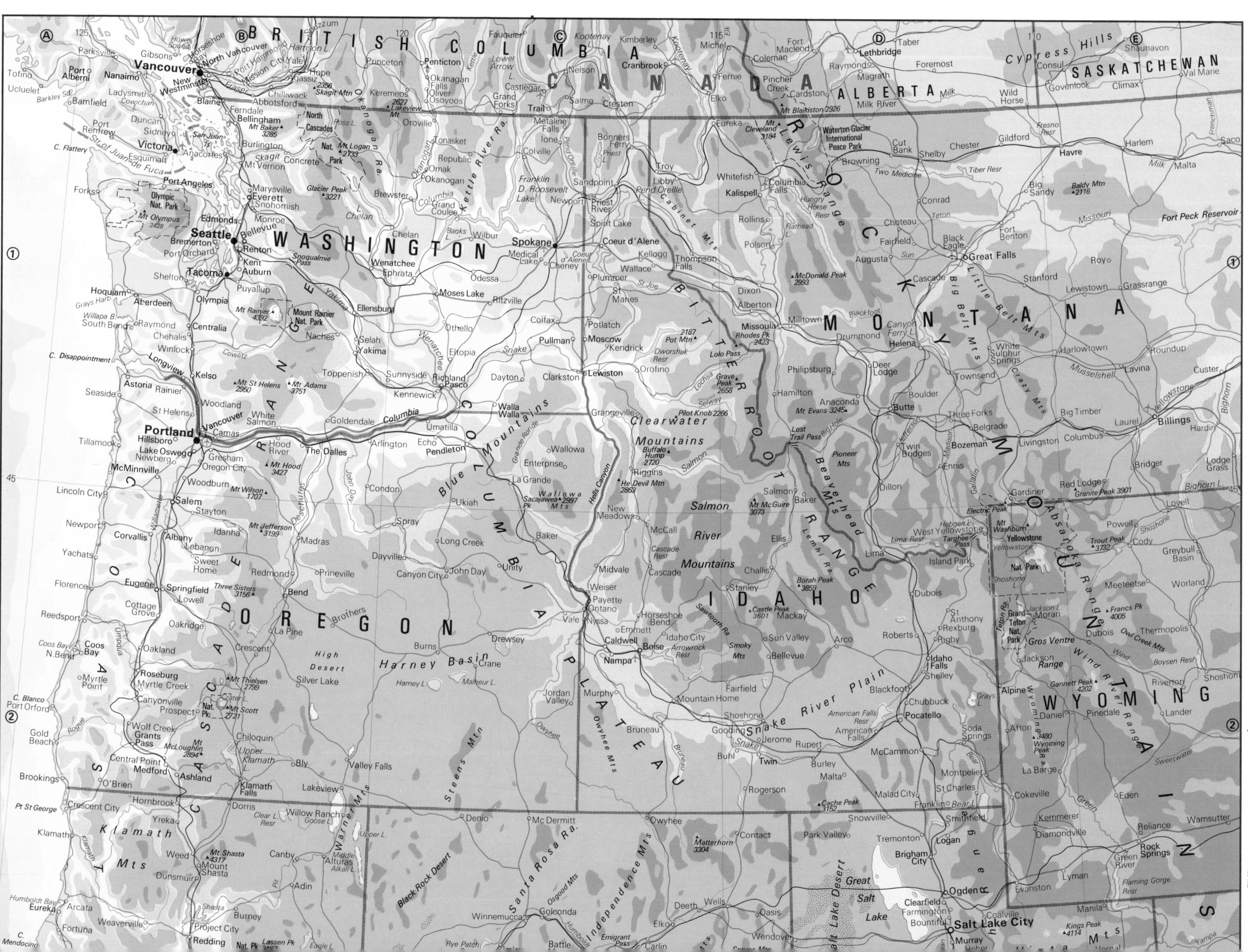
BRITISH COLUMBIA
ALBERTA
SASKATCHEWAN
WASHINGTON
OREGON
IDAHO
MONTANA
WYOMING
ROCKY MOUNTAINS
BITTERROOT RANGE
CASCADE RANGE
COLUMBIA PLATEAU
Seattle
Portland
Spokane
Vancouver
Victoria
Boise
Salt Lake City
Great Falls
Billings
Helena
Missoula
Salem
Eugene
Tacoma
Olympia
Pocatello
Butte
Bozeman
Yakima
Lewiston
Great Salt Lake
Great Salt Lake Desert
Salmon River Mountains
Clearwater Mountains
Blue Mountains
Wallowa Mts
Beaverhead Mts
Lemhi Ra.
Lewis Range
Big Belt Mts
Little Belt Mts
Absaroka Range
Wind River Range
Owyhee Mts
Independence Mts
Santa Rosa Ra.
Steens Mtn
Harney Basin
High Desert
Black Rock Desert
Klamath Mts
Snake River Plain
Yellowstone Nat. Park
Grand Teton Nat. Park
Mount Rainier Nat. Park
Olympic Nat. Park
Waterton-Glacier International Peace Park
Mt Rainier 4392
Mt Hood 3427
Mt Adams 3751
Mt Shasta 4317
Gannett Peak 4202
Borah Peak 3860
Kings Peak 4114

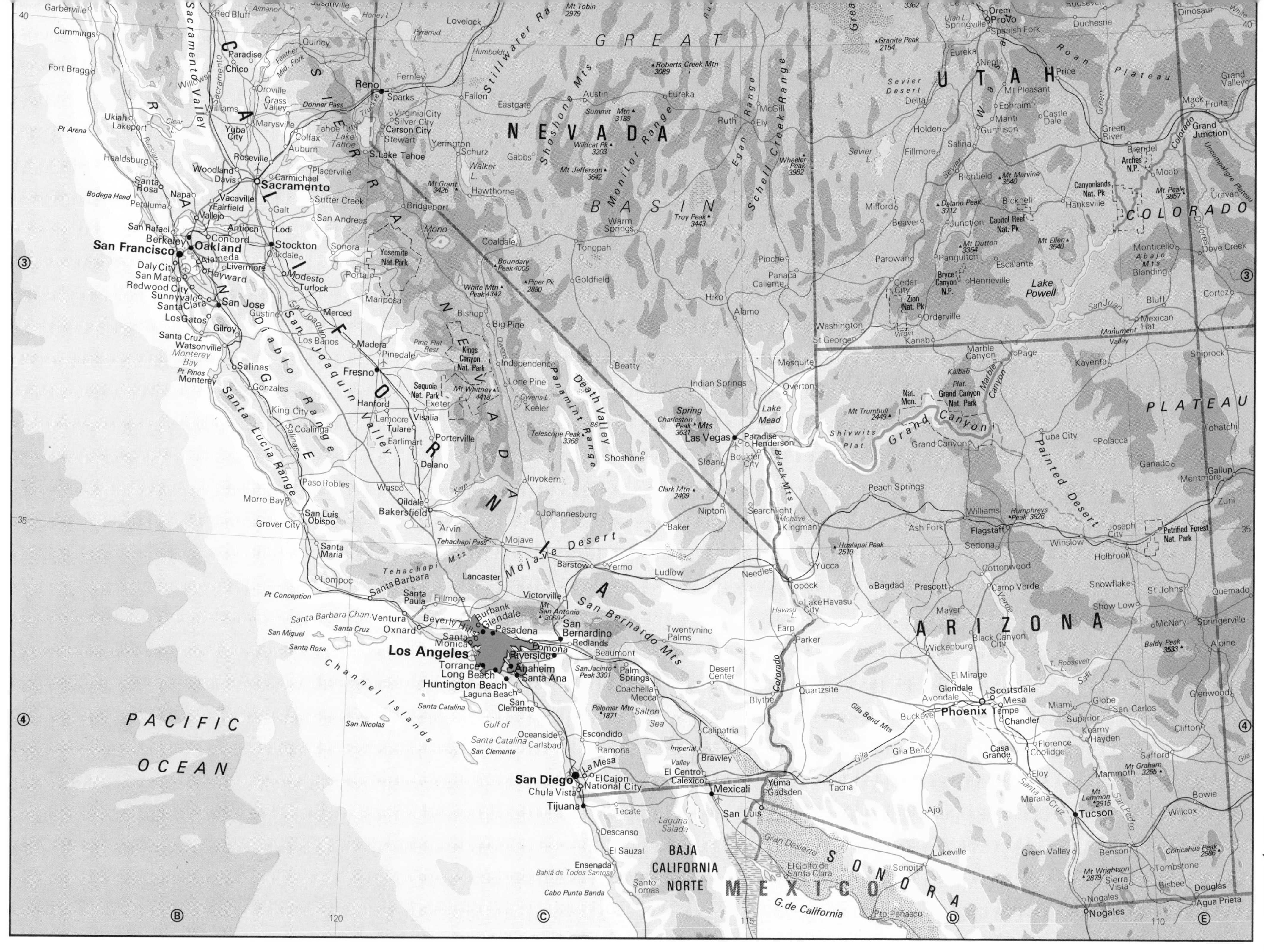
PACIFIC OCEAN
CALIFORNIA
NEVADA
UTAH
ARIZONA
COLORADO
SONORA
MEXICO
BAJA CALIFORNIA NORTE
GREAT BASIN
PLATEAU
SIERRA NEVADA
Mojave Desert
Painted Desert
Death Valley
Grand Canyon
Grand Canyon Nat. Park
Lake Mead
Lake Powell
Lake Tahoe
Salton Sea
Sacramento Valley
San Joaquin Valley
Santa Lucia Range
Diablo Range
Panamint Range
San Bernardino Mts
Black Mts
Spring Mts
Shoshone Mts
Monitor Range
Schell Creek Range
Egan Range
Stillwater Ra.
Channel Islands
Gulf of Santa Catalina
G. de California
El Golfo de Santa Clara
Gran Desierto
Yosemite Nat Park
Kings Canyon Nat. Park
Sequoia Nat. Park
Zion Nat. Pk
Bryce Canyon N.P.
Capitol Reef Nat. Pk
Canyonlands Nat. Pk
Arches N.P.
Petrified Forest Nat. Park
Mt Whitney 4418
Mt Trumbull 2449
Humphreys Peak 3826
Charleston Peak 3631
Telescope Peak 3368
White Mtn Peak 4342
Boundary Peak 4005
Wheeler Peak 3982
Mt Peale 3857
Mt Ellen 3540
Baldy Peak 3533
Mt Graham 3265
Chiricahua Peak 2986
Mt Lemmon 2915
Mt Wrightson 2879
Hualapai Peak 2519
Clark Mtn 2409
Palomar Mtn 1871
San Jacinto Peak 3301
Mt San Antonio 3068
Mt Grant 3426
Mt Jefferson 3642
Wildcat Pk 3203
Summit Mtn 3188
Roberts Creek Mtn 3089
Troy Peak 3443
Mt Tobin 2979
Granite Peak 2154
Delano Peak 3712
Mt Dutton 3364
Mt Marvine 3540
Piper Pk 2880
San Francisco
Oakland
San Jose
Sacramento
Stockton
Fresno
Bakersfield
Los Angeles
Long Beach
Pasadena
Anaheim
Santa Ana
Riverside
San Bernardino
San Diego
Tijuana
Mexicali
Calexico
El Centro
Las Vegas
Henderson
Reno
Carson City
Phoenix
Tucson
Flagstaff
Yuma
Provo
Orem
Grand Junction
Santa Barbara
Ventura
Oxnard
Santa Maria
San Luis Obispo
Monterey
Salinas
Santa Cruz
Modesto
Merced
Visalia
Tulare
Chico
Red Bluff
Ukiah
Santa Rosa
Napa
Vallejo
Berkeley
Palm Springs
Barstow
Victorville
Lancaster
Mojave
Needles
Kingman
Lake Havasu City
Prescott
Sedona
Williams
Winslow
Holbrook
Gallup
Page
Kayenta
Tuba City
Moab
Green River
Price
Richfield
Cedar City
St George
Kanab
Mesquite
Ely
Tonopah
Goldfield
Beatty
Bishop
Independence
Lone Pine
Hawthorne
Fallon
Lovelock
Fernley
Sparks
Bridgeport
Mammoth
Scottsdale
Mesa
Tempe
Chandler
Glendale
Casa Grande
Nogales
Douglas
Bisbee
Tombstone
Ensenada
Tecate
Chula Vista
National City
Escondido
Oceanside
Carlsbad
San Clemente
Huntington Beach
Torrance
Santa Monica
Burbank
Pt Conception
Pt Arena
Fort Bragg
Eureka
Austin
Eastgate
Gabbs
Pioche
Caliente
Indian Springs
Shoshone
Baker
Nipton
Searchlight
Boulder City
Blythe
Parker
Brawley
Calipatria
Ajo
Gila Bend
Wickenburg
Show Low
Globe
Safford
Willcox
Benson
Sierra Vista

0 25 50 75 100 km
0 25 50 mls

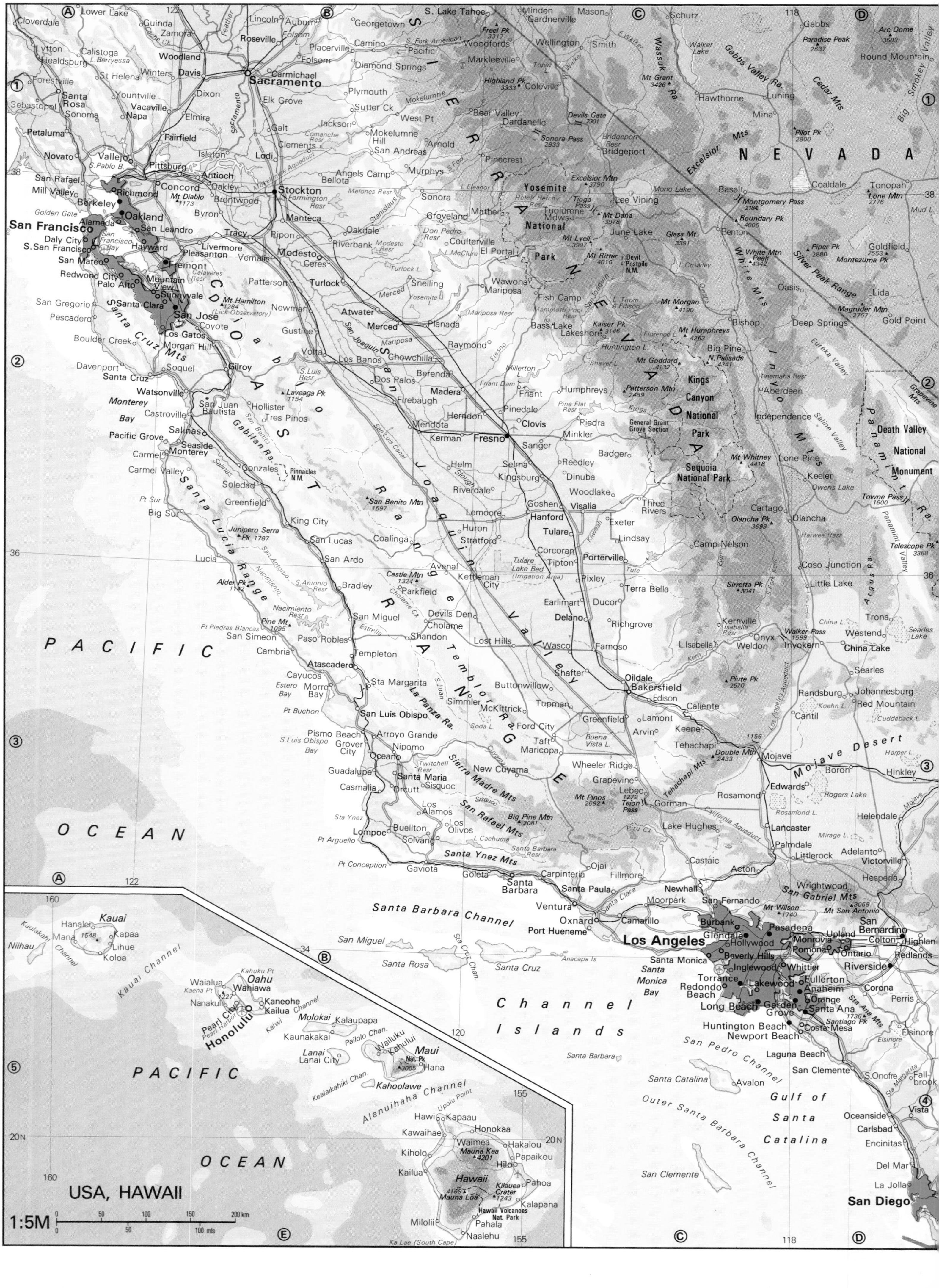

118

N E V A D A

Arc Dome 3589
Round Mountain
Paradise Peak 2637
Gabbs
Schurz
Mina
Luning
Hawthorne
Walker Lake
Mt Grant 3426
Coleville
Bridgeport
Mono Lake
Basalt
Montgomery Pass 2184
Boundary Pk 4005
Benton
Glass Mt 3391
Bishop
Big Pine
Deep Springs
Oasis
Lida
Gold Point
Goldfield
Montezuma Pk 2553
Silver Peak Range
Lone Mtn 2776
Tonopah
Coaldale
Mud Lake
Magruder Mtn 2757

S I E R R A   N E V A D A

Cloverdale
Lower Lake
Georgetown
S. Lake Tahoe
Minden
Gardnerville
Mason
Lincoln
Auburn
Roseville
Placerville
Woodfords
Wellington
Smith
Guinda
Zamora
Woodland
Camino
Pacific
Markleeville
Healdsburg
Calistoga
St Helena
Winters
Davis
Diamond Springs
Folsom
Highland Pk 3317
Freel Pk
Sacramento
Plymouth
Mokelumne
Dardanelle
Sonora Pass 2933
Napa
Elmira
Jackson
San Andreas
Arnold
Pinecrest
Yosemite
Vallejo
Pittsburg
Antioch
Oakley
Stockton
Angels Camp
Murphys
Sonora
Groveland
Mather
National
Richmond
Berkeley
Oakland
Concord
Brentwood
Manteca
Oakdale
Modesto
Riverbank
Coulterville
El Portal
Wawona
Mariposa
Park
San Francisco
Hayward
Fremont
Livermore
Tracy
Ripon
Turlock
Atwater
Merced
Planada
Raymond
Fresno
San Jose
Los Gatos
Morgan Hill
Gilroy
Los Banos
Dos Palos
Madera
Clovis
Pinedale
Santa Cruz
Watsonville
Hollister
King City
Coalinga
Mendota
Herndon
Kerman
Fresno
Sanger
Monterey
Salinas
Soledad
Greenfield
San Lucas
San Ardo
Bradley
Paso Robles
Shandon
Kettleman City
Bakersfield
Tulare
Visalia
Porterville
San Luis Obispo
Pismo Beach
Santa Maria
Lompoc
Solvang
Santa Barbara
Ventura
Oxnard
Los Angeles
Santa Monica
Long Beach
Anaheim
Santa Ana
Riverside
San Bernardino
San Diego
Oceanside
Carlsbad
Encinitas

P A C I F I C   O C E A N

Death Valley National Monument
Telescope Peak 3368
Panamint Range
Inyo Mts
Mojave Desert
Mojave
Lancaster
Palmdale
Victorville
Barstow

Channel Islands
Santa Barbara Channel
Santa Rosa
Santa Cruz
Anacapa Is
San Miguel
Gulf of Santa Catalina
Santa Catalina

P A C I F I C   O C E A N

Kauai
Hanalei
Kapaa
Lihue
Koloa
Niihau
Kauai Channel
Oahu
Waialua
Wahiawa
Kaneohe
Kailua
Pearl City
Honolulu
Molokai
Kalaupapa
Lanai
Lanai City
Maui
Wailuku
Kahului
Hana
Kahoolawe
Hawaii
Kailua
Waimea
Mauna Kea 4201
Hilo
Papaikou
Mauna Loa 4169
Kilauea Crater
Hawaii Volcanoes Nat. Park
Pahala
Naalehu
Ka Lae (South Cape)

0 50 100 150 200 km
0 50 100 mls

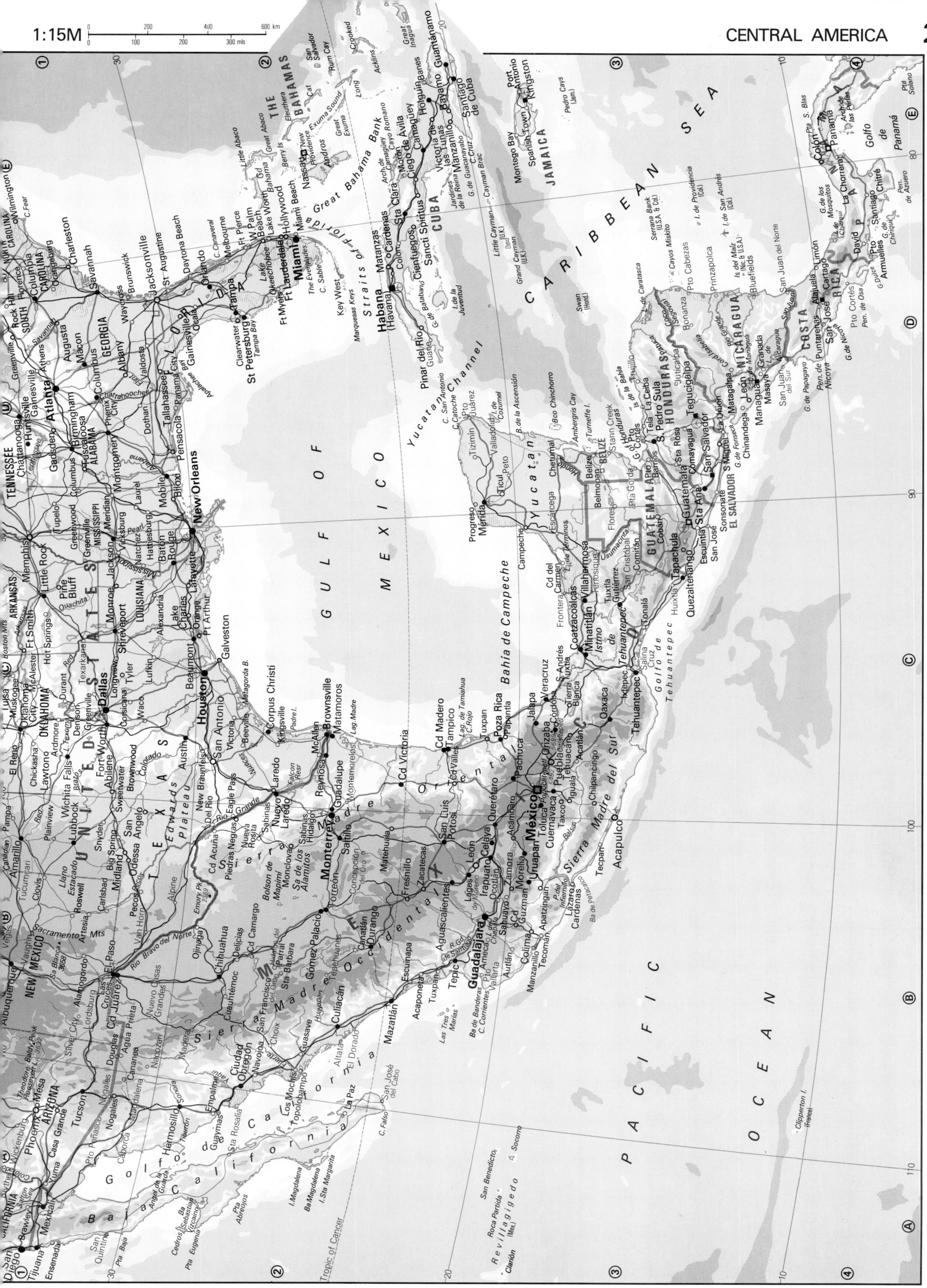

1:15M

0 200 400 600 km
0 100 200 300 mls

THE BAHAMAS

CUBA

JAMAICA

CARIBBEAN SEA

GULF OF MEXICO

PACIFIC OCEAN

UNITED STATES

MEXICO

BELIZE

GUATEMALA

EL SALVADOR

HONDURAS

NICARAGUA

COSTA RICA

PANAMA

NORTH CAROLINA
SOUTH CAROLINA
GEORGIA
FLORIDA
ALABAMA
TENNESSEE
MISSISSIPPI
LOUISIANA
ARKANSAS
OKLAHOMA
TEXAS
NEW MEXICO
ARIZONA
CALIFORNIA

Yucatan
Campeche
Bahía de Campeche
Straits of Florida
Yucatan Channel
Golfo de California

Miami
Ft Lauderdale
Hollywood
W Palm Beach
Ft Pierce
Melbourne
Orlando
Tampa
St Petersburg
Clearwater
Ft Myers
Key West
Jacksonville
St Augustine
Daytona Beach
Gainesville
Ocala
Tallahassee
Panama City
Pensacola
Mobile
New Orleans
Baton Rouge
Lafayette
Lake Charles
Beaumont
Orange
Port Arthur
Galveston
Houston
San Antonio
Austin
Corpus Christi
Brownsville
Matamoros
McAllen
Laredo
Dallas
Fort Worth
Waco
Abilene
San Angelo
Midland
Odessa
Lubbock
Amarillo
El Paso
Cd Juárez
Albuquerque
Tucson
Phoenix
Mexicali
Tijuana
San Diego
Ensenada
La Paz
Mazatlán
Culiacán
Hermosillo
Guaymas
Chihuahua
Torreón
Gómez Palacio
Durango
Monterrey
Saltillo
Zacatecas
Aguascalientes
Guadalajara
León
Guanajuato
Querétaro
San Luis Potosí
Tampico
Cd Madero
Cd Victoria
Veracruz
Poza Rica
Mexico
Toluca
Cuernavaca
Puebla
Orizaba
Córdoba
Acapulco
Oaxaca
Tehuantepec
Tuxtla Gutiérrez
Coatzacoalcos
Minatitlán
Villahermosa
Mérida
Campeche
Chetumal
Belize
Belmopan
Guatemala
Quezaltenango
Tapachula
Sta Ana
San Salvador
Tegucigalpa
S Pedro Sula
Managua
León
San José
Panamá
Colón
David

Habana (Havana)
Matanzas
Cárdenas
Pinar del Río
Cienfuegos
Sta Clara
Sancti Spíritus
Camagüey
Holguín
Bayamo
Santiago de Cuba
Guantánamo

Nassau
Freeport

Kingston
Montego Bay
Spanish Town

Tropic of Cancer

1:5M

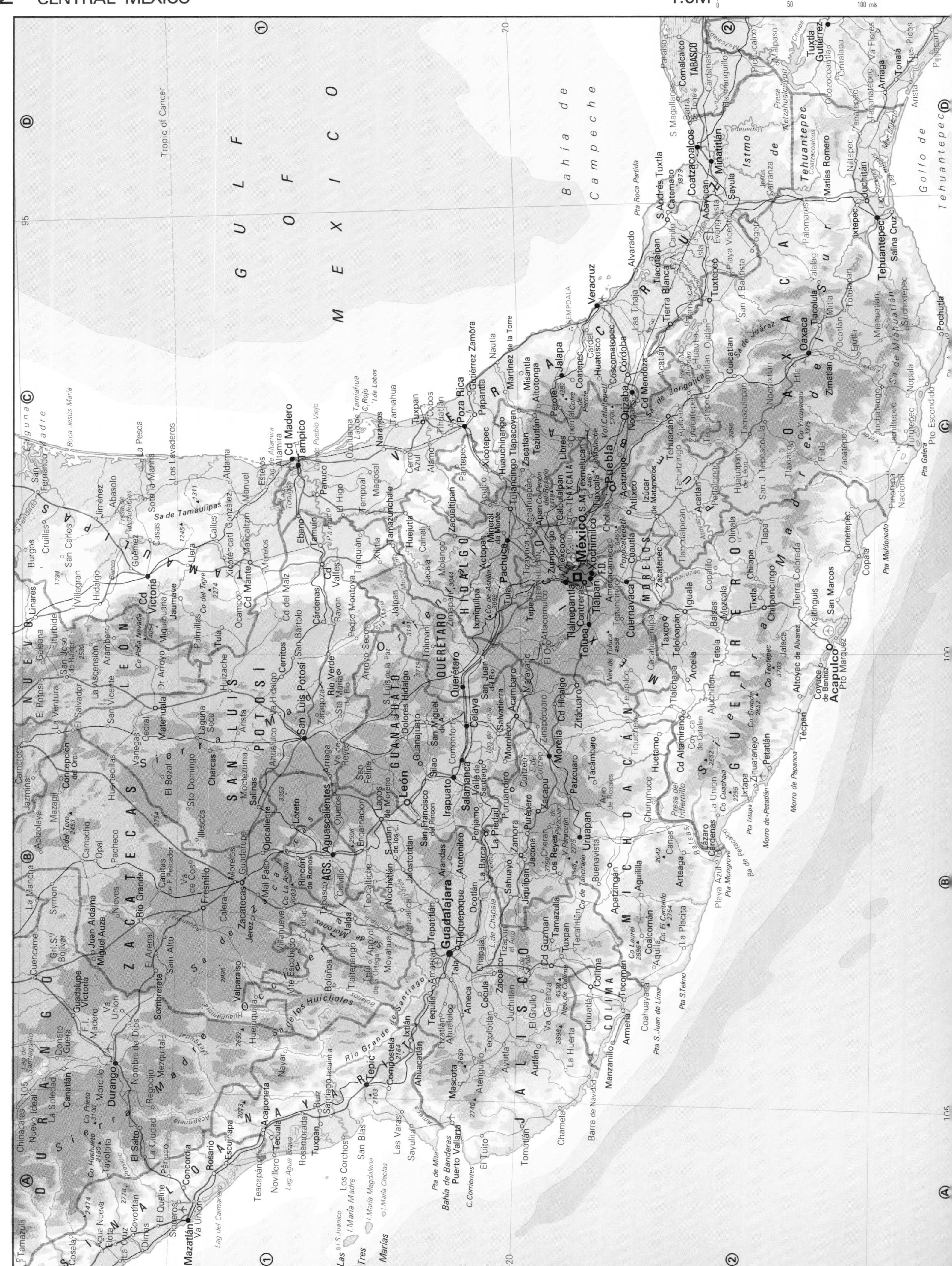
0 50 100 150 200 km
0 50 100 mls
GULF OF MEXICO
Bahía de Campeche
Golfo de Tehuantepec
Tropic of Cancer
DURANGO
ZACATECAS
SAN LUIS POTOSÍ
NUEVO LEÓN
TAMAULIPAS
AGUASCALIENTES
GUANAJUATO
QUERÉTARO
HIDALGO
JALISCO
COLIMA
MICHOACÁN
MÉXICO
MORELOS
PUEBLA
TLAXCALA
VERACRUZ
GUERRERO
OAXACA
TABASCO
Sierra Madre Occidental
Sierra Madre Oriental
Sierra Madre del Sur
Istmo de Tehuantepec
México
Guadalajara
Puebla
León
Aguascalientes
San Luis Potosí
Querétaro
Morelia
Toluca
Cuernavaca
Pachuca
Oaxaca
Acapulco
Veracruz
Tampico
Cd Madero
Cd Victoria
Durango
Zacatecas
Tepic
Colima
Mazatlán
Puerto Vallarta
Manzanillo
Jalapa
Orizaba
Coatzacoalcos
Tehuantepec
Salina Cruz
Tuxtla Gutiérrez
Poza Rica
Celaya
Irapuato
Salamanca
Uruapan
Chilpancingo
Tlaxcala
Tres Marías

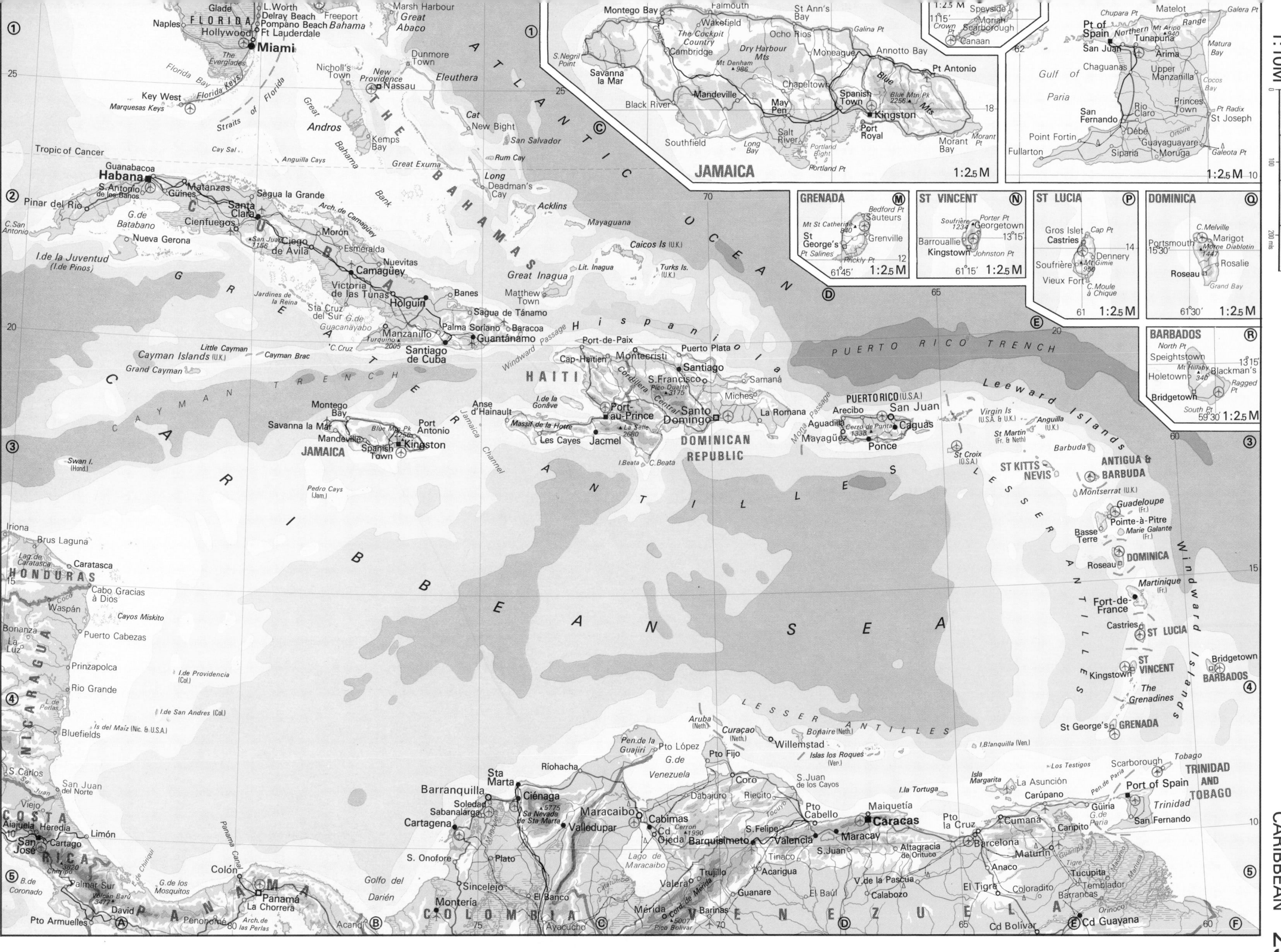

1:10M

100   200   300   400 km
100   200 mls

CARIBBEAN SEA

ATLANTIC OCEAN

PUERTO RICO TRENCH

CAYMAN TRENCH

Windward Islands

Leeward Islands

Lesser Antilles

Greater Antilles

Trinidad and Tobago (inset)
1:2.5M
Galera Pt, Matelot, Mt Aripo Range, Northern Range, Toco Pt, St Joseph, Galeota Pt, Chupara Pt, Cocos Bay, Matura Bay, Pt Radix, Mayaro, Arima, Tunapuna, Upper Manzanilla, Rio Claro, Debé, Guayaguayare, Siparia, San Juan, Pt. of Spain, Chaguanas, San Fernando, Gulf of Paria, Point Fortin, Point Fortin, Fullarton

Tobago (1:2.5M): Speyside, Scarborough, Canaan, Moriah, Plymouth, Crown Pt

Dominica
1:2.5M
C.Melville, Marigot, Morne Diablotin 1447, Portsmouth, Roseau, Grand Bay, 61°30'

Barbados
1:2.5M
North Pt, Speightstown, 13°15, Mt Hillaby 340, Blackman's, Ragged Pt, Holetown, Bridgetown, South Pt, 59°30'

St Lucia
1:2.5M
Gros Islet, Cap Pt, Castries, Dennery, Soufrière, Pitons 798, Vieux Fort, Moule à Chique, 61

St Vincent
1:2.5M
Porter Pt, Georgetown, 13°15', Soufrière 1234, Johnston Pt, Barrouallie, Kingstown, 61°15'

Grenada
1:2.5M
Bedford Pt, Sauteurs, Mt St Catherine 840, Grenville, St George's, Pt Salines, Prickly Pt, 61°45', 12

Jamaica (inset)
Montego Bay, St Ann's Bay, Pt Antonio, Annotto Bay, Morant Bay, Blue Mtn Pk 2256, Kingston, Port Royal, Spanish Town, Chapelton, May Pen, Mandeville, Dry Harbour Mts, Mt Denham 986, Cockpit Country, Falmouth, Wakefield, Cambridge, Black River, Southfield, Savanna la Mar, S. Negril Point

Main map labels
Miami, Naples, Key West, Marquesas Keys, Florida Keys, Key West, Hollywood, Ft Lauderdale, Pompano Beach, Delray Beach, L Worth, Freeport, Marsh Harbour, Great Abaco, Nicholl's Town, Andros, Nassau, New Providence, Eleuthera, Dunmore Town, Cat, Kemps Bay, Great Exuma, Long, Deadman's Cay, Rum Cay, San Salvador, New Bight, Cockburn Town, Great Inagua, Lit. Inagua, Matthew Town, Acklins, Mayaguana, Caicos Is (U.K.), Turks Is. (U.K.)

THE BAHAMAS

CUBA
Habana, Guanabacoa, Matanzas, Guines, Cienfuegos, Santa Clara, Nueva Gerona, I. de la Juventud (I. de Pinos), Pinar del Rio, C. San Antonio, Sagua la Grande, Sancti Spíritus, Morón, Camagüey, Victoria de las Tunas, Holguín, Banes, Nuevitas, Esmeralda, Ciego de Ávila, Manzanillo, Bayamo, Palma Soriano, Santiago de Cuba, Guantánamo, Baracoa

Cayman Islands (U.K.), Grand Cayman, Little Cayman, Cayman Brac

HAITI
Cap-Haïtien, Port-de-Paix, Gonaïves, Port-au-Prince, Jacmel, Les Cayes, Anse d'Hainault, Ile de la Gonâve, Massif de la Hotte, La Selle 2680

DOMINICAN REPUBLIC
Monte Cristi, Santiago, Puerto Plata, San Francisco, Samaná, La Vega, Santo Domingo, La Romana, Ponce, Barahona, I. Beata, C. Beata, Cordillera Central, Pico Duarte 3175

Hispaniola

PUERTO RICO (U.S.A.)
San Juan, Caguas, Arecibo, Aguadilla, Mayagüez, Ponce, Mona Passage

Virgin Is (U.S.A. & U.K.), St Croix (U.S.A.), Anguilla (U.K.), St Martin (Fr. & Neth.), St Kitts & Nevis, Montserrat (U.K.), Antigua & Barbuda, Barbuda, Guadeloupe (Fr.), Pointe-à-Pitre, Basse Terre, Marie Galante, Dominica, Roseau, Martinique (Fr.), Fort-de-France, St Lucia, Castries, St Vincent, Kingstown, The Grenadines, Grenada, St George's, Barbados, Bridgetown

Tobago, Trinidad, Port of Spain, San Fernando, Scarborough

Los Testigos, La Asunción, I.Margarita, Isla Margarita, I.Blanquilla (Ven.), I.La Tortuga, I.Los Roques (Neth.), Bonaire (Neth.), Curaçao (Neth.), Willemstad, Aruba (Neth.), Islas los Roques (Ven.), S. Juan de los Cayos

VENEZUELA
Caracas, Maiquetía, Maracay, Valencia, Puerto Cabello, Barquisimeto, Coro, Maracaibo, Lago de Maracaibo, Cabimas, Ciudad Ojeda, Mérida, Valera, Trujillo, Barinas, Guanare, Acarigua, San Felipe, Barcelona, Cumaná, Carúpano, Güiria, Maturín, Anaco, El Tigre, Carúpano, Tucupita, Temblador, Cd Guayana, Cd Bolívar, Orinoco, Barrancas

COLOMBIA
Sta Marta, Barranquilla, Cartagena, Cienaga, Riohacha, Valledupar, Montería, Sincelejo, El Banco, Plato, Soledad, Sabanalarga, S. Onofre, Pen. de la Guajira, Sierra Nevada de Sta Marta, Pico Cristóbal Colón 5775, G. de Venezuela, G.de Darién, Golfo del Darién

PANAMA
Panamá, La Chorrera, Colón, Panama Canal, Arch. de las Perlas

COSTA RICA
San José, Alajuela, Heredia, Cartago, Limón, Pto Armuelles, David, Pto Cortés

NICARAGUA
San Juan del Norte, Bluefields, Rio Grande, Prinzapolca, Puerto Cabezas, Cabo Gracias à Dios, Cayos Miskito, Lago de Nicaragua, San Carlos

HONDURAS
Brus Laguna, Iriona, Cabo Camarón, Bonanza, Waspán, Caratasca, L.de Caratasca

Swan I. (Hond.), I. de Providencia (Col.), I. de San Andrés (Col.), Pedro Cays (Jam.)

Tropic of Cancer

25, 20, 15, 70, 65, 60, 75

1:35M

Gulf of Mexico
U.S.A.
Miami
THE BAHAMAS
Habana
Tropic of Cancer
Mérida
CUBA
MEXICO
Guantanamo
DOMINICAN REP.
HAITI
BELIZE
Belmopan
JAMAICA
Kingston
Port au-Prince
Sto Domingo
Pto Rico (U.S.A.)
ANTIGUA & BARBUDA
GUATEMALA
Guatemala
HONDURAS
Tegucigalpa
ST KITTS-NEVIS
Guadeloupe (Fr.)
S.Salvador
EL SALVADOR
DOMINICA
Martinique (Fr.)
CARIBBEAN SEA
NICARAGUA
ST LUCIA
Managua
ST VINCENT
BARBADOS
GRENADA
COSTA RICA
S.José
Barranquilla
Sta Marta
Maracaibo
Caracas
Barcelona
TRINIDAD & TOBAGO
PANAMA
Panamá
Medellín
S.Cristóbal
Orinoco
Cd Bolivar
VENEZUELA
Georgetown
I. del Coco (C.R.)
Bogotá
GUYANA
Paramaribo
Cayenne
Malpelo (Col.)
Buenaventura
Cali
SURINAM
FR. GUIANA
Boa Vista
COLOMBIA
Popayán
S.Lorenzo
Quito
I. de Marajó
S.Pedro e S.Paulo (Braz.)
Galapagos Is (Ecu.)
ECUADOR
Negro
Santarem
Equator
Guayaquil
Belém
Manaus
Amazonas
Iquitos
São Luis
Xingu
Fortaleza
Tapajós
I.Fernando de Noronha (Braz.)
Teresina
Purus
Madeira
Ucayali
Natal
Trujillo
PERU
Pto Velho
Recife
BRAZIL
Maceió
Callao
Lima
Huancayo
Pto Maldonado
Salvador
Cuzco
Cuiabá
Brasília
SOUTH PACIFIC OCEAN
Arequipa
La Paz
São Francisco
Goiânia
BOLIVIA
Cochabamba
Sta Cruz
Sucre
Arica
Corumbá
Belo Horizonte
Campo Grande
Ribeirão Prêto
Campos
PARAGUAY
Rio de Janeiro
São Paulo
Santos
Trindade (Braz.)
Antofagasta
Asunción
Salta
Tropic of Capricorn
Curitiba
S.Félix (Chi.)
S.Miguel de Tucumán
Resistencia
Posadas
Paraná
CHILE
ARGENTINA
Pto Alegre
Córdoba
Sante Fe
Paraná
Pelotas
Mendoza
Rosario
URUGUAY
Valparaiso
Santiago
Buenos Aires
Montevideo
SOUTH ATLANTIC OCEAN
Is Juan Fernández (Chi.)
R. de la Plata
Concepción
Mar del Plata
Bahía Blanca
Valdivia
Pto Montt
Cmd. Rivadavia
G.San Jorge
Falkland Is (U.K.)
Stanley
Rio Gallegos
Punta Arenas
Tierra del Fuego
S.Georgia (U.K.)
S.Sandwich Is (U.K.)
S.Shetland Is (U.K.)
S.Orkney Is (U.K.)
ANTARCTICA

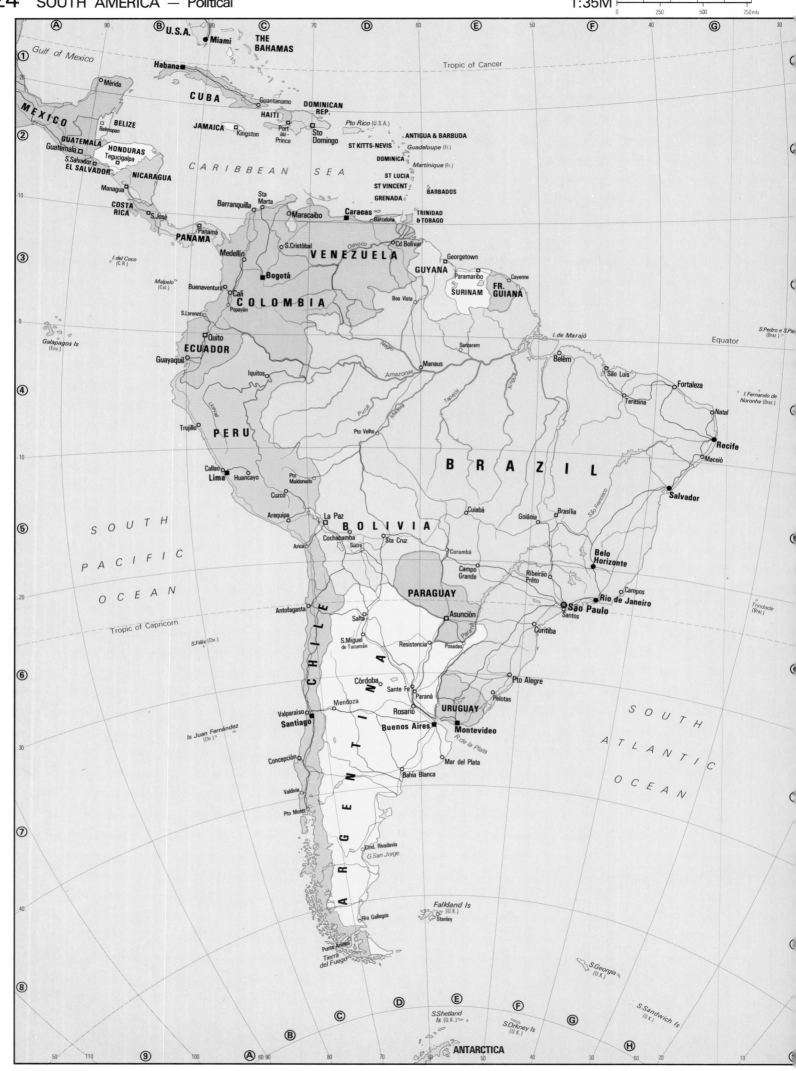

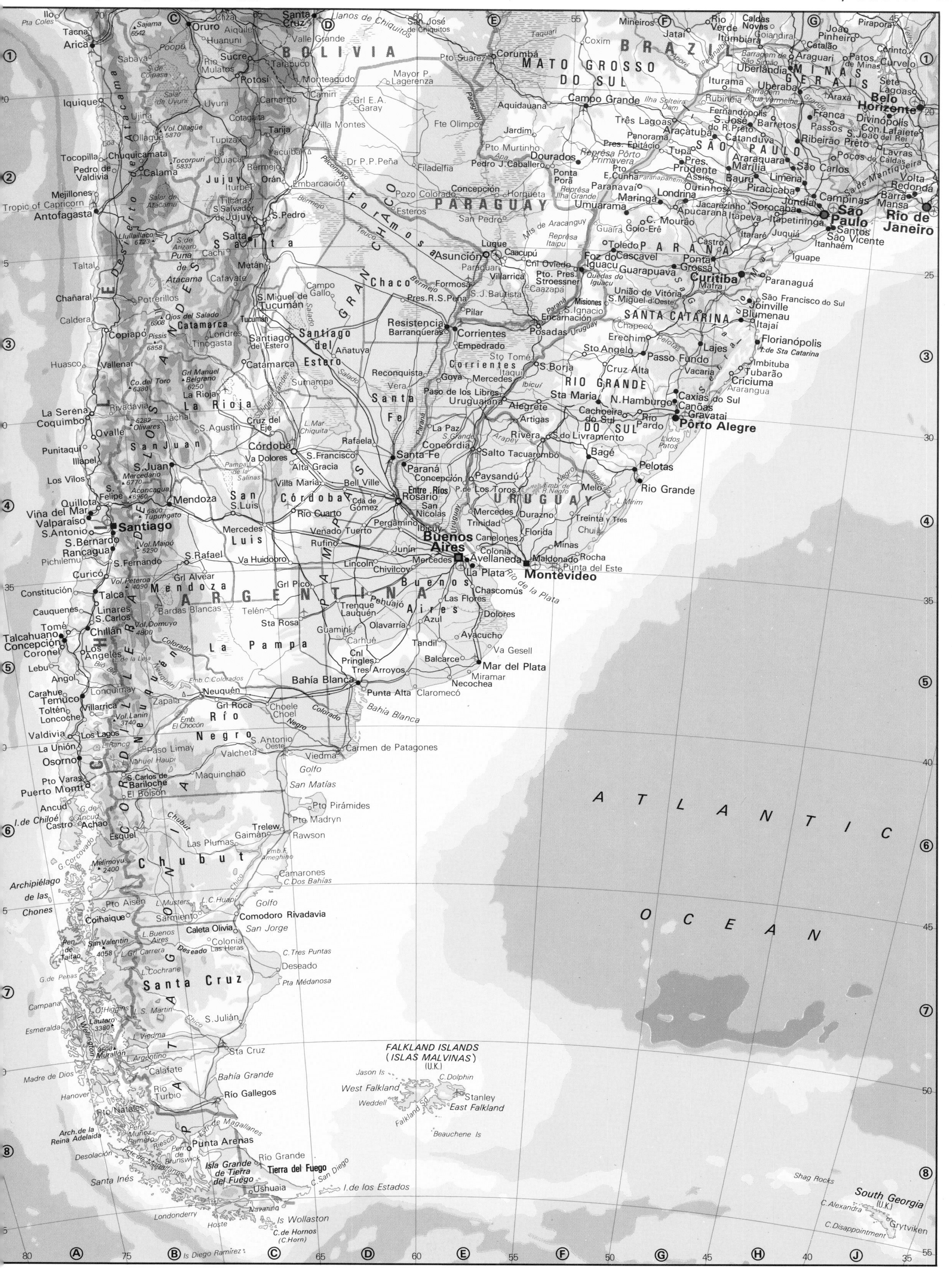
BOLIVIA
PARAGUAY
URUGUAY
ARGENTINA
ATLANTIC OCEAN
FALKLAND ISLANDS (ISLAS MALVINAS) (U.K.)
South Georgia (U.K.)
Buenos Aires
Montevideo
Santiago
Asunción
São Paulo
Rio de Janeiro
Pôrto Alegre
Curitiba
Tropic of Capricorn

1:15M

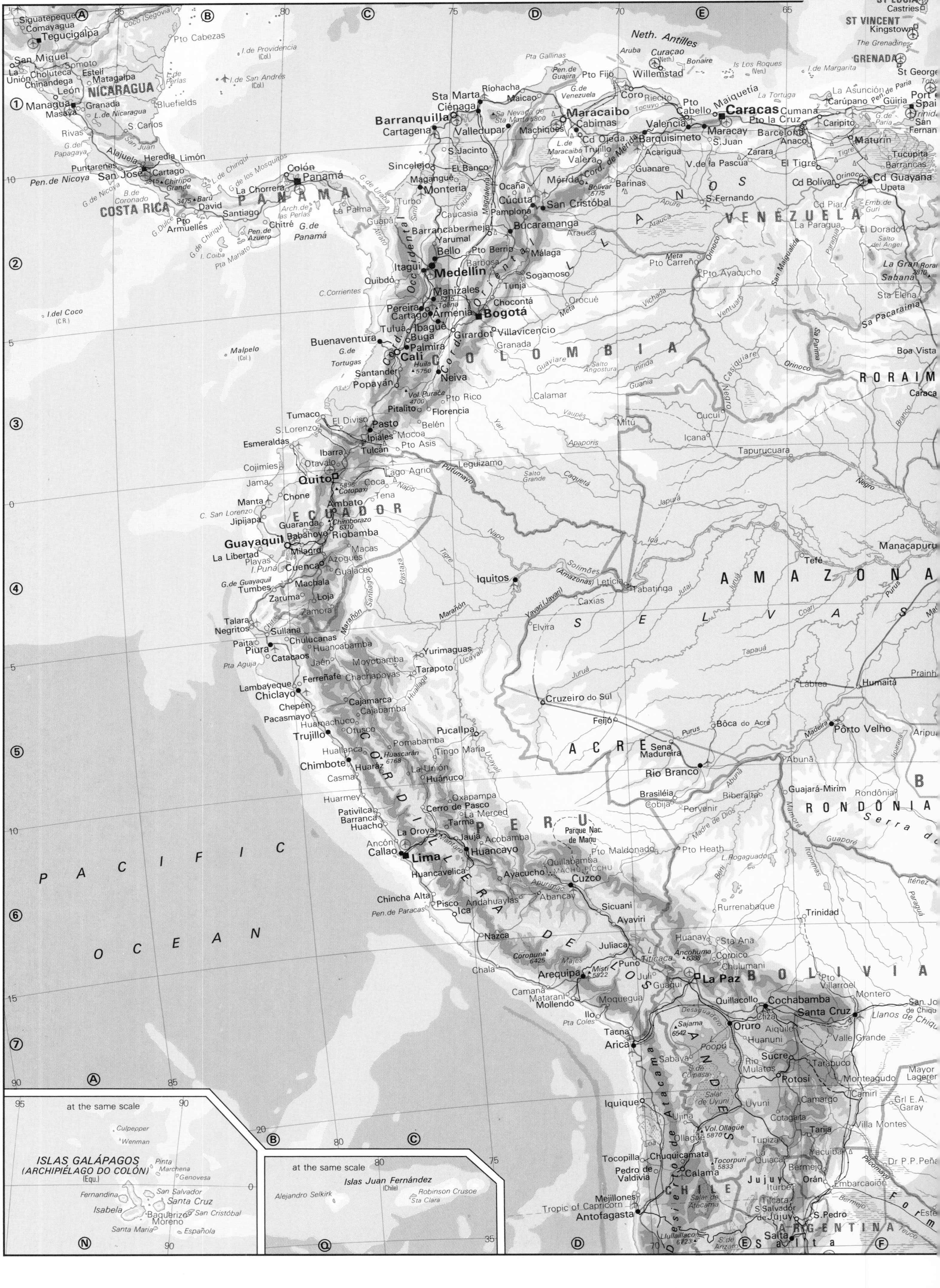

200   400   600 km
100   200   300 mls

A   B   C   75   D   70   E   65   F

Roseau
Fort-de-France
Martinique (Fr.)
ST LUCIA
Castries
ST VINCENT
Kingstown
The Grenadines
GRENADA
St George's

Siguatepeque
Comayagua
Tegucigalpa
San Miguel
La Unión   Somoto   Estelí   Matagalpa
Choluteca   Chinandega   León
NICARAGUA
Managua   Masaya   Granada
Rivas   L. de Nicaragua
S. Carlos
Bluefields
Coco (Segovia)
Pto Cabezas
I. de Providencia (Col.)
I. de San Andrés (Col.)
Arch. de las Perlas
Colón   Panamá
PANAMÁ
La Chorrera
G. de Panamá
Pen. de Azuero
Chitré   Santiago
David   Barú   3475
Chiriquí Grande   3815
Heredia   Limón
San José   Cartago   Chirripó Grande
COSTA RICA
Puntarenas
Pen. de Nicoya   G. de Nicoya
G. del Papagaya
B. de Coronado
I. del Coco (C.R.)
Malpelo (Col.)

Pta Gallinas
Pen. de Guajira   Pta Gallinas
Ríohacha
Sta Marta   Ciénaga
Barranquilla   Cartagena
Valledupar
Maicao
Sa Nevada de Sta Marta 5800
S. Jacinto   El Banco
Sincelejo
Magangué   Machiques
Montería
Turbo   Caucasia   Ocaña
Quibdó   Barrancabermeja
Yarumal   Pto Berrio   Málaga
Bello   Barbosa   Pamplona
Itagüí   Medellín   Sogamoso
Manizales   Chocontá
Pereira   Cartago   Tunja
Armenia   Bogotá
Buenaventura   Tuluá   Ibagué   Girardot
Buga   Villavicencio
Palmira   Granada
Cali   Santander   Neiva
Huila 5750
Popayán   Vol. Purace 4700   Pto Rico
Tumaco   Pitalito   Florencia
El Diviso   Pasto   Belén
S. Lorenzo   Ipiales   Mocoa
Esmeraldas   Tulcán   Pto Asis
Cojimíes   Ibarra   Leguizamo
Jama   Otavalo
Quito   5896 Cotopaxi   Coca
Manta   Chone   Tena
C. San Lorenzo   Ambato   Napo
ECUADOR
Jipijapa   Guaranda   Chimborazo 6310
Guayaquil   Babahoyo   Riobamba
La Libertad   Milagro   Macas
Playas   Cuenca   Azogues
I. Puná   Machala   Gualaceo
G. de Guayaquil   Tumbes
Zaruma   Loja
Talara   Zamora
Negritos
Paita   Sullana   Huancabamba
Piura   Chulucanas
Catacaos   Jaén   Moyobamba
Pta Aguja   Yurimaguas
Lambayeque   Chachapoyas   Tarapoto
Ferreñafe
Chiclayo   Cajamarca
Chepén   Cajabamba
Pacasmayo
Huamachuco   Otusco
Trujillo   Pomabamba
Huallanca   Tingo María
Chimbote   Huaráz   Huascarán 6768
Casma   La Unión
Huánuco
Huarmey   Oxapampa
Cerro de Pasco
Pativilca   La Merced
Barranca   Tarma
Huacho   La Oroya   Jauja   Acobamba
Ancón   Huancayo
Callao   Lima   Parque Nac. de Manu
Huancavelica
PERU
Chincha Alta   Ayacucho   Quillabamba   MACHU PICCHU
Pisco   Ica   Abancay   Cuzco
Pen. de Paracas   Andahuaylas   Sicuani
Nazca   Ayaviri
Chala   Juliaca   Sta Ana
Coropuna 6425   Puno   Titicaca   Ancohuma 6388
Arequipa   Misti 5822   Juli   Corocoro   Chulumani
Camaná   LA PAZ
Matarani   BOLIVIA
Mollendo   Moquegua   Quillacollo   Cochabamba
Ilo   Desaguadero   Oruro   Santa Cruz
Tacna   Sajama 6542   Aiquile   Llanos de Chiqu
Arica   Sabaya   Huanuni
Poopó   Sucre   Tarabuco
CHILE   Salar de Uyuni   Potosí
Iquique   Camargo   Tarija
Tocopilla   Chuquicamata   Villa Montes
Pedro de Valdivia   Tupiza   Yacuiba
Calama   S. Pedro   Tarija   Bermejo
Mejillones   Vol. Ollagüe 5870
Tropic of Capricorn   Tocorpuri 5833
Antofagasta   ARGENTINA
Salar de Atacama   JUJUY   Orán
S. Salvador de Jujuy
Llullaillaco 6723   Salta

VENEZUELA
Neth. Antilles
Aruba   Curaçao   Bonaire
Pen. de Paraguaná
Pto Fijo   Willemstad
Coro   Riecito   Pto Cabello   Maiquetía   Caracas
Cd Ojeda   Valencia   Maracay   Pto la Cruz   Cumaná
Maracaibo   Cabimas   Barcelona   Carúpano   Güiria
L. de Maracaibo   Barquisimeto   S. Juan   Anaco   Maturín
Valera   Acarigua   V. de la Pasqua   El Tigre   Tucupita
Cord. de Mérida   Guanare   Zaraza   Barrancas
Mérida   Bolívar 5775   Barinas   Cd Bolívar   Cd Guayana
Cúcuta   Apure   Upata
San Cristóbal   Arauca   S. Fernando   Emb. de Guri
Bucaramanga   La Paragua   El Dorado
LLANOS   Salto del Angel
Pto Carreño   Sta Elena
Orocué   Sa Pacaraima
COLOMBIA   RORAIM
Meta   Pto Ayacucho   Roraima 2810   La Gran Sabana
Calamar   Ventuari   Boa Vista
Inírida   Casiquiare   Caura
Salto Angostura   Guainía   Caroni
Mitú   Cucuí   Río Negro
Vaupés   Icana
Apaporis   Tapurucuara
Caquetá   CARACAS

AMAZONA
SELVAS
Iquitos   Leticia   Tabatinga
Marañón   Caxias   Tefé   Manacapuru
Solimões (Amazonas)   Jutaí
Yavari (Javari)   Purus
Ucayali   Juruá   Tapauá   Lábrea   Humaitá
Elvira   Coari   Prainh
Cruzeiro do Sul   Bôca do Acre
Feijó   Purus   Pôrto Velho   Aripu
ACRE   Sena Madureira   Madeira
Rio Branco   RONDÔNIA
Brasiléia   Riberalta   Guajará-Mirim
Cobija   Porvenir   Serra
Madre de Dios   Mamoré
Pto Maldonado   Pto Heath   Guaporé
R. Rogaguado   Iténez
Trinidad   Paraguay
Rurrenabaque
Huanay   Sta Ana   Itonamas

ISLAS GALÁPAGOS
(ARCHIPIÉLAGO DO COLÓN) (Ecu.)
at the same scale
Culpepper   Wenman
Pinta   Marchena   Genovesa
Fernandina   Santa Cruz   San Cristóbal
Isabela   Baquerizo Moreno
Santa Maria   Española

Islas Juan Fernández (Chile)
at the same scale
Alejandro Selkirk   Robinson Crusoe   Sta Clara

PACIFIC OCEAN

ATLANTIC

OCEAN

BARBADOS
⊕ Bridgetown

TRINIDAD AND TOBAGO

Mabaruma
Charity
Suddie
V-en Hoop
Bartica
Linden
GUYANA
Bonfim
Lethem
Georgetown
New Amsterdam
Paramaribo
Nieuw Nickerie
Totness
Albina
Nieuw Amsterdam
Marienburg
Apoera
Witagron
SURINAM
Julianatop 1280
Kaieteur Falls
Leguan I.
Sinnamary
Kourou
I. du Diable (Devil's I.)
Cayenne
FRENCH GUIANA
Blommestein-meer
Oiapoque
Cabo Orange
Serra Tumucumaque
AMAPÁ
Sa do Navio
Macapá
Pto Santana

Manaus
Careiro
Itacoatiara
Oriximiná
Obidos
Monte Alegre
Santarém
Amazonas
Pará
Xingu
I. de Marajó
B. de Marajó
Bragança
Salinópolis
Belém
Abaetetuba
Cametá
Capanema
Pinheiro
Alcântara
B. de São Marcos
São Luís
Rosário
Parnaíbao
Monção
Chapadinha
Bacabal
Coroatá
Codó
Caxias
Camocim
Acaraú
Itapipoca
Caucaia
Fortaleza (Ceará)

Aveiro
Itaituba
Parque Nacional Amazonia
Pimenta
PARÁ
Jácareacanga
Marabá
Imperatriz
Grajaú
Pto Franco
Carolina
S. Félix
MARANHÃO
Pindaré
Piripiri
Sobral
Sta Quitéria
Campo Maior
Teresina
Castelo
Crateus
Morada N.
Quixadá
Aracati
Areia Branca
Macau
Pta do Calcanhar
Rocas
I. Fernando de Noronha
Canindé
Mombaça
Tauá
CEARÁ
Iguatu
Acopiara
Patu
RIO GRANDE DO NORTE
Mossoró
Natal
Caicó

Serra do Cachimbo
Cachimbo
Teles Pires
Represa Tucuruí
Tucuruí
Araguaína
Floriano
Oeiras
PIAUÍ
Picos
J. do Norte
Crato
S.Raimundo Nonato
Paulistana
Ouricuri
Salgueiro
Sousa
Patos
Talhada
Limoeiro
Caruaru
PARAÍBA
Campina Grande
Cabedelo
João Pessoa
PERNAMBUCO
Olinda
Recife (Pernambuco)

C. do Araguaía
Balsas
Tocantins
TOCANTINS
Petrolina
Juazeiro
Garanhuns
Palmares
Palmeira dos Ind.
Caboatão
ALAGOAS
Maceió

MATO GROSSO
Parecis
Mato Grosso
Sa dos Caiabis
Sa Formosa
Pto Artur
São Félix
Ilha do Bananal
Rio Araguaia
Represa de Sobradinho
Barra
São Francisco
BAHIA
Sen. do Bonfim
Propriá
Arapiraca
Penedo
SERGIPE
Aracaju
Estância

Cuiabá
Cáceres
Fatima du Sul
Rondonópolis
Planalto de Mato Grosso
Aruanã
GOIÁS
Uruaçu
Barreiras
Ibotirama
Chapada Diamantina
Iaçu
Jacobina
Lagarto
Serrinha
Alagoinhas
R. de Jacuípe
Feira de S.
Cachoeira
Castro Alves
B. de T. os Santos
Salvador (Bahia)
Valença
Jequié

Pto Suarez
Corumbá
Planalto de
Formosa
Goiás
Jaraguá
Pirenópolis
Brasília
São Francisco
Januária
Porteirinha
Bom Jesus da Lapa
Caetité
Contas
Ipiaú
Vitória da Conquista
Itabuna
Ilhéus

San Matias
MATO GROSSO DO SUL
Cuiabá
Mato Grosso
Goiás
Ceres
Anápolis
Goiânia
Iporá
São Francisco
Montes Claros
Salinas
Araçuaí
Sa do Chifre
Itapetinga
Canavieiras
Belmonte
Pôrto Seguro
Itamaraju

Aquidauana
Campo Grande
Mineiros
Rio Verde
Caldas Novas
Paracatu
Pirapora
Teófilo Otôni
Nanuque
São Mateus

Corumbá
Jatai
Itumbiara
Goiandira
João Pinheiro
Diamantina
Gov. Valadares
ESPÍRITO
Linhares
Colatina

Jardim
Três Lagoas
Coxim
Taquari
Catalão
Patos de Minas
Corinto
Curvelo
Araçuaí
Fabriciano
Cnl
Caratinga
SANTO
Vitória
Vila Velha

Fte Olimpo
Ilha Solteira
S. José do R. Preto
Barretos
Uberlândia
Uberaba
Araguari
Sete Lagoas
MINAS GERAIS
Serra do Espinhaço
Rio Doce
Manhuaçu
Con. Ponte Nova
Cariacica
Cachoeiro de Itapemirim

Pto Murtinho
Dourados
Panorama
Pres. Epitácio
Araçatuba
Rubinéia
Fernandópolis
Araxá
Franca
Passos
Belo Horizonte
Divinópolis
Lafaiete
Caranggla
Itaperuna
S.João da Barra

Pedro J. Caballero
Represa Pôrto Primavera
Pres. Prudente
Tupã
Catanduva
Ribeirão Preto
S.João del Rei
Lavras
Pocos de Caldas
Barbacena
Juiz de Fora
Nova Friburgo
Campos

Ponta Porã
Paranavaí
Assis
Marília
Bauru
Araraquara
São Carlos
Limeira
Carangola
Volta Redonda
Petrópolis
Magé

PARAGUAY
Concepción
Adelfia
Apa
E.Cunha
Ourinhos
SÃO PAULO
Piracicaba
Jundiaí
Campinas
Barra Mansa
Niterói
Rio de Janeiro

Pozo
Luque
Asunción
San Pedro
Mts de Aracanguy
Represa Itaipu
Guaira
Umuarama
Maringá
Londrina
Apucarana
Jacarezinho
Sorocaba
Itapeva
São Paulo
Santos
São Vicente
Itanhaém

Cascavel
Toledo
Goio-Erê
C. Mourão
PARANÁ
Castro
Itararé
Juquiá
Iguape

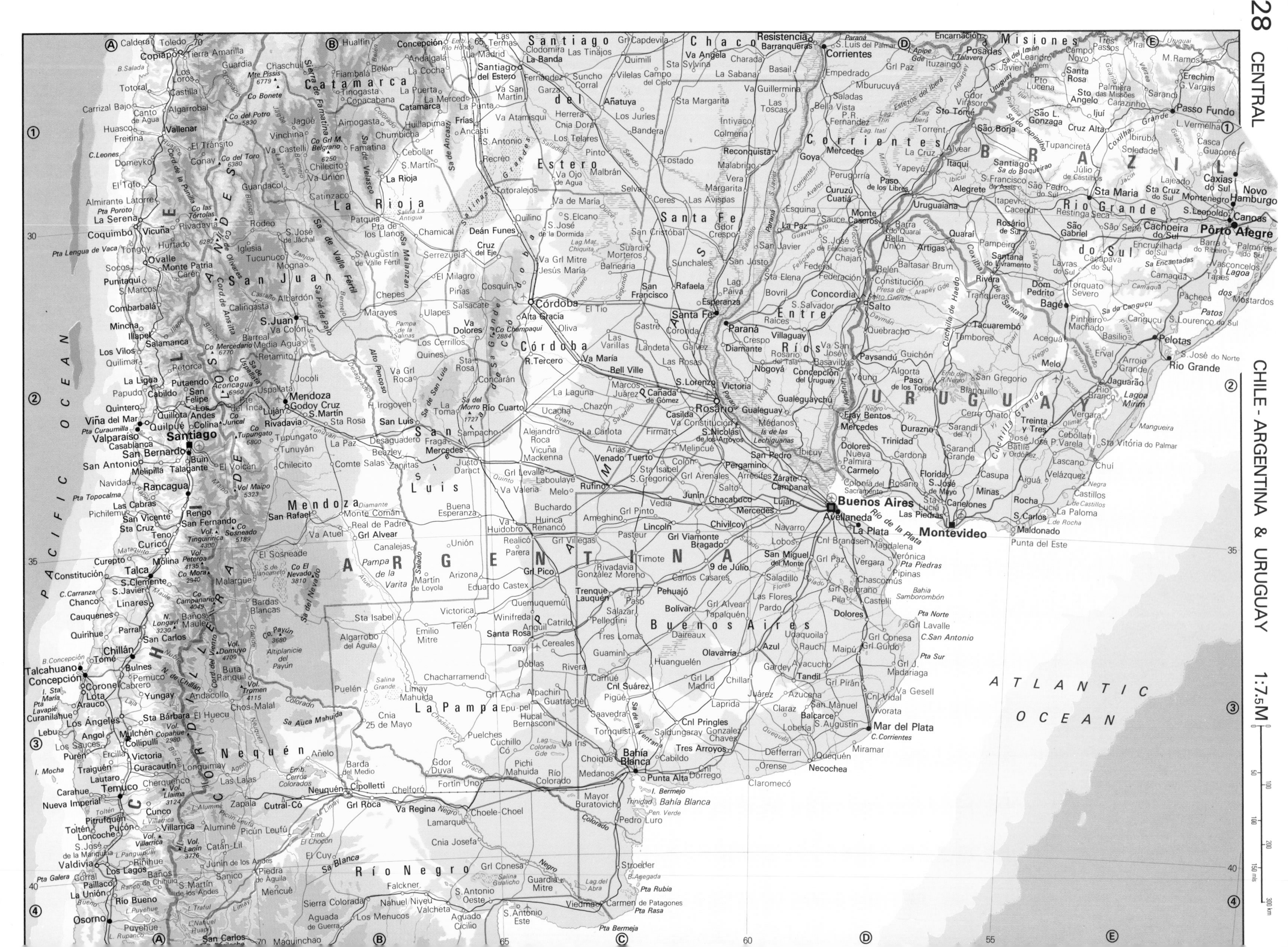
0 100 200 300 km
0 50 100 150 mls
ATLANTIC OCEAN
PACIFIC OCEAN
BRAZIL
URUGUAY
ARGENTINA
Buenos Aires
Montevideo
Santiago
Córdoba
Rosario
Mendoza
Mar del Plata
Bahía Blanca
Pôrto Alegre
Santa Fe
Paraná
Corrientes
Resistencia
Posadas
Salto
Paysandú
Concepción
Valparaíso
Talca
Temuco
Valdivia
Osorno
La Serena
Coquimbo
S.Juan
San Luis
La Rioja
Catamarca
Santiago del Estero
Neuquén
La Plata
Pelotas
Rio Grande
Santa Rosa
Viedma
Chaco
Corrientes
Entre Ríos
La Pampa
Buenos Aires
Río Negro
Misiones
Río de la Plata
Lagoa Mirim
Lagoa dos Patos
Cuchilla de Haedo
Cuchilla Grande

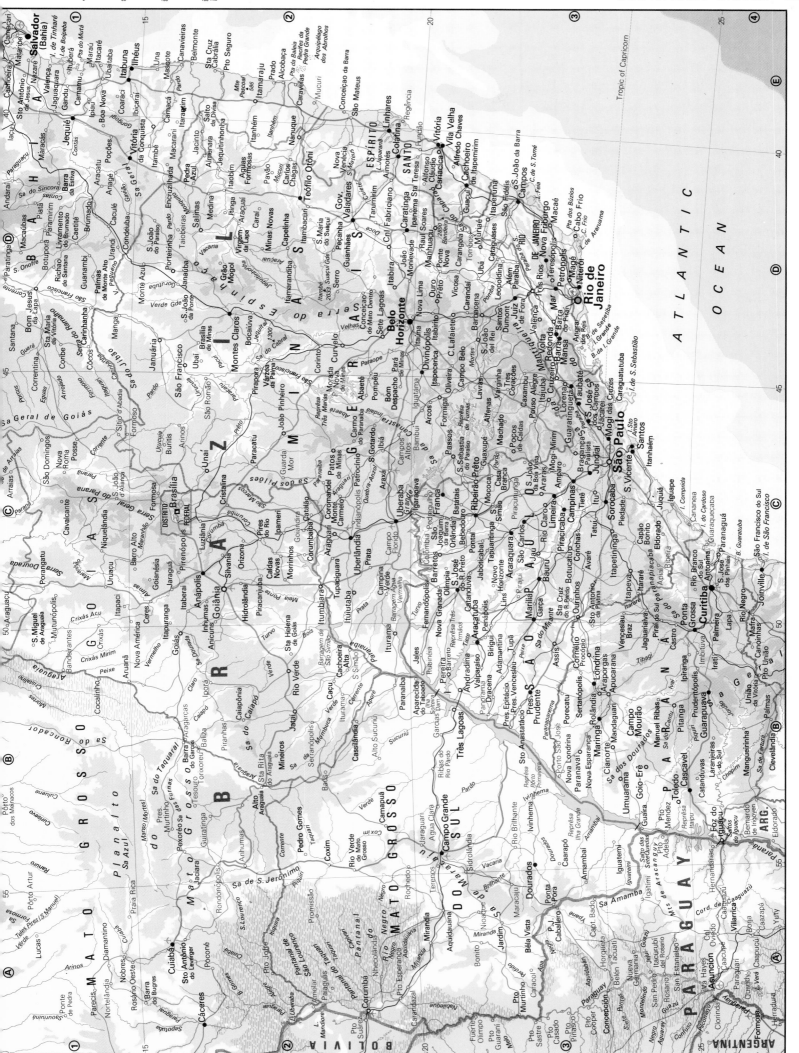

200   400   600 km
100   200   300 mils

A   40   B   2   30   C   20   70   D   10   E   0   F   10   G

Greenland
(Den.)
Kap Farvel

Jan Mayen
(Nor.)

ARCTIC

ICELAND
Reykjavík

Arctic Circle

NORWEGIAN

Vesterålen
Lofoten   Narvik
Sunds

SEA

Trondheim

③

Færøerne
(Den.)

Shetland

Orkney

Bergen
Stavanger

Oslo

Stockhol

50

Vänern

ATLANTIC

UNITED KINGDOM
OF GREAT BRITAIN AND
NORTHERN IRELAND
Glasgow   Aberdeen
Edinburgh

NORTH

Ålborg   Göteborg   Jonköping   Gotla

SWEDEN

Öland

OCEAN

Belfast
IRELAND

Newcastle

SEA

DENMARK
København   Malmö
Bornholm

Balti

Dublin
Cork

Liverpool   Manchester

Rostock   Gdańs

④

Birmingham

Cardiff
Bristol

London

Amsterdam
's-Gravenhage
Rotterdam
NETHERLANDS

Hamburg

Hannover

Poznań

GERMANY   Berlin

40

English Channel

Bruxelles
BELGIUM
Lille

Essen
Köln
Bonn   Frankfurt

Leipzig   Dresden   Wrocław

POL

Le Havre
Rouen
Seine

LUXEMBOURG

Praha   CZECHOSLO

50

Paris

Nürnberg

Strasbourg

Brno

Nantes
Loire   Tours

Stuttgart

München

Wien   Bratislava

Bay of
Biscay

Clermont-
Ferrand

Bern   Zurich
Genève   SWITZERLAND   LIECHTENSTEIN
Lyon

Salzburg
AUSTRIA   Graz

HUN

FRANCE

La Coruña

Bordeaux

Rhône

Milano

Trieste   Zagreb

Venezia

40

Porto
PORTUGAL

Bilbao
Valladolid

Toulouse

Marseille

ANDORRA
Zaragoza
Ebro

Torino

Genova

MONACO

Firenze
SAN
MARINO

ITALY

Corse
Bastia

Ajaccio

ADRIATIC   SEA
Split

YUGO

Lisboa
Tajo

SPAIN

Madrid
Toledo

Barcelona

Roma

Faro

Sevilla

Valencia   Is Baleares   Menorca   Sardegna   Olbia   Napoli   Taranto

⑤

Murcia

Ibiza

Mallorca

TYRRHENIAN
SEA

Cagliari

Madeira
(Port.)

Málaga

Tanger   Gibraltar (U.K.)
Ceuta (Sp.)

MEDITERRANEAN

Palermo   Messina
Reggio di Calabria

Melilla
(Sp.)

Oran

Sicilia

Casablanca   Rabat

Alger

Islas Canarias
(Sp.)

MOROCCO

Marrakech

ALGERIA

Tunis

TUNISIA

MALTA

SEA

D   10   E   F   10   G

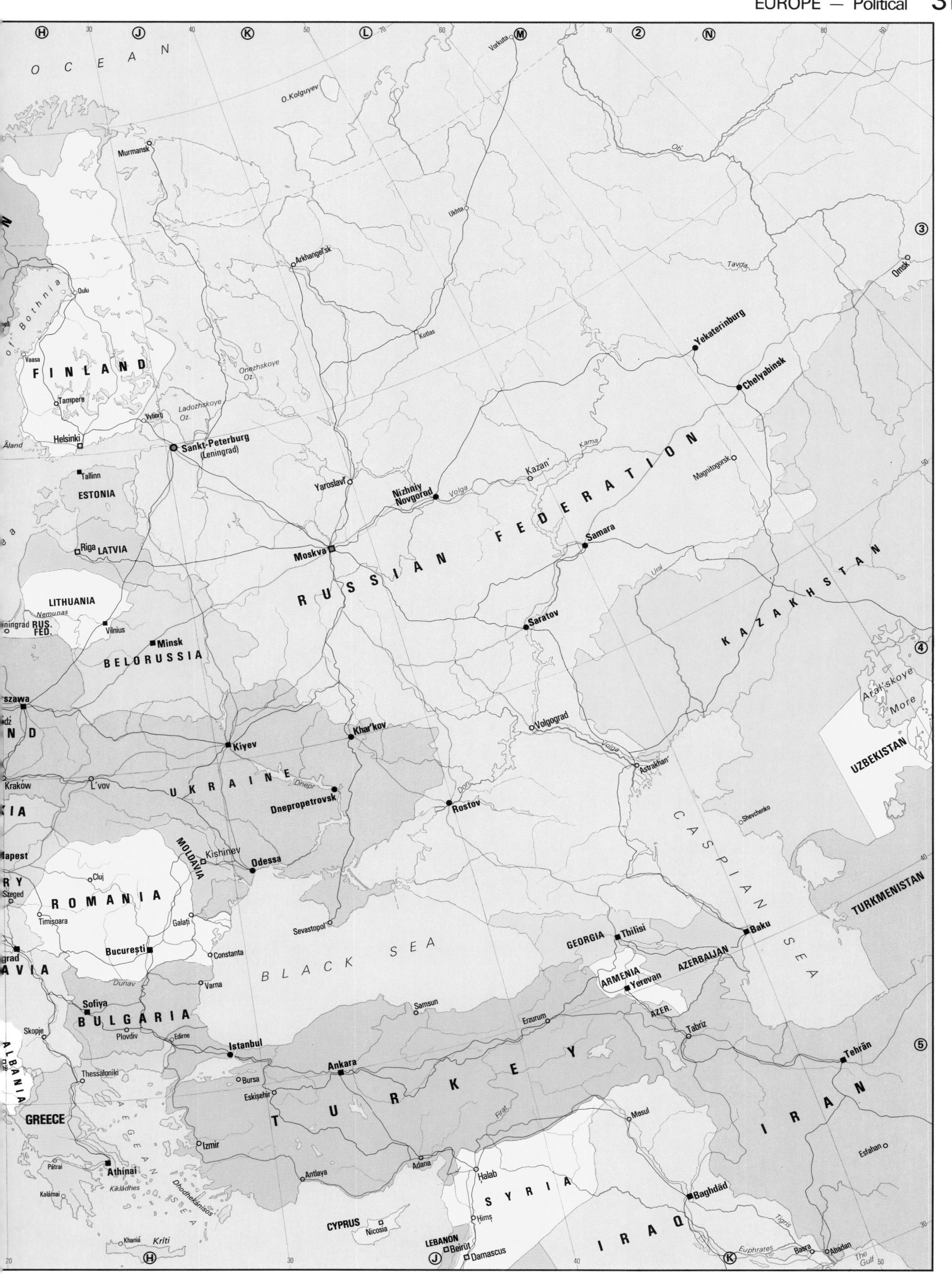

OCEAN

H 30 J 40 K 50 L 70 60 M 70 ② N 80

O.Kolguyev

Murmansk

Vorkuta

Ob'

Tavda

Omsk

③

Arkhangel'sk

Ukhta

F I N L A N D

Oulu

Vaasa

Onezhskoye
Oz.

Kotlas

Yekaterinburg

Tampere

Ladozhskoye
Oz.

Chelyabinsk

Åland

Helsinki

Vyborg

Sankt-Peterburg
(Leningrad)

Kazan'

Magnitogorsk

Tallinn

Yaroslavl'

ESTONIA

Nizhniy
Novgorod

Volga

R U S S I A N   F E D E R A T I O N

Riga LATVIA

Moskva

Samara

K A Z A K H S T A N

LITHUANIA

Nemunas

Saratov

Kaliningrad RUS.
FED.

Vilnius

④

Minsk

Aral'skoye
More

Szawa

B E L O R U S S I A

Volgograd

Krakow

Kiyev

Khar'kov

Shevchenko

UZBEKISTAN

L'vov

Dnepr

Astrakhan'

Volga

KIA

U K R A I N E

Don

Dnepropetrovsk

Rostov

C A S P I A N

apest

MOLDAVIA

Kishinev

RY

Szeged

Odessa

R O M A N I A

TURKMENISTAN

Cluj

Timisoara

S E A

Galati

Bucuresti

Sevastopol

40

Baku

AVIA

Constanta

GEORGIA Tbilisi

grad

Dunav

B L A C K   S E A

ARMENIA AZERBAIJAN

Varna

Sofiya

Yerevan

Samsun

AZER.

B U L G A R I A

Erzurum

Tabriz

Skopje

Plovdiv

Edirne

Istanbul

Tehran

⑤

ALBANIA

Thessaloniki

Ankara

Mosul

GREECE

Bursa

T U R K E Y

I R A N

Eskisehir

Firat

Izmir

Esfahan

Patrai

Antlaya

Adana

Halab

Athinai

Kalamai

Kikladhes

S E A

Dhodhekanisos

S Y R I A

Baghdad

Tigris

Khania Kriti

H CYPRUS

Nicosia

Hims

I R A Q

30

LEBANON

Beirut

J

Damascus

40

Euphrates

Basra

K

Abadan

The
Gulf 50

20

1:7.5M

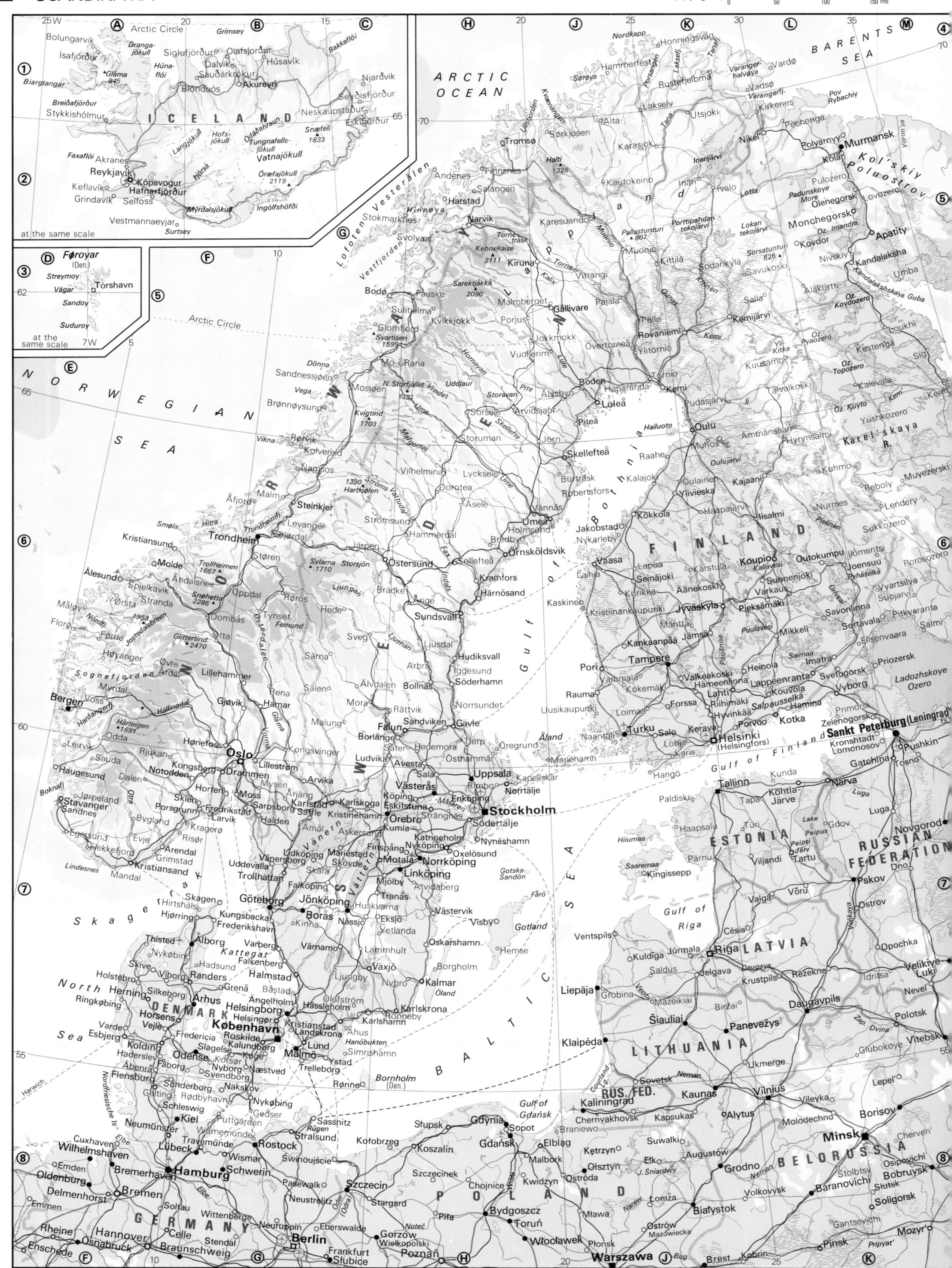

0 100 200 300 km
0 50 100 150 mls
ICELAND
Arctic Circle
Grimsey
Bolungarvik
Ísafjörður
Siglufjörður
Ólafsfjörður
Dalvík
Húsavík
Sauðárkrókur
Akureyri
Blönduós
Njarðvík
Seyðisfjörður
Neskaupstaður
Eskifjörður
Breiðafjörður
Stykkishólmur
Faxaflói
Akranes
Reykjavík
Kópavogur
Hafnarfjörður
Keflavík
Grindavík
Selfoss
Mýrdalsjökull
Ingólfshöfði
Vestmannaeyjar
Surtsey
Langjökull
Hofsjökull
Vatnajökull
Öræfajökull 2119
Snæfell 1833
at the same scale
Føroyar (Den.)
Streymoy
Vágar
Tórshavn
Sandoy
Suðuroy
ARCTIC OCEAN
BARENTS SEA
NORWEGIAN SEA
Arctic Circle
Nordkapp
Honningsvåg
Hammerfest
Sørøya
Vardø
Vadsø
Varangerfj.
Kirkenes
Lakselv
Alta
Utsjoki
Tromsø
Pechenga
Nikel
Polyarnyy
Murmansk
Kola
Kol'skiy Poluostrov
Olenegorsk
Monchegorsk
Apatity
Kovdor
Kandalaksha
Kandalakshskaya Guba
Umba
Finnsnes
Andenes
Harstad
Narvik
Hinnøya
Stokmarknes
Lofoten
Vesterålen
Vestfjorden
Svolvær
Kiruna
Kebnekaise 2111
Halti 1328
Kautokeino
Inari
Ivalo
Karesuando
Muonio
Kittilä
Sodankylä
Savukoski
Salla
Kemijärvi
Rovaniemi
Ylitornio
Tornio
Kemi
Gällivare
Malmberget
Porjus
Jokkmokk
Bodø
Fauske
Sulitjelma
Kvikkjokk
Glomfjord
Svartisen 1599
Mo i Rana
Mosjøen
Sandnessjøen
Dønna
Vega
Brønnøysund
Vikna
Rørvik
Kolvereid
Namsos
Steinkjer
Levanger
Stjørdal
Trondheim
Trondheimsfj.
Hitra
Smøla
Kristiansund
Molde
Ålesund
Åndalsnes
Trollheimen 1667
Snøhetta 2286
Oppdal
Røros
Støren
Dombås
Otta
Glittertind 2470
Jostedalsbreen
Stranda
Ørsta
Måløy
Florø
Førde
Nordfj.
Høyanger
Sognefjorden
Årdal
Lillehammer
Gjøvik
Hamar
Bergen
Voss
Myrdal
Hardangerfj.
Hallingdal
Hårteigen 1691
Odda
Leirvik
Sauda
Haugesund
Rjukan
Hønefoss
Oslo
Kongsberg
Notodden
Drammen
Lillestrøm
Kongsvinger
Dalen
Jørpeland
Stavanger
Sandnes
Egersund
Flekkefjord
Lindesnes
Mandal
Kristiansand
Grimstad
Arendal
Risør
Kragerø
Bygland
Evje
Skien
Porsgrunn
Larvik
Horten
Moss
Sarpsborg
Fredrikstad
Halden
Skagerrak
Skagen
Hirtshals
Hjørring
Frederikshavn
Thisted
Ålborg
Nykøbing
Skive
Viborg
Randers
Holstebro
Herning
Silkeborg
Århus
Grenå
Ringkøbing
Horsens
Vejle
Varde
Esbjerg
Kolding
Fredericia
Haderslev
Åbenrå
Flensburg
Sønderborg
Odense
Svendborg
Nyborg
Korsør
Slagelse
Kalundborg
Roskilde
København
Køge
Næstved
Nakskov
Nykøbing
Rødbyhavn
Gedser
DENMARK
North Sea
Kattegat
Nordfriesische Is
Harwich
Kiel
Schleswig
Neumünster
Lübeck
Travemünde
Puttgarden
Warnemünde
Rostock
Wismar
Schwerin
Hamburg
Cuxhaven
Wilhelmshaven
Bremerhaven
Emden
Oldenburg
Delmenhorst
Bremen
Emmen
Soltau
Rheine
Hannover
Osnabrück
Enschede
Celle
Braunschweig
Stendal
Wittenberge
Neuruppin
Berlin
Eberswalde
Frankfurt
Słubice
GERMANY
Elbe
Neustrelitz
Pasewalk
Szczecin
Stargard
Świnoujście
Stralsund
Sassnitz
Rügen
Kołobrzeg
Koszalin
Słupsk
Gdynia
Sopot
Gdańsk
Elbląg
Malbork
Chojnice
Kwidzyn
Szczecinek
Piła
Bydgoszcz
Toruń
Włocławek
Gorzów Wielkopolski
Poznań
Płońsk
Warszawa
Mława
Ostrów Mazowiecka
Łomża
Białystok
Olsztyn
Ostróda
Ełk
Suwałki
Augustów
Kętrzyn
POLAND
Gulf of Gdańsk
Kaliningrad
RUS. FED.
Chernyakhovsk
Sovetsk
Kaunas
Vilnius
Alytus
Klaipėda
Šiauliai
Panevežys
Ukmergė
LITHUANIA
Liepāja
Grobiņa
Mažeikiai
Biržai
Ventspils
Kuldīga
Jūrmala
Rīga
Jelgava
Saldus
LATVIA
Daugavpils
Rezekne
Krustpils
Cēsis
Valga
Gulf of Riga
Pärnu
Viljandi
Tartu
Võru
ESTONIA
Tallinn
Paldiski
Haapsalu
Kohtla-Järve
Narva
Hiiumaa
Saaremaa
Kingissepp
Peipsi Järv
Lake Peipus
Pskov
Ostrov
Gdov
Luga
Novgorod
RUSSIAN FEDERATION
Sankt Peterburg (Leningrad)
Kronshtadt
Lomonosov
Pushkin
Tosno
Gatchina
Zelenogorsk
Primorsk
Vyborg
Svetogorsk
Priozersk
Ladozhskoye Ozero
Sortavala
Pitkyaranta
Suojarvi
Salmi
Elisenvaara
Imatra
Lappeenranta
Hamina
Kotka
Kouvola
Lahti
Porvoo
Helsinki (Helsingfors)
Kerava
Hyvinkää
Riihimäki
Hämeenlinna
Forssa
Salo
Lohja
Karis
Hangö
Turku
Naantali
Uusikaupunki
Rauma
Pori
Loimaa
Kokemäki
Valkeakoski
Tampere
Kankaanpää
Jämsä
Jyväskylä
Mänttä
Mikkeli
Savonlinna
Pieksämäki
Varkaus
Kuopio
Outokumpu
Joensuu
Suonenjoki
Äänekoski
Seinäjoki
Kurikka
Lapua
Kristiinankaupunki
Kaskinen
Vaasa
Laihia
Nykarleby
Jakobstad
Kokkola
Kalajoki
Ylivieska
Oulainen
Raahe
Oulu
Muhos
Haapajärvi
Iisalmi
Kajaani
Nurmes
Kuhmo
Kuusamo
Pudasjärvi
Taivalkoski
Hailuoto
FINLAND
Åland
Mariehamn
Öregrund
Gulf of Finland
Gulf of Bothnia
Luleå
Boden
Haparanda
Piteå
Älvsbyn
Arvidsjaur
Sorsele
Storuman
Jörn
Skellefteå
Burträsk
Robertsfors
Lycksele
Vilhelmina
Dorotea
Åsele
Umeå
Vännäs
Holmsund
Bredbyn
Örnsköldsvik
Sollefteå
Kramfors
Härnösand
Strömsund
Hammerdal
Östersund
Järpen
Storsjön
Sylarna 1710
Bräcke
Ånge
Sundsvall
Hede
Sveg
Ljusdal
Hudiksvall
Iggesund
Söderhamn
Bollnäs
Sälen
Särna
Älvdalen
Mora
Rättvik
Falun
Borlänge
Sandviken
Gävle
Norrsundet
Säter
Hedemora
Avesta
Ludvika
Östhammar
Uppsala
Sala
Västerås
Enköping
Norrtälje
Kapellskär
Stockholm
Södertälje
Nynäshamn
Strängnäs
Eskilstuna
Köping
Örebro
Kumla
Karlskoga
Kristinehamn
Karlstad
Säffle
Arvika
Åmål
Vänern
Vättern
Askersund
Katrineholm
Nyköping
Oxelösund
Finspång
Norrköping
Motala
Linköping
Mjölby
Åtvidaberg
Tranås
Västervik
Lidköping
Mariestad
Skövde
Vänersborg
Uddevalla
Trollhättan
Falköping
Skara
Göteborg
Borås
Jönköping
Huskvarna
Nässjö
Eksjö
Kinna
Vetlanda
Kungsbacka
Varberg
Falkenberg
Halmstad
Värnamo
Ljungby
Växjö
Lammhult
Oskarshamn
Visby
Gotland
Fårö
Gotska Sandön
Hemse
Borgholm
Kalmar
Öland
Nybro
Karlskrona
Ronneby
Karlshamn
Olofström
Hässleholm
Kristianstad
Åhus
Hanöbukten
Landskrona
Helsingborg
Helsingør
Ängelholm
Båstad
Lund
Malmö
Trelleborg
Ystad
Simrishamn
Rønne
Bornholm (Den.)
BALTIC SEA
Minsk
BELORUSSIA
Vitebsk
Polotsk
Lepel'
Glubokoye
Molodechno
Borisov
Grodno
Volkovysk
Baranovichi
Slutsk
Soligorsk
Bobruysk
Osipovichi
Stolbtsy
Mozyr'
Pinsk
Brest
Kobrin
Gantsevichi
Velikiye Luki
Nevel'
Opochka
Idritsa
Dno

1:5M

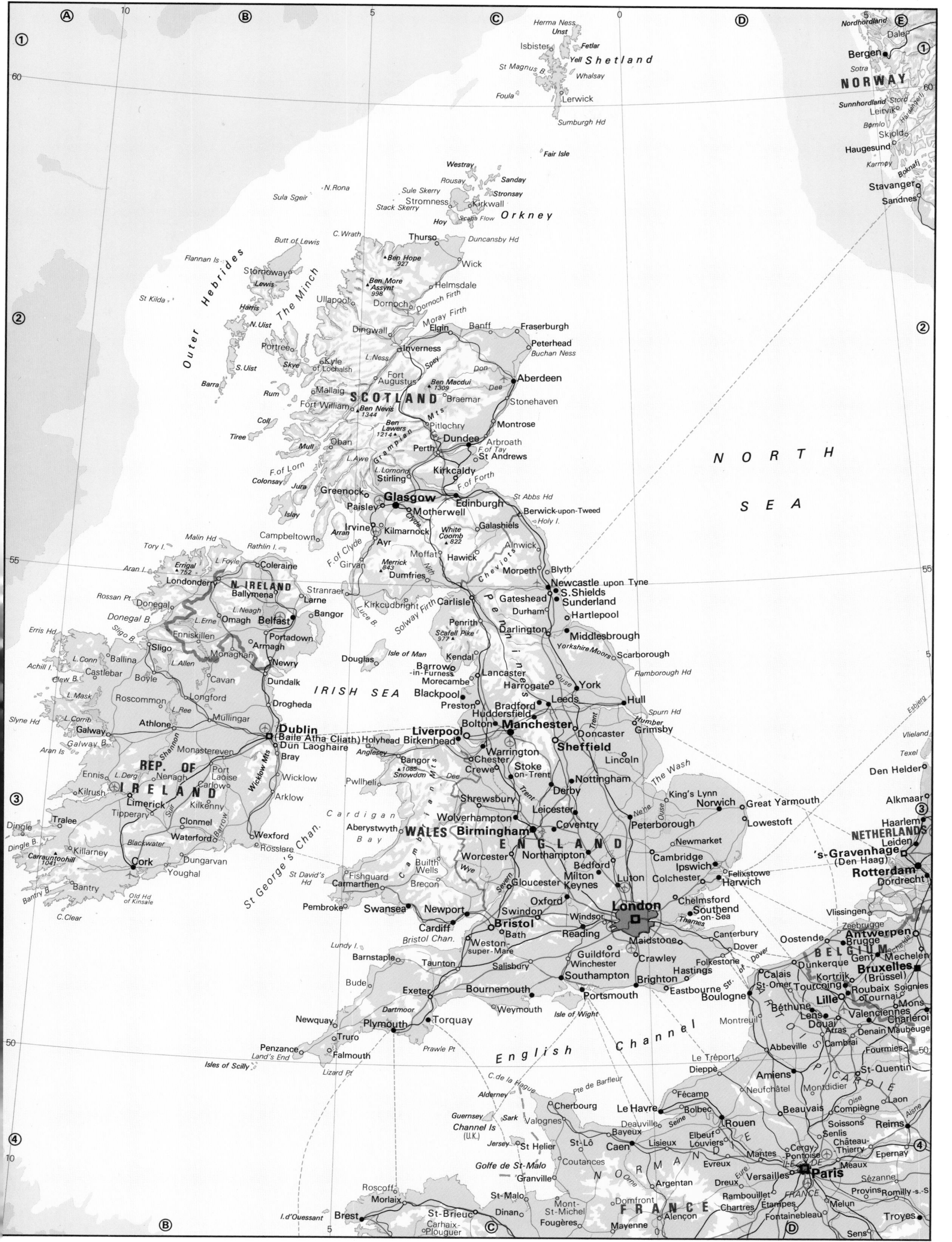

1:2.5M

0 25 50 75 100 km
0 25 50 mls

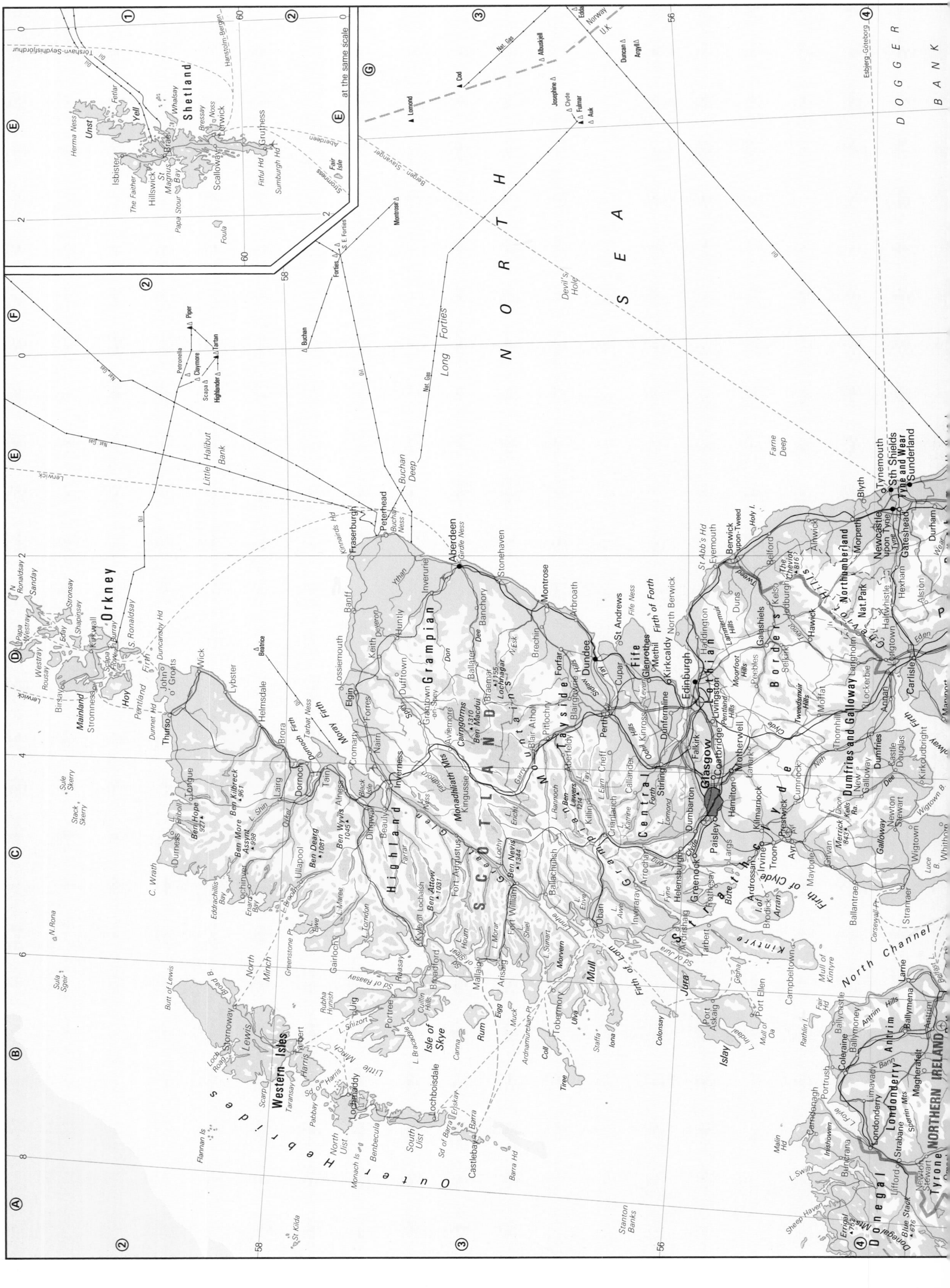

North Sea

Shetland

Herma Ness, Unst, Yell, Whalsay, Fetlar, Brae, St Magnus Bay, Bressay, Noss, Lerwick, The Faither, Hillswick, Papa Stour, Scalloway, Gruthess, Fitful Hd, Sumburgh Hd, Foula, Fair Isle, Istbister

Torshavn-Seydhisfjordhur Oil
Hanstholm-Bergen Gas
Bergen-Stavanger
at the same scale

Norway, U.K., Edda, Nat. Gas, Albuskjell, Duncan, Argyll, Cod, Lomond, Josephine, Clyde, Fulmar, Auk, Esbjerg-Goteborg, DOGGER BANK

Montrose, Forties, S.E. Forties, Buchan, Piper, Tartan, Claymore, Petronella, Scapa, Highlander, Little Halibut Bank, Nat. gas

Devil's Hole, Long Forties, Buchan Deep, Farne Deep

Orkney

N. Ronaldsay, Sanday, Papa Westray, Westray, Eday, Stronsay, Rousay, Shapinsay, Birsay, Mainland, Kirkwall, Stromness, Hoy, S. Ronaldsay, Burray, Scapa Flow, Duncansby Hd, Pentland Firth, Dunnet Hd, John o'Groats

N. Rona, Sula Sgeir, Stack Skerry, Sule Skerry, Stack Skerry, Lerwick, Nat. gas

Beatrice

C. Wrath, Durness, Ben Hope 927, Ben Loyal, Ben Kilbreck 961, Ben More Assynt 998, Ben Dearg 1081, Thurso, Wick, Lybster, Helmsdale, Brora, Dornoch Firth, Tarbat Ness, Cromarty Firth, Black Isle, Inverness, Nairn, Elgin, Forres, Lossiemouth, Buckie, Keith, Dufftown, Huntly, Banff, Inverurie

Eddrachillis Bay, Stack Skerry, Lochinver, Ullapool, L. Broom, Enard Bay, Gairloch, Greenstone Pt, L. Maree, L. Torridon, Achnasheen, Ben Attow 1031, Ben Wyvis 1045, Beauly, Farrar, Glen Mor, Loch Ness, Monadhliath Mts, Grantown-on-Spey, Aviemore, Cairngorms 1310, Ben Macdui, Braemar, Ballater, Don, Dee, Banchory

Grampian

Stonehaven, Aberdeen, Girdle Ness, Peterhead, Buchan Ness, Fraserburgh, Kinnairds Hd, Ythan, Deveron, Spey

Scotland

Highland

Rubha Hunish, L. Shizort, Portree, Raasay, Sd of Raasay, Isle of Skye, Cullin Hills, L. Bracadale, Canna, Rum, Eigg, Muck, Mallaig, Kyle of Lochalsh, L. Alsh, L. Hourn, L. Nevis, Knoydart, Glenfinnan, Fort Augustus, L. Oich, L. Lochy, Ben Nevis 1344, Fort William, L. Linnhe, L. Eil, L. Shiel, Ardgour, Sunart, Ballachulish, Glen Coe, Morvern, Tobermory, Ardnamurchan Pt, Coll, Tiree, Staffa, Iona, Ulva, Mull, Colonsay, Firth of Lorn, Oban, L. Awe, L. Etive, L. Creran

Outer Hebrides, Western Isles, Lewis, Butt of Lewis, Broad B., L. Roag, Loch Seaforth, Stornoway, Scarp, Taransay, Harris, Sd of Harris, Pabbay, North Uist, Benbecula, South Uist, Monach Is, St Kilda, Flannan Isles, Lochmaddy, Little Minch, L. Shizort, Barra Hd, Castlebay, Barra, Sd of Barra, Eriskay, Lochboisdale

Sea of the Hebrides, North Minch, The Minch

Tayside, Pitlochry, Blair Atholl, Braemar, Blairgowrie, Forfar, Brechin, Montrose, Arbroath, Esk, Lochnagar 1155, Glen Shee, Aberfeldy, Kirriemuir, Rannoch, L. Rannoch, L. Tay, L. Ericht, Ben Lawers 1214, Killin, Crieff, Comrie, L. Earn, Callander, Dunkeld, Perth, Cupar, St Andrews, Fife Ness, Leven, **Fife**, Glenrothes, Methil, Kirkcaldy, Dunfermline, Firth of Forth, North Berwick, Dundee, Tay

Central, Stirling, Falkirk, L. Katrine, L. Lomond, Dumbarton, **Glasgow**, Coatbridge, Livingston, Motherwell, Hamilton, Paisley, **Lothian**, Edinburgh, Haddington, Pentland Hills, Kinross, L. Leven

Strathclyde, Greenock, Helensburgh, Gourock, Largs, Arrochar, Inveraray, L. Fyne, Ardrossan, Irvine, Troon, Prestwick, Ayr, Maybole, Kilmarnock, Cumnock, Girvan, Ballantrae, L. Doon, Merrick 843, Galloway, Newton Stewart, Corsewall Pt, Stranraer, Wigtown, Newton Stewart, Nith, **Dumfries and Galloway**, Dumfries, Castle Douglas, Kirkcudbright, Whithorn

Kintyre, Mull of Kintyre, Jura, Paps of Jura, Islay, Port Askaig, Port Ellen, Mull of Oa, Gigha, Tarbert, Campbeltown, Sd of Jura, L. Tarbert, Sanda, Ailsa Craig, Firth of Clyde, Bute, Arran, Brodick, Rathlin I., Fair Hd, North Channel

Borders, Lammermuir Hills, Moorfoot Hills, Peebles, Galashiels, Selkirk, Hawick, Tweed, Ettrick, Teviot, Jedburgh, Kelso, The Cheviot 816, Cheviot Hills, St Abb's Hd, Eyemouth, Berwick-upon-Tweed, Duns, Holy I., Lauder

Northumberland, Nat. Park, Rothbury, Alnwick, Belford, Bamburgh, Morpeth, Blyth, Newcastle upon Tyne, Gateshead, Tynemouth, Sth Shields, **Tyne and Wear**, Sunderland, Hexham, Durham, Alston, Carlisle, Longtown, Langholm, Lockerbie, Annan, Moffat, Thornhill, Eden, Tweedsmuir Hills, Solway Firth

Northern Ireland, Londonderry, Tyrone, Strabane, Magherafelt, Coleraine, Portrush, Portstewart, Antrim, Ballymena, Larne, Ballymoney, Ballycastle, Antrim Hills, Carrickfergus, Sperrin Mts, Omagh, **Donegal**, Errigal 752, Bloody Foreland, L. Swilly, Letterkenny, L. Foyle, Malin Hd, Inishowen, Donegal, Blue Stack Mts, Sheep Haven, Derg, Stanton Banks, Main Hd

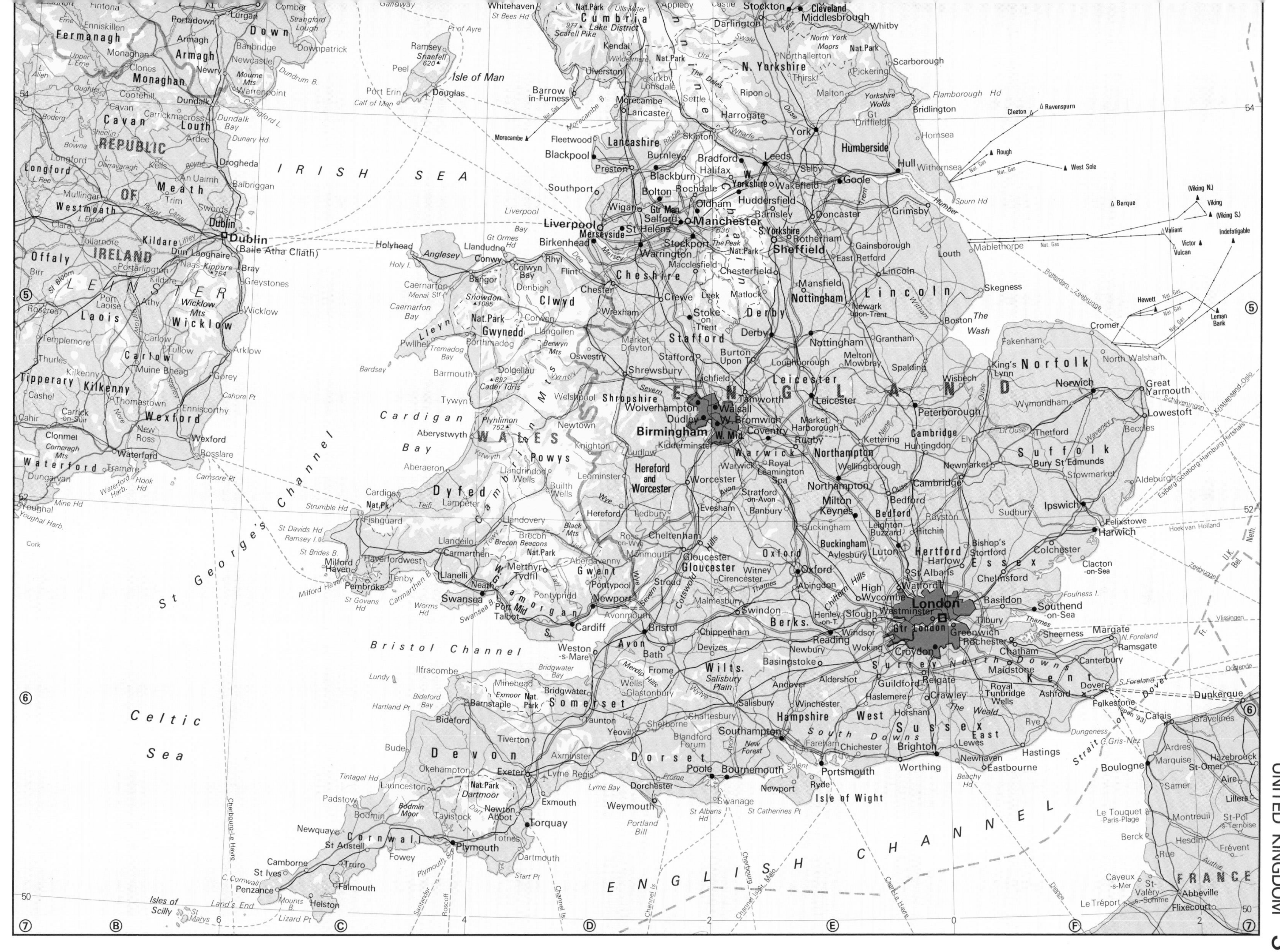
IRISH SEA
ENGLISH CHANNEL
Celtic Sea
St George's Channel
Bristol Channel
Cardigan Bay
ENGLAND
WALES
REPUBLIC OF IRELAND
LEINSTER
FRANCE
Isle of Man
Isle of Wight
Isles of Scilly
London
Gtr London
Birmingham
Manchester
Liverpool
Leeds
Sheffield
Bristol
Cardiff
Swansea
Plymouth
Southampton
Portsmouth
Brighton
Dover
Norwich
Ipswich
Cambridge
Oxford
Nottingham
Leicester
Derby
Coventry
Northampton
Peterborough
Hull
York
Middlesbrough
Stockton
Darlington
Scarborough
Dublin
(Baile Átha Cliath)
Wexford
Waterford
Dundalk
Drogheda
Douglas
Calais
Boulogne
Dunkerque
Abbeville
Norfolk
Suffolk
Essex
Kent
Surrey
West Sussex
East Sussex
Hampshire
Dorset
Devon
Cornwall
Somerset
Avon
Wilts.
Berks.
Oxford
Gloucester
Hereford and Worcester
Shropshire
Stafford
Cheshire
Lancashire
Cumbria
N. Yorkshire
Humberside
Cleveland
Lincoln
Nottingham
Leicester
Warwick
Northampton
Buckingham
Hertford
Bedford
Derby
Dyfed
Powys
Gwynedd
Clwyd
Gwent
Glamorgan
Merseyside
Meath
Louth
Monaghan
Armagh
Down
Fermanagh
Cavan
Westmeath
Longford
Offaly
Laois
Kildare
Wicklow
Carlow
Wexford
Kilkenny
Tipperary
Waterford
Lake District
The Dales
The Wash
Dartmoor
Exmoor
North Downs
South Downs
The Weald
Cotswold Hills
Chiltern Hills
Strait of Dover

1:2.5M 0 25 50 75 100 km 0 25 50 mls

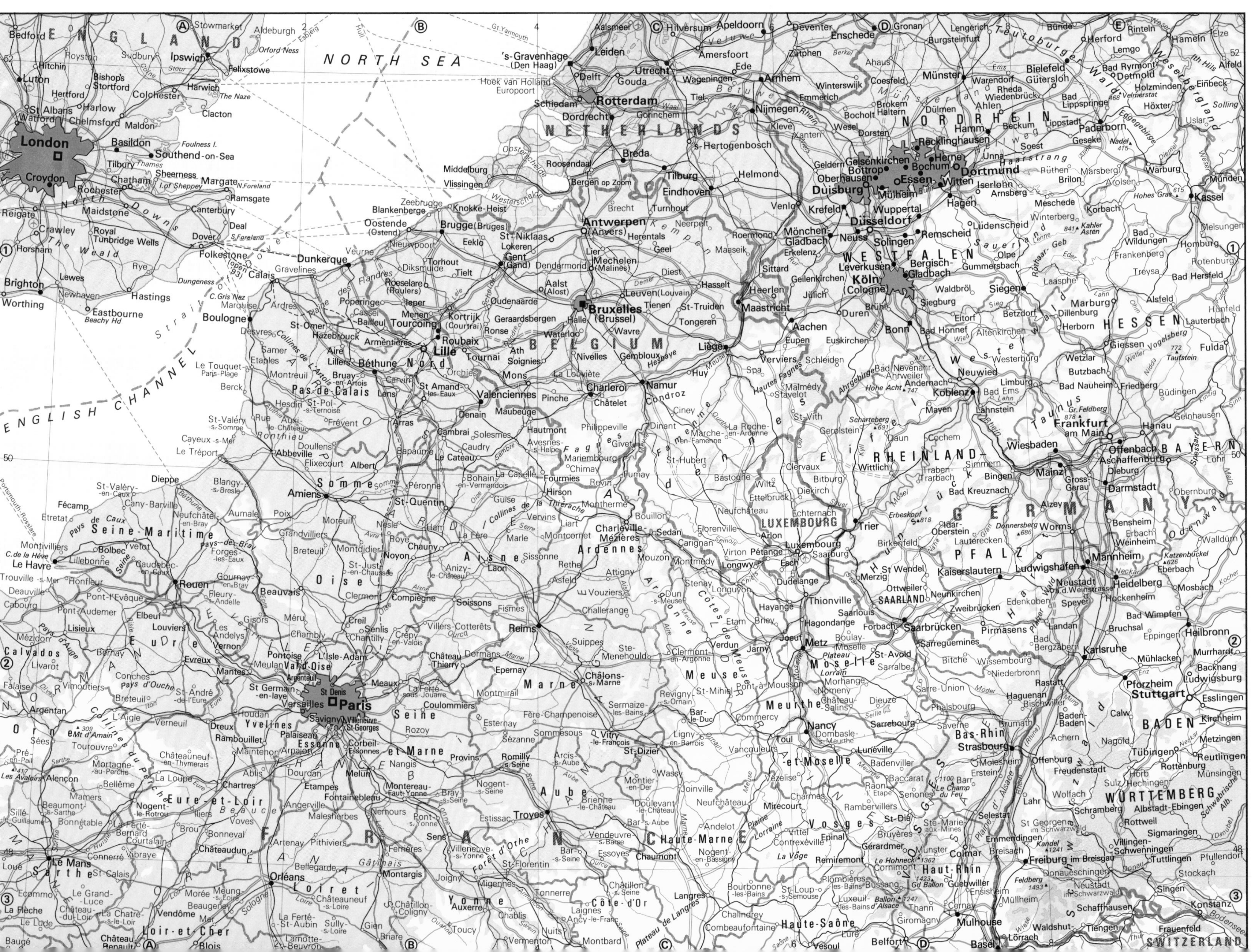
NORTH SEA
ENGLISH CHANNEL
ENGLAND
NETHERLANDS
BELGIUM
LUXEMBOURG
FRANCE
GERMANY
SWITZERLAND
London
Paris
Bruxelles (Brussel)
Rotterdam
's-Gravenhage (Den Haag)
Antwerpen (Anvers)
Köln (Cologne)
Bonn
Düsseldorf
Frankfurt am Main
Stuttgart
Strasbourg
Lille
Reims
Metz
Nancy
Rouen
Le Havre
Amiens
Orléans
Le Mans
Luxembourg
Liège
Aachen
Dortmund
Essen
Duisburg
Kassel
Mannheim
Karlsruhe
Saarbrücken
Trier
Koblenz
Mainz
Wiesbaden
Dunkerque
Calais
Boulogne
Dover
Brighton
Ipswich

25 50 75 100 km
25 50 mls

AUSTRIA

SALZBURG

KÄRNTEN

TIROL

VORALBERG

SWITZERLAND

LIECHTENSTEIN

YUGOSLAVIA

SLOVENIA

CROATIA

FRIULI VENEZIA GIULIA

VENETO

TRENTINO

LOMBARDIA

PIEMONTE

VALLE D'AOSTA

EMILIA ROMAGNA

TOSCANA

UMBRIA

MARCHE

LIGURIA

PROVENCE

SAN MARINO

MONACO

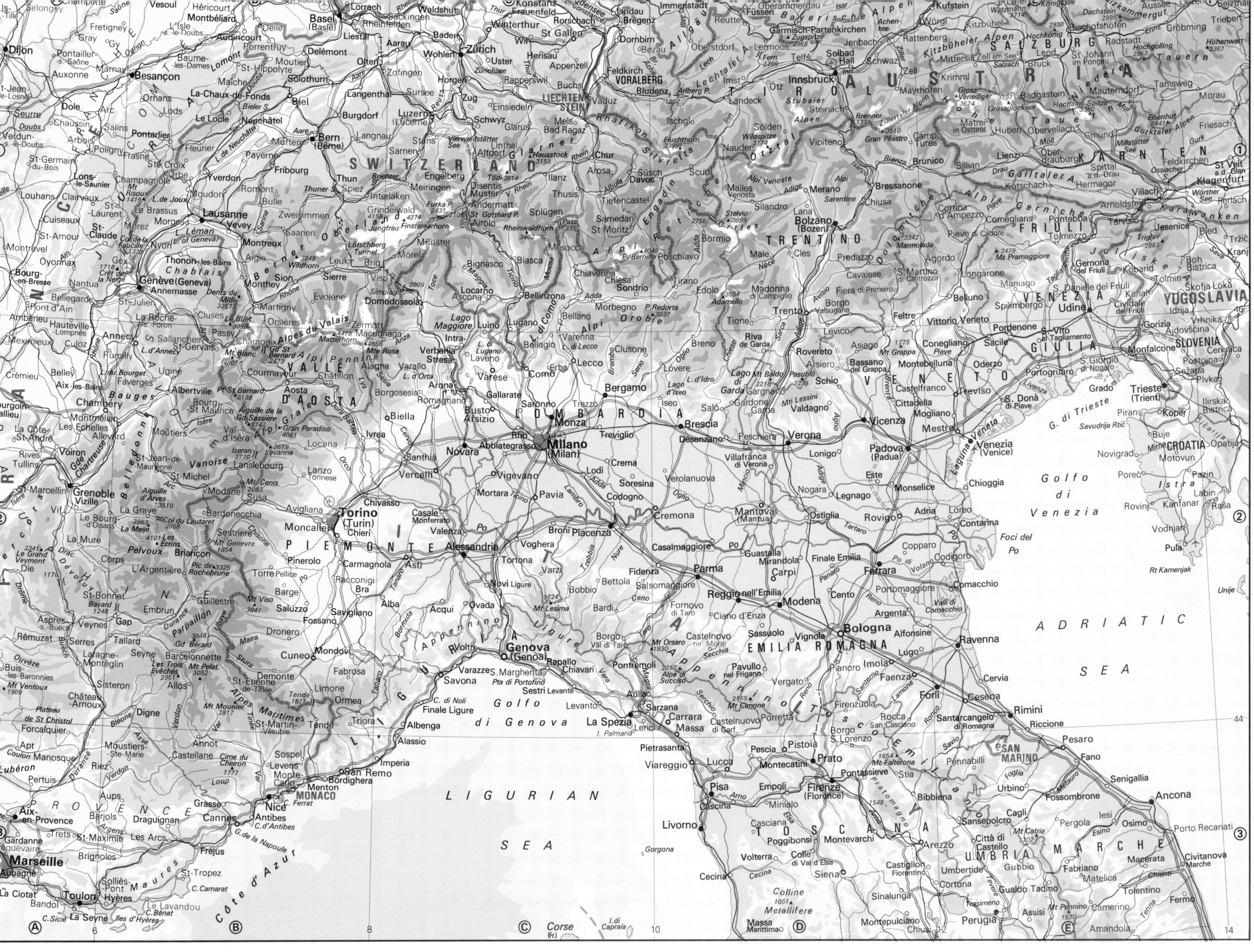

ADRIATIC SEA

LIGURIAN SEA

Golfo di Venezia

G. di Trieste

Golfo di Genova

Innsbruck · Klagenfurt · Salzburg · Kufstein
Zürich · Basel · Bern · Luzern · St Gallen · Chur · Davos · St Moritz
Genève (Geneva) · Lausanne · Montreux · Sion
Trieste (Trst) · Udine · Venezia (Venice) · Padova (Padua) · Vicenza · Verona · Treviso · Belluno · Bolzano (Bozen) · Trento · Rovereto
Milano (Milan) · Monza · Bergamo · Brescia · Como · Lecco · Sondrio · Pavia · Cremona · Mantova (Mantua) · Lodi · Crema
Torino (Turin) · Aosta · Novara · Vercelli · Alessandria · Asti · Cuneo · Biella · Ivrea
Bologna · Ferrara · Modena · Parma · Reggio nell'Emilia · Ravenna · Forlì · Cesena · Rimini · Piacenza · Faenza · Imola
Genova (Genoa) · Savona · Imperia · San Remo · La Spezia · Rapallo
Firenze (Florence) · Pisa · Livorno · Prato · Pistoia · Lucca · Arezzo · Siena · Massa · Carrara · Viareggio
Ancona · Pesaro · Fano · Senigallia · Urbino · Perugia · Foligno
Nice · Antibes · Cannes · Grasse · Menton · Toulon · Marseille · Aix-en-Provence · Grenoble · Chambéry · Annecy · Briançon · Digne · Gap
Besançon · Dijon · Dole

Po · Adige · Adda · Ticino · Rhône · Rhein · Drau · Sava · Tagliamento · Piave · Brenta

Lago Maggiore · Lago di Como · Lago di Garda · Lago d'Iseo · L. di Lugano

Côte d'Azur

Mt Rosa 4634 · Matterhorn · Mont Blanc 4807 · Gran Paradiso 4061 · Grossglockner

Corse (fr.)

1:5M 0 50 100 150 200 km 0 50 100 mls

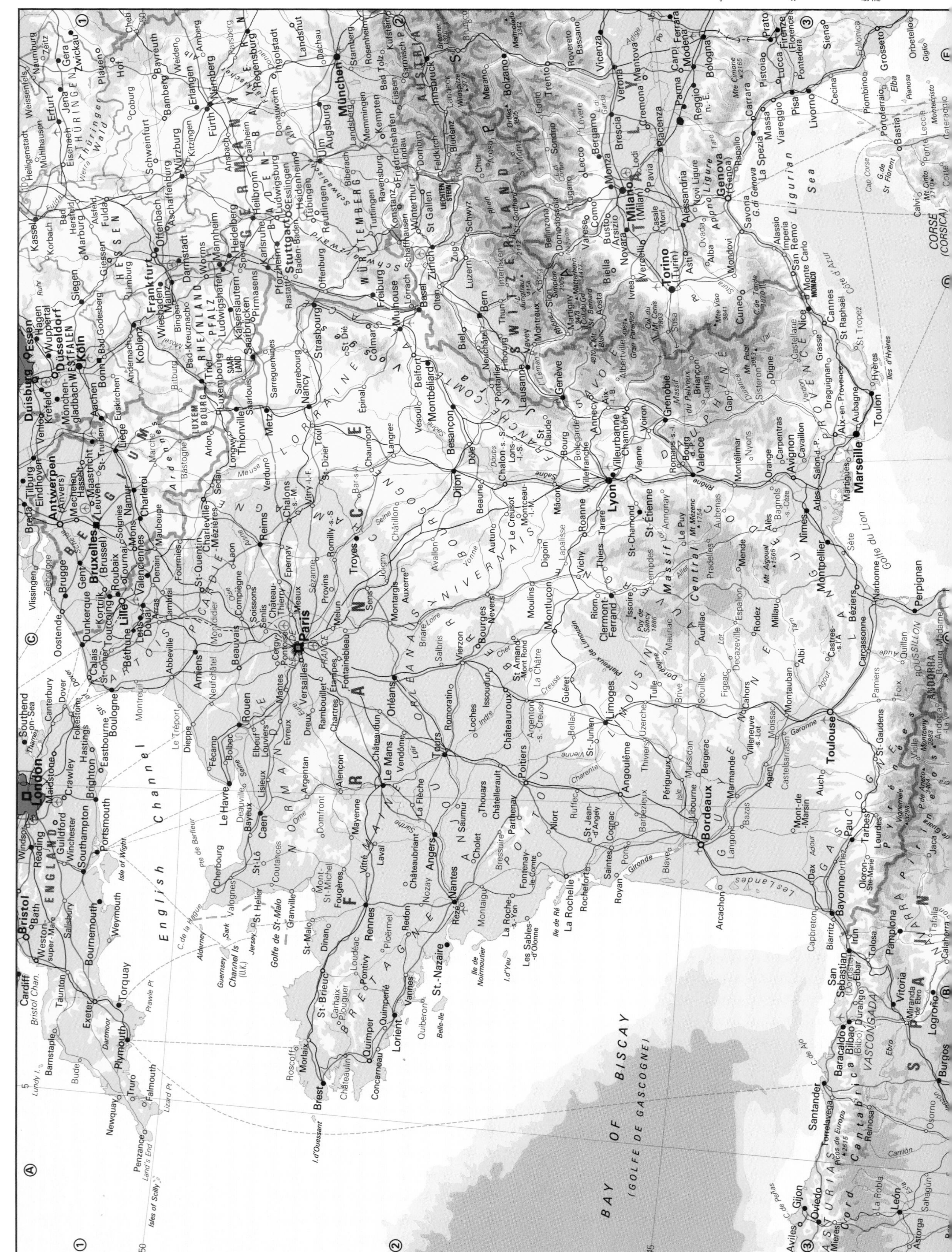
BAY OF BISCAY
(GOLFE DE GASCOGNE)
English Channel
Ligurian Sea
CORSE (CORSICA)
FRANCE
GERMANY
BELGIUM
SWITZERLAND
AUSTRIA
ITALY
SPAIN
ANDORRA
MONACO
LUXEMBOURG
LIECHTENSTEIN
ENGLAND
Paris
London
Lyon
Marseille
Bordeaux
Toulouse
Nantes
Brest
Rennes
Le Mans
Tours
Orléans
Limoges
Clermont-Ferrand
Dijon
Besançon
Strasbourg
Nancy
Metz
Reims
Lille
Rouen
Le Havre
Caen
Cherbourg
Amiens
Grenoble
Nice
Montpellier
Nîmes
Avignon
Toulon
Perpignan
Genève
Lausanne
Bern
Basel
Zürich
Torino (Turin)
Milano (Milan)
Genova (Genoa)
Bruxelles (Brussel)
Antwerpen (Anvers)
Köln
Frankfurt
Stuttgart
München
Bilbao
San Sebastián
Massif Central
Pyrénées
Les Landes
Golfe du Lion
Isles of Scilly
Channel Is (U.K.)

1:5M

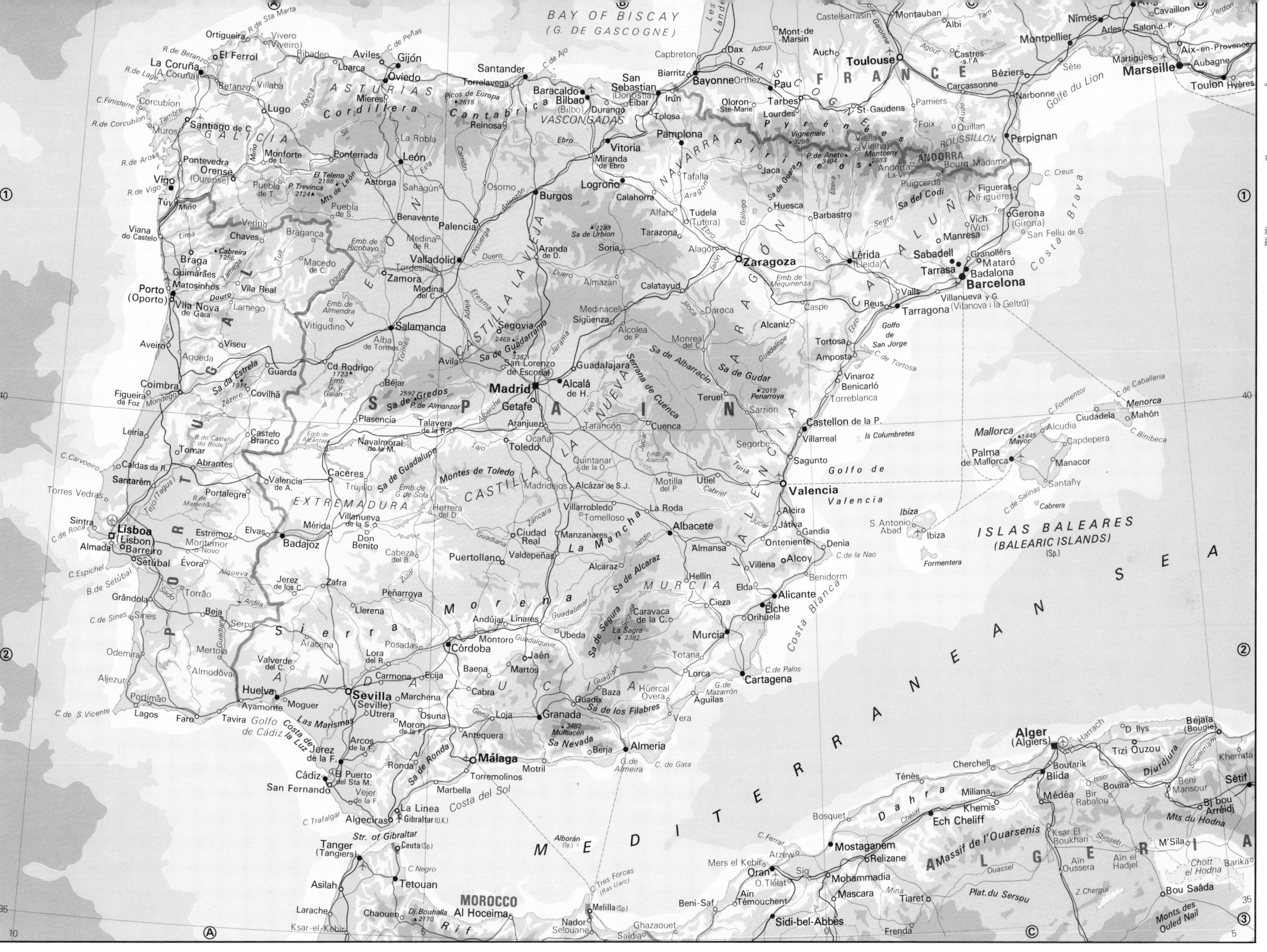

1:5M 0 50 100 150 200 km / 0 50 100 mls

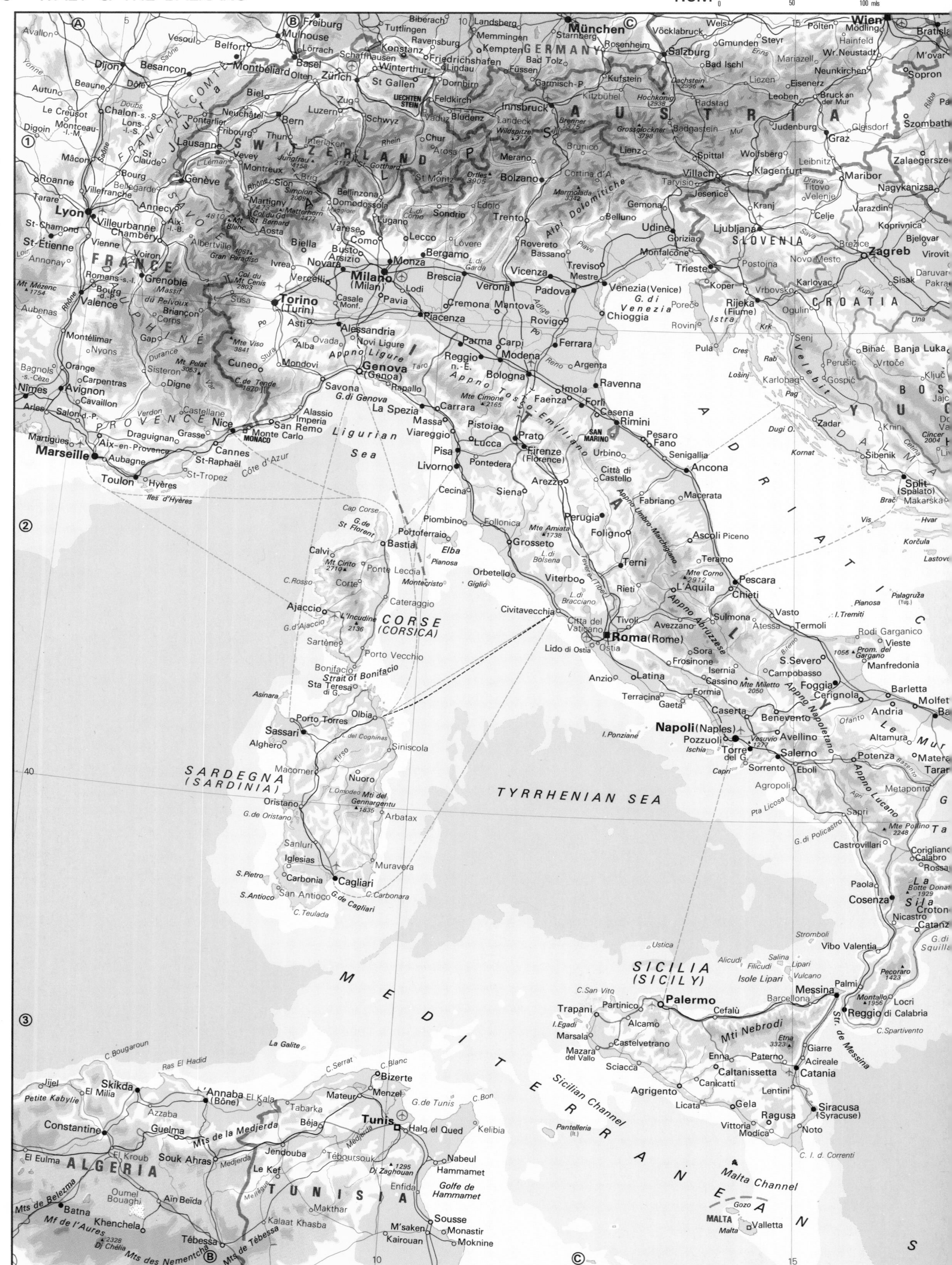

A
B
C
5
10
15
1
2
3
40
Freiburg
Mulhouse
Basel
Zürich
Biberach
Tuttlingen
Ravensburg
Konstanz
Schaffhausen
Winterthur
Friedrichshafen
Lindau
Landsberg
Memmingen
Kempten
Füssen
München
Starnberg
Rosenheim
Bad Tölz
Garmisch-P.
GERMANY
Vöcklabruck
Salzburg
Gmunden
Bad Ischl
Wels
Steyr
Pölten
Wien
Mödling
Hainfeld
Wr. Neustadt
Bratisla
Mariazell
Neunkirchen
M'ovar
Sopron
Dachstein 2996
Hochkönig 2938
Liezen
Eisenerz
Leoben
Bruck an der Mur
Radstad
Kitzbühel
Kufstein
Innsbruck
Landeck
Wildspitze 3774
Brenner 1375
Grossglockner 3798
Badgastein
Mur
Judenburg
Graz
Gleisdorf
Szombath
AUSTRIA
Lienz
Spittal
Wolfsberg
Klagenfurt
Leibnitz
Villach
Tarvisio
Jesenice
Drava
Maribor
Zalaegersze
Nagykanizsa
Kranj
Celje
Ljubljana
SLOVENIA
Varazdin
Koprivnica
Bjelovar
Brežice
Zagreb
Virovit
Novo Mesto
Postojna
Daruvar
Pakrac
Karlovac
Sisak
Kupa
Vrbovsko
Ogulin
CROATIA
Una
Rijeka (Fiume)
Koper
Trieste
Gorizia
Monfalcone
Udine
Gemona
Belluno
Cortina d'A.
Marmolada 3342
Alpi Dolomitiche
Bolzano
Merano
Brunico
Ortles 3905
St Moritz
Chur
Arosa
Vaduz
LIECHTENSTEIN
Feldkirch
Bludenz
Dornbirn
St Gallen
Schwyz
Zug
Luzern
Rhein
St Gotthard
Interlaken
Thun
Bern
Biel
Neuchâtel
Fribourg
Pontarlier
Lausanne
Vevey
Montreux
L. Léman
Genève
SWITZERLAND
Jungfrau 4158
Sion
Brig
Simplon 2009
Martigny
Matterhorn 4477
Col du Gd St Bernard
Mt Blanc 4810
Aosta
Domodossola
Bellinzona
Lugano
L. Maggiore
L. di Como
Sondrio
Edolo
Trento
Rovereto
Bassano
Piave
Treviso
Mestre
Venezia (Venice)
G. di Venezia
Chioggia
Padova
Vicenza
Verona
L. di Garda
Brescia
Bergamo
Lecco
Lóvere
Como
Varese
Busto Arsizio
Monza
Milano (Milan)
Novara
Vercelli
Biella
Ivrea
Lodi
Pavia
Casale Monf.
Torino (Turin)
Susa
Asti
Alessandria
Novi Ligure
Alba
Ovada
Piacenza
Cremona
Mantova
Adige
Rovigo
Po
Ferrara
Parma
Carpi
Modena
Reggio n.-E.
Bologna
Reno
Argenta
Imola
Faenza
Forlì
Ravenna
Cesena
Rimini
SAN MARINO
Pesaro
Fano
Urbino
Senigallia
Ancona
Macerata
Appno Tosco-Emiliano
Mte Cimone 2165
Genova (Genoa)
Savona
Appno Ligure
Rapallo
G. di Genova
La Spezia
Carrara
Massa
Viareggio
Pistoia
Lucca
Prato
Firenze (Florence)
Pisa
Pontedera
Livorno
Cecina
Siena
Arezzo
Città di Castello
Perugia
Foligno
Fabriano
Ascoli Piceno
Teramo
Terni
Rieti
Mte Amiata 1738
Grosseto
Follonica
Piombino
Portoferraio
Elba
Pianosa
Orbetello
Giglio
Montecristo
L. di Bolsena
Viterbo
L. di Bracciano
Tevere (Tiber)
Civitavecchia
Città del Vaticano
Roma (Rome)
Ostia
Lido di Ostia
Tivoli
Avezzano
L'Aquila
Mte Corno 2912
Pescara
Chieti
Sulmona
Appno Abruzzese
Appno Umbro-Marchigiano
Vasto
Atessa
Termoli
I. Tremiti
Pianosa
Palagruža (Yug.)
Rodi Garganico
Vieste
Prom. del Gargano 1056
Manfredonia
S. Severo
Campobasso
Foggia
Cerignola
Barletta
Molfet
Andria
Altamura
Sora
Frosinone
Isernia
Cassino
Mte Miletto 2050
Appno Napoletano
Latina
Anzio
Terracina
Gaeta
Formia
Caserta
Benevento
Avellino
Napoli (Naples)
Pozzuoli
Ischia
Vesuvio 1277
Torre del G.
Capri
Sorrento
Salerno
Eboli
Potenza
Ofanto
Matera
Agropoli
Pta Licosa
Appno Lucano
Metaponto
Sapri
G. di Policastro
Mte Pollino 2248
Castrovillari
Corigliano Calabro
Rossano
Paola
La Botte Donato 1929
Sila
Cosenza
Crotone
Nicastro
Catanzaro
Vibo Valentia
Stromboli
Salina
Alicudi
Filicudi
Lipari
Vulcano
Isole Lipari
Ustica
Messina
Palmi
Pecoraro 1423
Montalto 1956
Locri
Reggio di Calabria
Str. de Messina
C. Spartivento
SICILIA (SICILY)
Palermo
C. San Vito
Trapani
Partinico
Alcamo
Cefalù
Barcellona
Mti Nebrodi
Etna 3323
Giarre
Acireale
Catania
I. Egadi
Marsala
Castelvetrano
Mazara del Vallo
Sciacca
Agrigento
Enna
Paterno
Caltanissetta
Canicattì
Lentini
Licata
Gela
Ragusa
Vittoria
Modica
Siracusa (Syracuse)
Noto
C. I. d. Correnti
Pantelleria (It.)
Sicilian Channel
Malta Channel
Gozo
MALTA
Malta
Valletta
TYRRHENIAN SEA
MEDITERRANEAN SEA
Ligurian Sea
ADRIATIC SEA
I. Ponziane
CORSE (CORSICA)
Cap Corse
G. de St Florent
Bastia
Calvi
Mt Cinto 2710
Ponte Leccia
Corte
C. Rosso
Ajaccio
G. d'Ajaccio
L'Incudine 2136
Cateraggio
Sartène
Porto Vecchio
Bonifacio
Strait of Bonifacio
Sta Teresa di G.
Asinara
Porto Torres
Sassari
Olbia
Alghero
L. del Coghinas
Siniscola
Tirso
Macomer
Nuoro
L. Omodeo
Mti del Gennargentu 1835
Arbatax
Oristano
G. de Oristano
SARDEGNA (SARDINIA)
Sanluri
Iglesias
Muravera
S. Pietro
Carbonia
Cagliari
S. Antioco
San Antioco
G. de Cagliari
C. Carbonara
C. Teulada
La Galite
C. Bougaroun
Ras El Hadid
C. Serrat
C. Blanc
Bizerte
Mateur
Menzel
G. de Tunis
C. Bon
Tunis
Halq el Qued
Kelibia
Tabarka
Béja
Medjerda
Mts de la Medjerda
Jendouba
Téboursouk
Dj Zaghouan 1295
Nabeul
Hammamet
Golfe de Hammamet
Enfida
Le Kef
Makthar
Kalaat Khasba
Sousse
Monastir
M'saken
Kairouan
Moknine
TUNISIA
Tébessa
Mts de Tébessa
Mts des Nementcha
Dj Chélia 2328
Mf de l'Aures
Khenchela
Batna
Mts de Belezma
Oumel Bouaghi
Aïn Beïda
Souk Ahras
El Kroub
ALGERIA
El Eulma
Constantine
Guelma
Azzaba
'Annaba (Bône)
El Kala
Skikda
El Milia
Jijel
Petite Kabylie
Avallon
Vesoul
Belfort
Montbéliard
Besançon
Dijon
Saône
Yonne
Beaune
Dôle
Autun
Le Creusot
Chalon-s.-S.
Lons-l.-S.
Montceau-l.-M.
Digoin
Doubs
Jura
FRANCHE COMTÉ
Mâcon
St Claude
Bourg
Bellegarde
Roanne
Villefranche
Tarare
Lyon
Villeurbanne
St-Chamond
St-Étienne
Loire
Annonay
Vienne
Annecy
Aix-l.-B.
Chambéry
SAVOIE
Albertville
Voiron
Grenoble
Gran Paradiso 4061
Col du Mt Cenis 2803
FRANCE
Romans-s.-I.
Bourg-d.-P.
Valence
Mt Mézenc 1754
Rhône
Massif du Pelvoux
Briançon
Corps
DAUPHINÉ
Aubenas
Montélimar
Nyons
Gap
Durance
Mte Viso 3841
Stura
Mt Pelat 3053
Sisteron
Cuneo
Mondovi
C. de Tende 1870
Bagnols-s.-Cèze
Orange
Carpentras
Digne
Var
Nîmes
Avignon
Cavaillon
Arles
Salon-d.-P.
Verdon
Castellane
PROVENCE
Nice
Alassio
Imperia
San Remo
Monte Carlo
MONACO
Grasse
Draguignan
Martigues
Aix-en-Provence
Marseille
Aubagne
Cannes
St-Raphaël
Côte d'Azur
St-Tropez
Toulon
Hyères
Iles d'Hyères
Split (Spalato)
Makarska
Brač
Hvar
Vis
Korčula
Lastovo
Šibenik
Zadar
Knin
Cincer 2004
Dugi O.
Kornat
Pag
Karlobag
Gospić
Perušić
Velebit
Senj
Krk
Cres
Rab
Lošinj
Pula
Rovinj
Poreč
Istra
Bihać
Banja Luka
Vrtoče
Ključ
BOS
Jajc
DALMA
YU

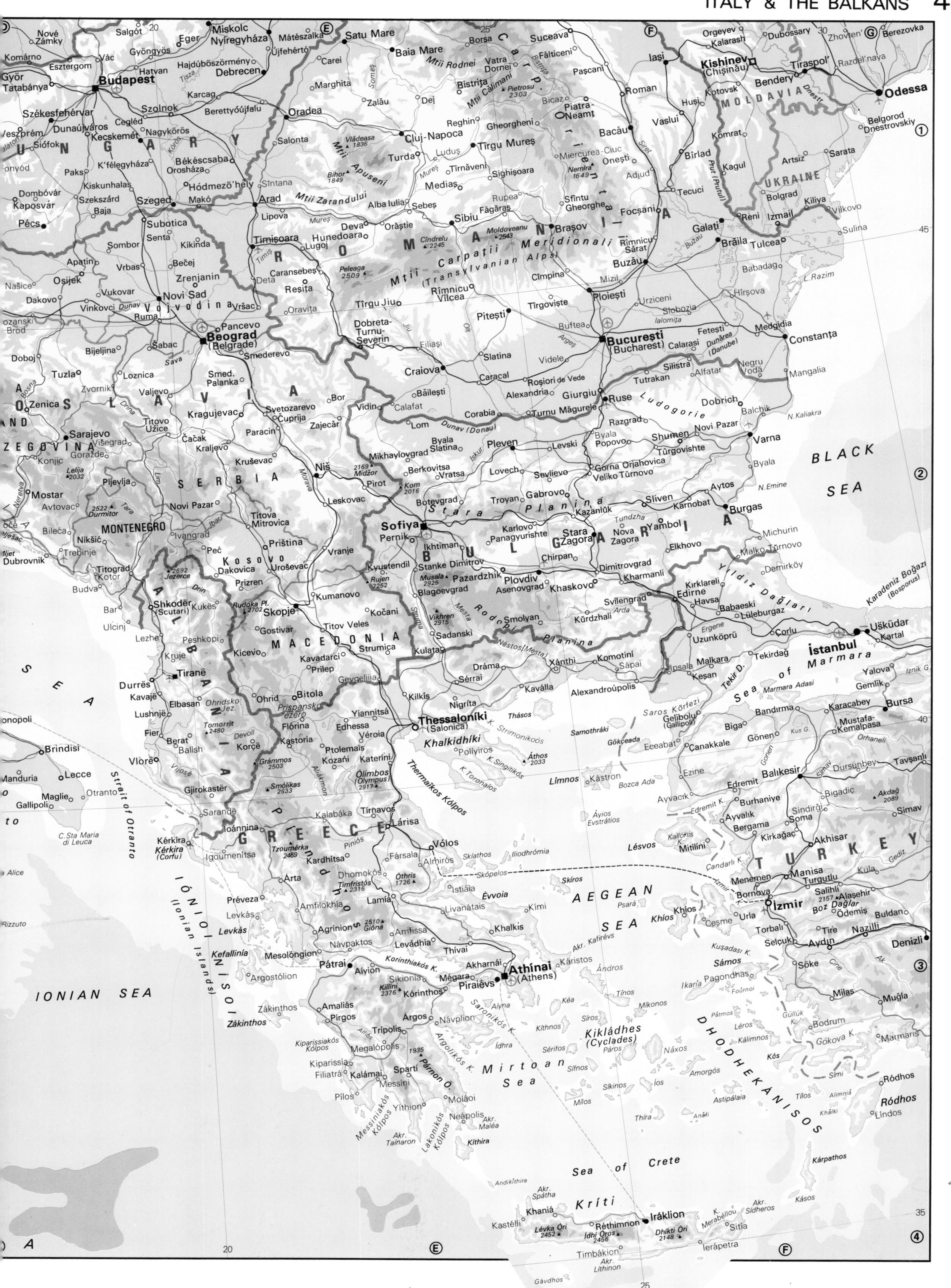
Budapest
Miskolc
Nyíregyháza
Debrecen
Szolnok
Kecskemét
Szeged
Pécs
Satu Mare
Baia Mare
Oradea
Cluj-Napoca
Tîrgu Mureş
Suceava
Iaşi
Kishinev
(Chişinău)
Tiraspol'
Odessa
Bacău
Roman
Arad
Timişoara
Sibiu
Braşov
Galaţi
Brăila
Tulcea
Buzău
Ploieşti
Bucureşti
(Bucharest)
Constanţa
Piteşti
Craiova
Ruse
Varna
Burgas
Pleven
Sofiya
Plovdiv
Stara Zagora
Novi Sad
Beograd
(Belgrade)
Niš
Sarajevo
Skopje
Tiranë
Shkodër
(Scutari)
Thessaloníki
(Salonica)
Lárisa
Vólos
Pátrai
Athínai
(Athens)
Piraiévs
Iráklion
Kríti
Edirne
İstanbul
Üsküdar
Bursa
İzmir
Denizli
Balıkesir
HUNGARY
ROMANIA
MOLDAVIA
UKRAINE
YUGOSLAVIA
SERBIA
MONTENEGRO
BULGARIA
ALBANIA
MACEDONIA
GREECE
TURKEY
Vojvodina
Kosovo
Mtii Carpaţii Meridionali
(Transylvanian Alps)
Stara Planina
Rodopi Planina
BLACK SEA
AEGEAN SEA
IONIAN SEA
Sea of Marmara
Sea of Crete
Mirtoan Sea
Strait of Otranto
IÓNIOI NÍSOI
(Ionian Islands)
Kikládhes
(Cyclades)
DHODHEKÁNISOS
Brindisi
Lecce
Rhódos

1:5M

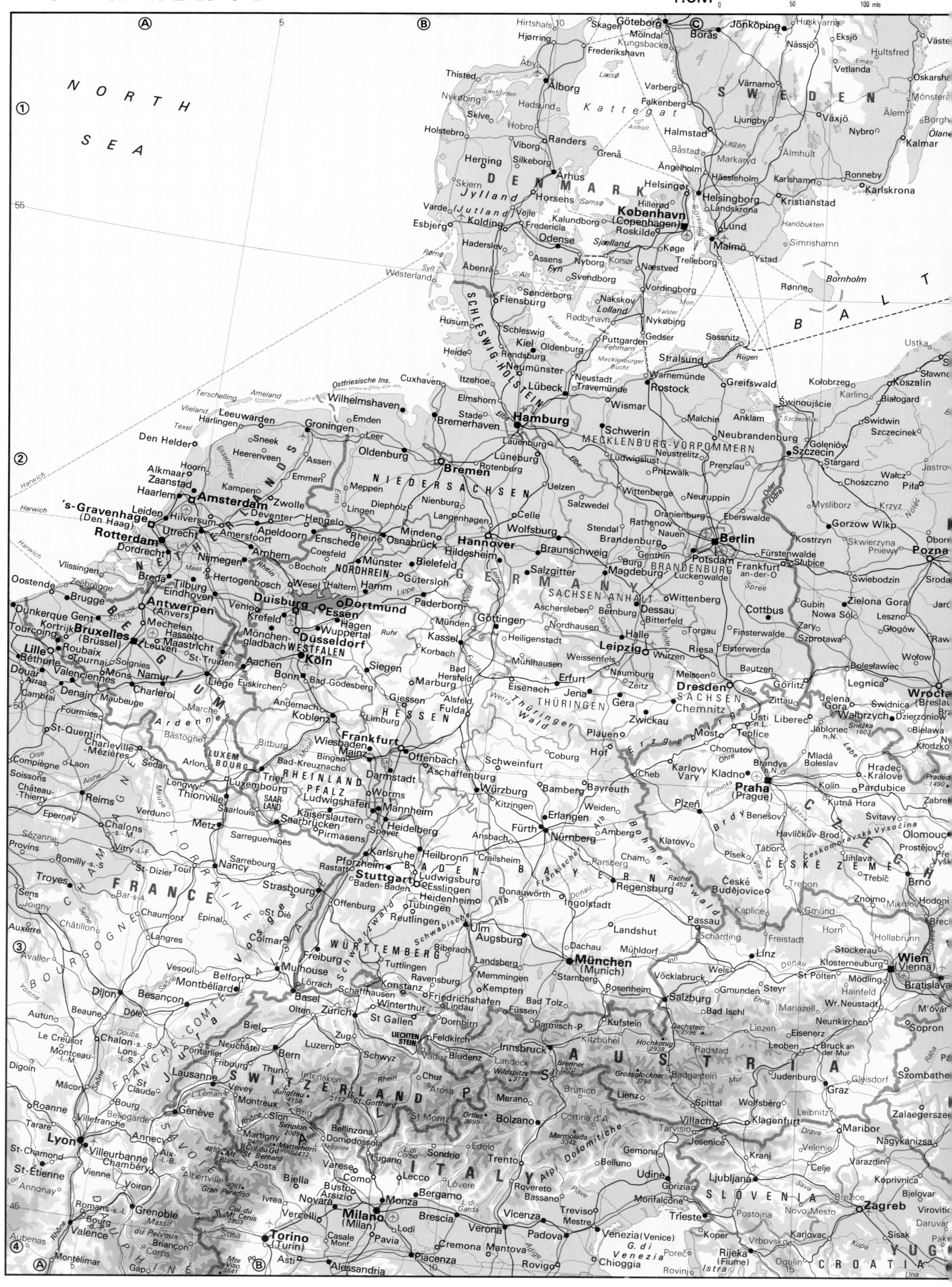

0 50 100 150 200 km
0 50 100 mls
NORTH SEA
BALTIC
DENMARK
SWEDEN
NETHERLANDS
BELGIUM
LUXEMBOURG
GERMANY
FRANCE
SWITZERLAND
AUSTRIA
ITALY
CZECH
SLOVENIA
CROATIA
SCHLESWIG-HOLSTEIN
MECKLENBURG-VORPOMMERN
NIEDERSACHSEN
NORDRHEIN-WESTFALEN
SACHSEN-ANHALT
BRANDENBURG
THÜRINGEN
SACHSEN
HESSEN
RHEINLAND PFALZ
SAARLAND
BADEN-WÜRTTEMBERG
BAYERN
ČESKÉ ZEMĚ
CHAMPAGNE
LORRAINE
ALSACE
BOURGOGNE
FRANCHE-COMTÉ
SAVOIE
DAUPHINÉ
Ardennes
Jura
ALPS
Kattegat
Jylland (Jutland)
Sjælland
Fyn
Lolland
Falster
Bornholm
Rügen
Fehmarn
Ostfriesische Ins.
Terschelling
Ameland
Vlieland
Texel
IJsselmeer
Thüringer Wald
Erzgebirge
Böhmer-wald
Schwarzwald
Schwäbische Alb
Vosges
Alpi Dolomitiche
Göteborg
Jönköping
Helsingborg
Malmö
København (Copenhagen)
Odense
Århus
Ålborg
Esbjerg
Kiel
Lübeck
Hamburg
Bremen
Bremerhaven
Wilhelmshaven
Rostock
Stralsund
Szczecin
Schwerin
Berlin
Potsdam
Frankfurt an-der-O
Hannover
Braunschweig
Magdeburg
Halle
Leipzig
Dresden
Chemnitz
Erfurt
Amsterdam
'S-Gravenhage (Den Haag)
Rotterdam
Utrecht
Groningen
Antwerpen (Anvers)
Bruxelles (Brüssel)
Liège
Lille
Duisburg
Essen
Dortmund
Düsseldorf
Köln
Bonn
Koblenz
Frankfurt
Wiesbaden
Mainz
Mannheim
Heidelberg
Karlsruhe
Stuttgart
Nürnberg
Würzburg
Regensburg
München (Munich)
Augsburg
Ulm
Strasbourg
Nancy
Metz
Reims
Luxembourg
Saarbrücken
Praha (Prague)
Plzeň
Brno
Wien (Vienna)
Bratislava
Linz
Salzburg
Innsbruck
Graz
Klagenfurt
Ljubljana
Zagreb
Zürich
Basel
Bern
Lausanne
Genève
Lyon
Grenoble
Dijon
Besançon
Torino (Turin)
Milano (Milan)
Bergamo
Brescia
Verona
Venezia (Venice)
Padova
Vicenza
Trieste
Bolzano
Trento
Wrocław
Poznań
Zielona Gora
Legnica

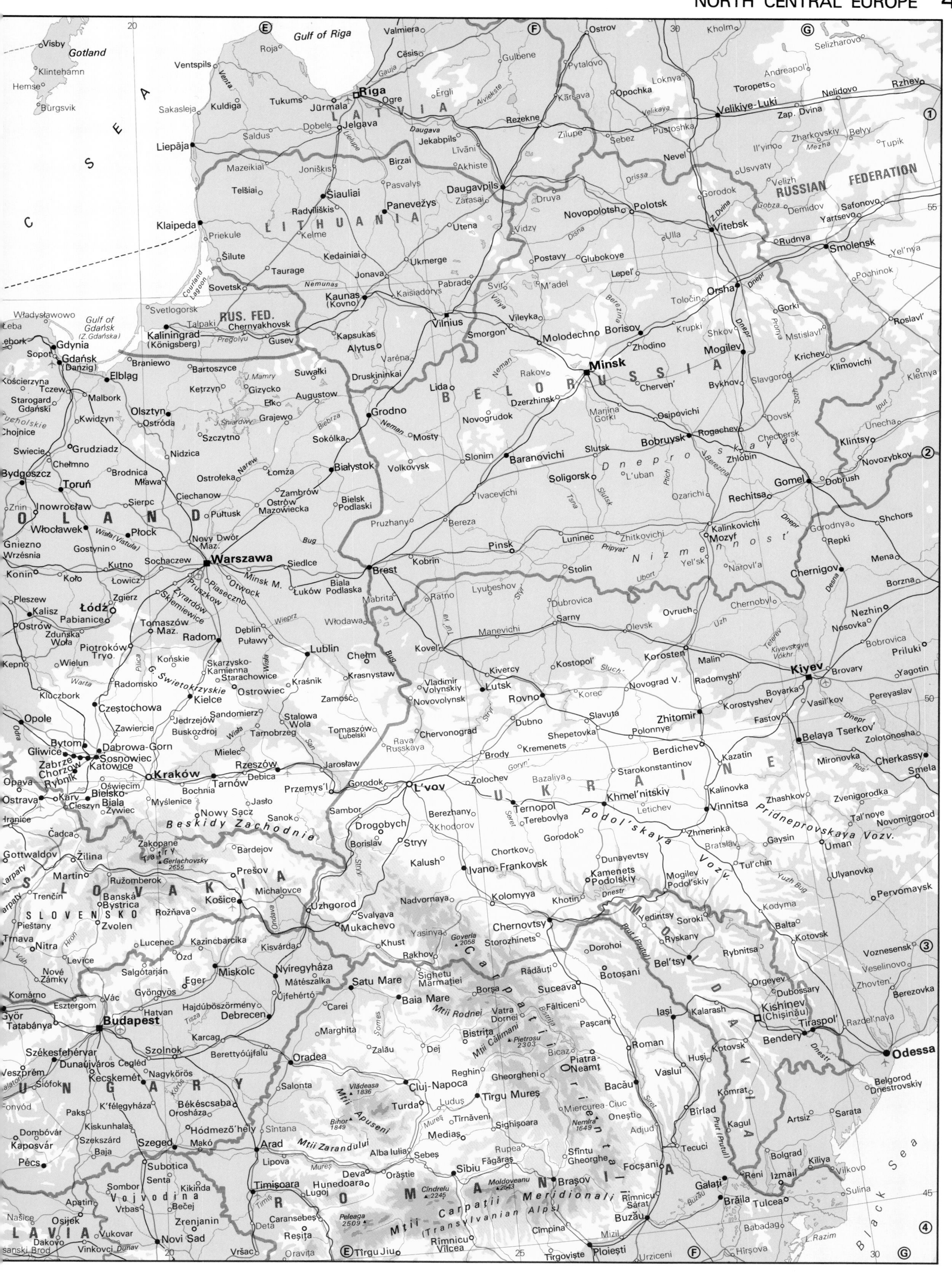

1:10M 0 100 200 300 400 km / 0 100 200 mls

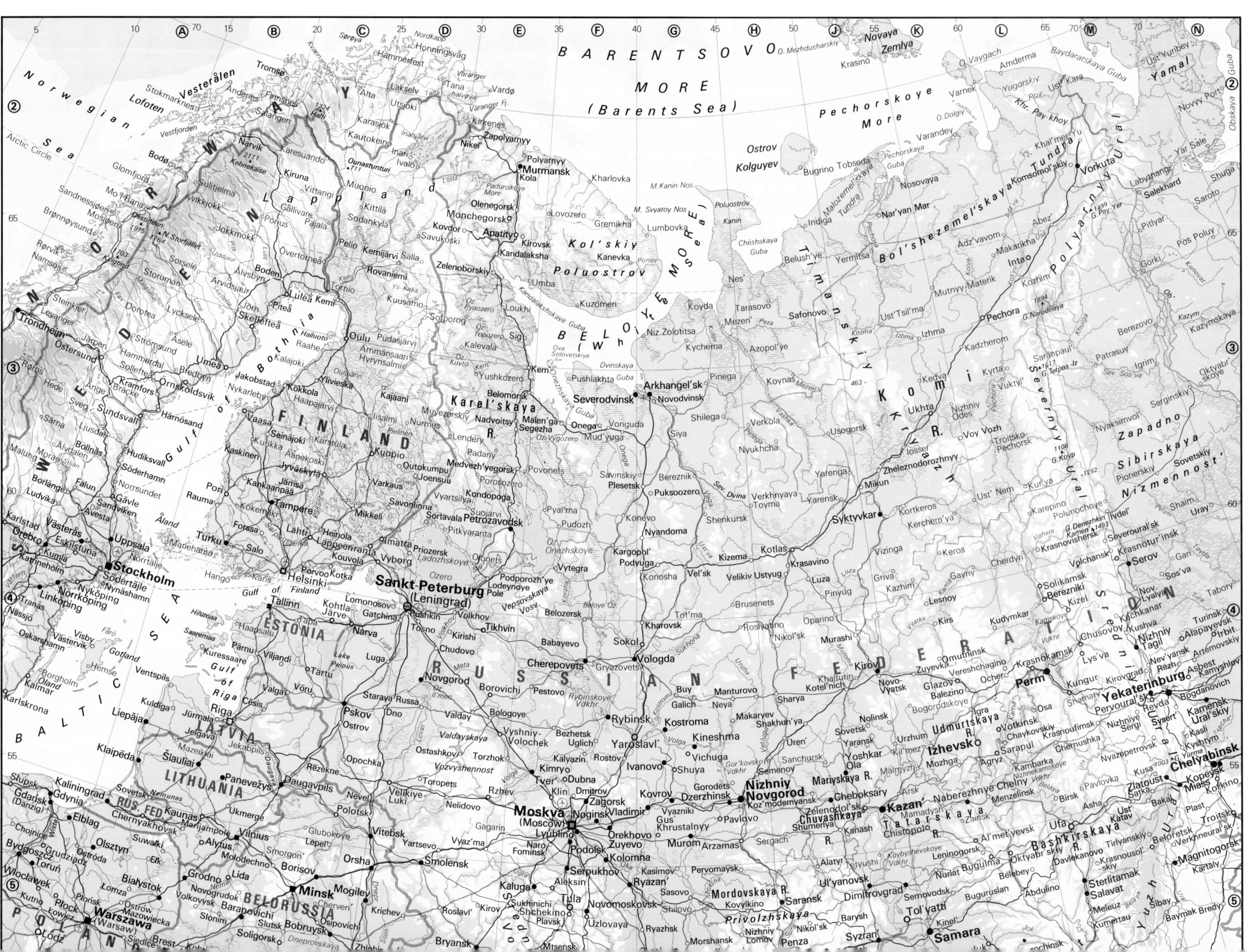
BARENTSOVO MORE
(Barents Sea)
Norwegian Sea
Pechorskoye More
FINLAND
ESTONIA
LATVIA
LITHUANIA
BELORUSSIA
RUSSIAN FEDERATION
Moskva
(Moscow)
Sankt-Peterburg
(Leningrad)
Stockholm
Helsinki
Tallinn
Riga
Vilnius
Minsk
Warszawa
(Warsaw)
Arkhangel'sk
Murmansk
Kazan'
Perm
Yekaterinburg
Chelyabinsk
Samara
Nizhniy Novgorod
Gulf of Finland
Gulf of Riga
Gulf of Bothnia
BALTIC SEA

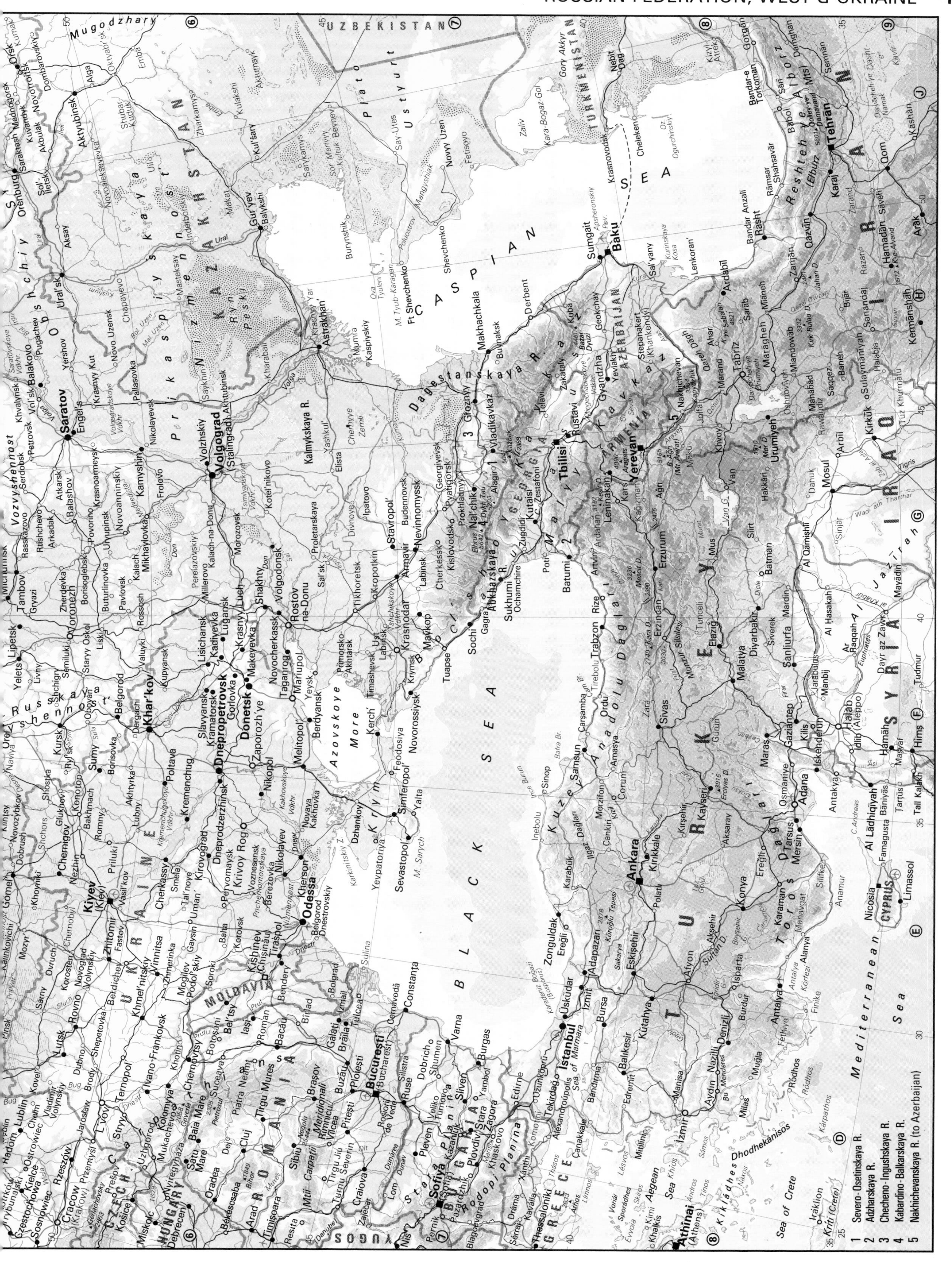

1 Severo-Osetinskaya R.
2 Adzharskaya R.
3 Checheno-Ingushskaya R.
4 Kabardino-Balkarskaya R.
5 Nakhichevanskaya R. (to Azerbaijan)

1:40M

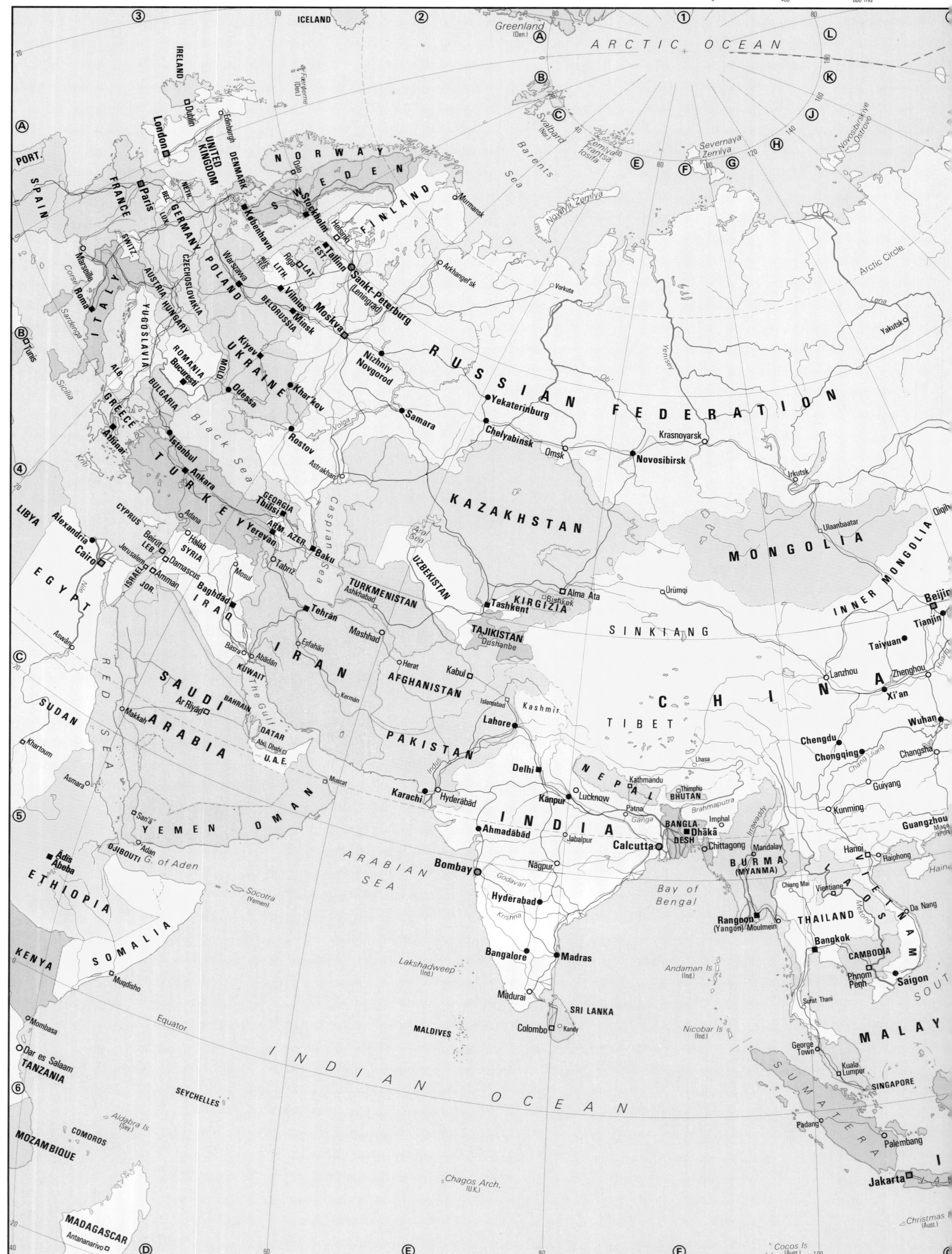
ARCTIC OCEAN
RUSSIAN FEDERATION
KAZAKHSTAN
MONGOLIA
CHINA
INDIA
IRAN
SAUDI ARABIA
TURKEY
UKRAINE
AFGHANISTAN
PAKISTAN
INDIAN OCEAN
ARABIAN SEA
Bay of Bengal
Moskva
Beijing
Delhi
Bombay
Calcutta
Tehrān
Novosibirsk
Krasnoyarsk
Irkutsk
Yakutsk
Ulaanbaatar
Tashkent
Alma Ata
Kabul
Karachi
Lahore
Baghdad
Ankara
İstanbul
Cairo
Jakarta
Bangkok
Rangoon (Yangon)
Saigon
Hanoi
Dhākā
Kathmandu
Colombo
Madras
Bangalore
Hyderabad
TIBET
SINKIANG
NEPAL
BHUTAN
BANGLADESH
BURMA (MYANMA)
THAILAND
CAMBODIA
VIETNAM
LAOS
SRI LANKA
MALDIVES
SEYCHELLES
SOMALIA
ETHIOPIA
KENYA
TANZANIA
MADAGASCAR
MOZAMBIQUE
EGYPT
SUDAN
LIBYA
YEMEN
OMAN
U.A.E.
QATAR
BAHRAIN
KUWAIT
IRAQ
SYRIA
JOR.
ISRAEL
LEB.
CYPRUS
GEORGIA
ARM.
AZER.
TURKMENISTAN
UZBEKISTAN
KIRGIZIA
TAJIKISTAN
INNER MONGOLIA
SUMATERA
SINGAPORE
Equator
Arctic Circle

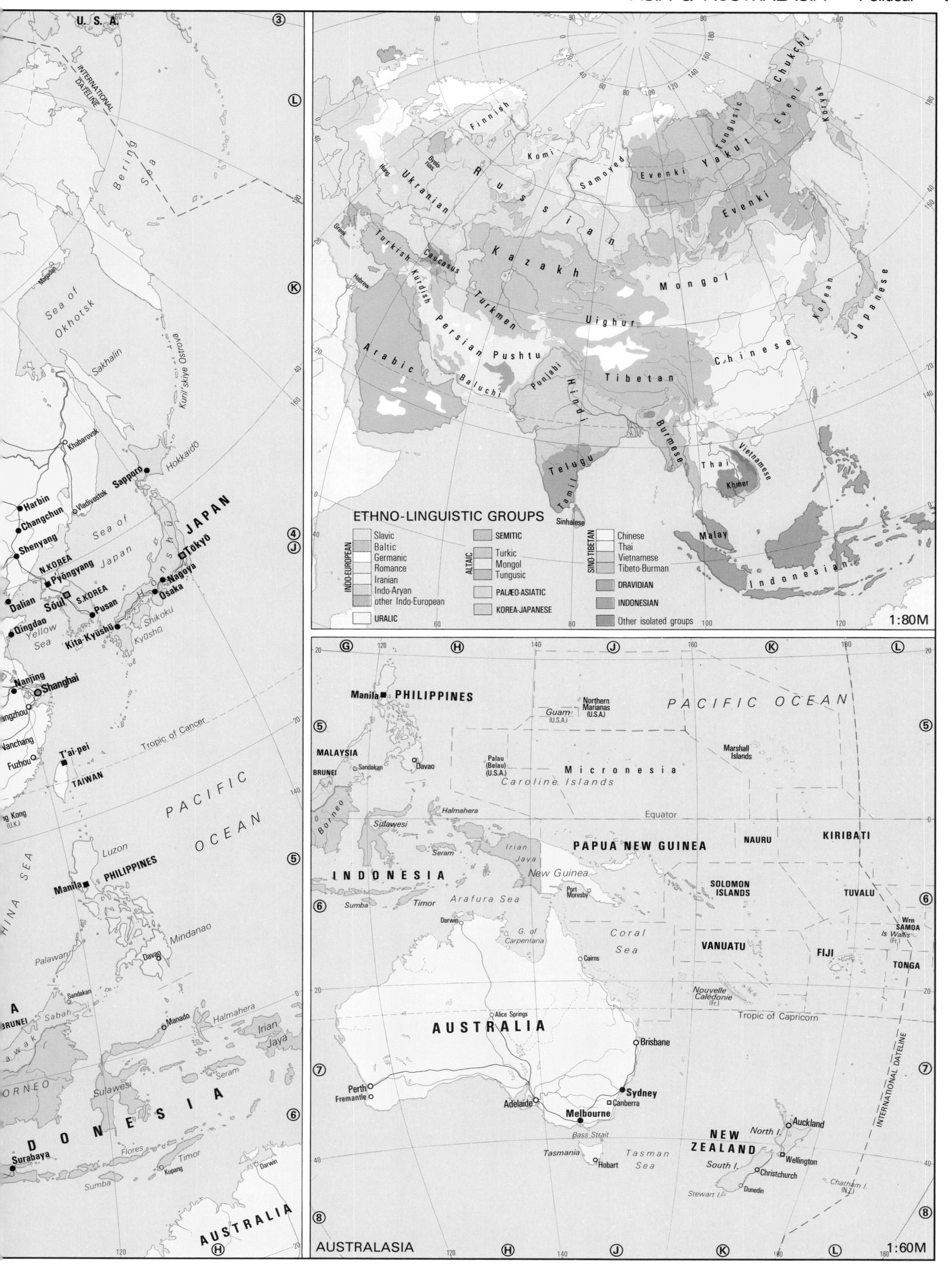

ETHNO-LINGUISTIC GROUPS

INDO-EUROPEAN
- Slavic
- Baltic
- Germanic
- Romance
- Iranian
- Indo-Aryan
- other Indo-European

URALIC

ALTAIC
- SEMITIC
- Turkic
- Mongol
- Tungusic

PALÆO-ASIATIC

KOREA-JAPANESE

SINO-TIBETAN
- Chinese
- Thai
- Vietnamese
- Tibeto-Burman

DRAVIDIAN

INDONESIAN

Other isolated groups

1:80M

AUSTRALASIA

1:60M

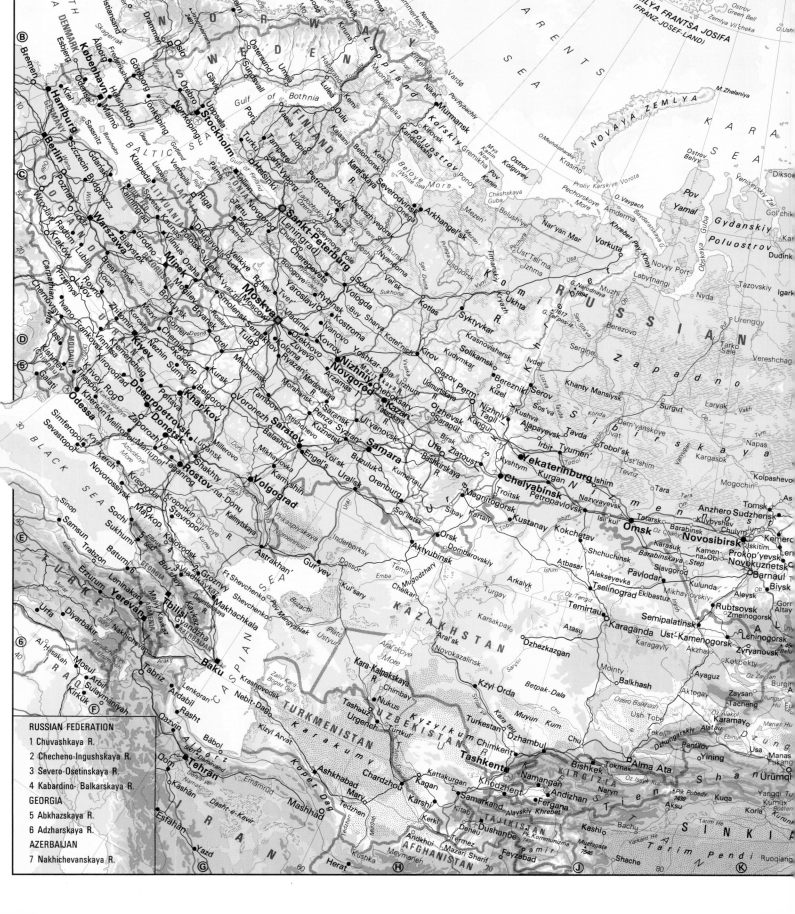

RUSSIAN FEDERATION
1 Chuvashkaya R.
2 Checheno-Ingushskaya R.
3 Severo-Osetinskaya R.
4 Kabardino-Balkarskaya R.
GEORGIA
5 Abkhazskaya R.
6 Adzharskaya R.
AZERBAIJAN
7 Nakhichevanskaya R.

SEVERNAYA ZEMLYA (NORTH LAND)
NOVOSIBIRSKYE OSTROVA (NEW SIBERIAN ISLANDS)
LAPTEV SEA
EAST SIBERIAN SEA
CHUKCHI SEA
BERING SEA
SEA OF OKHOTSK
SEA OF JAPAN
YELLOW SEA
OCEAN
FEDERATION
Yakutskaya R.
Sredne Sibirskoye Ploskogorye
Poluostrov Taymyr
Khrebet Cherskogo
Verkhoyanskiy Khrebet
Kolymskoye Nagor'ye
Koryakskoye Nagor'ye
Chukotskiy Khrebet
KAMCHATKA
Sredinnyy Khrebet
Stanovoy Khrebet
Aldanskoye Nagor'ye
Dzhugdzhur
SAKHALIN
Kuril'skiye Ostrova (Kuril Islands)
Sikhote Alin'
Buryatskaya R.
Tuvinskaya R.
MONGOLIA
GOBI
INNER MONGOLIA
MANCHURIA
NORTH KOREA
SOUTH KOREA
JAPAN
HOKKAIDO
HONSHU
SHIKOKU
KYŪSHŪ
Noril'sk
Yakutsk
Magadan
Petropavlovsk-Kamchatskiy
Irkutsk
Krasnoyarsk
Ulan Ude
Chita
Khabarovsk
Vladivostok
Ulaanbaatar
Harbin
Changchun
Shenyang
Beijing (Peking)
Tianjin (Tientsin)
P'yŏngyang
Sŏul (Seoul)
Pusan
Taegu
Tōkyō
Yokohama
Nagoya
Ōsaka
Kyōto
Kōbe
Sapporo
Fukuoka
Kita-Kyūshū
Hiroshima
Dalian
Jinan
Qingdao
Taiyuan
Baotou
Hohhot
Lanzhou
Yinchuan
Bering Str.
La Pérouse Strait
Korea Strait
Tsugaru-kaikyō
Bo Hai
Korea Bay

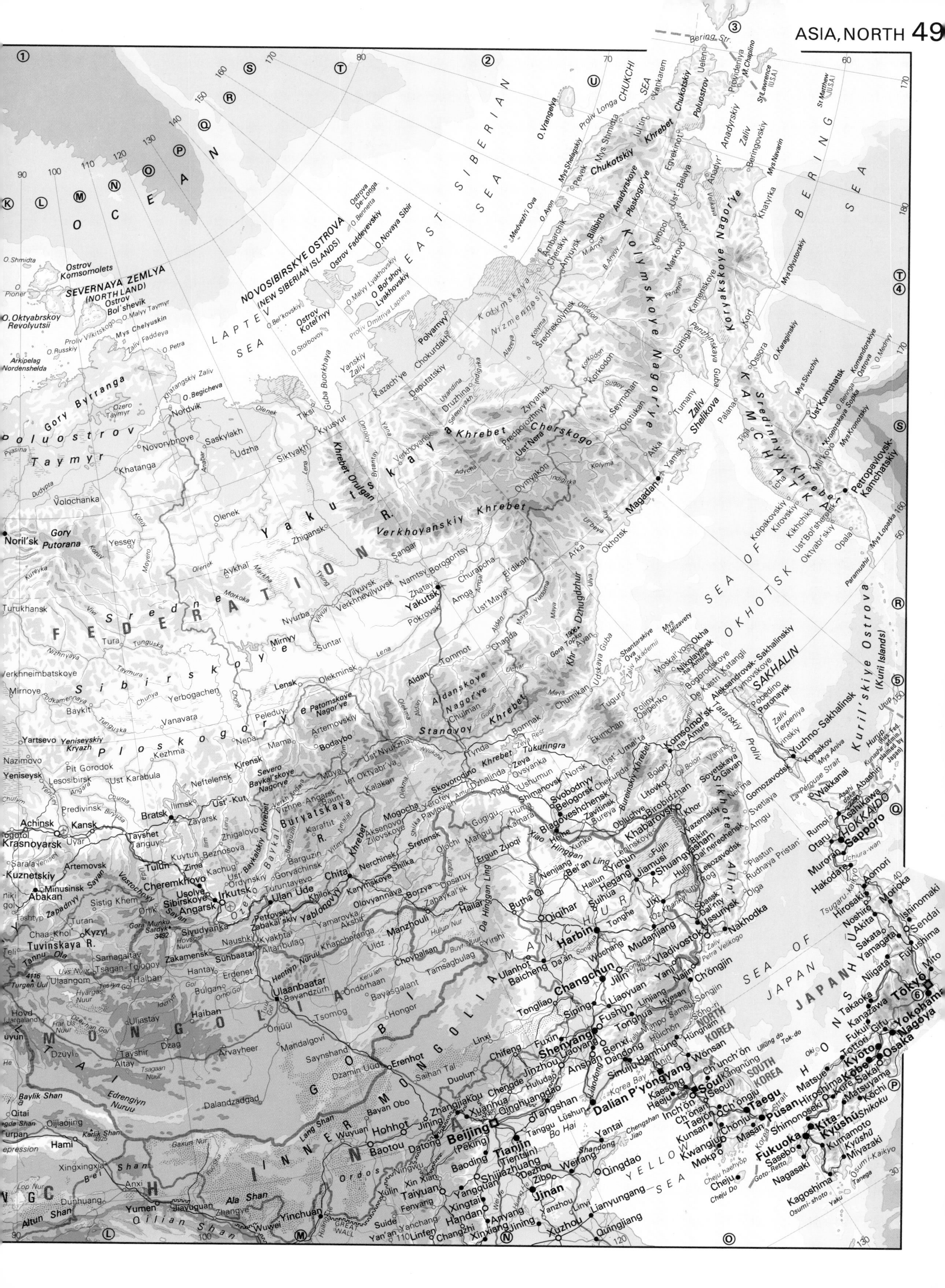

1:20M
0 200 400 600 800 km
0 200 400 mls

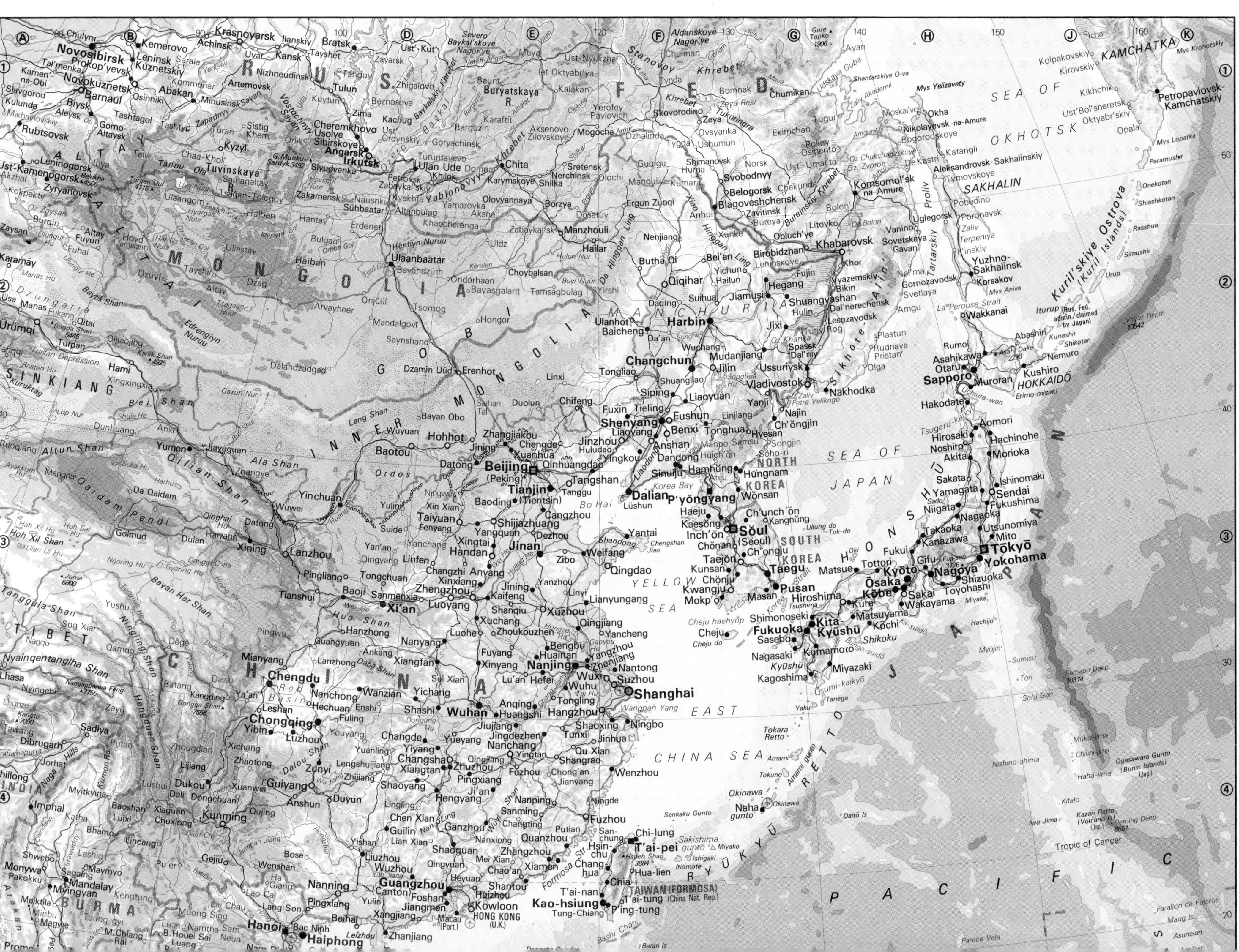
KAMCHATKA
Petropavlovsk-Kamchatskiy
SEA OF OKHOTSK
SAKHALIN
Kuril'skiye Ostrova (Kuril Islands)
HOKKAIDŌ
Sapporo
HONSHŪ
Tōkyō
Yokohama
Nagoya
Ōsaka
Kōbe
Kyōto
Hiroshima
Fukuoka
Kita-Kyūshū
SEA OF JAPAN
NORTH KOREA
SOUTH KOREA
P'yŏngyang
Sŏul (Seoul)
Pusan
Vladivostok
Khabarovsk
Harbin
Changchun
Shenyang
Dalian
Beijing (Peking)
Tianjin (Tientsin)
YELLOW SEA
EAST CHINA SEA
Shanghai
Nanjing
Wuhan
Chongqing
Chengdu
Xi'an
Lanzhou
Guangzhou (Canton)
HONG KONG (U.K.)
T'ai-pei
TAIWAN (FORMOSA)
Kao-hsiung
Hanoi
Haiphong
Ulaanbaatar
MONGOLIA
INNER MONGOLIA
GOBI
MANCHURIA
Hohhot
Baotou
Ürümqi
SINKIANG
TIBET
CHINA
Lhasa
BURMA
Mandalay
Kunming
RUSSIAN FED.
Novosibirsk
Krasnoyarsk
Irkutsk
Ulan Ude
Chita
Tropic of Cancer
PACIFIC
RYŪKYŪ RETTO
Okinawa

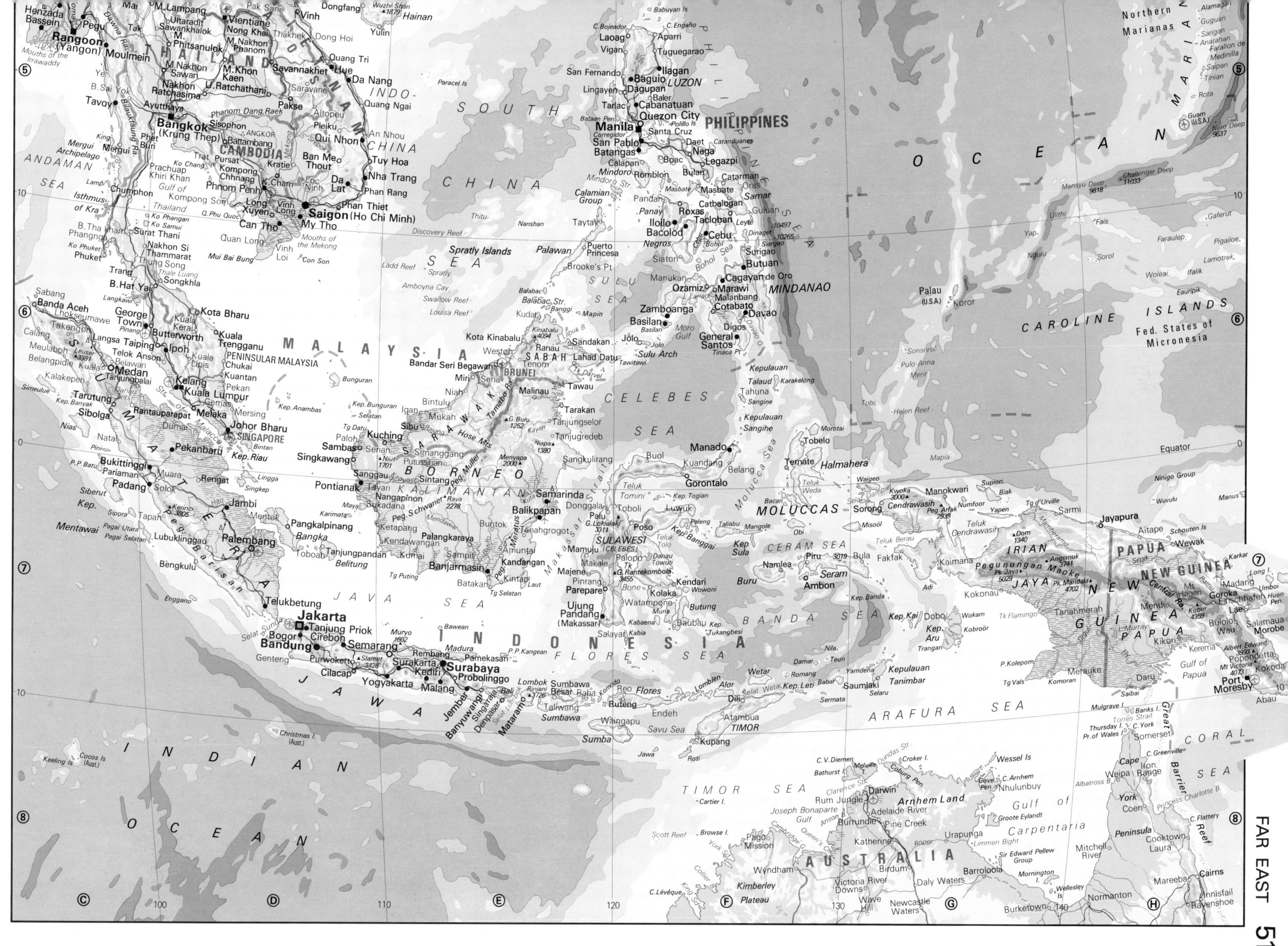
PHILIPPINES
MALAYSIA
INDONESIA
BORNEO
KALIMANTAN
SULAWESI (CELEBES)
MOLUCCAS
PAPUA NEW GUINEA
IRIAN JAYA
AUSTRALIA
CAMBODIA
SINGAPORE
BRUNEI
SOUTH CHINA SEA
CELEBES SEA
SULU SEA
JAVA SEA
BANDA SEA
FLORES SEA
ARAFURA SEA
TIMOR SEA
CORAL SEA
CERAM SEA
Molucca Sea
ANDAMAN SEA
INDIAN OCEAN
OCEAN
CAROLINE ISLANDS
Fed. States of Micronesia
Northern Marianas
Equator
Manila
Quezon City
Bangkok (Krung Thep)
Saigon (Ho Chi Minh)
Phnom Penh
Kuala Lumpur
Jakarta
Surabaya
Bandung
Semarang
Palembang
Medan
Kuching
Banjarmasin
Balikpapan
Ujung Pandang (Makassar)
Manado
Ambon
Davao
Zamboanga
Cebu
Jayapura
Port Moresby
Darwin
Rangoon (Yangon)
Moulmein
Vientiane
Da Nang
Hainan
Palau (U.S.A.)
Guam (U.S.A.)
Great Barrier Reef
Gulf of Carpentaria
Arnhem Land
Cape York Peninsula
TIMOR
Kupang
Dili

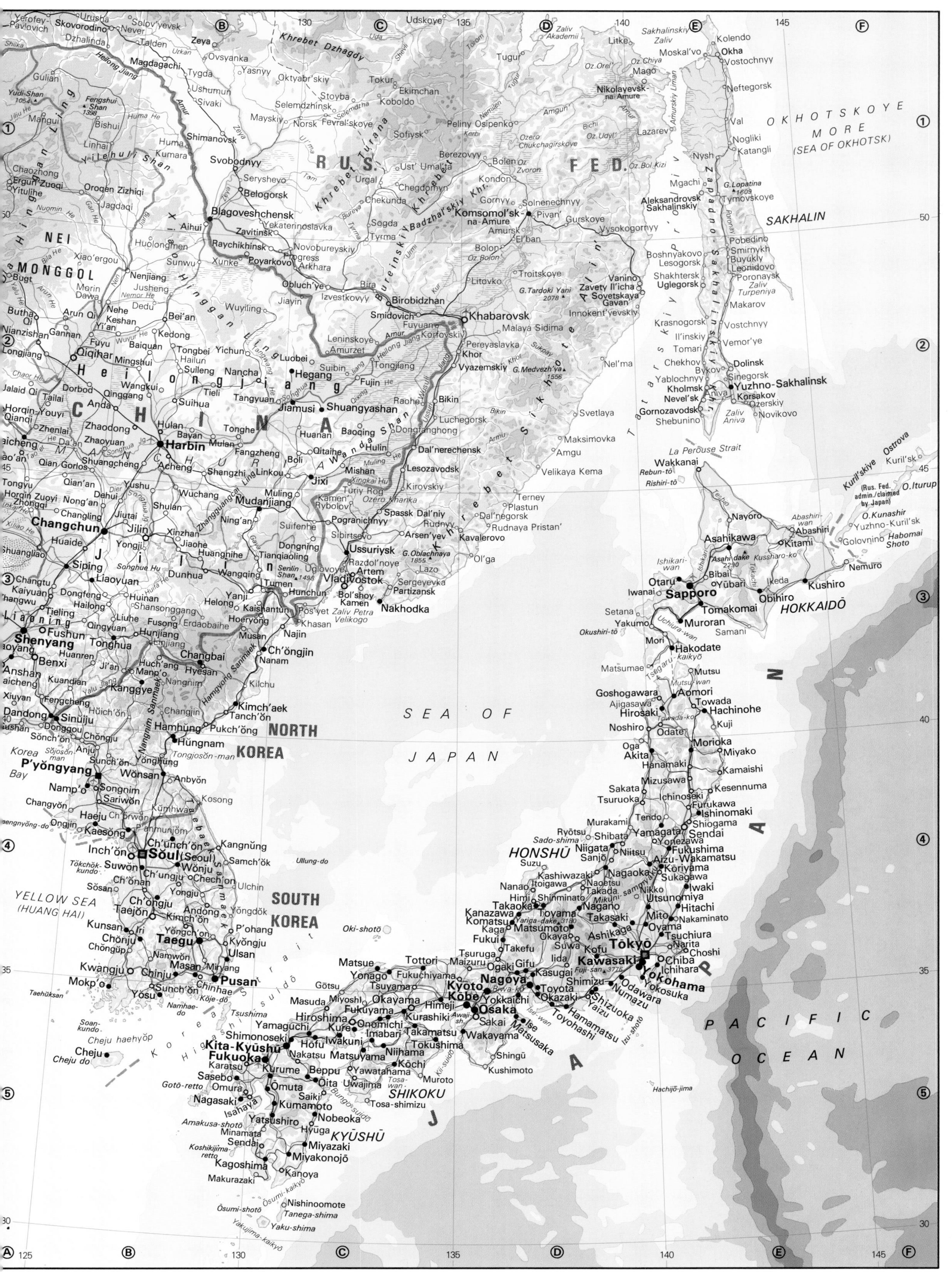

1:10M

1:5M

0 50 100 150 200 km
0 50 100 mls

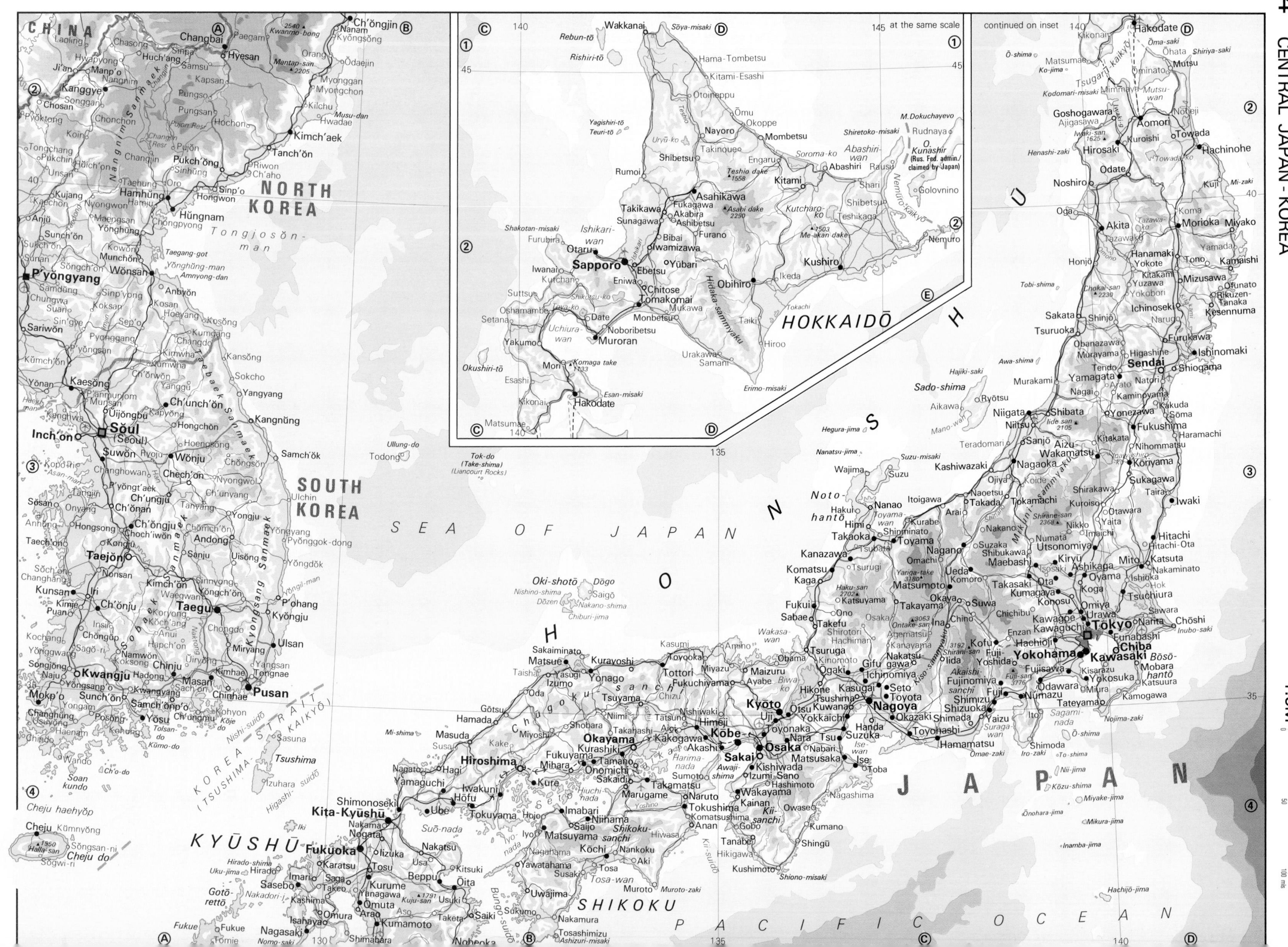

continued on inset
at the same scale
HOKKAIDŌ
SEA OF JAPAN
HONSHU
JAPAN
PACIFIC OCEAN
SHIKOKU
KYŪSHŪ
NORTH KOREA
SOUTH KOREA
CHINA
KOREA STRAIT (TSUSHIMA KAIKYŌ)
Tsushima
Oki-shotō
Sado-shima
Noto-hantō
Tōkyō
Yokohama
Kawasaki
Chiba
Nagoya
Kyōto
Ōsaka
Kōbe
Sakai
Hiroshima
Okayama
Fukuoka
Kita-Kyūshū
Sendai
Sapporo
Niigata
Kanazawa
Shizuoka
Hamamatsu
Sŏul (Seoul)
Inch'ŏn
P'yŏngyang
Pusan
Taegu
Kwangju
Taejŏn
Wŏnsan
Hamhŭng
Ch'ŏngjin
Hakodate
Asahikawa
Kushiro
Obihiro
Muroran
Wakkanai
Nemuro
Kunashir (Rus. Fed. admin./ claimed by Japan)
Tok-do (Take-shima) (Liancourt Rocks)
Ullung-do
Cheju
Cheju do

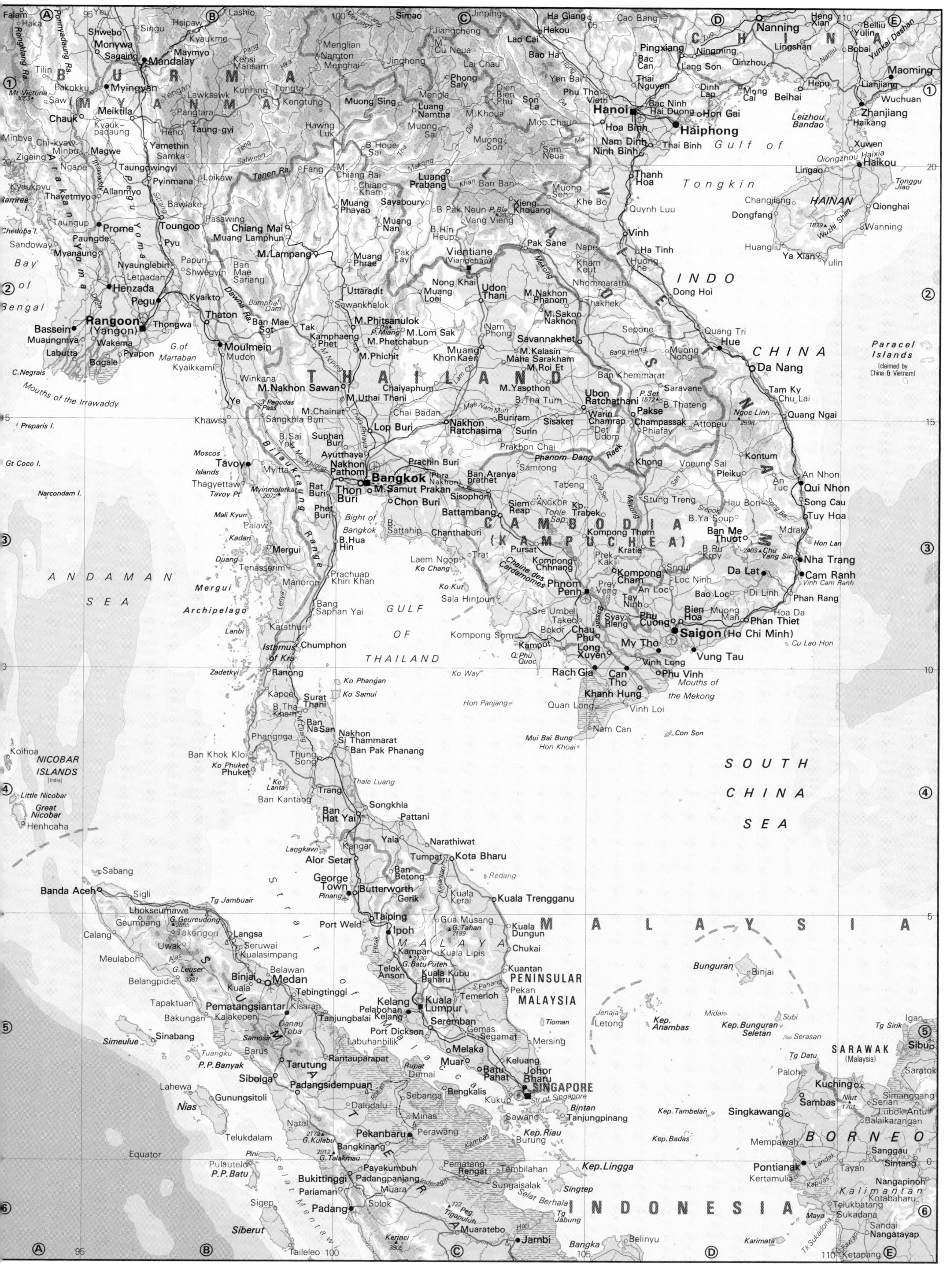
BURMA
MYANMAR
THAILAND
CAMBODIA (KAMPUCHEA)
LAOS
VIETNAM
CHINA
MALAYSIA
PENINSULAR MALAYSIA
INDONESIA
SUMATERA
BORNEO
Kalimantan
SARAWAK (Malaysia)
HAINAN
SINGAPORE
ANDAMAN SEA
Bay of Bengal
GULF OF THAILAND
SOUTH CHINA SEA
Gulf of Tongkin
Strait of Malacca
Selat Mentawai
Mouths of the Irrawaddy
Mouths of the Mekong
Paracel Islands (claimed by China & Vietnam)
NICOBAR ISLANDS (India)
Little Nicobar
Great Nicobar
Mergui Archipelago
Isthmus of Kra
Bight of Bangkok
Equator
Rangoon (Yangon)
Mandalay
Moulmein
Bassein
Pegu
Henzada
Prome
Toungoo
Meiktila
Myingyan
Monywa
Shwebo
Sagaing
Maymyo
Lashio
Taunggyi
Mergui
Tavoy
Bangkok
Thon Buri
Nakhon Pathom
Ayutthaya
Lop Buri
Nakhon Ratchasima
Chiang Mai
Chiang Rai
M.Lampang
M.Phitsanulok
M.Nakhon Sawan
Ubon Ratchathani
Udon Thani
Nong Khai
Chumphon
Ranong
Surat Thani
Nakhon Si Thammarat
Phuket
Songkhla
Ban Hat Yai
Pattani
Vientiane (Viangchan)
Luang Prabang
Savannakhet
Pakse
Phnom Penh
Battambang
Kompong Som
Kampot
Kompong Cham
Kratie
Siem Reap
ANGKOR
Tonle Sap
Hanoi
Haiphong
Nam Dinh
Ninh Binh
Thanh Hoa
Vinh
Hue
Da Nang
Quang Ngai
Qui Nhon
Nha Trang
Cam Ranh
Da Lat
Phan Thiet
Saigon (Ho Chi Minh)
Vung Tau
My Tho
Can Tho
Rach Gia
Nanning
Zhanjiang
Haikou
Maoming
Beihai
Kota Bharu
Alor Setar
George Town
Butterworth
Ipoh
Taiping
Kuala Lumpur
Kelang
Seremban
Melaka
Johor Bharu
Kuantan
Kuala Trengganu
Banda Aceh
Medan
Pematangsiantar
Sibolga
Padang
Pekanbaru
Jambi
Bukittinggi
Kuching
Pontianak
Singkawang
Nias
Siberut
Simeulue
Bunguran
Kep. Anambas
Kep. Riau
Kep. Lingga

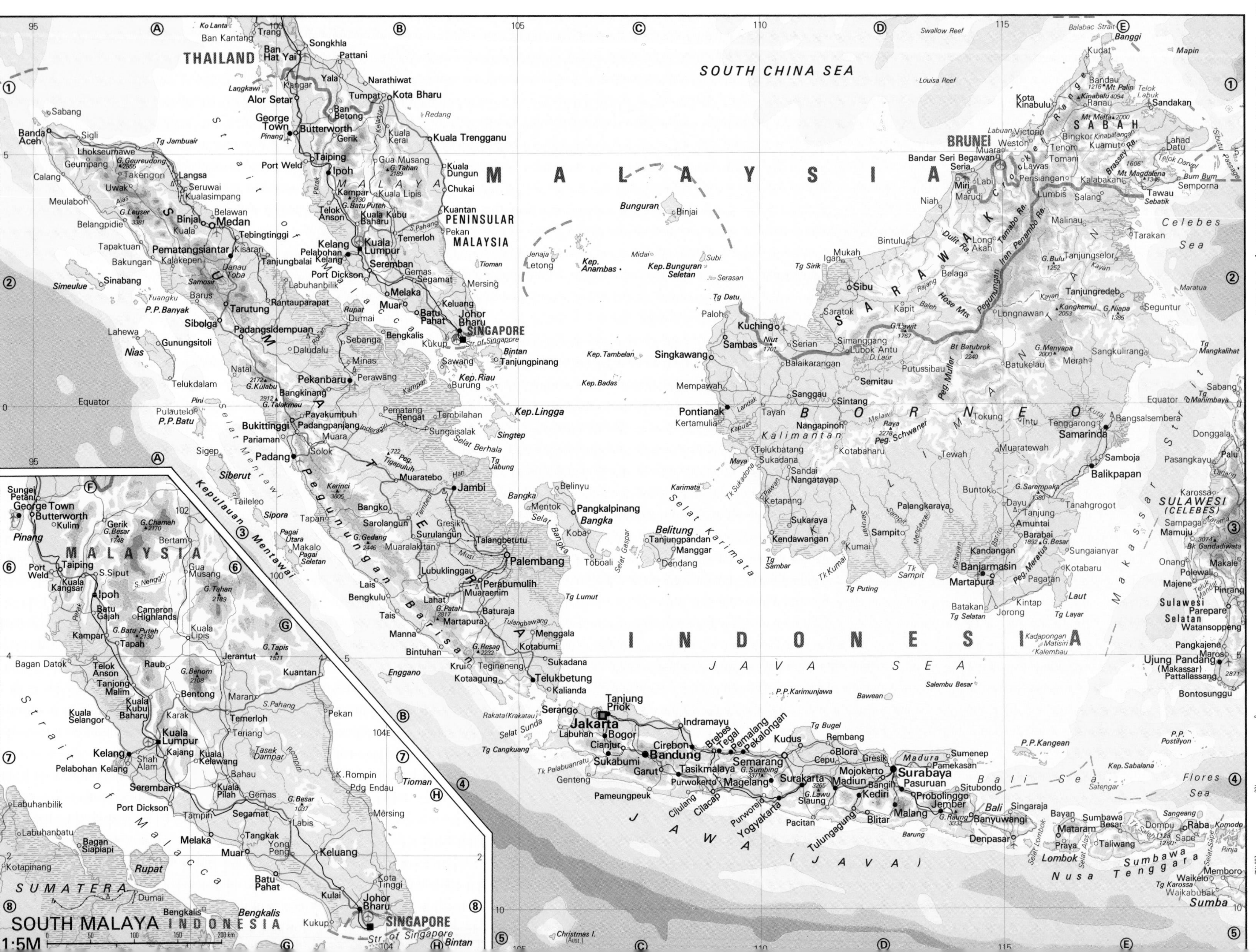

1:10M

SOUTH MALAYA
1:5M

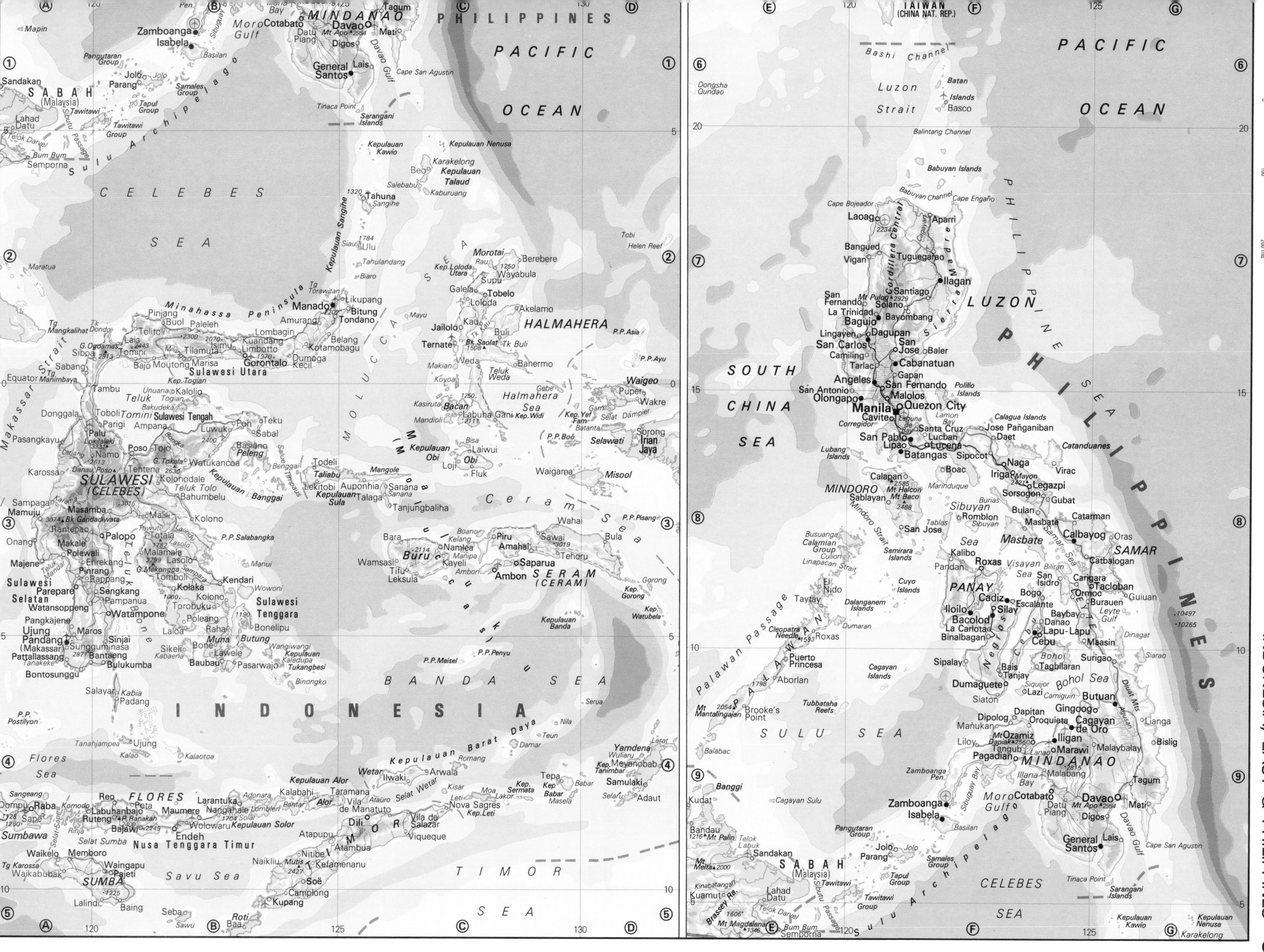
PACIFIC OCEAN
PHILIPPINES
PHILIPPINE SEA
LUZON
SOUTH CHINA SEA
SULU SEA
CELEBES SEA
MINDANAO
SAMAR
PANAY
MINDORO
MOLUCCA SEA
HALMAHERA
SERAM (CERAM)
BANDA SEA
INDONESIA
TIMOR SEA
Savu Sea
Flores Sea
SULAWESI (CELEBES)
FLORES
SUMBA
SABAH (Malaysia)
Manila
Quezon City
Cebu
Davao
Zamboanga
Manado
Ambon
Kupang
Dili
Ujung Pandang (Makassar)
Kendari
Ternate
TAIWAN (CHINA NAT. REP.)

1:20M

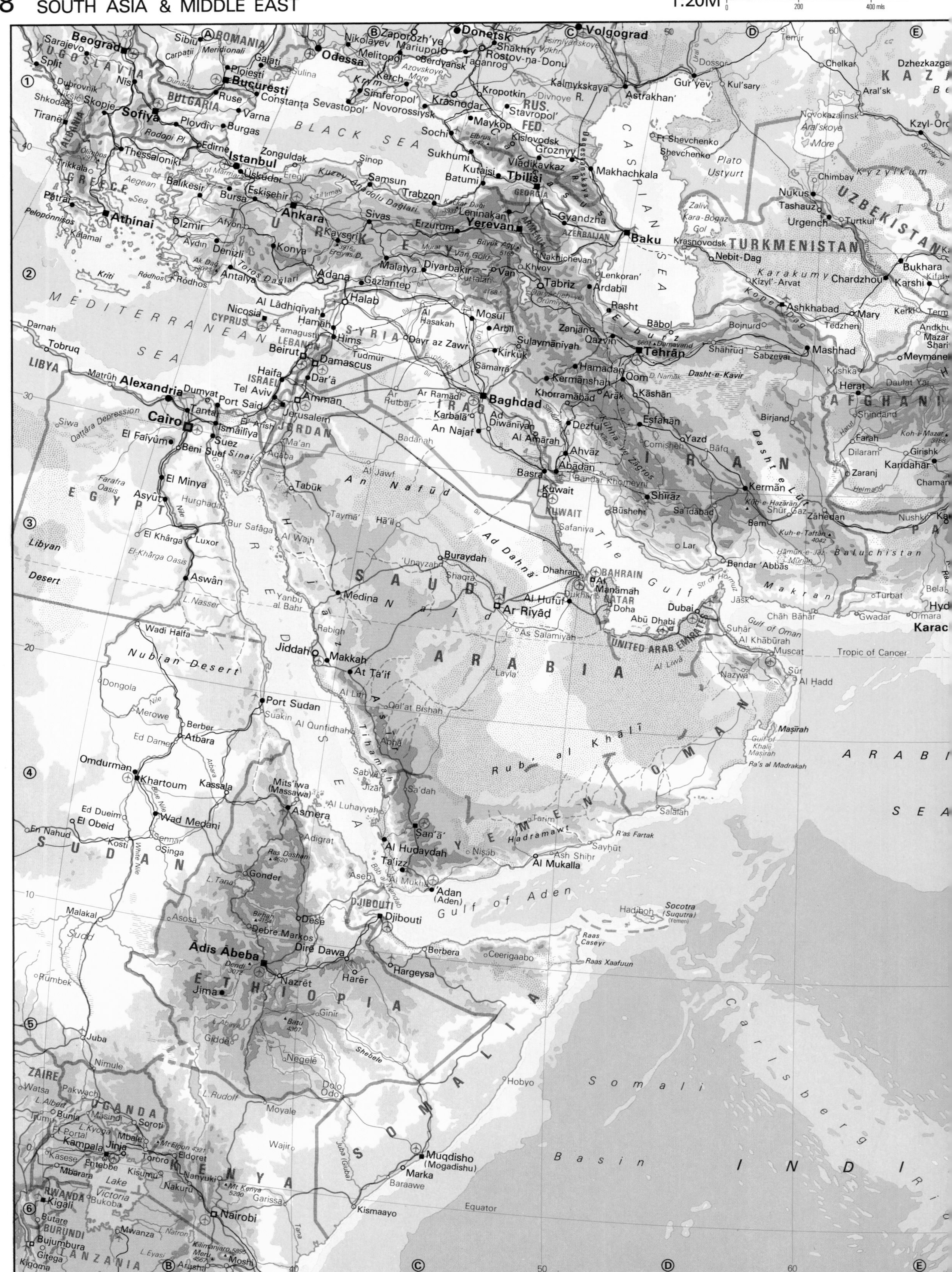

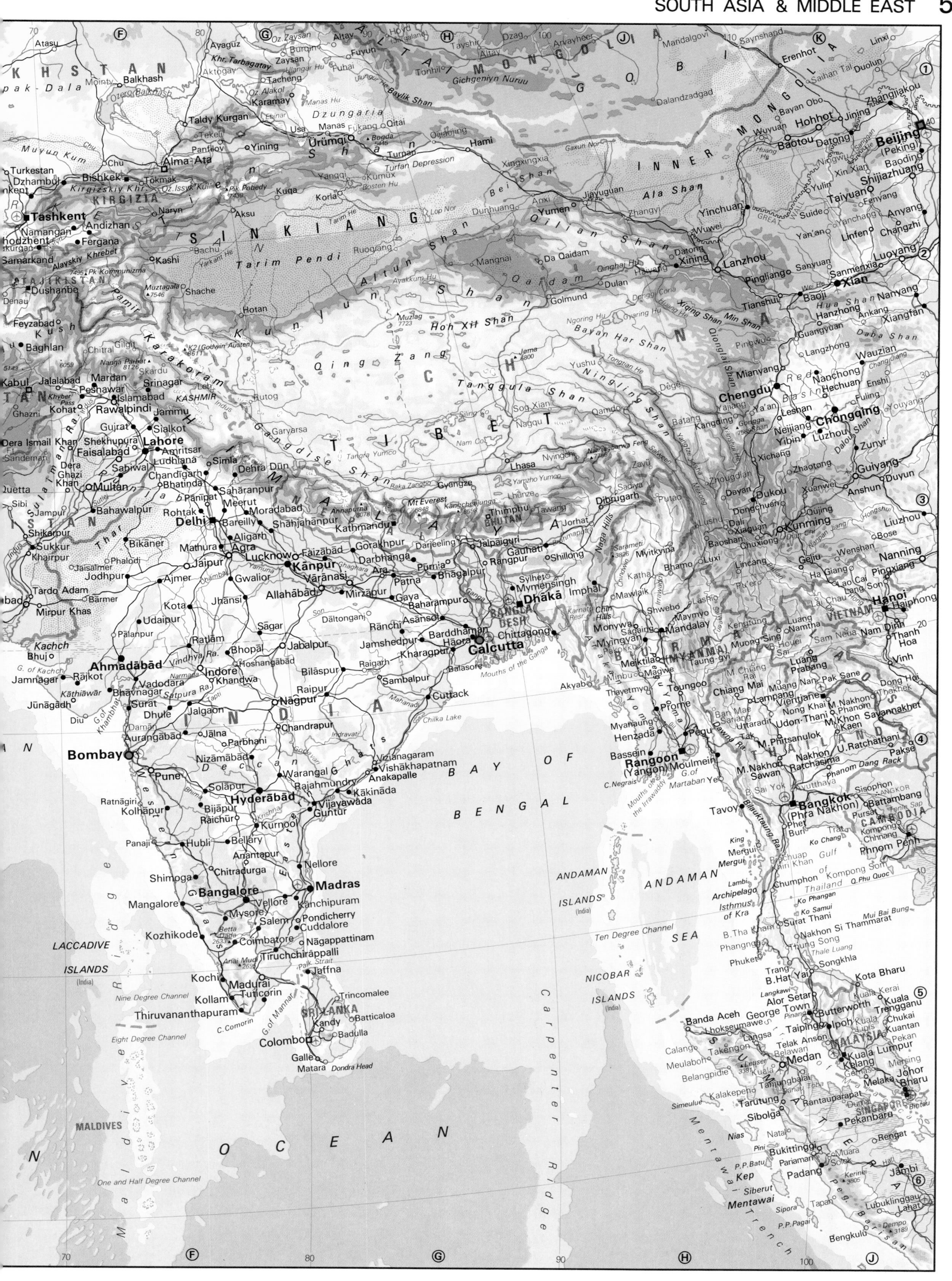

Atasu
Ayaguz
Oz. Zaysan
Zaysan
Burqin
Altay
Fuyun
Hoyd
Tayshir
Dzag
Arvayheer
Mandalgovi
Saynshand
Erenhot
Linxi
Duolun
Khr. Tarbagatay
Aktogay
Tacheng
Fuhai
Balkhash
Oz. Balkhash
Oz. Alakol
Karamay
Manas Hu
Baylik Shan
Gichgeniyn Nuruu
Dalandzadgad
Zhangjiakou
Bayan Obo
Hohhot
Jining
Beijing
(Peking)
Taldy Kurgan
Dzungaria
Usa
Manas
Fukang
Qitai
Bogda
Ürümqi
Turpan
Qijiaojing
Hami
Gaxun Nor
Wuyuan
Baotou
Datong
Baoding
Shijiazhuang
Tekeli
Panfilov
Yining
Alma-Ata
Muyun Kum
Chu
Turfan Depression
Xingxingxia
INNER MONGOLIA
Turkestan
Dzhambul
Bishkek
Tokmak
Oz. Issyk Kul
Pik Pobedy
7439
Kumux
Bosten Hu
Yanqqi
Kuqa
Korla
Bei Shan
Anxi
Jiayuguan
Ala Shan
Yulin
Xin Xian
Taiyuan
Fenyang
KIRGIZIA
Kirgizskiy Khr.
Naryn
Aksu
Lop Nor
Dunhuang
Yumen
Zhangye
Yinchuan
Suide
Yanchang
Anyang
Tashkent
Namangan
Andizhan
Fergana
Khodzhent
SINKIANG
Tarim He
Qilian Shan
Wuwei
Yan'an
Linfen
Changzhi
Samarkand
Alayskiy Khrebet
Kashi
Bachu
Yarkant He
Tarim Pendi
Ruoqiang
Mangnai
Da Qaidam
Qinghai Hu
Datong
Xining
Lanzhou
Luoyang
TAJIKISTAN
Pk Kommunizma
7495
Dushanbe
Muztagala
7546
Shache
Altun Shan
Ayakkum Hu
Qaidam
Dulan
Pingliang
Sanyuan
Sanmenxia
Xian
Wei He
Baoji
Tianshui
Hua Shan
Nanyang
Golmund
Denau
Pamir
Hotan
Kunlun Shan
Muzlag
7723
Hoh Xil Shan
Ngoring Hu
Gyaring Hu
Xiqing Shan
Min Shan
Hanzhong
Ankang
Xiangfan
Feyzabad
Hindu Kush
Baghlan
Chitral
Gilgit
Karakoram
K2 (Godwin Austen)
8611
Bayan Har Shan
Pingwu
Guangyuan
Daba Shan
Nanga Parbat
8126
Skardu
Qing Zang
Jama
6800
Yushu
Tongtian He
Langzhong
Wauzian
Kabul
Jalalabad
Mardan
Peshawar
Khyber Pass
Srinagar
Islamabad
KASHMIR
Rutog
Tanggula Shan
Ningjing Shan
Dêgê
Mianyang
Nanchong
Hechuan
Enshi
Ghazni
Kohat
Rawalpindi
Jammu
Indus
Sog Xian
Qamdo
Chengdu
Red Basin
Ya'an
Leshan
Chongqing
Fuling
Youyang
Gujrat
Sialkot
Garyarsa
Gangdise Shan
TIBET
Nagqu
Siling Co
Batang
Kangding
Gongga Shan
7556
Neijiang
Yibin
Luzhou
Dera Ismail Khan
Shekhupura
Lahore
Amritsar
Faisalabad
Ludhiana
Nam Co
Tangra Yumco
Namjagbarwa Feng
7756
Zayu
Salween
Yangtze
Xichang
Zunyi
Sandeman
Dera Ghazi Khan
Sahiwal
Chandigarh
Bhatinda
Simla
Dehra Dun
Lhasa
Nyingchi
Zhaotong
Guiyang
Duyun
Quetta
Multan
Sutlej
Panipat
Saharanpur
Raka Zangbo
Gyangze
Yamzho Yumco
Lhunze
Sadiya
Dibrugarh
Putao
Mekong
Zhougdian
Dayan
Dukou
Xuanwei
Anshun
Sibi
Jampur
Bahawalpur
Rohtak
Meerut
Moradabad
Annapurna
8078
Mt Everest
8848
Kanchenjunga
8598
Thimphu
Tawang
BHUTAN
Dongchuan
Qujing
Liuzhou
Shikarpur
Delhi
Bareilly
Shahjahanpur
Kathmandu
HIMALAYA
Jorhat
Naga Hills
Lushui
Dali
Xiaguan
Kunming
Sukkur
Khairpur
Thar
Bikaner
Aligarh
Mathura
Agra
Faizabad
Gorakhpur
Darjeeling
Jalpaiguri
Gauhati
Sarameti
3826
Myitkyina
Baoshan
Chuxiong
Wenshan
Bose
Nanning
Jaisalmer
Phalodi
Jodhpur
Jaipur
Lucknow
Kanpur
Darbhanga
Purnia
Rangpur
Shillong
Bhamo
Luxi
Lincang
Gejiu
Pingxiang
Ajmer
Gwalior
Yamuna
Chambal
Ghaghara
Ara
Patna
Bhagalpur
Sylhet
Mymensingh
Katha
Ha Giang
Lao Cai
Lang Son
Tardo Adam
Barmer
Mirpur Khas
Kota
Jhansi
Allahabad
Varanasi
Mirzapur
Gaya
Baharampur
Dhaka
Imphal
Mawlaik
Chindwin
Irrawaddy
Lashio
Pu'er
Lai Chau
Hanoi
Haiphong
Udaipur
Son
Daltonganj
Ranchi
Asansol
BANGLADESH
Karnafuli Resr.
Chin Hills
Shwebo
Maymyo
Kengtung
Luang Namtha
Palanpur
Sagar
Ratlam
Bhopal
Jabalpur
Jamshedpur
Barddhaman
Haora
Calcutta
Chittagong
Monywa
Sagaing
Mandalay
Muong Sing
Nam Dinh
Thanh Hoa
Kachch
Bhuj
G. of Kachch
Ahmadabad
Vindhya Ra.
Hoshangabad
Kharagpur
Raigarh
Myingyan
Pakokku
BURMA (MYANMAR)
Taunggyi
Sam Neua
Vinh
Jamnagar
Rajkot
Vadodara
Narmada
Indore
Khandwa
Bilaspur
Sambalpur
Balasore
Mouths of the Ganga
Meiktila
Minbu
Magwe
Luang Prabang
Kathiawar
Bhavnagar
Satpura Ra.
Tapti
Raipur
Cuttack
Akyab
Thayetmyo
Toungoo
Chiang Mai
Lampang
Muang Nan
Pak Sane
Vientiane
Dong Hoi
Junagadh
Surat
Dhule
Jalgaon
Nagpur
INDIA
Mahanadi
Chilka Lake
Prome
Nong Khai
M. Nakhon Phanom
Udon Thani
Savannakhet
Diu
G. of Khambhat
Daman
Aurangabad
Jalna
Chandrapur
Indravati
Myanaung
Henzada
Pegu
Uttaradit
M. Phitsanulok
M. Khon Kaen
THAILAND
Parbhani
Godavari
Bassein
Rangoon
(Yangon)
Moulmein
G. of Martaban
Ye
U. Ratchathani
Pakse
Bombay
Nizamabad
Deccan
Vizianagaram
Vishakhapatnam
Anakapalle
BAY OF BENGAL
Pune
Warangal
Rajahmundry
Kakinada
C. Negrais
Mouths of the Irrawaddy
M. Nakhon Sawan
Nakhon Ratchasima
Phanom Dang Rack
Ratnagiri
Kolhapur
Solapur
Hyderabad
Bijapur
Raichur
Krishna
Vijayawada
Guntur
Kurnool
Tavoy
Bangkok
(Phra Nakhon)
Sisophon
Battambang
Pursat
CAMBODIA
Kompong Chhnang
Phnom Penh
Panaji
Hubli
Bellary
Anantapur
Nellore
King
Mergui
Ko Chang
Gulf of Thailand
Shimoga
Chitradurga
Madras
ANDAMAN ISLANDS
(India)
ANDAMAN SEA
Chumphon
Kompong Som
Q. Phu Quoc
Mangalore
Bangalore
Vellore
Kanchipuram
Mysore
Pondicherry
Salem
Cuddalore
Lambi
Archipelago
Isthmus of Kra
Ko Phangan
Ko Samui
Surat Thani
Mui Bai Bung
LACCADIVE ISLANDS
(India)
Kozhikode
Coimbatore
Nagappattinam
Tiruchchirappalli
Ten Degree Channel
Nakhon Si Thammarat
Thung Song
Thale Luang
Songkhla
Phangnga
Phuket
Kochi
Madurai
Tuticorin
Palk Strait
Jaffna
NICOBAR ISLANDS
(India)
Trang
B. Hat Yai
Kota Bharu
Nine Degree Channel
Kollam
Trincomalee
Langkawi
Alor Setar
Kuala Kerai
Kuala Trengganu
Thiruvananthapuram
C. Comorin
G. of Mannar
SRI LANKA
Batticaloa
Kandy
Badulla
Banda Aceh
George Town
Butterworth
Chukai
Kuantan
Eight Degree Channel
Colombo
Galle
Matara
Dondra Head
Lhokseumawe
Taiping
Ipoh
MALAYSIA
Kuala Lumpur
Pekan
Calang
Meulaboh
Takengon
Leuser
3381
Medan
Kelang
Mersing
Belangpidie
Tanjungbalai
Melaka
Johor Bharu
Kalakepeng
Tarutung
Rantauparapat
SINGAPORE
Simeulue
Sibolga
Pekanbaru
MALDIVES
INDIAN OCEAN
Nias
Bukittinggi
Pariaman
Padang
Solok
Kerinci
3805
Rengat
Jambi
Maldive Ridge
Carpenter Ridge
One and Half Degree Channel
P.P. Batu
Kep
Siberut
Mentawai
Mentawai Trench
Sipora
P.P. Pagai
Tapan
Lubuklinggau
Lahat
Dempo
3189
Bengkulu
Barisan
70
80
90
100
110
40
30
20
10
F
G
H
J
K
1
2
3
4
5
6

1:7.5M 0 100 200 300 km 0 50 100 150 mls

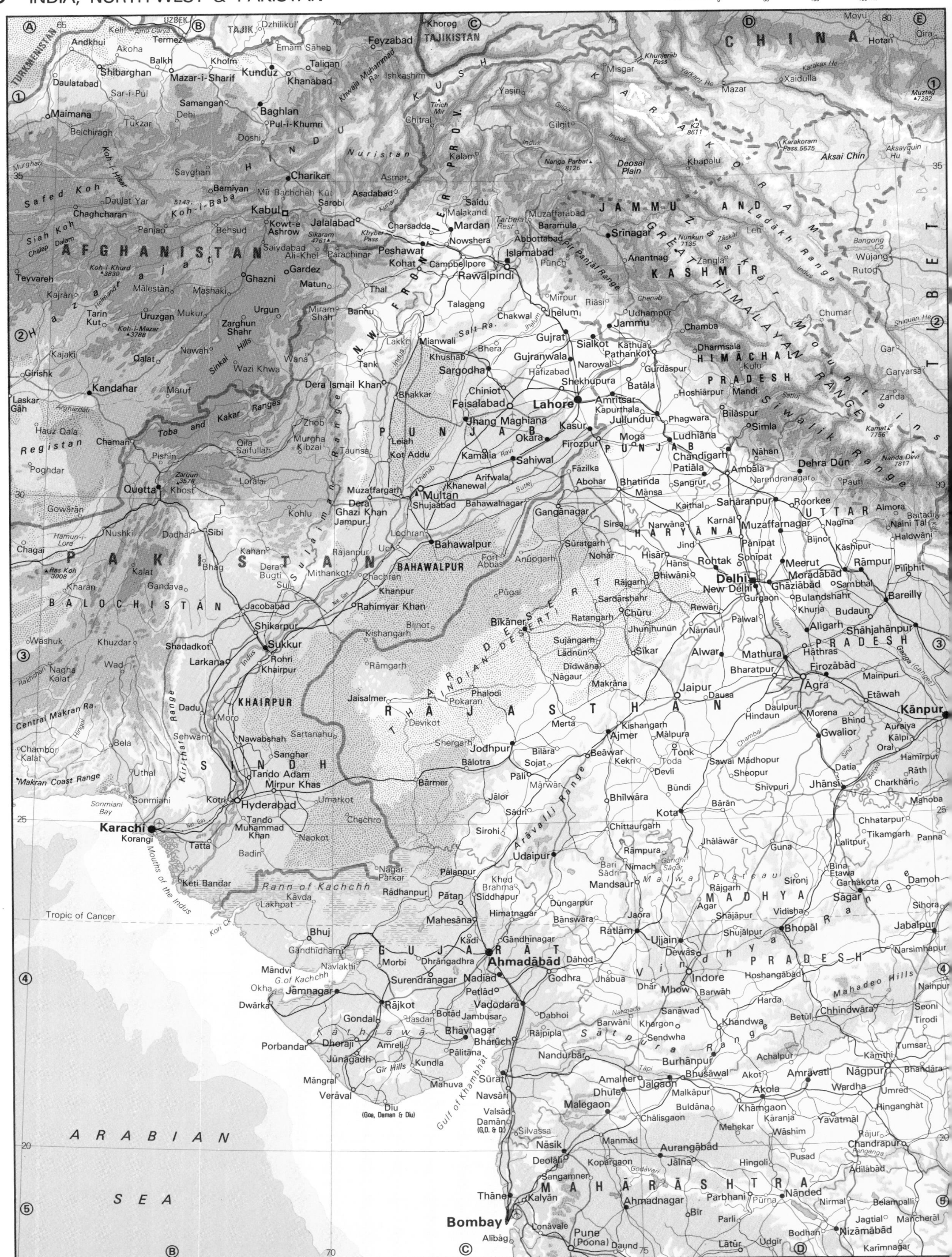

A
B
C
D
E
65
70
75
80
UZBEK
TAJIK
Dzhilikul'
Khorog
TAJIKISTAN
CHINA
Moyu
Hotan
Qira
TURKMENISTAN
Kelif
Amu Darya
Termez
Andkhui
Akoha
Balkh
Kholm
Emam Saheb
Taliqan
Feyzabad
Shibarghan
Mazar-i-Sharif
Kunduz
Khanabad
Ishkashim
Khwaja Muhammad Ra.
Daulatabad
Sar-i-Pul
Samangan
Baghlan
Pul-i-Khumri
Maimana
Tukzar
Dehi
Belchiragh
Doshi
Tirich Mir
Chitral
Yasin
Gilgit
Misgar
Khunjerab Pass
Yarkant He
Mazar
Karakax He
Xaidulla
Muztag 7282
K2 8611
Karakoram Pass 5575
Aksai Chin
Aksayqin Hu
HINDU KUSH
Nuristan
Kalam
Indus
Nanga Parbat 8126
Deosai Plain
Khapalu
KARAKORAM
Murghab
35
Koh-i-Hisar
Safed Koh
Sayghan
Charikar
Asmar
Bamiyan
Mir Bachcheh Kut
Asadabad
Daulat Yar
5143
Koh-i-Baba
Kabul
Sarobi
Saidu
Malakand
Chaghcharan
Kowt-e Ashrow
Jalalabad
Charsadda
Mardan
Tarbela Resr
Muzaffarabad
Baramula
JAMMU AND KASHMIR
Siah Koh
Chalap Dalam
Panjao
Behsud
Sikaram 4761
Khyber Pass
Nowshera
Abbottabad
Srinagar
Nunkun 7135
Leh
Ladakh Range
Bangong Co
AFGHANISTAN
Saiydabad
Ali-Khel
Parachinar
Peshawar
Kohat
Campbellpore
Islamabad
Rawalpindi
Punch
Pir Panjal Range
Anantnag
Zaskar
Zangla
Wujang
Rutog
Hazarajat
Koh-i-Khurd 3830
Gardez
KASHMIR
Teyvareh
Kajran
Helmand
Malestan
Mashaki
Ghazni
Matun
Thal
Mirpur
Riasi
Chenab
Udhampur
GREAT HIMALAYAN RANGE
Tarin Kut
Uruzgan
Mukur
Urgun
Miram Shah
Bannu
Talagang
Chakwal
Jhelum
Jammu
Chumar
Shiquan He
Koh-i-Mazar 3788
Zarghun Shahr
Salt Ra.
Gujrat
Sialkot
Kathua
Chamba
NORTH-WEST FRONTIER PROV.
Kajaki
Nawah
Sinkai Hills
Wana
Lakki
Mianwali
Khushab
Bhera
Gujranwala
Pathankot
Dharmsala
HIMACHAL PRADESH
Gar
Girishk
Qalat
Wazi Khwa
Tank
Sargodha
Hafizabad
Narowal
Gurdaspur
Kulu
Garyarsa
Kandahar
Maruf
Dera Ismail Khan
Bhakkar
Chiniot
Shekhupura
Batala
Hoshiarpur
Mandi
Laskar Gah
Arghandab
Faisalabad
Lahore
Amritsar
Kapurthala
Zanda
Toba and Kakar Ranges
Jhang Maghiana
Jullundur
Phagwara
Bilaspur
Hauz Qala
Chaman
Zhob
PUNJAB
Kasur
Moga
Ludhiana
Simla
Kamat 7756
Registan
Qila Saifullah
Murgha Kibzai
Leiah
Okara
Firozpur
Pishin
Taunsa
Kot Addu
Kamalia
Ravi
Sahiwal
Chandigarh
Nahan
Nanda Devi 7817
Poghdar
Patiala
Ambala
Dehra Dun
Zarghun 3578
Khost
Loralai
Chenab
Arifwala
Fazilka
Bhatinda
Sangrur
Narendranagar
Pauri
Quetta
Muzaffargarh
Khanewal
Multan
Abohar
Mansa
30
Dera Ghazi Khan
Shujaabad
Bahawalnagar
Sutlej
Kaithal
Saharanpur
Roorkee
Almora
Gowaran
Kohlu
Jampur
Ganganagar
Sirsa
Narwana
Karnal
Muzaffarnagar
Nagina
UTTAR PRADESH
Baitadi
Naini Tal
Haldwani
Hamun-i-Lora
Nushki
Dadhar
Sibi
Lodhran
Bahawalpur
Suratgarh
HARYANA
Panipat
Bijnor
Chagai
Kahan
Rajanpur
Uch
Fort Abbas
Nohar
Hisar
Jind
Rohtak
Sonipat
Kashipur
Meerut
Rampur
Pilibhit
Ras Koh 3008
PAKISTAN
Bhag
Dera Bugti
Sulaiman Range
Mithankot
Chachran
BAHAWALPUR
Anupgarh
Hansi
Bhiwani
Delhi
New Delhi
Ghaziabad
Moradabad
Sambhal
Kalat
Gandava
Sui
Khanpur
Pugal
Rajgarh
Gurgaon
Bulandshahr
Bareilly
Kharan
BALOCHISTAN
Jacobabad
Rahimyar Khan
Sardarshahr
Rewari
Khurja
Budaun
Shikarpur
Bijnot
Bikaner
Churu
Ratangarh
Palwal
Aligarh
Shahjahanpur
Washuk
Khuzdar
Shadadkot
Sukkur
Kishangarh
Rohri
Khairpur
Sujangarh
Jhunjhunun
Narnaul
Ladnun
Sikar
Alwar
Mathura
Hathras
Yamuna
Ganga (Ganges)
Larkana
Ramgarh
THAR
INDIAN DESERT
Didwana
Nagaur
Bharatpur
Firozabad
Mainpuri
Nagha Kalat
Wad
Rakhshan
Central Makran Ra.
KHAIRPUR
Jaisalmer
Phalodi
Pokaran
Makrana
Jaipur
Dausa
Agra
Etawah
Dadu
Moro
RAJASTHAN
Hindaun
Daulpur
Morena
Bhind
Kanpur
Hingol
Kirthar Range
Sehwan
Nawabshah
Sartanahu
Devikot
Merta
Kishangarh
Ajmer
Malpura
Chambal
Gwalior
Auraiya
Kalpi
Orai
Bela
Chambor Kalat
Sanghar
Shergarh
Jodhpur
Bilara
Beawar
Tonk
Toda
Sawai Madhopur
Hamirpur
Uthal
SINDH
Tando Adam
Mirpur Khas
Balotra
Sojat
Kekri
Devli
Sheopur
Sind
Datia
Rath
Makran Coast Range
Barmer
Pali
Marwar
Bundi
Shivpuri
Jhansi
Charkhari
Sonmiani Bay
Sonmiani
Kotri
Hyderabad
Umarkot
Jalor
Aravalli Range
Bhilwara
Kota
Baran
Betwa
Mahoba
25
Karachi
Korangi
Nat. Gas
Tando Muhammad Khan
Chachro
Naokot
Sirohi
Sadri
Chittaurgarh
Jhalawar
Chhatarpur
Tikamgarh
Panna
Tatta
Mouths of the Indus
Badin
Udaipur
Rampura
Gandhi Sagar
Lalitpur
Guna
Nagar Parkar
Palanpur
Bari Sadri
Nimach
Malwa Plateau
Sironj
Bina-Etawa
Keti Bandar
Rann of Kachchh
Radhanpur
Patan
Khed Brahma
Siddhapur
Mandsaur
Rajgarh
Garhakota
Damoh
Kavda
Lakhpat
Dungarpur
Agar
MADHYA PRADESH
Sagar
Tropic of Cancer
Kori Cr.
Mahesana
Himatnagar
Banswara
Jaora
Shajapur
Vidisha
Sihora
Bhuj
Kadi
Gandhinagar
Ratlam
Ujjain
Shujalpur
Bhopal
Jabalpur
Gandhidham
GUJARAT
Ahmadabad
Dahod
Dewas
Narsimhapur
Mandvi
Navlakhi
Morbi
Dhrangadhra
Vindhya Range
Indore
Hoshangabad
Mahadeo Hills
G. of Kachchh
Surendranagar
Nadiad
Godhra
Jhabua
Dhar
Mhow
Barwah
Nainpur
Okha
Jamnagar
Petlad
Dwarka
Rajkot
Vadodara
Narmada
Harda
Seoni
Botad
Jambusar
Dabhoi
Barwani
Khargon
Sanawad
Khandwa
Betul
Chhindwara
Gondal
Jasdan
Bhavnagar
Kathiawar
Rajpipla
Satpura Range
Sendhwa
Tirodi
Porbandar
Dhoraji
Amreli
Bharuch
Palitana
Nandurbar
Burhanpur
Achalpur
Tumsar
Junagadh
Gir Hills
Kundla
Surat
Tapi
Bhusawal
Amravati
Kamthi
Nagpur
Bhandara
Mangrol
Mahuva
Amalner
Jalgaon
Akot
Akola
Wardha
Umred
Veraval
Diu
(Goa, Daman & Diu)
Gulf of Khambhat
Navsari
Dhule
Malkapur
Valsad
Malegaon
Buldana
Khamgaon
Hinganghat
Daman (G.D. & D.)
Chalisgaon
Karanja
Yavatmal
ARABIAN SEA
Silvassa
Mehekar
Washim
Rajura
20
Nasik
Manmad
Aurangabad
Pusad
Chandrapur
Penganga
Deolali
Kopargaon
Jalna
Hingoli
Adilabad
Godavari
Sangamner
MAHARASHTRA
Thane
Kalyan
Ahmadnagar
Parbhani
Purna
Nanded
Nirmal
Belampalli
Bombay
Bir
Parli
Jagtial
Mancheral
Alibag
Conavale
Pune (Poona)
Daund
Latur
Udgir
Bodhan
Nizamabad
Karimnagar
TIBET
Siwalik Range
1
2
3
4
5

1:7.5M

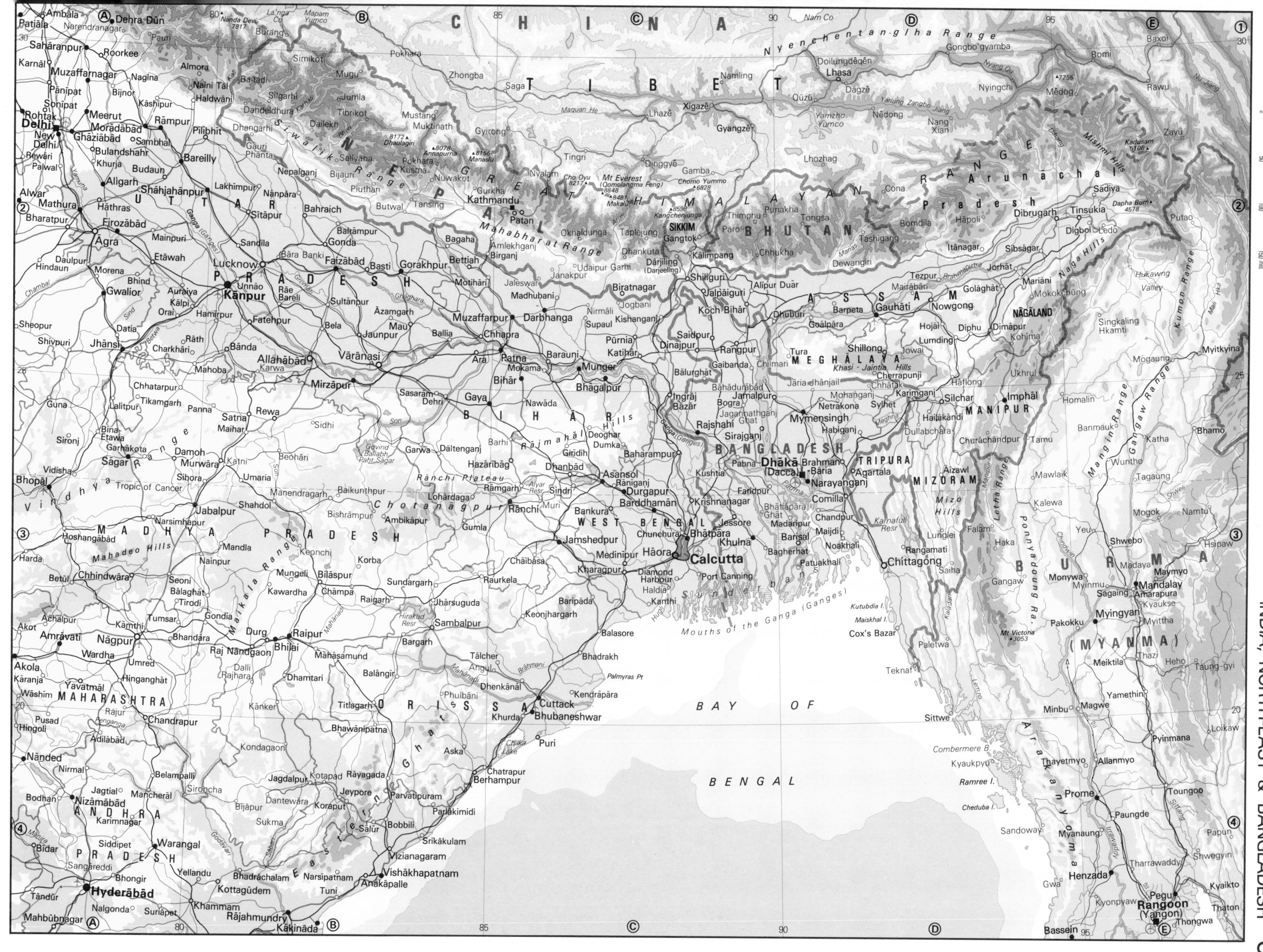

1:7.5M

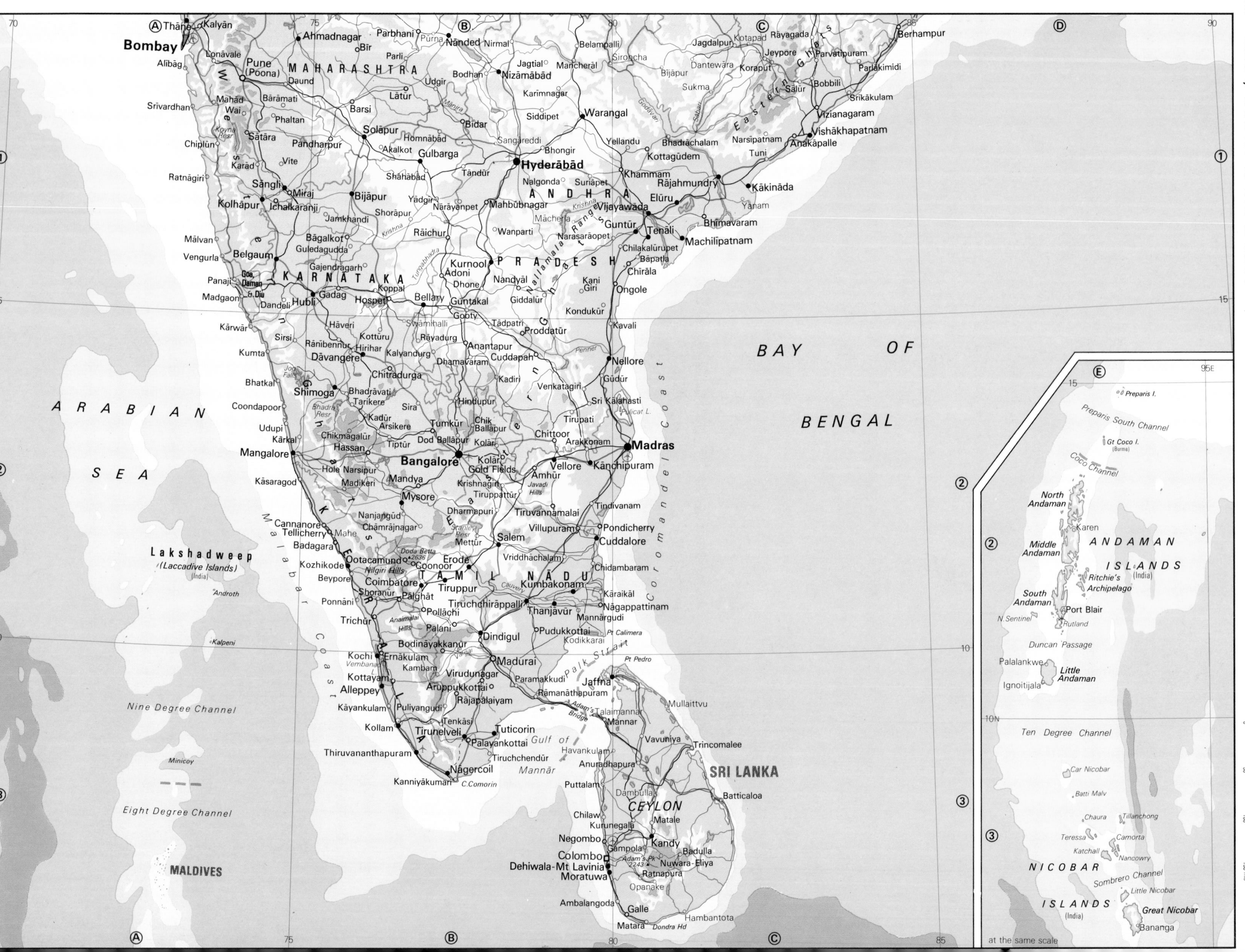

BAY OF BENGAL
ARABIAN SEA
SRI LANKA
CEYLON
MALDIVES
Lakshadweep
(Laccadive Islands)
(India)
MAHARASHTRA
KARNATAKA
ANDHRA PRADESH
TAMIL NADU
KERALA
Bombay
Pune (Poona)
Hyderābād
Bangalore
Madras
Mysore
Mangalore
Madurai
Colombo
Kandy
Jaffna
Trincomalee
Batticaloa
Galle
Coromandel Coast
Malabar Coast
Palk Strait
Gulf of Mannār
Adam's Bridge
C.Comorin
Nine Degree Channel
Eight Degree Channel
ANDAMAN ISLANDS (India)
North Andaman
Middle Andaman
South Andaman
Port Blair
Little Andaman
Duncan Passage
Ten Degree Channel
NICOBAR ISLANDS (India)
Car Nicobar
Great Nicobar
at the same scale

Scale bar: 100 200 300 km / 50 100 150 mls

TURKMENISTAN

AFGHANISTAN

PAKISTAN

IRAN

IRAQ

KUWAIT

SAUDI ARABIA

QATAR

BAHRAIN

Caspian Sea

The Gulf

Selected place names and features:

Gvan, Gurdak, Akcha, Shibarghan, Sar-i-Pul, Tukzar, Andkhui, Kelif, Kerki, Repetek, Burdalyk, Karakumskiy Kanal, Zakhmet, Bayram-Ali, Mary, Iolotan, Tedzhen, Dushak, Kaakhka, Ashkhabad, Bezmein, Bakharden, Kizyl Arvat, Kara Kum, Maimana, Qaisar, Bala Murghab, Qala Nau, Obeh, Herat, Shindand, Farah, Dilaram, Girishk, Lashkar Gah, Kandahar, Tarin Kut, Chaghcharan, Daulatabad

Mashhad, Neyshabur, Sabzevar, Quchan, Bojnurd, Shirvan, Gonbad-e Kavus, Gorgan, Sari, Babol, Amol, Tehran, Karaj, Qazvin, Rasht, Bandar Anzali, Ardabil, Tabriz, Urumiyeh, Zanjan, Hamadan, Arak, Malayer, Borujerd, Khorramabad, Dezful, Ahvaz, Abadan, Khorramshahr

Qom, Kashan, Esfahan, Najafabad, Shahr Kord, Yazd, Kerman, Bam, Zahedan, Shiraz, Fasa, Darab, Bandar Abbas, Qeshm, Strait of Hormuz, Jask, Chah Bahar, Iranshahr

Baghdad, Karbala, An Najaf, Al Hillah, Ad Diwaniyah, An Nasiriyah, Al Amarah, Al Basrah (Basra), Az Zubayr

Kuwait, Al Ahmadi, Ad Dammam, Al Hufuf, Al Manamah, Doha, Dubai, Sharjah, Abu Dhabi

Dasht-e Lut

Dasht-e Kavir

Kevir-i-Namak

Dasht-e Naomid

Dasht-i-Margo

Reg-i-Stan

Zagros Mountains

Elburz (Reshteh-ye Alborz Mts)

Paropamisus

Band-i-Turkestan

Makran Coast Range

Central Makran Range

Chagai Hills

Khrebet Kopet Dag

Kuh-e Hazar Masjed

Kuh-e Damavand 5604

100 200 300 km
50 100 150 mls

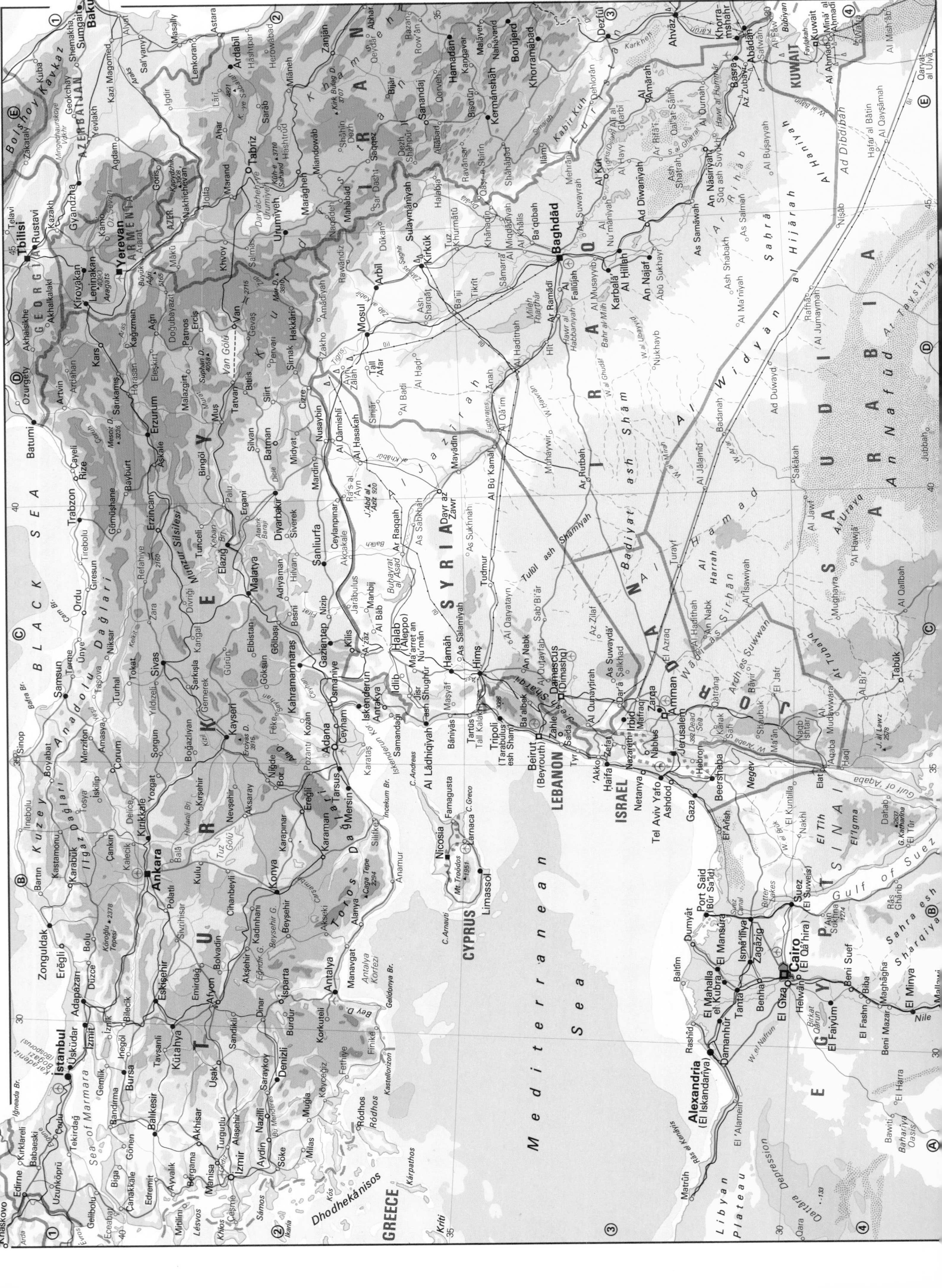

BLACK SEA

GEORGIA
Tbilisi
Batumi

AZERBATJAN
Baku
Sumqaiyt

ARMENIA
Yerevan

IRAN
Tabriz
Urumiyeh
Hamadān
Kermānshāh
Khorramābād
Borūjerd
Ahvāz
Khorramshahr
Abādān

T U R K E Y
Istanbul
Ankara
Izmir
Bursa
Konya
Kayseri
Sivas
Erzurum
Trabzon
Samsun
Zonguldak
Eskişehir
Antalya
Adana
Mersin
Gaziantep
Şanlıurfa
Diyarbakir
Malatya
Van
Kars

I R A Q
Baghdād
Mosul
Kirkūk
Arbil
Sulaymānīyah
Al Hillah
Karbalā
An Najaf
Ad Dīwānīyah
As Samāwah
An Nāsirīyah
Al 'Amārah
Al Kūt
Al Başrah (Basra)

KUWAIT
Kuwait

S Y R I A
Halab (Aleppo)
Hamāh
Hims
Dimashq (Damascus)
Ar Raqqah
Dayr az Zawr
Tudmur

LEBANON
Beirut (Beyrouth)
Tripoli (Tarabulus esh Sham)

ISRAEL
Tel Aviv Yafo
Jerusalem
Haïfa ('Hefa)
Gaza
Beersheba

JORDAN
Amman
Zarqa
Irbid

SAUDI ARABIA
Tabūk
Sakākah

C Y P R U S
Nicosia
Limassol
Famagusta

E G Y P T
Cairo (El Qâ'hira)
Alexandria (El Iskandarîya)
Suez
Port Said (Bûr Sa'îd)
El Mansûra
Tanta

S I N A I

Mediterranean Sea

GREECE
Kríti

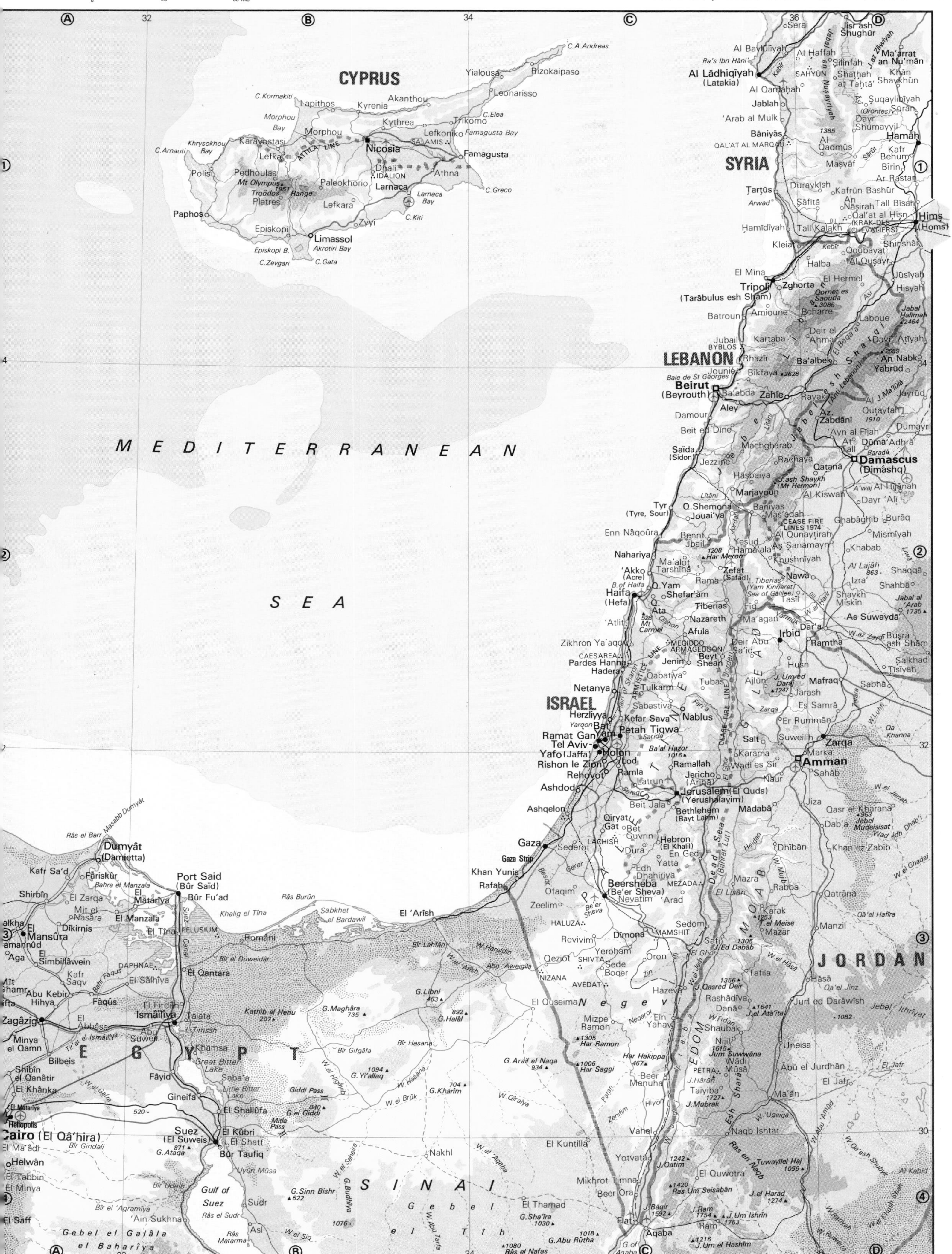

1:2.5M

25   50   75   100 km
25   50 mls

CYPRUS

C.A.Andreas

Yialousa
Rizokaipaso
C. Kormakiti
Lapithos   Kyrenia
Morphou   Akanthou
Bay   Leonarisso
C. Elea
Morphou   Kythrea   Trikomo   Lefkoniko   Famagusta Bay
Khrysokhou   ATTILA LINE   Nicosia   SALAMIS
Bay   Karavostasi   Lefka   Dhali   Famagusta
C. Arnauti   Pedhoulas   IDALION   Athna
Polis   Mt Olympus 1951   Paleokhorio   C. Greco
Paphos   Troödos Range   Larnaca
Platres   Lefkara   Larnaca Bay
Episkopi   Zyyi   C. Kiti
Limassol
Episkopi B.   Akrotiri Bay
C. Zevgari   C. Gata

MEDITERRANEAN

SEA

SYRIA

Al Bayluliyah   Jisr ash
Serai   Shughur
Ra's Ibn Hani   Al Haffah   Ma'arrat
Silinfah   an Nu'man
Al Lādhiqīyah   SAHYŪN   Shathah   Khan
(Latakia)   Al Qardâhā   at Tahtā   Shaykhūn
Jablah   'Arab al Mulk   Şuqaylibīyah   Qūrān
Bāniyās   (Orontes) `Asi   1385   Dayr Shumayyil
QAL'AT AL MARQAB   Al   **Hamâh**
Qadmûs   Maşyāf   Birin
Ţarţûs   Duraykīsh   Kafrūn Bashūr
Arwad   An   Ar Rastan
Şāfītā   Nasīrah   Tall Bīsah
Hamīdīyah   Qal'at al Hisn   **Hims**
Tall Kalakh   (KRAK-DES   (Homs)
CHEVALIERS)
Kleiat   Kebīr   Qoubayât   Shinshār
El Mîna   Halba   El Hermel   Jūsīyah
Tripoli   Zghorta   Ôornet es   Hisyah
(Tarâbulus esh Shām)   Saouda 3086   Jabal
Batroun   Amioune   Laboue   Halimah 2464
Jubail   Kartaba   Deir el   Dayr 'Aţīyah
BYBLOS   Rhazîr   Ba'albek   2659   An Nabk
LEBANON   Ba'abda   Jounié   2628   Yabrūd
Beirut   Bikfaya   Al Ma'lūla
(Beyrouth)   Ba'abda   Zahle   Rayak   Jayrūd
Baie de St Georges   Aley   'Ayn al Fijah   Dūmā 'Adhrā
Damour   Az   Qutayfah   Dumayr
Beit ed Dine   Zabdānī 1910
Saïda   Mâchgharab   **Damascus**
(Sidon)   Rachaya   (Dimâshq)
Jezzine   Qatana
Tyr   Q. Shemona   J. ash Shaykh   A'waj Al Hijānah
(Tyre, Sour)   Jouai'ya   (Mt Hermon)   Dayr 'Alī
Hāşbaiya   Mas'adah   Al Kiswan
Enn Nâqoûra   Marjayoun   Baniyâs   Ghabâghib   Burâq
Bennt   1208   CEASE FIRE   Mismīyah
Nahariya   Jbail   Hama'ala   LINES 1974   Khabab
Ma'alot   Yesud   As Sanamayn
'Akko   Tarshīhā   Har Meron   Al Qunayţirah   Al Lajāh
(Acre)   Zefat   Nawā   Izra'   Shaqqā
B. of Haifa   Rama   (Safad)   Tiberias   Shahbā
Haifa   Q. Yam   (Yam Kinneret)   Tasil   Jabal al
(Hefa)   Q.   Shefar'am   (Sea of Galilee)   Shaykh Miskīn   'Arab 1735
'Atlit   Ata   528   Fiq   As Suwaydā
Mt Carmel   Dishon   Nazareth   Ma'agan   Dar'a
Zikhron Ya'aqov   Afula   Deir Abu   Irbid   Ramtha
CAESAREA   MEGIDDO   Sa'id   W. az Zaydī   Buşrā   Şalkhad
Pardes Hanna   ARMAGEDDON   Jenin   Beyt   ash Shām   Tīsīyah
Hadera   Qabatiya   Shean   Husn
Netanya   Tulkarm   Tubas   Ajlun   Jarash   Mafraq
ISRAEL   Sabastiya   Fari'a   1247   Er Rummān   Qa' el
Herzliyya   Nablus   Zarqa   Es Samrā   Khanna
Kefar Sava   Sabhā
Ramat Gan   Petah Tiqwa   Salt   Suweilih   **Zarqa**
Tel Aviv-   Sarida   Karama   Marka
Yafo (Jaffa)   Ramallah   Wadi es Sir   **Amman**
Holon   Lod   Ba'al Hazor 1016   Jericho   Sahâb
Rishon le Zion   Ramla   (Arīhā)   Naur
Rehovot   Latrun   Jerusalem (El Quds)   Mādabā   Jiza   Qasr el Kharana
Ashdod   Beit Jala   (Yerushalayim)   Dab'a   Qasr Mudeisisat
Bethlehem   Dhab'i   Wad adh   Khan ez Zabīb
Ashqelon   Qiryat   (Bayt Lahm)
Bet   Hebron   En Gedi
Gat   Guvrin   (El Khalil)
Gaza   Sederot   LACHISH   Dura   Edh   Mazra
Gaza Strip   Yatta   Dhahiriya   MEZADA   Safi   Qatrāna
Khan Yunis   Ofaqim   Be'er   El Lisân   Karak   J. el Meise
Rafah   Sheva   **Beersheba**   Mazâr   Manzil
Zeelim   (Be'er Sheva)   Sedom   T. el Meise
Ofaqim   Nevatim   Arad   Qā'el Hafira
HALUZA   Dhîbân   Khan ez Zabīb
El 'Arîsh   Revivim   Dimona   MAMSHIT   Rabba

EGYPT

Dumyât   Ras el Barr   Masabb Dumyât
(Damietta)
Kafr Sa'd   Faraskûr   Bahra el Manzala   El
Shirbîn   Matariya   El   **Port Said**
El Zarqa   El Manzala   El   (Bûr Said)
alkha   Mit el   Tîna   Bûr Fu'ad
El Mansûra   Nasara   PELUSIUM   Ras Burûn
amannûd   El Simbillâwein   DAPHNAE   Sabkhet   El 'Arîsh
Aga   Kafr   El Firdân   el Bardawîl
Minya   Saqv   El Qantara   Bîr Lahfân   W. Hareidin
el Qamn   Fâqûs   Talata   Abu 'Aweigila
Zagâzig   El 'Abbâsa   Ismaïliya   Români   W. Arîsh
Bilbeis   Khamsa   Timsah   Bîr Hasana   Qeziot   SHIVTA
Shîbîn   Great Bitter   Kathîb el Henu   G. Libni   El Quseima   SEDE   AVEDAT
el Qanâtir   Lake   207   463   Mizpe   Boqer   Negev
El Khânka   Fâyid   Saba'a   G. Maghâra   892   Ramon
Minya   Gineifa   Little Bitter   735   G. Halâl   1305   Neqarot   Oron
el Qamn   Lake   Giddi Pass   Har Ramon   En Yahav
Heliopolis   Suez   El Shallûfa   Bîr Gifgâfa   1615
Cairo (El Qâ'hira)   (El Suweis)   G. el Giddi   G. Yi'allaq   1094   G. Kharîm   Har Hakippa   467
Ma'âdi   El Kûbri   840   G. Arâif el Naqa   1006   Beer
Helwân   Bîr Gindali   El Shatt   Midle Pass   W. el Brûk   934   Har Saggi   Menuha
El Tabbîn   Bûr Taufiq   Pass   J. Hârûn   PETRA
El Minya   Gulf of   Uyûn Mûsa   520   Zenifim   Vahel   Jum Suwwâna   Shaubak
El Saff   Suez   Nakhl   1242   J. el Atâ'ita
Bîr el   G. Sinn Bishr   J. Qatim   Elat   1082
'Agramîya   622   W. Sadr   1076   Beer Ora   1420   Tuwaiyilel Hâj 1095
Râs Matarma   Ras el Sudr   El Kuntilla   Mikhrot Timna   Ras en Naqb
Gebel el Galâla   Asl   G. Sha'îra   El Thamad   Yotvata   1274
el Baharîya   1030   1018   1216   Naqb Ishtar
Ain Sukhna   G. Abu Rûtha   Râs en Nafas   Aqaba   J. Um Ishrin

SINAI

Gebel   el Tîh

Gulf of   Aqaba

JORDAN

Dead Sea   (Bahret Lut)

EDOM   Esh Sharah

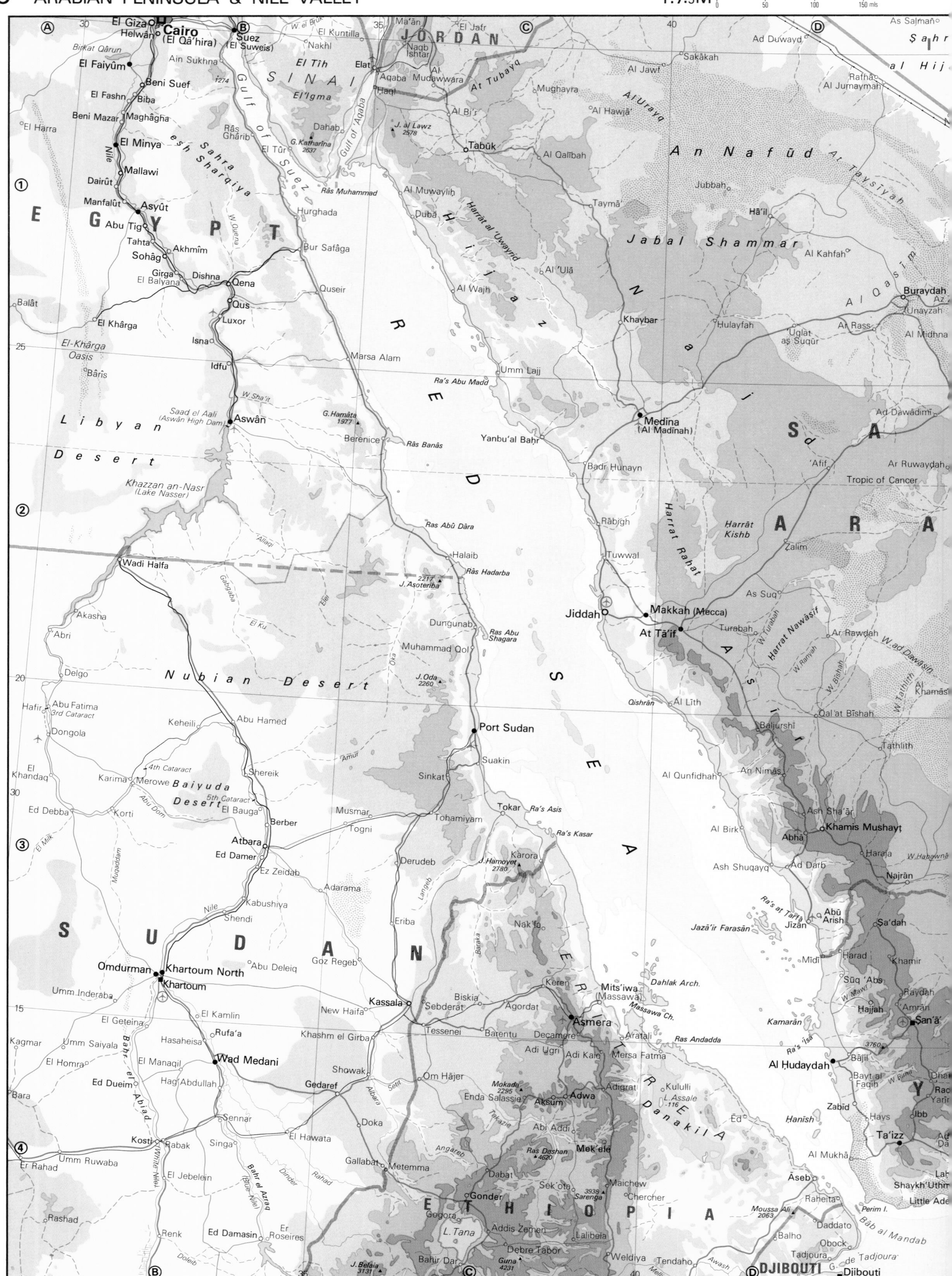
0 100 200 300 km
0 50 100 150 mls
EGYPT
Cairo (El Qâ'hira)
El Giza
Helwân
Suez (El Suweis)
Birkat Qârun
El Faiyûm
Ain Sukhna
Beni Suef
El Fashn
Biba
Beni Mazar
Maghâgha
El Harra
El Minya
Nile
Mallawi
Dairût
Manfalût
Asyût
Abu Tig
Tahta
Akhmîm
Sohâg
Girga
El Balyana
Dishna
Qena
Qus
Luxor
Isna
Idfu
Aswân
Saad el Aali (Aswân High Dam)
Balât
El Khârga
El-Khârga Oasis
Bâris
Libyan Desert
Khazzan an-Nasr (Lake Nasser)
esh Sahra esh Sharqiya
W. Quena
Râs Ghârib
Gulf of Suez
Râs Muhammad
Hurghada
Bur Safâga
Quseir
Marsa Alam
W. Sha'it
G. Hamâta 1977
Berenice
Râs Banâs
SINAI
El Tîh
El 'Igma
Nakhl
El Kuntilla
W. el Brûk
Dahab
G. Katharîna 2637
El Tûr
Gulf of Aqaba
Elat
Aqaba
Haql
JORDAN
Ma'ān
El Jafr
Naqb Ishtar
Mudawwara
J. al Lawz 2578
At Tubayq
Al Bi'r
Tabūk
Mughayra
Al Jawf
Sakākah
Ad Duwayd
As Salmān
Şahr al Hijārah
Rafhā
Al Jumaymah
Al 'Urayq
Al Hawjā'
An Nafūd
At Taysiyah
Al Qalībah
Jubbah
Taymā'
Hā'il
Jabal Shammar
Al Kahfah
Al Muwaylih
Dubā
Harrat al 'Uwayrid
Hijjaz
Al 'Ulā
Al Wajh
Khaybar
Ḥulayfah
Al Qasim
Buraydah
'Unayzah
Ar Rass
'Uglat aş Şuqūr
Al Midhnab
Umm Lajj
Ra's Abu Madd
Medina (Al Madīnah)
Yanbu'al Baḥr
Badr Ḥunayn
Ad Dawādimī
SAUDI ARABIA
Najd
'Afif
Ar Ruwaydah
Tropic of Cancer
Rābigh
Harrat Rahat
Ḥarrât Kishb
Zalim
Tuwwal
Jiddah
Makkah (Mecca)
At Ta'if
As Suq
Turabah
Harrat Nawāṣif
Ar Rawdah
W. ad Dawāsir
W. Turabah
W. Ranyah
W. Bishah
W. Tathlith
Al Khamāsīn
Qishrān
Al Līth
Qal'at Bīshah
Baljurshī
Asir
Tathlith
Al Qunfidhah
An Nimās
Ash Sha'ār
Al Birk
Abha
Khamis Mushayt
Haraja
W. Habawnā
Ash Shuqayq
Ad Darb
Najrān
Ra's at Tarfā
Abū Arīsh
Jizān
Jazā'ir Farasān
Sa'dah
Midi
Harad
Khamir
Sūq 'Abs
Raydah
Hajjah
Amrān
San'ā'
Kamarān
Ra's 'Īsā
3760
Al Ḥudaydah
Bājil
Bayt al Faqih
Zabīd
Hays
Ibb
Ḥanish
Ta'izz
Al Mukhā
Perim I.
Bāb al Mandab
Shaykh 'Uthmān
RED SEA
Wadi Halfa
Gabgaba
Allaqi
Halaib
Râs Hadarba
2217 J. Asoteriba
Elei
El Ku
Akasha
Abri
Delgo
Nubian Desert
Dungunab
Ras Abu Shagara
Muhammad Qol
Oka
J. Oda 2260
Port Sudan
Suakin
Hafir
Abu Fatima 3rd Cataract
Dongola
Keheili
Abu Hamed
Amur
El Khandaq
Karima
Merowe
4th Cataract
Shereik
Baiyuda Desert
5th Cataract
El Bauga
Sinkat
Ed Debba
Korti
Abu Dom
Berber
Musmar
Tohamiyam
Togni
Tokar
Ra's Asis
Ra's Kasar
W. El Milk
Muqaddam
Atbara
Ed Damer
Ez Zeidab
Derudeb
J. Hamoyet 2780
Karora
Adarama
Langeb
Kabushiya
Nile
Shendi
Eriba
Nak'fa
Baraka
SUDAN
Omdurman
Khartoum North
Khartoum
Abu Deleiq
Goz Regeb
Umm Inderaba
El Kamlin
Kassala
Sebderat
Biskia
Agordat
Keren
Mits'iwa (Massawa)
Dahlak Arch.
Massawa Ch.
El Geteina
New Haifa
Asmera
ERITREA
Kagmar
Umm Saiyala
Hasaheisa
Rufa'a
Khashm el Girba
Tessenei
Barentu
Decamere
Arafali
Ras Andadda
El Homra
El Manaqil
Wad Medani
Adi Ugri
Adi Kale
Mersa Fatma
Bahr el Abiad
Ed Dueim
Hag Abdullah
Showak
Om Hâjer
Setit
Gedaref
Mokada 2295
Enda Salassie
Aksum
Adwa
Adigrat
Kululli
L. Assale -116
Bara
Atbara
Tekezze
Abi Addi
Danakil
Sennar
Doka
Kosti
Rabak
Singa
El Hawata
Ed
Er Rahad
Umm Ruwaba
White Nile
Angareb
Ras Dashan 4620
Mek'ele
Gallabat
Metemma
Dinder
Rahad
El Jebelein
Bahr el Azraq (Blue Nile)
Dabat
Sek'ota
3936 Sarenga
Maichew
Chercher
Aseb
Gonder
ETHIOPIA
Gogora
L. Tana
Rashad
Renk
Ed Damasin
Er Roseires
Addis Zemen
Lalibela
Debre Tabor
Moussa Ali 2063
Raheita
Daddato
Balho
Obock
Tadjoura
G. de Tadjoura
Doleib
J. Belaia 3131
Bahir Dar
Guna 4231
Weldiya
Tendaho
Awash
Mille
DJIBOUTI
Djibouti
A B C D
1 2 3 4
30 35 40
25 20 15

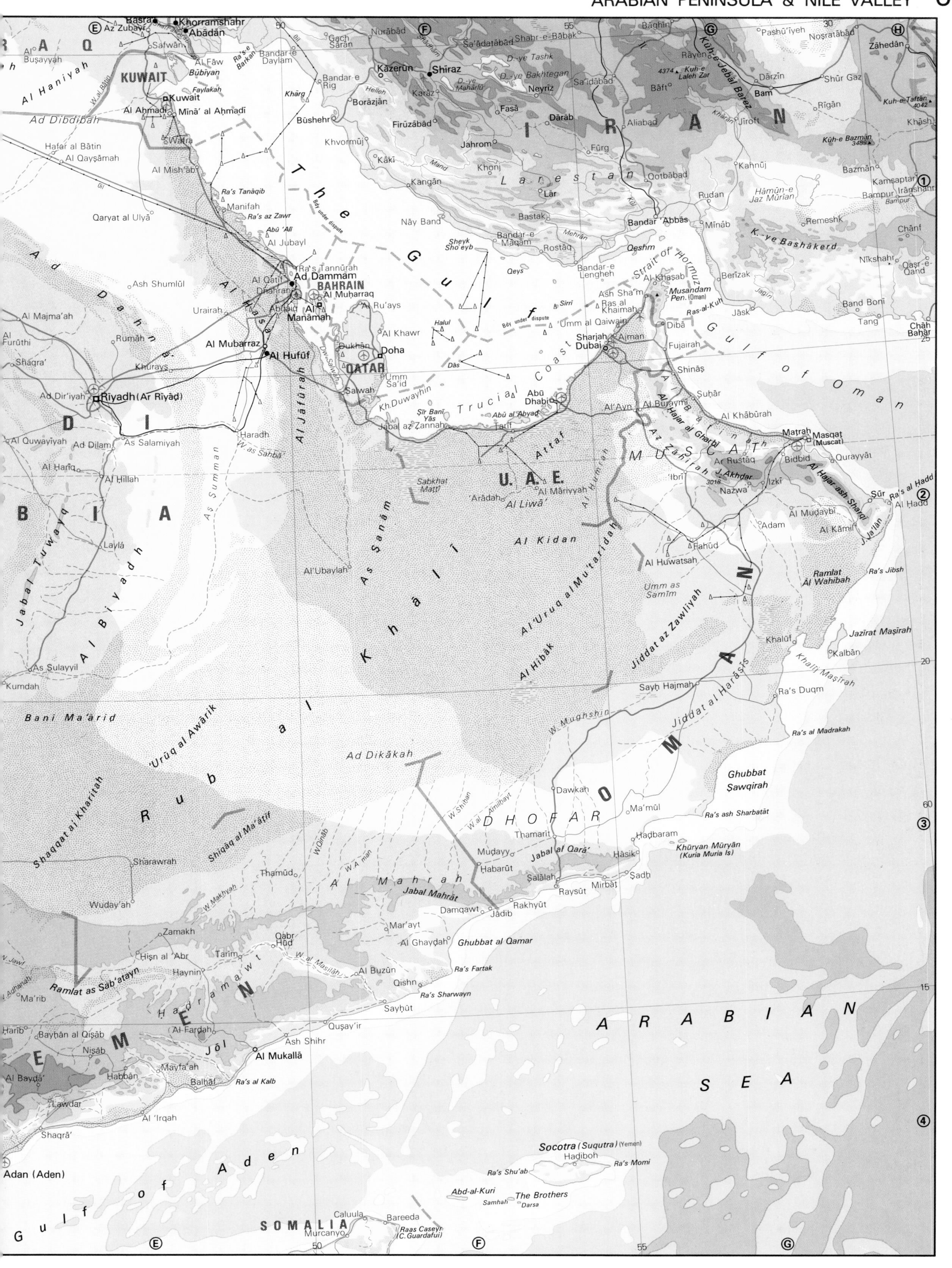
KUWAIT
BAHRAIN
QATAR
U. A. E.
MUSCAT
OMAN
DHOFAR
IRAN
The Gulf
Strait of Hormuz
Gulf of Oman
Trucial Coast
Rub al Khali
ARABIAN SEA
Gulf of Aden
SOMALIA
Riyadh (Ar Riyad)
Doha
Abu Dhabi
Dubai
Sharjah
Masqat (Muscat)
Manamah
Kuwait
Al Mukalla
Adan (Aden)
Shiraz
Bandar 'Abbas
Socotra (Suqutra) (Yemen)

1:40M

400 800 1200 1600 km
400 800 mls

A 2 30 B 20 60 C 10 D 0 E 10 F G 30 H 40 J 50 K 60 L 70 2 M

NORWAY
FINLAND
SWEDEN
Helsinki
Oslo Tallinn Sankt-Peterburg (Leningrad)
Stockholm EST. Nizhniy Novgorod
North Göteborg Riga Volga
Sea UNITED LAT. Moskva Samara
KINGDOM DENMARK LITH. RUSSIAN FEDERATION Ural
IRELAND København Minsk KAZAKHSTAN Oz. Balkhash
Edinburgh Hamburg Gdansk Vilnius BELORUSSIA Aral Syr-Darya
Dublin NETH. Berlin Warszawa Kiyev Khar'kov Sea UZBEKISTAN Tashkent
London 's Gravenhage GERMANY POLAND UKRAINE Volgograd KIR.
Bruxelles BELG. Bonn Praha Kraków Dnepr Caspian TAJ.
Paris LUX. CZECHOSLOVAKIA Rostov Odessa Don TURKMENISTAN
FRANCE Bern München Wien Budapest MOLD. Volga Georgia Tbilisi Baku Sea Mashhad
Bordeaux SWITZ. AUSTRIA HUNGARY ROMANIA Bucureşti Black Sea GEORGIA ARM. AZER. AFGHANISTAN
Bay of Milano Beograd Sofiya București Istanbul Tabriz
Biscay YUGOSLAVIA BULGARIA Ankara IRAN
Porto Marseille ITALY Roma Tiranë Athinai TURKEY Tehrān PAK.
Lisboa PORTUGAL Madrid Barcelona Corse Napoli ALB. GREECE Kriti CYPRUS Nicosia SYRIA Baghdād Shīrāz
SPAIN Islas Sardegna Beirût Damascus IRAQ Euphrates Basra
Acores (Port.) Tajo Baleares LEB. Jerusalem Amman Tigris KUWAIT Kuwait
Madeira (Port.) Tanger Oran Sicilia Mediterranean Sea Port Said ISR. JORDAN BAHRAIN Abū Dhabi Muscat
Rabat Fès Annaba Tunis Benghāzi Alexandria QATAR UNITED ARAB
Islas Marrakech Casablanca Constantine TUNISIA Cairo Suez EMIRATES
Canarias (Sp.) MOROCCO Béchar Sfax Tripoli SAUDI OMAN
La'youn ALGERIA Ghudamis Asyût Aswân ARABIA Ar Riyâd The Gulf
Nouadhibou Western Tindouf In Salah LIBYA EGYPT Nile Makkah
Sahara F'dérik Tropic of Cancer Ghât Sabha L. Nasser Wadi Halfa Muscat Kuria Muria Is
MAURITANIA SAHARA Tamanrasset Red Sea
Nouakchott Tombouctou Agadez Port Sudan San'â YEMEN Gulf of Aden
St-Louis Sénégal NIGER Omdurman Atbara Socotra (Yemen)
Dakar MALI Niger CHAD Khartoum Kassala Adan Djibouti
THE GAMBIA Banjul Bamako Niamey L. Chad Ndjamena El Obeid Blue Nile Asmara DJIBOUTI Hargeysa
GUINEA BISSAU Bissau BURKINA Kano Maiduguri SUDAN Ādīs Ābeba Diré Dawa
GUINEA Kankan Ouagadougou Kaduna White Nile ETHIOPIA Jimma SOMALIA
Conakry SIERRA Bobo Dioulasso BENIN NIGERIA Abuja Ngaoundéré Wau Juba Gulu
Freetown LEONE IVORY COAST Tamale Ilorin Niger CENTRAL Bambari L. Turkana Muqdisho
Monrovia Yamoussoukro GHANA TOGO Ibadan Onitsha AFRICAN REPUBLIC Wau UGANDA KENYA
LIBERIA Buchanan Kumasi Accra Lomé Lagos CAMEROON Bangui L. Albert Kampala Nairobi Kismaayo
Abidjan Port Harcourt Douala Yaoundé CONGO L. Edward Goma Lake INDIAN
Bioko Malabo EQUAT. GUINEA Bata ZAIRE Kisangani RWANDA Kigali Victoria Mwanza Mombasa Seychelles Arch.
Gulf of Guinea Principe GABON Libreville Mbandaka Kindu BURUNDI Bujumbura Dodoma Zanzibar OCEAN Amirante Is
SÃO TOMÉ & PRINCIPE Lambaréné Congo Ilebo Kigoma Lake Arusha SEYCHELLES Aldabra Is
São Tomé Annobon (Eq.G) Brazzaville Bandundu Kananga Kalemié Tanganyika TANZANIA Dar es Salaam Farquhar Is
Equator Kinshasa Mbuji-Mayi Kamina Mbala Dodoma
Cabinda (Ang.) Matadi Kasai Luluaba Mbeya
Luanda Malanje Lubumbashi Ruvuma COMOROS Mayotte (Fr.) Antseranana Tromelin (Fr.)
ANGOLA Kuito Ndola Lake Nyasa MALAWI Lichinga Moçambique Mahajanga
Lobito Zambezi Lusaka ZAMBIA Lilongwe MOZAMBIQUE Nampula
Namibe Cubango ZIMBABWE Zomba MADAGASCAR
St Helena (U.K.) Kunene Livingstone Harare Zambezi Beira Antananarivo MAURITIUS
Tsumeb Hwange Mutare Réunion (Fr.) Toamasina
Ascension (U.K.) BOTSWANA Bulawayo Gweru Limpopo Toliara
Walvis Bay (S.A.) Windhoek Serowe Inhambane Mozambique Channel
NAMIBIA Gaborone Maputo
Tropic of Capricorn Keetmanshoop Pretoria Mbabane SWAZILAND
Johannesburg
Kimberley Bloemfontein Maseru LESOTHO Durban
SOUTH AFRICA Orange East London
Cape Town Port Elizabeth

NORTH ATLANTIC OCEAN
SOUTH ATLANTIC OCEAN
Tristan da Cunha (U.K.)

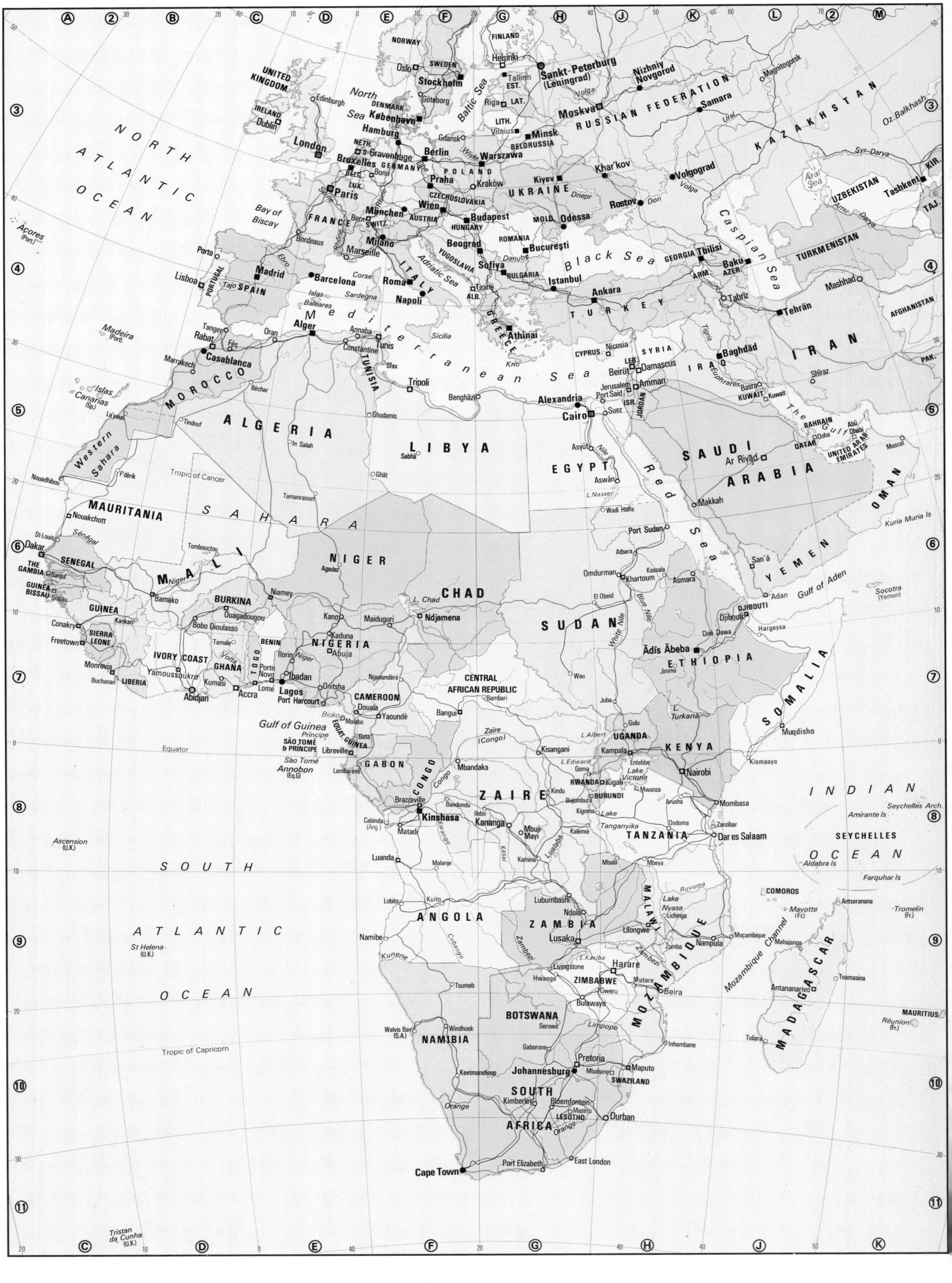

200 400 600 km
100 300 300 mls

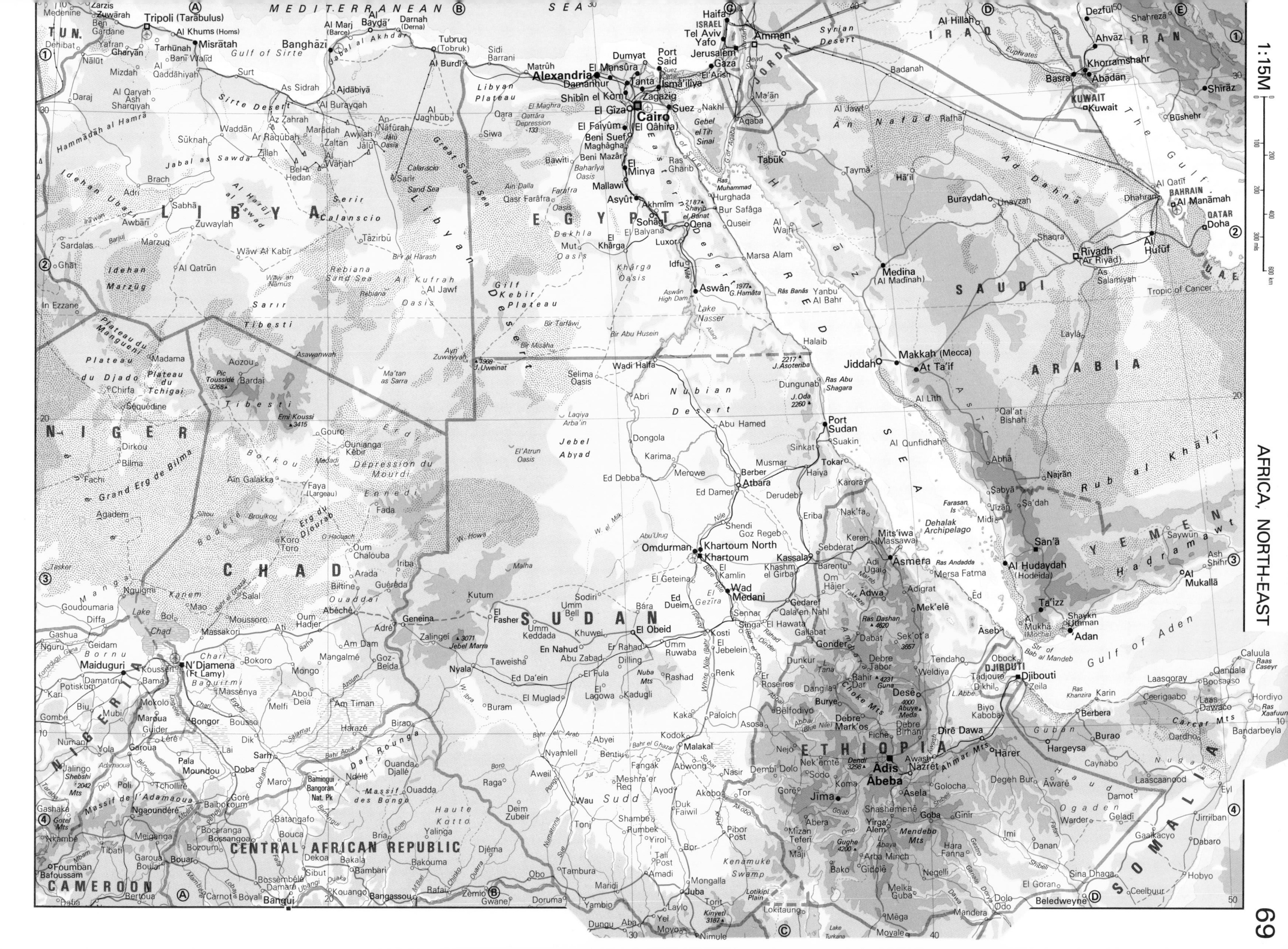

MEDITERRANEAN SEA

TUN. **LIBYA** **EGYPT** **SUDAN** **CHAD** **NIGER** **NIGERIA** **CAMEROON** **CENTRAL AFRICAN REPUBLIC** **ETHIOPIA** **SOMALIA** **SAUDI ARABIA** **YEMEN** **IRAN** **IRAQ** **ISRAEL** **JORDAN** **KUWAIT** **BAHRAIN** **QATAR** **UAE**

Tripoli (Tarābulus), Banghāzī, Alexandria, Cairo, Al Gīzah, Port Said, Suez, Jerusalem, Tel Aviv, Amman, Gaza, Haifa, Damascus

Khartoum, Omdurman, Khartoum North, Wad Medani, Kassala, Port Sudan, Atbara, Berber, Dongola, El Obeid, El Fasher, Nyala, Geneina, Juba, Wau, Malakal

N'Djamena (Ft Lamy), Abéché, Maiduguri, Bangui

Adis Abeba, Asmera, Jima, Nazrēt, Dirē Dawa, Harer, Gondar, Dese, Mek'elē

Djibouti, Berbera, Burao, Hargeysa, Hobyo

Makkah (Mecca), Medina (Al Madīnah), Jiddah, Ta'if, Riyadh (Ar Riyāḍ), Al Hufūf, Tabūk, Ḥā'il

Ṣan'ā, Ta'izz, Al Ḥudaydah (Hodeida), 'Adan, Al Mukallā

Kuwait, Al Manāmah, Doha, Abū Ẓaby, Dubayy, Baṣra, Abadan, Al Hillah, Shīrāz, Būshehr

Red Sea, The Gulf, Gulf of Aden, Gulf of Oman, Gulf of Sirte, Dead Sea, Lake Nasser, Lake Chad, Tropic of Cancer

Libyan Desert, Nubian Desert, Great Sand Sea, Rub' al Khālī, Ad Dahnā', An Nafūd, Syrian Desert, Tibesti, Emi Koussi 3415, Sudd

1:15M

200 400 600 km
100 200 300 mls

Inset (top left):
40 N 30 W
Corvo
Flores
São Jorge
Faial
Pico
Terceira
Angra Do Heroismo
Graciosa
Açores (Azores) (Portugal)
Santa Maria
São Miguel
Ponta Delgada
Formigas
Santa Maria
at the same scale

Inset (bottom left):
25 W
Sto Antão
S Vicente
S Luzia
S Nicolau
Sal
Boa Vista
CAPE VERDE
S Tiago
Maio
Fogo Brava
Praia
15 N
at the same scale

Main map labels:

MEDITERRANEAN SEA
PORTUGAL
Lisboa (Lisbon)
SPAIN
Madeira (Portugal)
Funchal
Islas Canarias (Canary Islands) (Spain)
Las Palmas De Gran Canaria
Santa Cruz De Tenerife
MOROCCO
Casablanca (Dar-el-Beida)
Rabat
Marrakech
Agadir
ALGERIA
Alger (Algiers)
Oran
Constantine
TUNISIA
Tunis
Western Sahara
Tropic of Cancer
S A H A R A
Grand Erg Occidental
Grand Erg Oriental
MAURITANIA
Nouakchott
Nouadhibou
Atar
MALI
Tombouctou
Gao
NIGER
Agadez
SENEGAL
Dakar
THE GAMBIA
Banjul
GUINEA-BISSAU
Bissau
GUINEA
Conakry
SIERRA LEONE
Freetown
LIBERIA
Monrovia
IVORY COAST
Yamoussoukro
Abidjan
BURKINA
Ouagadougou
Bobo Dioulasso
GHANA
Accra
Kumasi
TOGO
Lomé
BENIN
Porto Novo
Cotonou
NIGERIA
Lagos
Ibadan
Kano
Kaduna
Abuja
CAMEROON
Yaoundé
Douala
EQUATORIAL GUINEA
Libreville
S. TOME & PRINCIPE
GULF OF GUINEA
Bight of Benin
Bight of Biafra
Equator

1:7.5M

Scale bar: 100 200 300 km / 50 100 150 mls

A full-page reference map titled **North & West African Coasts**. Major countries and regions labelled include MOROCCO, ALGERIA, TUNISIA, LIBYA, MALI, NIGER, BURKINA, NIGERIA, BENIN, TOGO, GHANA, IVORY COAST, CAMEROON, CHAD, C.A.R., and SPAIN.

Selected labelled features and settlements:

Mediterranean Sea, Bight of Benin, Gold Coast

MALTA — Valletta; Tripoli; Tunis; La Goulette; Bizerte; Sousse; Sfax; Gabès; Gabes; Golfe de Gabès; Iles Kerkenna; I. de Jerba; Zuwārah; Al 'Azīziyah

Algeria: Alger (Algiers), Oran, Constantine, Sétif, Béjaïa (Bougie), Tlemcen, Sidi bel Abbès, Mostaganem, Ghardaia, Laghouat, Biskra, Touggourt, El Oued

Tunisia: Kairouan, Gafsa, Kasserine, Medenine

Morocco: Casablanca (Dar-el-Beida), Rabat, Salé, Fès, Meknès, Marrakech, Tanger (Tangier), Oujda, Kenitra, Essaouira, Safi; Haut Atlas, Moyen Atlas

Spain: Cádiz, Málaga, Marbella, Almeria, Gibraltar; Str. of Gibraltar; Ceuta (Sp.), Melilla (Sp.)

Nigeria states/cities: Lagos, Ibadan, Abeokuta, Ogbomosho, Oyo, Ilorin, Kaduna, Kano, Zaria, Maiduguri, Port Harcourt, Enugu, Onitsha, Benin City, Calabar, Aba, Owerri, Jos, Bauchi, Sokoto; BORNO, YOBE, JIGAWA, KATSINA, KANO, SOKOTO, KEBBI, NIGER, KWARA, OYO, OGUN, ONDO, OSUN, EDO, DELTA, RIVERS, IMO, ABIA, AKWA IBOM, CROSS RIVER, ENUGU, ANAMBRA, KOGI, BENUE, TARABA, ADAMAWA, PLATEAU, KADUNA

Niger: Niamey, Zinder, Maradi, Tessaoua

Burkina: Ouagadougou, Bobo Dioulasso, Ouahigouya

Ghana: Accra, Kumasi, Tema, Tamale, Sekondi, Takoradi, Cape Coast, Winneba; C. Three Points

Togo: Lomé; Benin: Cotonou, Porto Novo

Ivory Coast: Abidjan, Bouaké, Grand-Bassam

Cameroon: Garoua, Maroua, Ngaoundéré, Foumban; Massif de l'Adamaoua

Chad: Ndjamena (Ft Lamy), Lake Chad

Bight of Benin

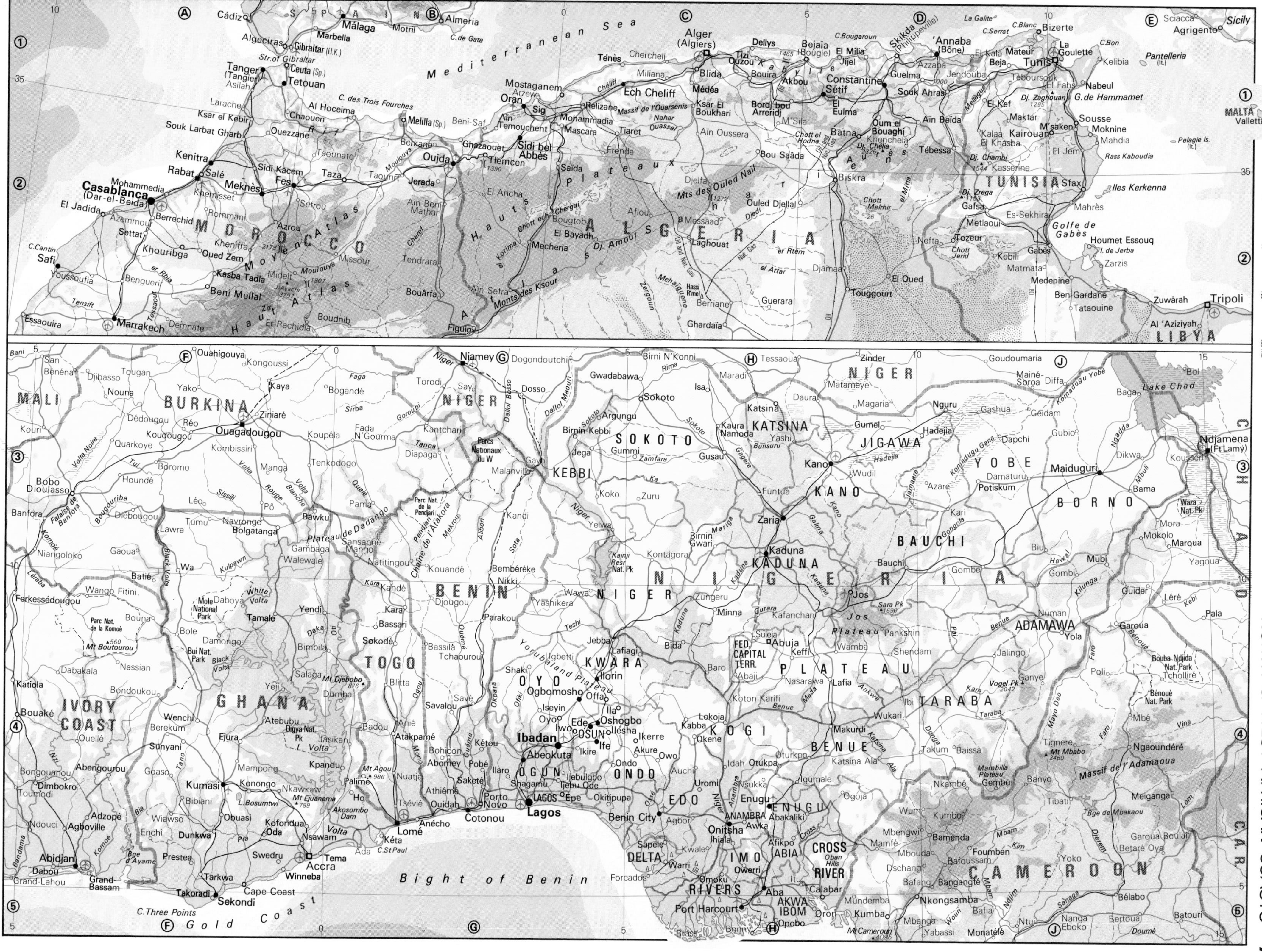

1:15M 0 200 400 600 km 0 100 200 300 mls

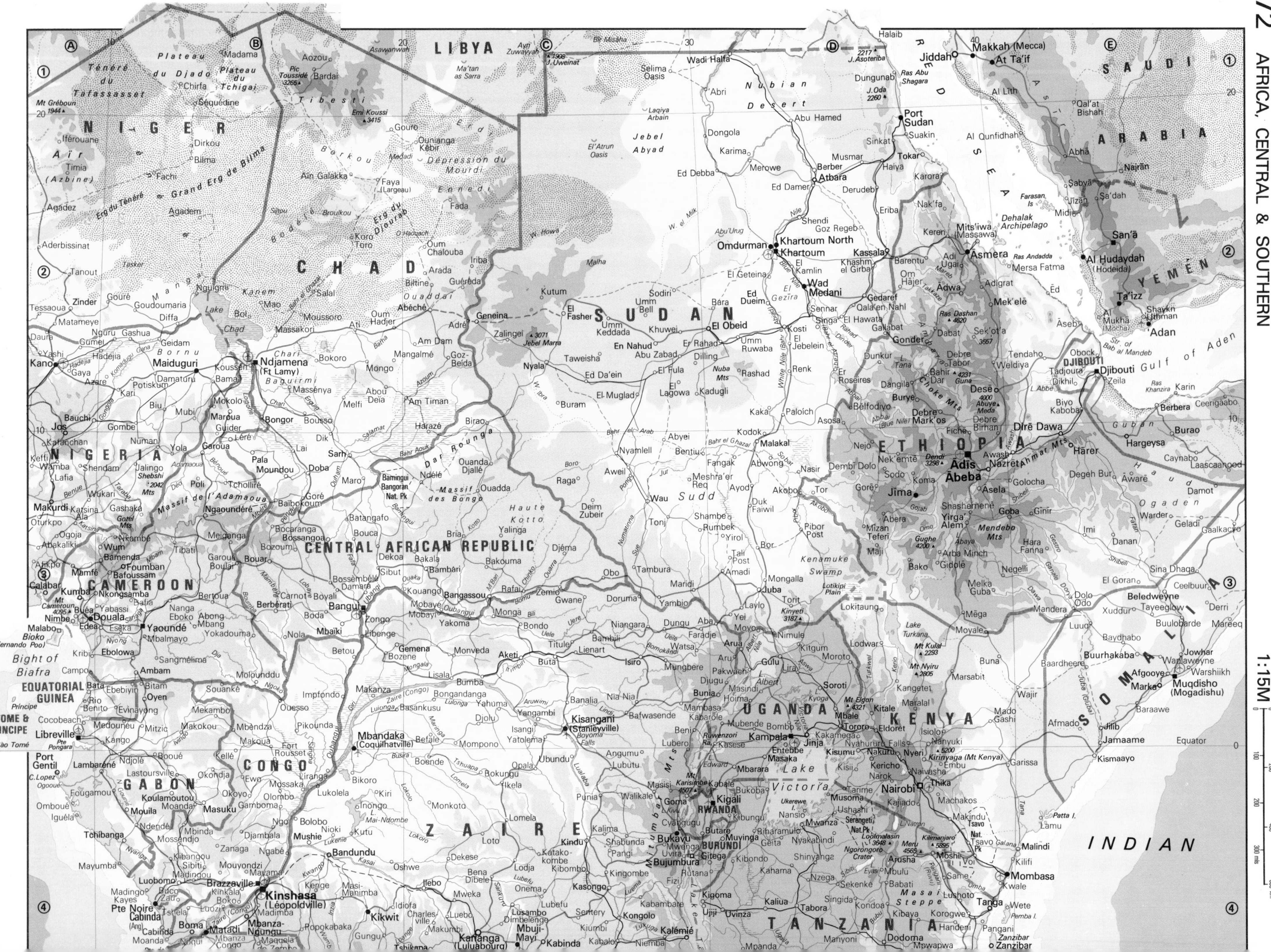
SAUDI ARABIA
YEMEN
ETHIOPIA
SOMALIA
SUDAN
CHAD
NIGER
LIBYA
NIGERIA
CAMEROON
CENTRAL AFRICAN REPUBLIC
UGANDA
KENYA
TANZANIA
RWANDA
BURUNDI
ZAIRE
CONGO
GABON
EQUATORIAL GUINEA
S.TOME & PRINCIPE
DJIBOUTI
INDIAN

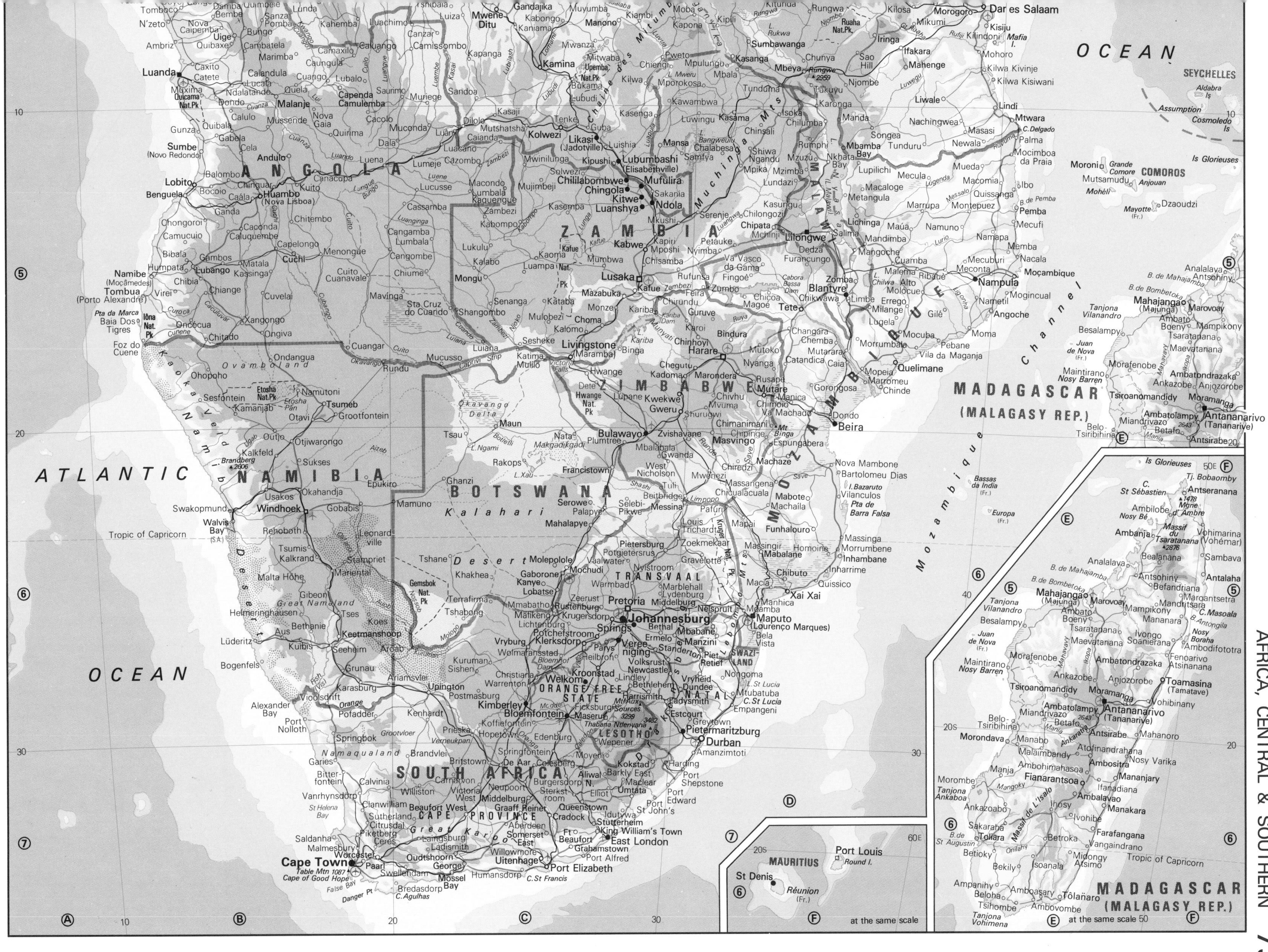
ATLANTIC
OCEAN
OCEAN
ANGOLA
ZAMBIA
NAMIBIA
BOTSWANA
ZIMBABWE
MOZAMBIQUE
MALAWI
SOUTH AFRICA
LESOTHO
SWAZILAND
TRANSVAAL
ORANGE FREE STATE
NATAL
CAPE PROVINCE
MADAGASCAR (MALAGASY REP.)
Mozambique Channel
Kalahari
Desert
Namib Desert
COMOROS
SEYCHELLES
MAURITIUS
Tropic of Capricorn
Luanda
Lobito
Benguela
Huambo (Nova Lisboa)
Lubumbashi (Elisabethville)
Ndola
Kitwe
Lusaka
Livingstone
Harare
Bulawayo
Lilongwe
Blantyre
Beira
Maputo (Lourenço Marques)
Windhoek
Walvis Bay
Gaborone
Pretoria
Johannesburg
Bloemfontein
Kimberley
Durban
Pietermaritzburg
Port Elizabeth
East London
Cape Town
Cape of Good Hope
Dar es Salaam
Nampula
Antananarivo (Tananarive)
Toamasina (Tamatave)
Port Louis
St Denis
Réunion (Fr.)
at the same scale

1:7.5M

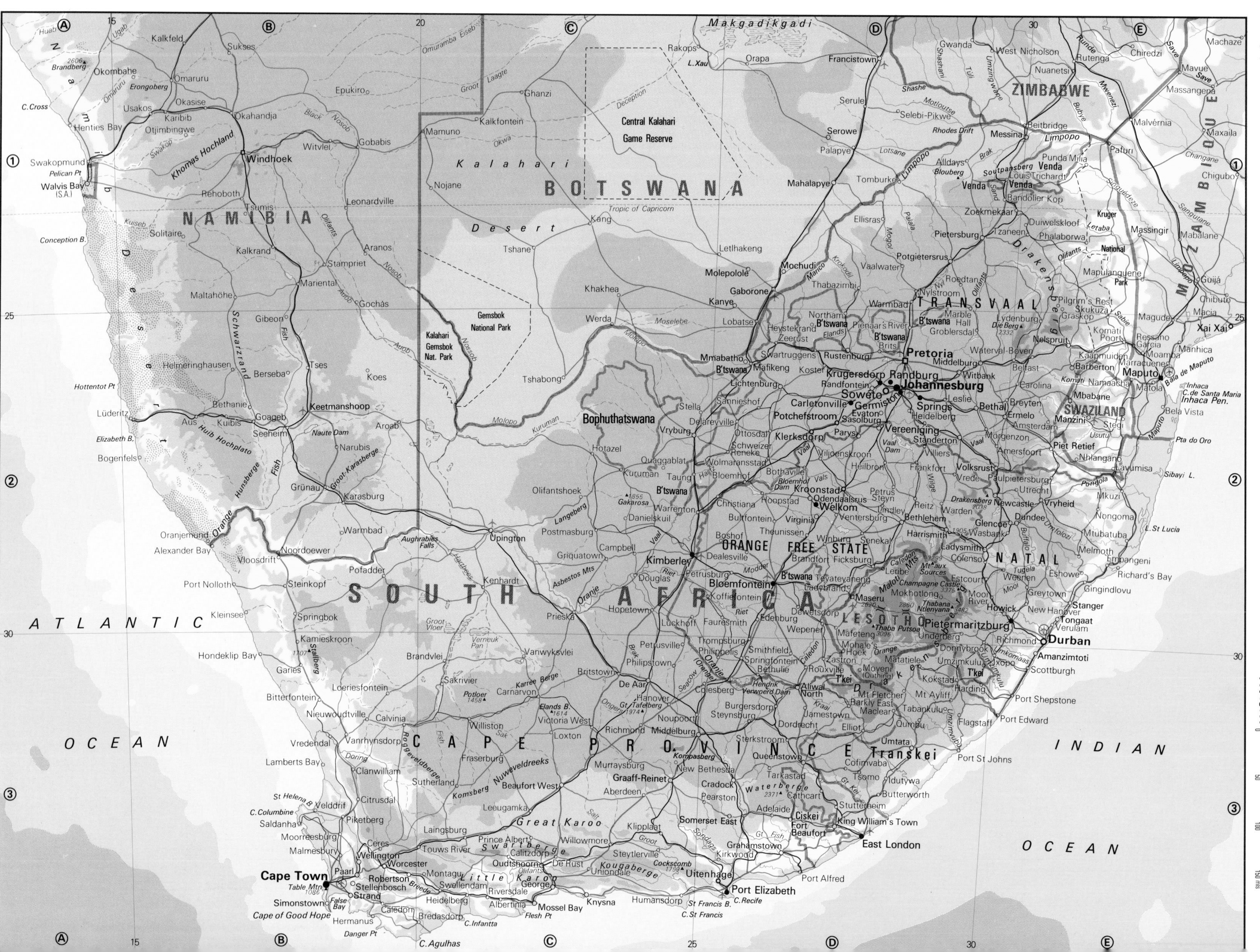

0 100 200 300 km
0 50 100 150 mls
SOUTH AFRICA
BOTSWANA
NAMIBIA
ZIMBABWE
MOZAMBIQUE
SWAZILAND
LESOTHO
TRANSVAAL
NATAL
ORANGE FREE STATE
CAPE PROVINCE
Transkei
Ciskei
Bophuthatswana
Venda
Kalahari Desert
Central Kalahari Game Reserve
Gemsbok National Park
Kalahari Gemsbok Nat. Park
Kruger National Park
Great Karoo
Drakensberg
ATLANTIC OCEAN
INDIAN OCEAN
Tropic of Capricorn
Pretoria
Johannesburg
Soweto
Durban
Pietermaritzburg
Bloemfontein
Kimberley
Port Elizabeth
East London
Cape Town
Windhoek
Gaborone
Maputo
Mbabane
Maseru
Walvis Bay (S.A.)
Swakopmund
Lüderitz
Upington
Cape of Good Hope
C. Agulhas
Orange
Vaal
Limpopo
Molopo

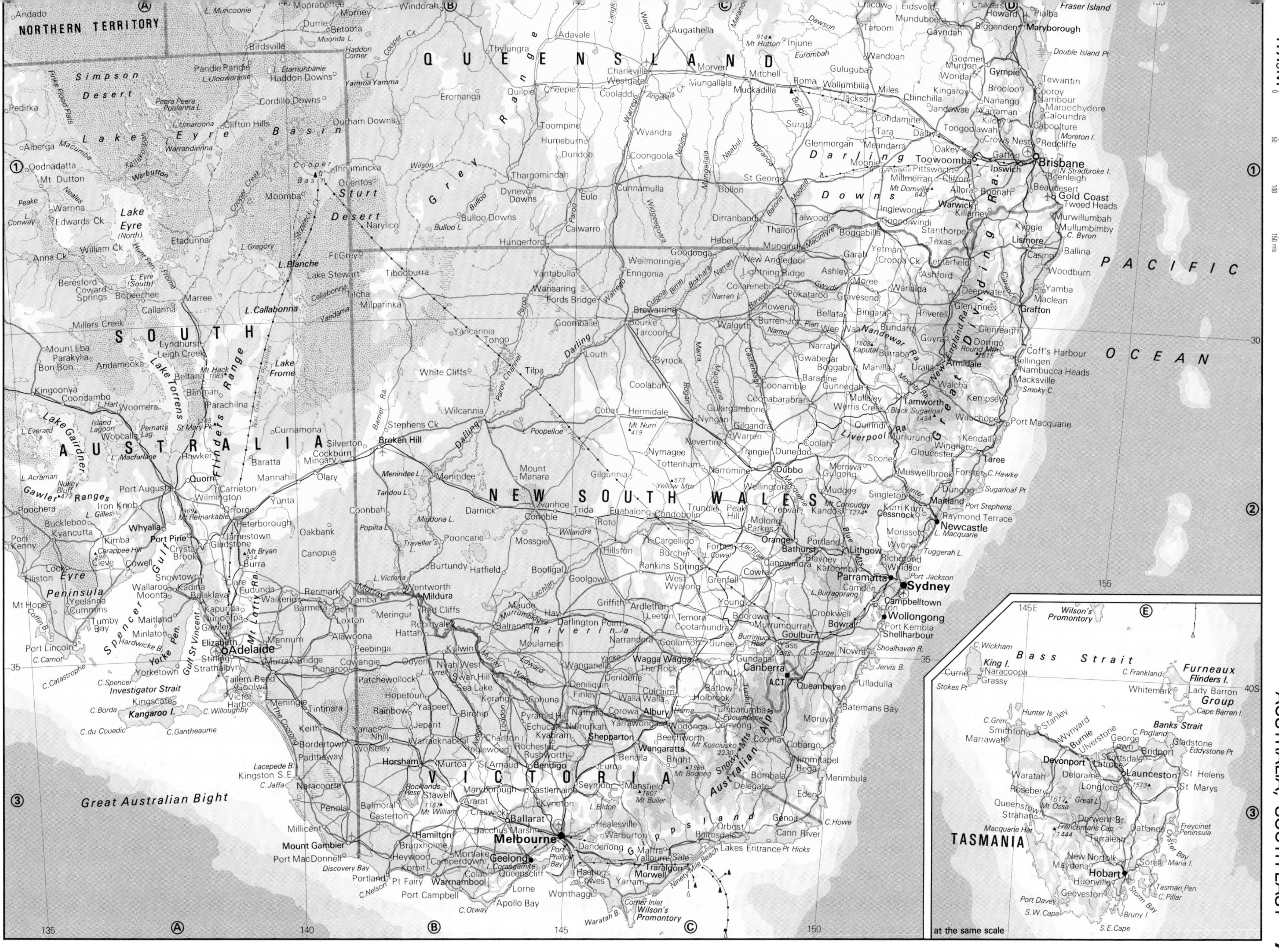

1:7.5M

100   200   300 km
50   100   150 mls

PACIFIC

OCEAN

TASMANIA

Furneaux Group Flinders I.

Bass Strait

Hobart

Great Australian Bight

NORTHERN TERRITORY

QUEENSLAND

NEW SOUTH WALES

VICTORIA

SOUTH AUSTRALIA

Brisbane

Newcastle

Sydney

Wollongong

Canberra

A.C.T.

Melbourne

Geelong

Ballarat

Adelaide

Broken Hill

Mildura

Darling River

Murray

Lake Eyre

Lake Torrens

Lake Gairdner

Simpson Desert

Sturt Desert

Great Dividing Range

Australian Alps

Flinders Ranges

Gulf of Carpentaria

1:20M

200 400 600 800 km
200 400 mils

Seas and Oceans

INDIAN OCEAN
Java Trench
Timor Sea
Arafura Sea
Banda Sea
Flores Sea
Molucca Sea
Ceram Sea
Bismarck Sea
Gulf of Carpentaria
Coral Sea
Timor Sea
Gulf of Papua
Torres Strait
Great Australian Bight
Bass Strait
Spencer Gulf

Countries / Regions

BORNEO
SULAWESI (CELEBES)
INDONESIA
IRIAN JAYA
NEW GUINEA
PAPUA NEW GUINEA
Bismarck Archipelago
WESTERN AUSTRALIA
NORTHERN TERRITORY
SOUTH AUSTRALIA
QUEENSLAND
NEW SOUTH WALES
VICTORIA
TASMANIA
A.C.T.
AUSTRALIA
Arnhem Land

Deserts and Ranges

Great Sandy Desert
Gibson Desert
Great Victoria Desert
Simpson Desert
Tanami
Nullarbor Plain
Barkly Tableland
Macdonnell Ranges
Hamersley Ra.
King Leopold Ra.
Kimberley Plateau
Great Dividing Range
Musgrave Ra.
Petermann Ra.
Flinders Ra.
Australian Alps
Lake Eyre Basin

Selected towns and cities

Manado, Tolitoli, Gorontalo, Palu, Poso, Kendari, Palopo, Parepare, Majene, Watampone, Banjarmasin, Samarinda, Balikpapan, Ujung Pandang (Makassar), Kintap, Tanjung

Dili, Kupang, Denpasar, Mataram, Raba, Reo, Ruteng, Waingapu, Ende

Jayapura, Sarmi, Aitape, Wewak, Manokwari, Sorong, Fakfak, Kaimana, Merauke, Kokonau, Tanahmerah, Mt Hagen, Mendi, Goroka, Mt Wilhelm, Madang, Lae, Morobe, Bulolo, Kerema, Kikori, Daru, Port Moresby, Kupiano, Samarai, Kokoda, Popondetta, Admiralty Is, Manus, Kavieng

Darwin, Adelaide River, Rum Jungle, Pine Creek, Katherine, Burrundie, Pago Mission, Wyndham, Daly Waters, Newcastle Waters, Borroloola, Wave Hill, Powell Creek, Tennant Creek, Barrow Creek, Alice Springs, Oodnadatta

Weipa, York, Coen, Cooktown, Laura, Mitchell River, Normanton, Croydon, Georgetown, Forsayth, Burketown, Camooweal, Cloncurry, Mount Isa, Dajarra, Richmond, Hughenden, Charters Towers, Townsville, Ayr, Bowen, Collinsville, Proserpine, Mackay, Winton, Longreach, Barcaldine, Blackall, Clermont, Emerald, Rockhampton, Mount Morgan, Windorah, Charleville, Quilpie, Roma, Toowoomba, Cunnamulla, St George, Goondiwindi, Warwick, Brisbane

Broome, Derby, Fitzroy Crossing, Hall's Creek, Port Hedland, Marble Bar, Shay Gap, Roebourne, Dampier, Onslow, Nullagine, Wittenoom, Paraburdoo, Newman, Carnarvon, Meekatharra, Wiluna, Cue, Sandstone, Mt Magnet, Leonora, Northampton, Mullewa, Geraldton, Dongara, Moora, Northam, Merredin, Bullfinch, Southern Cross, Kalgoorlie, Coolgardie, Norseman, Perth, Fremantle, Pinjarra, Collie, Bunbury, Narrogin, Wagin, Katanning, Busselton, Augusta, Albany, Esperance

Coober Pedy, Marree, Leigh Ck, Woomera, Tarcoola, Ooldea, Ceduna, Penong, Port Augusta, Whyalla, Port Pirie, Peterborough, Quorn, Port Lincoln, Elizabeth, Adelaide, Murray Bridge, Kingston, Victor Harbour, Mount Gambier, Naracoorte

Broken Hill, Wilcannia, Bourke, Walgett, Moree, Narrabri, Tamworth, Armidale, Dubbo, Nyngan, Cobar, Ivanhoe, Menindee, Hay, Griffith, Wagga Wagga, Albury, Deniliquin, Cootamundra, Goulburn, Sydney, Wollongong, Canberra, Bathurst, Orange, Newcastle, Maitland, Cessnock, Lithgow, Mt Kosciusko

Melbourne, Geelong, Ballarat, Bendigo, Horsham, Hamilton, Portland, Warrnambool, Colac, Morwell, Sale, Bairnsdale, Shepparton, Mildura, Swan Hill, Echuca

Hobart, Launceston, Devonport, Burnie, Smithton, Queenstown, Mt Ossa, Geeveston

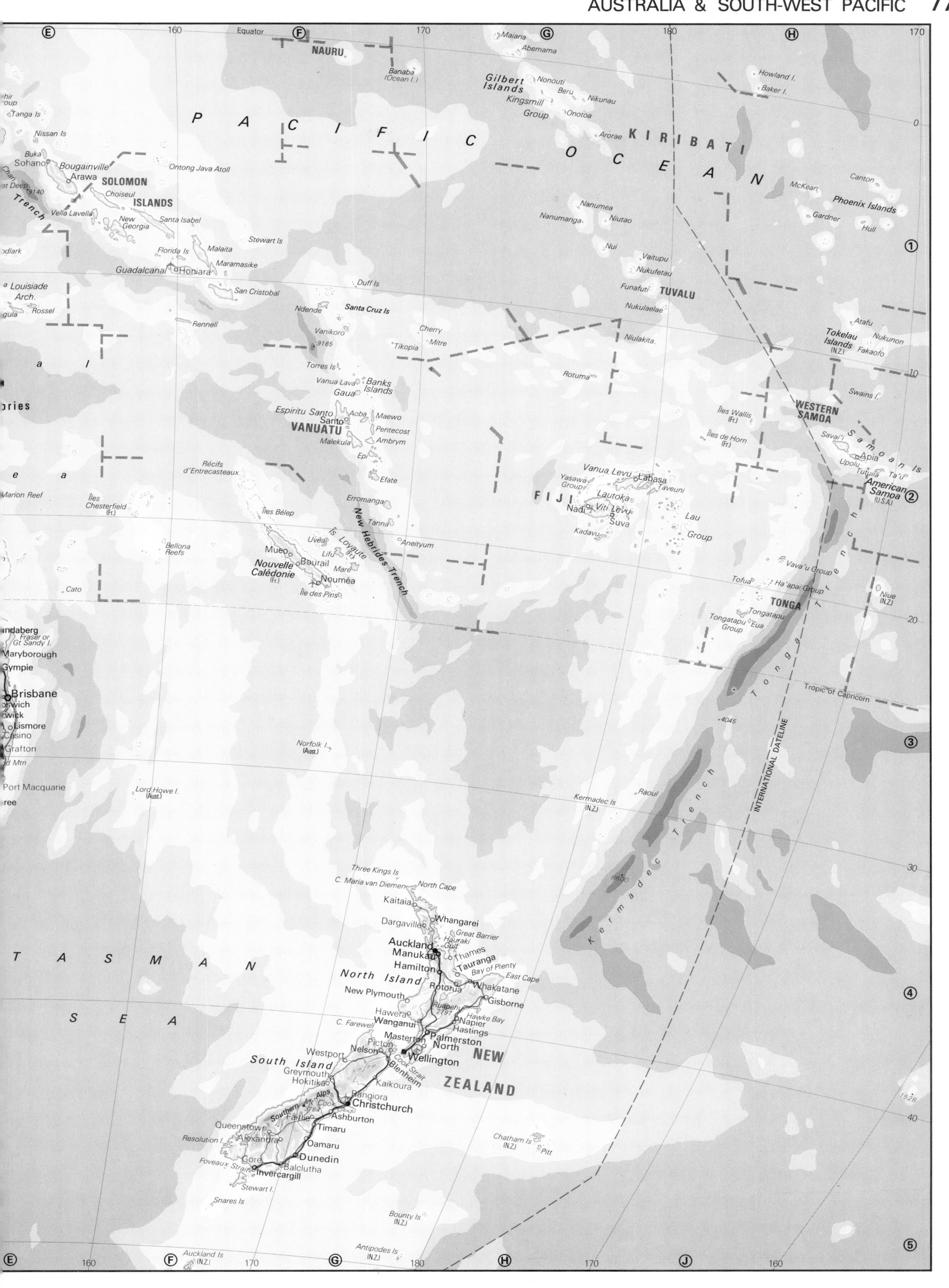

PACIFIC OCEAN

Equator

NAURU

Banaba
(Ocean I.)

Gilbert
Islands

Maiana
Abemama

Nonouti
Beru
Nikunau
Onotoa

Arorae

KIRIBATI

Howland I.
Baker I.

Canton

McKean

Phoenix Islands

Gardner
Hull

Tanga Is

Nissan Is

Buka
Sohano
Arawa
Bougainville
SOLOMON
ISLANDS
Choiseul

Chan Deep 9140

Vella Lavella
New
Georgia
Santa Isabel

Florida Is
Malaita

Guadalcanal
Honiara
Maramasike

San Cristobal

Ontong Java Atoll

Trench

Woodlark

Louisiade
Arch.

Rossel

Rennell

Duff Is

Ndende

Santa Cruz Is

Vanikoro
9165

Cherry
Mitre

Tikopia

Niulakita

Nanumea

Nanumanga
Niutao

Nui

Vaitupu
Nukufetau

Funafuti
TUVALU

Nukulaelae

Rotuma

Atafu
Nukunon

Tokelau
Islands
(N.Z.)
Fakaofo

Swains I.

WESTERN
SAMOA

Torres Is

Vanua Lava
Gaua
Banks
Islands

Espiritu Santo
Santo
Aoba
Maewo

VANUATU
Pentecost

Malekula
Ambrym
Epi

Récifs
d'Entrecasteaux

Îles Wallis
(Fr.)

Îles de Horn
(Fr.)

Savai'i

Apia
Upolu

Tutuila
American
Samoa
(U.S.A.)

Ta'u

Îles Chesterfield
(Fr.)

Marion Reef

Îles Bélep

Bellona
Reefs

Efate

Erromanga

Tanna

Aneityum

New Hebrides Trench

FIJI

Vanua Levu
Labasa

Yasawa
Group
Lautoka
Taveuni

Nadi
Viti Levu

Suva

Kadavu

Lau
Group

Vava'u Group

Tofua
Ha'apai Group

Niue
(N.Z.)

Muea
Bourail
Nouvelle
Calédonie
(Fr.)

Uvéa
Lifu
Maré

Îs Loyauté
(Fr.)

Nouméa

Île des Pins

Cato

Tongatapu

TONGA

Tongatapu
Group

'Eua

4045

Bundaberg
Fraser or
Gt Sandy I.

Maryborough

Gympie

Brisbane
Ipswich

Warwick

Lismore
Casino

Grafton

Port Macquarie

Tree

Norfolk I.
(Aust.)

Lord Howe I.
(Aust.)

Kermadec Is
(N.Z.)

Raoul

Tropic of Capricorn

INTERNATIONAL DATELINE

Tonga Trench

Kermadec Trench

TASMAN

SEA

Three Kings Is

C. Maria van Diemen
North Cape

Kaitaia

Dargaville

Whangarei

Great Barrier

Hauraki
Gulf

Auckland
Manukau

Hamilton

North Island

Thames

Tauranga

Bay of Plenty

East Cape

New Plymouth

Rotorua

Whakatane

Gisborne

Hawera

Ruapehu
2797

Wanganui

C. Farewell

Masterton

Napier

Hawke Bay

Hastings

Palmerston
North

Picton

Westport
Nelson

Cook Strait

Wellington

NEW

Greymouth

South Island

Blenheim

Kaikoura

ZEALAND

Hokitika

Alps
Cook
3764

Rangiora

Christchurch

Southern
Tasman

Ashburton

Queenstown

Timaru

Resolution I.

Alexandra

Oamaru

Gore

Dunedin

Foveaux Strait

Balclutha

Invercargill

Stewart I.

Snares Is

Chatham Is
(N.Z.)

Pitt

Bounty Is
(N.Z.)

1528

1:5M

50   100   150   200 km
0
50   100 mls

Three Kings Is   B

C. Maria van Diemen   North Cape

A   170   175   B

Ninety Mile Beach   Rangaunu B.
Doubtless B.

35   Ahipara B.   Kaitaia   Bay of Islands   35
Tauroa Pt   C. Brett
Kaikohe   Russell
Kawakawa
Hokianga Har.   Hikurangi
Whangarei
Dargaville   Hen & Chickens Is
Bream B.
Little Barrier I.   Great Barrier I.
Wellsford
Kaipara Har.   C. Colville
Manu   Mercury Is
① Hauraki   Takapuna   Mercury Bay   ①
Gulf   Coromandel
Auckland   Peninsula
Papatoetoe   Manukau
Papakura
Pukekohe   Thames
Waiuku   Mayor I.
NORTH   Paeroa   Waihi

Huntly   Te Aroha   White I.   C. Runaway   Hicks Bay
Glen Afton   Morrinsville   Matakana I.   East C
Ngaruawahia   Tauranga Har.
ISLAND   Hamilton   Cambridge   Tauranga   Bay of Plenty
Te   Te Puke   Whakatane
Awamutu   Putaruru   Rotorua   Opotiki   Taneatua
Kawhia   Otorohanga   Kawerau
Waitomo   Rotorua   Raukumara Ra.
Te Kuiti   Tokomaru Bay
Mangakino   Murupara
N. Taranaki Bight   Ohura   Taupo   Tolaga Bay
Waitara   Taumarunui   L. Taupo   Gisborne
New Plymouth   Poverty Bay
Inglewood   Mt   Tarawera
C. Egmont   Mt Egmont 2518   Stratford   Ngauruhoe 2291   Makorako 1727   Wairoa
Opunake   Eltham   Mt Ruapehu 2797   Eskdale   Mahia Peninsula
Hawera   Raetihi   Ohakune   Taradale   Napier   Portland I.
S. Taranaki Bight   Patea   Waiouru   Hastings   C. Kidnappers
Wanganui   Taihape   Havelock North

40   Marton   Waipukurau   40
Feilding   Dannevirke
Palmerston N.   Woodville
C. Farewell   Farewell Spit   Foxton   Pahiatua
Golden   Levin   Eketahuna   C. Turnagain
Collingwood   Bay   Separation Pt   Otaki   Herbertville
Rocks Pt   C. Stephens   Paraparaumu   Masterton
Takaka   D'Urville I.   Carterton
Tasman   Porirua   Upper Hutt
Karamea   Mts   Tasman   Tawa   Martinborough
Bight   The Twins   Bay   Wellington   Lower Hutt
1826   Motueka   Nelson   Palliser Bay   Mt Ross 983
Seddonville   Richmond   Picton   C. Palliser
Westport   Murchison   Richmond Ra.   Blenheim
C. Foulwind   Wairau   C. Campbell
Buller   L. Rotoroa   L. Potoiti
② Reefton   Victoria   Mt Travers   Kaikoura Ra.   ②
Ra.   2338   Tapuaenuku 2885
Runanga   Grey   Spenser   Clarence
Greymouth   Mts   Hanmer   Kaikoura
Brunner   Lewis   Springs   Kaikoura Pen.
Hokitika   Pass   Waiau
Ross   L. Sumner   Culverden   Cheviot
SOUTH   Arthurs   Waiau   Hurunui
Pass   Pukekerau Ra.   Pegasus
Abut Hd   Waimakariri   Waipara   Bay
ISLAND   Rangiora   Kaiapoi
Franz Josef Gl.   Coleridge   Christchurch
SOUTHERN   Methven   Hornby   Lyttelton   Banks
Mt Cook 3764   Rakaia   Lincoln   Peninsula
Mt Sefton 3157   Ashburton   Akaroa
Hermitage   L. Tekapo   L. Ellesmere
Jackson Hd   Geraldine   Canterbury
Cascade Pt   Pukaki   Temuka   Bight
L. Fairlie
Awarua Pt   Pollux 2542   Ohau   Pukaki   Timaru
Mt Aspiring 3027   Young Ra.   L. Benmore
Milford Sd   Wanaka   Omarama   Waimate
Milford Sd   L. Hawea   L. Aviemore
George Sd   Pyramid   Kurow   45
45   Homer Tunnel 2326   Arrowtown   Hawkdun Ra.   Oamaru
Caswell Sd   Wanaka   Waitaki
Secretary I.   Queenstown   Cromwell   Ranfurly
Fiordland   L. Wakatipu   Clyde   Hampden
Doubtful Sd   Te Anau   Alexandra   Palmerston
Nat. Park   L. Te Anau   Kingston   Roxburgh   Waikouaiti
Breaksea Sd   Manapouri   Lumsden   Port Chalmers
Resolution I.   718   Mt Ward   Otago Peninsula
Dusky Sd   Manapouri   Riversdale   Mosgiel   Dunedin
Ohai   Heriot   Clutha
Puysegur Pt   Te Waewae   Lumsden   Lawrence
Bay   Winton   Gore   Milton
Campbell   Mataura   Balclutha
Te Waewae   Edendale   Kaitangata
Riverton   Owaka

③ Foveaux Strait   Invercargill   ③
Solander I.   Bluff
Codfish I.   Paterson Inlet
Stewart Island   Oban   Shelter Pt
Mt Allen 730
A   Port Pegasus   B   175   C

TASMAN SEA

SOUTH

PACIFIC

OCEAN

COOK STRAIT

Canterbury Plains

1:40M

Antarctic Research Stations
1 Teniente Rodolfo Marsh Martín (Chile)
2 Comandante Ferraz (Brazil)
3 Capitán Arturo Prat (Chile)
4 Bellingshausen (Former USSR)
5 Jubany (Arg.)
6 Henryk Arctowski (Poland)
7 General Bernardo O'Higgins (Chile)
8 Esperanza (Arg.)
9 Vicecomodoro Marambio (Arg.)
10 Chang Cheng (Great Wall) (China)
11 Palmer (USA)
12 Faraday (UK)
13 Rothera (UK)
14 General San Martin (Arg.)

Abbreviations

Abbreviations used in Reference Map Section

	Full Form	English Form	Language
A			
a.d.	an der	on the	German
Akr.	Ákra, Akrotírion	cape	Greek
Appno	Appennino	mountain range	Italian
Arch.	Archipelago	archipelago	English
B			
B.	1. Baai, Bahía, Baia, Baie, Bay, Bucht, Bukhta, Bugt	bay	Dutch, Spanish, Portuguese, French, English, German, Russian, Danish
	2. Ban	village	Indo-Chinese
	3. Barrage	dam	French
Bol.	Bol'sh/aya, -oy, -oye	big	Russian
Br.	1. Branch	branch	English
	2. Bridge, Brücke	bridge	English, German
	3. Burun	cape	Turkish
Brj	Baraj,-i	dam	Turkish
C			
C.	Cabo, Cap, Cape	cape	Spanish, French, English
Can.	Canal	canal	English
Cd	Ciudad	town	Spanish
Chan.	Channel	channel	English
Ck	Creek	creek	English
Cord.	Cordillera	mountain range	Spanish
D			
D.	1. Dağ,Dâgh, Daği, Dağlari	mountain, range	Persian, Turkish
	2. Daryācheh	lake	Persian
Dj.	Djebel	mountain	Arabic
E			
E.	East	east	English
Emb.	Embalse	reservoir	Spanish
Escarp.	Escarpment	escarpment	English
Estr.	Estrecho	strait	Spanish
F			
F.	Firth	estuary	Gaelic
Fj.	1. Fjell	mountain	Norwegian
	2. Fjord, Fjorður	fjord	Norwegian, Icelandic
Ft	Fort	fort	English
G			
G.	1. Gebel	mountain	Arabic
	2. Göl, Gölü	lake	Turkish
	3. Golfe, Golfo, Gulf	gulf	French, Italian, Portuguese, Spanish, English
	4. Gora, -gory	mountain, range	Russian
	5. Gunung	mountain	Malay, Indonesian
Gd, Gde	Grand, Grande	grand	English, French
Geb.	Gebirge	mountain range	German
Gl.	Glacier	glacier	French, English
Grl	General	general	Spanish
Gt, Gtr	Great, Groot, -e, Greater	greater	English, Dutch
H			
Har.	Harbour	harbour	English
Hd	Head	head	English
I			
I.	Ile, Ilha, Insel, Isla, Island Isle, Isola, Isole	island	French, Portuguese, German Spanish, English, Italian
In.	1. Indre, Inner	inner	Norwegian, English
	2. Inlet	inlet	English
Is	Iles, Ilhas, Islands, Isles, Islas	islands	French, Portuguese, English, Spanish
Isth.	Isthmus	isthmus	English
J			
J.	Jabal, Jebel, Jibal	mountain	Arabic
K			
K.	1. Kaap, Kap, Kapp	cape	Dutch, German, Norwegian, Swedish
	2. Koh, Kuh, Kuhha	mountain	Persian
	3. Kolpos	gulf	Greek
Kep.	Kepulauan	islands	Indonesian
Khr.	Khrebet	mountain range	Russian
Kör.	Körfez, -i	gulf, bay	Turkish
L			
L.	1. Lac, Lago, Lagoa, Lake, Liman, Limni, Loch, Lough	lake	French, Italian, Spanish, Portuguese, English, Russian, Greek, Gaelic
Lag.	Lagoon, Laguna, -e, Lagôa	lagoon	English, Spanish, French, Portuguese
Ld	Land	land	English
Lit.	Little	little	English
M			
M.	1. Muang	town	Thai
	2. Mys	cape	Russian
m	metre, -s	metre(s)	English, French
Mal.	Mali, -o, -yy	small	Russian
Mf	Massif	mountain group	French
Mgne	Montagne(s)	mountain(s)	French
Mont	Monument	monument	English
Mt	Mont, Mount	mountain	French, English
Mte	Monte	mountain	Italian, Portuguese, Spanish
Mti	Monti	mountain, range	Italian
Mtn	Mountain	mountain	English
Mts	Monts, Mountains, Montañas, Montes	mountains	French, English, Spanish, Italian, Portuguese
N			
N.	1. Neu, Ny	new	German
	2. Nevado	snow capped mtns	Spanish
	3. Noord, Nord, Norte, Nørre, North	north	Danish, French, Portuguese, Spanish, Danish, English
Nat.	National	national	English
Nat. Pk	National Park	national park	English
Ndr	Neder, Nieder	lower	Dutch, Swedish, German
N.E.	North East	north east	English
N.M.	National Monument	national monument	English
N.P.	National Park	national park	English
N.W.	North West	north west	English
O			
O.	1. Oost, Ost	east	Dutch, German
	2. Ostrov	island	Russian
Ø	Øy	island	Norwegian
Oz.	Ozero, Ozera	lake(s)	Russian
P			
P.	1. Pass, Passo	pass	English, German, Italian
	2. Pic, Pico, Pizzo	peak	French, Portuguese, Spanish, Italian
	3. Pulau	island	Malay, Indonesian
P.P.	Pulau-pulau	islands	Indonesian
Pass.	Passage	passage	English
Peg.	Pegunungan	mountains	Indonesian
Pen.	Peninsula, Peninsola	peninsula	English, Italian
Pk	1. Park	park	English
	2. Peak, Pik	peak	English, Russian
Plat.	Plateau, Planalto	plateau	English, French, Portuguese
Pov	Poluostrov	peninsula	Russian
Pr.	Prince	prince	English
Pres.	President, Presidente	president	English, Spanish, Portuguese
Promy	Promontory	promontory	English
Pt	Point	point	English
Pta	1. Ponta, Punta	point	Portuguese, Italian, Spanish
	2. Puerta	pass	Spanish
Pte	Pointe	point	French
Pto	Porto, Puerto	port	Spanish
R			
R.	1. Rio, River, Rivière,	river	Portuguese, Spanish, English, French
	2. Ría	river mouth	Spanish
Ra.	Range	range	English
Rap.	Rapids	rapids	English
Res.	Reserve, Reservation	reserve, reservation	English
Resr	Reservoir	reservoir	English
Résr	Réservoir	reservoir	French
S			
S.	1. Salar, Salina	salt marsh	Spanish
	2. San, São	saint	Spanish, Portuguese
	3. See	sea, lake	German
	4. South, Sud	south	English, French
s.	sur	on	French
Sa	Serra, Sierra	mountain range	Portuguese, Spanish
Sd	Sound, Sund	sound	English, German, Swedish
S.E.	South East	south east	English
Sev.	Sever, Severnaya	north	Russian
Sp.	Spitze	peak	German
Spr.	Spring,(s)	spring(s)	English
St	Saint	saint	English
Sta	Santa	saint	Spanish
Sta.	Station	station	English
Ste	Sainte	saint	French
Sto	Santo	saint	Portuguese, Spanish
Str.	Strait	strait	English
S.W.	South West	south west	English
T			
T.	Tall, Tel	hill, mountain	Arabic, Hebrew
Tg	Tanjong, Tandjong	cape	Malay, Indonesian
Tk	Têluk, Têlok	bay	Indonesian
Tr.	Trench, Trough	trench, trough	English
U			
U.	Uad	wadi	Arabic
Ug	Ujung	cape	Malay
Upr	Upper	upper	English
V			
V.	1. Val, Valle	valley	French, Italian, Spanish
	2. Ville	town	French
Va	Villa	town	Spanish
Vdkhr.	Vodokhranilishche	reservoir	Russian
Vol.	Volcán, Volcano	volcano	Spanish, English
Vozv.	Vozvyshennost'	upland	Russian
W			
W.	1. Wadi	wadi	Arabic
	2. Water	water	English
	3. Well	well	English
	4. West	west	English
Y			
Yuzh.	Yuzhnaya, Yuzhno, Yuzhnyy	south	Russian
Z			
Z.	Zaliv	gulf, bay	Russian
Zap.	Zapadnyy, -aya, -o, -oye	western	Russian
Zem.	Zemlya	country, land	Russian

Index

Introduction to the index

In the index, the first number refers to the page, and the following letter and number to the section of the map in which the index entry can be found. For example, 38C2 **Paris** means that Paris can be found on page 38 where column C and row 2 meet.

Abbreviations used in the index

Afghan	Afghanistan	Hung	Hungary	Phil	Philippines	Arch	Archipelago
Alb	Albania	Ind	Indonesia	Pol	Poland	B	Bay
Alg	Algeria	Irish Rep	Irish Republic	Port	Portugal	C	Cape
Ant	Antarctica	N Ire	Ireland, Northern	Rom	Romania	Chan	Channel
Arg	Argentina	Leb	Lebanon	Russian Fed	Russian Federation	Gl	Glacier
Aust	Australia	Lib	Liberia	S Arabia	Saudi Arabia	I(s)	Island(s)
Bang	Bangladesh	Liech	Liechtenstein	Scot	Scotland	Lg	Lagoon
Belg	Belgium	Lux	Luxembourg	Sen	Senegal	L	Lake
Bol	Bolivia	Madag	Madagascar	S Africa	South Africa	Mt(s)	Mountain(s)
Bulg	Bulgaria	Malay	Malaysia	Switz	Switzerland	O	Ocean
Camb	Cambodia	Maur	Mauritania	Tanz	Tanzania	P	Pass
Can	Canada	Mor	Morocco	Thai	Thailand	Pass	Passage
CAR	Central African Republic	Mozam	Mozambique	Turk	Turkey	Pen	Peninsula
Czech	Czechoslovakia	Neth	Netherlands	USA	United States of America	Plat	Plateau
Den	Denmark	NZ	New Zealand	Urug	Uruguay	Pt	Point
Dom Rep	Dominican Republic	Nic	Nicaragua	Ven	Venezuela	Res	Reservoir
El Sal	El Salvador	Nig	Nigeria	Viet	Vietnam	R	River
Eng	England	Nor	Norway	Yugos	Yugoslavia	S	Sea
Eq Guinea	Equatorial Guinea	Pak	Pakistan	Zim	Zimbabwe	Sd	Sound
Eth	Ethiopia	PNG	Papua New Guinea			Str	Strait
Fin	Finland	Par	Paraguay			V	Valley

A

42B2 **Aachen** Germany
36C1 **Aalst** Belg
32K6 **Äänekoski** Fin
37C1 **Aarau** Switz
37B1 **Aare** *R* Switz
52A3 **Aba** China
71H4 **Aba** Nig
72D3 **Aba** Zaïre
63B2 **Ābādān** Iran
63C2 **Ābādeh** Iran
70B1 **Abadla** Alg
29C2 **Abaeté** Brazil
29C2 **Abaeté** *R* Brazil
27J4 **Abaetetuba** Brazil
52D1 **Abagnar Qi** China
71H4 **Abaji** Nig
19E3 **Abajo Mts** USA
71H4 **Abakaliki** Nig
49L4 **Abakan** Russian Fed
70C3 **Abala** Niger
70C2 **Abalessa** Alg
26D6 **Abancay** Peru
63C2 **Abarqū** Iran
53E3 **Abashiri** Japan
53E3 **Abashiri-wan** *B* Japan
22C1 **Abasolo** Mexico
51H7 **Abau** PNG
72D3 **Abaya** *L* Eth
72D2 **Abbai** *R* Eth
72E2 **Abbe** *L* Eth
38C1 **Abbeville** France
17D4 **Abbeville** Louisiana, USA
15C2 **Abbeville** S Carolina, USA
37C2 **Abbiategrasso** Italy
18B1 **Abbotsford** Can
12A2 **Abbotsford** USA
60C2 **Abbottabad** Pak
67F4 **Abd-al-Kuri** *I* Yemen
44J5 **Abdulino** Russian Fed
72C2 **Abéché** Chad
71F4 **Abengourou** Ivory Coast
32F7 **Åbenrå** Den
42B1 **Åbenra** Den
71G4 **Abeokuta** Nig
72D3 **Abera** Eth
35C5 **Aberaeron** Wales
20C2 **Aberdeen** California, USA
13D3 **Aberdeen** Maryland, USA
15B2 **Aberdeen** Mississippi, USA
74C3 **Aberdeen** S Africa
34D3 **Aberdeen** Scot
8D2 **Aberdeen** S Dakota, USA

8A2 **Aberdeen** Washington, USA
6J3 **Aberdeen L** Can
34D3 **Aberfeldy** Scot
35D6 **Abergavenny** Wales
35C5 **Aberystwyth** Wales
44L2 **Abez'** Russian Fed
66D3 **Abhā** S Arabia
63B1 **Abhar** Iran
71H4 **Abia** *State* Nigeria
66C4 **Abi Addi** Eth
71F4 **Abidjan** Ivory Coast
17C2 **Abilene** Kansas, USA
16C3 **Abilene** Texas, USA
35E6 **Abingdon** Eng
12C3 **Abingdon** USA
7K4 **Abitibi** *R* Can
7L5 **Abitibi,L** Can
45G7 **Abkhazskaya** Respublika, Georgia
36A2 **Ablis** France
60C2 **Abohar** India
71G4 **Abomey** Benin
72B3 **Abong Mbang** Cam
57E9 **Aborlan** Phil
72B2 **Abou Deïa** Chad
67E1 **Abqaiq** S Arabia
39A2 **Abrantes** Port
72D1 **'Abri** Sudan
76A3 **Abrolhos** *Is* Aust
8B2 **Absaroka Range** *Mts* USA
67F2 **Abū al Abyad** *I* UAE
67E1 **Abū 'Ali** *I* S Arabia
66D3 **Abū Arish** S Arabia
66B3 **Abu Deleiq** Sudan
67F2 **Abū Dhabi** UAE
66B3 **'Abu Dom** *Watercourse* Sudan
65C3 **Abū el Jurdhān** Jordan
66B3 **Abu Fatima** Sudan
72D2 **Abu Hamed** Sudan
68E7 **Abuja** Nigeria
65A3 **Abu Kebir Hihya** Egypt
26E5 **Abunã** Brazil
26E6 **Abuna** *R* Bol
64D3 **Abū Sukhayr** Iraq
65B3 **Abu Suweir** Egypt
78B2 **Abut Head** *C* NZ
66B1 **Abu Tig** Egypt
72D2 **Abu'Urug** *Well* Sudan
72D2 **Abuye Meda** *Mt* Eth
72C2 **Abu Zabad** Sudan
72D3 **Abwong** Sudan
42B1 **Åby** Den

65C3 **Aby 'Aweigïla** *Well* Egypt
72C3 **Abyei** Sudan
13F2 **Acadia Nat Pk** USA
21B2 **Acambaro** Mexico
23B5 **Acandi** Colombia
21B2 **Acaponeta** Mexico
21B3 **Acapulco** Mexico
27L4 **Acaraú** Brazil
26E2 **Acarigua** Ven
22C2 **Acatlán** Mexico
22C2 **Acatzingo** Mexico
22D2 **Acayucan** Mexico
71F4 **Accra** Ghana
28E2 **Aceguá** Urug
60D4 **Achalpur** India
25B6 **Achao** Chile
53B2 **Acheng** China
37D1 **Achensee** *L* Austria
36E2 **Achern** Germany
33A3 **Achill** *I* Irish Rep
49L4 **Achinsk** Russian Fed
40D3 **Acireale** Italy
11D3 **Ackley** USA
23C2 **Acklins** *I* Caribbean
26D6 **Acobamba** Peru
25B4 **Aconcagua** *Mt* Chile
27L5 **Acopiara** Brazil
68B4 **Açores** *Is* Atlantic O
A Coruña = La Coruña
37C2 **Acqui** Italy
75A2 **Acraman,L** Aust
Acre = 'Akko
26D5 **Acre** *State,* Brazil
20C3 **Acton** USA
22C1 **Actopan** Mexico
71G4 **Ada** Ghana
17C3 **Ada** USA
39B1 **Adaja** *R* Spain
10C6 **Adak** *I* USA
67G2 **Adam** Oman
72D3 **Adama** Eth
29B3 **Adamantina** Brazil
72B3 **Adamaoua** Region, Nig/Cam
71J4 **Adamawa** State, Nigeria
37D1 **Adamello** *Mt* Italy
14D1 **Adams** USA
62B3 **Adam's Bridge** India/Sri Lanka
3E3 **Adams L** Can
8A2 **Adams,Mt** USA
62C3 **Adam's Peak** *Mt* Sri Lanka
67E4 **'Adan** Yemen
45F8 **Adana** Turk

45E7 **Adapazari** Turk
66B3 **Adarama** Sudan
79F7 **Adare,C** Ant
57D4 **Adaut** Indon
75B1 **Adavale** Aust
37C2 **Adda** *R* Italy
67E1 **Ad Dahna'** Region, S Arabia
66D4 **Ad Dālī'** Yemen
67F1 **Ad Damman** S Arabia
66D3 **Ad Darb** S Arabia
66D2 **Ad Dawādimī** S Arabia
67E1 **Ad Dibdibah** Region, S Arabia
67F3 **Ad Dikākah** Region, S Arabia
67E2 **Ad Dilam** S Arabia
67E2 **Ad Dir'iyah** S Arabia
66C4 **Addis Zeman** Eth
64D3 **Ad Diwaniyah** Iraq
64D3 **Ad Duwayd** S Arabia
11D3 **Adel** USA
76C4 **Adelaide** Aust
6J3 **Adelaide Pen** Can
51G8 **Adelaide River** Aust
20D3 **Adelanto** USA
Aden = 'Adan
58C4 **Aden,G of** Yemen/Somalia
70C3 **Aderbissinat** Niger
65D2 **Adhra** Syria
51G7 **Adi** *I* Indon
40C1 **Adige** *R* Italy
72D2 **Adigrat** Eth
66C4 **Adi Kale** Eth
60D5 **Adilābād** India
18B2 **Adin** USA
13E2 **Adirondack Mts** USA
72D3 **Ādīs Ābeba** Eth
72D2 **Adi Ugai** Eth
64C2 **Adiyaman** Turk
41F1 **Adjud** Rom
10G1 **Admiralty B** USA
6E4 **Admiralty I** USA
7K2 **Admiralty Inlet** *B* Can
76D1 **Admiralty Is** PNG
57B4 **Adonara** *I* Indon
62B1 **Ādoni** India
38B3 **Adour** *R* France
70A2 **Adrar** Region, Maur
70C2 **Adrar** *Mts* Alg
70A2 **Adrar Soutouf** Region, Mor
72C2 **Adré** Chad
69A2 **Adri** Libya
37E2 **Adria** Italy

12C2 **Adrian** Michigan, USA
16B2 **Adrian** Texas, USA
40C2 **Adriatic S** Italy/Yugos
72D2 **Adwa** Eth
49P3 **Adycha** *R* Russian Fed
71F4 **Adzopé** Ivory Coast
44K2 **Adz'va** *R* Russian Fed
44K2 **Adz'vavom** Russian Fed
41E3 **Aegean** *S* Greece
58E2 **Afghanistan** Republic, Asia
72E3 **Afgooye** Somalia
66D2 **'Afif** S Arabia
71H4 **Afikpo** Nig
32G6 **Åfjord** Nor
71C2 **Aflou** Alg
72E3 **Afmado** Somalia
70A3 **Afollé** Region, Maur
14C1 **Afton** New York, USA
18D2 **Afton** Wyoming, USA
65C2 **Afula** Israel
45E8 **Afyon** Turk
65A3 **Aga** Egypt
72B2 **Agadem** Niger
70C3 **Agadez** Niger
70B1 **Agadir** Mor
60D4 **Agar** India
61D3 **Agartala** India
18B1 **Agassiz** Can
10A6 **Agattu** *I* USA
10A5 **Agattu Str** USA
71H4 **Agbor** Nig
71F4 **Agboville** Ivory Coast
64E1 **Agdam** Azerbaijan
54C3 **Agematsu** Japan
38C3 **Agen** France
63B2 **Āghā Jārī** Iran
45G8 **Ağn** Turk
37D2 **Agno** *R* Italy
66C3 **Agordat** Eth
37E1 **Agordo** Italy
71G4 **Agou,Mt** Togo
38C3 **Agout** *R* France
60D3 **Agra** India
64D2 **Ağri** Turk
40D2 **Agri** *R* Italy
40C3 **Agrigento** Italy
41E3 **Agrínion** Greece
28A3 **Agrio** *R* Chile
40C2 **Agropoli** Italy
44J4 **Agryz** Russian Fed
7N3 **Agto** Greenland
29B3 **Agua Clara** Brazil
28B4 **Aguada de Guerra** Arg
23D3 **Aguadilla** Puerto Rico

Aguado Cicilio   Al Qardāhah

28B4 Aguado Cicilio Arg
22B1 Aguanava R Mexico
5J3 Aguanish Can
5J3 Aguanus R Can
28D1 Aguapey R Arg
21B1 Agua Prieta Mexico
29A3 Aguaray Guazu Par
21B2 Aguascalientes Mexico
22B1 Aguascalientes State, Mexico
29D2 Aguas Formosas Brazil
25G1 Agua Vermelha, Barragem Res Brazil
39A1 Agueda Port
70C3 Aguelhok Mali
70A2 Agüenit Well Mor
39B2 Aguilas Spain
22B2 Aguililla Mexico
xxviiiC7 Agulhas Basin Indian O
73C7 Agulhas,C S Africa
xxviiiC6 Agulhas Plat Indian O
57G9 Agusan R Phil
Ahaggar = Hoggar
45H8 Ahar Iran
78B1 Ahipara B NZ
36D1 Ahlen Germany
60C4 Ahmadābād India
62A1 Ahmadnagar India
72E3 Ahmar Mts Eth
15D1 Ahoskie USA
36D1 Ahr R Germany
36D1 Ahrgebirge Region, Germany
22B1 Ahuacatlán Mexico
22B1 Ahualulco Mexico
32G7 Åhus Sweden
63C1 Ahuvān Iran
63B2 Ahvāz Iran
23A4 Aiajuela Costa Rica
37B1 Aigle Switz
28E2 Aiguá Urug
37B2 Aiguille d'Arves Mt France
37B2 Aiguille de la Grand Sassière Mt France
53B1 Aihui China
54C3 Aikawa Japan
15C2 Aiken USA
52A5 Ailao Shan Upland China
28B1 Aimogasta Arg
29D2 Aimorés Brazil
37A1 Ain R France
71D1 Aïn Beïda Alg
71B2 Aïn Beni Mathar Mor
69B2 Ain Dalla Well Egypt
39C2 Aïn el Hadjel Alg
72B2 Aïn Galakka Chad
71C1 Aïn Oussera Alg
71B2 Aïn Sefra Alg
64B4 'Ain Sukhna Egypt
11C3 Ainsworth USA
71B1 Aïn Temouchent Alg
54B4 Aioi Japan
70B2 Aioun Abd el Malek Well Maur
70B3 Aïoun El Atrouss Maur
26E7 Aiquile Bol
70C3 Aïr Desert Region Niger
3F3 Airdrie Can
36B1 Aire France
35E5 Aire R Eng
36C2 Aire R France
7L3 Airforce I Can
37C1 Airolo Switz
6E3 Aishihik Can
10L3 Aishihik L Can
36B2 Aisne Department, France
38C2 Aisne R France
76D1 Aitape PNG
43F1 Aiviekste R Latvia
52B2 Aixa Zuogi China
38D3 Aix-en-Provence France
37A2 Aix-les-Bains France
61C3 Aiyar Res India
41E3 Aíyion Greece
41E3 Aíyna I Greece
61D3 Āīzawl India
73B6 Aizeb R Namibia
53E4 Aizu-Wakamatsu Japan
40B2 Ajaccio Corse
22C2 Ajalpan Mexico
69B1 Ajdabiyak Libya
37E2 Ajdovščina Slovenia, Yugos
53E3 Ajigasawa Japan
65C2 Ajlūn Jordan
67G1 Ajman UAE
60C3 Ajmer India
19D4 Ajo USA
41F2 Ajtos Bulg
22B2 Ajuchitan Mexico
41F3 Ak R Turk
54D2 Akabira Japan
54C3 Akaishi-sanchi Mts Japan
62B1 Akalkot India
65B1 Akanthou Cyprus
78B2 Akaroa NZ
66B2 Akasha Sudan
54B4 Akashi Japan
71C1 Akbou Alg
45K5 Akbulak Russian Fed
64C2 Akçakale Turk
70A2 Akchar Watercourse Maur
41F3 Ak Dağ Mt Turk
57C2 Akelamo Indon
72C3 Aketi Zaïre
64D1 Akhalkalaki Georgia
64D1 Akhalsikhe Georgia
41E3 Akharnái Greece
10H4 Akhiok USA
64A2 Akhisar Turk
43F1 Akhiste Latvia
69C2 Akhmîm Egypt
45H6 Akhtubinsk Russian Fed
45E5 Akhtyrka Ukraine
54B4 Aki Japan
7K4 Akimiski I Can
53E4 Akita Japan
70A3 Akjoujt Maur
65C2 'Akko Israel
10L2 Aklavik Can
70B3 Aklé Aouana Desert Region Maur
72D3 Akobo Sudan
72D3 Akobo R Sudan
60B1 Akoha Afghan
60D4 Akola India
71G4 Akosombo Dam Ghana
60D4 Akot India
7M3 Akpatok I Can
41E3 Ákra Kafirévs C Greece
41E4 Ákra Líthinon C Greece
41E3 Ákra Maléa C Greece
32A2 Akranes Iceland
41F3 Ákra Sídheros C Greece
41E3 Ákra Spátha C Greece
41E3 Ákra Taínaron C Greece
9E2 Akron USA
65B1 Akrotiri B Cyprus
60D1 Aksai Chin Mts China
45E8 Aksaray Turk
45J5 Aksay Kazakhstan
60D1 Aksayquin Hu L China
64B2 Akşehir Turk
64B2 Akseki Turk
49N4 Aksenovo Zilovskoye Russian Fed
50E1 Aksha Russian Fed
59G1 Aksu China
66C4 Aksum Eth
48J5 Aktogay Kazakhstan
45K6 Aktumsyk Kazakhstan
45K5 Aktyubinsk Kazakhstan
4F1 Akulivik Can
71H4 Akure Nig
32B1 Akureyri Iceland
10E5 Akutan USA
10E5 Akutan I USA
10E5 Akutan Pass USA
71H5 Akwa Ibom State Nigeria
48K5 Akzhal Kazakhstan
9E3 Alabama State, USA
15B2 Alabama R USA
15B2 Alabaster USA
64C2 Ala Dağlari Mts Turk
45G7 Alagir Russian Fed
37B2 Alagna Italy
27L5 Alagoas State, Brazil
27L6 Alagoinhas Brazil
39B1 Alagón Spain
64E4 Al Ahmadi Kuwait
21D3 Alajuela Costa Rica
10F3 Alakanuk USA
48K5 Alakol, Ozero L Russian Fed/Kazakhstan
32L5 Alakurtti Russian Fed
64E3 Al Amārah Iraq
19B3 Alameda USA
22C1 Alamo Mexico
19C3 Alamo USA
16A3 Alamogordo USA
16C4 Alamo Heights USA
16A2 Alamosa USA
32H6 Åland I Fin
45E8 Alanya Turk
15C2 Alapaha R USA
44L4 Alapayevsk Russian Fed
56A2 Alas R Indon
64A2 Alaşehir Turk
50D3 Ala Shan Mts China
6C3 Alaska State, USA
6D4 Alaska,G of USA
10G4 Alaska Pen USA
6C3 Alaska Range Mts USA
40B2 Alassio Italy
37C3 Alássio Region, Italy
10H2 Alatna R USA
44H5 Alatyr' Russian Fed
75B2 Alawoona Aust
67G2 Al'Ayn UAE
59F2 Alayskiy Khrebet Mts Tajikistan
49R3 Alazeya R Russian Fed
71E2 Al'Azīzīyah Libya
38D3 Alba Italy
64C2 Al Bāb Syria
39B2 Albacete Spain
39A1 Alba de Tormes Spain
64D2 Al Badi Iraq
41E1 Alba Iulia Rom
41D2 Albania Republic, Europe
76A4 Albany Aust
15C2 Albany Georgia, USA
12B3 Albany Kentucky, USA
13E2 Albany New York, USA
8A2 Albany Oregon, USA
4E3 Albany R Can
66C4 Albara R Sudan
28B2 Albardón Arg
67G2 Al Batinah Region, Oman
51H8 Albatross B Aust
69B1 Al Bayḍā Libya
67E4 Al Bayḍā' Yemen
65C1 Al Baylūlīyah Syria
15C1 Albemarle USA
15D1 Albemarle Sd USA
37C2 Albenga Region, Italy
39B1 Alberche R Spain
75A1 Alberga Aust
36B1 Albert France
6G4 Alberta Province, Can
51H7 Albert Edward Mt PNG
74C3 Albertinia S Africa
72D3 Albert,L Uganda/Zaïre
9D2 Albert Lea USA
72D3 Albert Nile R Uganda
18D1 Alberton USA
5J4 Alberton Can
38D2 Albertville France
38C3 Albi France
17D1 Albia USA
27H2 Albina Surinam
12C2 Albion Michigan, USA
11C3 Albion Nebraska, USA
13D2 Albion New York, USA
64C4 Al Bi'r S Arabia
66D3 Al Birk S Arabia
67E2 Al Biyadh Region, S Arabia
39B2 Alborán I Spain
32G7 Ålborg Den
36E2 Albstadt-Ebingen Germany
64D3 Al Bū Kamāl Syria
37C1 Albula R Switz
8C3 Albuquerque USA
67G2 Al Buraymi Oman
69A1 Al Burayqah
69B1 Al Burdī Libya
76D4 Albury Aust
64E3 Al Buşayyah Iraq
34G3 Albuskjell Oilfield N Sea
67F3 Al Buzūn Yemen
39B1 Alcalá de Henares Spain
40C3 Alcamo Italy
39B1 Alcaniz Spain
27K4 Alcântara Brazil
39B2 Alcaraz Spain
39B2 Alcázar de San Juan Spain
39B2 Alcira Spain
29E2 Alcobaça Brazil
39B1 Alcolea de Pinar Spain
39B2 Alcoy Spain
39C2 Alcudia Spain
68J8 Aldabra Is Indian O
16A4 Aldama Mexico
22C1 Aldama Mexico
49O4 Aldan Russian Fed
49P4 Aldan R Russian Fed
49O4 Aldanskoye Nagor'ye Upland Russian Fed
35F5 Aldeburgh Eng
38B2 Alderney I UK
35E6 Aldershot Eng
70A3 Aleg Maur
29A2 Alegre R Brazil
25E3 Alegrete Brazil
28C2 Alejandro Roca Arg
49O4 Aleksandrovsk Sakhalinskiy Russian Fed
48J4 Alekseyevka Kazakhstan
44F5 Aleksin Russian Fed
42D1 Ålem Sweden
29D3 Além Paraíba Brazil
38C2 Alençon France
20E5 Alenuihaha Chan Hawaiian Is
Aleppo = Ḥalab
7M1 Alert Can
38C3 Alès France
40B2 Alessandria Italy
48B3 Ålesund Nor
10B5 Aleutian Is USA
10G4 Aleutian Range Mts USA
xxixL2 Aleutian Trench Pacific O
6E4 Alexander Arch USA
74B2 Alexander Bay S Africa
15B2 Alexander City USA
79G3 Alexander I Ant
78A3 Alexandra NZ
25J8 Alexandra,C South Georgia
7L2 Alexandra Fjord Can
69B1 Alexandria Egypt
9D3 Alexandria Louisiana, USA
9D2 Alexandria Minnesota, USA
9F3 Alexandria Virginia, USA
41F2 Alexandroúpolis Greece
5K3 Alexis R Can
3D3 Alexis Creek Can
65C2 Aley Leb
48K4 Aleysk Russian Fed
64D3 Al Fallūjah Iraq
67E4 Al Fardah Yemen
39B1 Alfaro Spain
41F2 Alfatar Bulg
64E3 Al Fāw Iraq
36E1 Alfeld Germany
29C3 Alfensas Brazil
41E3 Alfiós R Greece
37D2 Alfonsine Italy
29D3 Alfonzo Cláudio Brazil
29D3 Alfredo Chaves Brazil
67E1 Al Furūthi S Arabia
45K6 Alga Kazakhstan
28A1 Algarrobal Chile
28B3 Algarrobo del Águila Arg
39A2 Algeciras Spain
71C1 Alger Alg
70B2 Algeria Republic, Africa
67F3 Al Ghaydah Yemen
40B2 Alghero Sardegna
Algiers = Alger
11D3 Algona USA
13D1 Algonquin Park Can
4F4 Algonquin Prov Park Can
28D2 Algorta Urug
67G2 Al Hadd Oman
64D3 Al Hadithah Iraq
64C3 Al Hadithah S Arabia
64D2 Al Haḍr Iraq
65D1 Al Haffah Syria
67G2 Al Hajar al Gharbī Mts Oman
67G2 Al Hajar ash Sharqī Mts Oman
64C3 Al Hamad Desert Region Jordan/S Arabia
64E4 Al Haniyah Desert Region Iraq
67E2 Al Harīq S Arabia
64C3 Al Harrah Desert Region S Arabia
69A2 Al Harūj al Aswad Upland Libya
67E1 Al Hasa Region, S Arabia
64D2 Al Hasakah Syria
64C4 Al Hawjā' S Arabia
64E3 Al Hayy Iraq
67F2 Al Hibāk Region, S Arabia
65D2 Al Hījānah Syria
64D3 Al Hillah Iraq
67E2 Al Hillah S Arabia
71B1 Al Hoceima Mor
66D4 Al Hudaydah Yemen
67E1 Al Hufūf S Arabia
67F2 Al Humrah Region, UAE
67G2 Al Huwatsah Oman
63B1 Alīābad Iran
63D3 Aliabad Iran
41E2 Aliákmon R Greece
64E3 Alī al Gharbī Iraq
62A1 Alībāg India
71B3 Alibori R Benin
39B2 Alicante Spain
8D4 Alice USA
76C3 Alice Springs Aust
40C3 Alicudi I Italy
60D3 Aligarh India
63B2 Aligūdarz Iran
60B2 Ali-Khel Afghan
41F3 Alimniá I Greece
61C2 Alīpur Duār India
12C2 Aliquippa USA
67E4 Al'Irqah Yemen
64C3 Al'Īsawiyah S Arabia
74D3 Aliwal North S Africa
69B2 Al Jaghbūb Libya
64D3 Al Jālamīd S Arabia
69B2 Al Jawf Libya
64C4 Al Jawf S Arabia
45G8 Al Jazīrah Syria
64D2 Al Jazīrah Desert Region Syria/Iraq
39A2 Aljezur Port
67E1 Al Jubayl S Arabia
65D4 Al Kabid Desert Jordan
66D1 Al Kahfah S Arabia
67G2 Al Kāmil Oman
64D2 Al Khābūr R Syria
67G2 Al Khābūrah Oman
64D3 Al Khālis Iraq
66D2 Al Khamāsīn S Arabia
67G1 Al Khasab Oman
67F1 Al Khawr Qatar
69A1 Al Khums Libya
67F2 Al Kidan Region, S Arabia
65D2 Al Kiswah Syria
42A2 Alkmaar Neth
69B2 Al Kufrah Oasis Libya
64E3 Al Kūt Iraq
64C2 Al Lādhiqīyah Syria
61B2 Allahābād India
65D2 Al Lajāh Mt Syria
10H2 Allakaket USA
55B2 Allanmyo Burma
66B2 'Allaqi Watercourse Egypt
15C2 Allatoona L USA
74D1 Alldays S Africa
13D2 Allegheny R USA
9F3 Allegheny Mts USA
14A2 Allegheny Res USA
15C2 Allendale USA
78A3 Allen,Mt NZ
13D2 Allentown USA
62B3 Alleppey India
38C2 Aller R France
37D1 Allgäu Mts Germany
11B3 Alliance USA
66D2 Al Līth S Arabia
67F2 Al Liwā Region, UAE
75D1 Allora Aust
37B2 Allos France
12C2 Alma Michigan, USA
16C1 Alma Nebraska, USA
59F1 Alma Ata Kazakhstan
39A2 Almada Port
Al Madīnah = Medina S Arabia
51H5 Almagan I Pacific O
67F3 Al Mahrah Region, Yemen
67E1 Al Majma'ah S Arabia
67F1 Al Manāmah Bahrain
64D3 Al Ma'nīyah Iraq
19B2 Almanor,L USA
39B2 Almansa Spain
3C2 Alma Peak Mt Can
67F2 Al Māriyyah UAE
5G4 Alma Can
69B1 Al Marj Libya
39B1 Almazán Spain
36E1 Alme R Germany
29D2 Almenara Brazil
39B2 Almeria Spain
29C2 Almes R Brazil
44J5 Al'met'yevsk Russian Fed
42C1 Älmhult Sweden
66D1 Al Midhnab S Arabia
64E3 Al Miqdādīyah Iraq
79G3 Almirante Brown Base Ant
28A1 Almirante Latorre Chile
41E3 Almirós Greece
67E1 Al Mish'ab A Arabia
39A2 Almodôvar Port
60D3 Almora India
67E1 Al Mubarraz S Arabia
64C4 Al Mudawwara Jordan
67G2 Al Mudaybi Oman
67F1 Al Muharraq Bahrain
67E4 Al Mukallā Yemen
66D4 Al Mukhā Yemen
64D3 Al Musayyib Iraq
66C1 Al Muwaylih S Arabia
34C3 Alness Scot
64E3 Al Nu'mānīyah Iraq
34E4 Alnwick Eng
4B3 Alonsa Can
57B4 Alor I Indon
55C4 Alor Setar Malay
Alost = Aalst
76E2 Alotau PNG
76B3 Aloysius,Mt Aust
28C3 Alpachiri Arg
37D2 Alpe di Succiso Mt Italy
12C1 Alpena USA
37B1 Alpes du Valais Mts Switz
37B2 Alpes Maritimes Mts France
37E1 Alpi Carniche Mts Italy
40C1 Alpi Dolomitiche Mts Italy
37B2 Alpi Graie Mts Italy
19E4 Alpine Arizona, USA
16B3 Alpine Texas, USA
18D2 Alpine Wyoming, USA
37C1 Alpi Orobie Mts Italy
37B2 Alpi Penine Mts Italy
37C1 Alpi Retiche Mts Switz
37D1 Alpi Venoste Mts Italy
40B1 Alps Mts Europe
69A1 Al Qaddāhiyah Libya
65D1 Al Qadmūs Syria
64D3 Al Qā'im Iraq
64C4 Al Qalībah S Arabia
64D2 Al Qāmishlī Syria
65D1 Al Qardāhah Syria

Al Qaryah Ash Sharqiyah

Arad

69A1 **Al Qaryah Ash Sharqiyah** Libya
64C3 **Al Qaryatayn** Syria
66D1 **Al Qasīm** Region, S Arabia
67E1 **Al Qātif** S Arabia
69A2 **Al Qatrūn** Libya
67E1 **Al Qayṣāmah** S Arabia
65D2 **Al Quatayfah** Syria
39A2 **Alquera** *Res* Port/Spain
64C3 **Al Qunayṭirah** Syria
66D3 **Al Qunfidhah** S Arabia
64E3 **Al Qurnah** Iraq
65D1 **Al Quṣayr** Syria
64C3 **Al Qutayfah** Syria
67E2 **Al Quwayīyah** S Arabia
42B1 **Als** *I* Den
38D2 **Alsace** Region, France
42B2 **Alsfeld** Germany
34D4 **Alston** Eng
32J5 **Alta** Nor
25D4 **Alta Gracia** Arg
23D5 **Altagracia de Orituco** Ven
50B2 **Altai** *Mts* Mongolia
15C2 **Altamaha** *R* USA
27H4 **Altamira** Brazil
22C1 **Altamira** Mexico
40D2 **Altamura** Italy
50D1 **Altanbulag** Mongolia
49M5 **Altanbulag** Russian Fed
51H7 **Altape** PNG
21B2 **Altata** Mexico
48K5 **Altay** China
49L5 **Altay** Mongolia
48K4 **Altay** *Mts* Russian Fed
37C1 **Altdorf** Switz
36D1 **Altenkirchen** Germany
28B3 **Altiplanicie del Payún** *Plat* Arg
37B1 **Altkirch** France
29B2 **Alto Araguaia** Brazil
73D5 **Alto Molócue** Mozam
12A3 **Alton** USA
13D2 **Altoona** USA
28B2 **Alto Pencoso** *Mts* Arg
29B2 **Alto Sucuriú** Brazil
22C2 **Altotonga** Mexico
22B2 **Altoyac de Alvarez** Mexico
59G2 **Altun Shan** *Mts* China
18B2 **Alturas** USA
16C3 **Altus** USA
67F2 **Al'Ubaylah** S Arabia
66C1 **Al'Ulā** S Arabia
28A3 **Aluminé** Arg
64C4 **Al Urayq** *Desert Region* S Arabia
67F2 **Al'Uruq al Mu'taridah** Region, S Arabia
16C2 **Alva** USA
22C2 **Alvarado** Mexico
17C3 **Alvarado** USA
32G6 **Älvdalen** Sweden
28D1 **Alvear** Arg
17C4 **Alvin** USA
32J5 **Alvsbyn** Sweden
69A2 **Al Wāha** Libya
66C1 **Al Wajh** S Arabia
60D3 **Alwar** India
64D3 **Al Widyān** *Desert Region* Iraq/S Arabia
52A2 **Alxa Yougi** China
64E2 **Alyat** Azerbaijan
32J8 **Alytus** Lithuania
36E2 **Alzey** Germany
22C2 **Amacuzac** *R* Mexico
72D3 **Amadi** Sudan
64D2 **Amādīyah** Iraq
7L3 **Amadjuak L** Can
57C3 **Amahai** Indon
53B5 **Amakusa-shotō** *I* Japan
32G7 **Åmål** Sweden
49N4 **Amalat** *R* Russian Fed
41E3 **Amaliás** Greece
60C4 **Amalner** India
29A3 **Amambai** Brazil
29B3 **Amambai** *R* Brazil
50F4 **Amami** *I* Japan
50F4 **Amami gunto** *Arch* Japan
27H3 **Amapá** Brazil
27H3 **Amapá** State, Brazil
4B3 **Amaranth** Can
61E3 **Amarapura** Burma
16B2 **Amarillo** USA
45F7 **Amasya** Turk
22B1 **Amatitan** Mexico
22C1 **Amaulipas** Mexico
Amazonas = Solimões
27H4 **Amazonas** Brazil
26E4 **Amazonas** State, Brazil
24D4 **Amazonas** *R* Brazil
60D2 **Ambāla** India
62C3 **Ambalangoda** Sri Lanka
73E6 **Ambalavao** Madag
72B3 **Ambam** Cam
73E5 **Ambanja** Madag
49S3 **Ambarchik** Russian Fed
26C4 **Ambato** Ecuador
73E5 **Ambato-Boeny** Madag
73E5 **Ambatolampy** Madag
73E5 **Ambatondrazaka** Madag
42C3 **Amberg** Germany
21D3 **Ambergris Cay** *I* Belize
37A2 **Ambérieu** France
61B3 **Ambikāpur** India
73E5 **Ambilobe** Madag
73E6 **Amboasary** Madag
73E5 **Ambodifototra** Madag
73E6 **Ambohimahasoa** Madag
57C3 **Ambon** Indon
57C3 **Ambon** *I* Indon
73E6 **Ambositra** Madag
73E6 **Ambovombe** Madag
73B4 **Ambriz** Angola
77F2 **Ambrym** *I* Vanuatu
10B6 **Amchitka** USA
10B6 **Amchitka** *I* USA
10C6 **Amchitka Pass** USA
72C2 **Am Dam** Chad
44L2 **Amderma** Russian Fed
21B2 **Ameca** Mexico
22A1 **Ameca** *R* Mexico
22C2 **Amecacameca** Mexico
28C2 **Ameghino** Arg
42B2 **Ameland** *I* Neth
14D2 **Amenia** USA
18D2 **American Falls** USA
18D2 **American Falls Res** USA
19D2 **American Fork** USA
79F10 **American Highland** *Upland* Ant
xxixL5 **American Samoa** *Is* Pacific O
15C2 **Americus** USA
42B2 **Amersfoort** Neth
74D2 **Amersfoort** S Africa
11D2 **Amery** USA
79G10 **Amery Ice Shelf** Ant
11D3 **Ames** USA
14E1 **Amesbury** USA
4E4 **Ameson** Can
41E3 **Amfilokhía** Greece
41E3 **Amfissa** Greece
49P3 **Amga** Russian Fed
49P3 **Amgal** *R* Russian Fed
53D2 **Amgu** Russian Fed
10C2 **Amguema** *R* Russian Fed
53D1 **Amgun'** *R* Russian Fed
72D2 **Amhara** *Region* Eth
7M5 **Amherst** Can
14D1 **Amherst** Massachusetts, USA
13D3 **Amherst** Virginia, USA
62B2 **Amhūr** India
38C2 **Amiens** France
54C3 **Amino** Japan
65C1 **Amioune** Leb
68K8 **Amirante Is** Indian O
3H3 **Amisk L** Can
16B4 **Amistad Res** Mexico
61C2 **Amlekhgan** Nepal
10D6 **Amlia** *I* USA
64C3 **Amman** Jordan
32K6 **Ämmänsaario** Fin
54A3 **Amnyong-dan** *C* N Korea
63C1 **Amol** Iran
7L5 **Amos** Can
Amoy = Xiamen
57B3 **Ampana** Indon
73E6 **Ampanihy** Madag
29C3 **Amparo** Brazil
39C1 **Amposta** Spain
5H4 **Amqui** Can
66D3 **Amrān** Yemen
60D4 **Amrāvati** India
60C4 **Amreli** India
60C2 **Amritsar** India
42A2 **Amsterdam** Neth
74E2 **Amsterdam** S Africa
13E2 **Amsterdam** USA
72C2 **Am Timan** Chad
48H5 **Amu Darya** *R* Uzbekistan
10D6 **Amukta** *I* USA
10D6 **Amukta Pass** USA
7J2 **Amund Ringnes I** Can
6F2 **Amundsen G** Can
79F4 **Amundsen S** Ant
79E **Amundsen-Scott** *Base* Ant
56E3 **Amuntai** Indon
49O4 **Amur** *R* Russian Fed
66C3 **Amur** *Watercourse* Sudan
57B2 **Amurang** Indon
53D1 **Amursk** Russian Fed
53E1 **Amurskiy Liman** *Str* Russian Fed
53C2 **Amurzet** Russian Fed
49N2 **Anabar** *R* Russian Fed
26F2 **Anaco** Ven
8B2 **Anaconda** USA
18B1 **Anacortes** USA
16C2 **Anadarko** USA
49T3 **Anadyr'** Russian Fed
49T3 **Anadyr'** *R* Russian Fed
49U3 **Anadyrskiy Zaliv** *S* Russian Fed
49T3 **Anadyrskoye Ploskogor'ye** *Plat* Russian Fed
41F3 **Anáfi** *I* Greece
29D1 **Anagé** Brazil
64D3 **'Ānah** Iraq
19C4 **Anaheim** USA
62B2 **Anaimalai Hills** India
62C1 **Anakāpalle** India
10J2 **Anaktuvuk P** USA
73E5 **Analalaya** Madag
71H4 **Anambra** *State* Nig
71H4 **Anambra** *R* Nig
12A2 **Anamosa** USA
45E8 **Anamur** Turk
54B4 **Anan** Japan
62B2 **Anantapur** India
60D2 **Anantnag** India
27J7 **Anápolis** Brazil
63D2 **Anār** Iran
63C2 **Anārak** Iran
63E2 **Anardara** Afghan
51H5 **Anatahan** *I* Pacific O
25D3 **Añatuya** Arg
53B4 **Anbyŏn** N Korea
20C4 **Ancapa Is** USA
28B1 **Ancasti** Arg
6D3 **Anchorage** USA
26E7 **Ancohuma** *Mt* Bol
26C6 **Ancón** Peru
40C2 **Ancona** Italy
14D1 **Ancram** USA
25B6 **Ancud** Chile
36C3 **Ancy-le-Franc** France
26D6 **Andabuaylas** Peru
28A3 **Andacollo** Arg
75A1 **Andado** Aust
28B1 **Andagalá** Arg
32F6 **Andalsnes** Nor
39A2 **Andalucia** Region, Spain
15B2 **Andalusia** USA
59H4 **Andaman Is** Burma
59H4 **Andaman S** Burma
75A2 **Andamooka** Aust
29D1 **Andaraí** Brazil
35B5 **Andee** Irish Rep
36C2 **Andelot** France
32H5 **Andenes** Nor
37C1 **Andermatt** Switz
42B2 **Andernach** Germany
12B2 **Anderson** Indiana, USA
17D2 **Anderson** Missouri, USA
15C2 **Anderson** S Carolina, USA
6F3 **Anderson** *R* Can
62B1 **Andhra Pradesh** State, India
41E3 **Andikíthira** *I* Greece
48J5 **Andizhan** Uzbekistan
48H6 **Andkhui** Afghan
53B4 **Andong** S Korea
39C1 **Andorra** Principality, SW Europe
39C1 **Andorra-La-Vella** Andorra
35E6 **Andover** Eng
14E1 **Andover** New Hampshire, USA
14B1 **Andover** New York, USA
29B3 **Andradina** Brazil
10F3 **Andreafsky** USA
10C6 **Andreanof Is** USA
43G1 **Andreapol'** Russian Fed
64B2 **Andreas,C** Cyprus
16B3 **Andrews** USA
40D2 **Andria** Italy
9F4 **Andros** *I* Bahamas
41E3 **Ándros** *I* Greece
62A2 **Androth** *I* India
39B2 **Andújar** Spain
73B5 **Andulo** Angola
71G4 **Anécho** Togo
70C3 **Anéfis** Mali
77F3 **Aneityum** *I* Vanuatu
28B3 **Añelo** Arg
66C4 **Angareb** *Watercourse* Eth
49M4 **Angarsk** Russian Fed
44A3 **Ånge** Sweden
21A2 **Angel de la Guarda** *I* Mexico
57F7 **Angeles** Phil
32G7 **Angelholm** Sweden
75C1 **Angellala Creek** *R* Aust
20B1 **Angels Camp** USA
51G7 **Angemuk** *Mt* Indon
38B2 **Angers** France
36B2 **Angerville** France
55C3 **Angkor** *Hist Site* Camb
33C3 **Anglesey** *I* Wales
17C4 **Angleton** USA
7P3 **Angmagssalik** Greenland
73E5 **Angoche** Mozam
25B5 **Angol** Chile
12C2 **Angola** Indiana, USA
14A1 **Angola** New York, USA
73B5 **Angola** Republic, Africa
xxxJ5 **Angola Basin** Atlantic O
10M4 **Angoon** USA
38C2 **Angoulême** France
70A1 **Angra do Heroismo** Açores
29D3 **Angra dos Reis** Brazil
28C3 **Anguil** Arg
23E3 **Anguilla** *I* Caribbean
23B2 **Anguilla Cays** *Is* Caribbean
61C3 **Angul** India
72C4 **Angumu** Zaïre
42C1 **Anholt** *I* Den
52C4 **Anhua** China
52D3 **Anhui** Province, China
29B2 **Anhumas** Brazil
54A3 **Anhŭng** S Korea
10G3 **Aniak** USA
29C2 **Anicuns** Brazil
71G4 **Anié** Togo
16A2 **Animas** *R* USA
16A3 **Animas Peak** *Mt* USA
11D3 **Anita** USA
36B2 **Anizy-le-Château** France
38B2 **Anjou** Republic, France
73E5 **Anjouan** *I* Comoros
73E5 **Anjozorobe** Madag
53B4 **Anju** N Korea
52B3 **Ankang** China
45E8 **Ankara** Turk
73E5 **Ankaratra** *Mt* Madag
73E6 **Ankazoabo** Madag
73E5 **Ankazobe** Madag
11D3 **Ankeny** USA
42C2 **Anklam** Germany
71H4 **Ankwe** *R* Nig
55D3 **An Loc** Viet
52B4 **Anlong** China
52C3 **Anlu** China
12B3 **Anna** USA
71D1 **'Annaba** Alg
64C3 **An Nabk** S Arabia
64C3 **An Nabk** Syria
75A1 **Anna Creek** Aust
69B2 **An Nāfūrah** Libya
64D3 **An Najaf** Iraq
34D4 **Annan** Scot
13D3 **Annapolis** USA
61B2 **Annapurna** *Mt* Nepal
12C2 **Ann Arbor** USA
65D1 **An Nāsirah** Syria
64E3 **An Nāsirīyah** Iraq
37B2 **Annecy** France
37B1 **Annemasse** France
3B2 **Annette I** USA
55D3 **An Nhon** Viet
66D3 **An Nimās** S Arabia
52A5 **Anning** China
15B2 **Anniston** USA
70C4 **Annobon, I** Eq Guinea
38C2 **Annonay** France
37B3 **Annot** France
23J1 **Annotto Bay** Jamaica
52D3 **Anqing** China
52B2 **Ansai** China
42C3 **Ansbach** Germany
23C3 **Anse d'Hainault** Haiti
52E1 **Anshan** China
52B4 **Anshun** China
16C1 **Ansley** USA
16C3 **Anson** USA
51F8 **Anson B** Aust
70C3 **Ansongo** Mali
12C1 **Ansonville** Can
12C3 **Ansted** USA
45F8 **Antakya** Turk
73F5 **Antalaha** Madag
45E8 **Antalya** Turk
45E8 **Antalya Körfezi** *B* Turk
73E5 **Antananarivo** Madag
79G1 **Antarctic Circle** Ant
79G3 **Antarctic Pen** Ant
39B2 **Antequera** Spain
16A3 **Anthony** USA
70B1 **Anti-Atlas** *Mts* Mor
37B3 **Antibes** France
7M5 **Anticosti, Î d'** Can
5J4 **Anticosti Prov Park** Can
12B1 **Antigo** USA
23E3 **Antigua** *I* Caribbean
Anti Lebanon = Jebel esh Sharqi
19B3 **Antioch** USA
77G5 **Antipodes Is** NZ
17C3 **Antlers** USA
25B2 **Antofagasta** Chile
29C4 **Antonina** Brazil
16A2 **Antonito** USA
34B4 **Antrim** County, N Ire
34B4 **Antrim** N Ire
14E1 **Antrim** USA
34B4 **Antrim Hills** N Ire
73E5 **Antseranana** Madag
73E5 **Antsirabe** Madag
73E5 **Antsohiny** Madag
55D3 **An Tuc** Viet
28C1 **Añtuya** Arg
36C1 **Antwerpen** Belg
35B5 **An Uaimh** Irish Rep
54A3 **Anui** S Korea
60C3 **Anupgarh** India
62C3 **Anuradhapura** Sri Lanka
Anvers = Antwerpen
6B3 **Anvik** USA
10B6 **Anvil Pk** *Mt* USA
49L5 **Anxi** China
52C2 **Anyang** China
52A3 **A'nyêmaqên Shan** *Upland* China
49S3 **Anyuysk** Russian Fed
37C2 **Anza** *R* Italy
3F2 **Anzac** Can
48K4 **Anzhero-Sudzhensk** Russian Fed
40C2 **Anzio** Italy
77F2 **Aoba** *I* Vanuatu
53E3 **Aomori** Japan
40B1 **Aosta** Italy
70B3 **Aoukar** *Desert Region* Maur
70C2 **Aoulef** Alg
72B1 **Aozou** Chad
25E2 **Apa** *R* Brazil/Par
9E4 **Apalachee B** USA
15C3 **Apalachicola** USA
15B3 **Apalachicola B** USA
22C2 **Apan** Mexico
26D3 **Apaporis** *R* Colombia
29B3 **Aparecida do Taboado** Brazil
57F7 **Aparri** Phil
41D1 **Apatin** Croatia, Yugos
44E2 **Apatity** Russian Fed
21B3 **Apatzingan** Mexico
42B2 **Apeldoorn** Neth
77H2 **Apia** Western Samoa
29C3 **Apiai** Brazil
22B1 **Apizolaya** Mexico
27G2 **Apoera** Surinam
75B3 **Apollo Bay** Aust
57G9 **Apo,Mt** Phil
15C3 **Apopka,L** USA
27H7 **Aporé** *R* Brazil
12A1 **Apostle Is** USA
22B1 **Apozol** Mexico
9E3 **Appalachian Mts** USA
37D2 **Appenino Tosco-Emiliano** *Mts* Italy
40C2 **Appennino Abruzzese** *Mts* Italy
40B2 **Appennino Ligure** *Mts* Italy
40D2 **Appennino Lucano** *Mts* Italy
40D2 **Appennino Napoletano** *Mts* Italy
40C2 **Appennino Tosco-Emilliano** *Mts* Italy
40C2 **Appennino Umbro-Marchigiano** *Mts* Italy
37C1 **Appenzell** Switz
35D4 **Appleby** Eng
11C2 **Appleton** Minnesota, USA
12B2 **Appleton** Wisconsin, USA
45J7 **Apsheronskiy Poluostrov** *Pen* Azerbaijan
4F5 **Apsley** Can
37A3 **Apt** France
25F2 **Apucarana** Brazil
22C1 **Apulco** Mexico
26E2 **Apure** *R* Ven
26D6 **Apurimac** *R* Peru
64C4 **'Aqaba** Jordan
64B4 **'Aqaba,G of** Egypt/S Arabia
63C2 **'Aqdā** Iran
27G8 **Aqidauana** Brazil
22A1 **Aqua Nueva** Mexico
29A3 **Aquidabán** *R* Par
25E2 **Aquidauana** Brazil
29A2 **Aquidauana** *R* Brazil
22B2 **Aquila** Mexico
61B2 **Ara** India
15B2 **Arab** USA
65C1 **'Arab al Mulk** Syria
58E4 **Arabian** *S* Asia/Arabian Pen
xxviiiE4 **Arabian Basin** Indian O
27L6 **Aracajú** Brazil
25E2 **Aracanguy, Mts de** *Mts* Brazil
29A3 **Aracanguy, Mts de** Par
27L4 **Aracati** Brazil
29D1 **Aracatu** Brazil
27H8 **Araçatuba** Brazil
39A2 **Aracena** Spain
27K7 **Araçuai** Brazil
65C3 **Arad** Israel
45C6 **Arad** Rom

Arada Augustine I

72C2 Arada Chad
67F2 'Arādah UAE
76C1 Arafura S Indon/Aust
27H7 Aragarças Brazil
45G7 Aragats Mt Armenia
39B1 Aragón Region, Spain
39B1 Aragon R Spain
29C1 Araguaçu Brazil
27H6 Araguaia R Brazil
27J5 Araguaína Brazil
27J7 Araguari Brazil
29C2 Araguari R Brazil
54C3 Arai Japan
70C2 Arak Alg
63B2 Arāk Iran
10D3 Arakamchechen, Ostrov Is Russian Fed
55A2 Arakan Yoma Mts Burma
62B2 Arakkonam India
64E2 Araks R Azerbaijan
48H5 Aral'sk Kazakhstan
48G5 Aral'skoye More S Kazakhstan/Uzbekistan
22C1 Aramberri Mexico
33B2 Aran I Irish Rep
39B1 Aranda de Duero Spain
22B1 Arandas Mexico
39B1 Aranjuez Spain
74B1 Aranos Namibia
17F4 Aransas Pass USA
54B4 Arao Japan
70B3 Araouane Mali
16C1 Arapahoe USA
25E4 Arapey R Urug
28D2 Arapey Grande R Urug
27L6 Arapiraca Brazil
29B3 Araporgas Brazil
25G3 Araranguá Brazil
27J8 Araraquara Brazil
29C3 Araras Brazil
76D4 Ararat Aust
64D2 Ararat Armenia
64D1 Aras R Turk
45H8 Aras R Azerbaijan/Iran
66C3 Aratali Eth
54D3 Arato Japan
26E2 Arauca R Ven
28A3 Arauco Chile
26D2 Arauea Colombia
60C3 Arāvalli Range Mts India
77E1 Arawa PNG
27J7 Araxá Brazil
45G8 Araxes R Iran
72D3 Arba Minch Eth
40B3 Arbatax Sardegna
45G8 Arbīl Iraq
37A1 Arbois France
4B3 Arborg Can
32H6 Arbrå Sweden
34D3 Arbroath Scot
37A3 Arc R France
37B2 Arc R France
38B3 Arcachon France
14A1 Arcade USA
15E4 Arcadia USA
18B2 Arcata USA
20D1 Arc Dome, Mt USA
22B2 Arcelia Mexico
14C2 Archbald USA
20E3 Arches Nat Pk USA
23B2 Archipiélago de Camaguey Arch Cuba
25B8 Archipiélago de la Reina Adelaida Arch Chile
25B6 Archipiélago de las Chones Arch Chile
26C2 Archipiélago de las Perlas Arch Panama
36C2 Arcis-sur-Aube France
18D2 Arco USA
29C3 Arcos Brazil
39A2 Arcos de la Frontera Spain
37A1 Arc Senans France
79C1 Arctic Circle
6E3 Arctic Red Can
6E3 Arctic Red River Can
6D3 Arctic Village USA
79G2 Arctowski Base Ant
41F2 Arda R Bulg
45H8 Ardabīl Iran
45G7 Ardahan Turk
70C2 Ardar des Iforas Upland Alg/Mali
63C2 Ardekān Iran
32F6 Ardel Nor
36C2 Ardennes Department, France
42B2 Ardennes Region, Belg
63C2 Ardestan Iran
64C3 Ardh es Suwwan Desert Region Jordan
39A2 Ardila R Port
75C2 Ardlethan Aust
8D3 Ardmore USA
34B3 Ardnamurchan Pt Scot
35F6 Ardres France
36A1 Ardres France
34C3 Ardrishaig Scot
34C4 Ardrossan Scot
23D3 Arecibo Puerto Rico
27L4 Areia Branca Brazil
19B3 Arena,Pt USA
32F7 Arendal Nor
26D7 Arequipa Peru
40C2 Arezzo Italy
37B3 Argens R France
40C2 Argenta Italy
38C2 Argentan France
36B2 Argenteuil France
5L4 Argentia Can
24D7 Argentina Republic, S America
xxxF7 Argentine Basin Atlantic O
38C2 Argenton-sur-Creuse France
41F2 Argeşul R Rom
60B2 Arghardab R Afghan
41E3 Argolikós Kólpos G Greece
36C2 Argonne Region, France
41E3 Árgos Greece
41E3 Argostólion Greece
20B3 Arguello,Pt USA
71G3 Argungu Nig
20D3 Argus Range Mts USA
76B2 Argyle,L Aust
34G3 Argyll Oilfield N Sea
42C1 Århus Den
73C6 Ariamsvlei Namibia
39B1 Arian zón R Spain
28C2 Arias Venado Arg
70B3 Aribinda Burkina
25B1 Arica Chile
60C2 Arifwala Pak
Arihā = Jericho
16B2 Arikaree, R USA
23L1 Arima Trinidad
29C2 Arinos Brazil
27G6 Arinos R Brazil
22B2 Ario de Rosales Mexico
23L1 Aripo,Mt Trinidad
26F5 Aripuana Brazil
26F5 Aripuanã R Brazil
34C3 Arisaig Scot
62B2 Ariskere India
22B1 Arista Mexico
22D2 Arista Mexico
3C3 Aristazabal I Can
28B3 Arizona Arg
8B3 Arizona State, USA
32G7 Årjäng Sweden
49Q4 Arka Russian Fed
45G5 Arkadak Russian Fed
17D3 Arkadelphia USA
48H4 Arkalyk Kazakhstan
9D3 Arkansas State, USA
9D3 Arkansas R USA
17C2 Arkansas City USA
44G3 Arkhangel'sk Russian Fed
53C2 Arkhara Russian Fed
49K2 Arkipelag Nordenshelda Arch Russian Fed
33B3 Arklow Irish Rep
5G5 Arkville USA
37D1 Arlberg P Austria
38C3 Arles France
11C3 Arlington S Dakota, USA
17C3 Arlington Texas, USA
13D3 Arlington Virginia, USA
18B1 Arlington Washington, USA
12B2 Arlington Heights USA
42B3 Arlon Belg
Armageddon = Megido
35B4 Armagh County, N Ire
35B4 Armagh N Ire
41F3 Armagós I Greece
36B3 Armançon R France
45G7 Armavir Russian Fed
22B2 Armena Mexico
45G7 Armenia Republic Europe
26C3 Armenia Colombia
76E4 Armidale Aust
3E3 Armstrong Can
53D2 Armu R Russian Fed
7L3 Arnaud R Can
64B2 Arnauti C Cyprus
16C2 Arnett USA
42B2 Arnhem Neth
76C2 Arnhem,C Aust
76C2 Arnhem Land Aust
37D3 Arno R Italy
20B1 Arnold USA
37E1 Arnoldstein Austria
4B2 Arnot Can
4F4 Arnprior Can
36E1 Arnsberg Germany
74B2 Aroab Namibia
36E1 Arolsen Germany
37C2 Arona Italy
10F3 Aropuk L USA
77G1 Arorae I Kiribati
40B1 Arosa Switz
36B2 Arpajon France
29E2 Arquipélago dos Abrolhos Arch Brazil
70A3 Arquipélago dos Bijagós Arch Guinea-Bissau
29C1 Arraias Brazil
64D3 Ar Ramādī Iraq
34C4 Arran I Scot
64C2 Ar Raqqah Syria
69A2 Ar Rāqūbah Libya
38C1 Arras France
66D1 Ar Rass S Arabia
65D1 Ar Rastan Syria
66D2 Ar Rawdah S Arabia
70A2 Arrecife Canary Is
28C2 Arrecifes Arg
22B1 Arriaga Mexico
22D2 Arriaga Mexico
64E3 Ar Rifā't Iraq
64E3 Ar Rihāb Desert Region Iraq
Ar Rīyād = Riyadh
34C3 Arrochar Scot
28E2 Arroio Grande Brazil
29C1 Arrojado R Brazil
18C2 Arrowrock Res USA
78A2 Arrowtown NZ
20B3 Arroyo Grande USA
22C1 Arroyo Seco Mexico
67F1 Ar Ru'ays Qatar
67G2 Ar Rustaq Oman
64D3 Ar Rutbah Iraq
66D2 Ar Ruwaydah S Arabia
53C3 Arsen'yev Russian Fed
37D2 Arsiero Italy
38D2 Arsizio Italy
44H4 Arsk Russian Fed
41E3 Árta Greece
22B2 Arteaga Mexico
53C3 Artem Russian Fed
49L4 Artemovsk Russian Fed
49N4 Artemovskiy Russian Fed
36A2 Artenay France
8C3 Artesia USA
78B2 Arthurs P NZ
32G7 Århthus Den
7K2 Artic Bay Can
25E4 Artigas Urug
28D2 Artigas Urug
6H3 Artillery L Can
38C1 Artois Region, France
43F3 Artsiz Ukraine
79G2 Arturo Prat Base Ant
45G7 Artvin Turk
72D3 Aru Zaïre
27H6 Aruanã Brazil
23C4 Aruba I Caribbean
61C2 Arun R Nepal
61D2 Arunāchal Pradesh Union Territory, India
53A2 Arun He R China
53A2 Arun Qi China
62B3 Aruppukkottai India
72D4 Arusha Tanz
72C3 Aruwimi R Zaïre
16A2 Arvada USA
50D2 Arvayheer Mongolia
37B2 Arve R France
7L5 Arvida Can
32H5 Arvidsjaur Sweden
44B2 Arvidsjaur Sweden
32G7 Arvika Sweden
19C3 Arvin USA
65C1 Arwad I Syria
57C4 Arwala Indon
44G4 Arzamas Russian Fed
71B1 Arzew Alg
60C2 Asadabad Afghan
54B4 Asahi R Japan
53E3 Asahi dake Mt Japan
53E3 Asahikawa Japan
54A3 Asan-man B S Korea
61C3 Asansol India
69A2 Asawanwah Well Libya
44L4 Asbest Russian Fed
74C2 Asbestos Mts S Africa
13E2 Asbury Park USA
xxxH5 Ascension I Atlantic O
42B3 Aschaffenburg Germany
42C2 Aschersleben Germany
40C2 Ascoli Piceno Italy
37C1 Ascona Switz
72E2 Āseb Eth
70C2 Asedjirad Upland Alg
72D3 Asela Eth
32H6 Åsele Sweden
41E2 Asenovgrad Bulg
36C2 Asfeld France
44K4 Asha Russian Fed
15C2 Ashburn USA
77G5 Ashburton NZ
76A3 Ashburton R Aust
64B3 Ashdod Israel
17D3 Ashdown USA
15D1 Asheboro USA
4B3 Ashern Can
9E3 Asheville USA
75D1 Ashford Aust
35F6 Ashford Eng
19D3 Ash Fork USA
54D2 Ashibetsu Japan
53D4 Ashikaga Japan
54B4 Ashizuri-misaki Pt Japan
48G6 Ashkhabad Turkmenistan
16C2 Ashland Kansas, USA
9E3 Ashland Kentucky, USA
11A2 Ashland Montana, USA
17C1 Ashland Nebraska, USA
12C2 Ashland Ohio, USA
8A2 Ashland Oregon, USA
13D3 Ashland Virginia, USA
11D2 Ashland Wisconsin, USA
75C1 Ashley Aust
11C2 Ashley USA
14C2 Ashokan Res USA
65C3 Ashqelon Israel
64D3 Ash Shabakh Iraq
67G1 Ash Sha'm UAE
66D3 Ash Sh'ār S Arabia
64D2 Ash Sharqāt Iraq
64E3 Ash Shatrah Iraq
67E4 Ash Shihr Yemen
67E1 Ash Shumlul S Arabia
66D3 Ash Shuqayq S Arabia
12C2 Ashtabula USA
7M4 Ashuanipi L Can
5G4 Ashuapmushuan Prov Park Can
45F8 'Āsī R Syria
37D2 Asiago Italy
71A1 Asilah Mor
40B2 Asinara I Medit S
48K4 Asino Russian Fed
66D2 Asir Region, S Arabia
61B4 Aska India
64D2 Aşkale Turk
32G7 Askersund Sweden
65B4 Asl Egypt
60C1 Asmar Afghan
72D2 Asmera Eth
54B4 Aso Japan
72D2 Asosa Eth
16B3 Aspermont USA
78A2 Aspiring,Mt NZ
37A2 Aspres-sur-Buëch France
64C2 As Sabkhah Syria
67E2 As Salamiyah S Arabia
64C2 As Salamīyah Syria
66D4 Assale,L Eth
64D3 As Salmān Iraq
61D2 Assam State, India
64E3 As Samāwah Iraq
67F2 AsŞanām Region, S Arabia
65D2 As Sanamayn Syria
37B3 Asse R France
42B2 Assen Neth
42C1 Assens Den
69A1 As Sidrah Libya
6H5 Assiniboia Can
6G4 Assiniboine,Mt Can
4B4 Assiniboine R Can
5G3 Assinica Prov Park Can
37E3 Assissi Italy
64C3 As Sukhnah Syria
67E2 As Sulayyil S Arabia
67E2 As Summan Region, S Arabia
73E4 Assumption I Seychelles
66D2 As Suq S Arabia
64C3 As Suwaydā' Syria
64D3 As Suwayrah Iraq
64E2 Astara Azerbaijan
40B2 Asti Italy
41F3 Astipálaia I Greece
39A1 Astorga Spain
8A2 Astoria USA
45H6 Astrakhan' Russian Fed
39A1 Asturias Region, Spain
25E3 Asunción Par
72D3 Aswa R Uganda
66B2 Aswân Egypt
69C2 Aswân High Dam Egypt
69C2 Asyût Egypt
64C3 As Zilaf Syria
77H1 Atafu I Tokelau Is
71G4 Atakpamé Togo
57B5 Atambua Indon
7N3 Atangmik Greenland
57B4 Atapupu Indon
70A2 Atar Maur
20B3 Atascadero USA
48J5 Atasu Kazakhstan
57C4 Atauro I Indon
72D2 Atbara Sudan
48H4 Atbasar Kazakhstan
9D4 Atchafalaya B USA
9D3 Atchison USA
14C3 Atco USA
71F4 Atebubu Ghana
22B1 Atenguillo Mexico
40C2 Atessa Italy
36B1 Ath Belg
3F3 Athabasca Can
6G4 Athabasca R Can
6H4 Athabasca, L Can
Athens = Athínai
15B2 Athens Alabama, USA
9E3 Athens Georgia, USA
12C3 Athens Ohio, USA
14B2 Athens Pennsylvania, USA
15C1 Athens Tennessee, USA
17C3 Athens Texas, USA
71G4 Athiémé Benin
41E3 Athínai Greece
33B3 Athlone Irish Rep
65B1 Athna Cyprus
14D1 Athol USA
41E2 Áthos Mt Greece
35B5 Athy Irish Rep
72B2 Ati Chad
7J5 Atikoken Can
5J3 Atikonak L Can
49R3 Atka Russian Fed
10D6 Atka I USA
45G5 Atkarsk Russian Fed
17D2 Atkins USA
22C2 Atlacomulco Mexico
9E3 Atlanta Georgia, USA
12C2 Atlanta Michigan, USA
17C1 Atlantic USA
9F3 Atlantic City USA
14C2 Atlantic Highlands USA
xxxH8 Atlantic Indian Basin Atlantic O
xxxH7 Atlantic Indian Ridge Atlantic O
70C1 Atlas Saharien Mts Alg
6E4 Atlin Can
6E4 Atlin L Can
65C2 'Atlit Israel
22C2 Atlixco Mexico
9E3 Atmore USA
73E6 Atofinandrahana Madag
10H4 Atognak I USA
17C3 Atoka USA
22B1 Atotonilco Mexico
22C2 Atoyac R Mexico
26C2 Atrato R Colombia
67F2 Attaf Region, UAE
66D2 At Tā'if S Arabia
65D2 At Tall Syria
15B2 Attalla USA
7K4 Attawapiskat Can
4D3 Attawapiskat L Can
7K4 Attawapiskat R Can
64D3 At Taysīyah Desert Region S Arabia
12B2 Attica Indiana, USA
14A1 Attica New York, USA
36C2 Attigny France
5H2 Attikamagen L Can
65B1 Attila Line Cyprus
13E2 Attleboro Massachusetts, USA
55D3 Attopeu Laos
10A5 Attu USA
10A5 Attu I USA
64C4 At Tubayq Upland S Arabia
28B3 Atuel R Arg
32H7 Atvidaberg Sweden
20B2 Atwater USA
38D3 Aubagne France
36C2 Aube Department, France
36C2 Aube R France
38C3 Aubenas France
10N2 Aubry L Can
15B2 Auburn Alabama, USA
19B3 Auburn California, USA
12B2 Auburn Indiana, USA
13E2 Auburn Maine, USA
17C1 Auburn Nebraska, USA
13D2 Auburn New York, USA
18B1 Auburn Washington, USA
38C3 Auch France
71H4 Auchi Nig
77G4 Auckland NZ
xxixK7 Auckland Is NZ
38C3 Aude R France
7K4 Auden Can
37B1 Audincourt France
11D3 Audubon USA
75C1 Augathella Aust
74B2 Aughrabies Falls S Africa
42C3 Augsburg Germany
76A4 Augusta Aust
9E3 Augusta Georgia, USA
17C2 Augusta Kansas, USA
9G2 Augusta Maine, USA
18D1 Augusta Montana, USA
12A2 Augusta Wisconsin, USA
10H4 Augustine I USA

Augustow Bandolier Kop

43E2 Augustow Pol
76A3 Augustus,Mt Aust
34G3 Auk Oilfield N Sea
37C2 Aulla Italy
36A2 Aumale France
74B1 Auob R Namibia
5H2 Aupalak Can
57C3 Auponhia Indon
37B3 Aups France
60D3 Auraiya India
60D5 Aurangābād India
71D1 Aurès Mts Alg
38C3 Aurillac France
8C3 Aurora Colorado, USA
12B2 Aurora Illinois, USA
12C3 Aurora Indiana, USA
17D2 Aurora Mississippi, USA
17C1 Aurora Nebraska, USA
74B2 Aus Namibia
12C2 Au Sable USA
70A2 Ausert Well Mor
9D2 Austin Minnesota, USA
19C3 Austin Nevada, USA
14A2 Austin Pennsylvania, USA
8D3 Austin Texas, USA
76D4 Australian Alps Mts Aust
30G4 Austria, Fed Republic Europe
36A1 Authie R France
21B3 Autlán Mexico
38C2 Autun France
38C2 Auvergne Region, France
38C2 Auxerre France
36A1 Auxi-le-Château France
37A1 Auxonne France
38C2 Avallon France
20C4 Avalon USA
7N5 Avalon Pen Can
28D1 Avalos R Arg
29C3 Avaré Brazil
63E2 Avaz Iran
65C3 Avedat Hist Site Israel
27G4 Aveiro Brazil
39A1 Aveiro Port
25E4 Avellaneda Arg
40C2 Avellino Italy
20B3 Avenal USA
36B1 Avesnes-sur-Helpe France
32H6 Avesta Sweden
40C2 Avezzano Italy
34D3 Aviemore Scot
78B2 Aviemore,L NZ
37B2 Avigliana Italy
38C3 Avignon France
39B1 Avila Spain
39A1 Aviles Spain
37D1 Avisio R Italy
11C3 Avoca Iowa, USA
14B1 Avoca New York, USA
75B3 Avoca R Aust
35D6 Avon County, Eng
14B1 Avon USA
35E6 Avon R Dorset, Eng
35E5 Avon R Warwick, Eng
19D4 Avondale USA
35D6 Avonmouth Wales
15E4 Avon Park USA
36B2 Avre R France
41D2 Avtovac Bosnia & Herzegovina, Yugos
65D2 A'waj R Syria
53D5 Awaji-shima B Japan
72E3 Awarē Eth
78A2 Awarua Pt NZ
72E3 Awash Eth
72E3 Awash R Eth
54C3 Awa-shima I Japan
78B2 Awatere R NZ
69A2 Awbārī Libya
72C3 Aweil Sudan
69B2 Awjilah Libya
71H4 Awka Nig
10G2 Awuna R USA
7J1 Axel Heiberg I Can
35D6 Axminster Eng
54C3 Ayabe Japan
25E5 Ayacucho Arg
23C5 Ayacucho Colombia
26D6 Ayacucho Peru
48K5 Ayaguz Kazakhstan
59G2 Ayakkum Hu L China
39A2 Ayamonte Spain
49P4 Ayan Russian Fed
26D6 Ayauiri Peru
45D8 Aydin Turk
41F3 Áyios Evstrátios I Greece
49N3 Aykhal Russian Fed
35E5 Aylesbury Eng
3E3 Aylmer,Mt Can
65D2 'Ayn al Fījah Syria
64D2 Ayn Zālah Iraq
69B2 Ayn Zuwayyah Well Libya
72D3 Ayod Sudan
49S3 Ayon, Ostrov I Russian Fed
76D2 Ayr Aust
34C4 Ayr Scot
34C4 Ayr R Scot
35C4 Ayre,Pt of Eng
55C3 Aytthaya Thai
22B1 Ayutla Mexico
41F3 Ayvacik Turk
41F3 Ayvalik Turk
61B2 Āzamgarh India
70B3 Azaouad Desert Region Mali
71J3 Azare Nig
64C2 A'Zāz Syria
Azbine = Aïr
70A2 Azeffal, Watercourse Maur
71A2 Azemmour Mor
45H7 Azerbaijan Republic Europe
26C4 Azogues Ecuador
44H2 Azopol'ye Russian Fed
Azores = Açores
72C2 Azoum, R Chad
45F6 Azovskoye More S Russian Fed/Ukraine
71A2 Azrou Mor
16A2 Aztec USA
28D3 Azucena Arg
26B2 Azuero,Pen de Panama
25E5 Azúl Arg
71D1 Azzaba Alg
65D2 Az-Zabdānī Syria
67G2 Az Zāhirah Mts Oman
69A2 Az Zahrah Libya
66D1 Az Zilfi S Arabia
64E3 Az Zubayr Iraq

B

57B5 Baa Indon
65C2 Ba'abda Leb
64C3 Ba'albek Leb
65C3 Ba'al Hazor Mt Israel
72E3 Baardheere Somalia
41F2 Babadag Rom
64A1 Babaeski Turk
66D4 Bāb al Mandab Str Djibouti/Yemen
26C4 Babanoyo Ecuador
57C4 Babar I Indon
72D4 Babati Tanz
44F4 Babayevo Russian Fed
11D2 Babbitt USA
12C2 Baberton USA
3C2 Babine R Can
3C3 Babine L Can
76C1 Babo Indon
63C1 Bābol Iran
57F7 Babuyan Chan Phil
57F7 Babuyan Is Phil
27J4 Bacabal Brazil
57C3 Bacan I Indon
45D6 Bačau Rom
55D1 Bac Can Viet
36D2 Baccarat France
75B3 Bacchus Marsh Aust
59F2 Bachu China
6J3 Back R Can
10N3 Backbone Ranges Mts Can
36E2 Backnang Germany
55D1 Bac Ninh Viet
57F8 Bacolod Phil
57F8 Baco,Mt Phil
62B2 Badagara India
52A1 Badain Jaran Shamo Desert China
39A2 Badajoz Spain
39C1 Badalona Spain
64D3 Badanah S Arabia
37E1 Bad Aussee Austria
36E2 Bad Bergzabern Germany
36D1 Bad Ems Germany
38D2 Baden Region, Germany
37C1 Baden Switz
42B3 Baden-Baden Germany
36D2 Badenviller France
42B3 Baden-Württemberg State, Germany
42C3 Badgastein Austria
20C2 Badger USA
42B2 Bad-Godesberg Germany
42B2 Bad Hersfeld Germany
36D1 Bad Honnef Germany
60B4 Badin Pak
40C1 Bad Ischl Austria
64C3 Badiyat ash Sham Desert Region Jordan/Iraq
42B3 Bad-Kreuznach Germany
11B2 Badlands USA
36E1 Bad Lippspringe Germany
36E1 Bad Nauheim Germany
36D1 Bad Nevenahr-Ahrweiler Germany
71G4 Badou Togo
37C1 Bad Ragaz Switz
66C2 Badr Hunayn S Arabia
36E1 Bad Ryrmont Germany
42C3 Bad Tolz Germany
62C3 Badulla Sri Lanka
36E1 Bad Wildungen Germany
36E2 Bad Wimpfen Germany
53C1 Badzhal'skiy Khrebet Mts Russian Fed
39B2 Baena Spain
71J4 Bafang Cam
70A3 Bafatá Guinea-Bissau
7L2 Baffin B Greenland/Can
17F4 Baffin B USA
7L2 Baffin I Can
72B3 Bafia Cam
70A3 Bafing R Mali
70A3 Bafoulabé Mali
72B3 Bafoussam Cam
63D2 Bāfq Iran
45F7 Bafra Burun Pt Turk
63D3 Bāft Iran
72C3 Bafwasende Zaïre
71J3 Baga Nig
61B2 Bagaha India
62B1 Bāgalkot India
73D4 Bagamoyo Tanz
56F7 Bagan Datok Malay
56F7 Bagan Siapiapi Indon
19D4 Bagdad USA
25F4 Bagé Brazil
16A1 Baggs USA
64D3 Baghdād Iraq
61C3 Bagherhat Bang
63D2 Bāghīn Iran
60B1 Baghlan Afghan
11C2 Bagley USA
70B4 Bagnoa Ivory Coast
38C3 Bagnols-sur-Cèza France
70B3 Bagoé R Mali
57F7 Baguio Phil
61C2 Bāhādurābād India
9F4 Bahamas,The Is Caribbean
61C3 Baharampur India
64A4 Bahariya Oasis Egypt
56G7 Bahau Malay
60C3 Bahawahpur Province, Pak
60C3 Bahawalpur Pak
60C3 Bahawathagar Pak
Bahia = Salvador
27K6 Bahia State, Brazil
28C4 Bahia Anegada Arg
25D5 Bahía Blanca Arg
25D5 Bahia Blanca B Arg
28A3 Bahia Concepción B Chile
29D3 Bahia da Ilha Grande B Brazil
21B2 Bahia de Banderas B Mexico
21C2 Bahia de Campeche B Mexico
26B2 Bahia de Corando B Costa Rica
21D3 Bahia de la Ascension B Mexico
21B3 Bahia de Petacalco B Mexico
70A2 Bahia de Rio de Oro B Mor
29D3 Bahia de Sepetiba B Brazil
19C4 Bahiá de Todos Santos B Mexico
25C8 Bahía Grande B Arg
8B4 Bahia Kino Mexico
21A2 Bahia Magdalena B Mexico
28A1 Bahia Salada B Chile
28D3 Bahia Samborombon B Arg
21A2 Bahia Sebastia Vizcaino B Mexico
66C4 Bahir Dar Eth
65A3 Bahrael Manzala L Egypt
61B2 Bahraich India
58D3 Bahrain Sheikdom, Arabian Pen
64D3 Bahr al Milh L Iraq
72C3 Bahr Aouk R Chad/CAR
Bahrat Lut = Dead S
Bahr el Abiad = White Nile
66B4 Bahr el Abiad R Sudan
72C3 Bahr el Arab Watercourse Sudan
Bahr el Azraq = Blue Nile
66B4 Bahr el Azraq R Sudan
72D3 Bahr el Ghazal R Sudan
72B2 Bahr el Ghazal Watercourse Chad
65A3 Bahr Fāqûs R Egypt
63E3 Bāhū-Kalāt Iran
57B3 Bahumbelu Indon
5H2 Baie de Keglo B Can
5J4 Baie de Malbaie B Can
74E2 Baia de Maputo B Mozam
27J4 Baia de Marajó B Brazil
73E5 Baiá de Pemba B Mozam
27K4 Baia de São Marcos B Brazil
5H4 Baie des Chaleurs B Can
39A2 Baia de Setúbal B Port
27L6 Baia de Todos os Santos B Brazil
73B5 Baia dos Tigres Angola
29C4 Baiá Guaratuba Brazil
45C6 Baia Mare Rom
72B3 Baïbokoum Chad
53A2 Baicheng China
73F5 Baie Antongila B Madag
7M5 Baie-Comeau Can
73E5 Baie de Bombetoka B Madag
73E5 Baie de Mahajamba B Madag
73E6 Baie de St Augustin B Madag
65C2 Baie de St Georges B Leb
7L4 Baie-du-Poste Can
5F2 Baie Kogaluc B Can
5G4 Baie Saint Paul Can
7N5 Baie Verte Can
52B3 Baihe China
52C3 Bai He R China
64D3 Ba'ījī Iraq
61B3 Baikunthpur India
Baile Atha Cliath = Dublin
41E2 Băileşti Rom
36B1 Bailleul France
10N1 Baillie Is Can
52A3 Baima China
15C2 Bainbridge USA
57B5 Baing Indon
53B2 Baiquan China
10F3 Baird Inlet USA
6B3 Baird Mts USA
52D1 Bairin Youqi China
52D1 Bairin Zuoqi China
76D4 Bairnsdale Aust
57F9 Bais Phil
71J4 Baissa Nig
61B2 Baitadi Nepal
66B3 Baiyuda Desert Sudan
41D1 Baja Hung
21A1 Baja California Pen Mexico
19C4 Baja California Norte Mexico
57B4 Bajawi Indon
66D4 Bājil Yemen
57B2 Bajo Indon
44K5 Bakal Russian Fed
72C3 Bakala CAR
70A3 Bakel Sen
19C3 Baker California, USA
8C2 Baker Montana, USA
8B2 Baker Oregon, USA
7J3 Baker Foreland Pt Can
6J3 Baker L Can
6J3 Baker Lake Can
8A2 Baker,Mt USA
8B3 Bakersfield USA
63D1 Bakharden Turkmenistan
63D1 Bakhardok Turkmenistan
45E5 Bakhmach Ukraine
32C1 Bakkaflói B Iceland
72D3 Bako Eth
72C3 Bakouma CAR
45H7 Baku Azerbaijan
57B3 Bakudek I Indon
56A2 Bakungan Indon
64B2 Balâ Turk
57E9 Balabac I Phil
56E1 Balabac Str Malay
61B3 Bālāghāt India
56D2 Balaikarangan Indon
75A2 Balaklava Aust
45H5 Balakovo Russian Fed
63E1 Bala Murghab Afghan
61B3 Balāngīr India
45G5 Balashov Russian Fed
61C3 Balasore India
66A1 Balât Egypt
41D1 Balaton L Hung
35B5 Balbniggan Irish Rep
25E5 Balcarce Arg
41F2 Balchik Bulg
77F5 Balclutha NZ
17D2 Bald Knob USA
4B2 Baldock L Can
15C2 Baldwin USA
4D5 Baldwin Michigan, USA
18E1 Baldy Mt USA
8C3 Baldy Peak Mt USA
Balearic Is = Islas Baleares
56D2 Baleh, R Malay
57F7 Baler Phil
44J4 Balezino Russian Fed
67E4 Balhāf Yemen
66D4 Balho Djibouti
76A1 Bali I Indon
64A2 Balıkesir Turk
64C2 Balīkh R Syria
56E3 Balikpapan Indon
57F7 Balintang Chan Phil
56D4 Bali S Indon
29B2 Baliza Brazil
66D3 Baljurshī S Arabia
60B1 Balkh Afghan
48J5 Balkhash Kazakhstan
48J5 Balkhash, Ozero L Kazakhstan
34C3 Ballachulish Scot
34C4 Ballantrae Scot
6G2 Ballantyne Str Can
62B2 Ballapur India
76D4 Ballarat Aust
34D3 Ballater Scot
79F7 Balleny Is Ant
61B2 Ballia India
75D1 Ballina Aust
33B3 Ballina Irish Rep
16C3 Ballinger USA
36D3 Ballon d'Alsace Mt France
41D2 Ballsh Alb
14D1 Ballston Spa USA
34B4 Ballycastle N Ire
34B4 Ballymena N Ire
34B4 Ballymoney N Ire
35A4 Ballyshannon Irish Rep
75B3 Balmoral Aust
16B3 Balmorhea USA
28C2 Balnearia Arg
60B3 Balochistān Region, Pak
73B5 Balombo Angola
75C1 Balonn R Aust
60C3 Balotra India
61B2 Balrāmpur India
76D4 Balranald Aust
27J5 Balsas Brazil
22C2 Balsas Mexico
21B3 Balsas R Mexico
45D6 Balta Ukraine
28D2 Baltasar Brum Urug
32H7 Baltic S N Europe
64B3 Baltîm Egypt
9F3 Baltimore USA
61C2 Bālurghāt India
45J6 Balykshi Kazakhstan
63D3 Bam Iran
72B2 Bama Nig
70B3 Bamako Mali
72C3 Bambari CAR
15C2 Bamberg USA
42C3 Bamberg Germany
72C3 Bambili Zaïre
29C3 Bambui Brazil
72B3 Bamenda Cam
3C4 Bamfield Can
72B3 Bamingui R CAR
72B3 Bamingui Bangoran National Park, CAR
60B2 Bamiyan Afghan
63E3 Bampur Iran
63E3 Bampur R Iran
77F1 Banaba I Kiribati
72C3 Banalia Zaïre
70B3 Banamba Mali
62E3 Bananga Nicobar Is
55C3 Ban Aranyaprathet Thai
55C2 Ban Ban Laos
55C4 Ban Betong Thai
35B4 Banbridge N Ire
35E5 Banbury Eng
34D3 Banchory Scot
21D3 Banco Chinchorro Is Mexico
4F4 Bancroft Can
61B2 Bānda India
56A1 Banda Aceh Indon
70B4 Bandama R Ivory Coast
63D3 Bandar Abbās Iran
45H8 Bandar Anzalī Iran
63C3 Bandar-e Daylam Iran
63C3 Bandar-e Lengheh Iran
63C3 Bandar-e Māqām Iran
63C3 Bandar-e Rig Iran
45J8 Bandar-e Torkoman Iran
63B2 Bandar Khomeynī Iran
56D2 Bandar Seri Begawan Brunei
51F7 Banda S Indon
56E1 Bandau Malay
63D3 Band Bonī Iran
29D3 Bandeira Mt Brazil
28C1 Bandera Arg
29B1 Banderantes Brazil
70B3 Bandiagara Mali
63E2 Band-i-Baba Upland Afghan
45D7 Bandirma Turk
63E1 Band-i-Turkestan Mts Afghan
37A3 Bandol France
74D1 Bandolier Kop S Africa

Bandundu **Bei Shan**

72B4 **Bandundu** Zaïre
56C4 **Bandung** Indon
45H8 **Baneh** Iran
57C2 **Banermo** Indon
21E2 **Banes** Cuba
3E3 **Banff** Can
34D3 **Banff** Scot
6G4 **Banff** *R* Can
3E3 **Banff Nat Pk** Can
71F3 **Banfora** Burkina
62B2 **Bangalore** India
71J4 **Bangangté** Cam
72C3 **Bangassou** CAR
56E1 **Banggi** *I* Malay
55D2 **Bang Hieng** *R* Laos
56C3 **Bangka** *I* Indon
56B2 **Bangkinang** Indon
56B3 **Bangko** Indon
55C3 **Bangkok** Thai
59H3 **Bangladesh** Republic, Asia
60D2 **Bangong Co** *L* China
9G2 **Bangor** Maine, USA
34B4 **Bangor** N Ire
14C2 **Bangor** Pennsylvania, USA
35C5 **Bangor** Wales
56E3 **Bangsalsembera** Indon
55B3 **Bang Saphan Yai** Thai
57F7 **Bangued** Phil
72B3 **Bangui** CAR
73D5 **Bangweulu** *L* Zambia
55C4 **Ban Hat Yai** Thai
55C2 **Ban Hin Heup** Laos
55C1 **Ban Houei Sai** Laos
55B3 **Ban Hua Hin** Thai
70B3 **Bani** *R* Mali
70C3 **Bani Bangou** Niger
67E3 **Banī Ma'arid** Region, S Arabia
69A1 **Banī Walīd** Libya
64C2 **Bāniyās** Syria
65C2 **Baniyas** Syria
40D2 **Banja Luka** Bosnia & Herzegovina, Yugos
56D3 **Banjarmasin** Indon
70A3 **Banjul** The Gambia
55B4 **Ban Kantang** Thai
55D2 **Ban Khemmarat** Laos
55B4 **Ban Khok Kloi** Thai
77F2 **Banks** *Is* Vanuatu
51H8 **Banks I** Aust
6E4 **Banks I** British Columbia, Can
6F2 **Banks I** Northwest Territories, Can
18C1 **Banks L** USA
78B2 **Banks Pen** NZ
75E3 **Banks Str** Aust
61C3 **Bankura** India
55B2 **Ban Mae Sariang** Thai
55B2 **Ban Mae Sot** Thai
61E3 **Banmauk** Burma
55D3 **Ban Me Thuot** Viet
34B4 **Bann** *R* N Ire
55B4 **Ban Na San** Thai
60C2 **Bannu** Pak
28A4 **Baños de Chihuio** Chile
28A3 **Baños Maule** Chile
55C2 **Ban Pak Neun** Laos
55C4 **Ban Pak Phanang** Thai
55D3 **Ban Ru Kroy** Camb
55B3 **Ban Sai Yok** Thai
55C3 **Ban Sattahip** Thai
43D3 **Banská Bystrica** Czech
60C4 **Bānswāra** India
57B4 **Bantaeng** Indon
55B4 **Ban Tha Kham** Thai
55D2 **Ban Thateng** Laos
55C2 **Ban Tha Tum** Thai
33B3 **Bantry** Irish Rep
33A3 **Bantry** *B* Irish Rep
55D3 **Ban Ya Soup** Viet
71J4 **Banyo** Cam
56D4 **Banyuwangi** Indon
xxviiiE7 **Banzare Seamount** Indian O
52C3 **Baofeng** China
55C1 **Bao Ha** Viet
52B3 **Baoji** China
55D3 **Bao Loc** Viet
53C2 **Baoqing** China
50C4 **Baoshan** China
52C1 **Baotou** China
62C1 **Bāpatla** India
36B1 **Bapaume** France
64D3 **Ba'Qūbah** Iraq
41D2 **Bar** Montenegro, Yugos
57C3 **Bara** Indon
72D2 **Bara** Sudan
72E3 **Baraawe** Somalia
56E3 **Barabai** Indon
61B2 **Bāra Banki** India
48J4 **Barabinsk** Russian Fed
48J4 **Barabinskaya Step** *Steppe* Kazakhstan/Russian Fed
39B1 **Baracaldo** Spain
23C2 **Baracoa** Cuba
65D2 **Baradá** *R* Syria
75C2 **Baradine** Aust
66C3 **Baraka** *Watercourse* Eth
62A1 **Bārāmati** India
60C2 **Baramula** Pak
60D3 **Bārān** India
57F8 **Barangas** Phil
6E4 **Baranof I** USA
44D5 **Baranovichi** Belorussia
75A2 **Baratta** Aust
61C2 **Barauni** India
27K8 **Barbacena** Brazil
23F4 **Barbados** *I* Caribbean
39C1 **Barbastro** Spain
74E2 **Barberton** S Africa
38B2 **Barbezieux** France
26D2 **Barbòsa** Colombia
23E3 **Barbuda** *I* Caribbean
76D3 **Barcaldine** Aust
Barce = Al Marj
40D3 **Barcellona** Italy
39C1 **Barcelona** Spain
26F1 **Barcelona** Ven
37B2 **Barcelonnette** France
76D3 **Barcoo** *R* Aust
28B3 **Barda del Medio** Arg
72B1 **Bardai** Chad
25C5 **Bardas Blancas** Arg
61C3 **Barddhamān** India
43E3 **Bardejov** Czech
37C2 **Bardi** Italy
37B2 **Bardonecchia** Italy
35C5 **Bardsey** *I* Wales
12B3 **Bardstown** USA
67F4 **Bareeda** Somalia
60D3 **Bareilly** India
44F1 **Barentsovo More** *S* Russian Fed
48D2 **Barentsøya** *I* Barents S
Barents S = Barentsovo More
72D2 **Barentu** Eth
61B3 **Bargarh** India
37B2 **Barge** Italy
49M4 **Barguzin** Russian Fed
49N4 **Barguzin** *R* Russian Fed
13F2 **Bar Harbor** USA
61C3 **Barhi** India
40D2 **Bari** Italy
39D2 **Barika** Alg
26D2 **Barinas** Ven
61C3 **Baripāda** India
66B2 **Bârîs** Egypt
60C4 **Bari Sādri** India
61D3 **Barisal** Bang
56D3 **Barito** *R* Indon
37B3 **Barjols** France
69A2 **Barjuj** *Watercourse* Libya
52A3 **Barkam** China
17E2 **Barkley,L** USA
3C4 **Barkley Sd** Can
74D3 **Barkly East** S Africa
76C2 **Barkly Tableland** *Mts* Aust
36C2 **Bar-le-Duc** France
76A3 **Barlee,L** Aust
76A3 **Barlee Range** *Mts* Aust
40D2 **Barletta** Italy
60C3 **Barmer** India
75B2 **Barmera** Aust
35C5 **Barmouth** Wales
35E4 **Barnard Castle** Eng
48K4 **Barnaul** Russian Fed
14C3 **Barnegat** USA
14C3 **Barnegat B** USA
14A2 **Barnesboro** USA
7L2 **Barnes Icecap** Can
15C2 **Barnesville** Georgia, USA
12C3 **Barnesville** Ohio, USA
16B3 **Barnhart** USA
35E5 **Barnsley** Eng
35C6 **Barnstaple** Eng
71H4 **Baro** Nig
61D2 **Barpeta** India
26E1 **Barquisimeto** Ven
35F5 **Barqe** *Oilfield* N Sea
36D2 **Barr** France
27K6 **Barra** Brazil
34B3 **Barra** *I* Scot
75D2 **Barraba** Aust
29D1 **Barra da Estiva** Brazil
22B2 **Barra de Navidad** Mexico
29D3 **Barra de Pirai** Brazil
22D2 **Barra de Tonalá** Mexico
29A2 **Barra do Bugres** Brazil
29B2 **Barra do Garças** Brazil
28D2 **Barra do Quarai** Brazil
28E2 **Barra do Ribeiro** Brazil
71F4 **Barrage d'Ayama** Ivory Coast
71J4 **Barrage de Mbakaou** *Dam* Cam
27K6 **Barragem de Sobradinho** Brazil
39A2 **Barragem do Castelo do Bode** *Res* Port
39A2 **Barragem do Maranhão** Port
34B3 **Barra Head** *Pt* Scot
27K8 **Barra Mansa** Brazil
26C6 **Barranca** Peru
26D2 **Barrancabermeja** Colombia
26F2 **Barrancas** Ven
105E3 **Barranqueras** Arg
26D1 **Barranquilla** Colombia
34B3 **Barra,Sound of** *Chan* Scot
4F4 **Barraute** Can
14D1 **Barre** USA
28B2 **Barreal** Arg
27K6 **Barreiras** Brazil
39A2 **Barreiro** Port
27L5 **Barreiros** Brazil
76D5 **Barren,C** Aust
10H4 **Barren Is** USA
27J8 **Barretos** Brazil
3F3 **Barrhead** Can
4F5 **Barrie** Can
3D3 **Barrière** Can
75B2 **Barrier Range** *Mts* Aust
3H2 **Barrington L** Can
76E4 **Barrington,Mt** Aust
29C2 **Barro Alto** Brazil
51G8 **Barroloola** Aust
12A1 **Barron** USA
23N2 **Barrouaillie** St Vincent
6C2 **Barrow** USA
35B5 **Barrow** *R* Irish Rep
76C3 **Barrow Creek** Aust
76A3 **Barrow I** Aust
35D4 **Barrow-in-Furness** Eng
6C2 **Barrow,Pt** USA
7J2 **Barrow Str** Can
13D1 **Barry's Bay** Can
14C2 **Barryville** USA
62B1 **Barsi** India
8B3 **Barstow** USA
38C2 **Bar-sur-Aube** France
36C2 **Bar-sur-Seine** France
27G2 **Bartica** Guyana
64B1 **Bartın** Turk
76D2 **Bartle Frere,Mt** Aust
8D3 **Bartlesville** USA
11C3 **Bartlett** USA
73D6 **Bartolomeu Dias** Mozam
43E2 **Bartoszyce** Pol
26B2 **Barú** Panama
56D4 **Barung** *I* Indon
56A2 **Barus** Indon
60D4 **Barwāh** India
60C4 **Barwāni** India
75C1 **Barwon** *R* Aust
44H5 **Barysh** Russian Fed
28D1 **Basail** Arg
20C1 **Basalt** USA
72B3 **Basankusu** Zaïre
28D2 **Basavilbas** Arg
57F6 **Basco** Phil
36D3 **Basel** France
40B1 **Basel** Switz
40D2 **Basento** *R* Italy
3F3 **Bashaw** Can
57F6 **Bashi Chan** Phil
44J5 **Bashkirskaya** Respublika, Russian Fed
57B3 **Basiano** Indon
57F9 **Basilan** *I* Phil
35F6 **Basildon** Eng
28E2 **Basilio** Brazil
18E2 **Basin** USA
35E6 **Basingstoke** Eng
8B2 **Basin Region** USA
64E3 **Basra** Iraq
36D2 **Bas-Rhin** Department, France
55D3 **Bassac** *R* Camb
3F3 **Bassano** Can
40C1 **Bassano** Italy
37D2 **Bassano del Grappa** Italy
71G4 **Bassari** Togo
73D6 **Bassas da India** *I* Mozam Chan
55A2 **Bassein** Burma
23E3 **Basse Terre** Guadeloupe
11C3 **Bassett** USA
71G4 **Bassila** Benin
20C2 **Bass Lake** USA
76D5 **Bass Str** Aust
32G7 **Båstad** Sweden
63C3 **Bastak** Iran
61B2 **Basti** India
40B2 **Bastia** Corse
42B3 **Bastogne** Belg
17D3 **Bastrop** Louisiana, USA
17C3 **Bastrop** Texas, USA
72A3 **Bata** Eq Guinea
56D3 **Batakan** Indon
60D2 **Batala** India
50C3 **Batang** China
72B3 **Batangafo** CAR
57F6 **Batan Is** Phil
57D3 **Batanta** *I* Indon
29C3 **Batatais** Brazil
13D2 **Batavia** USA
75D3 **Batemans Bay** Aust
15C2 **Batesburg** USA
17D2 **Batesville** Arkansas, USA
17E3 **Batesville** Mississippi, USA
5H4 **Bath** Can
35D6 **Bath** Eng
13F2 **Bath** Maine, USA
13D2 **Bath** New York, USA
72B2 **Batha** *R* Chad
12C1 **Bathawana Mt** Can
76D4 **Bathurst** Aust
7M5 **Bathurst** Can
6F2 **Bathurst,C** Can
76C2 **Bathurst I** Aust
6H2 **Bathurst I** Can
6H3 **Bathurst Inlet** *B* Can
71F4 **Batié** Burkina
63C2 **Bātlāq-e-Gavkhūnī** *Salt Flat* Iran
75C3 **Batlow** Aust
64D2 **Batman** Turk
71D1 **Batna** Alg
9D3 **Baton Rouge** USA
65C1 **Batroun** Leb
55C3 **Battambang** Camb
62C3 **Batticaloa** Sri Lanka
62E3 **Batti Malv** *I* Indian O
3G3 **Battle** *R* Can
9E2 **Battle Creek** USA
7N4 **Battle Harbour** Can
18C2 **Battle Mountain** USA
56F6 **Batu Gajah** Malay
56E2 **Batukelau** Indon
45G7 **Batumi** Georgia
55C5 **Batu Pahat** Malay
56B3 **Baturaja** Indon
65C2 **Bat Yam** Israel
76B1 **Baubau** Indon
71H3 **Bauchi** Nig
71H3 **Bauchi** State, Nig
11D2 **Baudette** USA
37B2 **Bauges** *Mts* France
7N4 **Bauld,C** Can
37B1 **Baumes-les-Dames** France
49N4 **Baunt** Russian Fed
27J8 **Bauru** Brazil
29B2 **Baus** Brazil
42C2 **Bautzen** Germany
56D4 **Baween** *I* Indon
69B2 **Bawîti** Egypt
71F3 **Bawku** Ghana
55B2 **Bawlake** Burma
75A2 **Bawlen** Aust
15C2 **Baxley** USA
61E1 **Baxoi** China
21E2 **Bayamo** Cuba
53B2 **Bayan** China
56E4 **Bayan** Indon
50D2 **Bayandzürh** Mongolia
50C3 **Bayan Har Shan** *Mts* China
52A1 **Bayan Mod** China
52B1 **Bayan Obo** China
11B3 **Bayard** Nebraska, USA
16A3 **Bayard** New Mexico, USA
37B2 **Bayard** *P* France
10N4 **Bayard,Mt** Can
49N5 **Bayasgalant** Mongolia
57F8 **Baybay** Phil
64D1 **Bayburt** Turk
9E2 **Bay City** Michigan, USA
17C4 **Bay City** Texas, USA
64B2 **Bay Dağlari** Turk
44M2 **Baydaratskaya Guba** *B* Russian Fed
72E3 **Baydhabo** Somalia
38B2 **Bayeaux** France
37D1 **Bayerische Alpen** *Mts* Germany
42C3 **Bayern** State, Germany
12A1 **Bayfield** USA
67E4 **Bayhan al Qisāb** Yemen
64C3 **Bāyir** Jordan
49M6 **Baykal, Ozero** *L* Kazakhstan
50D1 **Baykalskiy Khrebet** *Mts* Russian Fed
49L3 **Baykit** Russian Fed
49L5 **Baylik Shan** *Mts* China/ Mongolia
44K5 **Baymak** Russian Fed
15B2 **Bay Minette** USA
57F7 **Bayombang** Phil
38B3 **Bayonne** France
63E1 **Bayram Ali** Turkmenistan
42C3 **Bayreuth** Germany
17E3 **Bay St Louis** USA
13E2 **Bay Shore** USA
13D1 **Bays,L of** Can
66D4 **Bayt al Faqīh** Yemen
50B2 **Baytik Shan** *Mts* China
Bayt Lahm = Bethlehem
17D4 **Baytown** USA
39B2 **Baza** Spain
43F3 **Bazaliya** Ukraine
45H7 **Bazar-Dyuzi** *Mt* Azerbaijan
38B3 **Bazas** France
52B3 **Bazhong** China
63E3 **Bazmān** Iran
65D1 **Bcharre** Leb
11B2 **Beach** USA
14C3 **Beach Haven** USA
35F6 **Beachy Head** Eng
14D2 **Beacon** USA
73E5 **Bealanana** Madag
18D2 **Bear** *R* USA
12A2 **Beardstown** USA
Bear I = Bjørnøya
18D2 **Bear L** USA
4C3 **Bearskin Lake** Can
20B1 **Bear Valley** USA
8D2 **Beatrice** USA
34D2 **Beatrice** *Oilfield* N Sea
3D2 **Beatton** *R* Can
6F4 **Beatton River** Can
8B3 **Beatty** USA
4F4 **Beattyville** Can
36A2 **Beauce** Region, France
25E8 **Beauchene Is** Falkland Is
75D1 **Beaudesert** Aust
79B5 **Beaufort S** Can
74C3 **Beaufort West** S Africa
36A3 **Beaugeney** France
13E1 **Beauharnois** Can
34C3 **Beauly** Scot
19C4 **Beaumont** California, USA
9D3 **Beaumont** Texas, USA
36A2 **Beaumont-sur-Sarthe** France
38C2 **Beaune** France
4B3 **Beauséjour** Can
38C2 **Beauvais** France
3G2 **Beauval** Can
10J2 **Beaver** Alaska, USA
19D3 **Beaver** Utah, USA
4D2 **Beaver** *R* Can
3G3 **Beaver** *R* Saskatchewan, Can
3C1 **Beaver** *R* Yukon, Can
6D3 **Beaver Creek** Can
10J2 **Beaver Creek** USA
12B3 **Beaver Dam** Kentucky, USA
12B2 **Beaver Dam** Wisconsin, USA
18D1 **Beaverhead Mts** USA
3F3 **Beaverhill L** Can
12B1 **Beaver I** USA
17D2 **Beaver L** USA
3E2 **Beaverlodge** Can
60C3 **Beawar** India
28B2 **Beazley** Arg
29C3 **Bebedouro** Brazil
35F5 **Beccles** Eng
41E1 **Bečej** Serbia, Yugos
70B1 **Béchar** Alg
10G4 **Becharof L** USA
10F4 **Bechevin B** USA
9E3 **Beckley** USA
36E1 **Beckum** Germany
35E5 **Bedford** County, Eng
35E5 **Bedford** Eng
12B3 **Bedford** Indiana, USA
14A3 **Bedford** Pennsylvania, USA
23M2 **Bedford Pt** Grenada
14B2 **Beech Creek** USA
6D2 **Beechey Pt** USA
75C3 **Beechworth** Aust
75D1 **Beenleigh** Aust
65C3 **Beer Menuha** Israel
65C4 **Beer Ora** Israel
64B3 **Beersheba** Israel
Beèr Sheva = Beersheba
65C3 **Beér Sheva**, *R* Israel
8D4 **Beeville** USA
72C3 **Befale** Zaïre
73E5 **Befandriana** Madag
75C3 **Bega** Aust
49N2 **Begicheva, Ostrov** *I* Russian Fed
63C2 **Behbehān** Iran
10M4 **Behm Canal** *Sd* USA
63C1 **Behshahr** Iran
60B2 **Behsud** Afghan
53B2 **Bei'an** China
52B5 **Beihai** China
55D1 **Beihai** China
52D2 **Beijing** China
55E1 **Beiliu** China
52B4 **Beipan Jiang** *R* China
52E1 **Beipiao** China
73D5 **Beira** Mozam
64C3 **Beirut** Leb
50C2 **Bei Shan** *Mts* China

Beitbridge Biratnagar

74E1 **Beitbridge** Zim
65C2 **Beit ed Dīne** Leb
65C3 **Beit Jala** Israel
39A2 **Beja** Port
71D1 **Beja** Tunisia
71D1 **Bejaïa** Alg
39A1 **Béjar** Spain
63D2 **Bejestān** Iran
43E3 **Békéscsaba** Hung
73E6 **Bekily** Madag
61B2 **Bela** India
60B3 **Bela** Pak
56D2 **Belaga** Malay
14B3 **Bel Air** USA
62B1 **Belamoalli** India
57B2 **Belang** Indon
56A2 **Belangpidie** Indon
xxviiiH4 **Belau** *I* Pacific O
Belau = Palau
74E2 **Bela Vista** Mozam
29A3 **Béla Vista** Par/Brazil
56A2 **Belawan** Indon
44K4 **Belaya** *R* Ukraine
43G3 **Belaya Tserkov'** Russian Fed
7J2 **Belcher Chan** Can
7L4 **Belcher Is** Can
60B1 **Belchiragh** Afghan
44J5 **Belebey** Russian Fed
72E3 **Beled Weyne** Somalia
27J4 **Belém** Brazil
28B1 **Belén** Arg
26C3 **Belén** Colombia
29A3 **Belén** Par
28D2 **Belén** Urug
8C3 **Belen** USA
28B1 **Belén** *R* Arg
34B4 **Belfast** N Ire
74E2 **Belfast** S Africa
5H5 **Belfast** USA
34B4 **Belfast Lough** *Estuary* N Ire
11B2 **Belfield** USA
72D2 **Bēlfodiyo** Eth
34E4 **Belford** Eng
38D2 **Belfort** France
62A1 **Belgaum** India
42A2 **Belgium** Kingdom, N W Europe
45F5 **Belgorod** Russian Fed
45E6 **Belgorod Dnestrovskiy** Ukraine
Belgrade = Beograd
18D1 **Belgrade** USA
69A2 **Bel Hedan** Libya
56C3 **Belinyu** Indon
56C3 **Belitung** *I* Indon
21D3 **Belize** Belize
21D3 **Belize** Republic, C America
49P2 **Bel'kovskiv, Ostrov** *I* Russian Fed
38C2 **Bellac** France
6F4 **Bella Coola** Can
37C2 **Bellagio** Italy
17C4 **Bellaire** USA
37C1 **Bellano** Italy
62B1 **Bellary** India
75C1 **Bellata** Aust
28D2 **Bella Union** Urug
28D1 **Bella Vista** Arg
37B2 **Belledonne** *Mts* France
14B2 **Bellefonte** USA
8C2 **Belle Fourche** USA
11B3 **Belle Fourche** *R* USA
38D2 **Bellegarde** France
15E4 **Belle Glade** USA
7N4 **Belle I** Can
38B2 **Belle-Ile** *I* France
7N4 **Belle Isle,Str of** Can
36A2 **Bellême** France
5K4 **Belleoram** Can
7L5 **Belleville** Can
12B3 **Belleville** Illinois, USA
17C2 **Belleville** Kansas, USA
18D2 **Bellevue** Idaho, USA
12A2 **Bellevue** Iowa, USA
18B1 **Bellevue** Washington, USA
37A2 **Belley** France
75D2 **Bellingen** Aust
8A2 **Bellingham** USA
79G2 **Bellingshausen** *Base* Ant
79G3 **Bellingshausen S** Ant
40B1 **Bellinzona** Switz
26C2 **Bello** Colombia
77E3 **Bellona Reefs** Nouvelle Calédonie
20B1 **Bellota** USA
13E2 **Bellows Falls** USA
7K3 **Bell Pen** Can
40C1 **Belluno** Italy
25D4 **Bell Ville** Arg
4C5 **Belmond** USA
14B1 **Belmont** USA
27L7 **Belmonte** Brazil
21D3 **Belmopan** Belize
53B1 **Belogorsk** Russian Fed
73E6 **Beloha** Madag
27K7 **Belo Horizonte** Brazil
16C2 **Beloit** Kansas, USA
9E2 **Beloit** Wisconsin, USA
44E3 **Belomorsk** Russian Fed
44K5 **Beloretsk** Russian Fed
44D5 **Belorussia** *Republic* Europe
73E5 **Belo-Tsiribihina** Madag
44F2 **Beloye More** *S*
44F3 **Beloye Ozero** *L* Russian Fed
44F3 **Belozersk** Russian Fed
12C3 **Belpre** USA
75A2 **Beltana** Aust
17C3 **Belton** USA
43F3 **Bel'tsy** Moldavia
48K5 **Belukha** *Mt* Russian Fed
44H2 **Belush'ye** Russian Fed
12B2 **Belvidere** Illinois, USA
14C2 **Belvidere** New Jersey, USA
48J2 **Belyy, Ostrov** *I* Russian Fed
73B4 **Bembe** Angola
71G3 **Bembéréke** Benin
9D2 **Bemidji** USA
15B1 **Bemis** USA
32G6 **Bena** Nor
72C4 **Bena Dibele** Zaïre
75C3 **Benalla** Aust
34C2 **Ben Attow** *Mt* Scot
39A1 **Benavente** Spain
34B3 **Benbecula** *I* Scot
76A4 **Bencubbin** Aust
8A2 **Bend** USA
69E3 **Bendarbeyla** Somalia
34C3 **Ben Dearg** *Mt* Scot
43F3 **Bendery** Moldavia
76D4 **Bendigo** Aust
71F3 **Bénéna** Mali
42C3 **Benešov** Czech
40C2 **Benevento** Italy
59G4 **Bengal,B of** Asia
69A1 **Ben Gardane** Libya
71E2 **Ben Gardane** Tunisia
52D3 **Bengbu** China
57B3 **Benggai** *I* Indon
69B1 **Benghāzī** Libya
56B2 **Bengkalis** Indon
56B3 **Bengkulu** Indon
73B5 **Benguela** Angola
71A2 **Benguerir** Mor
64B3 **Benha** Egypt
34C2 **Ben Hope** *Mt* Scot
72C3 **Beni** Zaïre
26E6 **Béni** *R* Bol
70B1 **Beni Abbes** Alg
39C1 **Benicarló** Spain
39B2 **Benidorm** Spain
39C2 **Beni Mansour** Alg
69C2 **Beni Mazar** Egypt
71A2 **Beni Mellal** Mor
70C4 **Benin** Republic, Africa
71H4 **Benin City** Nig
71B1 **Beni-Saf** Alg
69C2 **Beni Suef** Egypt
16B2 **Benkelman** USA
34C2 **Ben Kilbreck** *Mt* Scot
33C2 **Ben Lawers** *Mt* Scot
34D3 **Ben Macdui** *Mt* Scot
34C2 **Ben More Assynt** *Mt* Scot
78B2 **Benmore,L** NZ
49R2 **Bennetta, Ostrov** *I* Russian Fed
34C3 **Ben Nevis** *Mt* Scot
13E2 **Bennington** USA
65C2 **Bennt Jbail** Leb
72B3 **Bénoué** *R* Cam
71J4 **Bénoué Nat Pk** Cam
36E2 **Bensheim** Germany
8B3 **Benson** Arizona, USA
11C2 **Benson** Minnesota, USA
72C3 **Bentiu** Sudan
29A2 **Bento Gomes** *R* Brazil
17D3 **Benton** Arkansas, USA
20C2 **Benton** California, USA
12B3 **Benton** Kentucky, USA
12B2 **Benton Harbor** USA
71H4 **Benue** State, Nig
71H4 **Benue** *R* Nig
34C3 **Ben Wyvis** *Mt* Scot
52E1 **Benxi** China
57C2 **Beo** Indon
41E2 **Beograd** Serbia, Yugos
61B3 **Beohāri** India
53C5 **Beppu** Japan
41D2 **Berat** Alb
72D2 **Berber** Sudan
72E2 **Berbera** Somalia
72B3 **Berbérati** CAR
36A1 **Berck** France
43F3 **Berdichev** Ukraine
45F6 **Berdyansk** Ukraine
12C3 **Berea** USA
57C2 **Berebere** Indon
71F4 **Berekum** Ghana
20B2 **Berenda** USA
66C2 **Berenice** Egypt
4C3 **Berens** *R* Can
6J4 **Berens River** Can
75A1 **Beresford** Aust
11C3 **Beresford** USA
43E3 **Berettyoújfalu** Hung
43E2 **Bereza** Belorussia
43E3 **Berezhany** Ukraine
43F2 **Berezina** *R* Belorussia
44G3 **Bereznik** Russian Fed
44K4 **Berezniki** Russian Fed
45E6 **Berezovka** Ukraine
44L3 **Berezovo** Russian Fed
53D1 **Berezovyy** Russian Fed
64A2 **Bergama** Turk
40B1 **Bergamo** Italy
32F6 **Bergen** Nor
14B1 **Bergen** USA
36C1 **Bergen op Zoom** Neth
38C3 **Bergerac** France
36D1 **Bergisch-Gladbach** Germany
4D4 **Bergland** USA
62C1 **Berhampur** India
49S4 **Beringa, Ostrov** *I* Russian Fed
10K3 **Bering Gl** USA
49T3 **Beringovskiy** Russian Fed
xxixK2 **Bering S** Russian Fed/USA
79C6 **Bering Str** Russian Fed/ USA
63D3 **Berīzak** Iran
39B2 **Berja** Spain
71B2 **Berkane** Mor
8A3 **Berkeley** USA
14A3 **Berkeley Spring** USA
79F2 **Berkner I** Ant
41E2 **Berkovitsa** Bulg
35E6 **Berkshire** County, Eng
14D1 **Berkshire Hills** USA
3E3 **Berland** *R* Can
42C2 **Berlin** Germany
13E2 **Berlin** New Hampshire, USA
14A3 **Berlin** Pennsylvania, USA
42C2 **Berlin** State, Germany
26F8 **Bermejo** Bol
25E3 **Bermejo** *R* Arg
2M5 **Bermuda** *I* Atlantic O
40B1 **Bern** Switz
16A2 **Bernalillo** USA
29B4 **Bernardo de Irigoyen** Arg
14C2 **Bernardsville** USA
28C3 **Bernasconi** Arg
36A2 **Bernay** France
42C2 **Bernburg** Germany
37B1 **Berner Orberland** *Mts* Switz
7K2 **Bernier B** Can
42C3 **Berounka** *R* Czech
71A2 **Berrechid** Mor
75B2 **Berri** Aust
71C2 **Berriane** Alg
38C2 **Berry** Region, France
20A1 **Berryessa,L** USA
9F4 **Berry Is** Bahamas
14B3 **Berryville** USA
74B2 **Berseba** Namibia
56F6 **Bertam** Malay
16A2 **Berthoud P** USA
72B3 **Bertoua** Cam
77G1 **Beru** *I* Kiribati
13D2 **Berwick** USA
34D4 **Berwick-upon-Tweed** Eng
35D5 **Berwyn** *Mts* Wales
73E5 **Besalampy** Madag
38D2 **Besançon** France
43E3 **Beskidy Zachodnie** *Mts* Pol
3G2 **Besnard L** Can
64C2 **Besni** Turk
65C3 **Besor** *R* Israel
15B2 **Bessemer** Alabama, USA
12B1 **Bessemer** Michigan, USA
73E5 **Betafo** Madag
39A1 **Betanzos** Spain
71J4 **Betaré Oya** Cam
65C3 **Bet Guvrin** Israel
74D2 **Bethal** S Africa
74B2 **Bethanie** Namibia
17D1 **Bethany** Missouri, USA
17C2 **Bethany** Oklahoma, USA
6B3 **Bethel** Alaska, USA
14D2 **Bethel** Connecticut, USA
12C2 **Bethel Park** USA
13D3 **Bethesda** USA
65C3 **Bethlehem** Israel
74D2 **Bethlehem** S Africa
13D2 **Bethlehem** USA
74D3 **Bethulie** S Africa
38C1 **Bethune** France
36A2 **Béthune** *R* France
73E6 **Betioky** Madag
75B1 **Betoota** Aust
72B3 **Betou** Congo
59E1 **Betpak Dala** *Steppe* Kazakhstan
73E6 **Betroka** Madag
7M5 **Betsiamites** Can
12A2 **Bettendorf** USA
61B2 **Bettiah** India
10H2 **Bettles** USA
37C2 **Béttola** Italy
60D4 **Bētul** India
36C1 **Betuwe** Region, Neth
60D3 **Betwa** *R* India
36D1 **Betzdorf** Germany
10G4 **Beverley,L** USA
14E1 **Beverly** USA
20C3 **Beverly Hills** USA
70B4 **Beyla** Guinea
62B2 **Beypore** India
Beyrouth = Beirut
64B2 **Beyşehir** Turk
45E8 **Beysehir Gölü** *L* Turk
65C2 **Beyt Shean** Israel
37C1 **Bezan** Austria
44F4 **Bezhetsk** Russian Fed
38C3 **Béziers** France
63D1 **Bezmein** Turkmenistan
50D1 **Beznosova** Russian Fed
61C2 **Bhadgaon** Nepal
62C1 **Bhadrāchalam** India
61C3 **Bhadrakh** India
62B2 **Bhadra Res** India
62B2 **Bhadrāvati** India
60B3 **Bhag** Pak
61C2 **Bhāgalpur** India
60C2 **Bhakkar** Pak
61E3 **Bhamo** Burma
60D4 **Bhandāra** India
60D3 **Bharatpur** India
60C4 **Bharūch** India
61C3 **Bhātiāpāra Ghat** Bang
60C2 **Bhatinda** India
62A2 **Bhatkal** India
61C3 **Bhātpāra** India
60C4 **Bhāvnagar** India
61B4 **Bhawānipatna** India
60C2 **Bhera** Pak
61B2 **Bheri** *R* Nepal
61B3 **Bhilai** India
60C3 **Bhīlwāra** India
62C1 **Bhīmavaram** India
60D3 **Bhind** India
60D3 **Bhiwāni** India
62B1 **Bhongir** India
60D4 **Bhopāl** India
61C3 **Bhubaneshwar** India
60B4 **Bhuj** India
60D4 **Bhusāwal** India
59H3 **Bhutan** Kingdom, Asia
71F4 **Bia** *R* Ghana
51G7 **Biak** *I* Indon
43E2 **Biala Podlaska** Pol
42D2 **Bialograd** Pol
43E2 **Bialystok** Pol
32A1 **Biargtangar** *C* Iceland
63D1 **Bīarjmand** Iran
57C2 **Biaro** *I* Indon
38B3 **Biarritz** France
37C1 **Biasca** Switz
64B4 **Biba** Egypt
53E3 **Bibai** Japan
73B5 **Bibala** Angola
37D3 **Bibbiena** Italy
42B3 **Biberach** Germany
71F4 **Bibiani** Ghana
5H4 **Bic** Can
41F1 **Bicaz** Rom
53D1 **Bichi** *R* Russian Fed
19D3 **Bicknell** USA
71H4 **Bida** Nig
62B1 **Bīdar** India
67G2 **Bidbid** Oman
13E2 **Biddeford** USA
35C6 **Bideford** Eng
35C6 **Bideford B** Eng
70C2 **Bidon 5** Alg
43E2 **Biebrza** Pol
40B1 **Biel** Switz
42D2 **Bielawa** Pol
42B2 **Bielefeld** Germany
37B1 **Bieler See** *L* Switz
40B1 **Biella** Italy
43E2 **Bielsk Podlaski** Pol
55D3 **Bien Hoa** Viet
40C2 **Biferno** *R* Italy
64A1 **Biga** Turk
41F3 **Bigadiç** Turk
5H4 **Big Bald Mt** Can
4D3 **Big Beaver House** Can
16B4 **Big Bend Nat Pk** USA
18D1 **Big Belt Mts** USA
17E3 **Big Black** *R* USA
17C1 **Big Blue** *R* USA
15E4 **Big Cypress Swamp** USA
6D3 **Big Delta** USA
38D2 **Bigent** Germany
3G3 **Biggar** Can
75D1 **Biggenden** Aust
10L4 **Bigger,Mt** Can
18D1 **Big Hole** *R* USA
11A2 **Bighorn** *R* USA
11A2 **Bighorn L** USA
11A3 **Bighorn Mts** USA
55C3 **Bight of Bangkok** *B* Thai
70C4 **Bight of Benin** *B* W Africa
70C4 **Bight of Biafra** *B* Cam
7L3 **Big I** Can
10G4 **Big Koniuji** *I* USA
16B3 **Big Lake** USA
37C1 **Bignasco** Switz
70A3 **Bignona** Sen
19C3 **Big Pine** USA
15E4 **Big Pine Key** USA
20C3 **Big Pine Mt** USA
12B2 **Big Rapids** USA
6H4 **Big River** Can
4B2 **Big Sand L** Can
18D1 **Big Sandy** USA
3H3 **Big Sandy L** Can
11C3 **Big Sioux** *R* USA
20D1 **Big Smokey V** USA
8C3 **Big Spring** USA
16B1 **Big Springs** USA
11C2 **Big Stone City** USA
12C3 **Big Stone Gap** USA
4B3 **Bigstone L** Can
20B2 **Big Sur** USA
18E1 **Big Timber** USA
7J4 **Big Trout L** Can
4D3 **Big Trout Lake** Can
40D2 **Bihać** Bosnia & Herzegovina, Yugos
61C2 **Bihār** India
61C3 **Bihar** State, India
72D4 **Biharamulo** Tanz
45C6 **Bihor** *Mt* Rom
62B1 **Bijāpur** India
62C1 **Bijāpur** India
63B1 **Bījār** Iran
61B2 **Bijauri** Nepal
41D2 **Bijeljina** Bosnia & Herzegovina, Yugos
52B4 **Bijie** China
60D3 **Bijnor** India
60C3 **Bijnot** Pak
60C3 **Bikāner** India
65C2 **Bikfaya** Leb
53C2 **Bikin** Russian Fed
53D2 **Bikin** *R* Russian Fed
72B4 **Bikoro** Zaïre
53A2 **Bila He** *R* China
60C3 **Bilara** India
60D2 **Bilaspur** India
61B3 **Bilāspur** India
55B3 **Bilauktaung Range** *Mts* Thai
39B1 **Bilbao** Spain
65A3 **Bilbeis** Egypt
Bilbo = Bilbao
42D3 **Bilé** *R* Czech
41D2 **Bileća** Bosnia & Herzegovina, Yugos
64B1 **Bilecik** Turk
72C3 **Bili** *R* Zaïre
49S3 **Bilibino** Russian Fed
57F8 **Biliran** *I* Phil
8C2 **Billings** USA
72B2 **Bilma** Niger
9E3 **Biloxi** USA
72C2 **Biltine** Chad
71F4 **Bimbita** Ghana
60D4 **Bina-Etawa** India
57F8 **Binalbagan** Phil
73D5 **Bindura** Zim
73C5 **Binga** Zim
73D5 **Binga** *Mt* Zim
75D1 **Bingara** Aust
42B3 **Bingen** Germany
13F1 **Bingham** USA
9F2 **Binghamton** USA
56E1 **Bingkor** Malay
64D2 **Bingöl** Turk
52D3 **Binhai** China
56A2 **Binjai** Indon
56C2 **Binjai** Indon
57B4 **Binongko** *I* Indon
56B2 **Bintan** *I* Indon
56B3 **Bintuhan** Indon
56D2 **Bintulu** Malay
25B5 **Bió Bió** *R* Chile
xxxJ4 **Bioko** *I* Atlantic O
62B1 **Bīr** India
53C2 **Bira** Russian Fed
69B2 **Bīr Abu Husein** *Well* Egypt
69B2 **Bi'r al Harash** *Well* Libya
72C2 **Birao** CAR
61C2 **Biratnagar** Nepal

Bourg de Péage

Burundi

38D2 **Bourg de Péage** France
37A1 **Bourg-en-Bresse** France
38C2 **Bourges** France
38C3 **Bourg-Madame** France
38C2 **Bourgogne** Region, France
37A2 **Bourgoin-Jallieu** France
37B2 **Bourg-St-Maurice** France
75C2 **Bourke** Aust
35E6 **Bournemouth** Eng
71C1 **Bou Saâda** Alg
72B2 **Bousso** Chad
70A3 **Boutilimit** Maur
71F4 **Boutourou,Mt** Ivory Coast
xxxJ7 **Bouvet I** Atlantic O
28D2 **Bovril** Arg
3F3 **Bow** *R* Can
11B2 **Bowbells** USA
76D2 **Bowen** Aust
19E4 **Bowie** Arizona, USA
17C3 **Bowie** Texas, USA
3F4 **Bow Island** Can
9E3 **Bowling Green** Kentucky, USA
17D2 **Bowling Green** Missouri, USA
12C2 **Bowling Green** Ohio, USA
13D3 **Bowling Green** Virginia, USA
11B2 **Bowman** USA
13D2 **Bowmanville** Can
75D2 **Bowral** Aust
3D3 **Bowron** *R* Can
52D3 **Bo Xian** China
52D2 **Boxing** China
64B1 **Boyabat** Turk
72B3 **Boyali** CAR
43G2 **Boyarka** Ukraine
6J4 **Boyd** Can
14C2 **Boyertown** USA
3F3 **Boyle** Can
33B3 **Boyle** Irish Rep
35B5 **Boyne** *R* Irish Rep
15E4 **Boynoton Beach** USA
72C3 **Boyoma Falls** Zaïre
18E2 **Boysen Res** USA
41F3 **Bozcaada** *I* Turk
41F3 **Boz Dağlari** *Mts* Turk
8B2 **Bozeman** USA
Bozen = Bolzano
72B3 **Bozene** Zaïre
72B3 **Bozoum** CAR
37B2 **Bra** Italy
40D2 **Brač** *I* Croatia, Yugos
4F4 **Bracebridge** Can
69A2 **Brach** Libya
32H6 **Bräcke** Sweden
16B4 **Brackettville** USA
15E4 **Bradenton** USA
35E5 **Bradford** Eng
14A2 **Bradford** USA
20B3 **Bradley** USA
16C3 **Brady** USA
34E1 **Brae** Scot
34D3 **Braemar** Scot
39A1 **Braga** Port
28C3 **Bragado** Arg
39A1 **Bragana** Port
27J4 **Bragança** Brazil
29C3 **Bragança Paulista** Brazil
61D3 **Brahman-Baria** Bang
61C3 **Brāhmani** *R* India
61D2 **Brahmaputra** *R* India
45D6 **Brăila** Rom
9D2 **Brainerd** USA
74C3 **Brak** *R* S Africa
74D1 **Brak** *R* S Africa
70A3 **Brakna** Region, Maur
6F4 **Bralorne** Can
4F5 **Brampton** Can
26F3 **Branco** *R* Brazil
73B6 **Brandberg** *Mt* Namibia
42C2 **Brandenburg** Germany
42C2 **Brandenburg** State, Germany
74D2 **Brandfort** S Africa
8D2 **Brandon** Can
11C3 **Brandon** USA
74C3 **Brandvlei** S Africa
42C2 **Brandys nad Lebem** Czech
43D2 **Braniewo** Pol
9E2 **Brantford** Can
75B3 **Branxholme** Aust
7M5 **Bras d'Or L** Can
29D2 **Brasila de Minas** Brazil
26E6 **Brasiléia** Brazil
27J7 **Brasilia** Brazil
41F1 **Brasov** Rom
56E2 **Brassay Range** *Mts* Malay
42D3 **Bratislava** Czech
49M4 **Bratsk** Russian Fed
43F3 **Bratslav** Ukraine
13E2 **Brattleboro** USA
42C2 **Braunschweig** Germany
70A4 **Brava** *I* Cape Verde
8B3 **Brawley** USA
35B5 **Bray** Irish Rep
7L3 **Bray I** Can
36B2 **Bray-sur-Seine** France
3E3 **Brazeau** *R* Can
3E3 **Brazeau,Mt** Can
24E5 **Brazil** Republic, S America
xxxG5 **Brazil Basin** Atlantic O
8D3 **Brazos** *R* USA
72B4 **Brazzaville** Congo
42C3 **Brdy** *Upland* Czech
78A3 **Breaksea Sd** NZ
78B1 **Bream B** NZ
56C4 **Brebes** Indon
34D3 **Brechin** Scot
36C1 **Brecht** Belg
11C2 **Breckenridge** Minnesota, USA
16C3 **Breckenridge** Texas, USA
42D3 **Břeclav** Czech
35D6 **Brecon** Wales
35D6 **Brecon Beacons** *Mts* Wales
35C5 **Brecon Beacons Nat Pk** Wales
42A2 **Breda** Neth
74C3 **Bredasdorp** S Africa
32H6 **Bredby** Sweden
44B3 **Bredbyn** Sweden
44K5 **Bredy** Russian Fed
74B3 **Breede** *R* S Africa
13D2 **Breezewood** USA
37C1 **Bregenz** Austria
37C1 **Bregenzer Ache** *R* Austria
32A1 **Breiðafjörður** *B* Iceland
36D2 **Breisach** Germany
37C2 **Brembo** Italy
37C2 **Brembo** *R* Italy
15B2 **Bremen** USA
42B2 **Bremen** Germany
42B2 **Bremerhaven** Germany
18B1 **Bremerton** USA
19E3 **Brendel** USA
17C3 **Brenham** USA
38E2 **Brenner** *Mt* Austria
42C3 **Brenner** *P* Austria/Italy
37D2 **Breno** Italy
4F4 **Brent** Can
37D2 **Brenta** *R* Italy
20B2 **Brentwood** USA
40C1 **Brescia** Italy
Breslau = Wrocław
37D1 **Bressanone** Italy
34E1 **Bressay** *I* Scot
38B2 **Bressuire** France
38B2 **Brest** France
43E2 **Brest** Belorussia
38B2 **Bretagne** Region, France
36B2 **Breteuil** France
36A2 **Bretevil** France
15B3 **Breton Sd** USA
14C2 **Breton Woods** USA
78B1 **Brett,C** NZ
15C1 **Brevard** USA
75C1 **Brewarrina** Aust
13F2 **Brewer** USA
14D2 **Brewster** New York, USA
18C1 **Brewster** Washington, USA
15B2 **Brewton** USA
74D2 **Breyten** S Africa
40D1 **Brežice** Slovenia, Yugos
72C3 **Bria** CAR
38D3 **Briancon** France
38C2 **Briare** France
15B2 **Bridgeport** Alabama, USA
19C3 **Bridgeport** California, USA
13E2 **Bridgeport** Connecticut, USA
11B3 **Bridgeport** Nebraska, USA
17C3 **Bridgeport** Texas, USA
20C1 **Bridgeport Res** USA
18E1 **Bridger** USA
16A1 **Bridger Peak** USA
14C3 **Bridgeton** USA
23F4 **Bridgetown** Barbados
5H5 **Bridgetown** Can
7M5 **Bridgewater** Can
14E2 **Bridgewater** USA
35D6 **Bridgwater** Eng
35D6 **Bridgwater B** Eng
35E4 **Bridlington** Eng
75E3 **Bridport** Aust
36C2 **Brienne-le-Château** France
37B1 **Brienzer See** *L* Switz
36C2 **Briey** France
40B1 **Brig** Switz
8B2 **Brigham City** USA
75C3 **Bright** Aust
35E6 **Brighton** Eng
37B3 **Brignoles** France
29A3 **Brilhante** *R* Brazil
36E1 **Brilon** Germany
41D2 **Brindisi** Italy
17D3 **Brinkley** USA
77E3 **Brisbane** Aust
13E2 **Bristol** Connecticut, USA
35D6 **Bristol** Eng
13E2 **Bristol** Pennsylvania, USA
14E2 **Bristol** Rhode Island, USA
9E3 **Bristol** Tennessee, USA
10F4 **Bristol B** USA
35C6 **Bristol Chan** Eng/Wales
6F4 **British Columbia** Province, Can
7K1 **British Empire Range** *Mts* Can
10K2 **British Mts** USA/Can
74D2 **Brits** S Africa
74C3 **Britstown** S Africa
4E4 **Britt** Can
11C2 **Britton** USA
38C2 **Brive** France
42D3 **Brno** Czech
15C2 **Broad** *R* USA
14C1 **Broadalbin** USA
7L4 **Broadback** *R* Can
34B2 **Broad Bay** *Inlet* Scot
34C3 **Broadford** Scot
11A2 **Broadus** USA
11B1 **Broadview** Can
11B3 **Broadwater** USA
6H4 **Brochet** Can
6G2 **Brock I** Can
13D2 **Brockport** USA
14E1 **Brockton** USA
4F5 **Brockville** Can
14A2 **Brockway** USA
7K2 **Brodeur Pen** Can
34C4 **Brodick** Scot
43D2 **Brodnica** Pol
45D5 **Brody** Ukraine
36D1 **Brokem Haltern** Germany
16C1 **Broken Bow** Nebraska, USA
17D3 **Broken Bow** Oklahoma, USA
17D3 **Broken Bow L** USA
76D4 **Broken Hill** Aust
37C2 **Broni** Italy
32G5 **Brønnøysund** Nor
14D2 **Bronx** *Borough* New York, USA
57E9 **Brooke's Point** Phil
17D2 **Brookfield** Missouri, USA
12B2 **Brookfield** Wisconsin, USA
9D3 **Brookhaven** USA
18B2 **Brookings** Oregon, USA
8D2 **Brookings** South Dakota, USA
14E1 **Brookline** USA
11D3 **Brooklyn** USA
14D2 **Brooklyn** *Borough* New York, USA
11D2 **Brooklyn Center** USA
6G4 **Brooks** Can
10G4 **Brooks,L** USA
10E2 **Brooks Mt** USA
6C3 **Brooks Range** *Mts* USA
15C3 **Brooksville** USA
13E2 **Brookton** USA
75D1 **Brooloo** Aust
76B2 **Broome** Aust
34D2 **Brora** Scot
18B2 **Brothers** USA
67F4 **Brothers,The** *Is* Yemen
36A2 **Brou** France
72B2 **Broulkou** *Well* Chad
43G2 **Brovary** Ukraine
11D2 **Browerville** USA
16B3 **Brownfield** USA
3F4 **Browning** USA
8D4 **Brownsville** USA
8D3 **Brownwood** USA
51F8 **Browse** *I* Aust
36B1 **Bruay-en-Artois** France
76A3 **Bruce,Mt** Aust
4E5 **Bruce Pen** Can
36E2 **Bruchsal** Germany
37E1 **Bruck** Austria
42D3 **Bruck an der Mur** Austria
Bruges = Brugge
36B1 **Brugge** Belg
36D1 **Brühl** Germany
29D1 **Brumado** Brazil
36D2 **Brumath** France
18C2 **Bruneau** USA
18C2 **Bruneau** *R* USA
56D2 **Brunei** Sultanate, S E Asia
40C1 **Brunico** Italy
78B2 **Brunner,L** NZ
9E3 **Brunswick** Georgia, USA
13F2 **Brunswick** Maine, USA
17D2 **Brunswick** Mississippi, USA
25B8 **Brunswick,Pen de** Chile
75E3 **Bruny I** Aust
44G3 **Brusenets** Russian Fed
16B1 **Brush** USA
23A3 **Brus Laguna** Honduras
Brussel = Bruxelles
42A2 **Bruxelles** Belg
36D2 **Bruyères** France
8D3 **Bryan** USA
75A2 **Bryan,Mt** Aust
44E5 **Bryansk** Russian Fed
17D3 **Bryant** USA
20D3 **Bryce Canyon Nat Pk** USA
42D2 **Brzeg** Pol
64E4 **Būbīyan** *I* Kuwait/Iraq
72D4 **Bubu** *R* Tanz
74E1 **Bubye** *R* Zim
26D2 **Bucaramanga** Colombia
34E3 **Buchan** *Oilfield* N Sea
70A4 **Buchanan** Lib
16C3 **Buchanan,L** USA
34E3 **Buchan Deep** N Sea
7L2 **Buchan G** Can
33C2 **Buchan Ness** *Pen* Scot
7N5 **Buchans** Can
28C2 **Buchardo** Arg
Bucharest = Bucureşti
20B3 **Buchon, Pt** USA
37C1 **Buchs** Switz
19D4 **Buckeye** USA
35E5 **Buckingham** Eng
10F2 **Buckland** USA
10F2 **Buckland** *R* USA
75A2 **Buckleboo** Aust
13F2 **Bucksport** USA
72B4 **Buco Zau** Congo
5J4 **Buctouche** Can
41F2 **Bucureşti** Rom
43D3 **Budapest** Hung
60D3 **Budaun** India
35C6 **Bude** Eng
17D3 **Bude** USA
45G7 **Budennovsk** Russian Fed
36E1 **Büdingen** Germany
41D2 **Budva** Montenegro, Yugos
72A3 **Buéa** Cam
37A2 **Buech** *R* France
20B3 **Buellton** USA
28B2 **Buena Esperanza** Arg
26C3 **Buenaventura** Colombia
16A4 **Buenaventura** Mexico
16A2 **Buena Vista** Colorado, USA
22B2 **Buenavista** Mexico
13D3 **Buena Vista** Virginia, USA
20C3 **Buena Vista L** USA
28A4 **Bueno** *R* Chile
25E4 **Buenos Aires** Arg
25E5 **Buenos Aires** State, Arg
17D2 **Buffalo** Mississipi, USA
9F2 **Buffalo** New York, USA
11B2 **Buffalo** South Dakota, USA
17C3 **Buffalo** Texas, USA
8C2 **Buffalo** Wyoming, USA
74E2 **Buffalo** *R* S Africa
3E2 **Buffalo Head Hills** *Mts* Can
18C1 **Buffalo Hump** USA
3F3 **Buffalo L** Alberta, Can
3E1 **Buffalo L** Northwest Territories, Can
6H4 **Buffalo Narrows** Can
15C2 **Buford** USA
41F2 **Buftea** Rom
43E2 **Bug** *R* Pol/Ukraine
26C3 **Buga** Colombia
63C1 **Bugdayli** Turkmenistan
44H2 **Bugrino** Russian Fed
53A2 **Bugt** China
44J5 **Bugulma** Russian Fed
44J5 **Buguruslan** Russian Fed
64C2 **Buhayrat al Asad** *Res* Syria
18D2 **Buhl** Idaho, USA
11D2 **Buhl** Minnesota, USA
71F4 **Bui Dam** Ghana
35D5 **Builth Wells** Wales
28A2 **Buin** Chile
37A2 **Buis-les-Baronnies** France
37E2 **Buje** Croatia, Yugos
72C4 **Bujumbura** Burundi
77E1 **Buka** *I* PNG
73C4 **Bukama** Zaïre
72C4 **Bukavu** Zaïre
58E2 **Bukhara** Uzbekistan
56D2 **Bukit Batubrok** *Mt* Indon
56B3 **Bukittinggi** Indon
72D4 **Bukoba** Tanz
57B3 **Buku Gandadiwata** *Mt* Indon
57C2 **Buku Saolat** *Mt* Indon
51G7 **Bula** Indon
57F8 **Bulan** Phil
60D3 **Bulandshahr** India
73C6 **Bulawayo** Zim
41F3 **Buldan** Turk
60D4 **Buldāna** India
10B6 **Buldir I** USA
50D2 **Bulgan** Mongolia
41E2 **Bulgaria** Republic, Europe
57C2 **Buli** Indon
37B1 **Bulle** Switz
78B2 **Buller** *R* NZ
75C3 **Buller,Mt** Aust
76A4 **Bullfinch** Aust
75B1 **Bulloo** *R* Aust
75B1 **Bulloo Downs** Aust
75B1 **Bulloo L** Aust
17D2 **Bull Shoals Res** USA
28A3 **Bulnes** Chile
76D1 **Bulolo** PNG
74D2 **Bultfontein** S Africa
57B4 **Bulukumba** Indon
72C3 **Bumba** Zaïre
56E2 **Bum Bum** *I* Malay
45D8 **Bu Menderes** *R* Turk
55B2 **Bumphal Dam** Thai
72D3 **Buna** Kenya
76A4 **Bunbury** Aust
34B4 **Buncrana** Irish Rep
77E3 **Bundaberg** Aust
75D2 **Bundarra** Aust
60D3 **Būndi** India
75C1 **Bungil** *R* Aust
73B4 **Bungo** Angola
54B4 **Bungo-suidō** *Str* Japan
56C2 **Bunguran** *I* Indon
72D3 **Bunia** Zaïre
17D2 **Bunker** USA
17D3 **Bunkie** USA
15C3 **Bunnell** USA
71H3 **Bunsuru** *R* Nig
56D3 **Buntok** Indon
57B2 **Buol** Indon
65D2 **Burāg** Syria
72C2 **Buram** Sudan
61B1 **Burang** China
72E3 **Burao** Somalia
57G8 **Burauen** Phil
66D1 **Buraydah** S Arabia
19C4 **Burbank** USA
75C2 **Burcher** Aust
63E1 **Burdalyk** Turkmenistan
45E8 **Burdur** Turk
53C1 **Bureinskiy Khrebet** *Mts* Russian Fed
50F2 **Bureya** Russian Fed
53C1 **Bureya** *R* Russian Fed
65B3 **Bûr Fu'ad** Egypt
42C2 **Burg** Germany
41F2 **Burgas** Bulg
15D2 **Burgaw** USA
37B1 **Burgdorf** Switz
5K4 **Burgeo** Can
74D3 **Burgersdorp** S Africa
48K5 **Burgin** China
22C1 **Burgos** Mexico
39B1 **Burgos** Spain
43D1 **Burgsvik** Sweden
41F3 **Burhaniye** Turk
60D4 **Burhānpur** India
57F8 **Burias** *I* Phil
5K4 **Burin Pen** Can
55C2 **Buriram** Thai
29C2 **Buritis** Brazil
3C3 **Burke Chan** Can
76C2 **Burketown** Aust
70B3 **Burkina** Republic, Africa
13D1 **Burk's Falls** Can
8B2 **Burley** USA
4F5 **Burlington** Can
16B2 **Burlington** Colorado, USA
9D2 **Burlington** Iowa, USA
14C2 **Burlington** New Jersey, USA
15D1 **Burlington** North Carolina, USA
9F2 **Burlington** Vermont, USA
18B1 **Burlington** Washington, USA
4D5 **Burlington** Wisconsin, USA
59H3 **Burma** Republic, Asia
16C3 **Burnet** USA
18B2 **Burney** USA
14B2 **Burnham** USA
76D5 **Burnie** Aust
35D5 **Burnley** Eng
18C2 **Burns** USA
6F4 **Burns Lake** Can
59G1 **Burqin** China
75A2 **Burra** Aust
75D2 **Burragorang,L** Aust
34D2 **Burray** *I* Scot
75C2 **Burren Junction** Aust
75C2 **Burrinjuck Res** Aust
51G8 **Burrundie** Aust
45D7 **Bursa** Turk
66B1 **Bur Safâga** Egypt
Bûr Sa'îd = Port Said
65B4 **Bûr Taufiq** Egypt
12C2 **Burton** USA
35E5 **Burton upon Trent** Eng
32J6 **Burtrask** Sweden
75B2 **Burtundy** Aust
57C3 **Buru** Indon
72C4 **Burundi** Republic, Africa

Burung Cap-Haitien

56B2 Burung Indon
11C3 Burwell USA
49N4 Buryatskaya Respublika, Russian Fed
72D2 Burye Eth
45J6 Burynshik Kazakhstan
35F5 Bury St Edmunds Eng
63C3 Būshehr Iran
72B4 Busira R Zaïre
43E2 Buskozdroj Pol
65D2 Busrā ash Shām Syria
36D3 Bussang France
76A4 Busselton Aust
38D2 Busto Italy
40B1 Busto Arsizio Italy
57E8 Busuanga I Phil
72C3 Buta Zaïre
28B3 Buta Ranquil Arg
72C4 Butare Rwanda
34C4 Bute I Scot
53A2 Butha Qi China
13D2 Butler USA
8B2 Butte USA
55C4 Butterworth Malay
74D3 Butterworth S Africa
33B2 Butt of Lewis C Scot
7M3 Button Is Can
20C3 Buttonwillow USA
57G9 Butuan Phil
57B4 Butung I Indon
45G5 Buturlinovka Russian Fed
61B2 Butwal Nepal
36E1 Butzbach Germany
72E3 Buulobarde Somalia
72E3 Buurhaakaba Somalia
44G4 Buy Russian Fed
52B1 Buyant Ovvo Mongolia
45H7 Buynaksk Russian Fed
49N5 Buyr Nuur L Mongolia
45G8 Büyük Ağri Daği Mt Turk
53E2 Buyukly Russian Fed
64A2 Büyük Menderes R Turk
41F1 Buzău Rom
41F1 Buzău R Rom
44J5 Buzuluk Russian Fed
14E2 Buzzards B USA
41F2 Byala Bulg
41E2 Byala Slatina Bulg
6H2 Byam Martin Chan Can
6H2 Byam Martin I Can
65C1 Byblos Hist. Site Leb
43D2 Bydgoszcz Pol
16B2 Byers USA
32F7 Bygland Nor
43G2 Bykhov Belorussia
53E2 Bykov Russian Fed
7K2 Bylot I Can
75C2 Byrock Aust
20B2 Byron USA
75D1 Byron,C Aust
49P3 Bytantay R Russian Fed
43D2 Bytom Pol

C

25E3 Caacupé Par
29A4 Caaguazú Par
73B5 Caála Angola
3C3 Caamano Sd Can
29A4 Caapucú Par
29B3 Caarapó Brazil
25E3 Caazapá Par
16A3 Caballo Res USA
57F7 Cabanatuan Phil
13F1 Cabano Can
27M5 Cabedelo Brazil
39A2 Cabeza del Buey Spain
28C3 Cabildo Arg
28A2 Cabildo Chile
26D1 Cabimas Ven
72B4 Cabinda Angola
72B4 Cabinda Province, Angola
18C1 Cabinet Mts USA
23C3 Cabo Beata Dom Rep
39C2 Cabo Binibeca C Spain
71A2 Cabo Cantin C Mor
40B3 Cabo Carbonara C Sardegna
28A3 Cabo Carranza C Chile
39A2 Cabo Carvoeiro C Port
8B3 Cabo Colnett C Mexico
28D3 Cabo Corrientes C Arg
26C2 Cabo Corrientes C Colombia
21B2 Cabo Corrientes C Mexico
23B3 Cabo Cruz C Cuba
39B1 Cabo de Ajo C Spain
39C1 Cabo de Caballeria C Spain
39C1 Cabo de Creus C Spain
25C9 Cabo de Hornos C Chile
39C2 Cabo de la Nao C Spain
39A1 Cabo de Peñas C Spain
39A2 Cabo de Roca C Port
39C2 Cabo de Salinas C Spain
74E2 Cabo de Santa Maria C Mozam
29D3 Cabo de São Tomé C Brazil
39A2 Cabo de São Vicente C Port
39B2 Cabo de Sata C Spain
39A2 Cabo de Sines C Port
39C1 Cabo de Tortosa C Spain
25C6 Cabo Dos Bahias C Arg
39A2 Cabo Espichel C Port
8B4 Cabo Falso C Mexico
39B2 Cabo Ferrat C Alg
39A1 Cabo Finisterre C Spain
39C1 Cabo Formentor C Spain
29D3 Cabo Frio Brazil
29D3 Cabo Frio C Brazil
23A4 Cabo Gracias à Dios Honduras
28A1 Cabo Leones C Chile
27J4 Cabo Maguarinho C Brazil
39A2 Cabo Negro C Mor
75D1 Caboolture Aust
27H3 Cabo Orange C Brazil
19C4 Cabo Punta Banda C Mexico
73D5 Cabora Bassa Dam Mozam
21A1 Caborca Mexico
21C2 Cabo Rojo C Mexico
22C1 Cabos Mexico
28D3 Cabo San Antonio C Arg
23A2 Cabo San Antonio C Cuba
25C8 Cabo San Diego C Arg
26B4 Cabo San Lorenzo C Ecuador
40B3 Cabo Teulada C Sardegna
39A2 Cabo Trafalgar C Spain
39B2 Cabo Tres Forcas C Mor
25C7 Cabo Tres Puntas C Arg
7M5 Cabot Str Can
39B2 Cabra Spain
39A1 Cabreira Mt Port
39C2 Cabrera I Spain
28A3 Cabrero Chile
39B2 Cabriel R Spain
22C2 Cacahuamilpa Mexico
41E2 Čačak Serbia, Yugos
28E2 Cacapava do Sul Brazil
14A3 Cacapon R USA
22C2 C A Carillo Mexico
28E1 Caceoul Brazil
27G7 Cáceres Brazil
39A2 Caceres Spain
17D2 Cache R USA
3D3 Cache Creek Can
20A1 Cache Creek, R USA
18D2 Cache Peak Mt USA
25C3 Cachi Arg
27G5 Cachimbo Brazil
27L6 Cachoeira Brazil
29B2 Cachoeira Alta Brazil
27L5 Cachoeira de Paulo Afonso Waterfall Brazil
25F4 Cachoeira do Sul Brazil
27K8 Cachoeiro de Itapemirim Brazil
20C3 Cachuma, L USA
73B5 Cacolo Angola
73B5 Caconda Angola
16B2 Cactus USA
29B2 Caçu Brazil
29D1 Caculé Brazil
73B5 Caculuvar R Angola
37B3 Čadca Czech
35D5 Cader Idris Mts Wales
11A2 Cadillac Can
9E2 Cadillac USA
57F8 Cadiz Phil
39A2 Cadiz Spain
27K6 Caeité Brazil
38B2 Caen France
35C5 Caernarfon Wales
35C5 Caernarfon B Wales
65C2 Caesarea Hist Site Israel
29D1 Caetité Brazil
25C3 Cafayate Arg
64B2 Caga Tepe Turk
57F7 Cagayan R Phil
57F9 Cagayan de Oro Phil
57F9 Cagayan Is Phil
37E3 Cagli Italy
40B3 Cagliari Sardegna
23D3 Caguas Puerto Rico
15B2 Cahaba R USA
35B5 Cahir Irish Rep
35B5 Cahone Pt Irish Rep
38C3 Cahors France
73D5 Caia Mozam
73C5 Caianda Angola
29B2 Caiapó R Brazil
29B2 Caiapônia Brazil
27L5 Caicó Brazil
23C2 Caicos Is Caribbean
9F4 Caicos Pass Bahamas
10G3 Cairn Mt USA
76D2 Cairns Aust
64B3 Cairo Egypt
9E3 Cairo USA
75B1 Caiwarro Aust
26C5 Cajabamba Peru
26C5 Cajamarca Peru
23D5 Calabozo Ven
41E2 Calafat Rom
25B8 Calafate Arg
57F8 Calagua Is Phil
39B1 Calahorra Spain
38C1 Calais France
13F1 Calais USA
25C2 Calama Chile
26D3 Calamar Colombia
57E8 Calamian Group Is Phil
73B4 Calandula Angola
56A2 Calang Indon
69B2 Calanscio Sand Sea Libya
57F8 Calapan Phil
41F2 Calarasi Rom
39B1 Calatayud Spain
20B2 Calaveras Res USA
57F8 Calbayog Phil
17D4 Calcasieu L USA
61C3 Calcutta India
39A2 Caldas da Rainha Port
27J7 Caldas Novas Brazil
25B3 Caldera Chile
8B2 Caldwell USA
74B3 Caledon S Africa
74D3 Caledon R S Africa
12A2 Caledonia Minnesota, USA
14B1 Caledonia New York, USA
5H4 Caledonia Hills Can
22B1 Calera Mexico
25C7 Caleta Olivia Arg
8B3 Calexico USA
6G4 Calgary Can
15C2 Calhoun USA
15C2 Calhoun Falls USA
26C3 Cali Colombia
20C3 Caliente California, USA
8B3 Caliente Nevada, USA
16A2 Caliente New Mexico, USA
20C3 California Aqueduct USA
8A3 California State, USA
62B2 Calimera,Pt India
28B2 Calingasta Arg
19C4 Calipatria USA
74C3 Calitzdorp S Africa
75B1 Callabonna R Aust
75A1 Callabonna,L Aust
13D1 Callander Can
34C3 Callander Scot
75A1 Callanna Aust
26C6 Callao Peru
22C1 Calles Mexico
14C2 Callicoon USA
3F2 Calling L Can
22C1 Calnali Mexico
15E4 Caloosahatchee R USA
75D1 Caloundra Aust
22C2 Calpulalpan Mexico
40C3 Caltanissetta Italy
73B4 Caluango Angola
73B5 Calulo Angola
73B5 Caluquembe Angola
67F4 Caluula Somalia
3C3 Calvert I Can
40B2 Calvi Corse
22B1 Calvillo Mexico
74B3 Calvinia S Africa
36E2 Calw Germany
29E1 Camacari Brazil
22B1 Camacho Mexico
28E2 Camaguã Brazil
28E2 Camaguã R Brazil
21E2 Camagüey Cuba
21E2 Camagüey,Arch de Is Cuba
29E1 Camamu Brazil
26D7 Camaná Peru
10N5 Camania I Can
29B2 Camapuã Brazil
26E8 Camargo Bol
20C3 Camarillo USA
25C6 Camarones Arg
18B1 Camas USA
73B4 Camaxilo Angola
73B4 Cambatela Angola
55C3 Cambodia Republic, S E Asia
35C6 Camborne Eng
38C1 Cambrai France
20B3 Cambria USA
35D5 Cambrian Mts Wales
12C2 Cambridge Can
35E5 Cambridge County, Eng
35F5 Cambridge Eng
23H1 Cambridge Jamaica
13D3 Cambridge Maryland, USA
13E2 Cambridge Massachussets, USA
11D2 Cambridge Minnesota, USA
78C1 Cambridge NZ
12C2 Cambridge Ohio, USA
6H3 Cambridge Bay Can
51F8 Cambridge G Aust
45F7 Cam Burun Pt Turk
9D3 Camden Arkansas, USA
75D2 Camden Aust
13E3 Camden New Jersey, USA
14C1 Camden New York, USA
15C2 Camden South Carolina, USA
10J1 Camden B USA
37E3 Camerino Italy
17D2 Cameron Missouri, USA
17C3 Cameron Texas, USA
56F6 Cameron Highlands Malay
6H2 Cameron I Can
78A3 Cameron Mts NZ
72B3 Cameroon Federal Republic, Africa
72A3 Cameroun Mt Cam
27J4 Cametá Brazil
57F9 Camiguin I Phil
57F7 Camiling Phil
15C2 Camilla USA
20B1 Camino USA
26F8 Camiri Bol
73C4 Camissombo Angola
27K4 Camocim Brazil
76C2 Camooweal Aust
62E3 Camorta I Indian O
28D2 Campana Arg
25A7 Campana I Chile
3C3 Campania I Can
74C2 Campbell S Africa
78B2 Campbell,C NZ
3C3 Campbell I Can
xxixN7 Campbell I NZ
10M2 Campbell L Can
6E3 Campbell,Mt Can
60C2 Campbellpore Pak
6F5 Campbell River Can
12B3 Campbellsville USA
7M5 Campbellton Can
75D2 Campbelltown Aust
34C4 Campbeltown Scot
21C3 Campeche Mexico
75B3 Camperdown Aust
27L5 Campina Grande Brazil
27J8 Campinas Brazil
29C2 Campina Verde Brazil
57B5 Camplong Indon
20C2 Camp Nelson USA
72A3 Campo Cam
40C2 Campobasso Italy
29C3 Campo Belo Brazil
28C1 Campo del Cielo Arg
29C2 Campo Florido Brazil
25D3 Campo Gallo Arg
25F2 Campo Grande Brazil
27K4 Campo Maior Brazil
25F2 Campo Mourão Brazil
28E1 Campo Novo Brazil
29D3 Campos Brazil
29C2 Campos Altos Brazil
37D1 Campo Tures Italy
19D4 Camp Verde USA
55D3 Cam Ranh Viet
6G4 Camrose Can
73B5 Camucuio Angola
23K1 Canaan Tobago
14D1 Canaan USA
73B5 Canacupa Angola
2F3 Canada Dominion, N America
25D4 Cañada de Gomez Arg
14C2 Canadensis USA
16B2 Canadian USA
8C3 Canadian R USA
45D7 Canakkale Turk
28B3 Canalejas Arg
3E3 Canal Flats Can
14B1 Canandaigua USA
14B1 Canandaigua L USA
21A1 Cananea Mexico
29C4 Cananeia Brazil
xxxG3 Canary Basin Atlantic O
Canary Is = Islas Canarias
22B2 Canas Mexico
21B2 Canatlán Mexico
9E4 Canaveral,C USA
27L7 Canavieriras Brazil
76D4 Canberra Aust
18B2 Canby California, USA
11C3 Canby Minnesota, USA
41F3 Çandarli Körfezi B Turk
3G3 Candle L Can
14D2 Candlewood,L USA
11C2 Cando USA
14B1 Candor USA
25E4 Canelones Urug
17C2 Caney USA
73C5 Cangamba Angola
73C5 Cangombe Angola
28E2 Canguçu Brazil
52D2 Cangzhou China
7M4 Caniapiscau R Can
7M4 Caniapiscau, Réservoir Res Can
40C3 Canicatti Italy
27L4 Canindé Brazil
14B1 Canisteo USA
14B1 Canisteo R USA
22B1 Canitas de Felipe Pescador Mexico
16A2 Canjilon USA
64B1 Çankırı Turk
3E3 Canmore Can
34B3 Canna I Scot
62B2 Cannanore India
38D3 Cannes France
11B2 Cannonball R USA
75C3 Cann River Aust
25F3 Canõas Brazil
3G2 Canoe L Can
29B4 Canoinhas Brazil
16A2 Canon City USA
75B2 Canopus Aust
6H4 Canora Can
75C2 Canowindra Aust
5J4 Canso Can
35B5 Cansore Pt Irish Rep
35F6 Canterbury Eng
78B2 Canterbury Bight B NZ
78B2 Canterbury Plains NZ
55D4 Can Tho Viet
20D3 Cantil USA
28A1 Canto de Augua Chile
Canton = Guangzhou
17E3 Canton Mississippi, USA
12A2 Canton Missouri, USA
9E2 Canton Ohio, USA
14B2 Canton Pensylvania, USA
11C3 Canton S Dakota, USA
77H1 Canton I Phoeniz Is
10J3 Cantwell USA
36A2 Cany-Barville France
16B3 Canyon USA
18C2 Canyon City USA
18D1 Canyon Ferry L USA
19D3 Canyonlands Nat Pk USA
10N3 Canyon Range Mts Can
18B2 Canyonville USA
73C4 Canzar Angola
55D1 Cao Bang Viet
27J4 Capanema Brazil
29C3 Capão Bonito Brazil
37B3 Cap Bénat C France
71D1 Cap Blanc C Tunisia
71E1 Cap Bon C Tunisia
71D1 Cap Bougaron C Alg
38B3 Capbreton France
37B3 Cap Camarat C France
5H4 Cap Chat Can
22A1 Cap Corrientes C Mexico
40B2 Cap Corse C Corse
73E5 Cap d'Ambre C Madag
37B3 Cap d'Antibes C France
5J4 Cap de Gaspé C Can
38B2 Cap de la Hague C France
5G4 Cap-de-la-Madeleine Can
7L3 Cap de Nouvelle-France C Can
39C2 Capdepera Spain
22B2 Cap de Tancitiario C Mexico
71B1 Cap des Trois Fourches C Mor
75E3 Cape Barren I Aust
xxxJ6 Cape Basin Atlantic O
7N5 Cape Breton I Can
71F4 Cape Coast Ghana
13E2 Cape Cod B USA
7M3 Cape Dyer Can
79F7 Cape Evans Base Ant.
15D2 Cape Fear R USA
17E2 Cape Girardeau USA
Cape Horn = Cabo de Hornos
xxviiiH4 Cape Johnston Depth Pacific O
29D2 Capelinha Brazil
10E2 Cape Lisburne USA
73B5 Capelongo Angola
13E3 Cape May USA
73B4 Capenda Camulemba Angola
6F2 Cape Parry Can
74C3 Cape Province S Africa
74B3 Cape Town S Africa
xxxG4 Cape Verde Is Atlantic O
xxxG4 Cape Verde Basin Atlantic O
10K4 Cape Yakataga USA
76D2 Cape York Pen Aust
37B3 Cap Ferrat C France
36A1 Cap Gris Nez C France
23C3 Cap-Haitien Haiti

Capim Champa

27J4 **Capim** *R* Brazil
29A3 **Capitán Bado** Par
20D3 **Capitol Reef Nat Pk** USA
29A2 **Capivari** *R* Brazil
5K3 **Cap Mécatina** *C* Can
23P2 **Cap Moule à Chique** *C* St Lucia
37C2 **Capo di Noli** *C* Italy
40D3 **Capo Isola de Correnti** *C* Italy
40D3 **Capo Rizzuto** *C* Italy
41D3 **Capo Santa Maria di Leuca** *C* Italy
40C3 **Capo San Vito** Italy
40D3 **Capo Spartivento** *C* Italy
23P2 **Cap Pt** St Lucia
40C2 **Capri** *I* Italy
73C5 **Caprivi Strip** Region, Namibia
40B2 **Cap Rosso** *C* Corse
71D1 **Cap Serrat** *C* Tunisia
37A3 **Cap Sicié** *C* France
70A3 **Cap Vert** *C* Sen
26D4 **Caquetá** *R* Colombia
41E2 **Caracal** Rom
26F3 **Caracaraí** Brazil
26E1 **Caracas** Ven
29A3 **Caracol** Brazil
29C3 **Caraguatatuba** Brazil
25B5 **Carahue** Chile
29D2 **Caraí** Brazil
29D3 **Carandaí** Brazil
29A2 **Carandazal** Brazil
27K8 **Carangola** Brazil
41E1 **Caransebeş** Rom
75A2 **Carappee Hill** *Mt* Aust
23A3 **Caratasca** Honduras
29D2 **Caratinga** Brazil
39B2 **Caravaca** Spain
29E2 **Caravelas** Brazil
28E1 **Carazinho** Brazil
12B3 **Carbondale** Illinois, USA
14C2 **Carbondale** Pennsylvania, USA
7N5 **Carbonear** Can
40B3 **Carbonia** Sardegna
6G4 **Carcajou** Can
69D3 **Carcar Mts** Somalia
38C3 **Carcassonne** France
6E3 **Carcross** Can
22C2 **Cardel** Mexico
21D2 **Cardenas** Cuba
22C1 **Cárdenas** Mexico
22D2 **Cárdenas** Mexico
35D6 **Cardiff** Wales
35C5 **Cardigan** Wales
35C5 **Cardigan B** Wales
28D2 **Cardóna** Urug
3F4 **Cardston** Can
3G2 **Careen L** Can
41E1 **Carei** Rom
27G4 **Careiro** Brazil
28A2 **Carén** Chile
12C2 **Carey** USA
38B2 **Carhaix-Plouguer** France
25D5 **Carhué** Arg
27K8 **Cariacica** Brazil
24C2 **Caribbean S** C America
4B2 **Caribou** Can
13F1 **Caribou** USA
10N3 **Caribou** *R* Can
6G4 **Caribou Mts** Alberta, Can
6F4 **Caribou Mts** British Columbia, Can
57F8 **Carigara** Phil
36C2 **Carignan** France
36B1 **Carin** France
29D1 **Carinhanha** Brazil
29D1 **Carinhanha** *R* Brazil
26F1 **Caripito** Ven
4F4 **Carleton Place** Can
74D2 **Carletonville** S Africa
18C2 **Carlin** USA
12B3 **Carlinville** USA
34D4 **Carlisle** Eng
13D2 **Carlisle** USA
10D5 **Carlisle** *I* USA
28C3 **Carlos** Arg
29D2 **Carlos Chagas** Brazil
35B5 **Carlow** County, Irish Rep
35B5 **Carlow** Irish Rep
19C4 **Carlsbad** California, USA
8C3 **Carlsbad** New Mexico, USA
16B3 **Carlsbad Caverns Nat Pk** USA
xxviiiE4 **Carlsberg Ridge** Indian O
6H5 **Carlyle** Can
10L3 **Carmacks** Can
37B2 **Carmagnola** Italy
35C6 **Carmarthen** Wales
35C6 **Carmarthen B** Wales
20B2 **Carmel** California, USA
14D2 **Carmel** New York, USA
65C2 **Carmel,Mt** Israel
28D2 **Carmelo** Urug
20B2 **Carmel Valley** USA
8B4 **Carmen** *I* Mexico
25D6 **Carmen de Patagones** Arg
12B3 **Carmi** USA
19B3 **Carmichael** USA
29C2 **Carmo do Paranaiba** Brazil
39A2 **Carmona** Spain
76A3 **Carnarvon** Aust
74C3 **Carnarvon** S Africa
29E2 **Carncacá** Brazil
34B4 **Carndonagh** Irish Rep
76B3 **Carnegi,L** Aust
34D3 **Carngorms** *Mts* Scot
62E3 **Car Nicobar** *I* Indian O
72B3 **Carnot** CAR
75A2 **Carnot,C** Aust
10N2 **Carnwath** *R* Can
15E4 **Carol City** USA
27J5 **Carolina** Brazil
74E2 **Carolina** S Africa
15D2 **Carolina Beach** USA
xxviiiJ4 **Caroline Is** Pacific O
45C6 **Carpathians** *Mts* E Europe
43F3 **Carpatii Orientali** *Mts* Rom
76C2 **Carpentaria,G of** Aust
59H5 **Carpenter Ridge** Indian O
38D3 **Carpentras** France
40C2 **Carpi** Italy
20C3 **Carpinteria** USA
15C3 **Carrabelle** USA
40C2 **Carrara** Italy
33B3 **Carrauntoohill** *Mt* Irish Rep
35B5 **Carrickmacross** Irish Rep
35B5 **Carrick-on-Suir** Irish Rep
75A2 **Carrieton** Aust
8D2 **Carrington** USA
39B1 **Carrión** *R* Spain
28A1 **Carrizal Bajo** Chile
17F4 **Carrizo Spring** USA
16A3 **Carrizozo** USA
9D2 **Carroll** USA
15B2 **Carrollton** Georgia, USA
12B3 **Carrollton** Kentucky, USA
17D2 **Carrollton** Missouri, USA
3H3 **Carrot** *R* Can
17E2 **Carruthersville** USA
45F7 **Carsamba** Turk
45E8 **Carsamba** *R* Turk
8B3 **Carson City** USA
12C2 **Carsonville** USA
23B4 **Cartagena** Colombia
39B2 **Cartagena** Spain
26C3 **Cartago** Colombia
21D4 **Cartago** Costa Rica
20C2 **Cartago** USA
26D1 **Cartegena** Colombia
78C2 **Carterton** NZ
17D2 **Carthage** Missouri, USA
13D2 **Carthage** New York, USA
17D3 **Carthage** Texas, USA
76B2 **Cartier I** Timor S
7N4 **Cartwright** Can
27L5 **Caruaru** Brazil
26F1 **Carúpano** Ven
15D1 **Cary** USA
28A2 **Casablanca** Chile
71A2 **Casablanca** Mor
29C3 **Casa Branca** Brazil
8B3 **Casa Grande** USA
40B1 **Casale Monferrato** Italy
37D2 **Casalmaggiore** Italy
28C3 **Casares** Arg
22C1 **Casas** Mexico
28E1 **Casca** Brazil
18D1 **Cascade** USA
3D4 **Cascade Mts** Can/USA
78A2 **Cascade Pt** NZ
8A2 **Cascade Range** *Mts* USA
18C2 **Cascade Res** USA
25F2 **Cascavel** Brazil
37D3 **Casciana** Italy
37D3 **Cascina** Italy
40C2 **Caserta** Italy
79G9 **Casey** *Base* Ant
35B5 **Cashel** Irish Rep
28C2 **Casilda** Arg
77E3 **Casino** Aust
26C5 **Casma** Peru
20B3 **Casmalia** USA
39C1 **Caspe** Spain
8C2 **Casper** USA
45H7 **Caspian S** Asia/Europe
13D3 **Cass** USA
73C5 **Cassamba** Angola
36B1 **Cassel** France
11C2 **Casselton** USA
3C2 **Cassiar** Can
6E3 **Cassiar Mts** Can
29B2 **Cassilândia** Brazil
40C2 **Cassino** Italy
11D2 **Cass Lake** USA
20C3 **Castaic** USA
28B2 **Castaño** *R* Arg
37D2 **Castelfranco** Italy
38D3 **Castellane** France
28D3 **Castelli** Arg
39C1 **Castellon de la Plana** Spain
37D2 **Castelnovo ne'Monti** Italy
37D2 **Castelnuovo di Garfagnana** Italy
27K5 **Castelo** Brazil
39A2 **Castelo Branco** Port
38C3 **Castelsarrasin** France
40C3 **Castelvetrano** Italy
75B3 **Casterton** Aust
37D3 **Castiglion Fiorentino** Italy
28A1 **Castilla** Chile
39B2 **Castilla La Nueva** Region, Spain
39B1 **Castilla La Vieja** Region, Spain
28E2 **Castillos** Urug
33B3 **Castlebar** Irish Rep
34B3 **Castlebay** Scot
19D3 **Castle Dale** USA
34D4 **Castle Douglas** Scot
18C1 **Castlegar** Can
75B3 **Castlemain** Aust
20B3 **Castle,Mt** USA
18D2 **Castle Peak** USA
75C2 **Castlereagh** Aust
16B2 **Castle Rock** USA
38C3 **Castres-sur-l'Agout** France
23E4 **Castries** St Lucia
25B6 **Castro** Arg
25F2 **Castro** Brazil
27L6 **Castro Alves** Brazil
40D3 **Castrovillari** Italy
20B2 **Castroville** USA
28D2 **Casupa** Urug
78A2 **Caswell Sd** NZ
21E2 **Cat** *I* Bahamas
57F8 **Catabalogan** Phil
26B5 **Catacaos** Peru
29D3 **Cataguases** Brazil
17D3 **Catahoula L** USA
29C2 **Catalão** Brazil
39C1 **Cataluña** Region, Spain
25C3 **Catamarca** Arg
25C3 **Catamarca** State, Arg
73D5 **Catandica** Mozam
57F8 **Catanduanes** *I* Phil
25G2 **Catanduva** Brazil
29B4 **Catanduvas** Brazil
40D3 **Catania** Italy
28A3 **Catan-Lil** Arg
40D3 **Catanzaro** Italy
17F4 **Catarina** USA
57F8 **Catarman** Phil
75A2 **Catastrophe,C** Aust
23C5 **Catatumbo** *R* Ven
14B2 **Catawissa** USA
22C2 **Catemaco** Mexico
38D3 **Cater** Corse
40B2 **Cateraggio** Corse
73B4 **Catete** Angola
74D3 **Cathcart** S Africa
28B1 **Catinzaco** Arg
70A3 **Catió** Guinea-Bissau
4C3 **Cat L** Can
4C3 **Cat Lake** Can
77E3 **Cato** *I* Aust
21D2 **Catoche,C** Mexico
14B3 **Catoctin Mt** USA
13D3 **Catonsville** USA
28C3 **Catrilo** Arg
13E2 **Catskill** USA
13E2 **Catskill Mts** USA
5J2 **Caubvick,Mt** Can
26D2 **Cauca** *R* Colombia
27L4 **Caucaia** Brazil
26C2 **Caucasia** Colombia
45G7 **Caucasus** *Mts* Georgia
36A2 **Caudebec-en-Caux** France
36B1 **Caudry** France
73B4 **Caungula** Angola
25B5 **Cauquenes** Chile
13F1 **Causapscal** Can
62B2 **Cauvery** *R* India
38D3 **Cavaillon** France
29C1 **Cavalcanta** Brazil
37D1 **Cavalese** italy
11C2 **Cavalier** USA
70B4 **Cavally** *R* Lib
35B5 **Cavan** County, Irish Rep
35B5 **Cavan** Irish Rep
57F8 **Cavite** Phil
26D4 **Caxias** Brazil
27K4 **Caxias** Brazil
25F3 **Caxias do Sul** Brazil
73B4 **Caxito** Angola
15C2 **Cayce** USA
64D1 **Çayeli** Turk
27H3 **Cayenne** French Guiana
36A1 **Cayeux-sur-Mer** France
21E3 **Cayman Brac** *I* Caribbean
23A3 **Cayman Is** Caribbean
23A3 **Cayman Trench** Caribbean
72E3 **Caynabo** Somalia
20B3 **Cayncos** USA
21E2 **Cayo Romana** *I* Cuba
21D3 **Cayos Mistikos** *Is* Nic
23A2 **Cay Sal** *I* Caribbean
14B1 **Cayuga L** USA
14C1 **Cazenovia** USA
73C5 **Cazombo** Angola
5J4 **C Breton Highlands** Can
Ceará = Fortaleza
27K5 **Ceara State,** Brazil
28B1 **Cebollar** Arg
28E2 **Cebollati** Urug
57F8 **Cebu** Phil
57F8 **Cebu** *I* Phil
14C3 **Cecilton** USA
40C2 **Cecina** Italy
37D3 **Cecina** *R* Italy
11D3 **Cedar** *R* USA
8B3 **Cedar City** USA
17C3 **Cedar Creek Res** USA
11D3 **Cedar Falls** USA
6H4 **Cedar L** Can
20D1 **Cedar Mts** USA
9D2 **Cedar Rapids** USA
15B2 **Cedartown** USA
22B1 **Cedral** Mexico
21A2 **Cedros** *I* Mexico
76C4 **Ceduna** Aust
72E3 **Ceelbuur** Somalia
69D3 **Ceerigaabo** Somalia
40C3 **Cefalù** Italy
43D3 **Cegléd** Hung
73B5 **Cela** Angola
21B2 **Celaya** Mexico
Celebes = Sulawesi
51F6 **Celebes S** S E Asia
12C2 **Celina** USA
40D1 **Celje** Slovenia, Yugos
42C2 **Celle** Germany
35B6 **Celtic S** UK
51G7 **Cendrawasih** *Pen* Indon
37C2 **Ceno** *R* Italy
17D3 **Center** USA
15B1 **Center Hill L** USA
14D2 **Center Moriches** USA
37D2 **Cento** Italy
34C3 **Central** Region, Scot
16A3 **Central** USA
72B3 **Central African Republic** Africa
17C1 **Central City** Nebraska, USA
14A2 **Central City** Pennsylvania, USA
12B3 **Centralia** Illinois, USA
8A2 **Centralia** Washington, USA
74C1 **Central Kalahari Game Res** Botswana
63E3 **Central Makran Range** *Mts* Pak
18B2 **Central Point** USA
51H7 **Central Range** *Mts* PNG
14B1 **Central Square** USA
15B2 **Centre Point** USA
15B2 **Centreville** Alabama, USA
14B3 **Centreville** Maryland, USA
56D4 **Cepu** Indon
Ceram = Seram
51F7 **Ceram Sea** Indonesia
28C3 **Cereales** Arg
28C1 **Ceres** Arg
27J7 **Ceres** Brazil
74B3 **Ceres** S Africa
20B2 **Ceres** USA
38C2 **Cergy-Pontoise** France
40D2 **Cerignola** Italy
45D7 **Cernavodă** Rom
36D3 **Cernay** France
8C4 **Cerralvo** *I* Mexico
22B1 **Cerritos** Mexico
28B2 **Cerro Aconcagua** *Mt* Arg
22C1 **Cerro Azul** Mexico
28B1 **Cerro Boneta** *Mt* Arg
28A3 **Cerro Campanario** *Mt* Chile
28C2 **Cerro Champaqui** *Mt* Arg
28D2 **Cerro Chatto** Urug
22B2 **Cerro Cuachaia** *Mt* Mexico
22C1 **Cerro de Astillero** Mexico
28B1 **Cerro del Potro** *Mt* Chile/Arg
22C1 **Cerro del Tigre** *Mt* Mexico
28B1 **Cerro del Toro** *Mt* Chile/Arg
28B2 **Cerro de Olivares** *Mt* Arg
26C6 **Cerro de Pasco** Peru
23D3 **Cerro de Punta** *Mt* Puerto Rico
22B2 **Cerro El Cantado** *Mt* Mexico
28B3 **Cerro El Nevado** Arg
28B1 **Cerro General M Belgrano** *Mt* Arg
22B2 **Cerro Grande** *Mts* Mexico
22A1 **Cerro Huehueto** *Mt* Mexico
28A2 **Cerro Juncal** *Mt* Arg/Chile
22B1 **Cerro la Ardilla** *Mts* Mexico
28A1 **Cerro las Tortolas** *Mt* Chile
22B2 **Cerro Laurel** *Mt* Mexico
28A2 **Cerro Mercedario** *Mt* Arg
28A3 **Cerro Mora** *Mt* Chile
23C4 **Cerron** *Mt* Ven
28B3 **Cerro Payún** *Mt* Arg
22C1 **Cerro Peña Nevada** *Mt* Mexico
22C2 **Cerro Penón del Rosario** *Mt* Mexico
28B2 **Cerro Sosneado** *Mt* Arg
22B2 **Cerro Teotepec** *Mt* Mexico
28B2 **Cerro Tupungato** *Mt* Arg
22C2 **Cerro Yucuyacau** *Mt* Mexico
37E2 **Cervia** Italy
37C2 **Cervo** *R* Italy
40C2 **Cesena** Italy
44D4 **Cēsis** Latvia
42C3 **České Budějovice** Czech
42C3 **České Zemé** Region, Czech
42D3 **Českomoravská Vysočina** *Mts* Czech
41F3 **Çeşme** Turk
76E4 **Cessnock** Aust
40D2 **Cetina** *R* Croatia, Yugos
71A1 **Ceuta** N W Africa
64C2 **Ceyham** Turk
64C2 **Ceyhan** *R* Turk
64C2 **Ceylanpınar** Turk
Ceylon = Sri Lanka
49L4 **Chaa-Khol** Russian Fed
38C2 **Chaâteaudun** France
37B1 **Chablais** Region, France
36B3 **Chablis** France
28C2 **Chacabuco** Arg
26C5 **Chachapoyas** Peru
28B3 **Chacharramendi** Arg
60C3 **Chachran** Pak
25D3 **Chaco** State, Arg
72B2 **Chad** Republic, Africa
72B2 **Chad** *L* C Africa
28B3 **Chadileuvu** *R* Arg
8C2 **Chadron** USA
17E2 **Chaffee** USA
60A3 **Chagai** Pak
63E3 **Chagai Hills** Pak
49P4 **Chagda** Russian Fed
60B2 **Chaghcharan** Afghan
xxviiiE5 **Chagos Arch** Indian O
23L1 **Chaguanas** Trinidad
63E2 **Chahah Burjak** Afghan
63E3 **Chāh Bahār** Iran
54A2 **Ch'aho** N Korea
55C2 **Chai Badan** Thai
61C3 **Chāībāsa** India
71G3 **Chaîne de l'Atakor** *Mts* Benin
55C3 **Chaine des Cardamomes** *Mts* Camb
73C4 **Chaine des Mitumba** *Mts* Zaïre
55C2 **Chaiyaphum** Thai
28D2 **Chajari** Arg
63E2 **Chakhansur** Afghan
60C2 **Chakwal** Pak
26D7 **Chala** Peru
73D5 **Chalabesa** Zambia
60A2 **Chalap Dalam** *Mts* Afghan
36C3 **Chalindrey** France
52C4 **Chaling** China
60D4 **Chālisgaon** India
10K2 **Chalkyitsik** USA
36C2 **Challerange** France
18D2 **Challis** USA
36C2 **Châlons sur Marne** France
38C2 **Chalon sur Saône** France
42C3 **Cham** Germany
16A2 **Chama** USA
60B2 **Chaman** Pak
60D2 **Chamba** India
60D3 **Chambal** *R* India
11C3 **Chamberlain** USA
10J2 **Chamberlin,Mt** USA
13D3 **Chambersburg** USA
38D2 **Chambéry** France
36B2 **Chambly** France
13E1 **Chambord** Can
60A3 **Chambor Kalat** Pak
22A2 **Chamela** Mexico
63C2 **Chamgordan** Iran
28B2 **Chamical** Arg
37B2 **Chamonix** France
61B3 **Champa** India

Champagne Chukchi S

38C2 **Champagne** Region, France
74D2 **Champagne Castle** *Mt* Lesotho
37A1 **Champagnole** France
9E2 **Champaign** USA
55D3 **Champassak** Laos
9F2 **Champlain,L** USA
37A1 **Champlitte** France
62B2 **Chāmrājnagar** India
25B3 **Chañaral** Chile
28A3 **Chanco** Chile
6D3 **Chandalar** USA
6D3 **Chandalar** *R* USA
15B3 **Chandeleur Is** USA
60D2 **Chandīgarh** India
5J4 **Chandler** Can
19D4 **Chandler** USA
61D3 **Chandpur** Bang
60D5 **Chandrapur** India
63E3 **Chānf** Iran
74E1 **Changane** *R* Mozam
73D5 **Changara** Mozam
53B3 **Changbai** China
53B3 **Changchun** China
52C4 **Changde** China
54A3 **Changdo** N Korea
54A3 **Changhang** S Korea
54A3 **Changhowan** S Korea
50E4 **Chang-hua** Taiwan
54A4 **Changhung** S Korea
55D2 **Changjiang** China
52D3 **Chang Jiang** *R* China
53B3 **Changjin** N Korea
54A2 **Changjin** *R* N Korea
54A2 **Changjin Res** N Korea
53A3 **Changling** China
52C4 **Changsha** China
52E3 **Changshu** China
53A3 **Changtu** China
52B2 **Changwu** China
53B4 **Changyŏn** N Korea
52C2 **Changzhi** China
52E3 **Changzhou** China
38B2 **Channel Is** UK
8B3 **Channel Is** USA
7N5 **Channel Port-aux-Basques** Can
4D4 **Channing** USA
55C3 **Chanthaburi** Thai
36B2 **Chantilly** France
7J3 **Chantrey Inlet** *B* Can
17C2 **Chanute** USA
48J4 **Chany, Ozero** *L* Russian Fed
52D5 **Chaoàn** China
52D5 **Chao'an** China
52D3 **Chao Hu** *L* China
55C3 **Chao Phraya** *R* Thai
53A2 **Chaor He** *R* China
71A1 **Chaouen** Mor
52E1 **Chaoyang** China
53A1 **Chaozhong** China
27K6 **Chapada Diamantina** *Mts* Brazil
27K4 **Chapadinha** Brazil
22B1 **Chapala** Mexico
22B1 **Chapala,Lac de** *L* Mexico
45J5 **Chapayevo** Kazakhstan
25F3 **Chapecó** Brazil
15D1 **Chapel Hill** USA
23H1 **Chapeltown** Jamaica
7K5 **Chapleau** Can
44G5 **Chaplygin** Russian Fed
16B1 **Chappell** USA
28D1 **Charada** Arg
79G3 **Charcot I** Ant
58E2 **Chardzhou** Turkmenistan
71B2 **Charef** Mor
38C2 **Charente** *R* France
72B2 **Chari** *R* Chad
72B2 **Chari Baguirmi** Region, Chad
60B1 **Charikar** Afghan
17D1 **Chariton** *R* USA
27G2 **Charity** Guyana
60D3 **Charkhāri** India
36C1 **Charleroi** Belg
5G4 **Charlesbourg** Can
9F3 **Charles,C** USA
12B3 **Charleston** Illinois, USA
17E2 **Charleston** Missouri, USA
9F3 **Charleston** S Carolina, USA
9E3 **Charleston** W Virginia, USA
19C3 **Charleston Peak** *Mt* USA
14B3 **Charles Town** USA
14D1 **Charlestown** USA
72C4 **Charlesville** Zaïre
76D3 **Charleville** Aust
38C2 **Charleville-Mézières** France
12B1 **Charlevoix** USA
12C2 **Charlotte** Michigan, USA
9E3 **Charlotte** N Carolina, USA
15E4 **Charlotte Harbor** *B* USA
9F3 **Charlottesville** USA
7M5 **Charlottetown** Can
23K1 **Charlotteville** Tobago
75B3 **Charlton** Aust
4F3 **Charlton I** Can
36D2 **Charmes** France
60C2 **Charsadda** Pak
76D3 **Charters Towers** Aust
38C2 **Chartres** France
28B1 **Chaschuil** Arg
25E5 **Chascomús** Arg
3E3 **Chase** Can
54A2 **Chasong** N Korea
37A2 **Château-Arnoux** France
38B2 **Châteaubriant** France
36A3 **Château-du-Loir** France
36A2 **Châteaudun** France
38B2 **Châteaulin** France
36A2 **Châteauneuf-en Thymerais** France
36B3 **Châteauneuf-sur-Loire** France
36A3 **Château Renault** France
38C2 **Châteauroux** France
36D2 **Château-Salins** France
38C2 **Château-Thierry** France
3E2 **Chateh** Can
36C1 **Châtelet** Belg
38C2 **Châtellerault** France
11D3 **Chatfield** USA
35F6 **Chatham** Eng
14E2 **Chatham** Massachusets, USA
7M5 **Chatham** New Brunswick, Can
14D1 **Chatham** New York, USA
4E5 **Chatham** Ontario, Can
13D3 **Chatham** Virginia, USA
77H5 **Chatham Is** NZ
3B3 **Chatham Sd** Can/USA
10M4 **Chatham Str** USA
5J4 **Chéticamp** Can
38C2 **Châtillon** France
36B3 **Châtillon-Coligny** France
36C3 **Châtillon-sur-Siene** France
61B4 **Chatrapur** India
14C3 **Chatsworth** USA
15C2 **Chattahoochee** USA
15B2 **Chattahoochee** *R* USA
9E3 **Chattanooga** USA
37B2 **Châttilon** Italy
55A1 **Chauk** Burma
38D2 **Chaumont** France
36B2 **Chauny** France
55D3 **Chau Phu** Viet
62E3 **Chaura** *I* Indian O
37A1 **Chaussin** France
39A1 **Chaves** Port
44J4 **Chaykovskiy** Russian Fed
39B2 **Chazaouet** Alg
28C2 **Chazón** Arg
26D2 **Chcontá** Colombia
42C2 **Cheb** Czech
44H4 **Cheboksary** Russian Fed
43G2 **Chechersk** Belorussia
53B4 **Chech'on** S Korea
60C3 **Chechro** Pak
17C2 **Checotah** USA
55A2 **Cheduba** *I* Burma
75B1 **Cheepie** Aust
53C1 **Chegdomyn** Russian Fed
70B2 **Chegga** Maur
73D5 **Chegutu** Zim
10D2 **Chegytun'** Russian Fed
18B1 **Chehalis** USA
53B5 **Cheju** S Korea
53B5 **Cheju do** *I* S Korea
53B5 **Cheju-haehyŏp** *Str* S Korea
53E2 **Chekhov** Russian Fed
49P4 **Chekunda** Russian Fed
3D4 **Chelan** USA
18B1 **Chelan,L** USA
45J8 **Cheleken** Turkmenistan
28B3 **Chelforo** Arg
71C1 **Chéliff** *R* Alg
58D1 **Chelkar** Kazakhstan
43E2 **Chelm** Pol
43D2 **Chelmno** Pol
35F6 **Chelmsford** Eng
35D6 **Cheltenham** Eng
44L4 **Chelyabinsk** Russian Fed
73D5 **Chemba** Mozam
42C2 **Chemnitz** USA
14B1 **Chemung** *R* USA
60D2 **Chenab** *R* India/Pak
70B2 **Chenachen** Alg
14C1 **Chenango** *R* USA
18C1 **Cheney** USA
17C2 **Cheney Res** USA
52D1 **Chengda** China
52A3 **Chengdu** China
52E2 **Chengshan Jiao** *Pt* China
52C4 **Chenxi** China
52C4 **Chen Xian** China
52D3 **Cheo Xian** China
26C5 **Chepén** Peru
28B2 **Chepes** Arg
12A1 **Chequamegon B** USA
38C2 **Cher** *R* France
22B2 **Cheran** Mexico
15D2 **Cheraw** USA
38B2 **Cherbourg** France
22B1 **Chercas** Mexico
71C1 **Cherchell** Alg
66C4 **Cherchér** Eth
44K3 **Cherdyn** Russian Fed
49M4 **Cheremkhovo** Russian Fed
44F4 **Cherepovets** Russian Fed
45E6 **Cherkassy** Ukraine
45G7 **Cherkessk** Russian Fed
45E5 **Chernigov** Ukraine
43G2 **Chernobyl** Ukraine
45D6 **Chernovtsy** Ukraine
44K4 **Chernushka** Russian Fed
44C5 **Chernyakhovsk** Russian Fed
45H6 **Chernyye Zemli** *Region* Russian Fed
11C3 **Cherokee** Iowa, USA
16C2 **Cherokee** Oklahoma, USA
17C2 **Cherokees,L o'the** USA
28A3 **Cherquenco** Chile
61D2 **Cherrapunji** India
77F2 **Cherry** *I* Solomon Is
49S3 **Cherskiy** Russian Fed
44D5 **Cherven'** Belorussia
43E2 **Chervonograd** Ukraine
13D3 **Chesapeake** USA
13D3 **Chesapeake B** USA
35D5 **Cheshire** County, Eng
14D1 **Cheshire** USA
44H2 **Chëshskaya Guba** *B* Russian Fed
19B2 **Chester** California, USA
35D5 **Chester** Eng
12B3 **Chester** Illinois, USA
14D1 **Chester** Massachusetts, USA
18D1 **Chester** Montana, USA
13D3 **Chester** Pennsylvania, USA
15C2 **Chester** S Carolina, USA
3F4 **Chester** USA
14D1 **Chester** Vermont, USA
14B3 **Chester** *R* USA
35E5 **Chesterfield** Eng
7J3 **Chesterfield Inlet** Can
14B3 **Chestertown** USA
13F1 **Chesuncook L** USA
21D3 **Chetumal** Mexico
3D2 **Chetwynd** Can
10E3 **Chevak** USA
78B2 **Cheviot** NZ
33C2 **Cheviots** *Hills* Eng/Scot
3E4 **Chewelah** USA
16B1 **Cheyenne** USA
11B3 **Cheyenne** *R* USA
16B2 **Cheyenne Wells** USA
61B2 **Chhapra** India
61D2 **Chhātak** Bang
60D4 **Chhatarpur** India
60D4 **Chhindwāra** India
61C2 **Chhuka** Bhutan
52E5 **Chia'i** Taiwan
73B5 **Chiange** Angola
55C2 **Chiang Kham** Thai
55B2 **Chiang Mai** Thai
22D2 **Chiapa** *R* Mexico
37C2 **Chiavari** Italy
37C1 **Chiavenna** Italy
53E4 **Chiba** Japan
73B5 **Chibia** Angola
7L4 **Chibougamau** Can
5G4 **Chibougamau L** Can
54B3 **Chiburi-jima** *I* Japan
74E1 **Chibuto** Mozam
9E2 **Chicago** USA
12B2 **Chicago Heights** USA
10L4 **Chichagof I** USA
35E6 **Chichester** Eng
54C3 **Chichibu** Japan
50H4 **Chichi-jima** *I* Japan
9E3 **Chickamauga L** USA
17E3 **Chickasawhay** *R* USA
8D3 **Chickasha** USA
10K3 **Chicken** USA
26B5 **Chiclayo** Peru
8A3 **Chico** USA
25C6 **Chico** *R* Arg
73D5 **Chicoa** Mozam
13E2 **Chicopee** USA
7L5 **Chicoutimi** Can
73D6 **Chicualacuala** Mozam
62B2 **Chidambaram** India
7M3 **Chidley,C** Can
3D2 **Chief** *R* Can
15C3 **Chiefland** USA
70B4 **Chiehn** Lib
73C4 **Chiengi** Zambia
37E3 **Chienti** *R* Italy
37B2 **Chieri** Italy
36C2 **Chiers** *R* France
37C1 **Chiesa** Italy
37D2 **Chiese** *R* Italy
40C2 **Chieti** Italy
52D1 **Chifeng** China
10G4 **Chiginigak,Mt** USA
6C3 **Chigmit Mts** USA
22C2 **Chignahuapán** Mexico
5J4 **Chignecto B** Can
10G4 **Chignik** USA
74E1 **Chigubo** Mozam
21B2 **Chihuahua** Mexico
16A4 **Chihuahua** State, Mexico
62B2 **Chik Ballāpur** India
62B2 **Chikmagalūr** India
10G3 **Chikuminuk L** USA
73D5 **Chikwawa** Malawi
55A1 **Chi-kyaw** Burma
62C1 **Chilakalūrupet** India
22C2 **Chilapa** Mexico
62B3 **Chilaw** Sri Lanka
75D1 **Childers** Aust
16B3 **Childress** USA
24C6 **Chile** Republic
28B1 **Chilecito** La Rioja, Arg
28B2 **Chilecito** Mendoza, Arg
73C5 **Chililabombwe** Zambia
61C3 **Chilka** *L* India
3D3 **Chilko** *R* Can
6F4 **Chilko L** Can
3D3 **Chilkotin** *R* Can
28A3 **Chillán** Chile
28C3 **Chillar** Arg
17D2 **Chillicothe** Missouri, USA
12C3 **Chillicothe** Ohio, USA
3D4 **Chilliwack** Can
61C2 **Chilmari** India
26C4 **Chilmborazo** *Mt* Ecuador
73D5 **Chilongozi** Zambia
18B2 **Chiloquin** USA
21C3 **Chilpancingo** Mexico
35E6 **Chiltern Hills** *Upland* Eng
12B2 **Chilton** USA
73D5 **Chilumba** Malawi
50F4 **Chi-lung** Taiwan
73D5 **Chilwa** *L* Malawi
73D5 **Chimanimani** Zim
36C1 **Chimay** Belg
48G5 **Chimbay** Uzbekistan
26C5 **Chimbote** Peru
48H5 **Chimkent** Kazakhstan
73D5 **Chimoio** Mozam
46F4 **China** Republic, Asia
22A1 **Chinacates** Mexico
20D3 **China L** USA
20D3 **China Lake** USA
China National Republic = Taiwan
21D3 **Chinandega** Nic
16B4 **Chinati Peak** *Mt* USA
26C6 **Chincha Alta** Peru
3E2 **Chinchaga** *R* Can
75D1 **Chinchilla** Aust
73D5 **Chinde** Mozam
54A4 **Chindo** S Korea
61D3 **Chindwin** *R* Burma
73C5 **Chingola** Zambia
73B5 **Chinguar** Angola
70A2 **Chinguetti** Maur
53B4 **Chinhae** S Korea
73D5 **Chinhoyi** Zim
10H4 **Chiniak,C** USA
60C2 **Chiniot** Pak
53B4 **Chinju** S Korea
72C3 **Chinko** *R* CAR
54C3 **Chino** Japan
73D5 **Chinsali** Zambia
40C1 **Chioggia** Italy
73D5 **Chipata** Zambia
4E3 **Chipie** *R* Can
73D6 **Chipinge** Zim
62A1 **Chiplūn** India
3H2 **Chipman** *R* Can
35D6 **Chippenham** Eng
12A1 **Chippewa** *R* USA
9D2 **Chippewa Falls** USA
12A1 **Chippewa,L** USA
26B4 **Chira** *R* Peru
62C1 **Chīrāla** India
73D6 **Chiredzi** Zim
72B1 **Chirfa** Niger
19E4 **Chiricahua Peak** *Mt* USA
10G4 **Chirikof I** USA
41F2 **Chirpan** Bulg
26B2 **Chirrípo Grande** *Mt* Costa Rica
77G5 **Chirstchurch** NZ
73C5 **Chirundu** Zim
73C5 **Chisamba** Zambia
7L4 **Chisasibi** Can
11D2 **Chisholm** USA
52B4 **Chishui He** *R* China
68J8 **Chisimaio** Somalia
Chişinău = Kishinev
37B2 **Chisone** Italy
44J4 **Chistopol** Russian Fed
50E1 **Chita** Russian Fed
73B5 **Chitado** Angola
4B3 **Chitek L** Can
73B5 **Chitembo** Angola
10K3 **Chitina** USA
10K3 **Chitina** *R* USA
54D2 **Chitose** Japan
62B2 **Chitradurga** India
60C1 **Chitral** Pak
26B2 **Chitré** Panama
61D3 **Chittagong** Bang
60C4 **Chittaurgarh** India
62B2 **Chittoor** India
73C5 **Chiume** Angola
37D1 **Chiusa** Italy
37D3 **Chiusi** Italy
37B2 **Chivasso** Italy
25D4 **Chivilcoy** Arg
73D5 **Chivu** Zim
53E1 **Chiya, Ozero** *L* Russian Fed
54B3 **Chizu** Japan
54A3 **Choch'iwŏn** S Korea
54A4 **Ch'o-do** *I* S Korea
25C5 **Choele Choel** Arg
28C3 **Choique** Arg
77E1 **Choiseul** *I* Solomon Is
21B2 **Choix** Mexico
43D2 **Chojnice** Pol
54D3 **Chokai-san** *Mt* Japan
72D2 **Choke** *Mts* Eth
49Q2 **Chokurdakh** Russian Fed
20B3 **Cholame** USA
20B3 **Cholame Creek** *R* USA
38B2 **Cholet** France
22C2 **Cholula** Mexico
26A1 **Choluteca** Honduras
73C5 **Choma** Zambia
54A3 **Chŏmch'ŏn** S Korea
61C2 **Chomo Yummo** *Mt* China/India
42C2 **Chomutov** Czech
49M3 **Chona** *R* Russian Fed
53B4 **Ch'ŏnan** S Korea
55C3 **Chon Buri** Thai
54A2 **Chonchon** N Korea
26C4 **Chone** Ecuador
54A3 **Chongdo** S Korea
53B3 **Ch'ŏngjin** N Korea
53B4 **Chongju** N Korea
53B4 **Ch'ŏngju** S Korea
73B5 **Chongoroi** Angola
54A3 **Chongpyong** N Korea
52B4 **Chongqing** China
54A3 **Chŏngsŏn** S Korea
53B4 **Chŏngŭp** S Korea
53B4 **Chŏnju** S Korea
61C2 **Chooyu** *Mt* China/Nepal
29B4 **Chopim** *R* Brazil
43F3 **Chortkov** Ukraine
53B4 **Ch'ŏrwŏn** N Korea
43D2 **Chorzow** Pol
54A2 **Chosan** N Korea
53E4 **Choshi** Japan
28A3 **Chos-Malal** Arg
42D2 **Choszczno** Pol
61B3 **Chotanāgpur** Region, India
18D1 **Choteau** USA
71B2 **Chott ech Chergui** Alg
71D1 **Chott el Hodna** Alg
71D2 **Chott Jerid** Tunisia
71D2 **Chott Melrhir** Alg
20B2 **Chowchilla** USA
49N5 **Choybalsan** Mongolia
78B2 **Christchurch** NZ
74D2 **Christiana** S Africa
7M2 **Christian,C** Can
10M4 **Christian Sd** USA
7N3 **Christianshåb** Greenland
xxviiiG5 **Christmas I** Indian O
48J5 **Chu** Kazakhstan
48J5 **Chu** *R* Kazakhstan
18D2 **Chubbuck** USA
25C6 **Chubut** State, Arg
25C6 **Chubut** *R* Arg
44E4 **Chudovo** Russian Fed
44D1 **Chudskoye, Ozero** *L* Estonia/Russian Fed
6D3 **Chugach Mts** USA
10J3 **Chugiak** USA
10E5 **Chuginadak** *I* USA
54B3 **Chūgoku-sanchi** *Mts* Japan
11B3 **Chugwater** USA
28E2 **Chuí** Brazil
25B5 **Chuillán** Chile
55C5 **Chukai** Malay
Chukchagirskoye, Ozero *L* Russian Fed
10E2 **Chukchi S** Russian Fed/USA

Chukotskiy Khrebet Contreras

49T3 Chukotskiy Khrebet Mts Russian Fed
49U3 Chukotskiy Poluostrov Pen Russian Fed
55D2 Chu Lai Viet
19C4 Chula Vista USA
10J3 Chulitna USA
50F1 Chulman Russian Fed
26B5 Chulucanas Peru
26E7 Chulumani Bol
48K4 Chulym Russian Fed
49K4 Chulym R Russian Fed
49L4 Chuma R Russian Fed
60D2 Chumar India
28B1 Chumbicha Arg
49P4 Chumikan Russian Fed
55B3 Chumphon Thai
53B4 Ch'unch'ŏn S Korea
61C3 Chunchura India
53B4 Ch'ungju S Korea
Chungking = Chongqing
54A4 Ch'ungmu S Korea
54A3 Chungwa N Korea
73D4 Chunya Tanz
49M3 Chunya R Russian Fed
54A3 Ch'unyang S Korea
23L1 Chupara Pt Trinidad
25C2 Chuquicamata Chile
40B1 Chur Switz
61D3 Churāchāndpur India
49P3 Churapcha Russian Fed
7J4 Churchill Can
7M4 Churchill R Labrador, Can
7J4 Churchill R Manitoba, Can
7J4 Churchill,C Can
7M4 Churchill Falls Can
6H4 Churchill L Can
60C3 Chūru India
22B2 Churumuco Mexico
44K4 Chusovoy Russian Fed
44H4 Chuvashkaya Respublika, Russian Fed
50C4 Chuxiong China
55D3 Chu Yang Sin Mt Viet
56C4 Cianjur Indon
37D2 Ciano d'Enza Italy
29B3 Cianorte Brazil
43E2 Ciechanow Pol
22B2 Ciedad Altamirano Mexico
26D1 Ciedad Ojeda Ven
21E2 Ciego de Avila Cuba
26D1 Ciénaga Colombia
21D2 Cienfuegos Cuba
43D3 Cieszyn Pol
39B2 Cieza Spain
64B2 Cihanbeyli Turk
22B2 Cihuatlán Mexico
56C4 Cijulang Indon
56C4 Cilacap Indon
16B2 Cimarron USA
16C2 Cimarron R USA
37B3 Cime du Cheiron Mt France
41F1 Cîmpina Rom
39C1 Cinca R Spain
40D2 Činčer Mt Bosnia & Herzegovina, Yugos
9E3 Cincinnati USA
41E1 Cindrelu Mt Rom
41F3 Cine R Turk
36C1 Ciney Belg
22D2 Cintalapa Mexico
28B3 Cipolletti Arg
6D3 Circle Alaska, USA
11A2 Circle Montana, USA
12C3 Circleville USA
56C4 Cirebon Indon
35E6 Cirencester Eng
16C3 Cisco USA
37D2 Citadella Italy
21C3 Citlaltepetl Mt Mexico
74B3 Citrusdal S Africa
40C2 Citta del Vaticano Italy
40C2 Città di Castello Italy
21B2 Ciudad Acuña Mexico
26F2 Ciudad Bolivar Ven
21B2 Ciudad Camargo Mexico
21C3 Ciudad del Carmen Mexico
39C2 Ciudadela Spain
26F2 Ciudad Guayana Ven
21B3 Ciudad Guzman Mexico
22B2 Ciudad Hidalgo Mexico
21B1 Ciudad Juárez Mexico
8C4 Ciudad Lerdo Mexico
21C2 Ciudad Madero Mexico
22C2 Ciudad Mendoza Mexico
21B2 Ciudad Obregon Mexico
23C4 Ciudad Ojeda Ven
26F2 Ciudad Piar Ven
39B2 Ciudad Real Spain
39A1 Ciudad Rodrigo Spain
21C2 Ciudad Valles Mexico
21C2 Ciudad Victoria Mexico
37E1 Cividale del Friuli Italy
37E3 Civitanova Marche Italy
40C2 Civitavecchia Italy
64D2 Cizre Turk
35F6 Clacton-on-Sea Eng
6G4 Claire,L Can
13D2 Clairton USA
37A1 Clairvaux France
15B2 Clanton USA
74B3 Clanwilliam S Africa
35B5 Clara Irish Rep
28D3 Claraz Arg
12C2 Clare USA
13E2 Claremont USA
17C2 Claremore USA
75D1 Clarence R Aust
78B2 Clarence R NZ
76C2 Clarence Str Aust
10M4 Clarence Str USA
17D3 Clarendon USA
5L4 Clarenville Can
7N5 Clarenville Can
6G4 Claresholm Can
17C1 Clarinda USA
11D3 Clarion Iowa, USA
13D2 Clarion Pennsylvania, USA
21A3 Clarión I Mexico
13D2 Clarion R USA
xxixM4 Clarion Fracture Zone Pacific O
9E3 Clark Hill Res USA
10O3 Clark,Mt Can
19C3 Clark Mt USA
12C2 Clark,Pt Can
12C3 Clarksburg USA
9D3 Clarksdale USA
10G4 Clarks Point USA
18C1 Clarkston USA
17D2 Clarksville Arkansas, USA
15B1 Clarksville Tennessee, USA
29B2 Claro R Brazil
25E5 Claromecó Arg
17C2 Clay Center USA
34E2 Claymore Oilfield N Sea
3C4 Clayoquot Sd Can
8C3 Clayton New Mexico, USA
13D2 Clayton New York, USA
33B3 Clear C Irish Rep
10J4 Cleare,C USA
14A2 Clearfield Pennsylvania, USA
18D2 Clearfield Utah, USA
3E2 Clear Hills Mts Can
19B3 Clear L USA
11D3 Clear Lake USA
18B2 Clear Lake Res USA
11A3 Clearmont USA
3D3 Clearwater Can
9E4 Clearwater USA
3F2 Clearwater R Can
3D3 Clearwater L Can
18C1 Clearwater Mts USA
8D3 Cleburne USA
35F4 Cleeton Oilfield N Sea
20B1 Clements USA
57E8 Cleopatra Needle Mt Phil
76D3 Clermont Aust
36B2 Clermont France
36C2 Clermont-en-Argonne France
38C2 Clermont-Ferrand France
36D1 Clervaux Germany
37D1 Cles Italy
75A2 Cleve Aust
35E4 Cleveland County, Eng
17D3 Cleveland Mississippi, USA
9E2 Cleveland Ohio, USA
15C1 Cleveland Tennessee, USA
17C3 Cleveland Texas, USA
29B4 Clevelândia Brazil
18D1 Cleveland,Mt USA
33B3 Clew B Irish Rep
19E4 Clifton Arizona, USA
75D1 Clifton Aust
14C2 Clifton New Jersey, USA
75A1 Clifton Hills Aust
3J2 Clifton L Can
3G4 Climax Can
15C1 Clinch R USA
15C1 Clinch Mts USA
17D2 Clinton Arkansas, USA
6F4 Clinton Can
14D2 Clinton Connecticut, USA
12A2 Clinton Iowa, USA
14E1 Clinton Massachusetts, USA
17D3 Clinton Mississippi, USA
17D2 Clinton Missouri, USA
15D2 Clinton N Carolina, USA
14C2 Clinton New Jersey, USA
16C2 Clinton Oklahoma, USA
6H3 Clinton-Colden L Can
21B3 Clipperton I Pacific O
26E7 Cliza Bol
28C1 Clodomira Arg
76D3 Cloncurry Aust
35B4 Clones Irish Rep
35B5 Clonmel Irish Rep
9D2 Cloquet USA
29A4 Clorinda Arg
11A3 Cloud Peak Mt USA
10G3 Cloudy Mt USA
20A1 Cloverdale USA
20C2 Clovis California, USA
8C3 Clovis New Mexico, USA
45C6 Cluj Rom
41E1 Cluj-Napoca Rom
37B1 Cluses France
37C2 Clusone Italy
78A3 Clutha R NZ
35D5 Clwyd County, Wales
7M2 Clyde Can
78A3 Clyde NZ
14B1 Clyde USA
34C4 Clyde R Scot
19C4 Coachella USA
22B2 Coahuayana Mexico
16B4 Coahuila State, Mexico
10N3 Coal R Can
22B2 Coalcomán Mexico
3F4 Coaldale Can
19C3 Coaldale USA
19B3 Coalinga USA
18D2 Coalville USA
29E1 Coaraci Brazil
26F5 Coari R Brazil
15B2 Coastal Plain USA
6E4 Coast Mts Can
8A2 Coast Ranges Mts USA
34C4 Coatbridge Scot
22C2 Coatepec Mexico
14C3 Coatesville USA
13E1 Coaticook Can
7K3 Coats I Can
79F1 Coats Land Region, Ant
21C3 Coatzacoalcas Mexico
22D2 Coatzacoalcos R Mexico
7L5 Cobalt Can
21C3 Cobán Guatemala
76D4 Cobar Aust
75C3 Cobargo Aust
4C3 Cobham R Can
26E6 Cobija Bol
14C1 Cobleskill USA
39B2 Cobo de Palos C Spain
7L5 Cobourg Can
76C2 Cobourg Pen Aust
42C2 Coburg Germany
26C4 Coca Ecuador
15C3 Coca USA
29B1 Cocalinho Brazil
26E7 Cochabamba Bol
36D1 Cochem Germany
3F3 Cochrane Alberta, Can
7K5 Cochrane Ontario, Can
3H2 Cochrane R Can
75B2 Cockburn Aust
14B3 Cockeysville USA
23H1 Cockpit Country,The Jamaica
74C3 Cockscomb Mt S Africa
21D3 Coco R Honduras/Nic
72A3 Cocobeach Gabon
62E2 Coco Channel Andaman Is
29D1 Côcos Brazil
23L1 Cocos B Trinidad
xxviiiF5 Cocos Is Indian O
xxixP4 Cocos Ridge Pacific O
22B1 Cocula Mexico
34G3 Cod Oilfield N Sea
9F2 Cod,C USA
78A3 Codfish I NZ
7M4 Cod I Can
37E2 Codigoro Italy
27K4 Codó Brazil
37C2 Codogno Italy
8C2 Cody USA
51H8 Coen Aust
42B2 Coesfeld Germany
3E4 Coeur d'Alene USA
8D3 Coffeyville USA
75A2 Coffin B Aust
75D2 Coff's Harbour Aust
74D3 Cofimvaba S Africa
22C2 Cofre de Perote Mt Mexico
38B2 Cognac France
14B1 Cohocton USA
14B1 Cohocton R USA
13E2 Cohoes USA
75B3 Cohuna Aust
25B7 Coihaique Chile
62B2 Coimbatore India
39A1 Coimbra Port
26B3 Cojimies Ecuador
18D2 Cokeville USA
76D4 Colac Aust
27K7 Colatina Brazil
79F6 Colbeck,C Ant
16B2 Colby USA
35F6 Colchester Eng
14D2 Colchester USA
37B1 Col de la Faucille France
3F3 Cold L Can
40B1 Col du Grand St Bernard P Switz/Italy
37B2 Col du Lautaret P France
40B1 Col du Mont Cenis P Italy/France
38D2 Col du Mt Cenis P Italy
12C2 Coldwater USA
4D4 Coldwell Can
10K2 Coleen R USA
18D1 Coleman Can
12C2 Coleman Michigan, USA
16C3 Coleman Texas, USA
74D2 Colenso S Africa
34B4 Coleraine N Ire
78B2 Coleridge,L NZ
74D3 Colesberg S Africa
20C1 Coleville USA
19B3 Colfax California, USA
17D3 Colfax Louisiana, USA
18C1 Colfax Washington, USA
21B3 Colima Mexico
22B2 Colima State, Mexico
28A2 Colina Chile
34B3 Coll I Scot
75C1 Collarenebri Aust
40B2 Colle de Tende P Italy/France
37D3 Colle di Val d'Elsa Italy
10J3 College USA
15C2 College Park Georgia, USA
14B3 College Park Washington, USA
17C3 College Station USA
76A4 Collie Aust
76B2 Collier B Aust
37D3 Colline Metallifere Mts Italy
36A1 Collines de L'Artois Mts France
36B2 Collines De Thiérache France
36A2 Collines du Perche Mts France
4E5 Collingwood Can
78B2 Collingwood NZ
17E3 Collins Mississippi, USA
14A1 Collins New York, USA
6H2 Collinson Pen Can
76D3 Collinsville Aust
12B3 Collinsville Illinois, USA
17C2 Collinsville Oklahoma, USA
28A3 Collipulli Chile
38D2 Colmar France
28C1 Colmena Arg
36A1 Colne R Eng
Cologne = Köln
29C3 Colômbia Brazil
26D3 Colombia Republic, S America
13D3 Colombia USA
62B3 Colombo Sri Lanka
25E4 Colón Arg
21D2 Colon Cuba
26C2 Colón Panama
25E4 Colonia Urug
28D2 Colonia del Sacramento Urug
28B3 Colonia 25 de Mayo Arg
28C1 Colonia Dora Arg
28B3 Colonia Josefa Arg
25C7 Colonia Las Heras Arg
13D3 Colonial Heights USA
34B3 Colonsay I Scot
23E5 Coloradito Ven
8C3 Colorado State, USA
8B3 Colorado R Arizona, USA
25D5 Colorado R Buenos Aires, Arg
28B1 Colorado R La Rioja, Arg
8D3 Colorado R Texas, USA
16B3 Colorado City USA
8B3 Colorado Plat USA
8C3 Colorado Springs USA
22B1 Colptlán Mexico
14B3 Columbia Maryland, USA
17E3 Columbia Mississippi, USA
9D3 Columbia Missouri, USA
13D2 Columbia Pennsylvania, USA
9E3 Columbia S Carolina, USA
9E3 Columbia Tennessee, USA
3E3 Columbia R Can
8A2 Columbia R USA
18D1 Columbia Falls USA
6G4 Columbia,Mt Can
18C1 Columbia Plat USA
74B3 Columbine,C S Africa
9E3 Columbus Georgia, USA
12B3 Columbus Indiana, USA
9E3 Columbus Mississippi, USA
18E1 Columbus Montana, USA
8D2 Columbus Nebraska, USA
16A3 Columbus New Mexico, USA
9E2 Columbus Ohio, USA
17C4 Columbus Texas, USA
12B2 Columbus Wisconsin, USA
18C1 Colville USA
6C3 Colville R USA
78C1 Colville,C NZ
6F3 Colville L Can
35D5 Colwyn Bay Wales
37E2 Comacchio Italy
22D2 Comalcalco Mexico
16C3 Comanche USA
20B1 Comanche Res USA
21D3 Comayagua Honduras
28A2 Combarbalá Chile
35C4 Comber N Ire
61D4 Combermere B Burma
36C3 Combeufontaine France
37E1 Comeglians Italy
35B5 Comeragh Mts Irish Rep
16C3 Comfort USA
61D3 Comilla Bang
21C3 Comitán Mexico
36C2 Commercy France
7K3 Committee B Can
40B1 Como Italy
25C7 Comodoro Rivadavia Arg
22B1 Comonfort Mexico
62B3 Comorin,C India
73E5 Comoros Is Indian O
38C2 Compiègne France
22B1 Compostela Mexico
28B2 Comte Salas Arg
61D2 Cona China
70A4 Conakry Guinea
28A1 Conay Chile
28B2 Concarán Arg
38B2 Concarneau France
29E2 Conceiçao da Barra Brazil
27J5 Conceição do Araguaia Brazil
29D2 Conceiçao do Mato Dentro Brazil
28B1 Concepción Arg
29A3 Concepción Brazil/Par
25B5 Concepción Chile
25E2 Concepción Par
25E4 Concepción R Arg
21B2 Concepcion del Oro Mexico
28D2 Concepcion del Uruguay Arg
74A1 Conception B Namibia
8A3 Conception,Pt USA
29C3 Conchas Brazil
16B2 Conchas L USA
36A2 Conches France
8C4 Conchos R Mexico
19B3 Concord California, USA
9F2 Concord New Hampshire, USA
15C1 Concord North Carolina, USA
25E4 Concordia Arg
22A1 Concordia Mexico
8D3 Concordia USA
18B1 Concrete USA
75D1 Condamine Aust
29D1 Condeuba Brazil
76D4 Condobolin Aust
18B1 Condon USA
36C1 Condroz, Mts Belg
27H8 Condrina Brazil
15B2 Conecuh R USA
37E2 Conegliano Italy
14B1 Conesus L USA
29A3 Confuso R Par
68F8 Congo Republic, Africa
68F8 Congo R Congo
Congo,R = Zaïre,R
12C1 Coniston Can
12C2 Conneaut USA
9F2 Connecticut State, USA
13E2 Connecticut R USA
13D2 Connellsville USA
36A2 Connerré France
12B3 Connersville USA
75B2 Conoble Aust
18D1 Conrad USA
17C3 Conroe USA
29D3 Conselheiro Lafaiete Brazil
55D4 Con Son Is Viet
Constance,L = Bodensee
45D7 Constanta Rom
71D1 Constantine Alg
10G4 Constantine,C USA
25B5 Constitución Chile
28D2 Constitución Urug
3G4 Consul Can
18D2 Contact USA
37E2 Contarina Italy
27K6 Contas R Brazil
22C2 Contreras Mexico

Dalay **Dibrugarh**

52A1 **Dalay** Mongolia
63E3 **Dalbandin** Pak
76E3 **Dalby** Aust
15B1 **Dale Hollow L** USA
32F7 **Dalen** Nor
35D4 **Dales,The** *Upland* Eng
15B2 **Daleville** USA
8C3 **Dalhart** USA
5H4 **Dalhousie** Can
6E2 **Dalhousie,C** Can
52E2 **Dalian** China
65B1 **Dalion** *Hist Site* Cyprus
8D3 **Dallas** USA
18B1 **Dalles,The** USA
10M5 **Dall I** USA
61B3 **Dalli Rajhara** India
70C3 **Dallol** *R* Niger
71G3 **Dallol Bosso** *R* Niger
71G3 **Dallol Maouri** *R* Niger
40D2 **Dalmatia** *Region* Bosnia & Herzegovina, Yugos
53D3 **Dal'negorsk** Russian Fed
53C2 **Dal'nerechensk** Russian Fed
70B4 **Daloa** Ivory Coast
52B4 **Dalou Shan** *Mts* China
61B3 **Dāltenganj** India
4E4 **Dalton** Can
15C2 **Dalton** Georgia, USA
14D1 **Dalton** Massachusetts, USA
56B2 **Daludalu** Indon
76C2 **Daly** *R* Aust
19B3 **Daly City** USA
76C2 **Daly Waters** Aust
57F9 **Damaguete** Phil
60C4 **Damān** India
64B3 **Damanhûr** Egypt
76B1 **Damar** *I* Indon
72B3 **Damara** CAR
64C3 **Damascus** Syria
14B3 **Damascus** USA
71J3 **Damaturu** Nig
63C1 **Damavand** Iran
73B4 **Damba** Angola
62C3 **Dambulla** Sri Lanka
63C1 **Damghan** Iran
Damietta = Dumyât
60D4 **Damoh** India
71F4 **Damongo** Ghana
72E3 **Damot** Eth
65C2 **Damour** Leb
76A3 **Dampier** Aust
67F3 **Damqawt** Yemen
65C3 **Danā** Jordan
66D4 **Danakil** Region, Eth
20C2 **Dana,Mt** USA
70B4 **Danané** Lib
55D2 **Da Nang** Viet
57F8 **Danao** Phil
57B3 **Danau Poso** *Mt* Indon
56A2 **Danau Tobu** *L* Indon
57B3 **Danau Tuwuti** *L* Indon
52A3 **Danbu** China
13E2 **Danbury** USA
14D1 **Danby** USA
61B2 **Dandeldhura** Nepal
62A1 **Dandeli** India
75C3 **Dandenong** Aust
53A3 **Dandong** China
74B3 **Danger Pt** S Africa
72D2 **Dangila** Eth
18D2 **Daniel** USA
7N4 **Daniel's Harbour** Can
74C2 **Danielskuil** S Africa
7P3 **Dannebrogs Øy** *I* Greenland
78C2 **Dannevirke** NZ
14B1 **Dansville** USA
62C1 **Dantewāra** India
Danube = Dunărea
Danube = Donau
45G8 **Danuk** Iraq
9E2 **Danville** Illinois, USA
9E3 **Danville** Kentucky, USA
14B2 **Danville** Pennsylvania, USA
9F3 **Danville** Virginia, USA
Danzig = Gdańsk
52C4 **Dao Xian** China
52B4 **Daozhen** China
71J3 **Dapchi** Nig
61E2 **Dapha Bum** *Mt* India
65B3 **Daphnae** *Hist Site* Egypt
57F9 **Dapiak,Mt** Phil
57F9 **Dapitan** Phil
50C3 **Da Qaidam** China
53B2 **Daqing** China
65D2 **Dar'a** Syria
63C3 **Dārāb** Iran
69A1 **Daraj** Libya
63C2 **Dārān** Iran
64C3 **Dar'ā Salkhad** Syria
61C2 **Darbhanga** India
20C1 **Dardanelle** USA
17D2 **Dardanelle,L** USA
Dar-el-Beida = Casablanca Mor
73D4 **Dar Es Salaam** Tanz
78B1 **Dargaville** NZ
15C2 **Darien** USA
Darjeeling = Dārjiling
61C2 **Dārjiling** India
76D4 **Darling** *R* Aust
75C1 **Darling Downs** Aust
7L1 **Darling Pen** Can
75B2 **Darlington** Aust
35E4 **Darlington** Eng
15D2 **Darlington** USA
42B3 **Darmstadt** Germany
69B1 **Darnah** Libya
75B2 **Darnick** Aust
6F3 **Darnley B** Can
79G10 **Darnley,C** Ant
39B1 **Daroca** Spain
72C3 **Dar Rounga** Region, CAR
67F4 **Darsa** *I* Yemen
35D6 **Dart** *R* Eng
33C3 **Dartmoor** *Moorland* Eng
35D6 **Dartmoor Nat Pk** Eng
7M5 **Dartmouth** Can
35D6 **Dartmouth** Eng
76D1 **Daru** PNG
40D1 **Daruvar** Croatia, Yugos
63E2 **Darweshan** Afghan
76C2 **Darwin** Aust
63C3 **Daryacheh-ye Bakhtegan** *L* Iran
63C3 **Daryacheh-ye Mahārlū** *L* Iran
63C2 **Daryācheh-ye Namak** *Salt Flat* Iran
63E2 **Daryacheh-ye-Sistan** *Salt Lake* Iran/Afghan
63C3 **Daryacheh-ye Tashk** *L* Iran
45H8 **Daryācheh-ye Urumīyeh** *L* Iran
63D3 **Dārzīn** Iran
67F1 **Das** *I* UAE
52C3 **Dashennonglia** *Mt* China
63D1 **Dasht** Iran
63E3 **Dasht** *R* Pak
63C2 **Dasht-e-Kavir** *Salt Desert* Iran
63D2 **Dasht-e Lut** *Salt Desert* Iran
63E2 **Dasht-e Naomid** *Desert Region* Iran
63E2 **Dasht-i-Margo** *Desert* Afghan
54D2 **Date** Japan
60D3 **Datia** India
52A2 **Datong** China
52C1 **Datong** China
52A2 **Datong He** *R* China
57F9 **Datu Piang** Phil
44D4 **Daugava** *R* Latvia
44D4 **Daugavpils** Latvia
38D2 **Dauphiné** Region, France
7M1 **Dauguard Jensen Land** Greenland
60A1 **Daulatabad** Afghan
60D3 **Daulpur** India
36D1 **Daun** Germany
62A1 **Daund** India
6H4 **Dauphin** Can
14B2 **Dauphin** USA
15B2 **Dauphin I** USA
4B3 **Dauphin L** Can
70C3 **Daura** Nig
60D3 **Dausa** India
63E3 **Dāvah Panāh** Iran
62B2 **Dāvangere** India
57G9 **Davao** Phil
57G9 **Davao G** Phil
20A2 **Davenport** California, USA
9D2 **Davenport** Iowa, USA
26B2 **David** Panama
3G3 **Davidson** Can
6D3 **Davidson Mts** USA
3H2 **Davin L** Can
19B3 **Davis** USA
79G10 **Davis** *Base* Ant
7M4 **Davis Inlet** Can
7N3 **Davis Str** Greenland/Can
44K5 **Davlekanovo** Russian Fed
37C1 **Davos** Switz
3G2 **Davy L** Can
72E3 **Dawa** *R* Eth
52A4 **Dawan** China
60B2 **Dawat Yar** Afghan
67F1 **Dawḥat Salwah** *B* Qatar/S Arabia
67F3 **Dawkah** Oman
55B2 **Dawna Range** *Mts* Burma
6E3 **Dawson** Can
15C2 **Dawson** Georgia, USA
11C2 **Dawson** N Dakota, USA
76D3 **Dawson** *R* Aust
6F4 **Dawson Creek** Can
3F1 **Dawson Landing** Can
3E3 **Dawson,Mt** Can
10L3 **Dawson Range** *Mts* Can
52A3 **Dawu** China
52C3 **Dawu** China
38B3 **Dax** France
52B3 **Daxian** China
52B5 **Daxin** China
52A3 **Daxue Shan** *Mts* China
28D2 **Dayman** *R* Urug
52C4 **Dayong** China
65D2 **Dayr'Ali** Syria
65D1 **Dayr'Atīyah** Syria
64D2 **Dayr az Zawr** Syria
65D1 **Dayr Shumayyil** Syria
9E3 **Dayton** Ohio, USA
15B1 **Dayton** Tennessee, USA
17D4 **Dayton** Texas, USA
18C1 **Dayton** Washington, USA
9E4 **Daytona Beach** USA
52C4 **Dayu** China
56E3 **Dayu** Indon
52D2 **Da Yunhe** China
52D2 **Da Yunhe** *R* China
18C2 **Dayville** USA
52B3 **Dazhu** China
74C3 **De Aar** S Africa
23C2 **Deadman's Cay** Bahamas
64C3 **Dead S** Israel/Jordan
11B3 **Deadwood** USA
36A1 **Deal** Eng
74D2 **Dealesville** S Africa
3C3 **Dean** *R* Can
3C3 **Dean Chan** Can
28C2 **Deán Funes** Arg
12C2 **Dearborn** USA
3B2 **Dease Lake** Can
3C2 **Dease** *R* Can
6F3 **Dease Arm** *B* Can
8B3 **Death V** USA
20D2 **Death Valley Nat Mon** USA
38C2 **Deauville** France
71F4 **Debakala** Ivory Coast
10F3 **Debauch Mt** USA
3G3 **Debden** Can
23L1 **Débé** Trinidad
43E2 **Debica** Pol
43E2 **Deblin** Pol
70B3 **Débo,L** Mali
72D3 **Debre Birhan** Eth
43E3 **Debrecen** Hung
72D2 **Debre Mark'os** Eth
72D2 **Debre Tabor** Eth
66C3 **Decamere** Eth
9E3 **Decatur** Alabama, USA
15C2 **Decatur** Georgia, USA
9E3 **Decatur** Illinois, USA
12C2 **Decatur** Indiana, USA
38C3 **Decazeville** France
74C1 **Deception** *R* Botswana
52A4 **Dechang** China
11D3 **Decorah** USA
71F3 **Dedougou** Burkina
53B2 **Dedu** China
73D5 **Dedza** Malawi
34C4 **Dee** *R* Dumfries and Galloway, Scot
35D5 **Dee** *R* Eng/Wales
34D3 **Dee** *R* Grampian, Scot
4F4 **Deep River** Can
14D2 **Deep River** USA
20D2 **Deep Springs** USA
75D1 **Deepwater** Aust
10F5 **Deer I** USA
7N5 **Deer Lake** Can
8B2 **Deer Lodge** USA
26E7 **Deésaguadero** *R* Bol
18C2 **Deeth** USA
28D3 **Defferrari** Arg
4E5 **Defiance** USA
15B2 **De Funiak Springs** USA
50C3 **Dêgê** China
76A3 **De Grey** *R* Aust
66D3 **Dehalak** *Arch* Eth
63C2 **Deh Bīd** Iran
60B1 **Dehi** Afghan
70D1 **Dehibat** Tunisia
62B3 **Dehiwala-Mt Lavinia** Sri Lanka
63B2 **Dehlorān** Iran
60D2 **Dehra Dūn** India
61B3 **Dehri** India
53B3 **Dehui** China
72C3 **Deim Zubeir** Sudan
65C2 **Deir Abu Sa'id** Jordan
65D1 **Deir el Ahmar** Leb
45C6 **Dej** Rom
12B2 **De Kalb** Illinois, USA
17D3 **De Kalb** Texas, USA
49Q4 **De Kastri** Russian Fed
72C4 **Dekese** Zaïre
72B3 **Dekoa** CAR
8B3 **Delano** USA
19D3 **Delano Peal** *Mt* USA
74D2 **Delareyville** S Africa
10C6 **Delarof Is** USA
9F3 **Delaware** State, USA
12C2 **Delaware** USA
13D2 **Delaware** *R* USA
9F3 **Delaware B** USA
75C3 **Delegate** Aust
37B1 **Delemont** Switz
73E5 **Delgado** *C* Mozam
66B2 **Delgo** Sudan
16B2 **Delhi** Colorado, USA
60D3 **Delhi** India
13E2 **Delhi** New York, USA
64B1 **Delice** Turk
21B2 **Delicias** Mexico
63C2 **Delījān** Iran
37B1 **Delle** France
11C3 **Dell Rapids** USA
71C1 **Dellys** Alg
20D4 **Del Mar** USA
32F8 **Delmenhorst** Germany
10F2 **De Long Mts** USA
49R2 **De-Longa, Ostrov** *I* Russian Fed
75E3 **Deloraine** Aust
6H5 **Deloraine** Can
15E4 **Delray Beach** USA
8C4 **Del Rio** USA
8B3 **Delta** USA
10J3 **Delta** *R* USA
71H4 **Delta** *State* Nigeria
10J3 **Delta Junction** USA
14C1 **Delta Res** USA
72D3 **Dembī Dolo** Eth
36C1 **Demer** *R* Belg
43G1 **Demidov** Russian Fed
16A3 **Deming** USA
41F2 **Demirköy** Turk
71A2 **Demnate** Mor
37B2 **Demonte** Italy
15B2 **Demopolis** USA
48H4 **Demyanskoya** Russian Fed
38C1 **Denain** France
59E2 **Denau** Uzbekistan
35D5 **Denbigh** Wales
10F3 **Denbigh,C** USA
56C3 **Dendang** Indon
36C1 **Dendermond** Belg
72D3 **Dendi** *Mt* Eth
36B1 **Dèndre** *R* Belg
52B1 **Dengkou** China
52C3 **Deng Xian** China
Den Haag = 's-Gravenhage
23H1 **Denham,Mt** Jamaica
42A2 **Den Helder** Neth
39C2 **Denia** Spain
76D4 **Deniliquin** Aust
18C2 **Denio** USA
11C3 **Denison** Iowa, USA
8D3 **Denison** Texas, USA
10H4 **Denison,Mt** USA
45D8 **Denizli** Turk
32F7 **Denmark** Kingdom, Europe
79C1 **Denmark Str** Greenland/ Iceland
23P2 **Dennery** St Lucia
56E4 **Denpasar** Indon
14C3 **Denton** Maryland, USA
8D3 **Denton** Texas, USA
76E1 **D'Entrecasteaux Is** PNG
37B1 **Dents du Midi** *Mt* Switz
8C3 **Denver** USA
4F2 **Denys** *R* Can
72B3 **Déo** *R* Cam
61C3 **Deoghar** India
60C5 **Deolāli** India
60D1 **Deosai Plain** India
14A1 **Depew** USA
14C1 **Deposit** USA
72C2 **Dépression du Mourdi** *Desert Region* Chad
49P3 **Deputatskiy** Russian Fed
17D3 **De Queen** USA
60C3 **Dera** Pak
60B3 **Dera Bugti** Pak
60B2 **Dera Ismail Khan** Pak
45H7 **Derbent** Russian Fed
76B2 **Derby** Aust
14D2 **Derby** Connecticut, USA
35E5 **Derby** County, Eng
35E5 **Derby** Eng
17C2 **Derby** Kansas, USA
45F5 **Dergachi** Ukraine
17D3 **De Ridder** USA
69B1 **Derna** Libya
72E3 **Derri** Somalia
14E1 **Derry** USA
72D2 **Derudeb** Sudan
74C3 **De Rust** S Africa
14C1 **De Ruyter** USA
75E3 **Derwent Bridge** Aust
28B2 **Desaguadero** Arg
28B2 **Desaguadero** *R* Arg
19C4 **Descanso** Mexico
3H3 **Deschambault L** Can
18B2 **Deschutes** *R* USA
72D2 **Desē** Eth
25C7 **Deseado** Arg
25C7 **Deseado** *R* Arg
37D2 **Desenzano** Italy
70A1 **Deserta Grande** *I* Medeira
19C4 **Desert Centre** USA
19D2 **Desert Peak** *Mt* USA
63E2 **Deshu** Afghan
25C2 **Desierto de Atacama** *Desert* Chile
17D2 **Desloge** USA
9D2 **Des Moines** Iowa, USA
16B2 **Des Moines** New Mexico, USA
11D3 **Des Moines** *R* USA
45E5 **Desna** *R* Russian Fed
25B8 **Desolación** *I* Chile
12B2 **Des Plaines** USA
42C2 **Dessau** Germany
10L3 **Destruction Bay** Can
36A1 **Desvres** France
41E1 **Deta** Rom
73C5 **Dete** Zim
36E1 **Detmold** Germany
9E2 **Detroit** USA
5J4 **Détroit d'Honguedo** *Str* Can
5J3 **Détroit de Jacques Cartier** *Str* Can
11C2 **Detroit Lakes** USA
55D3 **Det Udom** Thai
41E1 **Deva** Rom
42B2 **Deventer** Neth
34D3 **Deveron** *R* Scot
60C3 **Devikot** India
20C2 **Devil Postpile Nat Mon** USA
20C3 **Devils Den** USA
20C1 **Devils Gate** *P* USA
34F3 **Devil's Hole** *Region* N Sea
Devil's Island = Isla du Diable
11C2 **Devils L** N Dakota, USA
16B4 **Devils L** Texas, USA
8D2 **Devils Lake** USA
10M4 **Devils Paw** *Mt* Can
35E6 **Devizes** Eng
60D3 **Devli** India
41E2 **Devoll** *R* Alb
37A2 **Dévoluy** *Mts* France
35C6 **Devon** County, Eng
7J2 **Devon I** Can
76D5 **Devonport** Aust
61D2 **Dewangiri** Bhutan
60D4 **Dewās** India
74D2 **Dewetsdorp** S Africa
9E3 **Dewey Res** USA
17D3 **De Witt** USA
17E2 **Dexter** Missouri, USA
16B3 **Dexter** New Mexico, USA
52A3 **Deyang** China
63D2 **Deyhuk** Iran
63B2 **Dezfūl** Iran
52D2 **Dezhou** China
63B1 **Dezh Shāhpūr** Iran
67F1 **Dhahran** S Arabia
61D3 **Dhākā** Bang
65B1 **Dhali** Cyprus
66D4 **Dhamār** Yemen
62B2 **Dhamavaram** India
61B3 **Dhamtari** India
61C3 **Dhanbād** India
61B2 **Dhangarhi** Nepal
61C2 **Dhankuta** Nepal
60D4 **Dhār** India
62B2 **Dharmapuri** India
60D2 **Dharmsāla** India
70B3 **Dhar Oualata** *Desert Region* Maur
61B2 **Dhaulagiri** *Mt* Nepal
61C3 **Dhenkānāi** India
65C3 **Dhibah** Jordan
41F3 **Dhíkti Óri** *Mt* Greece
67F3 **Dhofar** Region, Oman
41E3 **Dhomokós** Greece
62B1 **Dhone** India
60C4 **Dhoraji** India
60C4 **Dhrāngadhra** India
61C2 **Dhuburi** India
60C4 **Dhule** India
20B2 **Diablo,Mt** USA
19B3 **Diablo Range** *Mts* USA
28C2 **Diamante** Arg
28B2 **Diamante** *R* Arg
27K7 **Diamantina** Brazil
76D3 **Diamantina** *R* Aust
29A1 **Diamantino** Brazil
61C3 **Diamond Harbours** India
20B1 **Diamond Springs** USA
18D2 **Diamondville** USA
71G3 **Diapaga** Burkina
67G1 **Dibā** UAE
73C4 **Dibaya** Zaïre
61D2 **Dibrugarh** India

Dickens Durham

16B3 **Dickens** USA
8C2 **Dickinson** USA
15B1 **Dickson** USA
13D2 **Dickson City** USA
45G8 **Dicle** *R* Turk
3F3 **Didsbury** Can
60C3 **Dīdwāna** India
37A2 **Die** France
74E2 **Die Berg** *Mt* S Africa
71F3 **Diebougou** Burkina
36E2 **Dieburg** Germany
3G3 **Diefenbaker,L** Can
36D2 **Diekirch** Lux
70B3 **Diéma** Mali
55C1 **Dien Bien Phu** Viet
42B2 **Diepholz** Germany
38C2 **Dieppe** France
53B3 **Dier Songhua Jiang** *R* China
36C1 **Diest** Belg
36D2 **Dieuze** France
71J3 **Diffa** Niger
61E2 **Digboi** India
7M5 **Digby** Can
38D3 **Digne** France
38C2 **Digoin** France
57G9 **Digos** Phil
76C1 **Digul** *R* Indon
71F4 **Digya Nat Pk** Ghana
61D2 **Dihang** *R* India
Dijlah = Tigris
37A1 **Dijon** France
72B3 **Dik** Chad
72E2 **Dikhil** Djibouti
65A3 **Dikirnis** Egypt
36B1 **Diksmuide** Belg
48K2 **Dikson** Russian Fed
71J3 **Dikwa** Nig
63E2 **Dilaram** Afghan
57C4 **Dili** Indon
55D3 **Di Linh** Viet
36E1 **Dillenburg** Germany
17F4 **Dilley** USA
72C2 **Dilling** Sudan
10G4 **Dillingham** USA
8B2 **Dillon** USA
14B2 **Dillsburg** USA
73C5 **Dilolo** Zaïre
22A1 **Dimas** Mexico
Dimashq = Damascus
72C4 **Dimbelenge** Zaïre
71F4 **Dimbokro** Ivory Coast
41F2 **Dimitrovgrad** Bulg
44H5 **Dimitrovgrad** Russian Fed
65C3 **Dimona** Israel
61D2 **Dimpāpur** India
57G8 **Dinagat** *I* Phil
61C2 **Dinajpur** India
38B2 **Dinan** France
36C1 **Dinant** Belg
64B2 **Dinar** Turk
72D2 **Dinder** *R* Sudan
62B2 **Dindigul** India
52B2 **Dingbian** China
61C2 **Dinggyê** China
33A3 **Dingle** Irish Rep
33A3 **Dingle** *B* Irish Rep
70A3 **Dinguiraye** Guinea
34C3 **Dingwall** Scot
52A2 **Dingxi** China
52D2 **Ding Xian** China
55D1 **Dinh Lap** Viet
11D2 **Dinorwic L** Can
16A1 **Dinosaur** USA
20C2 **Dinuba** USA
10E2 **Diomede Is** Russian Fed/USA
70A3 **Diouloulou** Sen
61D2 **Diphu** India
72E3 **Diredawa** Eth
76A3 **Dirk Hartog** *I* Aust
72B2 **Dirkou** Niger
75C1 **Dirranbandi** Aust
25J8 **Disappointment,C** South Georgia
18B1 **Disappointment,C** USA
76B3 **Disappointment,L** Aust
75B3 **Discovery B** Aust
xxxJ6 **Discovery Tablemount** Atlantic O
37C1 **Disentis Muster** Switz
66B1 **Dishna** Egypt
7N3 **Disko** *I* Greenland
7N3 **Disko Bugt** *B* Greenland
7N3 **Diskofjord** Greenland
13D3 **Dismal Swamp** USA
43F1 **Disna** *R* Belorussia
29C2 **Distrito Federal** Federal District, Brazil
60C4 **Diu** India
57G9 **Diuat Mts** Phil
36A2 **Dives** *R* France
27K8 **Divinópolis** Brazil
45G6 **Divnoye** Russian Fed
64C2 **Divriği** Turk
20B1 **Dixon** California, USA
12B2 **Dixon** Illinois, USA
18D1 **Dixon** Montana, USA
6E4 **Dixon Entrance** *Sd* Can/USA
3E2 **Dixonville** Can
64E3 **Diyālā** *R* Iraq
45G8 **Diyarbakir** Turk
63E3 **Diz** Pak
63B2 **Diz** *R* Iran
72B3 **Dja** *R* Cam
71C2 **Djadi** *R* Alg
72B1 **Djado,Plat du** Niger
71D2 **Djamaa** Alg
72B4 **Djambala** Congo
70C2 **Djanet** Alg
71C2 **Djebel Amour** *Mts* Alg
39A2 **Djebel Bouhalla** *Mt* Mor
71D1 **Djebel Chambi** *Mt* Tunisia
71D1 **Djebel Chélia** *Mts* Alg
71E1 **Djebel Zaghouan** *Mt* Tunisia
71D2 **Djebel Zrega** *Mt* Tunisia
71G4 **Djebobo** *Mt* Ghana
71C2 **Djelfa** Alg
72C3 **Djéma** CAR
70B3 **Djenné** Mali
71J4 **Djerem** *R* Cam
71F3 **Djibasso** Burkina
70B3 **Djibo** Burkina
72E2 **Djibouti** Djibouti
72E2 **Djibouti** Republic, E Africa
72C3 **Djolu** Zaïre
71G4 **Djougou** Benin
72D3 **Djugu** Zaïre
32C2 **Djúpivogur** Iceland
39C2 **Djurdjura** *Mts* Alg
44F4 **Dmitrov** Russian Fed
45E6 **Dnepr** *R* Ukraine
45E6 **Dneprodzerzhinsk** Ukraine
45F6 **Dnepropetrovsk** Ukraine
44D5 **Dneprovskaya Nizmennost'** Region, Belorussia
45C6 **Dnestr** *R* Ukraine
44E4 **Dno** Russian Fed
72B3 **Doba** Chad
43E1 **Dobele** Latvia
28C3 **Doblas** Arg
76C1 **Dobo** Indon
41D2 **Doboj** Bosnia & Herzegovina, Yugos
41F2 **Dobrich** Bulg
45E5 **Dobrush** Belorussia
27K7 **Doce** *R* Brazil
25D2 **Doctor R P Peña** Arg
62B2 **Dod** India
62B2 **Doda Betta** *Mt* India
Dodecanese = Sporádhes
8C3 **Dodge City** USA
3G2 **Dodge L** Can
12A2 **Dodgeville** USA
72D4 **Dodoma** Tanz
34G4 **Dogger Bank** *Sand-bank* N Sea
12B1 **Dog L** Can
12C1 **Dog L** Can
54B3 **Dōgo** *I* Japan
70C3 **Dogondoutchi** Niger
64D2 **Doğubayazit** Turk
67F1 **Doha** Qatar
61D2 **Doilungdêqên** China
66C4 **Doka** Sudan
76C1 **Dolak** *I* Indon
11C3 **Doland** USA
7L5 **Dolbeau** Can
38D2 **Dôle** France
66B4 **Doleib** *Watercourse* Sudan
35D5 **Dolgellau** Wales
14C1 **Dolgeville** USA
44K2 **Dolgiy, Ostrov** *I* Russian Fed
53E2 **Dolinsk** Russian Fed
37D1 **Dolomitche** *Mts* Italy
72E3 **Dolo Odo** Eth
25E5 **Dolores** Arg
28D2 **Dolores** Urug
16A2 **Dolores** *R* USA
22B1 **Dolores Hidalgo** Mexico
6G3 **Dolphin and Union Str** Can
25E8 **Dolphin,C** Falkland Is
51G7 **Dom** *Mt* Indon
45K5 **Dombarovskiy** Russian Fed
32F6 **Dombas** Nor
36D2 **Dombasle-sur-Meurthe** France
41D1 **Dombóvár** Hung
28A1 **Domeyko** Chile
38B2 **Domfront** France
23E3 **Dominica** *I* Caribbean
23C3 **Dominican Republic** Caribbean
7L3 **Dominion,C** Can
7N4 **Domino** Can
50E1 **Domna** Russian Fed
40B1 **Domodossola** Italy
28E2 **Dom Pedrito** Brazil
56E4 **Dompu** Indon
25B5 **Domuyo** *Mt* Arg
75D1 **Domville,Mt** Aust
34D3 **Don** *R* Scot
45G6 **Don** *R* Russian Fed
34B4 **Donaghadee** N Ire
22B1 **Donato Guerta** Mexico
Donau = Dunav Bulg
42C3 **Donau, R** Austria
42C3 **Donau** *R* Germany
36E3 **Donaueschingen** Germany
42C3 **Donauwörth** Germany
39A2 **Don Benito** Spain
35E5 **Doncaster** Eng
73B4 **Dondo** Angola
73D5 **Dondo** Mozam
62C3 **Dondra Head** *C* Sri Lanka
34B4 **Donegal** County, Irish Rep
33B3 **Donegal** Irish Rep
33B3 **Donegal** *B* Irish Rep
34A4 **Donegal** *Mts* Irish Rep
45F6 **Donetsk** Ukraine
71J4 **Donga** *R* Nig
52C4 **Dong'an** China
76A3 **Dongara** Aust
52A4 **Dongchuan** China
55D2 **Dongfang** China
53B3 **Dongfeng** China
76A1 **Donggala** Indon
50C3 **Donggi Cona** *L* China
53A4 **Donggou** China
52C5 **Donghai Dao** *I* China
52A1 **Dong He** *R* China
55D2 **Dong Hoi** Viet
52C5 **Dong Jiang** *R* China
53C2 **Donglanghong** China
53C3 **Dongning** China
72D2 **Dongola** Sudan
52D5 **Dongshan** China
50E4 **Dongsha Qundao** *I* China
52C2 **Dongsheng** China
52E3 **Dongtai** China
52C4 **Dongting Hu** *L* China
52B5 **Dongxing** China
52D3 **Dongzhi** China
17D2 **Doniphan** USA
40D2 **Donji Vakuf** Bosnia & Herzegovina, Yugos
32G5 **Dönna** *I* Nor
19B3 **Donner** *P* USA
36D2 **Donnersberg** *Mt* Germany
74D2 **Donnybrook** S Africa
38B3 **Donostia** Spain
20B2 **Don Pedro Res** USA
10H2 **Doonerak,Mt** USA
57F9 **Dopolong** Phil
52A3 **Do Qu** *R* China
37B2 **Dora Baltea** *R* Italy
38D2 **Dorbirn** Austria
53A2 **Dorbod** China
35D6 **Dorchester** Eng
7L3 **Dorchester,C** Can
38C2 **Dordogne** *R* France
42A2 **Dordrecht** Neth
74D3 **Dordrecht** S Africa
3G3 **Doré L** Can
3G3 **Doré Lake** Can
14D1 **Dorest Peak** *Mt* USA
70B3 **Dori** Burkina
74B3 **Doring** *R* S Africa
36B2 **Dormans** France
42B3 **Dornbirn** Austria
34C3 **Dornoch** Scot
34C3 **Dornoch Firth** *Estuary* Scot
32H6 **Dorotea** Sweden
75D2 **Dorrigo** Aust
18B2 **Dorris** USA
35D6 **Dorset** County, Eng
36D1 **Dorsten** Germany
42B2 **Dortmund** Germany
72C3 **Doruma** Zaïre
49N4 **Dosatuy** Russian Fed
60B1 **Doshi** Afghan
20B2 **Dos Palos** USA
71G3 **Dosso** Niger
48G5 **Dossor** Kazakhstan
9E3 **Dothan** USA
38C1 **Douai** France
72A3 **Douala** Cam
75D1 **Double Island Pt** Aust
5K3 **Double Mer** *B* Can
16B3 **Double Mountain Fork** *R* USA
20C3 **Double Mt** USA
38D2 **Doubs** *R* France
78A3 **Doubtful Sd** NZ
70B3 **Douentza** Mali
3B2 **Douglas** Alaska, USA
8C3 **Douglas** Arizona, USA
35C4 **Douglas** Eng
15C2 **Douglas** Georgia, USA
74C2 **Douglas** S Africa
8C2 **Douglas** Wyoming, USA
10E2 **Douglas,C** USA
3C3 **Douglas Chan** Can
15C1 **Douglas L** USA
10H4 **Douglas,Mt** USA
36C2 **Doulevant-le-Château** France
36B1 **Doullens** France
35B4 **Doun** County, N Ire
27H8 **Dourados** Brazil
29B3 **Dourados** *R* Brazil
36B2 **Dourdan** France
39A1 **Douro** *R* Port
16A2 **Dove Creek** USA
13D3 **Dover** Delaware, USA
35F6 **Dover** Eng
13E2 **Dover** New Hampshire, USA
14C2 **Dover** New Jersey, USA
12C2 **Dover** Ohio, USA
35E5 **Dover** *R* Eng
35F6 **Dover,Str of** Eng/France
43G2 **Dovsk** Belorussia
14C3 **Downington** USA
35C4 **Downpatrick** N Ire
14C1 **Downsville** USA
3D3 **Downton,Mt** Can
14C2 **Doylestown** USA
54B3 **Dōzen** *I* Japan
70A2 **Dr'aa** *R* Mor
37A2 **Drac** *R* France
29B3 **Dracena** Brazil
14E1 **Dracut** USA
38D3 **Draguignan** France
11B2 **Drake** USA
73D6 **Drakensberg** *Mts* S Africa
xxxE7 **Drake Pass** Pacific/Atlantic O
41E2 **Dráma** Greece
32G6 **Drammen** Nor
32A1 **Drangajökull** Iceland
22B1 **Dr Arroyo** Mexico
37E1 **Drau** *R* Austria
40D1 **Drava** *R* Slovenia, Yugos
3F3 **Drayton Valley** Can
38C2 **Dreaux** France
42C2 **Dresden** Germany
36A2 **Dreux** France
18C2 **Drewsey** USA
4E4 **Driftwood** Can
14A2 **Driftwood** USA
41E2 **Drin** *R* Alb
41D2 **Drina** *R* Bosnia & Herzegovina/Serbia
43F1 **Drissa** *R* Belorussia
35B5 **Drogheda** Irish Rep
43E3 **Drogobych** Ukraine
37A2 **Drôme** *R* France
37B2 **Dronera** Italy
79F12 **Dronning Maud Land** Region, Ant
26F8 **Dr P.P. Pená** Par
6G4 **Drumheller** Can
18D1 **Drummond** USA
12C1 **Drummond I** USA
5G4 **Drummondville** Can
43E2 **Druskininksi** Lithuania
49Q3 **Druzhina** Russian Fed
10L4 **Dry B** USA
11D2 **Dryberry L** Can
7J5 **Dryden** Can
14B1 **Dryden** USA
23H1 **Dry Harbour Mts** Jamaica
71J4 **Dschang** Cam
55B3 **Duang** *I* Burma
66C1 **Dubā** S Arabia
67G1 **Dubai** UAE
6H3 **Dubawnt** *R* Can
6H3 **Dubawnt L** Can
76D4 **Dubbo** Aust
35B5 **Dublin** County, Irish Rep
35B5 **Dublin** Irish Rep
15C2 **Dublin** USA
44F4 **Dubna** Russian Fed
45D5 **Dubno** Ukraine
18D2 **Dubois** Idaho, USA
13D2 **Du Bois** USA
18E2 **Dubois** Wyoming, USA
3C3 **Dubose,Mt** Can
43F3 **Dubossary** Moldavia
43F2 **Dubrovica** Ukraine
41D2 **Dubrovnik** Croatia, Yugos
9D2 **Dubuque** USA
19D2 **Duchesne** USA
15B1 **Duck** *R* USA
3H3 **Duck Mts** Can
20C3 **Ducor** USA
36D2 **Dudelange** Lux
48K3 **Dudinka** Russian Fed
35D5 **Dudley** Eng
49L2 **Dudypta** *R* Russian Fed
70B4 **Duekoué** Ivory Coast
39B1 **Duero** *R* Spain
77F1 **Duff Is** Solomon Is
34D3 **Dufftown** Scot
40C2 **Dugi Otok** *I* Croatia, Yugos
5G2 **Du Gué** *R* Can
42B2 **Duisburg** Germany
74E1 **Duiwelskloof** S Africa
64E3 **Dūkan** Iraq
10M5 **Duke I** USA
72D3 **Duk Faiwil** Sudan
67F1 **Dukhān** Qatar
52A4 **Dukou** China
50C3 **Dulan** China
28C2 **Dulce** *R* Arg
56D2 **Dulit Range** *Mts* Malay
61D3 **Dullabchara** India
36D1 **Dülmen** Germany
9D2 **Duluth** USA
65D2 **Dūmā** Syria
56B2 **Dumai** Indon
57E8 **Dumaran** *I* Phil
8C3 **Dumas** USA
65D2 **Dumayr** Syria
71G4 **Dumbai** Ghana
34C4 **Dumbarton** Scot
34D4 **Dumfries** Scot
34C4 **Dumfries and Galloway** Region, Scot
61C3 **Dumka** India
57B2 **Dumoga Kecil** Indon
13D1 **Dumoine,L** Can
79G8 **Dumont d'Urville** *Base* Ant
69C1 **Dumyât** Egypt
41F2 **Dunărea** *R* Rom
35B5 **Dunary Head** *Pt* Irish Rep
41E2 **Dunav** *R* Bulg
41D1 **Dunav** *R* Croatia/Serbia
43F3 **Dunayevtsy** Ukraine
3D4 **Duncan** Can
17C3 **Duncan** USA
4E3 **Duncan,C** Can
4F3 **Duncan L** Can
14B2 **Duncannon** USA
62E2 **Duncan Pass** Andaman Is
34D2 **Duncansby Head** *Pt* Scot
35B4 **Dundalk** Irish Rep
14B3 **Dundalk** USA
35B5 **Dundalk B** Irish Rep
7M2 **Dundas** Greenland
10M5 **Dundas I** Can
6G2 **Dundas Pen** Can
51G8 **Dundas Str** Aust
74E2 **Dundee** S Africa
34D3 **Dundee** Scot
14B1 **Dundee** USA
75B1 **Dundoo** Aust
35C4 **Dundrum** *B* N Ire
77G5 **Dunedin** NZ
15C3 **Dunedin** USA
75C2 **Dunedoo** Aust
34D3 **Dunfermline** Scot
60C4 **Dungarpur** India
35B5 **Dungarvan** Irish Rep
35F6 **Dungeness** Eng
75D2 **Dungog** Aust
72C3 **Dungu** Zaïre
72D1 **Dungunab** Sudan
53B3 **Dunhua** China
50C2 **Dunhuang** China
36B1 **Dunkerque** France
9F2 **Dunkirk** USA
72D2 **Dunkur** Eth
71F4 **Dunkwa** Ghana
33B3 **Dun Laoghaire** Irish Rep
14C2 **Dunmore** USA
23B1 **Dunmore Town** Bahamas
15D1 **Dunn** USA
34D2 **Dunnet Head** *Pt* Scot
11B3 **Dunning** USA
34D4 **Duns** Scot
11B2 **Dunseith** USA
18B2 **Dunsmuir** USA
78A2 **Dunstan Mts** NZ
36C2 **Dun-sur-Meuse** France
52D1 **Duolun** China
11B2 **Dupree** USA
73B4 **Duque de Braganca** Angola
12B3 **Du Quoin** USA
65C3 **Dura** Israel
38D3 **Durance** *R* France
12A2 **Durand** USA
21B2 **Durango** Mexico
39B1 **Durango** Spain
22A1 **Durango** State, Mexico
8C3 **Durango** USA
8D3 **Durant** USA
65D1 **Duraykīsh** Syria
25E4 **Durazho** Urug
74E2 **Durban** S Africa
36D1 **Duren** Germany
61B3 **Durg** India
61C3 **Durgapur** India
34E4 **Durham** County, Eng
34E4 **Durham** Eng

Durham Embarras Portage

9F3 Durham N Carolina, USA
14E1 Durham New Hampshire, USA
75B1 Durham Downs Aust
41D2 Durmitor *Mt* Montenegro, Yugos
34C2 Durness Scot
41D2 Durrës Alb
75B1 Durrie Aust
41F3 Dursunbey Turk
78B2 D'Urville I NZ
63E1 Dushak Turkmenistan
52B4 Dushan China
59E2 Dushanbe Tajikistan
14B2 Dushore USA
78A3 Dusky Sd NZ
42B2 Düsseldorf Germany
10E5 Dutch Harbor USA
19D3 Dutton,Mt USA
52B4 Duyun China
64B1 Düzce Turk
44F2 Dvinskaya Guba *B* Russian Fed
60B4 Dwārka India
18C1 Dworshak Res USA
9E3 Dyersburg USA
35C5 Dyfed County, Wales
45G7 Dykh Tau *Mt* Russian Fed
75B1 Dynevor Downs Aust
50C2 Dzag Mongolia
50D2 Dzamïn Üüd Mongolia
73E5 Dzaoudzi Mayotte
50C2 Dzavhan Gol *R* Mongolia
44G4 Dzerzhinsk Russian Fed
49O4 Dzhalinda Russian Fed
48J5 Dzhambul Kazakhstan
45E6 Dzhankoy Ukraine
48H5 Dzhezkazgan Kazakhstan
60B1 Dzhilikul' Tajikistan
48J5 Dzhungarskiy Alatau *Mts* Kazakhstan
42D2 Dzierzoniow Pol
59G1 Dzungaria Basin, China
49L5 Dzüyl Mongolia

E

7K4 Eabamet L Can
10K3 Eagle Alaska, USA
16A2 Eagle Colorado, USA
5K3 Eagle *R* Can
11B2 Eagle Butte USA
18B2 Eagle L California, USA
11D2 Eagle L Can
13F1 Eagle L Maine, USA
13F1 Eagle Lake USA
17C3 Eagle Mountain L USA
8C4 Eagle Pass USA
16A3 Eagle Peak *Mt* USA
6E3 Eagle Plain Can
10J3 Eagle River USA
11D1 Ear Falls Can
19C3 Earlimart USA
19D4 Earp USA
16B3 Earth USA
15C2 Easley USA
13D2 East Aurora USA
15B3 East B USA
35F6 Eastbourne Eng
14C1 East Branch Delaware *R* USA
77G4 East,C NZ
10B6 East C USA
12B2 East Chicago USA
50F3 East China Sea China/ Japan
61B4 Eastern Ghats *Mts* India
4B3 Easterville Can
25E8 East Falkland *I* Falkland Is
10J2 East Fork *R* USA
19C3 Eastgate USA
11C2 East Grand Forks USA
14D1 Easthampton USA
14D2 East Hampton USA
12B2 East Lake USA
12C2 East Liverpool USA
74D3 East London S Africa
7L4 Eastmain Can
7L4 Eastmain *R* Can
15C2 Eastman USA
12A2 East Moline USA
13D3 Easton Maryland, USA
13D2 Easton Pennsylvania, USA
14C2 East Orange USA
xxixO5 East Pacific Ridge Pacific O
xxixO4 East Pacific Rise Pacific O
15C2 East Point USA
13F2 Eastport USA
35E5 East Retford Eng
15B1 East Ridge USA
9D3 East St Louis USA
49R2 East Siberian S Russian Fed
35F6 East Sussex County, Eng
13D3 Eastville USA
20C1 East Walker USA
15C2 Eatonton USA
11D3 Eau Claire USA
51H6 Eauripik *I* Pacific O
22C1 Ebano Mexico
72B3 Ebebiyin Eq Guinea
14A2 Ebensburg USA
36E2 Eberbach Germany
42C2 Eberswalde Germany
54D2 Ebetsu Japan
52A4 Ebian China
48K5 Ebinur *L* China
40D2 Eboli Italy
72B3 Ebolowa Cam
39B1 Ebro *R* Spain
64A1 Eceabat Turk
71C1 Ech Cheliff Alg
52D2 Eching China
18C1 Echo USA
Echo Bay = Port Radium
6G3 Echo Bay Can
36D2 Echternach Lux
75B3 Echuca Aust
39A2 Ecija Spain
7K2 Eclipse Sd Can
36A3 Ecommoy France
26C4 Ecuador Republic, S America
34D2 Eday *I* Scot
72E2 Ed Eth
34G3 Edda *Oilfield* N Sea
72C2 Ed Da'ein Sudan
66B4 Ed Damasin Sudan
72D2 Ed Damer Sudan
72D2 Ed Debba Sudan
34C2 Eddrachillis *B* Scot
72D2 Ed Dueim Sudan
75E3 Eddystone Pt Aust
71G4 Ede Nig
72A3 Edea Cam
75C3 Eden Aust
16C3 Eden Texas, USA
18E2 Eden Wyoming, USA
34D4 Eden *R* Eng
74D2 Edenburg S Africa
78A3 Edendale NZ
36D2 Edenkoben Germany
36E1 Eder *R* Germany
11C2 Edgeley USA
7M3 Edgell I Can
11B3 Edgemont USA
48D2 Edgeøya *I* Barents S
14B3 Edgewood USA
65C3 Edh Dhahiriya Israel
41E2 Edhessa Greece
17F4 Edinburg USA
34D3 Edinburgh Scot
45D7 Edirne Turk
20C3 Edison USA
15C2 Edisto *R* USA
18B1 Edmonds USA
6G4 Edmonton Can
11C2 Edmore USA
7M5 Edmundston Can
17C4 Edna USA
10M4 Edna Bay USA
71H4 Edo *State* Nigeria
40C1 Edolo Italy
65C3 Edom Region, Jordan
45D8 Edremit Turk
41F3 Edremit Körfezi *B* Turk
50C2 Edrengiyn Nuruu *Mts* Mongolia
6G4 Edson Can
28C3 Eduardo Castex Arg
10N3 Eduni,Mt Can
75B3 Edward *R* Aust
72C4 Edward,L Zaïre/Uganda
20D3 Edwards USA
75A1 Edwards Creek Aust
8C3 Edwards Plat USA
12B3 Edwardsville USA
3B2 Edziza,Mt Can
10F3 Eek USA
36B1 Eeklo Belg
77F2 Efate *I* Vanuatu
9E3 Effingham USA
19D3 Egan Range *Mts* USA
7N3 Egedesminde Greenland
10G4 Egegik USA
3H2 Egenolf L Can
43E3 Eger Hung
32F7 Egersund Nor
36E1 Eggegebirge Region, Germany
14C3 Egg Harbor City USA
6G2 Eglinton I Can
78B1 Egmont,C NZ
78B1 Egmont,Mt NZ
64B2 Eğridir Gölü *L* Turk
29C1 Eguas *R* Brazil
49U3 Egvekinot Russian Fed
69B2 Egypt Republic, Africa
32K6 Ehsenvaara Fin
39B1 Eibar Spain
38C2 Eibeuf France
75D1 Eidsvolo Aust
36D1 Eifel Region, Germany
34B3 Eigg *I* Scot
59F5 Eight Degree Chan Indian O
76B2 Eighty Mile Beach Aust
75C3 Eildon,L Aust
36E1 Einbeck Germany
42B2 Eindhoven Neth
37C1 Einsiedeln Switz
65C3 Ein Yahav Israel
42C2 Eisenach Germany
42C3 Eisenerz Austria
37E1 Eisenhut *Mt* Austria
36D1 Eitorf Germany
52A1 Ejin qi China
71F4 Ejuanema,Mt Ghana
71F4 Ejura Ghana
22C2 Ejutla Mexico
11B2 Ekalaka USA
78C2 Eketahuna NZ
48J4 Ekibastuz Kazakhstan
49P4 Ekimchan Russian Fed
64B3 Ek Mahalla el Kubra Egypt
32H7 Eksjo Sweden
4D3 Ekwan *R* Can
65A3 El Abbâsa Egypt
64A3 El'Alamein Egypt
74D2 Elands *R* S Africa
74C3 Elands Berg S Africa
22B1 El Arenal Mexico
71B2 El Aricha Alg
64B3 El'Arish Egypt
64B4 Elat Israel
72C2 El' Atrun Oasis Sudan
71C2 el Attar *R* Alg
45F8 Elazig Turk
64C3 El Azraq Jordan
40C2 Elba *I* Italy
69C2 El Balyana Egypt
53D1 El'ban Russian Fed
26D2 El Banco Colombia
41E2 Elbasan Alb
66B3 El Bauga Sudan
23D5 El Baúl Ven
71C2 El Bayadh Alg
42C2 Elbe *R* Germany
65D1 El Bega'a *R* Leb
12B2 Elberta USA
8C3 Elbert,Mt USA
15C2 Elberton USA
36A2 Elbeuf France
64C2 Elbistan Turk
43D2 Elblag Pol
25B6 El Bolson Arg
11C2 Elbow Lake USA
22B1 El Bozal Mexico
45G7 Elbrus *Mt* Russian Fed
Elburz Mts = Reshteh-ye Alborz
19C4 El Cajon USA
17C4 El Campo USA
19C4 El Centro USA
39B2 Elche Spain
4D4 Elcho USA
28B3 El Cuy Arg
39B2 Elda Spain
49P3 El'dikan Russian Fed
26C3 El Diviso Colombia
70B2 El Djouf *Desert* Region Maur
17D2 Eldon USA
29B4 Eldorado Arg
9D3 El Dorado Arkansas, USA
29C3 Eldorado Brazil
3G2 Eldorado Can
8D3 El Dorado Kansas, USA
21B2 El Dorado Mexico
16B3 Eldorado Texas, USA
26F2 El Dorado Ven
72D3 Eldoret Kenya
14A2 Eldred USA
65C1 Elea,C Cyprus
18D2 Electric Peak *Mt* USA
70B2 El Eglab Region, Alg
66B2 Elel *Watercourse* Egypt
16A3 Elephant Butte Res USA
39B1 El Escorial Spain
64D2 Eleşkirt Turk
71D1 El Eulma Alg
9F4 Eleuthera *I* Bahamas
71D1 El Fahs Tunisia
64B4 El Faiyûm Egypt
70B2 El Farsia *Well* Mor
72C2 El Fasher Sudan
64B4 El Fashn Egypt
39A1 El Ferrol del Caudillo Spain
65B3 El Firdân Egypt
72C2 El Fula Sudan
70C1 El Gassi Alg
72D2 El Geteina Sudan
72D2 El Gezîra Region, Sudan
65C3 El Ghor *V* Israel/Jordan
9E2 Elgin Illinois, USA
11B2 Elgin N Dakota, USA
34D3 Elgin Scot
64B3 El Gîza Egypt
70C1 El Golea Alg
19D4 El Golfo de Santa Clara Mexico
72D3 Elgon,Mt Uganda/Kenya
72E3 El Goran Eth
22B2 El Grullo Mexico
70B2 El Guettara *Well* Mali
70B2 El Haricha *Desert Region* Mali
64A4 El Harra Egypt
39C2 El Harrach Alg
66B4 El Hawata Sudan
22C1 El Hig Mexico
66B4 El Homra Sudan
28A3 El Huecu Arg
64B4 El'Igma *Desert Region* Egypt
10F3 Elim USA
Elisabethville = Lubumbashi
32K6 Elisenvaara Russian Fed
El Iskandarîya = Alexandria Egypt
45G6 Elista Russian Fed
76C4 Elizabeth Aust
13E2 Elizabeth USA
74B2 Elizabeth B Namibia
9F3 Elizabeth City USA
14E2 Elizabeth Is USA
15C1 Elizabethton Tennessee, USA
12B3 Elizabethtown Kentucky, USA
15D2 Elizabethtown N Carolina, USA
14B2 Elizabethtown Pennsylvania, USA
71A2 El Jadida Mor
64C3 El Jafr Jordan
65D3 El Jafr *L* Jordan
72D2 El Jebelein Sudan
71E1 El Jem Tunisia
43E2 Ełk Pol
14C3 Elk *R* Maryland, USA
12C3 Elk *R* W Virginia, USA
11D3 Elkader USA
71D1 El Kala Alg
72D2 El Kamlin Sudan
71D1 El Kef Tunisia
20B1 Elk Grove USA
El Khalil = Hebron Israel
66B3 El Khandaq Sudan
65A3 El Khânka Egypt
66B1 El Khârga Egypt
66B1 El-Khârga Oasis Egypt
12B2 Elkhart USA
70B2 El Khenachich *Desert* Region Mali
11C3 Elkhorn *R* USA
41F2 Elkhovo Bulg
13D3 Elkins USA
14B2 Elkland USA
11A3 Elk Mt USA
18C1 Elko Can
8B2 Elko USA
71B2 el Korima *R* Alg
14C3 Elkton USA
66B2 El Ku *Watercourse* Egypt
65B3 El Kûbri Egypt
64B3 El Kuntilla Egypt
72C2 El Lagowa Sudan
6H2 Ellef Ringnes I Can
11C2 Ellendale USA
19D3 Ellen,Mt USA
8A2 Ellensburg USA
14C2 Ellenville USA
7K2 Ellesmere I Can
78B2 Ellesmere,L NZ
14B3 Ellicott City USA
74D3 Elliot S Africa
7K5 Elliot Lake Can
18D2 Ellis USA
65C3 El Lisan *Pen* Jordan
74D1 Ellisras S Africa
13F2 Ellsworth USA
79F3 Ellsworth Land *Region* Ant
65A4 El Ma'âdi Egypt
69B1 El Maghra *L* Egypt
66B4 El Manaqil Sudan
64B3 El Mansûra Egypt
65A3 El Manzala Egypt
65A3 El Matarîya Egypt
65B3 El Matarîya Egypt
14C3 Elmer USA
70B3 El Merelé *Desert Region* Maur
28B2 El Milagro Arg
71D1 El Milia Alg
66B3 El Milk *Watercourse* Sudan
65C1 El Mîna Leb
64B4 El Minya Egypt
20B1 Elmira California, USA
9F2 Elmira New York, USA
19D4 El Mirage USA
71D2 el Mitta *R* Alg
17F4 El Moral Mexico
70B2 El Mreitl *Well* Maur
42B2 Elmsborn Germany
72C2 El Muglad Sudan
70B2 El Mzereb *Well* Mali
57E8 El Nido Phil
72D2 El Obeid Sudan
22B2 El Oro Mexico
22A1 Elota Mexico
71D2 El Oued Alg
19D4 Eloy USA
8C3 El Paso USA
19B3 El Porta USA
20C2 El Portal USA
16A3 El Porvenir Mexico
22B1 El Potosí Mexico
39A2 El Puerto del Sta Maria Spain
El Qâhira = Cairo
65B3 El Qantara Egypt
El Quds = Jerusalem
22A1 El Quelite Mexico
65C3 El Quseima Egypt
65C4 El Quwetra Jordan
8D3 El Reno USA
6E3 Elsa Can
37D3 Elsa *R* Italy
65A4 El Saff Egypt
65B3 El Sâlhîya Egypt
22A1 El Salto Mexico
21D3 El Salvador Republic, C America
4E4 Elsas Can
19C4 El Sauzal Mexico
65B3 El Shallûfa Egypt
65B4 El Shatt Egypt
65A3 El Simbillâwein Egypt
20D4 Elsinore L USA
28B3 El Sosneade Arg
42C2 Elsterwerde Germany
16A4 El Sueco Mexico
El Suweis = Suez
65A4 El Tabbin Egypt
39A1 El Teleno *Mt* Spain
78B1 Eltham NZ
65C4 El Thamad Egypt
26F2 El Tigre Ven
64B4 El Tîh *Desert Region* Egypt
65B3 El Tîna Egypt
28C2 El Tio Arg
18C1 Eltopia USA
28A1 El Toro Chile
28A1 El Transito Chile
22A1 El Tuito Mexico
64B4 El Tûr Egypt
62C1 Elūru India
39A2 Elvas Port
26D5 Elvira Brazil
6H2 Elvira,C Can
28A2 El Volcán Chile
12B2 Elwood USA
35F5 Ely Eng
9D2 Ely Minnesota, USA
8B3 Ely Nevada, USA
12C2 Elyria USA
65A3 El Zarqa Egypt
63D1 Emāmrūd Iran
60B1 Emām Sāheb Afghan
42D1 Eman *R* Sweden
45K6 Emba Kazakhstan
45K6 Emba *R* Kazakhstan
25C5 Embalse Cerros Colorados *L* Arg
39B2 Embalse de Alarcón *Res* Spain
39A2 Embalse de Alcántarà *Res* Spain
39A1 Embalse de Almendra *Res* Spain
39A2 Embalse de Garcia de Sola *Res* Spain
26F2 Embalse de Guri *L* Ven
39B1 Embalse de Mequinenza *Res* Spain
39A1 Embalse de Ricobayo *Res* Spain
25E4 Embalse de Rio Negro *Res* Urug
28B3 Embalse El Choc1on *Res* Arg
25C5 Embalse Ezequil Ramos Mexia *L* Arg
25C6 Embalse Florentine Ameghino *L* Arg
39A1 Embalse Gabriel y Galan *Res* Spain
28B1 Embalse Rio Hondo *Res* Arg
25D2 Embarcación Arg
6G4 Embarras Portage Can

Embrun **Femund**

37B2 **Embrun** France
72D4 **Embu** Kenya
42B2 **Emden** Germany
52A4 **Emei** China
76D3 **Emerald** Aust
7M4 **Emeril** Can
6J5 **Emerson** Can
18C2 **Emigrant P** USA
72B1 **Emi Koussi** *Mt* Chad
28B3 **Emilo Mitre** Arg
64B2 **Emirdağ** Turk
14C2 **Emmaus** USA
42B2 **Emmen** Neth
36D2 **Emmendingen** Germany
36D1 **Emmerich** Germany
18C2 **Emmett** USA
14B3 **Emmitsburg** USA
10F3 **Emmonak** USA
8C4 **Emory Peak** *Mt* USA
21A2 **Empalme** Mexico
74E2 **Empangeni** S Africa
25E3 **Empedrado** Arg
xxixK2 **Emperor Seamount Chain** Pacific O
37D3 **Empoli** Italy
17C2 **Emporia** Kansas, USA
13D3 **Emporia** Virginia, USA
14A2 **Emporium** USA
42B2 **Ems** *R* Germany
4F4 **Emsdale** Can
34C2 **Enard** *B* Scot
22B1 **Encarnacion** Mexico
25E3 **Encarnación** Par
71F4 **Enchi** Ghana
17F4 **Encinal** USA
20D4 **Encinitas** USA
29D2 **Encruzilhada** Brazil
28E2 **Encruzilhada do Sul** Brazil
66C4 **Enda Salassie** Eth
76B1 **Endeh** Indon
3E3 **Enderby** Can
79G11 **Enderby Land** Region, Ant
11C2 **Enderlin** USA
13D2 **Endicott** USA
10H2 **Endicott Mts** USA
15D1 **Enfield** USA
37D1 **Engadin** *Mts* Switz
57F7 **Engaño,C** Phil
54D2 **Engaru** Japan
65C3 **En Gedi** Israel
37C1 **Engelberg** Switz
45H5 **Engel's** Russian Fed
56B4 **Enggano** *I* Indon
33C3 **England** Country, UK
7N4 **Englee** Can
15D1 **Englehard** USA
13D1 **Englehart** Can
16B2 **Englewood** USA
11D1 **English** *R* Can
33C3 **English Channel** Eng/France
4C4 **English River** Can
17C2 **Enid** USA
54D2 **Eniwa** Japan
70B3 **Enji** *Well* Maur
32H7 **Enkoping** Sweden
40C3 **Enna** Italy
72C2 **En Nahud** Sudan
72C2 **Ennedi** *Desert Region* Chad
10C2 **Ennelen** Russian Fed
75C1 **Enngonia** Aust
11B3 **Enning** USA
33B3 **Ennis** Irish Rep
18D1 **Ennis** Montana, USA
17C3 **Ennis** Texas, USA
35B5 **Enniscorthy** Irish Rep
35B4 **Enniskillen** N Ire
65C2 **Enn Nâqoûra** Leb
42C3 **Enns** *R* Austria
57A3 **Enrekang** Indon
32F8 **Enschede** Neth
21A1 **Ensenada** Mexico
52B3 **Enshi** China
36D3 **Ensisheim** France
72D4 **Entebbe** Uganda
15B2 **Enterprise** Alabama, USA
3E1 **Enterprise** Can
18C1 **Enterprise** Oregon, USA
71H4 **Enugu** Nig
71H4 **Enugu** *State* Nig
10D2 **Enurmino** Russian Fed
36E2 **Enz** *R* w Germ
54C3 **Enzan** Japan
71G4 **Epe** Nig
38C2 **Epernay** France
19D3 **Ephraim** USA
14B2 **Ephrata** Pennsylvania, USA
18C1 **Ephrata** Washington, USA
77F2 **Epi** *I* Vanuatu
38D2 **Épinal** France
65B1 **Episkopi** Cyprus
65B1 **Episkopi B** Cyprus
36E2 **Eppingen** Germany
36A2 **Epte** *R* France
74B1 **Epukiro** Namibia
28C3 **Epu pel** Arg
63C2 **Eqlid** Iran
68D7 **Equator**
72A3 **Equatorial Guinea** Republic, Africa
14D1 **Equinox Mt** USA
14C2 **Equinunk** USA
37C2 **Erba** Italy
36E2 **Erbach** Germany
36D2 **Erbeskopf** *Mt* Germany
28A3 **Ercilla** Chile
64D2 **Erciş** Turk
45F8 **Erciyas Daglari** *Mt* Turk
53B3 **Erdaobaihe** China
52C1 **Erdene** Mongolia
50D2 **Erdenet** Mongolia
72C2 **Erdi** *Desert Region* Chad
25F3 **Erechim** Brazil
64B1 **Ereğli** Turk
64B2 **Ereğli** Turk
50E2 **Erenhot** China
39B1 **Eresma** *R* Spain
36D1 **Erft** *R* Germany
42C2 **Erfurt** Germany
64C2 **Ergani** Turk
70B2 **Erg Chech** *Desert Region* Alg
72B2 **Erg du Djourab** *Desert Region* Chad
70D3 **Erg Du Ténéré** *Desert Region* Niger
64A1 **Ergene** *R* Turk
70B2 **Erg Iguidi** *Region* Alg
43F1 **Ergli** Latvia
72B2 **Erguig** *R* Chad
50E1 **Ergun** *R* China/Russian Fed
49O4 **Ergun Zuoqi** China
10C2 **Erguveyem** *R* Russian Fed
72D2 **Eriba** Sudan
9F2 **Erie** USA
9E2 **Erie,L** USA/Can
4B3 **Eriksdale** Can
54D2 **Erimo-misaki** *C* Japan
35C4 **Erin Port** Eng
34B3 **Eriskay** *I* Scot
66C3 **Eritrea** Region, Eth
36D1 **Erkelenz** Germany
42C3 **Erlangen** Germany
17D3 **Erling,L** USA
74D2 **Ermelo** S Africa
62B3 **Ernākulam** India
62B2 **Erode** India
75B1 **Eromanga** Aust
74B1 **Erongoberg** *Mt* Namibia
71B2 **Er Rachidia** Mor
72D2 **Er Rahad** Sudan
73D5 **Errego** Mozam
33B2 **Errigal** *Mt* Irish Rep
33A3 **Erris Head** *Pt* Irish Rep
77F2 **Erromanga** *I* Vanuatu
72D2 **Er Roseires** Sudan
71C2 **er Rtem** *R* Alg
65C2 **Er Rummān** Jordan
11C2 **Erskine** USA
36D2 **Erstein** France
28E2 **Erval** Brazil
42C2 **Erzgebirge** *Upland* Germany
45F8 **Erzincan** Turk
45G8 **Erzurum** Turk
54D2 **Esan-misaki** *C* Japan
38C3 **Esara** *R* Spain
54D2 **Esashi** Japan
42B1 **Esbjerg** Den
19D3 **Escalante** USA
8C4 **Escalón** Mexico
9E2 **Escanaba** USA
21C3 **Escárcega** Mexico
36C2 **Esch** Luxembourg
19C4 **Escondido** USA
21B2 **Escuinapa** Mexico
21C3 **Escuintla** Guatemala
72B3 **Eséka** Cam
39C1 **Esera** *R* Spain
63C2 **Eşfahān** Iran
74E2 **Eshowe** S Africa
65C3 **Esh Sharā** *Upland* Jordan
37E3 **Esino** Italy
78C1 **Eskdale** NZ
32C1 **Eskifjörður** Iceland
32H7 **Eskilstuna** Sweden
6E3 **Eskimo L** Can
7J3 **Eskimo Point** Can
45E8 **Eskisehir** Turk
39A1 **Esla** *R* Spain
26C3 **Esmeraldas** Ecuador
23B2 **Esmerelda** Cuba
25A7 **Esmerelda** *I* Chile
38C3 **Espalion** France
4E4 **Espanola** Can
16A2 **Espanola** USA
76B4 **Esperance** Aust
28C2 **Esperanza** Arg
79G2 **Esperanza** *Base* Ant
29D2 **Espírito Santo** State, Brazil
77F2 **Espiritu Santo** *I* Vanuatu
73D6 **Espungabera** Mozam
25B6 **Esquel** Arg
18B1 **Esquimalt** Can
28D2 **Esquina** Arg
65D2 **Es Samra** Jordan
71A2 **Essaourira** Mor
71E2 **Es-Sekhira** Tunisia
42B2 **Essen** Germany
27G3 **Essequibo** Guyana
35F6 **Essex** County, Eng
12C2 **Essexville** USA
42B3 **Esslingen** Germany
36B2 **Essonne** France
36C2 **Essoyes** France
27L6 **Estância** Brazil
74D2 **Estcourt** S Africa
37D2 **Este** Italy
26A1 **Esteli** Nic
36B2 **Esternay** France
20B3 **Estero B** USA
22C1 **Esteros** Mexico
25D2 **Esteros** Par
28D1 **Esteros del Iberá** *Swamp* Arg
16A1 **Estes Park** USA
6H5 **Estevan** Can
11D3 **Estherville** USA
15C2 **Estill** USA
36B2 **Estissac** France
44C4 **Estonia** *Republic* Europe
25B8 **Estrecho de Magallanes** *Str* Chile
20B3 **Estrella** *R* USA
39A2 **Estremoz** Port
43D3 **Esztergom** Hung
75A1 **Etadunna** Aust
7L2 **Etah** Can
36C2 **Etam** France
5K3 **Etamamiou** Can
38C2 **Etampes** France
75A1 **Etamunbanie,L** Aust
36A1 **Etaples** France
60D3 **Etāwah** India
72D3 **Ethiopia** Republic, Africa
22C2 **Etla** Mexico
40C3 **Etna** *Mt* Italy
10M4 **Etolin I** USA
10E3 **Etolin Str** USA
73B5 **Etosha Nat Pk** Namibia
73B5 **Etosha Pan** *Salt L* Namibia
15C2 **Etowah** *R* USA
36A2 **Etretat** France
3D2 **Etsha Plateau** Can
36C2 **Ettelbruck** Lux
77H3 **Eua** *I* Tonga
75C2 **Euabalong** Aust
12C2 **Euclid** USA
75C3 **Eucumbene,L** Aust
75A2 **Eudunda** Aust
17C2 **Eufala L** USA
15B2 **Eufaula** USA
8A2 **Eugene** USA
75C1 **Eulo** Aust
17D3 **Eunice** Louisiana, USA
16B3 **Eunice** New Mexico, USA
36D1 **Eupen** Germany
64D3 **Euphrates** *R* Iraq
17E3 **Eupora** USA
36A2 **Eure** Department, France
38C2 **Eure** *R* France
36A2 **Eure-et-Loir** Department, France
18B2 **Eureka** California, USA
7K1 **Eureka** Can
18C1 **Eureka** Montana, USA
8B3 **Eureka** Nevada, USA
11C2 **Eureka** S Dakota, USA
19D3 **Eureka** Utah, USA
7K2 **Eureka Sound** Can
20D2 **Eureka V** USA
75C3 **Euroa** Aust
75C1 **Eurombah** *R* Aust
73E6 **Europa** *I* Mozam Chan
36C1 **Europort** Neth
42B2 **Euskirchen** Germany
15B2 **Eutaw** USA
3C3 **Eutsuk L** Can
3F3 **Evansburg** Can
7K1 **Evans,C** Can
7L4 **Evans,L** Can
16A2 **Evans,Mt** Colorado, USA
18D1 **Evans,Mt** Montana, USA
7K3 **Evans Str** Can
12B2 **Evanston** Illinois, USA
8B2 **Evanston** Wyoming, USA
9E3 **Evansville** Indiana, USA
11A3 **Evansville** Wyoming, USA
74D2 **Evaton** S Africa
76C4 **Everard,L** Aust
59G3 **Everest,Mt** Nepal/China
14A2 **Everett** Pennsylvania, USA
8A2 **Everett** Washington, USA
14D1 **Everett,Mt** USA
9E4 **Everglades,The** *Swamp* USA
15B2 **Evergreen** USA
35E5 **Evesham** Eng
72B3 **Evinayong** Eq Guinea
32F7 **Evje** Nor
37B1 **Evolène** Switz
39A2 **Évora** Port
38C2 **Evreux** France
41E3 **Évvoia** *I* Greece
72B4 **Ewo** Congo
20C1 **Excelisor Mt** USA
20C1 **Excelisor Mts** USA
17D2 **Excelsior Springs** USA
19C3 **Exeter** California, USA
35D6 **Exeter** Eng
13E2 **Exeter** New Hampshire, USA
35D6 **Exmoor Nat Pk** Eng
35D6 **Exmouth** Eng
39A2 **Extremadura** Region, Spain
21E2 **Exuma Sd** Bahamas
72D4 **Eyasi** *L* Tanz
34D4 **Eyemouth** Scot
69D4 **Eyl** Somalia
76B4 **Eyre** Aust
76C3 **Eyre Creek** *R* Aust
76C3 **Eyre,L** Aust
76C4 **Eyre Pen** Aust
3H2 **Eyrie L** Can
57F8 **Eyte** *I* Phil
22B1 **Ezatlan** Mexico
41F3 **Ezine** Turk
66B3 **Ez Zeidab** Sudan

F

4G3 **Faber L** Can
32F7 **Fåborg** Den
40C2 **Fabriano** Italy
37B2 **Fabrosa** Italy
72B2 **Fachi** Niger
72C2 **Fada** Chad
71G3 **Fada N'Gourma** Burkina
49Q2 **Faddeyevskiy, Ostrov** *I* Russian Fed
40C2 **Faenza** Italy
7N3 **Faeringehavn** Greenland
30E2 **Faeroerne** Is, N Atlantic
72B3 **Fafa** *R* CAR
72E3 **Fafan** *R* Eth
71G3 **Faga** *R* Burkina
41E1 **Făgăraş** Rom
36C1 **Fagnes** Region, Belg
70B3 **Faguibine,L** Mali
67G2 **Fahud** Oman
70A1 **Faiol** *I* Açores
16A3 **Fairacres** USA
6D3 **Fairbanks** USA
12C3 **Fairborn** USA
8D2 **Fairbury** USA
14B3 **Fairfax** USA
19B3 **Fairfield** California, USA
14D2 **Fairfield** Connecticut, USA
18D2 **Fairfield** Idaho, USA
18D1 **Fairfield** Montana, USA
12C3 **Fairfield** Ohio, USA
34B4 **Fair Head** *Pt* N Ire
33C2 **Fair Isle** *I* Scot
78B2 **Fairlie** NZ
11D3 **Fairmont** Minnesota, USA
12C3 **Fairmont** W Virginia, USA
14B1 **Fairport** USA
3E2 **Fairview** Can
16C2 **Fairview** USA
6E4 **Fairweather,Mt** USA
51H6 **Fais** *I* Pacific O
60C2 **Faisalabad** Pak
11B2 **Faith** USA
34E1 **Faither,The** *Pen* Scot
61B2 **Faizābād** India
77H1 **Fakaofo** *I* Tokeau Is
35F5 **Fakenham** Eng
76C1 **Fakfak** Indon
32G7 **Faköping** Sweden
71F3 **Falaise de Banfora** Burkina
61D3 **Falam** Burma
28B4 **Falckner** Arg
21C2 **Falcon Res** USA/Mexico
70A3 **Falémé** *R* Mali/Sen
17F4 **Falfurrias** USA
3E2 **Falher** Can
32G7 **Falkenberg** Sweden
34D4 **Falkirk** Scot
25D8 **Falkland Is** Dependency, S Atlantic
25E8 **Falkland Sd** Falkland Is
20D4 **Fallbrook** USA
8B3 **Fallon** USA
13E2 **Fall River** USA
16A1 **Fall River P** USA
17C1 **Falls City** USA
35C6 **Falmouth** Eng
23H1 **Falmouth** Jamaica
13E2 **Falmouth** Maine, USA
14E2 **Falmouth** Massachusetts, USA
74B3 **False B** S Africa
21A2 **Falso,C** Mexico
42C2 **Falster** *I* Den
41F1 **Fălticeni** Rom
32H6 **Falun** Sweden
64B2 **Famagusta** Cyprus
65B1 **Famagusta B** Cyprus
28B1 **Famatina** Arg
36C1 **Famenne** Region, Belg
4B3 **Family L** Can
20C3 **Famoso** USA
55B2 **Fang** Thai
72D3 **Fangak** Sudan
52E5 **Fang liao** Taiwan
53B2 **Fangzheng** China
40C2 **Fano** Italy
65A3 **Fâqûs** Egypt
79G3 **Faraday** *Base* Ant
72C3 **Faradje** Zaïre
73E6 **Farafangana** Madag
69B2 **Farafra Oasis** Egypt
63E2 **Farah** Afghan
63E2 **Farah** *R* Afghan
51H5 **Farallon de Medinilla** *I* Pacific O
70A3 **Faranah** Guinea
51H6 **Faraulep** *I* Pacific O
35E6 **Fareham** Eng
Farewell,C = Kap Farvel
77G5 **Farewell,C** NZ
78B2 **Farewell Spit** *Pt* NZ
8D2 **Fargo** USA
65C2 **Fari'a** *R* Israel
9D2 **Faribault** USA
61C3 **Faridpur** Bang
63D1 **Farīmān** Iran
65A3 **Fâriskûr** Egypt
13E2 **Farmington** Maine, USA
17D2 **Farmington** Missouri, USA
14E1 **Farmington** New Hampshire, USA
8C3 **Farmington** New Mexico, USA
18D2 **Farmington** Utah, USA
20B2 **Farmington Res** USA
34E4 **Farne Deep** N Sea
3E3 **Farnham,Mt** Can
10M3 **Faro** Can
39A2 **Faro** Port
32H7 **Fåro** *I* Sweden
71J4 **Faro** *R* Cam
68K8 **Farquhar** *Is* Indian O
34C3 **Farrar** *R* Scot
12C2 **Farrell** USA
41E3 **Fársala** Greece
63E2 **Farsi** Afghan
16B3 **Farwell** USA
63C3 **Fasā** Iran
45D5 **Fastov** Ukraine
61B2 **Fatehpur** India
27H7 **Fatima du Sul** Brazil
18C1 **Fauquier** Can
74D2 **Fauresmith** S Africa
37B2 **Faverges** France
4C3 **Fawcett L** Can
7K4 **Fawn** *R* Can
32H6 **Fax** *R* Sweden
32A2 **Faxaflóri** *B* Iceland
72B2 **Faya** Chad
15B2 **Fayette** USA
9D3 **Fayetteville** Arkansas, USA
9F3 **Fayetteville** N Carolina, USA
15B1 **Fayetteville** Tennessee, USA
65B3 **Fâyid** Egypt
64E4 **Faylakah** *I* Kuwait
60C2 **Fāzilka** India
70A2 **Fdérik** Maur
9F3 **Fear,C** USA
19B3 **Feather Middle Fork** *R* USA
36A2 **Fécamp** France
28D2 **Federación** Arg
28D2 **Federal** Arg
71H4 **Federal Capital Territory** Nig
51H6 **Federated States of Micronesia** *Is* Pacific O
42C2 **Fehmarn** *I* Germany
26D5 **Feijó** Brazil
52C5 **Feilai Xai Bei Jiang** *R* China
78C2 **Feilding** NZ
73D5 **Feira** Zambia
27L6 **Feira de Santan** Brazil
64C2 **Feke** Turk
36D3 **Feldberg** *Mt* Germany
42B3 **Feldkirch** Austria
28D2 **Feliciano** *R* Arg
33D3 **Felixstowe** Eng
37D1 **Feltre** Italy
32G6 **Femund** *L* Nor

Fengcheng Funafuti

53A3 **Fengcheng** China
52B4 **Fengdu** China
52D1 **Fenging** China
52B3 **Fengjie** China
53A1 **Fengshui Shan** *Mt* China
52B3 **Feng Xian** China
52C1 **Fengzhen** China
52C2 **Fen He** *R* China
10C6 **Fenimore Pass** USA
73E5 **Fenoarivo Atsinanana** Madag
45F7 **Feodosiya** Ukraine
63D2 **Ferdow** Iran
36B2 **Fère** France
36B2 **Fère-Champenoise** France
59F2 **Fergana** Uzbekistan
3J2 **Fergus** *R* Can
11C2 **Fergus Falls** USA
35B4 **Fermanagh** County, N Ire
37E3 **Fermo** Italy
37D1 **Fern** *Mt* Austria
28C1 **Fernandez** Arg
15C2 **Fernandina Beach** USA
xxxG5 **Fernando de Noronha** *I* Atlantic O
29B3 **Fernandópolis** Brazil
70C4 **Fernando Poo** *I* Eq Guinea
18B1 **Ferndale** USA
18C1 **Fernie** Can
19C3 **Fernley** USA
40C2 **Ferrara** Italy
26C5 **Ferreñafe** Peru
17D3 **Ferriday** USA
36B2 **Ferriéres** France
71A2 **Fès** Mor
5G4 **Festubert** Can
17D2 **Festus** USA
41F2 **Feteşti** Rom
64A2 **Fethiye** Turk
45J7 **Fetisovo** Kazakhstan
34E1 **Fetlar** *I* Scot
53C1 **Fevral'skoye** Russian Fed
48J6 **Feyzabad** Afghan
28B1 **Fiambalá** Arg
73E6 **Fianarantsoa** Madag
72D3 **Fichē** Eth
74D2 **Ficksburg** S Africa
37D2 **Fidenza** Italy
41D2 **Fier** Alb
37D1 **Fiera Di Primeiro** Italy
34D3 **Fife** Region, Scot
34D3 **Fife Ness** *Pen* Scot
38C3 **Figeac** France
39A1 **Figueira da Foz** Port
39C1 **Figueras** Spain
Figueres = Figueras
71B2 **Figuig** Mor
77G2 **Fiji** *Is* Pacific O
27G8 **Filadelpia** Par
41E2 **Filiaşi** Rom
41E3 **Filiatrá** Greece
40C3 **Filicudi** *I* Italy
19C4 **Fillmore** California, USA
19D3 **Fillmore** Utah, USA
37C2 **Finale Ligure** Italy
34C3 **Findhorn** *R* Scot
9E2 **Findlay** USA
3E3 **Findlay,Mt** Can
13D2 **Finger Lakes** USA
73D5 **Fingoè** Mozam
45E8 **Finike** Turk
76C3 **Finke** *R* Aust
75A1 **Finke Flood Flats** Aust
44C3 **Finland** Republic, N Europe
32J7 **Finland,G of** N Europe
6F4 **Finlay** *R* Can
6F4 **Finlay Forks** Can
75C3 **Finley** Aust
32H5 **Finnsnes** Nor
51H7 **Finschhafen** PNG
37C1 **Finsteraarhorn** *Mt* Switz
42C2 **Finsterwalde** Germany
35B4 **Fintona** N Ire
78A3 **Fiordland Nat Pk** NZ
65C2 **Fiq** Syria
45F8 **Firat** *R* Turk
3F2 **Firebag** *R* Can
20B2 **Firebaugh** USA
40C2 **Firenze** Italy
37D2 **Firenzuola** Italy
3C2 **Fireside** Can
28C2 **Firmat** Arg
60D3 **Firozābād** India
60C2 **Firozpur** India
32H7 **Firspång** Sweden
34C4 **Firth of Clyde** *Estuary* Scot
34D3 **Firth of Forth** *Estuary* Scot
34B3 **Firth of Lorn** *Estuary* Scot
33C2 **Firth of Tay** *Estuary* Scot
63C3 **Firūzābād** Iran
74B2 **Fish** *R* Namibia
74C3 **Fish** *R* S Africa
20C2 **Fish Camp** USA
14D2 **Fishers I** USA
7K3 **Fisher Str** Can
35C6 **Fishguard** Wales
10O3 **Fish L** Can
7N3 **Fiskenaesset** Greenland
36B2 **Fismes** France
13E2 **Fitchburg** USA
34E2 **Fitful Head** *Pt* Scot
15C2 **Fitzgerald** USA
3F2 **Fitzgerald** Can
76B2 **Fitzroy** *R* Aust
76B2 **Fitzroy Crossing** Aust
12C1 **Fitzwilliam I** Can
Fiume = Rijeka
72C4 **Fizi** Zaïre
74D3 **Flagstaff** S Africa
8B3 **Flagstaff** USA
13E1 **Flagstaff L** USA
35E4 **Flamborough Head** *C* Eng
8C2 **Flaming Gorge Res** USA
34B2 **Flannan Isles** *Is* Scot
10N3 **Flat** *R* Can
3F4 **Flathead** *R* USA
8B2 **Flathead L** USA
17D2 **Flat River** USA
51H8 **Flattery,C** Aust
8A2 **Flattery,C** USA
35D5 **Fleetwood** Eng
32F7 **Flekkefjord** *Inlet* Nor
50H4 **Fleming Deep** Pacific Oc
14C2 **Flemington** USA
42B2 **Flensburg** Germany
5K3 **Fleur-de-Lys** Can
37B1 **Fleurier** Switz
36A2 **Fleury-sur-Andelle** France
76C4 **Flinders I** Aust
76D5 **Flinders** *I* Aust
76C4 **Flinders Range** *Mts* Aust
6H4 **Flin Flon** Can
9E2 **Flint** USA
35D5 **Flint** Wales
9E3 **Flint** *R* USA
36B1 **Flixecourt** France
12A1 **Floodwood** USA
15B2 **Florala** USA
Florence = Firenze
9E3 **Florence** Alabama, USA
19D4 **Florence** Arizona, USA
16A2 **Florence** Colorado, USA
17C2 **Florence** Kansas, USA
18B2 **Florence** Oregon, USA
9F3 **Florence** S Carolina, USA
20C2 **Florence,L** USA
26C3 **Florencia** Colombia
36C2 **Florenville** Belg
21D3 **Flores** Guatemala
70A1 **Flores** *I* Açores
76B1 **Flores** *I* Indon
28D3 **Flores** *R* Arg
51E7 **Flores S** Indon
27K5 **Floriano** Brazil
25G3 **Florianópolis** Brazil
21D2 **Florida** State, USA
25E4 **Florida** Urug
15E4 **Florida B** USA
15E4 **Florida City** USA
77E1 **Florida Is** Solomon Is
9E4 **Florida Keys** *Is* USA
9E4 **Florida,Strs of** USA
41E2 **Flórina** Greece
32F6 **Florø** Nor
16B3 **Floydada** USA
37D1 **Fluchthorn** *Mt* Austria
57C3 **Fluk** Indon
76D1 **Fly** *R* PNG
37E2 **Foci del Po** *Delta* Italy
41F1 **Focsani** Rom
40D2 **Foggia** Italy
37E3 **Foglia** *R* Italy
5L4 **Fogo** Can
5L4 **Fogo I** Can
70A4 **Fogo** *I* Cape Verde
38C3 **Foix** France
4E4 **Foleyet** Can
7L3 **Foley I** Can
40C2 **Foligno** Italy
35F6 **Folkestone** Eng
15C2 **Folkston** USA
40C2 **Follonica** Italy
20B1 **Folsom** USA
14C1 **Fonda** USA
6H4 **Fond-du-Lac** Can
9E2 **Fond du Lac** USA
38C2 **Fontainebleau** France
3D2 **Fontas** *R* Can
17D2 **Fontenac** USA
38B2 **Fontenay-le-Comte** France
41D1 **Fonyód** Hung
Foochow = Fuzhou
10H3 **Foraker,Mt** USA
36D2 **Forbach** France
75C2 **Forbes** Aust
71H4 **Forcados** Nig
37A3 **Forcalquier** France
20C3 **Ford City** USA
32F6 **Forde** Nor
75C1 **Fords Bridge** Aust
17D3 **Fordyce** USA
70A4 **Forécariah** Guinea
7P3 **Forel,Mt** Greenland
18D1 **Foremost** Can
12C2 **Forest** Can
15B2 **Forest** USA
11D3 **Forest City** Iowa, USA
14C2 **Forest City** Pennsylvania, USA
15C2 **Forest Park** USA
20A1 **Forestville** USA
36B2 **Forêt d'Othe** France
34D3 **Forfar** Scot
16B2 **Forgan** USA
36A2 **Forges-les-Eaux** France
18B1 **Forks** USA
40C2 **Forli** Italy
39C2 **Formentera** *I* Spain
40C2 **Formia** Italy
70A1 **Formigas** *I* Açores
Formosa = Taiwan
25E3 **Formosa** Arg
27J7 **Formosa** Brazil
25D2 **Formosa** State, Arg
52D5 **Formosa Str** Taiwan/China
29C1 **Formoso** Brazil
29C1 **Formoso** *R* Brazil
37D2 **Fornovo di Taro** Italy
34D3 **Forres** Scot
76B4 **Forrest** Aust
9D3 **Forrest City** USA
3G2 **Forrest L** Can
76D2 **Forsayth** Aust
32J6 **Forssa** Fin
75D2 **Forster** Aust
17D2 **Forsyth** Missouri, USA
11A2 **Forsyth** Montana, USA
60C3 **Fort Abbas** Pak
7K4 **Fort Albany** Can
27L4 **Fortaleza** Brazil
34C3 **Fort Augustus** Scot
74D3 **Fort Beaufort** S Africa
18D1 **Fort Benton** USA
19B3 **Fort Bragg** USA
3F2 **Fort Chipewyan** Can
16C2 **Fort Cobb Res** USA
8C2 **Fort Collins** USA
4F4 **Fort Coulonge** Can
16B3 **Fort Davis** USA
23E4 **Fort de France** Martinique
15B2 **Fort Deposit** USA
9D2 **Fort Dodge** USA
76A3 **Fortescue** *R* Aust
7J5 **Fort Frances** Can
6F3 **Fort Franklin** Can
6F3 **Fort Good Hope** Can
75B1 **Fort Grey** Aust
34C3 **Forth** *R* Scot
16A3 **Fort Hancock** USA
7K4 **Fort Hope** Can
34F3 **Forties** *Oilfield* N Sea
28B3 **Fortin Uno** Arg
13F1 **Fort Kent** USA
70C1 **Fort Lallemand** Alg
Fort Lamy = Ndjamena
11B3 **Fort Laramie** USA
9E4 **Fort Lauderdale** USA
3D1 **Fort Liard** Can
6G4 **Fort Mackay** Can
6G5 **Fort Macleod** Can
6G4 **Fort McMurray** Can
6E3 **Fort McPherson** Can
12A2 **Fort Madison** USA
8C2 **Fort Morgan** USA
9E4 **Fort Myers** USA
6F4 **Fort Nelson** Can
3D2 **Fort Nelson** *R* Can
6F3 **Fort Norman** Can
15B2 **Fort Payne** USA
11A2 **Fort Peck** USA
8C2 **Fort Peck Res** USA
9E4 **Fort Pierce** USA
11B3 **Fort Pierre** USA
14C1 **Fort Plain** USA
6G3 **Fort Providence** Can
3H3 **Fort Qu'Appelle** Can
10F4 **Fort Randall** USA
6G3 **Fort Resolution** Can
72B4 **Fort Rousset** Congo
6F4 **Fort St James** Can
3D2 **Fort St John** Can
3F3 **Fort Saskatchewan** Can
17D2 **Fort Scott** USA
6E3 **Fort Selkirk** Can
7K4 **Fort Severn** Can
45J7 **Fort Shevchenko** Kazakhstan
6F3 **Fort Simpson** Can
6G3 **Fort Smith** Can
9D3 **Fort Smith** USA
6F3 **Fort Smith** Region, Can
8C3 **Fort Stockton** USA
16B3 **Fort Sumner** USA
16C2 **Fort Supply** USA
18B2 **Fortuna** California, USA
11B2 **Fortuna** N Dakota, USA
5K4 **Fortune B** Can
6G4 **Fort Vermilion** Can
15B2 **Fort Walton Beach** USA
9E2 **Fort Wayne** USA
34C3 **Fort William** Scot
16A2 **Fort Wingate** USA
8D3 **Fort Worth** USA
10K3 **Fortymile** *R* USA
10J2 **Fort Yukon** USA
52C5 **Foshan** China
7K2 **Fosheim** *Pen* Can
37B2 **Fossano** Italy
37E3 **Fossombrone** Italy
11C2 **Fosston** USA
3G2 **Foster L** Can
10L4 **Foster,Mt** USA
72B4 **Fougamou** Gabon
38B2 **Fougères** France
34D1 **Foula** *I* Scot
35F6 **Foulness I** Eng
78B2 **Foulwind,C** NZ
72B3 **Foumban** Cam
38C1 **Fourmies** France
10E5 **Four Mountains,Is of** USA
41F3 **Foúrnoi** *I* Greece
70A3 **Fouta Djallon** *Mts* Guinea
77F5 **Foveaux Str** NZ
35C6 **Fowey** Eng
16B2 **Fowler** USA
12B2 **Fox** *R* USA
3E3 **Fox Creek** Can
7K3 **Foxe Basin** *G* Can
7K3 **Foxe Chan** Can
7L3 **Foxe Pen** Can
10E5 **Fox Is** USA
3F2 **Fox Lake** Can
16A1 **Foxpark** USA
78C2 **Foxton** NZ
3G3 **Fox Valley** Can
73B5 **Foz do Cuene** Angola
25F3 **Foz do Iquaçu** Brazil
22B1 **Fracisco I Madero** Mexico
14B2 **Frackville** USA
28B2 **Fraga** Arg
14E1 **Framingham** USA
27J8 **Franca** Brazil
38C2 **France** Republic, Europe
10N3 **Frances** *R* Can
4D5 **Francesville** USA
38D2 **Franche Comté** Region, France
74D1 **Francistown** Botswana
3C3 **Francois L** Can
18E2 **Francs Peak** *Mt* USA
36E1 **Frankenberg** Germany
12B2 **Frankfort** Indiana, USA
9E3 **Frankfort** Kentucky, USA
14C1 **Frankfort** New York, USA
42B2 **Frankfurt** Germany
74D2 **Frankfurt** S Africa
36E1 **Frankfurt am Main** Germany
42C2 **Frankfurt-an-der-Oder** Germany
42C3 **Fränkischer Alb** *Upland* Germany
18D2 **Franklin** Idaho, USA
12B3 **Franklin** Indiana, USA
17D4 **Franklin** Louisiana, USA
14E1 **Franklin** Massachusetts, USA
15C1 **Franklin** N Carolina, USA
14E1 **Franklin** New Hampshire, USA
14C2 **Franklin** New Jersey, USA
13D2 **Franklin** Pennsylvania, USA
15B1 **Franklin** Tennessee, USA
13D3 **Franklin** Virginia, USA
6F2 **Franklin B** Can
18C1 **Franklin D Roosevelt** *L* USA
6F3 **Franklin Mts** Can
10G1 **Franklin,Pt** USA
6J2 **Franklin Str** Can
14A1 **Franklinville** USA
4E4 **Franz** Can
78B2 **Franz Josef Glacier** NZ
Franz-Joseph-Land = Zemlya Franza Josifa
4F5 **Fraser** *R* Can
74C3 **Fraserburg** S Africa
34D3 **Fraserburgh** Scot
75D1 **Fraser I** Aust
3C3 **Fraser Lake** Can
5J2 **Fraser** *R* Can
37B1 **Frasne** France
37C1 **Frauenfield** Switz
28D2 **Fray Bentos** Urug
33C2 **Frazerburgh** Scot
14C3 **Frederica** USA
42B1 **Fredericia** Den
13D3 **Frederick** Maryland, USA
16C3 **Frederick** Oklahoma, USA
16C3 **Fredericksburg** Texas, USA
13D3 **Fredericksburg** Virginia, USA
10M4 **Frederick Sd** USA
17D2 **Fredericktown** USA
7M5 **Fredericton** Can
7N3 **Frederikshåb** Greenland
32G7 **Frederikshavn** Den
13D2 **Fredonia** USA
32G7 **Fredrikstad** Nor
14C2 **Freehold** USA
20C1 **Freel Peak** *Mt* USA
5L4 **Freels,C** Can
11C3 **Freeman** USA
23B1 **Freeport** Bahamas
5H5 **Freeport** Can
12B2 **Freeport** Illinois, USA
17C4 **Freeport** Texas, USA
17F4 **Freer** USA
70A4 **Freetown** Sierra Leone
42B3 **Freiburg** Germany
36D2 **Freiburg im Breisgau** Germany
28A1 **Freirina** Chile
42C3 **Freistadt** Austria
37B3 **Fréjus** France
76A4 **Fremantle** Aust
20B2 **Fremont** California, USA
17C1 **Fremont** Nebraska, USA
12C2 **Fremont** Ohio, USA
27H3 **French Guiana** Dependency, S America
11A2 **Frenchman** *R* USA
75E3 **Frenchmans Cap** *Mt* Aust
xxixM5 **French Polynesia** *Is* Pacific O
71C1 **Frenda** Alg
21B2 **Fresnillo** Mexico
8B3 **Fresno** USA
20C2 **Fresno** *R* USA
18D1 **Fresno Res** USA
37A1 **Fretigney** France
36E2 **Freudenstadt** Germany
36B1 **Frévent** France
75E3 **Freycinet Pen** Aust
70A3 **Fria** Guinea
20C2 **Friant** USA
20C2 **Friant Dam** USA
28B1 **Frías** Arg
40B1 **Fribourg** Switz
36E1 **Friedberg** Germany
42B3 **Friedrichshafen** Germany
16C4 **Frio** *R* USA
16B3 **Friona** USA
37E1 **Friuli** Region, Italy
7M3 **Frobisher B** Can
7M3 **Frobisher Bay** Can
6H4 **Frobisher L** Can
45G6 **Frolovo** Russian Fed
35D6 **Frome** Eng
75A1 **Frome** *R* Aust
35D6 **Frome** *R* Eng
76C4 **Frome,L** Aust
21C3 **Frontera** Mexico
13D3 **Front Royal** USA
40C2 **Frosinone** Italy
14A3 **Frostburg** USA
16A2 **Fruita** USA
52C5 **Fuchuan** China
52E4 **Fuding** China
21B2 **Fuerte** *R* Mexico
29A3 **Fuerte Olimpo** Brazil
25E2 **Fuerte Olimpo** Par
70A2 **Fuerteventura** *I* Canary Is
52C2 **Fugu** China
50B2 **Fuhai** China
67G1 **Fujairah** UAE
54C3 **Fuji** Japan
52D4 **Fujian** Province, China
53C2 **Fujin** China
54C3 **Fujinomiya** Japan
53D4 **Fuji-san** *Mt* Japan
54C3 **Fujisawa** Japan
54C3 **Fuji-Yoshida** Japan
54D2 **Fukagawa** Japan
48K5 **Fukang** China
53C4 **Fukuchiyima** Japan
54A4 **Fukue** Japan
54A4 **Fukue** *I* Japan
53D4 **Fukui** Japan
53C5 **Fukuoka** Japan
53E4 **Fukushima** Japan
53C5 **Fukuyama** Japan
11C3 **Fulda** USA
42B2 **Fulda** Germany
42B2 **Fulda** *R* Germany
52B4 **Fuling** China
23L1 **Fullarton** Trinidad
20D4 **Fullerton** USA
12A2 **Fulton** Illinois, USA
12B3 **Fulton** Kentucky, USA
13D2 **Fulton** New York, USA
36C1 **Fumay** France
54D3 **Funabashi** Japan
77G1 **Funafuti** *I* Tuvalu

Glåma

Great Slave L

32G6 **Glåma** *R* Nor
36D2 **Glan** *R* Germany
37C1 **Glarner** *Mts* Switz
37C1 **Glarus** Switz
17C2 **Glasco** USA
12B3 **Glasgow** Kentucky, USA
11A2 **Glasgow** Montana, USA
34C4 **Glasgow** Scot
14C3 **Glassboro** USA
20C2 **Glass Mt** USA
35D6 **Glastonbury** Eng
44J4 **Glazov** Russian Fed
42D3 **Gleisdorf** Austria
78C1 **Glen Afton** NZ
14B3 **Glen Burnie** USA
74E2 **Glencoe** S Africa
19D4 **Glendale** Arizona, USA
20C3 **Glendale** California, USA
11B2 **Glendive** USA
11B3 **Glendo Res** USA
10J3 **Glenhallen** USA
75D1 **Glen Innes** Aust
75C1 **Glenmorgan** Aust
75D2 **Glenreagh** Aust
14B3 **Glen Rock** USA
17C3 **Glen Rose** USA
14D1 **Glens Falls** USA
17D3 **Glenwood** Arkansas, USA
11C2 **Glenwood** Minnesota, USA
16A3 **Glenwood** New Mexico, USA
16A2 **Glenwood Springs** USA
12A1 **Glidden** USA
32F6 **Glittertind** *Mt* Nor
43D2 **Gliwice** Pol
19D4 **Globe** USA
42D2 **Głogów** Pol
32G5 **Glomfjord** Nor
75D2 **Gloucester** Aust
35D6 **Gloucester** Eng
14E1 **Gloucester** USA
14C1 **Gloversville** USA
43F1 **Glubokoye** Belorussia
45E5 **Glukhov** Russian Fed
42D3 **Gmünd** Austria
42C3 **Gmunden** Austria
43D2 **Gniezno** Pol
74B2 **Goabeg** Namibia
62A1 **Goa, Daman and Diu** Union Territory, India
61D2 **Goālpāra** India
71F4 **Goaso** Ghana
72D3 **Goba** Eth
74B1 **Gobabis** Namibia
28C2 **Gobernador Crespo** Arg
28B3 **Gobernador Duval** Arg
52B1 **Gobi** *Desert* China/Mongolia
54C4 **Gobo** Japan
43G1 **Gobza** *R* Russian Fed
74B1 **Gochas** Namibia
62B1 **Godag** India
62C1 **Godāvari** *R* India
5H4 **Godbout** Can
20C2 **Goddard,Mt** USA
4E5 **Goderich** Can
7N3 **Godhavn** Greenland
60C4 **Godhra** India
28B2 **Godoy Cruz** Arg
4C2 **Gods** *R* Can
7J4 **Gods L** Can
7N3 **Godthåb** Greenland
Godwin Austen = K2
14E1 **Goffstown** USA
4E4 **Gogama** Can
66C4 **Gogora** Eth
29C2 **Goiandira** Brazil
29C2 **Goianésia** Brazil
29C2 **Goiânia** Brazil
29B2 **Goiás** Brazil
27J6 **Goiás** State, Brazil
29B3 **Goio-Erê** Brazil
72D3 **Gojab** *R* Eth
41F2 **Gökçeada** *I* Turk
45F8 **Goksu** *R* Turk
64C2 **Göksun** Turk
49M5 **Gol** *R* Mongolia
61D2 **Golāghāt** India
64C2 **Gölbaşi** Turk
48K2 **Gol'chikha** Russian Fed
18C2 **Golconda** USA
14B2 **Gold** USA
18B2 **Gold Beach** USA
75D1 **Gold Coast** Aust
3E3 **Golden** Can
78B2 **Golden B** NZ
18B1 **Goldendale** USA
20A2 **Golden Gate** *Chan* USA
17D4 **Golden Meadow** USA
19C3 **Goldfield** USA
4C3 **Goldpines** Can
20D2 **Gold Point** USA
4A2 **Goldsand L** Can
16C3 **Goldthwaite** USA
42C2 **Goleniów** Pol
20C3 **Goleta** USA
40B2 **Golfe d'Ajaccio** *G* Corse
71E2 **Golfe de Gabes** *G* Tunisia
Golfe de Gascogne = Biscay,Bay of
71E1 **Golfe de Hammamet** *G* Tunisia
37B3 **Golfe de la Napoule** *G* France
40B2 **Golfe de St Florent** *G* Corse
38B2 **Golfe de St-Malo** *B* France
38C3 **Golfe du Lion** *G* France
25B6 **Golfo Corcovado** *G* Chile
39B2 **Golfo de Almeira** *G* Spain
25B6 **Golfo de Ancud** *G* Chile
21D2 **Golfo de Batabano** *G* Cuba
23A2 **Golfo de Batano** *G* Cuba
39A2 **Golfo de Cadiz** *G* Spain
40B3 **Golfo de Cagliari** *G* Sardegna
21A1 **Golfo de California** *G* Mexico
21D4 **Golfo de Chiriqui** *G* Panama
21D3 **Golfo de Fonseca** Honduras
23B2 **Golfo de Guacanayabo** *G* Cuba
26B4 **Golfo de Guayaquil** *G* Ecuador
23B5 **Golfo del Darien** *G* Colombia/Panama
26B2 **Golfo de los Mosquitos** *G* Panama
26A1 **Golfo del Papagaya** *G* Nic
39B2 **Golfo de Mazarrón** *G* Spain
26A2 **Golfo de Nicoya** *G* Costa Rica
40B3 **Golfo de Oristano** *G* Sardegna
21E4 **Golfo de Panamá** *G* Panama
21D3 **Golfo de Papagayo** *G* Costa Rica
23E4 **Golfo de Paria** *G* Ven
26F1 **Golfo de Paris** *G* Ven
25B7 **Golfo de Penas** *G* Chile
38D3 **Golfo de St Florent** Corse
39C1 **Golfo de San Jorge** *G* Spain
21C3 **Golfo de Tehuantepec** *G* Mexico
26C3 **Golfo de Torugas** *G* Colombia
26C2 **Golfo de Uraba** *G* Colombia
39C2 **Golfo de Valencia** *G* Spain
37E2 **Golfo de Venezia** *G* Italy
23C4 **Golfo de Venezuela** *G* Ven
40B2 **Golfo di Genova** *G* Italy
40D3 **Golfo di Policastro** *G* Italy
40D3 **Golfo di Squillace** *G* Italy
40D2 **Golfo di Taranto** *G* Italy
37E2 **Golfo di Trieste** *G* Italy
40C1 **Golfo di Venezia** *G* Italy
21D4 **Golfo Dulce** *G* Costa Rica
25C7 **Golfo San Jorge** *G* Arg
25D6 **Golfo San Matías** *G* Arg
50C3 **Golmud** China
72E3 **Golocha** Eth
10F3 **Golovin B** USA
53F3 **Golovnino** Russian Fed
72C4 **Goma** Zaïre
71J3 **Gombe** Nig
71J3 **Gombi** Nig
43G2 **Gomel** Belorussia
70A2 **Gomera** *I* Canary Is
21B2 **Gómez Palacio** Mexico
49O4 **Gonam** *R* Russian Fed
63D1 **Gonbad-e Kāvūs** Iran
61B2 **Gonda** India
60C4 **Gondal** India
72D2 **Gonder** Eth
61B3 **Gondia** India
64A1 **Gönen** Turk
41F3 **Gonen** *R* Turk
35B5 **Goney** Irish Rep
61D1 **Gongbo'gyamba** China
52A4 **Gongga Shan** *Mt* China
52A2 **Gonghe** China
29D1 **Gongogi** *R* Brazil
71J3 **Gongola** *R* Nig
20B2 **Gonzales** California, USA
17C4 **Gonzales** Texas, USA
22C1 **Gonzalez** Mexico
28C3 **Gonzalez Chaves** Arg
74B3 **Good Hope,C of** S Africa
3D3 **Good Hope Mt** Can
18D2 **Gooding** USA
16B2 **Goodland** USA
10F4 **Goodnews Bay** USA
75C1 **Goodooga** *R* Aust
35E5 **Goole** Eng
75C2 **Goolgowi** Aust
75A3 **Goolwa** Aust
76A4 **Goomalling** Aust
75C2 **Goombalie** Aust
75D1 **Goomer** Aust
75D1 **Goomeri** Aust
75D1 **Goondiwindi** Aust
7N4 **Goose Bay** Can
15D2 **Goose Creek** USA
5J3 **Goose** *R* Can
18B2 **Goose L** USA
62B1 **Gooty** India
76D1 **Goraka** PNG
44K3 **Gora Koyp** *Mt* Russian Fed
49M4 **Gora Munku Sardyk** *Mt* Mongolia/Russian Fed
44K3 **Gora Narodnaya** *Mt* Russian Fed
44L2 **Gora Pay-Yer** *Mt* Russian Fed
44K3 **Gora Telpos-Iz** *Mt* Russian Fed
41D2 **Goražde** Bosnia & Herzegovina, Yugos
10K2 **Gordon** USA
3F2 **Gordon L** Can
13D3 **Gordonsville** USA
72B3 **Goré** Chad
72D3 **Gorē** Eth
78A3 **Gore** NZ
49P4 **Gore Topko** *Mt* Russian Fed
63C1 **Gorgān** Iran
37C3 **Gorgona** *I* Italy
36C1 **Gorinchem** Neth
64E2 **Goris** Armenia
40C1 **Gorizia** Italy
43G2 **Gorki** Belorussia
44M2 **Gorki** Russian Fed
44G4 **Gor'kovskoye Vodokhranilishche** *Res* Russian Fed
42C2 **Gorlitz** Germany
45F6 **Gorlovka** Ukraine
20C3 **Gorman** USA
41F2 **Gorna Orjahovica** Bulg
50B1 **Gorno-Altaysk** Russian Fed
53E1 **Gorno Lopatina** *Mt* Russian Fed
53D2 **Gorno Medvezh'ya** *Mt* Russian Fed
53C3 **Gorno Oblachnaya** *Mt* Russian Fed
53D2 **Gorno Tardoki Yani** *Mt* Russian Fed
53E2 **Gornozavodsk** Russian Fed
53D1 **Gornyy** Russian Fed
44K3 **Goro Denezhkin Kamen'** *Mt* Russian Fed
44G4 **Gorodets** Russian Fed
43G2 **Gorodnya** Ukraine
43F1 **Gorodok** Belorussia
43E3 **Gorodok** Ukraine
43F3 **Gorodok** Ukraine
51H7 **Goroka** PNG
61B2 **Gorokhpur** India
57D3 **Gorong** *I* Indon
73D5 **Gorongosa** Mozam
57B2 **Gorontalo** Indon
71G3 **Goroubi** *R* Burkina
44L4 **Goro Yurma** *Mt* Russian Fed
29D2 **Gorutuba** *R* Brazil
49M4 **Goryachinsk** Russian Fed
45J7 **Gory Akkyr** *Upland* Turkmenistan
49L2 **Gory Byrranga** *Mts* Russian Fed
43F3 **Goryn'** *R* Ukraine
49L3 **Gory Putorana** *Mts* Russian Fed
43E2 **Góry Świetokrzyskie** *Upland* Pol
32H8 **Gorzow Wielkopolski** Pol
20C2 **Goshen** USA
53E3 **Goshogawara** Japan
45F8 **Gosku** *R* Turk
40D2 **Gospić** Croatia, Yugos
41E2 **Gostivar** Macedonia, Yugos
43D2 **Gostynin** Pol
32G7 **Göteborg** Sweden
72B3 **Gotel** *Mts* Nig
16B1 **Gothenburg** USA
32H7 **Gotland** *I* Sweden
53B5 **Gotō-retto** *I* Japan
32H7 **Gotska Sandön** *I* Sweden
53C4 **Gōtsu** Japan
43D3 **Gottwaldov** Czech
36C1 **Gouda** Neth
72B2 **Goudoumaria** Niger
xxxH7 **Gough I** Atlantic O
75C2 **Goulburn** Aust
70B3 **Goumbou** Mali
70B3 **Goundam** Mali
72B2 **Gouré** Niger
70B3 **Gourma Rharous** Mali
36A2 **Gournay-en-Bray** France
72B2 **Gouro** Chad
18E1 **Govenlock** Can
51G8 **Gove Pen** Aust
45C6 **Goverla** *Mt* Ukraine
29D2 **Governador Valadares** Brazil
28D1 **Governador Virasoro** Arg
61B3 **Govind Ballabh Paht Sāgar** *L* India
14A1 **Gowanda** USA
60B3 **Gowārān** Afghan
28D1 **Goya** Arg
72C2 **Goz-Beïda** Chad
40C3 **Gozo** *I* Medit S
66C3 **Goz Regeb** Sudan
74C3 **Graaff-Reinet** S Africa
13D1 **Gracefield** Can
37E2 **Grado** Italy
75D1 **Grafton** Aust
11C2 **Grafton** N Dakota, USA
12C3 **Grafton** W Virginia, USA
3D2 **Graham** *R* Can
3B3 **Graham I** Can
3F2 **Graham L** Can
19E4 **Graham,Mt** USA
74D3 **Grahamstown** S Africa
27J5 **Grajaú** Brazil
43E2 **Grajewo** Pol
41E2 **Grámmos** *Mt* Greece/Alb
34D3 **Grampian** Region, Scot
34C3 **Grampian** *Mts* Scot
26D3 **Granada** Colombia
26A1 **Granada** Nic
39B2 **Granada** Spain
5G4 **Granby** Can
16A1 **Granby** USA
70A2 **Gran Canaria** *I* Canary Is
25D3 **Gran Chaco** *Region* Arg
12B2 **Grand** *R* Michigan, USA
17D1 **Grand** *R* Missouri, USA
23O2 **Grand B** Dominica
9F4 **Grand Bahama** *I* Bahamas
36D3 **Grand Ballon** *Mt* France
7N5 **Grand Bank** Can
xxxF1 **Grand Banks** Atlantic O
71F4 **Grand Bassam** Ivory Coast
37B2 **Grand Bérard** *Mt* France
19D3 **Grand Canyon** USA
19D3 **Grand Canyon Nat Pk** USA
23A3 **Grand Cayman** *I* Caribbean
3F3 **Grand Centre** Can
18C1 **Grand Coulee** USA
28B3 **Grande** *R* Arg
27K6 **Grande** *R* Bahia, Brazil
29C2 **Grande** *R* Minas Gerais/São Paulo, Brazil
3E3 **Grande Cache** Can
5H4 **Grande Cascapédia** Can
37A2 **Grande Chartreuse** Region, France
73E5 **Grande Comore** *I* Comoros
3E2 **Grande Prairie** Can
17C3 **Grande Prairie** USA
72B2 **Grand Erg de Bilma** *Desert Region* Niger
70B2 **Grand erg Occidental** *Mts* Alg
70C2 **Grand erg Oriental** *Mts* Alg
5J4 **Grande Rivière** Can
7L4 **Grande Rivière de la Baleine** *R* Can
18C1 **Grande Ronde** *R* USA
19D4 **Gran Desierto** USA
5H4 **Grande Vallée** Can
7M5 **Grand Falls** New Brunswick, Can
7N5 **Grand Falls** Newfoundland, Can
18C1 **Grand Forks** Can
11C2 **Grand Forks** USA
14C1 **Grand Gorge** USA
12B2 **Grand Haven** USA
16C1 **Grand Island** USA
17E3 **Grand Isle** USA
16A2 **Grand Junction** USA
5K4 **Grand L** Can
17D4 **Grand L** USA
5H5 **Grand Manan I** Can
12A1 **Grand Marais** USA
5G4 **Grand Mère** Can
5K3 **Grandois** Can
39A2 **Grândola** Port
6J4 **Grand Rapids** Can
12B2 **Grand Rapids** Michigan, USA
12A1 **Grand Rapids** Minnesota, USA
37B2 **Grand St Bernard** *P* Italy/Switz
8B2 **Grand Teton** *Mt* USA
18D2 **Grand Teton Nat Pk** USA
16A2 **Grand Valley** USA
36A2 **Grandvilliers** France
21D1 **Grangeburg** USA
18C1 **Grangeville** USA
4B5 **Granite Falls** USA
18E1 **Granite Peak** *Mt* Montana, USA
19D2 **Granite Peak** *Mt* Utah, USA
39C1 **Granollérs** Spain
40B1 **Gran Paradiso** *Mt* Italy
37D1 **Gran Pilastro** *Mt* Austria/Italy
35E5 **Grantham** Eng
20C1 **Grant,Mt** USA
34D3 **Grantown-on-Spey** Scot
16A2 **Grants** USA
18B2 **Grants Pass** USA
38B2 **Granville** France
14D1 **Granville** USA
6H4 **Granville L** Can
29D2 **Grão Mogol** Brazil
20C3 **Grapevine** USA
20D2 **Grapevine Mts** USA
74E1 **Graskop** S Africa
38D3 **Grasse** France
18E1 **Grassrange** USA
19B3 **Grass Valley** USA
5L4 **Grates Pt** Can
25F4 **Gravatai** Brazil
6H5 **Gravelbourg** Can
36B1 **Gravelines** France
73D6 **Gravelotte** S Africa
4F5 **Gravenhurst** Can
18D1 **Grave Peak** *Mt* USA
75D1 **Gravesend** Aust
10M4 **Gravina I** USA
37A1 **Gray** France
10F3 **Grayling** USA
4E5 **Grayling** Michigan, USA
18B1 **Grays Harbor** *B* USA
18D2 **Grays L** USA
12C3 **Grayson** USA
12B3 **Grayville** USA
42D3 **Graz** Austria
23H1 **Great** *R* Jamaica
9F4 **Great Abaco** *I* Bahamas
76B4 **Great Australian Bight** *G* Aust
14E1 **Great B** New Hampshire, USA
14C3 **Great B** New Jersey, USA
21E2 **Great Bahama Bank** Bahamas
78C1 **Great Barrier I** NZ
76D2 **Great Barrier Reef** *Is* Aust
14D1 **Great Barrington** USA
19C2 **Great Basin** USA
10O2 **Great Bear** *R* Can
6F3 **Great Bear L** Can
16C2 **Great Bend** USA
65B3 **Great Bitter L** Egypt
14A3 **Great Cacapon** USA
62E2 **Great Coco I** Burma
76D3 **Great Dividing Range** *Mts* Aust
35E4 **Great Driffield** Eng
14C3 **Great Egg Harbor** *B* USA
79F10 **Greater Antarctic** Region, Ant
23B2 **Greater Antilles** *Is* Caribbean
35E6 **Greater London** County, Eng
35D5 **Greater Manchester** County, Eng
21E2 **Great Exuma** *I* Bahamas
18D1 **Great Falls** USA
74D3 **Great Fish** *R* S Africa
34C3 **Great Glen** *V* Scot
61C2 **Great Himalayan Range** *Mts* Asia
9F4 **Great Inagua** *I* Bahamas
74C3 **Great Karroo** *Mts* S Africa
74D3 **Great Kei** *R* S Africa
75E3 **Great L** Aust
73B6 **Great Namaland** Region, Namibia
62E3 **Great Nicobar** *I* Indian O
35D5 **Great Ormes Head** *C* Wales
14E2 **Great Pt** USA
9F4 **Great Ragged** *I* Bahamas
73D4 **Great Ruaha** *R* Tanz
13E2 **Great Sacandaga L** USA
18D2 **Great Salt L** USA
18D2 **Great Salt Lake Desert** USA
69B2 **Great Sand Sea** Libya/Egypt
76B3 **Great Sandy Desert** Aust
8A2 **Great Sandy Desert** USA
Great Sandy I = Fraser I
10C6 **Great Sitkin, I** USA
6G3 **Great Slave L** Can

Great Smoky Mts

Halkett,C

15C1 **Great Smoky Mts** USA
15C1 **Great Smoky Mts Nat Pk** USA
3D2 **Great Snow Mt** Can
14D2 **Great South B** USA
74C3 **Great Tafelberg** *Mt* S Africa
76B3 **Great Victoria Desert** Aust
52B2 **Great Wall** China
35F5 **Great Yarmouth** Eng
65C1 **Greco,C** Cyprus
41E3 **Greece** Republic, Europe
13D2 **Greece** USA
16B1 **Greeley** USA
7K1 **Greely Fjord** Can
12B3 **Green** *R* Kentucky, USA
19D3 **Green** *R* Utah, USA
12B1 **Green B** USA
12B2 **Green Bay** USA
48H1 **Green Bell, Ostrov** *I* Russian Fed
12B3 **Greencastle** Indiana, USA
14B3 **Greencastle** Pennsylvania, USA
14C1 **Greene** USA
15C1 **Greeneville** USA
20B2 **Greenfield** California, USA
20C3 **Greenfield** California, USA
14D1 **Greenfield** Massachusetts, USA
12B2 **Greenfield** Wisconsin, USA
5G4 **Greening** Can
3G3 **Green Lake** Can
7O2 **Greenland** Dependency, N Atlantic
xxxH1 **Greenland Basin** Greenland S
79B1 **Greenland S** Greenland
34C4 **Greenock** Scot
14D2 **Greenport** USA
19D3 **Green River** Utah, USA
18E2 **Green River** Wyoming, USA
14C3 **Greensboro** Maryland, USA
15D1 **Greensboro** N Carolina, USA
16C2 **Greensburg** Kansas, USA
12B3 **Greensburg** Kentucky, USA
13D2 **Greensburg** Pennsylvania, USA
34C3 **Greenstone** *Pt* Scot
12B3 **Greenup** USA
19D4 **Green Valley** USA
15B2 **Greenville** Alabama, USA
70B4 **Greenville** Lib
17D3 **Greenville** Mississippi, USA
15D1 **Greenville** N Carolina, USA
14E1 **Greenville** N Hampshire, USA
12C2 **Greenville** Ohio, USA
15C2 **Greenville** S Carolina, USA
17C3 **Greenville** Texas, USA
51H8 **Greenville,C** Aust
35F6 **Greenwich** Eng
14D2 **Greenwich** USA
14C3 **Greenwood** Delaware, USA
17D3 **Greenwood** Mississippi, USA
15C2 **Greenwood** S Carolina, USA
17D2 **Greers Ferry L** USA
11C3 **Gregory** USA
75A1 **Gregory,L** Aust
76D2 **Gregory Range** *Mts* Aust
42C2 **Greifswald** Germany
44F2 **Gremikha** Russian Fed
42C1 **Grenå** Den
17E3 **Grenada** USA
23E4 **Grenada** *I* Caribbean
23E4 **Grenadines,The** *Is* Caribbean
75C2 **Grenfell** Aust
3H3 **Grenfell** Can
38D2 **Grenoble** France
23M2 **Grenville** Grenada
76D2 **Grenville,C** Aust
18B1 **Gresham** USA
56D4 **Gresik** Jawa, Indon
56B3 **Gresik** Sumatera, Indon
17D4 **Gretna** USA
78B2 **Grey** *R* NZ
18E2 **Greybull** USA
10L3 **Grey Hunter Pk** *Mt* Can
7N4 **Grey Is** Can
14D1 **Greylock,Mt** USA
78B2 **Greymouth** NZ
76D3 **Grey Range** *Mts* Aust
35B5 **Greystones** Irish Rep
74E2 **Greytown** S Africa
74C2 **Griekwastad** S Africa
15C2 **Griffin** USA
75C2 **Griffith** Aust
76D5 **Grim,C** Aust
13D2 **Grimsby** Can
35E5 **Grimsby** Eng
32B1 **Grimsey** *I* Iceland
3E2 **Grimshaw** Can
32F7 **Grimstad** Nor
37C1 **Grindelwald** Switz
11D3 **Grinnell** USA
7J2 **Grinnell Pen** Can
7K2 **Grise Fjord** Can
44J3 **Griva** Russian Fed
10O2 **Grizzly Bear** *Mt* Can
32J7 **Grobina** Latvia
74D2 **Groblersdal** S Africa
37E1 **Gröbming** Austria
43E2 **Grodno** Belorussia
61B2 **Gromati** *R* India
42B2 **Groningen** Neth
16B2 **Groom** USA
74C3 **Groot** *R* S Africa
76C2 **Groote Eylandt** *I* Aust
73B5 **Grootfontein** Namibia
74B2 **Groot-Karasberge** *Mts* Namibia
74C1 **Groot Laagte** *R* Botswana
74C2 **Groot Vloer** *Salt L* S Africa
23P2 **Gros Islet** St Lucia
5K4 **Gros Morne Nat Park** Can
36E1 **Grosser Feldberg** *Mt* Germany
40C2 **Grosseto** Italy
36E2 **Gross-Gerau** Germany
42C3 **Grossglockner** *Mt* Austria
37E1 **Gross Venediger** *Mt* Austria
10G4 **Grosvenor,L** USA
18D2 **Gros Ventre Range** *Mts* USA
5K3 **Groswater B** Can
11C2 **Groton** USA
4E4 **Groundhog** *R* Can
15B2 **Grove Hill** USA
20B2 **Groveland** USA
20B3 **Grover City** USA
13E2 **Groveton** USA
45H7 **Groznyy** Russian Fed
43D2 **Grudziadz** Pol
74B2 **Grünau** Namibia
34E2 **Grutness** Scot
45G5 **Gryazi** Russian Fed
44G4 **Gryazovets** Russian Fed
25J8 **Grytviken** South Georgia
29D3 **Guaçuí** Brazil
22B1 **Guadalajara** Mexico
39B1 **Guadalajara** Spain
77E1 **Guadalcanal** *I* Solomon Is
39B2 **Guadalimar** *R* Spain
39B1 **Guadalope** *R* Spain
39B2 **Guadalqivir** *R* Spain
21B2 **Guadalupe** Mexico
20B3 **Guadalupe** USA
2G6 **Guadalupe** *I* Mexico
16C4 **Guadalupe** *R* USA
16B3 **Guadalupe Nat Pk** USA
16B3 **Guadalupe Peak** *Mt* USA
22B1 **Guadalupe Victoria** Mexico
22B1 **Guadarupe** Mexico
23E3 **Guadeloupe** *I* Caribbean
39B2 **Guadian** *R* Spain
39A2 **Guadiana** *R* Port
39B2 **Guadian** *R* Spain
39B2 **Guadix** Spain
29B3 **Guaíra** Brazil
26E6 **Guajará Mirim** Brazil
26D1 **Guajira,Pen de** Colombia
26C4 **Gualaceo** Ecuador
37E3 **Gualdo Tadino** Italy
28D2 **Gualeguay** Arg
28D2 **Gualeguaychú** Arg
51H5 **Guam** *I* Pacific O
28C3 **Guamini** Arg
55C5 **Gua Musang** Malay
22B1 **Guanajuato** Mexico
22B1 **Guanajuato** State, Mexico
29D1 **Guanambi** Brazil
26E2 **Guanare** Ven
28B1 **Guandacol** Arg
21D2 **Guane** Cuba
52C5 **Guangdong** Province, China
52A3 **Guanghan** China
52C3 **Guanghua** China
52A4 **Guangmao Shan** *Mt* China
52A5 **Guangnan** China
52B3 **Guangyuan** China
52D4 **Guangze** China
52C5 **Guangzhon** China
46G4 **Guangzhou** China
29D2 **Guanhães** Brazil
26E3 **Guania** *R* Colombia
23E5 **Guanipa** *R* Ven
23B2 **Guantánamo** Cuba
52D1 **Guanting Shuiku** *Res* China
52B5 **Guanxi** Province, China
52A3 **Guan Xian** China
26C2 **Guapa** Colombia
28E1 **Guaporé** Brazil
28E1 **Guaporé** *R* Brazil
26F6 **Guaporé** *R* Brazil/Bol
26E7 **Guaquí** Bol
29D1 **Guará** *R* Brazil
29B4 **Guarapuava** Brazil
29C4 **Guaraqueçaba** Brazil
29C3 **Guaratinguetá** Brazil
39A1 **Guarda** Port
29C2 **Guarda Mor** Brazil
28B1 **Guardia** Chile
28C4 **Guardia Mitre** Arg
28E1 **Guarita** *R* Brazil
8C4 **Guasave** Mexico
37D2 **Guastalla** Italy
21C3 **Guatemala** Guatemala
21C3 **Guatemala** Republic, C America
28C3 **Guatraché** Arg
26D3 **Guavrare** *R* Colombia
29C3 **Guaxupé** Brazil
23L1 **Guayaguayare** Trinidad
26B4 **Guayaquil** Ecuador
21A2 **Guaymas** Mexico
28D2 **Guayquiraro** *R* Arg
73C5 **Guba** Zaïre
49P2 **Guba Buorkhaya** *B* Russian Fed
72E3 **Guban** *Region* Somalia
57F8 **Gubat** Phil
37E3 **Gubbio** Italy
42C2 **Gubin** Pol
71J3 **Gubio** Nig
62B2 **Güdūr** India
36D3 **Guebwiller** France
71D1 **Guelma** Alg
4E5 **Guelph** Can
70A2 **Guelta Zemmur** Mor
22C1 **Güemez** Mexico
23A2 **Guenabacoa** Cuba
71C2 **Guerara** Alg
72C2 **Guéréda** Chad
38C2 **Guéret** France
11B3 **Guernsey** USA
38B2 **Guernsey** *I* UK
22B2 **Guerrero** State, Mexico
72D3 **Gughe** *Mt* Eth
49O4 **Gugigu** China
51H5 **Guguan** *I* Pacific O
75C2 **Guiargambone** Aust
28D2 **Guichón** Urug
71J4 **Guider** Cam
52C4 **Guidong** China
70B4 **Guiglo** Ivory Coast
74E1 **Guija** Mozam
52C5 **Gui Jiang** *R* China
35E6 **Guildford** Eng
52C4 **Guilin** China
37B2 **Guillestre** France
52A2 **Guinan** China
20A1 **Guinda** USA
70A3 **Guinea** Republic, Africa
xxxH4 **Guinea Basin** Atlantic O
70A3 **Guinea-Bissau** Republic, Africa
70C4 **Guinea,G of** W Africa
23A2 **Güines** Cuba
70B3 **Guir** *Well* Mali
60C2 **Guiranwala** Pak
29B2 **Guiratinga** Brazil
26F1 **Güiria** Ven
36B2 **Guise** France
57G8 **Guiuan** Phil
52B5 **Gui Xian** China
52B4 **Guiyang** China
52B4 **Guizhou** Province, China
60C4 **Gujarāt** State, India
60C2 **Gujrat** Pak
62B1 **Gulbarga** India
43F1 **Gulbene** Latvia
62B1 **Guledagudda** India
15B2 **Gulfport** USA
58D3 **Gulf,The** S W Asia
75C2 **Gulgong** Aust
53A1 **Gulian** China
52B4 **Gulin** China
10J3 **Gulkana** USA
10J3 **Gulkana** *R* USA
3F3 **Gull L** Can
3G3 **Gull Lake** Can
72D3 **Gulu** Uganda
75C1 **Guluguba** Aust
56F6 **Gulung Chamah** *Mt* Malay
71H3 **Gumel** Nig
36D1 **Gummersbach** Germany
71H3 **Gummi** Nig
61B3 **Gumpla** India
64C1 **Gümüşhane** Turk
60D4 **Guna** India
72D2 **Guna** *Mt* Eth
75C3 **Gundagai** Aust
72B4 **Gungu** Zaïre
4B3 **Gunisao** *R* Can
4B3 **Gunisao L** Can
7Q3 **Gunnbjørn Fjeld** *Mt* Greenland
75D2 **Gunnedah** Aust
16A2 **Gunnison** USA
16A2 **Gunnison** *R* USA
62B1 **Guntakal** India
15B2 **Guntersville** USA
15B2 **Guntersville L** USA
62C1 **Guntūr** India
55C5 **Gunung Batu Putch** *Mt* Malay
56G7 **Gunung Benom** *Mt* Malay
56E3 **Gunung Besar** *Mt* Indon
56F6 **Gunung Besar** *Mt* Malay
56G7 **Gunung Besar** *Mt* Malay
56E2 **Gunung Bulu** *Mt* Indon
56B3 **Gunung Gedang** *Mt* Indon
56A2 **Gunung Geureudong** *Mt* Indon
56A2 **Gunung Kulabu** *Mt* Indon
56D2 **Gunung Lawit** *Mt* Malay
56D4 **Gunung Lawu** *Mt* Indon
56A2 **Gunung Leuser** *Mt* Indon
57B3 **Gunung Lokilalaka** *Mt* Indon
57B3 **Gunung Mekongga** *Mt* Indon
56E2 **Gunung Menyapa** *Mt* Indon
56E2 **Gunung Niapa** *Mt* Indon
57B2 **Gunung Ogoamas** *Mt* Indon
56B3 **Gunung Patah** *Mt* Indon
56D4 **Gunung Raung** *Mt* Indon
56B3 **Gunung Resag** *Mt* Indon
56E3 **Gunung Sarempaka** *Mt* Indon
56A2 **Gunungsitoli** Indon
56D4 **Gunung Sumbing** *Mt* Indon
55C5 **Gunung Tahan** *Mt* Malay
56B2 **Gunung Talakmau** *Mt* Indon
56G7 **Gunung Tapis** *Mt* Malay
57B3 **Gunung Tokala** *Mt* Indon
73B5 **Gunza** Angola
52D3 **Guoyang** China
26C4 **Guranda** Ecuador
71H4 **Gurara** Nig
60D2 **Gurdāspur** India
60D3 **Gurgaon** India
61B2 **Gurkha** Nepal
37E1 **Gurktaler Alpen** *Mts* Austria
53D1 **Gurskoye** Russian Fed
64C2 **Gürün** Turk
27J4 **Gurupi** *R* Brazil
73D5 **Guruve** Zim
52A1 **Gurvan Sayhan Uul** *Upland* Mongolia
45J6 **Gur'yev** Kazakhstan
71H3 **Gusau** Nig
43E2 **Gusev** Russian Fed
53A4 **Gushan** China
44G4 **Gus'Khrustalnyy** Russian Fed
10L4 **Gustavus** USA
20B2 **Gustine** USA
42B2 **Gütersloh** Germany
12B3 **Guthrie** Kentucky, USA
17C2 **Guthrie** Oklahoma, USA
16B3 **Guthrie** Texas, USA
22C1 **Gutiérrez Zamora** Mexico
11D3 **Guttenberg** USA
27G3 **Guyana** Republic, S America
xxxF4 **Guyana Basin** Atlantic O
52C1 **Guyang** China
38B3 **Guyenne** Region, France
16B2 **Guymon** USA
75D2 **Guyra** Aust
52B2 **Guyuan** China
63F1 **Guzar** Turkmenistan
61D4 **Gwa** Burma
75C2 **Gwabegar** Aust
71H3 **Gwadabawa** Nig
60D3 **Gwalior** India
74D1 **Gwanda** Zim
72C3 **Gwane** Zaïre
63E3 **Gwardar** Pak
68G9 **Gwelo** Zim
35D6 **Gwent** County, Wales
73C5 **Gweru** Zim
75C1 **Gwydir** *R* Aust
35D4 **Gwynedd** Wales
45H7 **Gyandzha** Azerbaijan
61C2 **Gyangzê** China
50C3 **Gyaring Hu** *L* China
48J2 **Gydanskiy Poluostrov** *Pen* Russian Fed
61C2 **Gyirong** China
7O3 **Gyldenløves** *Fjord* Greenland
75D1 **Gympie** Aust
43D3 **Gyöngyös** Hung
43D3 **Györ** Hung
4B3 **Gypsumville** Can

H

77H2 **Ha'apai Group** *Is* Tonga
32K6 **Haapajärvi** Fin
44C4 **Haapsalu** Estonia
42A2 **Haarlem** Neth
36D1 **Haarstrang** Region, Germany
21D2 **Habana** Cuba
67F3 **Habarūt** Oman
67E4 **Habbān** Yemen
61D3 **Habiganj** Bang
53F3 **Habomai Shoto** *I* Russian Fed
53D5 **Hachijō-jima** *I* Japan
54C3 **Hachiman** Japan
53E3 **Hachinohe** Japan
54C3 **Hachioji** Japan
14C2 **Hackettstown** USA
75A2 **Hack,Mt** Aust
67G3 **Hadbaram** Oman
34D4 **Haddington** Scot
75B1 **Haddon Corner** Aust
75B1 **Haddon Downs** Aust
71J3 **Hadejia** Nig
71H3 **Hadejia** *R* Nig
65C2 **Hadera** Israel
42B1 **Haderslev** Den
67F4 **Hadiboh** Socotra
6H2 **Hadley B** Can
54A3 **Hadong** S Korea
52B5 **Hadong** Vietnam
67E3 **Haḑramawt** Region, Yemen
42C1 **Hadsund** Den
53B4 **Haeju** N Korea
54A3 **Haeju-man** *B* N Korea
54A4 **Haenam** S Korea
67E1 **Hafar al Bātin** S Arabia
7M2 **Haffners Bjerg** *Mt* Greenland
66B3 **Hafir** Sudan
60C2 **Hafizabad** Pak
61D2 **Hāflong** India
32A2 **Hafnafjörður** Iceland
66B4 **Hag'Abdullah** Sudan
10F4 **Hagemeister** *I* USA
42B2 **Hagen** Germany
14B3 **Hagerstown** USA
54B4 **Hagi** Japan
52A5 **Ha Giang** Vietnam
36D2 **Hagondange** France
36D2 **Haguenan** France
70A2 **Hagunia** *Well* Mor
50H4 **Haha-jima** *I* Japan
50C3 **Hah Xil Hu** *L* China
53A3 **Haicheng** China
55D1 **Hai Duong** Viet
65C2 **Haifa** Israel
65C2 **Haifa,B of** Israel
52D2 **Hai He** *R* China
52C5 **Haikang** China
55E1 **Haikou** China
66D1 **Ha'il** S Arabia
61D3 **Hailākāndi** India
49N5 **Hailar** China
53B3 **Hailong** China
53B2 **Hailun** China
32J5 **Hailuoto** *I* Fin
55D2 **Hainan** *I* China
10L4 **Haines** USA
10L3 **Haines Junction** Can
42D3 **Hainfeld** Austria
52B5 **Haiphong** Vietnam
23C3 **Haiti** Republic, Caribbean
20D2 **Haiwee Res** USA
72D2 **Haiya** Sudan
52A2 **Haiyan** China
52B2 **Haiyuan** China
52D3 **Haizhou Wan** *B* China
43E3 **Hajdúböszörmény** Hung
66D3 **Hajfah** Yemen
54C3 **Hajiki-saki** *Pt* Japan
61D3 **Haka** Burma
20E5 **Hakalau** Hawaiian Is
64D2 **Hakkâri** Turk
53E3 **Hakodate** Japan
54C3 **Hakui** Japan
54C3 **Haku-san** *Mt* Japan
45F8 **Ḩalab** Syria
64E3 **Halabja** Iraq
72D1 **Halaib** Sudan
65D1 **Halba** Leb
50C2 **Halban** Mongolia
42C2 **Halberstadt** Germany
57F8 **Halcon,Mt** Phil
32G7 **Halden** Nor
61C3 **Haldia** India
60D3 **Haldwāni** India
3D2 **Halfway** *R* Can
4F4 **Haliburton** Can
4F4 **Haliburton Highlands** Can
7M5 **Halifax** Can
35E5 **Halifax** Eng
13D3 **Halifax** USA
10H1 **Halkett,C** USA

Halla-San High Hill

54A4 **Halla-San** *Mt* S Korea
7M1 **Hall Basin** *Sd* Can/ Greenland
7K3 **Hall Beach** Can
36C1 **Halle** Belg
42C2 **Halle** Germany
79F1 **Halley** *Base* Ant
13D1 **Halleybury** Can
10D3 **Hall I** USA
11B2 **Halliday** USA
32F6 **Hallingdal** *R* Nor
11C2 **Hallock** USA
7M3 **Hall Pen** Can
76B2 **Hall's Creek** Aust
14C2 **Hallstead** USA
57C2 **Halmahera** *I* Indon
57C3 **Halmahera S** Indon
32G7 **Halmstad** Sweden
42B2 **Haltern** Germany
32J5 **Haltia** *Mt* Nor
34D4 **Haltwhistle** Eng
67F1 **Halul** *I* Qatar
65C3 **Haluza** *Hist Site* Israel
54B4 **Hamada** Japan
70C2 **Hamada de Tinrhert** *Desert Region* Alg
70B2 **Hamada du Dra** *Upland* Alg
63B2 **Hamadān** Iran
70B2 **Hamada Tounassine** Region, Alg
45F8 **Ḩamāh** Syria
54C4 **Hamamatsu** Japan
32G6 **Hamar** Nor
54D1 **Hama-Tombetsu** Japan
62C3 **Hambantota** Sri Lanka
17D3 **Hamburg** Arkansas, USA
17C1 **Hamburg** Iowa, USA
14A1 **Hamburg** New York, USA
14C2 **Hamburg** Pennsylvania, USA
42B2 **Hamburg** Germany
14D2 **Hamden** USA
32J6 **Hämeeninna** Fin
76A3 **Hamersley Range** *Mts* Aust
53B3 **Hamgyong Sanmaek** *Mts* N Korea
53B3 **Hamhŭng** N Korea
50C2 **Hami** China
65C1 **Hamīdīyah** Syria
15B2 **Hamilton** Alabama, USA
75B3 **Hamilton** Aust
4F5 **Hamilton** Can
18D1 **Hamilton** Montana, USA
14C1 **Hamilton** New York, USA
78C1 **Hamilton** NZ
12C3 **Hamilton** Ohio, USA
34C4 **Hamilton** Scot
20B2 **Hamilton,Mt** USA
32K6 **Hamina** Fin
61B2 **Hamirpur** India
54A3 **Hamju** N Korea
42B2 **Hamm** Germany
69A2 **Hammādāh al Hamra** *Upland* Libya
32H6 **Hammerdal** Sweden
32J4 **Hammerfest** Nor
4F5 **Hammond** Can
12B2 **Hammond** Illinois, USA
17D3 **Hammond** Louisiana, USA
11B2 **Hammond** Montana, USA
14C3 **Hammonton** USA
78B3 **Hampden** NZ
35E6 **Hampshire** County, Eng
17D3 **Hampton** Arkansas, USA
11D3 **Hampton** Iowa, USA
14E1 **Hampton** New Hampshire, USA
13D3 **Hampton** Virginia, USA
63D3 **Hāmūn-e Jaz Mūrīan** *L* Iran
60B3 **Hamun-i-Lora** *Salt L* Pak
63E3 **Hamun-i Mashkel** *Salt Plain* Pak
54A3 **Han** *R* S Korea
20E5 **Hana** Hawaiian Is
20E5 **Hanalei** Hawaiian Is
53E4 **Hanamaki** Japan
36E1 **Hanau** Germany
52C2 **Hancheng** China
52C3 **Hanchuan** China
13D3 **Hancock** Maryland, USA
12B1 **Hancock** Michigan, USA
14C2 **Hancock** New York, USA
54C4 **Handa** Japan
52C2 **Handan** China
72D4 **Handeni** Tanz
20C2 **Hanford** USA
52B2 **Hanggin Qi** China
32J7 **Hangö** Fin
52E3 **Hangzhou** China
52E3 **Hangzhou Wan** *B* China
66D4 **Hanīsh** *I* Yemen
11C2 **Hankinson** USA
19D3 **Hanksville** USA
78B2 **Hanmer Springs** NZ
3F3 **Hanna** Can
4E3 **Hannah B** Can
17D2 **Hannibal** USA
42B2 **Hannover** Germany
32G7 **Hanöbukten** *B* Sweden
55D1 **Hanoi** Viet
74C3 **Hanover** S Africa
14B3 **Hanover** USA
25B8 **Hanover** *I* Chile
52B3 **Han Shui** China
52C3 **Han Shui** *R* China
60D3 **Hānsi** India
50D2 **Hantay** Mongolia
52B3 **Hanzhong** China
61C3 **Hāora** India
32J5 **Haparanda** Sweden
54A3 **Hapch'on** S Korea
28D1 **Hapevi** Brazil
61D2 **Hāpoli** India
5J3 **Happy Valley** Can
64C4 **Haql** S Arabia
66D3 **Harad** Yemen
67E2 **Haradh** S Arabia
72E3 **Hara Fanna** Eth
66D3 **Haraja** S Arabia
54D3 **Haramachi** Japan
72E3 **Harar** Eth
73D5 **Harare** Zim
72C2 **Harazé** Chad
53B2 **Harbin** China
12C2 **Harbor Beach** USA
5K3 **Harbour Deep** Can
5L4 **Harbour Grace** Can
60D4 **Harda** India
32F6 **Hardangerfjord** *Inlet* Nor
11A2 **Hardin** USA
36D2 **Hardt** Region, Germany
75A2 **Hardwicke B** Aust
17D2 **Hardy** USA
5K3 **Hare B** Can
72E3 **Harer** Eth
72E3 **Hargeysa** Somalia
65C3 **Har Hakippa** *Mt* Israel
50C3 **Harhu** *L* China
56B3 **Hari** *R* Indon
67E4 **Harīb** Yemen
54B4 **Harima-nada** *B* Japan
12C3 **Harlan** USA
18E1 **Harlem** USA
42B2 **Harlingen** Neth
17F4 **Harlingen** USA
35F6 **Harlow** Eng
18E1 **Harlowtown** USA
65C2 **Har Meron** *Mt* Israel
18C2 **Harney Basin** USA
18C2 **Harney L** USA
32H6 **Härnösand** Sweden
49L5 **Har Nuur** *L* Mongolia
70B4 **Harper** Lib
20D3 **Harper L** USA
10K3 **Harper,Mt** USA
13D3 **Harpers Ferry** USA
65C3 **Har Ramon** *Mt* Israel
66C1 **Harrāt al 'Uwayrid** *Upland* Region, S Arabia
66D2 **Harrāt Kishb** Region, S Arabia
66D2 **Harrat Nawāsīf** Region, S Arabia
66D2 **Harrat Rahat** Region, S Arabia
7L4 **Harricana** *R* Can
5J2 **Harrigan,C** Can
15C1 **Harriman** USA
14D1 **Harriman Res** USA
14C3 **Harrington** USA
7N4 **Harrington Harbour** Can
34B3 **Harris** *District* Scot
12B3 **Harrisburg** Illinois, USA
14B2 **Harrisburg** Pennsylvania, USA
74D2 **Harrismith** S Africa
17D2 **Harrison** USA
10H1 **Harrison B** USA
13D3 **Harrisonburg** USA
7N4 **Harrison,C** Can
3D4 **Harrison L** Can
17D2 **Harrisonville** USA
34B3 **Harris,Sound of** *Chan* Scot
12C2 **Harrisville** USA
35E4 **Harrogate** Eng
65C3 **Har Saggi** *Mt* Israel
32H5 **Harstad** Nor
10L3 **Hart** *R* Can
74C2 **Hartbees** *R* S Africa
32F6 **Hårteigen** *Mt* Nor
14D2 **Hartford** Connecticut, USA
12B2 **Hartford** Michigan, USA
11C3 **Hartford** S Dakota, USA
32G6 **Hartkjølen** *Mt* Nor
75A2 **Hart,L** Aust
5H4 **Hartland** Can
35C6 **Hartland Pt** Eng
34E4 **Hartlepool** Eng
16B2 **Hartley** USA
15B2 **Hartselle** USA
17C3 **Hartshorne** USA
15C2 **Hartwell Res** USA
74C2 **Hartz** *R* S Africa
50C2 **Har Us Nuur** *L* Mongolia
63E2 **Harut** *R* Afghan
16A2 **Harvard,Mt** USA
11B2 **Harvey** USA
35F6 **Harwich** Eng
60D3 **Haryāna** State, India
65C3 **Hāsā** Jordan
66B4 **Hasaheisa** Sudan
65C2 **Hāsbaiya** Leb
35E6 **Haselmere** Eng
54C4 **Hashimoto** Japan
63B1 **Hashtpar** Iran
63B1 **Hashtrūd** Iran
67G3 **Hāsik** Oman
16C3 **Haskell** USA
62B2 **Hassan** India
42B2 **Hasselt** Belg
70C2 **Hassi Inifel** Alg
70B2 **Hassi Mdakane** *Well* Alg
70C1 **Hassi Messaoud** Alg
71C2 **Hassi R'mel** Alg
32G4 **Hassleholm** Sweden
75C3 **Hastings** Aust
35F6 **Hastings** Eng
11D3 **Hastings** Minnesota, USA
8D2 **Hastings** Nebraska, USA
78C1 **Hastings** NZ
3H2 **Hatchet L** Can
15B1 **Hatchie** *R* USA
75B2 **Hatfield** Aust
10F2 **Hatham Inlet** USA
60D3 **Hāthras** India
55D2 **Ha Tinh** Viet
75B2 **Hattah** Aust
9F3 **Hatteras,C** USA
17E3 **Hattiesburg** USA
43D3 **Hatvan** Hung
55D3 **Hau Bon** Viet
72E3 **Haud** Region, Eth
32F7 **Haugesund** Nor
78C1 **Hauhungaroa Range** *Mts* NZ
3G2 **Haultain** *R* Can
78B1 **Hauraki G** NZ
78A3 **Hauroko,L** NZ
37C1 **Hausstock** *Mt* Switz
71A2 **Haut Atlas** *Mts* Mor
72C3 **Haute Kotto** Region, CAR
36C2 **Haute-Marne** Department, France
5H4 **Hauterive** Can
36C3 **Haute-Saône** Department, France
36C1 **Hautes Fagnes** *Mts* Belg
37A2 **Hauteville-Lompnès** France
36C1 **Hautmont** Belg
36D3 **Haut-Rhin** Department, France
71B2 **Hauts Plateaux** *Mts* Alg
63E2 **Hauzdar** Iran
60A2 **Hauz Qala** Afghan
12A2 **Havana** USA
Havana = Habana
62B3 **Havankulam** Sri Lanka
19D4 **Havasu L** USA
15D2 **Havelock** USA
78C1 **Havelock North** NZ
35C6 **Haverfordwest** West
14E1 **Haverhill** USA
62B2 **Hāveri** India
14D2 **Haverstraw** USA
42D3 **Havlíčkův Brod** Czech
18E1 **Havre** USA
14B3 **Havre de Grace** USA
7M4 **Havre-St-Pierre** Can
41F2 **Havsa** Turk
20E5 **Hawaii** Hawaiian Is
20E5 **Hawaii Volcanoes Nat Pk** Hawaiian Is
71J3 **Hawal** *R* Nig
78A2 **Hawea,L** NZ
78B1 **Hawera** NZ
20E5 **Hawi** Hawaiian Is
34D4 **Hawick** Scot
78A2 **Hawkdun Range** *Mts* NZ
78C1 **Hawke B** NZ
75D2 **Hawke,C** Aust
75A2 **Hawker** Aust
14C2 **Hawley** USA
55B1 **Hawng Luk** Burma
64D3 **Hawr al Habbaniyah** *L* Iraq
64E3 **Hawr al Hammár** *L* Iraq
20C1 **Hawthorne** USA
75B2 **Hay** Aust
6G3 **Hay** *R* Can
36C2 **Hayange** France
6B3 **Haycock** USA
19D4 **Hayden** Arizona, USA
16A1 **Hayden** Colorado, USA
4C2 **Hayes** *R* Can
7J4 **Hayes** *R* Can
7M2 **Hayes Halvø** *Region* Greenland
10J3 **Hayes,Mt** USA
14B3 **Haymarket** USA
67E3 **Haynin** Yemen
6G3 **Hay River** Can
16C2 **Hays** USA
66D4 **Hays** Yemen
17C2 **Haysville** USA
12A1 **Hayward** Wisconsin, USA
12C3 **Hazard** USA
61C3 **Hazārībāg** India
36B1 **Hazebrouck** France
17D3 **Hazelhurst** USA
6F4 **Hazelton** Can
3C2 **Hazelton Mts** Can
10E3 **Hazen B** USA
7M1 **Hazen L** Can
6G2 **Hazen Str** Can
65C3 **Hazeva** Israel
14C2 **Hazleton** USA
75C3 **Healesville** Aust
10J3 **Healy** USA
xxviiiE7 **Heard I** Indian O
17C3 **Hearne** USA
4E4 **Hearst** Can
11B2 **Heart** *R* USA
17F4 **Hebbronville** USA
52D2 **Hebei** Province, China
75C1 **Hebel** Aust
18D2 **Heber City** USA
18D2 **Hebger L** USA
52C2 **Hebi** China
52C2 **Hebian** China
7M4 **Hebron** Can
65C3 **Hebron** Israel
11B2 **Hebron** N. Dakota, USA
17C1 **Hebron** Nebraska, USA
3B3 **Hecate Str** Can
10M4 **Heceta I** USA
52B5 **Hechi** China
36E2 **Hechingen** Germany
6G2 **Hecla and Griper B** Can
78C2 **Hector,Mt** NZ
32G6 **Hede** Sweden
32H6 **Hedemora** Sweden
18C1 **He Devil Mt** USA
42B2 **Heerenveen** Neth
36C1 **Heerlen** Neth
Hefa = Haifa
52D3 **Hefei** China
52B4 **Hefeng** China
53C2 **Hegang** China
54C3 **Hegura-jima** *I* Japan
61E3 **Heho** Burma
65C3 **Heidan** *R* Jordan
42B2 **Heide** Germany
74C3 **Heidelberg** Cape Province, S Africa
74D2 **Heidelberg** Transvaal, S Africa
42B3 **Heidelberg** Germany
49O4 **Heihe** China
74D2 **Heilbron** S Africa
42B3 **Heilbronn** Germany
42C2 **Heiligenstadt** Germany
53B2 **Heilongjiang** Province, China
53A1 **Heilong Jiang** *R* China
32K6 **Heinola** Fin
52B4 **Hejiang** China
7R3 **Hekla** *Mt* Iceland
55C1 **Hekou** Viet
52A5 **Hekou Yaozou Zizhixian** China
52B2 **Helan** China
52B2 **Helan Shan** *Mt* China
17D3 **Helena** Arkansas, USA
18D1 **Helena** Montana, USA
20D3 **Helendale** USA
57D2 **Helen Reef** *I* Pacific O
34C3 **Helensburgh** Scot
65A3 **Heliopolis** Egypt
63C3 **Helleh** *R* Iran
39B2 **Hellin** Spain
18C1 **Hells Canyon** *R* USA
36D1 **Hellweg** Region, Germany
20B2 **Helm** USA
63E2 **Helmand** *R* Afghan
74B2 **Helmeringhausen** Namibia
36C1 **Helmond** Neth
34D2 **Helmsdale** Scot
53B3 **Helong** China
32G7 **Helsingborg** Sweden
Helsingfors = Helsinki
42C1 **Helsingør** Den
32J6 **Helsinki** Fin
35C6 **Helston** Eng
64B4 **Helwân** Egypt
17C3 **Hempstead** USA
32H7 **Hemse** Sweden
52A3 **Henan** China
52C3 **Henan** Province, China
78B1 **Hen and Chicken Is** NZ
54C2 **Henashi-zaki** *C* Japan
12B3 **Henderson** Kentucky, USA
15D1 **Henderson** N. Carolina, USA
19D3 **Henderson** Nevada, USA
17D3 **Henderson** Texas, USA
15C1 **Hendersonville** N. Carolina, USA
15B1 **Hendersonville** Tennessee, USA
74D3 **Hendrik Verwoerd Dam** S Africa
52E5 **Heng-ch'un** Taiwan
50C4 **Hengduan Shan** *Mts* China
42B2 **Hengelo** Neth
52B2 **Hengshan** China
52D2 **Hengshui** China
55D1 **Heng Xian** China
52C4 **Hengyang** China
55A4 **Henhoaha** Nicobar Is
35E6 **Henley-on-Thames** Eng
14C3 **Henlopen,C** USA
14E1 **Henniker** USA
16C3 **Henrietta** USA
7K4 **Henrietta Maria,C** Can
19D3 **Henrieville** USA
17C2 **Henryetta** USA
7M3 **Henry Kater Pen** Can
74A1 **Henties Bay** Namibia
50D2 **Hentiyn Nuruu** *Mts* Mongolia
55B2 **Henzada** Burma
52B5 **Hepu** China
63E2 **Herat** Afghan
6H4 **Herbert** Can
10D5 **Herbert** *I* USA
78C2 **Herbertville** NZ
36E1 **Herborn** Germany
23A4 **Heredia** Costa Rica
35D5 **Hereford** Eng
16B3 **Hereford** USA
35D5 **Hereford & Worcester** County, Eng
36C1 **Herentals** Belg
37B1 **Héricourt** France
17C2 **Herington** USA
78A3 **Heriot** NZ
37C1 **Herisau** Switz
14C1 **Herkimer** USA
37E1 **Hermagor** Austria
34E1 **Herma Ness** *Pen* Scot
74B3 **Hermanus** S Africa
75C2 **Hermidale** Aust
78B2 **Hermitage** NZ
76D1 **Hermit Is** PNG
Hermon,Mt = Jebel ash Shaykh
21A2 **Hermosillo** Mexico
29B4 **Hernandarias** Par
14B2 **Herndon** USA
36D1 **Herne** Germany
42B1 **Herning** Den
4D4 **Heron Bay** Can
63B1 **Herowābad** Iran
29A4 **Herradura** Arg
28C1 **Herrera** Arg
39B2 **Herrera del Duque** Spain
10L2 **Herschel I** Can
14B2 **Hershey** USA
35E6 **Hertford** County, Eng
65C2 **Herzliyya** Israel
36C1 **Hesbaye** Region, Belg
36A1 **Hesdin** France
52B2 **Heshui** China
20D3 **Hesperia** USA
10M3 **Hess** *R* Can
42B2 **Hessen** State, Germany
20C2 **Hetch Hetchy Res** USA
11B2 **Hettinger** USA
35F5 **Heweth** *Oilfield* N Sea
34D4 **Hexham** Eng
52C5 **He Xian** China
74D2 **Heystekrand** S Africa
52C5 **Heyuan** China
75B3 **Heywood** Aust
52D2 **Heze** China
15E4 **Hialeah** USA
11D2 **Hibbing** USA
15C1 **Hickory** USA
78C1 **Hicks Bay** NZ
75C3 **Hicks,Pt** Aust
17C3 **Hico** USA
54D2 **Hidaka-sammyaku** *Mts* Japan
22C1 **Hidalgo** Mexico
22C1 **Hidalgo** State, Mexico
21B2 **Hidalgo del Parral** Mexico
29C2 **Hidrolândia** Brazil
70A2 **Hierro** *I* Canary Is
54D3 **Higashine** Japan
53B5 **Higashi-suidō** *Str* Japan
18B2 **High Desert** USA
4B2 **High Hill** *R* Can

High Island Hyvikää

17D4 High Island USA
34C2 Highland Region, Scot
20D3 Highland USA
20C1 Highland Peak *Mt* USA
14C2 Highland Falls USA
3E2 High Level Can
15C1 High Point USA
3E2 High Prairie Can
6G4 High River Can
3G2 Highrock L Can
4A2 Highrock L Can
15C3 High Springs USA
14C2 Hightstown USA
35E6 High Wycombe Eng
32J7 Hiiumaa *I* Estonia
66C1 Hijaz Region, S Arabia
54C4 Hikigawa Japan
19C3 Hiko USA
54C3 Hikone Japan
78B1 Hikurangi NZ
8C4 Hildago del Parral Mexico
42B2 Hildesheim Germany
23Q2 Hillaby,Mt Barbados
16C2 Hill City USA
42C1 Hillerød Den
3G1 Hill Island L Can
11C2 Hillsboro N. Dakota, USA
14E1 Hillsboro New Hampshire, USA
16A3 Hillsboro New Mexico, USA
12C3 Hillsboro Ohio, USA
18B1 Hillsboro Oregon, USA
17C3 Hillsboro Texas, USA
4D4 Hillsport Can
75C2 Hillston Aust
12C3 Hillsville USA
34E1 Hillswick Scot
20E5 Hilo Hawaiian Is
14B1 Hilton USA
64C2 Hilvan Turk
42B2 Hilversum Neth
60D2 Himachal Pradesh State, India
59G3 Himalaya, Mts Asia
60C4 Himatnagar India
53C5 Himeji Japan
53D4 Himi Japan
45F9 Hims Syria
10J3 Hinchinbrook Entrance USA
10J3 Hinchinbrook I USA
11D2 Hinckley Minnesota, USA
14C1 Hinckley Res USA
60D3 Hindaun India
60B1 Hindu Kush *Mts* Afghan
62B2 Hindupur India
3E2 Hines Creek Can
60D4 Hinganghāt India
53B2 Hinggan Ling *Upland* China
60B3 Hingol *R* Pak
60D5 Hingoli India
20D3 Hinkley USA
32H5 Hinnøya *I* Nor
14D1 Hinsdale USA
3E3 Hinton Can
16C2 Hinton USA
28B2 Hipolito Itrogoyen Arg
54A4 Hirado Japan
54A4 Hirado-shima *I* Japan
61B3 Hirakud Res India
64B2 Hirfanli Baraji *Res* Turk
62B2 Hirihar India
54D2 Hiroo Japan
53E3 Hirosaki Japan
53C5 Hiroshima Japan
36C2 Hirson France
41F2 Hîrşova Rom
42B1 Hirtshals Den
60D3 Hisār India
67E3 Hisn al 'Abr Yemen
23C3 Hispaniola *I* Caribbean
65D1 Hisyah Syria
64D3 Hīt Iraq
53E4 Hitachi Japan
54D3 Hitachi-Ota Japan
35E6 Hitchin Eng
32F6 Hitra *I* Nor
54B4 Hiuchi-nada *B* Japan
54B4 Hiwasa Japan
65C3 Hiyon *R* Israel
42B1 Hjørring Den
55B1 Hka *R* Burma
71G4 Ho Ghana
55D1 Hoa Binh Viet
55D3 Hoa Da Viet
75E3 Hobart Aust
16C3 Hobart USA
16B3 Hobbs USA
42B1 Hobro Den
3D3 Hobson L Can
69D4 Hobyo Somalia
37E1 Hochalm Spitze *Mt* Austria
37E1 Hochgolling *Mt* Austria
Ho Chi Minh = Saigon
42C3 Hochkonig, Mt Austria
54A2 Hochon N Korea
36E2 Hockenheim Germany
37E1 Hockönig *Mt* Austria
4B3 Hodgson Can
41E1 Hódmezó'hely Hung
42D3 Hodonin Czech
36C1 Hoek van Holland Neth
54A3 Hoengsŏng S Korea
53B3 Hoeryong N Korea
54A3 Hoeyang N Korea
42C2 Hof Germany
32B2 Hofsjökull *Mts* Iceland
7R3 Höfn Iceland
53C5 Hōfu Japan
70C2 Hoggar *Upland* Alg
36D1 Hohe Acht *Mt* Germany
36E1 Hohes Gras *Mts* Germany
37E1 Hohe Tauern *Mts* Austria
52C1 Hohhot China
50C3 Hoh Sai Hu *L* China
59G2 Hoh Xil Shan *Mts* China
72D3 Hoima Uganda
61D2 Hojāi India
54B4 Hojo Japan
78B1 Hokianga Harbour *B* NZ
78B2 Hokitika NZ
53E3 Hokkaidō Japan
63D1 Hokmābād Iran
54D3 Hokota Japan
75C3 Holbrook Aust
19D4 Holbrook USA
19D3 Holden USA
17C2 Holdenville USA
16C1 Holdrege USA
62B2 Hole Narsipur India
23Q2 Holetown Barbados
23B2 Holguín Cuba
78B2 Holitika NZ
10G3 Holitna *R* USA
42D3 Hollabrunn Austria
12B2 Holland USA
14A2 Hollidaysburg USA
16C3 Hollis USA
20B2 Hollister USA
17E3 Holly Springs USA
20C3 Hollywood California, USA
15E4 Hollywood Florida, USA
6G2 Holman Island Can
32J6 Holmsund Sweden
65C2 Holon Israel
42B1 Holstebro Den
11C3 Holstein USA
7N3 Holsteinsborg Greenland
15C1 Holston *R* USA
12C2 Holt USA
17C2 Holton USA
10G3 Holy Cross USA
35C5 Holyhead Wales
34E4 Holy I Eng
35C5 Holy I Wales
16B1 Holyoke Colorado, USA
14D1 Holyoke Massachusetts, USA
36E1 Holzminden Germany
61D3 Homalin Burma
36E1 Homburg Germany
7M3 Home B Can
10H4 Homer Alaska, USA
17D3 Homer Louisiana, USA
78A2 Homer Tunnel NZ
15C2 Homerville USA
15E4 Homestead USA
15B2 Homewood USA
62B1 Homnābād India
73D6 Homoine Mozam
74B3 Hondeklip B S Africa
16A3 Hondo New Mexico, USA
16C4 Hondo Texas, USA
21C3 Hondo *R* Mexico
21D3 Honduras Republic, C America
21D3 Honduras,G of Honduras
32G6 Hønefoss Nor
14C2 Honesdale USA
19B2 Honey L USA
36A2 Honfleur France
55C1 Hong, R Viet
55D1 Hon Gai Viet
54A3 Hongchŏn S Korea
52A4 Hongguo China
52C4 Hong Hu *L* China
52B2 Honghui China
52C4 Hongjiang China
52C5 Hong Kong Colony, S E Asia
50E2 Hongor Mongolia
52B5 Hongshui He *R* China
54A3 Hongsong S Korea
54A3 Hongwon N Korea
52A3 Hongyuan China
52D3 Hongze Hu *L* China
77E1 Honiara Solomon Is
54D3 Honjō Japan
55C4 Hon Khoai *I* Camb
55D3 Hon Lan *I* Viet
32K4 Honnigsvåg Nor
44D1 Honningsvåg Nor
20E5 Honokaa Hawaiian Is
20E5 Honolulu Hawaiian Is
55C4 Hon Panjang *I* Viet
53D4 Honshu *I* Japan
18B1 Hood,Mt USA
18B1 Hood River USA
16B2 Hooker USA
35B5 Hook Head *C* Irish Rep
10L4 Hoonah USA
10E3 Hooper Bay USA
74D2 Hoopstad S Africa
42A2 Hoorn Neth
14D1 Hoosick Falls USA
8B3 Hoover Dam USA
10J3 Hope Alaska, USA
17D3 Hope Arkansas, USA
3D4 Hope Can
7M4 Hopedale Can
48D2 Hopen *I* Barents S
7M3 Hopes Advance,C Can
75B3 Hopetoun Aust
74C2 Hopetown S Africa
14A2 Hopewell Pennsylvania, USA
13D3 Hopewell Virginia, USA
12B3 Hopkinsville USA
18B1 Hoquiam USA
64D2 Horasan Turk
36E2 Horb Germany
69E3 Hordiyo Somalia
37C1 Horgen Switz
xxixL6 Horizon Depth Pacific O
67G1 Hormuz,Str of Oman/Iran
42D3 Horn Austria
7Q3 Horn *C* Iceland
10O2 Hornaday *R* Can
32H5 Hornavan *L* Sweden
17D3 Hornbeck USA
18B2 Hornbrook USA
78B2 Hornby NZ
20C2 Horndon USA
14B1 Hornell USA
7K5 Hornepayne Can
15B2 Horn I USA
6F3 Horn Mts Can
35E5 Hornsea Eng
52B1 Horn Uul *Mt* Mongolia
53A2 Horqin-Youyi Qianqi China
53A3 Horqin Zuoyi China
25E2 Horqueta Par
14B1 Horseheads USA
42C1 Horsens Den
18B1 Horseshoe Bay Can
18C2 Horseshoe Bend USA
75B3 Horsham Aust
35E6 Horsham Eng
32G7 Horten Nor
10O2 Horton *R* Can
56D2 Hose Mts Malay
63E3 Hoshab Pak
60D4 Hoshangābād India
60D2 Hoshiārpur India
16C2 Hosington USA
62B1 Hospet India
25C9 Hoste *I* Chile
59F2 Hotan China
74C2 Hotazel S Africa
17D3 Hot Springs Arkansas, USA
11B3 Hot Springs S. Dakota, USA
6G3 Hottah L Can
74A2 Hottentot Pt Namibia
36A2 Houdan France
12B1 Houghton USA
13F1 Houlton USA
52C2 Houma China
17D4 Houma USA
71E2 Houmet Essouq Tunisia
71F3 Houndé Burkina
53A3 Houqi China
14D2 Housatonic *R* USA
3C3 Houston Can
17E3 Houston Mississippi, USA
17C4 Houston Texas, USA
76A3 Houtman *Is* Aust
14A2 Houtzdale USA
50C2 Hovd Mongolia
50D1 Hövsgol Nuur *L* Mongolia
75D1 Howard Aust
12B2 Howard City USA
10G2 Howard P USA
75C3 Howe,C Aust
18B1 Howe Sd Can
74E2 Howick S Africa
13F1 Howland USA
36E1 Höxter Germany
34D2 Hoy *I* Scot
32F6 Høyanger Nor
11D2 Hoyt Lakes USA
42D2 Hradeç-Králové Czech
43D3 Hranice Czech
43D3 Hron *R* Czech
52E5 Hsin-chu Taiwan
61E3 Hsipaw Burma
52E5 Hsüeh Shan *Mt* Taiwan
54A4 Hsuyong S Korea
74A1 Huab *R* Namibia
52B2 Huachi China
26C6 Huacho Peru
52C1 Huade China
52D3 Huaibei China
52D3 Huaibin China
53A3 Huaide China
52D3 Huai He *R* China
52C4 Huaihua China
52C5 Huaiji China
52D3 Huainan China
19D3 Hualapai Peak *Mt* USA
28B1 Hualfin Arg
50F4 Hua-lien Taiwan
26C5 Huallaga *R* Peru
26C5 Huallanca Peru
26C5 Huamachuco Peru
73B5 Huambo Angola
53C2 Huanan China
26E7 Huanay Bol
26C5 Huancabamba Peru
26C6 Huancavelica Peru
26C6 Huancayo Peru
52D3 Huangchuan China
52A3 Huange He *R* China
Huang Hai = Yellow Sea
52D2 Huang He, R China
52B2 Huangling China
55D2 Huangliu China
53B3 Huangnihe China
52C3 Huangpi China
52D3 Huangshi China
28C3 Huanguelén Arg
52E4 Huangyan China
53B3 Huanren China
26C5 Huānuco Peru
25C1 Huanuni Bol
52B2 Huan Xian China
26C5 Huaráz Peru
26C6 Huarmey Peru
26C5 Huascarán *Mt* Peru
28A1 Huasco Chile
28A1 Huasco *R* Chile
22C2 Huatusco Mexico
22C1 Huauchinango Mexico
22B1 Huaunamota *R* Mexico
22C2 Huautla Mexico
52C2 Hua Xian China
21B2 Huayapan *R* Mexico
52C3 Hubei Province, China
37E1 Huben Austria
62B1 Hubli India
28C3 Hucal Arg
53B3 Huch'ang N Korea
35E5 Huddersfield Eng
32H6 Hudiksvall Sweden
15C3 Hudson Florida, USA
12C2 Hudson Michigan, USA
14D1 Hudson New York, USA
14D1 Hudson *R* USA
7K4 Hudson B Can
6H4 Hudson Bay Can
14D1 Hudson Falls USA
3D2 Hudson's Hope Can
7L3 Hudson Str Can
55D2 Hue Viet
22B1 Huejuqvilla Mexico
22C1 Huejutla Mexico
39A2 Huelva Spain
22B2 Hueramo Mexico
39B2 Húercal Overa Spain
22B1 Huertecillas Mexico
39B1 Huesca Spain
22C2 Huexotla *Hist Site* Mexico
76D3 Hughenden Aust
10H2 Hughes USA
3H2 Hughes *R* Can
61C3 Hugli *R* India
17C3 Hugo USA
16B2 Hugoton USA
52D4 Hui'an China
78C1 Huiarau Range *Mts* NZ
74B2 Huib hochplato *Plat* Namibia
53B3 Hüich'ön N Korea
53B3 Huifa He *R* China
52D5 Huilai China
52A4 Huili China
28B1 Huillapima Arg
22D2 Huimanguillo Mexico
53B3 Huinan China
28C2 Huinca Renancó Arg
36A2 Huisne *R* France
21C3 Huixtla Mexico
22B1 Huizache Mexico
52A4 Huize China
52C5 Huizhou China
22C2 Hujuápan de Léon Mexico
61E2 Hukawng Valley Burma
53B2 Hulan China
66D1 Hulayfah S Arabia
53C2 Hulin China
4F4 Hull Can
35E5 Hull Eng
77H1 Hull *I* Phoenix Is
26C3 Hulla *Mt* Colombia
42D1 Hultsfred Sweden
49N5 Hulun Nur *L* China
53B1 Huma China
53A1 Huma He *R* China
26F5 Humaita Brazil
74C3 Humansdorp S Africa
35E5 Humber *R* Eng
35E5 Humberside County, Eng
6H4 Humboldt Can
11D3 Humboldt Iowa, USA
15B1 Humboldt Tennessee, USA
18C2 Humboldt *R* USA
18B2 Humboldt B USA
7M2 Humboldt Gletscher *Gl* Greenland
19C3 Humboldt L USA
75C1 Humeburn Aust
75C3 Hume,L Aust
73B5 Humpata Angola
20C2 Humphreys USA
20C2 Humphreys,Mt California, USA
19D3 Humphreys Peak *Mt* Arizona, USA
32A1 Húnaflóri *B* Iceland
52C4 Hunan Province, China
53C3 Hunchun China
3D3 Hundred Mile House Can
41E1 Hunedoara Rom
36E1 Hünfeld Germany
43D3 Hungary Republic, Europe
75B1 Hungerford Aust
53B4 Hŭngnam N Korea
18D1 Hungry Horse Res USA
53B3 Hunjiang China
74B2 Hunsberge *Mts* Namibia
36D2 Hunsrück Mts, Germany
75D2 Hunter *R* Aust
3C3 Hunter I Can
75E3 Hunter Is Aust
10H3 Hunter,Mt USA
12B3 Huntingburg USA
35E5 Huntingdon Eng
12B2 Huntingdon Indiana, USA
14A2 Huntingdon Pennsylvania, USA
12C3 Huntington USA
20C4 Huntington Beach USA
20C2 Huntington L USA
78C1 Huntly NZ
34D3 Huntly Scot
10N3 Hunt,Mt Can
75A1 Hunt Pen Aust
15B2 Huntsville Alabama, USA
4F4 Huntsville Can
17C3 Huntsville Texas, USA
53B2 Huolongmen China
55D2 Huong Khe Viet
51H7 Huon Peninsula *Pen* PNG
75E3 Huonville Anst
12C1 Hurd,C Can
66B1 Hurghada Egypt
12A1 Hurley USA
20B2 Huron California, USA
11C3 Huron S. Dakota, USA
12C1 Huron,L USA/Can
28A2 Hurtado Chile
78B2 Hurunui *R* NZ
32B1 Husavik Iceland
41F1 Huşi Rom
32G7 Huskvarna Sweden
10G2 Huslia USA
65C2 Husn Jordan
42B2 Husum Germany
17C2 Hutchinson USA
75C1 Hutton,Mt Aust
52D2 Hutuo He *R* China
36C1 Huy Belg
52A2 Huzhu China
40D2 Hvar *I* Croatia, Yugos
54A2 Hwadae N Korea
73C5 Hwange Zim
73C5 Hwange Nat Pk Zim
54A2 Hwapyong N Korea
14E2 Hyannis Massachusetts, USA
11B3 Hyannis Nebraska, USA
50C2 Hyaryas Nuur *L* Mongolia
3B2 Hydaburg USA
14D2 Hyde Park USA
62B1 Hyderābād India
60B3 Hyderabad Pak
37B3 Hyères France
10N3 Hyland *R* Can
14A3 Hyndman USA
8B2 Hyndman Peak *Mt* USA
44D3 Hyrynsalmi Fin
3E2 Hythe Can
53C5 Hyūga Japan
32J6 Hyvikää Fin

Iaçu Isle of Wight

I

27K6 Iaçu Brazil
41F2 Ialomiţa *R* Rom
32G6 Iärpen Sweden
41F1 Iaşi Rom
71G4 Ibadan Nig
26C3 Ibagué Colombia
41E2 Ibar *R* Montenegro/Serbia
26C3 Ibarra Ecuador
66D4 Ibb Yemen
71H4 Ibi Nig
29C2 Ibiá Brazil
29E1 Ibicaraí Brazil
28D1 Ibicui *R* Brazil
28D2 Ibicuy Arg
28E1 Ibirubá Brazil
39C2 Ibiza Spain
39C2 Ibiza *I* Spain
73E5 Ibo Mozam
27K6 Ibotirama Brazil
67G2 'Ibrī Oman
26C6 Ica Peru
26E4 Icá *R* Brazil
26E3 Icana Brazil
32A1 Iceland Republic, N Atlantic O
3D3 Ice Mt Can
49R4 Icha Russian Fed
62A1 Ichalkaranji India
53E4 Ichihara Japan
54C3 Ichinomiya Japan
53E4 Ichinoseki Japan
10K4 Icy B USA
10F1 Icy C USA
3A2 Icy Str USA
17D3 Idabell USA
11C3 Ida Grove USA
71H4 Idah Nig
18D2 Idaho State, USA
18C2 Idaho City USA
18D2 Idaho Falls USA
16A2 Idaho Springs USA
18B2 Idanha USA
36D2 Idar Oberstein Germany
69A2 Idehan Marzūg *Desert* Libya
69A2 Idehan Ubari *Desert* Libya
70C2 Idelés Alg
50C2 Iderlym Gol *R* Mongolia
66B2 Idfu Egypt
41E3 Ídhi Óros *Mt* Greece
41E3 Ídhra *I* Greece
72B4 Idiofa Zaïre
10G3 Iditarod *R* USA
64C2 Idlib Syria
37E2 Idrija Slovenia, Yugos
32K7 Idritsa Russian Fed
74D3 Idutywa S Africa
36B1 Ieper Belg
41F3 Ierápetra Greece
37E3 Iesi Italy
73D4 Ifakara Tanz
51H6 Ifalik *I* Pacific
73E6 Ifanadiana Madag
71G4 Ife Nig
70C3 Iférouane Niger
56D2 Igan Malay
29C3 Igaranava Brazil
48K3 Igarka Russian Fed
29A3 Igatimi Par
71G4 Igbetti Nig
64E2 Igdir Iran
32H6 Iggesund Sweden
28B2 Iglesia Arg
40B3 Iglesias Sardegna
7K3 Igloolik Can
4C4 Ignace Can
64A1 Iğneada Burun *Pt* Turk
62E2 Ignoitijala Andaman Is
41E3 Igoumenítsa Greece
44J4 Igra Russian Fed
44L3 Igrim Russian Fed
22C2 Iguala Mexico
25G2 Iguape Brazil
29C3 Iguatama Brazil
29B3 Iguatemi Brazil
29A3 Iguatemi *R* Brazil
27L5 Iguatu Brazil
72A4 Iguéla Gabon
71H4 Igumale Nig
71H4 Ihiala Nig
73E6 Ihosy Madag
53D4 Iida Japan
54C3 Iide-san *Mt* Japan
32K6 Iisalmi Fin
54B4 Iizuka Japan
71G4 Ijebulgbo Nig
71G4 Ijebu Ode Nig
42B2 Ijsselmeer *S* Neth
28E1 Ijuí Brazil
28D1 Ijui *R* Brazil
41F3 Ikaría *I* Greece
53E3 Ikeda Japan
72C4 Ikela Zaïre
71H4 Ikerre Nig
41E2 Ikhtiman Bulg
54A4 Iki *I* Japan
71G4 Ikire Nig
10H4 Ikolik,C USA
73E5 Ikopa *R* Madag
71G4 Ila Nig
57F7 Ilagan Phil
63B2 Ilām Iran
50C1 Ilanskiy Russian Fed
37C1 Ilanz Switz
71G4 Ilaro Nig
3G2 Île à la Crosse Can
3G2 Île à la Crosse,L Can
68G8 Ilebo Zaire
36B2 Île De France Region, France
71E2 Île de Jerba *I* Tunisia
38B2 Ile de Noirmoutier *I* France
38B2 Ile de Ré *I* France
77F3 Île des Pins *I* Nouvelle Calédonie
13E1 Ile d'Orleans Can
38A2 Ile d'Ouessant *I* France
38B2 Ile d'Yeu *I* France
45K5 Ilek *R* Russian Fed
22A1 Ile María Cleofas *I* Mexico
22A1 Ile María Madre *I* Mexico
22A1 Ile María Magdalena Mexico
22A1 Ile San Juanico *I* Mexico
77F2 Îles Bélèp Nouvelle Calédonie
77E2 Îles Chesterfield Nouvelle Calédonie
77H2 Îles de Horn *Is* Pacific O
38D3 Iles d'Hylères *Is* France
71G4 Ilesha Nig
71E2 Iles Kerkenna *Is* Tunisia
4B2 Ilford Can
35C6 Ilfracombe Eng
64B1 Ilgaz Dağları *Mts* Turk
73D6 Ilha Bazaruto *I* Mozam
29C3 Ilha Comprida *I* Brazil
29E1 Ilha de Boipeba *I* Brazil
27H3 Ilha De Maracá *I* Brazil
27H4 Ilha de Marajó *I* Brazil
29C4 Ilha de São Francisco *I* Brazil
29C3 Ilha de São Sebastião *I* Brazil
29E1 Ilha de Tinharé *I* Brazil
27H6 Ilha do Bananal *Region* Brazil
29C4 Ilha do Cardoso *I* Brazil
25F2 Ilha Grande, Reprêsa *Res* Brazil
29D3 Ilha Grande *I* Brazil
29B3 Ilha Grande ou Sete Quedas *I* Brazil
29C3 Ilha Santo Amaro *I* Brazil
29B3 Ilha Solteira Dam Brazil
70A2 Ilhas Selvegens *I* Atlantic O
27L6 Ilhéus Brazil
48J5 Ili *R* Kazakhstan
10G4 Iliamna L USA
10H3 Iliamna V USA
36A2 Iliers France
57F9 Iligan Phil
49M4 Ilim *R* Russian Fed
49M4 Ilimsk Russian Fed
53E2 Il'inskiy Russian Fed
41E3 Iliodhrómia *I* Greece
14C1 Ilion USA
57F9 Illana B Phil
28A2 Illapel Chile
28A2 Illapel *R* Chile
70C3 Illéla Niger
37D1 Iller *R* Germany
22B1 Illescas Mexico
77H2 Îles Wallis *Is* Pacific O
12B2 Illinois State, USA
12A3 Illinois *R* USA
70C2 Illizi Alg
44E4 Il'men, Ozero *L* Russian Fed
26D7 Ilo Peru
57F8 Iloilo Phil
32L6 Ilomantsi Fin
71G4 Ilorin Nig
57C4 Ilwaki Indon
43G1 Il'yino Russian Fed
54B4 Imabari Japan
54C3 Imalchi Japan
32L5 Imandra, Ozero *L* Russian Fed
54A4 Imari Japan
44D3 Imatra Fin
25G3 Imbituba Brazil
29B4 Imbitura Brazil
72E3 Imi Eth
54A3 Imjin *R* N Korea
18C2 Imlay USA
37D1 Immenstadt Germany
71H4 Imo State, Nig
40C2 Imola Italy
27J5 Imperatriz Brazil
40B2 Imperia Italy
16B1 Imperial USA
19C4 Imperial V USA
72B3 Impfondo Congo
61D3 Imphāl India
37D1 Imst Austria
10F2 Imuruk L USA
54C3 Ina Japan
70C2 In Afahleleh *Well* Alg
54C4 Inamba-jima *I* Japan
70C2 In Amenas Alg
32K5 Inari Fin
32K5 Inarijärvi *L* Fin
54D3 Inawashiro-ko *L* Japan
70C2 In Belbel Alg
45F7 Ince Burun *Pt* Turk
64B2 Incekum Burun *Pt* Turk
53B4 Inch'ŏn S Korea
70B2 In Dagouber *Well* Mali
29C2 Indaiá *R* Brazil
32H6 Indals *R* Sweden
35G5 Indefatigable *Gasfield* N Sea
20C2 Independence California, USA
11D3 Independence Iowa, USA
17C2 Independence Kansas, USA
17D2 Independence Missouri, USA
18C2 Independence Mts USA
56B3 Inderagiri *R* Indon
45J6 Inderborskiy Kazakhstan
59F4 India Federal Republic, Asia
12B2 Indiana State, USA
13D2 Indiana USA
xxviiiF7 Indian-Antarctic Basin Indian O
xxviiiF7 Indian-Antarctic Ridge Indian O
12B3 Indianapolis USA
Indian Desert = Thar Desert
7N4 Indian Harbour Can
3H3 Indian Head Can
xxviiiE5 Indian O
17D1 Indianola Iowa, USA
17D3 Indianola Mississippi, USA
29C2 Indianópolis Brazil
19C3 Indian Springs USA
44H2 Indiga Russian Fed
49Q3 Indigirka *R* Russian Fed
55D2 Indo China Region, S E Asia
51F7 Indonesia Republic, S E Asia
60D4 Indore India
56C4 Indramayu Indon
38C2 Indre *R* France
60B3 Indus *R* Pak
45E7 Inebdu Turk
70C2 In Ebeggi *Well* Alg
64B1 Inebolu Turk
70C2 In Ecker Alg
64A1 Inegöl Turk
70D2 In Ezzane Alg
74C3 Infante,C S Africa
70C3 Ingal Niger
12C2 Ingersoll Can
76D2 Ingham Aust
7M2 Inglefield Land *Region* Greenland
78B1 Inglewood NZ
75D1 Inglewood Queensland, Aust
20C4 Inglewood USA
75B3 Inglewood Victoria, Aust
32B2 Ingólfshöfði *I* Iceland
42C3 Ingolstadt Germany
61C3 Ingrāj Bāzār India
70C3 In-Guezzam *Well* Alg
74E2 Inhaca *I* Mozam
74E2 Inhaca Pen Mozam
73D6 Inhambane Mozam
73D6 Inharrime Mozam
29C2 Inhumas Brazil
26E3 Inirida *R* Colombia
34B4 Inishowen District, Irish Rep
75C1 Injune Aust
3B2 Inklin Can
10M4 Inklin *R* Can
10G2 Inland L USA
37D1 Inn *R* Austria
75B1 Innamincka Aust
50D2 Inner Mongolia Autonomous Region, China
76D2 Innisfail Aust
53E2 Innokent'yevskiy Russian Fed
10G3 Innoko *R* USA
42C3 Innsbruck Austria
72B4 Inongo Zaïre
43D2 Inowrocław Pol
70C2 In Salah Alg
54A3 Insil S Korea
44L2 Inta Russian Fed
37B1 Interlaken Switz
77H3 International Date Line
11D2 International Falls USA
28C1 Intiyaco Arg
37C2 Intra Italy
56E3 Intu Indon
54D3 Inubo-saki *C* Japan
7L4 Inukjuak Can
6E3 Inuvik Can
6E3 Inuvik Region, Can
34C3 Inveraray Scot
78A3 Invercargill NZ
75D1 Inverell Aust
3E3 Invermere Can
34C2 Inverness Scot
34D3 Inverurie Scot
75A3 Investigator Str Aust
50B1 Inya Russian Fed
49Q3 Inya *R* Russian Fed
73D5 Inyanga Zim
20D3 Inyokern USA
20C2 Inyo Mts USA
72B4 Inzia *R* Zaïre
41E3 Ioánnina Greece
17C2 Iola USA
63E1 Iolotan Turkmenistan
34B3 Iona *I* Scot
73B5 Iôna Nat Pk Angola
18C1 Ione USA
Ionian Is = Ioníoi Nísoi
41D3 Ionian S Italy/Greece
41E3 Ioníoi Nísoi *Is* Greece
10D2 Ioniveyem *R* Russian Fed
41F3 Íos *I* Greece
44J3 Iosser Russian Fed
11D3 Iowa State, USA
11D3 Iowa *R* USA
12A2 Iowa City USA
11D3 Iowa Falls USA
29C2 Ipameri Brazil
29D2 Ipanema Brazil
45G6 Ipatovo Russian Fed
26C3 Ipiales Colombia
29E1 Ipiaú Brazil
29B4 Ipiranga Brazil
55C5 Ipoh Malay
27H7 Iporá Brazil
41F2 Ipsala Turk
75D1 Ipswich Aust
35F5 Ipswich Eng
14E1 Ipswich USA
43G2 Iput *R* Russian Fed
29C3 Iquape Brazil
25B2 Iquique Chile
26D4 Iquitos Peru
28E1 Irai Brazil
41F3 Iráklion Greece
58D2 Iran Republic, S W Asia
63E3 Irānshahr Iran
22B1 Irapuato Mexico
64D3 Iraq Republic, S W Asia
29B4 Irati Brazil
69A2 Irā Wan *Watercourse* Libya
65C2 Irbid Jordan
44L4 Irbit Russian Fed
27G3 Ireng *R* Guyana
53B4 Iri S Korea
51G7 Irian Jaya Province, Indon
72C2 Iriba Chad
57F8 Iriga Phil
73D4 Iringa Tanz
50F4 Iriomote *I* Japan
23A3 Iriona Honduras
27H5 Iriri *R* Brazil
35C5 Irish S Eng/Irish Rep
10H2 Irkillik *R* USA
49M4 Irkutsk Russian Fed
75A2 Iron Knob Aust
12B1 Iron Mountain USA
76D2 Iron Range Aust
12B1 Iron River USA
12C3 Irontown USA
12A1 Ironwood USA
4E4 Iroquois Falls Can
54C4 Iro-zaki *C* Japan
61E4 Irrawaddy *R* Burma
55A2 Irrawaddy,Mouths of the Burma
48H4 Irtysh *R* Russian Fed
39B1 Irun Spain
34C4 Irvine Scot
17C3 Irving USA
71H3 Isa Nig
57F9 Isabela Phil
20C3 Isabella Res USA
6H2 Isachsen Can
6H2 Isachsen,C Can
7Q3 Ísafjörður Iceland
53C5 Isahaya Japan
72C3 Isangi Zaïre
37D1 Isar *R* Germany
37D1 Isarco *R* Italy
34E1 Isbister Scot
37D1 Ischgl Austria
40C2 Ischia *I* Italy
54C4 Ise Japan
37D2 Iseo Italy
37A2 Isère *R* France
36D1 Iserlohn Germany
40C2 Isernia Italy
54C4 Ise-wan *B* Japan
71G4 Iseyin Nig
50F4 Ishigaki *I* Japan
53E3 Ishikari *R* Japan
53E3 Ishikari-wan *B* Japan
48H4 Ishim Russian Fed
48H4 Ishim *R* Kazakhstan
53E4 Ishinomaki Japan
54D3 Ishioka Japan
60C1 Ishkashim Afghan
12B1 Ishpeming USA
48J4 Isil'kul' Russian Fed
57B2 Isimu Indon
72D3 Isiolo Kenya
72C3 Isiro Zaïre
64C2 Iskenderun Turk
64C2 Iskenferun Körfezi *B* Turk
64B1 İskilip Turk
48K4 Iskitim Russian Fed
41E2 Iskur *R* Bulg
10M4 Iskut *R* Can/USA
22C2 Isla Mexico
28D1 Isla Apipe Grande Arg
23C3 Isla Beata Dom Rep
28C3 Isla Bermejo *I* Arg
23E4 Isla Blanquilla Ven
26B2 Isla Coiba *I* Panama
8B4 Isla de Cedros *I* Mexico
25B6 Isla de Chiloé *I* Chile
21D2 Isla de Cozumel *I* Mexico
23C3 Isla de la Gonâve Cuba
23A2 Isla de la Juventud *I* Cuba
28D2 Isla de las Lechiguanas *I* Arg
2K8 Isla del Coco *I* Costa Rica
21D3 Isla del Maiz *I* Caribbean
22C1 Isla de Lobos *I* Mexico
25D8 Isla de los Estados *I* Arg
24F4 Isla de Marajó *I* Brazil
xxixO6 Isla de Pascua *I* Pacific O
23A4 Isla de Providencia *I* Caribbean
23A4 Isla de San Andres *I* Caribbean
25G3 Isla de Santa Catarina *I* Brazil
27H2 Isla du Diable *I* French Guiana
27M4 Isla Fernando de Noronha *I* Brazil
25C8 Isla Grande de Tierra del Fuego *I* Arg/Chile
23D4 Isla la Tortuga *I* Ven
60C2 Islamabad Pak
21A2 Isla Magdalena *I* Mexico
23E4 Isla Margarita Ven
28A3 Isla Mocha Chile
15E4 Islamorada USA
4C3 Island L Can
75A2 Island Lg Aust
18D2 Island Park USA
5K4 Islands,B of Can
78B1 Islands,B of NZ
26B1 Isla Providencia *I* Colombia
26B4 Isla Puná *I* Ecuador
xxxD6 Isla San Ambrosia *I* Pacific O
xxxD6 Isla San Felix *I* Pacific O
21A2 Isla Santa Margarita *I* Mexico
28A3 Isla Santa Maria *I* Chile
39C2 Islas Baleares *Is* Spain
70A2 Islas Canarias *Is* Atlantic O
39C2 Islas Columbretes *Is* Spain
21D3 Islas de la Bahia *Is* Honduras
23A4 Islas del Maíz *Is* Caribbean
26F1 Islas de Margarita *Is* Ven
25C9 Islas Diego Ramírez *Is* Chile
26N0 Islas Galapagos *Is* Pacific O
26Q0 Islas Juan Fernandez *Is* Pacific O
26E1 Islas los Roques *Is* Ven
Islas Malvinas = Falkland Is
xxixO4 Islas Revilla Gigedo *Is* Pacific O
25C9 Islas Wollaston *Is* Chile
70A3 Isla Tidra *I* Maur
25B7 Isla Wellington *I* Chile
34B4 Islay *I* Scot
38C2 Isle *R* France
xxviiiE6 Isle Amsterdam *I* Indian O
13F2 Isle au Haut *I* USA
35E6 Isle of Wight *I* Eng

Jīroft Karacabey

63D3 Jīroft Iran
69D4 Jirriban Somalia
52B4 Jishou China
64C2 Jisr ash Shughūr Syria
41E2 Jiu R Rom
52D4 Jiujiang China
52A4 Jiulong China
52D4 Jiulong Jiang R China
53B3 Jiutai China
63E3 Jiwani Pak
53C2 Jixi China
65C3 Jiza Jordan
66D3 Jīzan S Arabia
70A3 Joal Sen
29D2 João Monlevade Brazil
27M5 João Pessoa Brazil
29C2 João Pinheiro Brazil
29C3 Joboticabal Brazil
28B2 Jocoli Arg
60C3 Jodhpur India
32K6 Joensuu Fin
36C2 Joeuf France
3E3 Joffre,Mt Can
61C2 Jogbani India
62A2 Jog Falls India
74D2 Johannesburg S Africa
19C3 Johannesburg USA
7L2 Johan Pen Can
10H2 John R USA
18C2 John Day USA
18B1 John Day R USA
3E2 John d'Or Prairie Can
13D3 John H. Kerr Res USA
16B2 John Martin Res USA
34D2 John O'Groats Scot
17C2 John Redmond Res USA
14A2 Johnsonburg USA
14C1 Johnson City New York, USA
15C1 Johnson City Tennessee, USA
15C2 Johnston USA
23N2 Johnston Pt St Vincent
14C1 Johnstown New York, USA
13D2 Johnstown Pennsylvania, USA
55C5 Johor Bharu Malay
38C2 Joigny France
25G3 Joinville Brazil
36C2 Joinville France
44J5 Jok R Russian Fed
32H5 Jokkmokk Sweden
67E4 Jōl Mts Yemen
45H8 Jolfa Iran
9E2 Joliet USA
7L5 Joliette Can
57F9 Jolo Phil
57F9 Jolo I Phil
59H2 Joma Mt China
43E1 Jonava Lithuania
52A3 Jonê China
9D3 Jonesboro Arkansas, USA
17D3 Jonesboro Louisiana, USA
7K2 Jones Sd Can
43E1 Joniškis Lithuania
32G7 Jönköping Sweden
5G4 Jonquière Can
9D3 Joplin USA
64C3 Jordan Kingdom, S W Asia
11A2 Jordan Montana, USA
14B1 Jordan New York, USA
65C2 Jordan R Israel
18C2 Jordan Valley USA
29B4 Jordão R Brazil
61D2 Jorhāt India
44C2 Jörn Sweden
56D3 Jorong Indon
32F7 Jørpeland Nor
71H4 Jos Nig
28E2 José Batlle y Ordoñez Urug
57F8 Jose Pañganiban Phil
28E2 José Pedro Varela Urug
76B2 Joseph Bonaparte G Aust
19D3 Joseph City USA
34G3 Josephine Oilfield N Sea
71H4 Jos Plat Nig
48B3 Jotunheimen Mt Nor
65C2 Jouai'ya Leb
65C2 Jounié Leb
61D2 Jowal India
72E3 Jowhar Somalia
10M3 Joy,Mt Can
27K5 Juàjeiro Brazil
22B1 Juan Aldama Mexico
6F5 Juan de Fuca,Str of USA/Can
73E5 Juan de Nova I Mozam Chan
28D3 Juárez Arg
27L5 Juazeiro do Norte Brazil
72D3 Juba Sudan
72E3 Juba R Somalia
65C1 Jubail Leb
64D3 Jubbah S Arabia
39B2 Jucar R Spain
22C2 Juchatengo Mexico
22B1 Juchipila R Mexico
22C2 Juchitán Mexico
22B1 Juchitlan Mexico
42C3 Judenburg Austria
26D7 Juilaca Peru
52C4 Juiling Shan Hills China
27K8 Juiz de Fora Brazil
25C2 Jujuy State, Arg
16B1 Julesburg USA
26E7 Juli Peru
27G3 Julianatop Mt Surinam
7O3 Julianehåb Greenland
36D1 Jülich Germany
37E1 Julijske Alpen Mts Slovenia, Yugos
28E1 Júlio de Castilhos Brazil
60D2 Jullundur India
61B2 Jumla Nepal
65C3 Jum Suwwāna Mt Jordan
60C4 Jūnāgadh India
52D2 Junan China
16C3 Junction Texas, USA
19D3 Junction Utah, USA
8D3 Junction City USA
25G2 Jundiaí Brazil
6E4 Juneau USA
76D4 Junee Aust
20C2 June Lake USA
40B1 Jungfrau Mt Switz
14B2 Juniata R USA
25D4 Junín Arg
28A3 Junin de los Andes Arg
20B2 Junipero Serra Peak Mt USA
52A4 Junlian China
25G2 Juquiá Brazil
72C3 Jur R Sudan
34C4 Jura I Scot
38D2 Jura Mts France
34C3 Jura,Sound of Chan Scot
65C3 Jurf ed Darāwīsh Jordan
48K4 Jurga Russian Fed
44C4 Jūrmala Latvia
26E4 Juruá R Brazil
27G6 Juruena R Brazil
53B2 Jusheng China
65D1 Jūsīyah Syria
28B2 Justo Daract Arg
26E4 Jutai R Brazil
21D3 Juticalpa Honduras
Jutland = Jylland
63D2 Jūymand Iran
42B1 Jylland Pen Den
32K6 Jyväskylä Fin

K

59F2 K2 Mt China/India
71H3 Ka R Nig
63D1 Kaakhka Turkmenistan
74E2 Kaapmuiden S Africa
76B1 Kabaena I Indon
70A4 Kabala Sierra Leone
72D4 Kabale Rwanda
72C4 Kabalo Zaïre
72C4 Kabambare Zaïre
72D3 Kabarole Uganda
71H4 Kabba Nig
76B1 Kabia I Indon
12C1 Kabinakagami L Can
4E3 Kabinakagami R Can
72C4 Kabinda Zaïre
65C1 Kabīr R Syria
63B2 Kabir Kuh Mts Iran
73C5 Kabompo Zambia
73C5 Kabompo R Zambia
73C4 Kabongo Zaïre
60B2 Kabul Afghan
57C2 Kaburuang I Indon
66B3 Kabushiya Sudan
60B4 Kachchh,G of India
44K4 Kachkanar Russian Fed
49M4 Kachug Russian Fed
55B3 Kadan Burma
56E3 Kadapongan I Indon
77G2 Kadavu I Fiji
60C4 Kadi India
75A2 Kadina Aust
64B2 Kadınhanı Turk
62B2 Kadiri India
45F6 Kadiyevka Ukraine
11B3 Kadoka USA
73C5 Kadoma Zim
72C2 Kadugli Sudan
71H3 Kaduna Nig
71H3 Kaduna State, Nig
71H3 Kaduna R Nig
62B2 Kadūr India
61E2 Kadusam Mt China
44K3 Kadzherom Russian Fed
54A3 Kaechon N Korea
70A3 Kaédi Maur
20E5 Kaena Pt Hawaiian Is
53B4 Kaesŏng N Korea
71H4 Kafanchan Nig
70A3 Kaffrine Sen
65D1 Kafr Behum Syria
65A3 Kafr Sa'd Egypt
65A3 Kafr Saqv Egypt
65D1 Kafrūn Bashūr Syria
73C5 Kafue Zambia
73C5 Kafue R Zambia
73C5 Kafue Nat Pk Zambia
53D4 Kaga Japan
10C6 Kagalaska I USA
48H6 Kagan Uzbekistan
45G7 Kağizman Turk
66B4 Kagmar Sudan
53C5 Kagoshima Japan
43F3 Kagul Moldavia
63D1 Kāhak Iran
72D4 Kahama Tanz
60B3 Kahan Pak
56D3 Kahayan R Indon
73B4 Kahemba Zaïre
36E1 Kahler Asten Mt Germany
63D3 Kahnūj Iran
12A2 Kahoka USA
20E5 Kahoolawe I Hawaiian Is
64C2 Kahramanmaraş Turk
20E5 Kahuku Pt Hawaiian Is
20E5 Kahului Hawaiian Is
78B2 Kaiapoi NZ
19D3 Kaibab Plat USA
27G2 Kaieteur Fall Guyana
52C3 Kaifeng China
78B1 Kaikohe NZ
77G5 Kaikoura NZ
78B2 Kaikoura Pen NZ
78B2 Kaikoura Range Mts NZ
52B4 Kaili China
20E5 Kailua Hawaiian Is
51G7 Kaimana Indon
54C4 Kainan Japan
71G3 Kainji Res Nig
78B1 Kaipara Harbour B NZ
52C5 Kaiping China
71E1 Kairouan Tunisia
20C2 Kaiser Peak Mt USA
42B3 Kaiserslautern Germany
53B3 Kaishantun China
43E2 Kaisiadorys Lithuania
78B1 Kaitaia NZ
78A3 Kaitangata NZ
60D3 Kaithal India
20E5 Kaiwi Chan Hawaiian Is
52B3 Kai Xian China
52A5 Kaiyuan Liaoning, China
53A3 Kaiyuan Yunnan, China
10G3 Kaiyuh Mts USA
32K6 Kajaani Fin
60B2 Kajaki Afghan
56F7 Kajang Malay
72D4 Kajiado Kenya
60B2 Kajrān Afghan
72D2 Kaka Sudan
12B1 Kakabeka Falls Can
72D3 Kakamega Kenya
54B4 Kake Japan
10M4 Kake USA
10H4 Kakhonak USA
45E6 Kakhovskoye Vodokhranilishche Res Ukraine
63C3 Kākī Iran
62C1 Kākināda India
3E1 Kakiska L Can
54B4 Kakogawa Japan
10K1 Kaktovik USA
54D3 Kakuda Japan
71D1 Kalaa El Khasba Tunisia
57B4 Kalabahi Indon
41E3 Kalabáka Greece
56E2 Kalabakan Malay
73C5 Kalabo Zambia
45G5 Kalach Russian Fed
45G6 Kalach-na-Donu Russian Fed
61D3 Kaladan R Burma
20E5 Ka Lae C Hawaiian Is
73C6 Kalahari Desert Botswana
74C2 Kalahari Gemsbok Nat Pk S Africa
63E1 Kalai-Mor Turkmenistan
44C3 Kalajoki Fin
49N4 Kalakan Russian Fed
56A2 Kalakepen Indon
60C1 Kalam Pak
41E3 Kalámai Greece
9E2 Kalamazoo USA
57B4 Kalao I Indon
57B4 Kalaotoa I Indon
20E5 Kalapana Hawaiian Is
43F3 Kalarsh Moldavia
60B3 Kalat Pak
20E5 Kalaupapa Hawaiian Is
67G2 Kalbān Oman
64B1 Kalecik Turk
57B4 Kaledupa I Indon
56E3 Kalembau I Indon
72C4 Kalémié Zaïre
44E2 Kalevala Russian Fed
61D3 Kalewa Burma
10H3 Kalgin I USA
76B4 Kalgoorlie Aust
61B2 Kali R India
56C4 Kalianda Indon
57F8 Kalibo Phil
72C4 Kalima Zaïre
56D3 Kalimantan Province, Indon
41F3 Kálimnos I Greece
61C2 Kālimpang India
32J8 Kaliningrad Russian Fed
45D5 Kalinkovichi Belorussia
43F3 Kalinovka Ukraine
8B2 Kalispell USA
43D2 Kalisz Pol
72D4 Kaliua Tanz
32J5 Kalix R Sweden
73B6 Kalkfeld Namibia
74C1 Kalkfontein Botswana
74B1 Kalkrand Namibia
75A1 Kallakoopah R Aust
32K6 Kallávesi L Fin
41F3 Kallonis Kólpos B Greece
32H7 Kalmar Sweden
45H6 Kalmytskaya Respublika, Russian Fed
57B3 Kalolio Indon
73C5 Kalomo Zambia
12A2 Kalona USA
3C3 Kalone Peak Mt Can
62A2 Kalpeni I India
60D3 Kālpi India
10F3 Kalskag USA
10G3 Kaltag USA
44F5 Kaluga Russian Fed
32G7 Kalundborg Den
43E3 Kalush Ukraine
62A1 Kalyān India
62B2 Kalyandurg India
44F4 Kalyazin Russian Fed
71J4 Kam R Nig
44J3 Kama R Russian Fed
53E4 Kamaishi Japan
60C2 Kamalia Pak
78C1 Kamanawa Mts NZ
73B5 Kamanjab Namibia
49O4 Kamara China
66D3 Kamarān I Yemen
5J2 Kamarsuk Can
60D2 Kamat Mt India
62B3 Kamban India
44J4 Kambarka Russian Fed
70A4 Kambia Sierra Leone
49S4 Kamchatka Pen Russian Fed
43F3 Kamenets Podolskiy Ukraine
44G5 Kamenka Russian Fed
48K4 Kamen-na-Obi Russian Fed
53C3 Kamen' Rybolov Russian Fed
49S3 Kamenskoya Russian Fed
44L4 Kamensk-Ural'skiy Russian Fed
74B3 Kamieskroon S Africa
6H3 Kamilukuak L Can
73C4 Kamina Zaïre
7J3 Kaminak L Can
54D3 Kaminoyama Japan
6F4 Kamloops Can
64E1 Kamo Armenia
54D3 Kamogawa Japan
72D3 Kampala Uganda
55C5 Kampar Malay
56B2 Kampar R Indon
42B2 Kampen Neth
55B2 Kamphaeng Phet Thai
55C3 Kampot Camb
Kampuchea = Cambodia
3H3 Kamsack Can
63E3 Kamsaptar Iran
44K4 Kamskoye Vodokhranilishche Res Russian Fed
60D4 Kāmthi India
3H2 Kamuchawie L Can
45H5 Kamyshin Russian Fed
44L4 Kamyshlov Russian Fed
7L4 Kanaaupscow R Can
19D3 Kanab USA
10C6 Kanaga I USA
37E1 Kanal Slovenia, Yugos
72C4 Kananga Zaïre
44H4 Kanash Russian Fed
54C3 Kanayama Japan
53D4 Kanazawa Japan
62B2 Kānchipuram India
60B2 Kandahar Afghan
5J3 Kanairiktok R Can
44E2 Kandalaksha Russian Fed
32L5 Kandalakshskaya Guba B Russian Fed
71G4 Kandé Togo
36D2 Kandel Mt Germany
71G3 Kandi Benin
75C2 Kandos Aust
62C3 Kandy Sri Lanka
13D2 Kane USA
7L1 Kane Basin B Can
72B2 Kanem Desert Region Chad
20E5 Kaneohe Hawaiian Is
44F2 Kanevka Russian Fed
37E2 Kanfanar Slovenia, Yugos
74C1 Kang Botswana
70B3 Kangaba Mali
64C2 Kangal Turk
7N3 Kangâmiut Greenland
63C3 Kangān Iran
55C4 Kangar Malay
76C4 Kangaroo I Aust
7N3 Kangâtsiaq Greenland
63B2 Kangavar Iran
52C1 Kangbao China
59G3 Kangchenjunga Mt Nepal
52A4 Kangding China
7P3 Kangerdlugssuaq B Greenland
7P3 Kangerdlugssuatsaiq B Greenland
72D3 Kangetet Kenya
53B3 Kanggye N Korea
7M4 Kangiqsualujjuaq Can
7L3 Kangiqsujuak Can
7L3 Kangirsuk Can
53B4 Kangnŭng S Korea
72B3 Kango Gabon
50C4 Kan94gto Mt China
52B3 Kang Xian China
55D4 Kanh Hung Viet
73C4 Kaniama Zaïre
62B1 Kani Giri India
44G2 Kanin, Poluostrov Pen Russian Fed
32J6 Kankaanpää Fin
12B2 Kankakee USA
12B2 Kankakee R USA
70B3 Kankan Guinea
61B3 Kānker India
15C1 Kannapolis USA
62B3 Kanniyākuman India
71H3 Kano Nig
71H3 Kano State, Nig
71H3 Kano R Nig
16B2 Kanorado USA
53C5 Kanoya Japan
61B2 Kānpur India
8D3 Kansas State, USA
17C2 Kansas R USA
9D3 Kansas City USA
52D5 Kanshi China
49L4 Kansk Russian Fed
54A3 Kansŏng S Korea
71G3 Kantchari Burkina
61C3 Kanthi India
10H3 Kantishna USA
10H3 Kantishna R USA
74D1 Kanye Botswana
50E4 Kao-hsiung Taiwan
73B5 Kaoka Veld Plain Namibia
70A3 Kaolack Sen
73C5 Kaoma Zambia
20E5 Kapaa Hawaiian Is
20E5 Kapaau Hawaiian Is
73C4 Kapanga Zaïre
7O3 Kap Cort Adelaer C Greenland
7Q3 Kap Dalton C Greenland
32H7 Kapellskär Sweden
7O4 Kap Farvel C Greenland
7P3 Kap Gustav Holm C Greenland
73C5 Kapiri Zambia
4E3 Kapiskau R Can
56D2 Kapit Malay
17D3 Kaplan USA
42C3 Kaplice Czech
55B4 Kapoe Thai
73C4 Kapona Zaïre
41D1 Kaposvár Hung
7L2 Kap Parry C Greenland
7Q3 Kap Ravn C Greenland
54A2 Kapsan N Korea
44C5 Kapsukas Lithuania
56C3 Kapuas R Indon
75A2 Kapunda Aust
60D2 Kapurthala India
7K5 Kapuskasing Can
12C1 Kapuskasing R Can
75D2 Kaputar Mt Aust
45H8 Kapydzhik Mt Armenia
54A3 Kapyŏng S Korea
7M2 Kap York C Greenland
71G4 Kara Togo
71G4 Kara R Togo
64B1 Karabük Turk
41F2 Karacabey Turk

Karachi
Khanka, Ozero

60B4 **Karachi** Pak
62A1 **Karād** India
45F7 **Kara Daglari** *Mt* Turk
45D7 **Karadeniz Boğazi** *Sd* Turk
50E1 **Karaftit** Russian Fed
48J5 **Karaganda** Kazakhstan
48J5 **Karagayly** Kazakhstan
49S4 **Karaginskiy, Ostrov** *I* Russian Fed
62B2 **Kāraikāl** India
63C1 **Karaj** Iran
64C3 **Karak** Jordan
56F7 **Karak** Malay
48G5 **Kara Kalpakskaya** Respublika, Uzbekistan
60D1 **Karakax He** *R* China
57C2 **Karakelong** *I* Indon
60D1 **Karakoram** *Mts* India
60D1 **Karakoram** *P* India/China
70A3 **Karakoro** *R* Maur/Sen
63E1 **Karakumskiy Kanal** Turkmenistan
48G6 **Karakumy** *Desert* Russian Fed
65C3 **Karama** Jordan
57A3 **Karama** *R* Indon
45E8 **Karaman** Turk
48K5 **Karamay** China
78B2 **Karamea** NZ
78B2 **Karamea Bight** *B* NZ
45E8 **Karanhk** *R* Turk
60D4 **Kāranja** India
64B2 **Karapınar** Turk
48J2 **Kara S** Russian Fed
74B2 **Karasburg** Namibia
32K5 **Karasjok** Nor
48J4 **Karasuk** Russian Fed
64C2 **Karataş** Turk
48H5 **Kara Tau** *Mts* Kazakhstan
55B3 **Karathuri** Burma
53B5 **Karatsu** Japan
48K2 **Karaul** Russian Fed
65B1 **Karavostasi** Cyprus
37E1 **Karawanken** *Mts* Austria
63C3 **Karāz** Iran
64D3 **Karbalā'** Iraq
43E3 **Karcag** Hung
41E3 **Kardhítsa** Greece
44E3 **Karel'skaya** Respublika, Russian Fed
62E2 **Karen** Andaman Is
44K3 **Karepino** Russian Fed
32J5 **Karesvando** Sweden
70B2 **Karet** *Desert Region* Maur
48K4 **Kargasok** Russian Fed
44F3 **Kargopol'** Russian Fed
45G8 **Karh** *R* Turk
71J3 **Kari** Nig
73C5 **Kariba** Zim
73C5 **Kariba** *L* Zim/Zambia
73C5 **Kariba Dam** Zim/Zambia
74B1 **Karibib** Namibia
72D2 **Karima** Sudan
56C3 **Karimata** *I* Indon
61D3 **Karimganj** Bang
62B1 **Karīmnagar** India
72E2 **Karin** Somalia
32J6 **Karis** Fin
72C4 **Karishimbe** *Mt* Zaïre
41E3 **Káristos** Greece
62A2 **Kārkal** India
51H7 **Karkar** *I* PNG
63B2 **Karkheh** *R* Iran
45E6 **Karkinitskiy Zaliv** *B* Ukraine
49L5 **Karlik Shan** *Mt* China
42D2 **Karlino** Pol
40D2 **Karlobag** Croatia, Yugos
40D1 **Karlovac** Croatia, Yugos
41E2 **Karlovo** Bulg
42C2 **Karlovy Vary** Czech
32G7 **Karlshamn** Sweden
32G7 **Karlskoga** Sweden
32H7 **Karlskrona** Sweden
42B3 **Karlsruhe** Germany
32G7 **Karlstad** Sweden
11C2 **Karlstad** USA
10H4 **Karluk** USA
61D3 **Karnafuli Res** Bang
60D3 **Karnal** India
62A1 **Karnataka** State, India
41F2 **Karnobat** Bulg
37E1 **Kärnten** Province, Austria
73C5 **Karoi** Zim
73D4 **Karonga** Malawi
72D2 **Karora** Sudan
57A3 **Karossa** Indon
41F3 **Kárpathos** *I* Greece
7N2 **Karrats Fjord** Greenland
74C3 **Karree Berge** S Africa
45G7 **Kars** Turk
48H5 **Karsakpay** Kazakhstan
43F1 **Kārsava** Latvia
58E2 **Karshi** Uzbekistan
32J6 **Karstula** Fin
65C1 **Kartaba** Leb
41F2 **Kartal** Turk
44L5 **Kartaly** Russian Fed
14A2 **Karthaus** USA
63B2 **Kārūn** *R* Iran
61B2 **Karwa** India
62A2 **Kārwār** India
50E1 **Karymskoye** Russian Fed
72B4 **Kasai** *R* Zaïre
73C5 **Kasaji** Zaïre
73D5 **Kasama** Zambia
73D4 **Kasanga** Tanz
62A2 **Kāsaragod** India
6H3 **Kasba L** Can
71A2 **Kasba Tadla** Mor
10F1 **Kasegaluk Lg** USA
73C5 **Kasempa** Zambia
73C5 **Kasenga** Zaïre
72D3 **Kasese** Uganda
63C2 **Kāshān** Iran
10G3 **Kashegelok** USA
59F2 **Kashi** China
54B4 **Kashima** Japan
60D3 **Kāshipur** India
53D4 **Kashiwazaki** Japan
63D1 **Kashmar** Iran
46E4 **Kashmir** State, India
44G5 **Kasimov** Russian Fed
57C3 **Kasiruta** *I* Indon
12B3 **Kaskaskia** *R* USA
4C2 **Kaskattama** *R* Can
32J6 **Kasko** Fin
44L4 **Kasli** Russian Fed
6G5 **Kaslo** Can
3H2 **Kasmere L** Can
72C4 **Kasonga** Zaïre
73B4 **Kasongo-Lunda** Zaïre
41F3 **Kásos** *I* Greece
45H6 **Kaspiyskiy** Russian Fed
72D2 **Kassala** Sudan
42B2 **Kassel** Germany
71D1 **Kasserine** Tunisia
73B5 **Kassinga** Angola
64B1 **Kastamonou** Turk
41E3 **Kastélli** Greece
64A2 **Kastellorizon** *I* Greece
41E2 **Kastoría** Greece
41F3 **Kástron** Greece
53D4 **Kasugai** Japan
54B3 **Kasumi** Japan
73D5 **Kasungu** Malawi
60C2 **Kasur** Pak
73C5 **Kataba** Zambia
13F1 **Katahdin,Mt** USA
72C4 **Katako-kombe** Zaïre
6D3 **Katalla** USA
49O4 **Katangli** Russian Fed
76A4 **Katanning** Aust
62E3 **Katchall** *I* Indian O
41E2 **Kateríni** Greece
6E4 **Kates Needle** *Mt* Can/USA
61E3 **Katha** Burma
76C2 **Katherine** Aust
60C4 **Kāthiāwār** *Pen* India
65B3 **Kathib El Henu** Egypt
61C2 **Kathmandu** Nepal
60D2 **Kathua** India
61C2 **Katihār** India
73C5 **Katima Mulilo** Namibia
6C4 **Katmai,Mt** USA
10H4 **Katmai Nat Mon** USA
61B3 **Katni** India
75D2 **Katoomba** Aust
43D2 **Katowice** Pol
32H7 **Katrineholm** Sweden
71H3 **Katsina** Nig
71H3 **Katsina** *Region* Nig
71H3 **Katsina** *State* Nig
71H4 **Katsina Ala** Nig
54D3 **Katsuta** Japan
54D3 **Katsuura** Japan
54C3 **Katsuy** Japan
48H6 **Kattakurgan** Uzbekistan
32G7 **Kattegat** *Str* Denmark/Sweden
36E2 **Katzenbuckel** *Mt* Germany
57C2 **Kau** Indon
20E5 **Kauai** *I* Hawaiian Is
20E5 **Kauai Chan** Hawaiian Is
20E5 **Kaulakahi Chan** Hawaiian Is
20E5 **Kaunakaki** Hawaiian Is
44C5 **Kaunas** Lithuania
71H3 **Kaura Namoda** Nig
32J5 **Kautokeino** Nor
41E2 **Kavadarci** Macedonia, Yugos
41D2 **Kavajë** Alb
53D3 **Kavalerovo** Russian Fed
62B2 **Kavali** India
41E2 **Kavália** Greece
60B4 **Kāvda** India
76E1 **Kavieng** PNG
54C3 **Kawagoe** Japan
54C3 **Kawaguchi** Japan
20E5 **Kawaihae** Hawaiian Is
78B1 **Kawakawa** NZ
73C4 **Kawambwa** Zambia
61B3 **Kawardha** India
13D2 **Kawartha Lakes** Can
53D4 **Kawasaki** Japan
20C2 **Kaweah** *R* USA
78C1 **Kawerau** NZ
78B1 **Kawhia** NZ
71F3 **Kaya** Burkina
10K4 **Kayak I** USA
56E2 **Kayan** *R* Indon
62B3 **Kāyankulam** India
11A3 **Kaycee** USA
57C3 **Kayeli** Indon
19D3 **Kayenta** USA
70A3 **Kayes** Mali
45F8 **Kayseri** Turk
49P2 **Kazach'ye** Russian Fed
64E1 **Kazakh** Azerbaijan
48G5 **Kazakhstan** *Republic* Europe
44H4 **Kazan'** Russian Fed
41F2 **Kazanlŭk** Bulg
50H4 **Kazan Retto** *Is* Japan
43F3 **Kazatin** Ukraine
45G7 **Kazbek** *Mt* Georgia
63C3 **Kāzerūn** Iran
44J3 **Kazhim** Russian Fed
64E1 **Kazi Magomed** Azerbaijan
43E3 **Kazincbarcika** Hung
44M3 **Kazym** *R* Russian Fed
44M3 **Kazymskaya** Russian Fed
41E3 **Kéa** *I* Greece
20E5 **Kealaikahiki Chan** Hawaiian Is
8D2 **Kearney** USA
19D4 **Kearny** USA
64C2 **Keban Baraji** *Res* Turk
71G3 **Kebbi** *State* Nig
70A3 **Kébémer** Sen
71J4 **Kebi** *R* Chad
71D2 **Kebili** Tunisia
65D1 **Kebīr** *R* Syria/Leb
32H5 **Kebrekaise** *Mt* Sweden
3C2 **Kechika** *R* Can
43D3 **Kecskemet** Hung
43E1 **Kedainiai** Lithuania
5H4 **Kedgwick** Can
53B2 **Kedong** China
70A3 **Kédougou** Sen
44J3 **Kedva** Russian Fed
10N4 **Keechiga** *R* Can
10N3 **Keele** *R* Can
10M3 **Keele Pk** *Mt* Can
19C3 **Keeler** USA
20C3 **Keene** California, USA
13E2 **Keene** New Hampshire, USA
74B2 **Keetmanshoop** Namibia
12B2 **Keewanee** USA
4C4 **Keewatin** Can
12A1 **Keewatin** USA
6J3 **Keewatin** *Region* Can
41E3 **Kefallinía** *I* Greece
57B4 **Kefamenanu** Indon
65C2 **Kefar Sava** Israel
71H4 **Keffi** Nig
32A2 **Keflavik** Iceland
6G4 **Keg River** Can
66B3 **Keheili** Sudan
55B1 **Kehsi Mansam** Burma
75B3 **Keith** Aust
34D3 **Keith** Scot
6F3 **Keith Arm** *B* Can
7M3 **Kekertuk** Can
60D3 **Kekri** India
55C5 **Kelang** Malay
57C3 **Kelang** *I* Indon
55C4 **Kelantan** *R* Malay
71E1 **Kelibia** Tunisia
60B1 **Kelif** Turkmenistan
64C1 **Kelkit** *R* Turk
72B4 **Kellé** Congo
10O3 **Keller L** Can
6F2 **Kellet,C** Can
18C1 **Kellogg** USA
48D3 **Kelloselka** Fin
35B5 **Kells** Irish Rep
34C4 **Kells Range** *Hills* Scot
43E1 **Kelme** Lithuania
6G5 **Kelowna** Can
6F4 **Kelsey Bay** Can
34D4 **Kelso** Scot
18B1 **Kelso** USA
3H3 **Kelvington** Can
44E3 **Kem'** Russian Fed
44E3 **Kem'** *R* Russian Fed
70B3 **Ke Macina** Mali
3C3 **Kemano** Can
48K4 **Kemerovo** Russian Fed
32J5 **Kemi** Fin
32K5 **Kemi** *R* Fin
32K5 **Kemijärvi** Fin
18D2 **Kemmerer** USA
36C1 **Kempen** Region, Belg
16C3 **Kemp,L** USA
23B2 **Kemps Bay** Bahamas
75D2 **Kempsey** Aust
42C3 **Kempten** Germany
10H3 **Kenai** USA
10H4 **Kenai Mts** USA
10H3 **Kenai Pen** USA
72D3 **Kenamuke Swamp** Sudan
35D4 **Kendal** Eng
75D2 **Kendall** Aust
76B1 **Kendari** Indon
56D3 **Kendawangan** Indon
61C3 **Kendrāpāra** India
18C1 **Kendrick** USA
17F4 **Kenedy** USA
70A4 **Kenema** Sierra Leone
72B4 **Kenge** Zaïre
55B1 **Kengtung** Burma
74C2 **Kenhardt** S Africa
70A3 **Kéniéba** Mali
71A2 **Kenitra** Mor
11B2 **Kenmare** USA
16B3 **Kenna** USA
13F1 **Kennebec** *R* USA
14E1 **Kennebunk** USA
14A1 **Kennedy** USA
17D4 **Kenner** USA
17E2 **Kennett** USA
14C3 **Kennett Square** USA
18C1 **Kennewick** USA
6F4 **Kenny Dam** Can
4D3 **Kenogami** *R* Can
7J5 **Kenora** Can
9E2 **Kenosha** USA
35F6 **Kent** County, Eng
16B3 **Kent** Texas, USA
18B1 **Kent** Washington, USA
12B2 **Kentland** USA
12C2 **Kenton** USA
6H3 **Kent Pen** Can
9E3 **Kentucky** State, USA
12C3 **Kentucky** *R* USA
9E3 **Kentucky L** USA
5J4 **Kentville** Can
17D3 **Kentwood** Louisiana, USA
12B2 **Kentwood** Michigan, USA
72D3 **Kenya** Republic, Africa
72D4 **Kenya,Mt** Kenya
12A2 **Keokuk** USA
61B3 **Keonchi** India
61C3 **Keonjhargarh** India
51G7 **Kepaluan Tanimbar** *Arch* Indon
43D2 **Kepno** Pol
57C3 **Kepualuan Widi** *Arch* Indon
57B4 **Kepulauan Alor** *Arch* Indon
56C2 **Kepulauan Anambas** *Arch* Indon
51G7 **Kepulauan Aru** *Arch* Indon
76B1 **Kepulauan Babar** *I* Indon
56C2 **Kepulauan Badas** *Is* Indon
51G7 **Kepulauan Banda** *Arch* Indon
76B1 **Kepulauan Banggai** *I* Indon
76B1 **Kepulauan Barat Daya** *Is* Indon
56C2 **Kepulauan Bunguran Seletan** *Arch* Indon
57D3 **Kepulauan Gorong** *Arch* Indon
51G7 **Kepulauan Kai** *Arch* Indon
57C2 **Kepulauan Kawio** *Arch* Indon
76B1 **Kepulauan Leti** *I* Indon
56B3 **Kepulauan Lingga** *Is* Indon
57C2 **Kepulauan Loloda** *Arch* Indon
56A3 **Kepulauan Mentawi** *Arch* Indon
57C2 **Kepulauan Nenusa** *Arch* Indon
57C3 **Kepulauan Obi** *Arch* Indon
56B2 **Kepulauan Riau** *Arch* Indon
56E4 **Kepulauan Sabalana** *Arch* Indon
57C2 **Kepulauan Sangihe** *Arch* Indon
76B1 **Kepulauan Sermata** *I* Indon
76B1 **Kepulauan Sula** *I* Indon
57C2 **Kepulauan Talaud** *Arch* Indon
56C2 **Kepulauan Tambelan** *Is* Indon
76C1 **Kepulauan Tanimbar** *I* Indon
76B1 **Kepulauan Togian** *I* Indon
76B1 **Kepulauan Tukangbesi** *Is* Indon
57D3 **Kepulauan Watubela** *Arch* Indon
57C3 **Kepulauan Yef Fam** *Arch* Indon
57B4 **Kepulaun Solor** *Arch* Indon
62B2 **Kerala** State, India
75B3 **Kerang** Aust
32J6 **Kerava** Fin
53D1 **Kerbi** *R* Russian Fed
45F6 **Kerch'** Ukraine
44J3 **Kerchem'ya** Russian Fed
76D1 **Kerema** PNG
18C1 **Keremeps** Can
72D2 **Keren** Eth
xxviiiE7 **Kerguelen Ridge** Indian O
72D4 **Kericho** Kenya
56B3 **Kerinci** *Mt* Indon
72D3 **Kerio** *R* Kenya
58E2 **Kerki** Turkmenistan
41D3 **Kérkira** Greece
41D3 **Kérkira** *I* Greece
77H3 **Kermadec Is** NZ
77H4 **Kermadec Trench** Pacific O
63D2 **Kerman** Iran
20B2 **Kerman** USA
63B2 **Kermānshāh** Iran
41F3 **Kerme Körfezi** *B* Turk
16B3 **Kermit** USA
19C3 **Kern** *R* USA
20C3 **Kernville** USA
44J3 **Keros** Russian Fed
3G3 **Kerrobert** Can
16C3 **Kerrville** USA
15C2 **Kershaw** USA
56C3 **Kertamulia** Indon
49N5 **Kerulen** *R* Mongolia
70B2 **Kerzaz** Alg
4F3 **Kesagami L** Can
41F2 **Keşan** Turk
53E4 **Kesennuma** Japan
53B2 **Keshan** China
45G7 **Kesir Daglari** *Mt* Turk
32L5 **Kesten'ga** Russian Fed
35D4 **Keswick** Eng
71G4 **Kéta** Ghana
56D3 **Ketapang** Indon
6E4 **Ketchikan** USA
70C3 **Ketia** Niger
60B4 **Keti Bandar** Pak
71G4 **Kétou** Benin
43E2 **Ketrzyn** Pol
35E5 **Kettering** Eng
12C3 **Kettering** USA
4D2 **Kettle** *R* Manitoba, Can
18C1 **Kettle** *R* British Columbia, Can
20C2 **Kettleman City** USA
18C1 **Kettle River Range** *Mts* USA
7L3 **Kettlestone B** Can
14B1 **Keuka L** USA
63D2 **Kevir-i Namak** *Salt Flat* Iran
12B2 **Kewaunee** USA
12B1 **Keweenaw B** USA
12B1 **Keweenaw Pen** USA
4E4 **Key Harbour** Can
15E4 **Key Largo** USA
14A3 **Keyser** USA
9E4 **Key West** USA
49M4 **Kezhma** Russian Fed
41D1 **K'félegháza** Hung
10F3 **Kgun L** USA
65D2 **Khabab** Syria
53D2 **Khabarovsk** Russian Fed
45G8 **Khabur** *R* Syria
60B3 **Khairpur** Pak
60B3 **Khairpur** Region, Pak
74C1 **Khakhea** Botswana
65B3 **Khalig El Tina** *B* Egypt
67G2 **Khalīj Maşīrah** *B* Oman
41F3 **Khálki** *I* Greece
41E2 **Khalkidhíki** *Pen* Greece
41E3 **Khalkís** Greece
44L2 **Khal'mer-Yu** Russian Fed
44H4 **Khalturin** Russian Fed
67G2 **Khalūf** Oman
60C4 **Khambhāt,G of** India
60D4 **Khāmgaon** India
66D3 **Khamir** Yemen
66D3 **Khamis Mushayt** S Arabia
55C2 **Kham Keut** Laos
62C1 **Khammam** India
65B3 **Khamsa** Egypt
63B1 **Khamseh** *Mts* Iran
55C2 **Khan** *R* Laos
60B1 **Khanabad** Afghan
64E3 **Khānaqīn** Iraq
60D4 **Khandwa** India
60C2 **Khanewal** Pak
65D3 **Khan ez Zabib** Jordan
55D4 **Khanh Hung** Viet
41E3 **Khaniá** Greece
53C3 **Khanka, Ozero** *L* China

Khankendy

Koma

Khankendy = Stepanakert
60C3 **Khanpur** Pak
65D1 **Khān Shaykhūn** Syria
48H3 **Khanty-Mansiysk** Russian Fed
65C3 **Khan Yunis** Egypt
60D1 **Khapalu** India
50E2 **Khapcheranga** Russian Fed
45H6 **Kharabali** Russian Fed
61C3 **Kharagpur** India
63D3 **Khārān** Iran
60B3 **Kharan** Pak
63C2 **Kharānaq** Iran
63C3 **Khārg** *Is* Iran
69C2 **Khârga Oasis** Egypt
60D4 **Khargon** India
45F6 **Khar'kov** Ukraine
44F2 **Kharlovka** Russian Fed
41F2 **Kharmanli** Bulg
44G4 **Kharovsk** Russian Fed
72D2 **Khartoum** Sudan
72D2 **Khartoum North** Sudan
53C3 **Khasan** Russian Fed
63E2 **Khash** Afghan
63E3 **Khāsh** Iran
63E2 **Khash** *R* Afghan
72D2 **Khashm el Girba** Sudan
61D2 **Khasi-Jaīntia Hills** India
41F2 **Khaskovo** Bulg
49M2 **Khatanga** Russian Fed
49N2 **Khatangskiy Zaliv** *Estuary* Russian Fed
49T3 **Khatyrka** Russian Fed
55B3 **Khawsa** Burma
66C1 **Khaybar** S Arabia
66B2 **Khazzan an-Nasr** *L* Egypt
55C2 **Khe Bo** Viet
60C4 **Khed Brahma** India
39C2 **Khemis** Alg
71A2 **Khemisset** Mor
71D1 **Khenchela** Alg
71A2 **Khenifra** Mor
39D2 **Kherrata** Alg
45E6 **Kherson** Ukraine
49N4 **Khilok** Russian Fed
41F3 **Khíos** Greece
41F3 **Khíos** *I* Greece
45D6 **Khmel'nitskiy** Ukraine
43E3 **Khodorov** Ukraine
59E1 **Khodzhent** Taji
60B1 **Kholm** Afghan
43G1 **Kholm** Russian Fed
53E2 **Kholmsk** Russian Fed
74B1 **Khomas Hochland, Mts** Namibia
55D3 **Khong** Laos
63C3 **Khonj** Iran
53C2 **Khor** Russian Fed
53D2 **Khor** *R* Russian Fed
63B2 **Khoramshahr** Iran
67F2 **Khōr Duwayhin** *B* UAE
60C1 **Khorog** Tajikistan
63B2 **Khorramābad** Iran
63D2 **Khosf** Iran
60B2 **Khost** Pak
45D6 **Khotin** Ukraine
10G3 **Khotol** *Mt* USA
71A2 **Khouribga** Mor
45D5 **Khoyniki** Belorussia
49Q3 **Khrebet Cherskogo** *Mts* Russian Fed
53B1 **Khrebet Dzhagdy** *Mts* Russian Fed
49P4 **Khrebet Dzhugdzhur** *Mts* Russian Fed
10C2 **Khrebet Iskamen** *Mts* Russian Fed
49O3 **Khrebet Orulgan** *Mts* Russian Fed
44L2 **Khrebet Pay-khoy** *Mts* Russian Fed
53D2 **Khrebet Sikhote Alin'** *Mts* Russian Fed
59G1 **Khrebet Tarbagatay** *Mts* Kazakhstan
49O4 **Khrebet Tukuringra** *Mts* Russian Fed
53C1 **Khrebet Turana** *Upland* Russian Fed
65B1 **Khrysokhou B** Cyprus
44L3 **Khulga** *R* Russian Fed
61C3 **Khulna** Bang
60D1 **Khunjerab** *P* China/India
63C2 **Khunsar** Iran
67E1 **Khurays** S Arabia
61C3 **Khurda** India
60D3 **Khurja** India
67G3 **Khūryan Mūryān** *Is* Oman
60C2 **Khushab** Pak
65C2 **Khushnīyah** Syria
43E3 **Khust** Ukraine
72C2 **Khuwei** Sudan
60B3 **Khuzdar** Pak
63E2 **Khvāf** Iran
45H5 **Khvalynsk** Russian Fed
63D2 **Khvor** Iran
63C3 **Khvormūj** Iran
45G8 **Khvoy** Iran
60C1 **Khwaja Muhammad** *Mts* Afghan
60C2 **Khyber P** Afghan/Pak
73C4 **Kiambi** Zaïre
17C3 **Kiamichi** *R* USA
10F2 **Kiana** USA
72B4 **Kibangou** Congo
72D4 **Kibaya** Tanz
72C4 **Kibombo** Zaïre
72D4 **Kibondo** Tanz
72D4 **Kibungu** Rwanda
41E2 **Kičevo** Macedonia, Yugos
6G4 **Kicking Horse P** Can
70C3 **Kidal** Mali
35D5 **Kidderminster** Eng
70A3 **Kidira** Sen
78C1 **Kidnappers,C** NZ
42C2 **Kiel** Germany
43E2 **Kielce** Pol
42C2 **Kieler Bucht** *B* Germany
Kiev = Kiyev
58E2 **Kifab** Uzbekistan
70A3 **Kiffa** Maur
68H8 **Kigali** Rwanda
5J2 **Kiglapatt,C** Can
10E3 **Kigluaik Mts** USA
72C4 **Kigoma** Tanz
20E5 **Kiholo** Hawaiian Is
54C4 **Kii-sanchi** *Mts* Japan
53C5 **Kii-suido** *B* Japan
49R4 **Kikhchik** Russian Fed
41E1 **Kikinda** Serbia, Yugos
41E3 **Kikládhes** *Is* Greece
76D1 **Kikon** PNG
54D2 **Kikonai** Japan
51H7 **Kikori** PNG
72B4 **Kikwit** Zaïre
20E5 **Kilauea Crater** *Mt* Hawaiian Is
6C3 **Kilbuck Mts** USA
53B3 **Kilchu** N Korea
75D1 **Kilcoy** Aust
35B5 **Kildane** County, Irish Rep
35B5 **Kildare** Irish Rep
17D3 **Kilgore** USA
72E4 **Kilifi** Kenya
72D4 **Kilimanjaro** *Mt* Tanz
73D4 **Kilindoni** Tanz
64C2 **Kilis** Turk
43F3 **Kiliya** Ukraine
35B5 **Kilkenny** County, Irish Rep
35B5 **Kilkenny** Irish Rep
41E2 **Kilkís** Greece
75D1 **Killarney** Aust
33B3 **Killarney** Irish Rep
17C3 **Killeen** USA
10H2 **Killik** *R* USA
34C3 **Killin** Scot
5J1 **Killinek I** Can
41E3 **Killíni** *Mt* Greece
34C4 **Kilmarnock** Scot
44J4 **Kil'mez** Russian Fed
73D4 **Kilosa** Tanz
33B3 **Kilrush** Irish Rep
71J4 **Kilunga** *R* Nig
73C4 **Kilwa** Zaïre
73D4 **Kilwa Kisiwani** Tanz
73D4 **Kilwa Kivinje** Tanz
71J4 **Kim** *R* Cam
75A2 **Kimba** Aust
16B1 **Kimball** USA
10K3 **Kimball,Mt** USA
3E4 **Kimberley** Can
74C2 **Kimberley** S Africa
76B2 **Kimberley Plat** Aust
53B3 **Kimch'aek** N Korea
53B4 **Kimch'ŏn** S Korea
54A3 **Kimhae** S Korea
41E3 **Kími** Greece
54A3 **Kimje** S Korea
44F4 **Kimry** Russian Fed
54A3 **Kimwha** N Korea
56E1 **Kinabalu** *Mt* Malay
56E1 **Kinabatangan** *R* Malay
4E5 **Kincardine** Can
3C2 **Kincolith** Can
17D3 **Kinder** USA
3G3 **Kindersley** Can
70A3 **Kindia** Guinea
72C4 **Kindu** Zaïre
44J5 **Kinel'** Russian Fed
44G4 **Kineshma** Russian Fed
75D1 **Kingaroy** Aust
19B3 **King City** USA
6F4 **Kingcome Inlet** Can
10F4 **King Cove** USA
17C2 **Kingfisher** USA
7L4 **King George Is** Can
76D5 **King I** Aust
3C3 **King I** Can
76B2 **King Leopold Range** *Mts* Aust
8B3 **Kingman** USA
72C4 **Kingombe** Zaïre
75A2 **Kingoonya** Aust
20C2 **Kingsburg** USA
19C3 **Kings Canyon Nat Pk** USA
75A3 **Kingscote** Aust
76B2 **King Sd** Aust
12B1 **Kingsford** USA
15C2 **Kingsland** USA
35F5 **King's Lynn** Eng
77G1 **Kingsmill Group** *Is* Kiribati
14D2 **Kings Park** USA
8B2 **Kings Peak** *Mt* USA
15C1 **Kingsport** USA
76C4 **Kingston** Aust
7L5 **Kingston** Can
21E3 **Kingston** Jamaica
13E2 **Kingston** New York, USA
78A3 **Kingston** NZ
14C2 **Kingston** Pennsylvania, USA
23E4 **Kingstown** St Vincent
8D4 **Kingsville** USA
5J2 **Kingurutik** *R* Can
34C3 **Kingussie** Scot
6J3 **King William I** Can
74D3 **King William's Town** S Africa
72B4 **Kinkala** Congo
32G7 **Kinna** Sweden
34D3 **Kinnairds Head** *Pt* Scot
54C3 **Kinomoto** Japan
34D3 **Kinross** Scot
72B4 **Kinshasa** Zaïre
16C2 **Kinsley** USA
15D1 **Kinston** USA
56E3 **Kintap** Indon
34C4 **Kintyre** *Pen* Scot
3E2 **Kinuso** Can
72D3 **Kinyeti** *Mt* Sudan
36E1 **Kinzig** *R* Germany
3H2 **Kipahigan L** Can
41E3 **Kiparissía** Greece
41E3 **Kiparissiakós Kólpos** *G* Greece
13D1 **Kipawa,L** Can
73D4 **Kipili** Tanz
10F4 **Kipnuk** USA
35B5 **Kippure** *Mt* Irish Rep
73C5 **Kipushi** Zaïre
36E2 **Kirchheim** Germany
49M4 **Kirensk** Russian Fed
48J5 **Kirgizia** *Republic* Europe
59F1 **Kirgizskiy Khrebet** *Mts* Kirgizia
72B4 **Kiri** Zaïre
77G1 **Kiribati** *Is* Pacific O
64B2 **Kırıkkale** Turk
44E4 **Kirishi** Russian Fed
60B3 **Kirithar Range** *Mts* Pak
41F3 **Kirkağaç** Turk
45H8 **Kirk Bulāg Dāgh** *Mt* Iran
35D4 **Kirkby** Eng
34D3 **Kirkcaldy** Scot
34C4 **Kirkcudbright** Scot
32K5 **Kirkenes** Nor
7K5 **Kirkland Lake** Can
64A1 **Kırklarelı** Turk
79E **Kirkpatrick,Mt** Ant
9D2 **Kirksville** USA
64D2 **Kirkūk** Iraq
34D2 **Kirkwall** Scot
17D2 **Kirkwood** USA
74D3 **Kirkwood** *R* S Africa
44E5 **Kirov** Russian Fed
44H4 **Kirov** Russian Fed
64D1 **Kirovakan** Armenia
44K4 **Kirovgrad** Russian Fed
45E6 **Kirovograd** Ukraine
44E2 **Kirovsk** Russian Fed
49R4 **Kirovskiy** Kamchatka, Russian Fed
53C2 **Kirovskiy** Primorskiykray, Russian Fed
44J4 **Kirs** Russian Fed
64B2 **Kirşehir** Turk
42C2 **Kiruna** Sweden
54C3 **Kiryū** Japan
72C3 **Kisangani** Zaïre
57C4 **Kisar** *I* Indon
56A2 **Kisaran** Indon
54C3 **Kisarazu** Japan
61C2 **Kishanganj** India
60C3 **Kishangarh** India
43F3 **Kishinev** Moldavia
54C4 **Kishiwada** Japan
72D4 **Kisii** Kenya
73D4 **Kisiju** Tanz
10B6 **Kiska** *I* USA
4B3 **Kiskitto L** Can
43D3 **Kiskunhalas** Hung
45G7 **Kislovodsk** Russian Fed
72E4 **Kismaayo** Somalia
54C3 **Kiso-sammyaku** *Mts* Japan
70B4 **Kissidougou** Guinea
15C3 **Kissimmee,L** USA
3H2 **Kississing L** Can
72D4 **Kisumu** Kenya
43E3 **Kisvárda** Hung
70B3 **Kita** Mali
48H6 **Kitab** Uzbekistan
54D3 **Kitakami** Japan
54D3 **Kitakami** *R* Japan
54D3 **Kitakata** Japan
53C5 **Kita-Kyūshū** Japan
72D3 **Kitale** Kenya
50H4 **Kitalo** *I* Japan
53E3 **Kitami** Japan
54D2 **Kitami-Esashi** Japan
16B2 **Kit Carson** USA
7K5 **Kitchener** Can
4F3 **Kitchigama** *R* Can
72D3 **Kitgum** Uganda
41E3 **Kíthira** *I* Greece
41E3 **Kíthnos** *I* Greece
65B1 **Kiti,C** Cyprus
6G2 **Kitikmeot** Region, Can
6F4 **Kitimat** Can
32K5 **Kitnen** *R* Fin
54B4 **Kitsuki** Japan
13D2 **Kittanning** USA
13E2 **Kittery** USA
32J5 **Kittilä** Fin
15D1 **Kitty Hawk** USA
73D4 **Kitunda** Tanz
10N4 **Kitwanga** Can
73C5 **Kitwe** Zambia
42C3 **Kitzbühel** Austria
37E1 **Kitzbühler Alpen** *Mts* Austria
42C3 **Kitzingen** Germany
72C4 **Kiumbi** Zaïre
10F2 **Kivalina** USA
43F2 **Kivercy** Ukraine
72C4 **Kivu,L** Zaïre/Rwanda
6B3 **Kiwalik** USA
45E5 **Kiyev** Ukraine
43G2 **Kiyevskoye Vodokhranilishche** *Res* Ukraine
44K4 **Kizel** Russian Fed
44G3 **Kizema** Russian Fed
64C2 **Kizil** *R* Turk
58D2 **Kizyl-Arvat** Turkmenistan
45J8 **Kizyl-Atrek** Turkmenistan
42C2 **Kladno** Czech
42C3 **Klagenfurt** Austria
44C4 **Klaipēda** Lithuania
18B2 **Klamath** USA
8A2 **Klamath** *R* USA
8A2 **Klamath Falls** USA
18B2 **Klamath Mts** USA
3C2 **Klappan** *R* Can
42C3 **Klatovy** Czech
10M4 **Klawak** USA
65C1 **Kleiat** Leb
74B2 **Kleinsee** S Africa
74D2 **Klerksdorp** S Africa
43G2 **Kletnya** Russian Fed
36D1 **Kleve** Germany
43G2 **Klimovichi** Belorussia
44F4 **Klin** Russian Fed
43D1 **Klintehamn** Sweden
45E5 **Klintsy** Russian Fed
74C3 **Klipplaat** S Africa
40D2 **Ključ** Bosnia & Herzegovina, Yugos
42D2 **Kłodzko** Pol
10L3 **Klondike** *R* USA/Can
6D3 **Klondike Plat** USA/Can
42D3 **Klosterneuburg** Austria
10L3 **Kluane** *R* Can
10L3 **Kluane L** Can
10L3 **Kluane Nat Pk** Can
43D2 **Kluczbork** Pol
10L4 **Klukwan** USA
10J3 **Klutina L** USA
10J3 **Knight I** USA
35D5 **Knighton** Wales
40D2 **Knin** Croatia, Yugos
76A4 **Knob,C** Aust
36B1 **Knokke-Heist** Belg
10M5 **Knox,C** Can
79G9 **Knox Coast** Ant
11D3 **Knoxville** Iowa, USA
9E3 **Knoxville** Tennessee, USA
7O3 **Knud Ramsussens Land** *Region* Greenland
74C3 **Knysna** S Africa
56C3 **Koba** Indon
7O3 **Kobberminebugt** *B* Greenland
53D5 **Kobe** Japan
42C1 **København** Den
37E1 **Kobiard** Slovenia, Yugos
42B2 **Koblenz** Germany
53C1 **Koboldo** Russian Fed
44C5 **Kobrin** Russian Fed
51G7 **Kobroör** *I* Indon
10G2 **Kobuk** *R* USA
41E2 **Kočani** Macedonia, Yugos
54A3 **Kŏch'ang** S Korea
55C3 **Ko Chang** *I* Thai
61C2 **Koch Bihār** India
37D1 **Kochel** Germany
36E2 **Kocher** *R* Germany
7L3 **Koch I** Can
62B3 **Kochi** India
53C5 **Kōchi** Japan
10H4 **Kodiak** USA
10H4 **Kodiak I** USA
62B2 **Kodikkarai** India
72D3 **Kodok** Sudan
54D2 **Kodomari-misaki** *C* Japan
43F3 **Kodyma** Ukraine
20D3 **Koehn L** USA
74B2 **Koes** Namibia
74D2 **Koffiefontein** S Africa
71F4 **Koforidua** Ghana
53D4 **Kōfu** Japan
54C3 **Koga** Japan
5J2 **Kogaluk** *R* Can
32G7 **Køge** Den
71H4 **Kogi** *State* Nig
60C2 **Kohat** Pak
60B2 **Koh-i-Baba** *Mts* Afghan
60B1 **Koh-i-Hisar** *Mts* Afghan
60B2 **Koh-i-Khurd** *Mt* Afghan
61D2 **Kohīma** India
60B1 **Koh-i-Mazar** *Mt* Afghan
63E2 **Koh-i-Qaisar** *Mt* Afghan
60B3 **Kohlu** Pak
44D4 **Kohtla Järve** Estonia
54A4 **Kohung** S Korea
54A4 **Kohyon** S Korea
54C3 **Koide** Japan
10K3 **Koidern** Can
55A4 **Koihoa** *Is* Nicobar Is
54A2 **Koin** N Korea
53B5 **Kōje-do** *I* S Korea
54C2 **Ko-jima** *I* Japan
48H4 **Kokchetav** Kazakhstan
32J6 **Kokemaki** *L* Fin
32J6 **Kokkola** Fin
71G3 **Koko** Nig
76D1 **Kokoda** PNG
12B2 **Kokomo** USA
51G7 **Kokonau** Indon
50B2 **Kokpekty** Kazakhstan
54A3 **Koksan** N Korea
7M4 **Koksoak** *R* Can
54A3 **Koksŏng** S Korea
74D3 **Kokstad** S Africa
55C3 **Ko Kut** *I* Thai
44E2 **Kola** Russian Fed
57B3 **Kolaka** Indon
55B4 **Ko Lanta** *I* Thai
62B2 **Kolār** India
62B2 **Kolār Gold Fields** India
70A3 **Kolda** Sen
32F7 **Kolding** Den
53E1 **Kolendo** Russian Fed
44H2 **Kolguyev, Ostrov** *I* Russian Fed
62A1 **Kolhāpur** India
10G4 **Koliganek** USA
42D2 **Kolín** Czech
62B3 **Kollam** India
42B2 **Köln** Germany
43D2 **Kolo** Pol
20E5 **Koloa** Hawaiian Is
42D2 **Kolobrzeg** Pol
70B3 **Kolokani** Mali
44F4 **Kolomna** Russian Fed
45D6 **Kolomyya** Ukraine
57B3 **Kolono** Indon
57B3 **Kolonodale** Indon
49R4 **Kolpakovskiy** Russian Fed
48K4 **Kolpashevo** Russian Fed
41F3 **Kólpos Merabéllou** *B* Greece
41E2 **Kólpos Singitikós** *G* Greece
41E2 **Kólpos Strimonikós** *G* Greece
41E2 **Kólpos Toronaíos** *G* Greece
44F2 **Kol'skiy Poluostrov** *Pen* Russian Fed
44K2 **Kolva** *R* Russian Fed
32G6 **Kolvereid** Nor
73C5 **Kolwezi** Zaïre
49R3 **Kolyma** *R* Russian Fed
49R3 **Kolymskaya Nizmennost** *Lowland* Russian Fed
49S3 **Kolymskoye Nagor'ye** *Mts* Russian Fed
10D2 **Kolyuchinskaya Guba** *B* Russian Fed
41E2 **Kom** *Mt* Bulg/Serbia
72D3 **Koma** Eth

Koma Kyaukpyu

54D3 **Koma** Japan
71J3 **Komaduga Gana** *R* Nig
71J3 **Komadugu Yobé** *R* Nig
54D2 **Komaga take** *Mt* Japan
49S4 **Komandorskiye Ostrova** *I* Russian Fed
43D3 **Komárno** Czech
74E2 **Komati,R** S Africa
74E2 **Komati Poort** S Africa
53D4 **Komatsu** Japan
54B4 **Komatsushima** Japan
71F3 **Kombissiri** Burkina
44J3 **Komi** Respublika, Russian Fed
50B1 **Kommunar** Russian Fed
57A4 **Komodo** *I* Indon
71F4 **Komoé** *R* Ivory Coast
51G7 **Komoran** *I* Indon
54C3 **Komoro** Japan
41F2 **Komotiní** Greece
74C3 **Kompasberg** *Mt* S Africa
55D3 **Kompong Cham** Camb
55C3 **Kompong Chhnang** *Mts* Camb
55C3 **Kompong Som** Camb
55D3 **Kompong Thom** Camb
55D3 **Kompong Trabek** Camb
43F3 **Komrat** Moldavia
74C3 **Komsberg** *Mts* S Africa
49Li **Komsomolets, Ostrov** *I* Russian Fed
44L2 **Komsomol'skiy** Russian Fed
49P4 **Komsomol'sk na Amure** Russian Fed
48H4 **Konda** *R* Russian Fed
61B4 **Kondagaon** India
72D4 **Kondoa** Tanz
53D1 **Kondon** Russian Fed
44E3 **Kondopoga** Russian Fed
62B1 **Kondukūr** India
10C2 **Konergino** Russian Fed
44F3 **Konevo** Russian Fed
7P3 **Kong Christian IX Land** *Region* Greenland
7O3 **Kong Frederik VI Kyst** *Region* Greenland
54A3 **Kongju** S Korea
48D2 **Kong Karls Land** *Is* Barents S
56E2 **Kongkemul** *Mt* Indon
72C4 **Kongolo** Zaïre
71F3 **Kongoussi** Burkina
32F7 **Kongsberg** Den
32G6 **Kongsvinger** Nor
Königsberg = Kaliningrad
37E1 **Königsee, L** Germany
43D2 **Konin** Pol
41D2 **Konjic** Bosnia & Herzegovina, Yugos
71F4 **Konongo** Ghana
44G3 **Konosha** Russian Fed
54C3 **Konosu** Japan
45E5 **Konotop** Ukraine
43E2 **Końskie** Pol
36E3 **Konstanz** Germany
71H3 **Kontagora** Nig
55D3 **Kontum** Viet
10B2 **Konus** *Mt* Russian Fed
45E8 **Konya** Turk
18C1 **Kootenay** *L* Can
3E4 **Kootenay** *R* Can
60C5 **Kopargaon** India
7R3 **Kópasker** Iceland
32A2 **Kópavogur** Iceland
40C1 **Koper** Slovenia, Yugos
58D2 **Kopet Dag** *Mts* Iran/Turkmenistan
44L4 **Kopeysk** Russian Fed
55C4 **Ko Phangan** *I* Thai
55B4 **Ko Phuket** *I* Thai
32H7 **Köping** Sweden
54A3 **Kopo-ri** S Korea
62B1 **Koppal** India
40D1 **Koprivnica** Croatia, Yugos
60B4 **Korangi** Pak
62C1 **Koraput** India
61B3 **Korba** India
42B2 **Korbach** Germany
41E2 **Korçë** Alb
40D2 **Korčula** *I* Croatia, Yugos
52E2 **Korea B** China/Korea
53B5 **Korea Str** S Korea/Japan
43F2 **Korec** Ukraine
49S3 **Korf** Russian Fed
64B1 **Körğlu Tepesi** *Mt* Turk
70B4 **Korhogo** Ivory Coast
60B4 **Kori Creek** India
41E3 **Korinthiakós Kólpos** *G* Greece
41E3 **Kórinthos** Greece
53E4 **Kōriyama** Japan
44L5 **Korkino** Russian Fed
49R3 **Korkodon** Russian Fed
49R3 **Korkodon** *R* Russian Fed
64B2 **Korkuteli** Turk
59G1 **Korla** China
65B1 **Kormakiti,C** Cyprus
40D2 **Kornat** *I* Croatia, Yugos
45E7 **Köroğlu Tepesi** *Mt* Turk
72D4 **Korogwe** Tanz
75B3 **Koroit** Aust
51G6 **Koror** Palau Is, Pacific O
43E3 **Körös** *R* Hung
45D5 **Korosten** Ukraine
43F2 **Korostyshev** Ukraine
72B2 **Koro Toro** Chad
10F4 **Korovin** *I* USA
53E2 **Korsakov** Russian Fed
32G7 **Korsør** Den
66B3 **Korti** Sudan
44J3 **Kortkeroz** Russian Fed
42A2 **Kortrijk** Belg
49S3 **Koryakskoye Nagor'ye** *Mts* Russian Fed
54A3 **Koryong** S Korea
41F3 **Kós** *I* Greece
10D2 **Kosa Belyaka** *B* Russian Fed
55C4 **Ko Samui** *I* Thai
54A3 **Kosan** N Korea
43D2 **Koscierzyna** Pol
15B2 **Kosciusko** USA
76D4 **Kosciusko** *Mt* Aust
10M4 **Kosciusko I** USA
53B5 **Koshikijima-retto** *I* Japan
43E3 **Kosiče** Czech
44J2 **Kosma** *R* Russian Fed
53B4 **Kosong** N Korea
41E2 **Kosovo** *Aut Republic* Serbia, Yugos
70B4 **Kossou** *L* Ivory Coast
74D2 **Koster** S Africa
72D2 **Kosti** Sudan
43F2 **Kostopol'** Ukraine
44G4 **Kostroma** Russian Fed
42C2 **Kostrzyn** Pol
44K2 **Kos'yu** *R* Russian Fed
32H8 **Koszalin** Pol
60D3 **Kota** India
56B4 **Kotaagung** Indon
56D3 **Kotabaharu** Indon
56E3 **Kotabaru** Indon
55C4 **Kota Bharu** Malay
56C3 **Kotabum** Indon
60C2 **Kot Addu** Pak
56E1 **Kota Kinabulu** Malay
57B2 **Kotamobagu** Indon
62C1 **Kotapad** India
56F7 **Kotapinang** *I* Indon
56G8 **Kota Tinggi** Malay
44H4 **Kotel'nich** Russian Fed
45G6 **Kotel'nikovo** Russian Fed
49P2 **Kotel'nyy, Ostrov** *I* Russian Fed
32K6 **Kotka** Fin
44H3 **Kotlas** Russian Fed
10F3 **Kotlik** USA
71H4 **Koton Karifi** Nig
41D2 **Kotor** Montenegro, Yugos
45D6 **Kotovsk** Ukraine
60B3 **Kotri** Pak
37E1 **Kötschach** Austria
62C1 **Kottagūdem** India
62B3 **Kottayam** India
72C3 **Kotto** *R* CAR
62B2 **Kottūru** India
49L3 **Kotuy** *R* Russian Fed
10F2 **Kotzebue** USA
6B3 **Kotzebue Sd** USA
71G3 **Kouande** Benin
72C3 **Kouango** CAR
71F3 **Koudougou** Burkina
74C3 **Kougaberge** *Mts* S Africa
72B4 **Koulamoutou** Gabon
70B3 **Koulikoro** Mali
71F3 **Koupéla** Burkina
71F3 **Kouri** Mali
27H2 **Kourou** French Guiana
70B3 **Kouroussa** Guinea
72B2 **Kousséri** Cam
32K6 **Kouvola** Fin
32L5 **Kovdor** Russian Fed
32L5 **Kovdozero, Ozero** *L* Russian Fed
43E2 **Kovel'** Ukraine
Kovno = Kaunas
44G4 **Kovrov** Russian Fed
44G5 **Kovylkino** Russian Fed
44F3 **Kovzha** *R* Russian Fed
55C4 **Ko Way** *I* Thai
52C5 **Kowloon** Hong Kong
54A3 **Kowŏn** N Korea
60B2 **Kowt-e-Ashrow** Afghan
64A2 **Köyceğiz** Turk
44G2 **Koyda** Russian Fed
62A1 **Koyna Res** India
44H3 **Koynas** Russian Fed
57C2 **Koyoa** *I* Indon
10F3 **Koyuk** USA
10F2 **Koyuk** *R* USA
10G3 **Koyukuk** USA
10G2 **Koyukuk** *R* USA
64C2 **Kozan** Turk
41E2 **Kozańi** Greece
62B2 **Kozhikode** India
44K2 **Kozhim** Russian Fed
44H4 **Koz'modemyansk** Russian Fed
54C4 **Kōzu-shima** *I* Japan
71G4 **Kpandu** Ghana
74D3 **Kraai** *R* S Africa
32F7 **Kragerø** Nor
41E2 **Kragujevac** Serbia, Yugos
55B3 **Kra,Isthmus of** Burma/Malay
Krakatau = Rakata
65D1 **Krak des Chevaliers** *Hist Site* Syria
Kraków = Cracow Pol
41E2 **Kraljevo** Serbia, Yugos
45F6 **Kramatorsk** Ukraine
32H6 **Kramfors** Sweden
40C1 **Kranj** Slovenia, Yugos
44H3 **Krasavino** Russian Fed
44J1 **Krasino** Russian Fed
43E2 **Kraśnik** Pol
45H5 **Krasnoarmeysk** Russian Fed
45F6 **Krasnodar** Russian Fed
53E2 **Krasnogorsk** Russian Fed
44K4 **Krasnokamsk** Russian Fed
44L4 **Krasnotur'insk** Russian Fed
44K4 **Krasnoufimsk** Russian Fed
44K5 **Krasnousol'-skiy** Russian Fed
44K3 **Krasnovishersk** Russian Fed
45J7 **Krasnovodsk** Turkmenistan
49L4 **Krasnoyarsk** Russian Fed
43E2 **Krasnystaw** Pol
45H5 **Krasnyy Kut** Russian Fed
45F6 **Krasnyy Luch** Ukraine
45H6 **Krasnyy Yar** Russian Fed
55D3 **Kratie** Camb
7N2 **Kraulshavn** Greenland
42B2 **Krefeld** Germany
45E6 **Kremenchug** Ukraine
45E6 **Kremenchugskoye Vodokhranilische** *Res* Ukraine
43F2 **Kremenets** Ukraine
16A1 **Kremming** USA
10E5 **Krenitzin Is** USA
72A3 **Kribi** Cam
44E5 **Krichev** Belorussia
37E1 **Krimml** Austria
32J6 **Krinstinestad** Fin
62B1 **Krishna** *R* India
62B2 **Krishnagiri** India
61C3 **Krishnangar** India
32F7 **Kristiansand** Nor
32G7 **Kristianstad** Sweden
48B3 **Kristiansund** Nor
32G7 **Kristineham** Sweden
41E3 **Kríti** *I* Greece
45E6 **Krivoy Rog** Ukraine
40C1 **Krk** *I* Croatia, Yugos
74D1 **Krokodil** *R* S Africa
49S4 **Kronotskaya Sopka** *Mt* Russian Fed
7P3 **Kronpris Frederik Bjerge** *Mts* Greenland
32K7 **Kronshtadt** Russian Fed
74D2 **Kroonstad** S Africa
45G6 **Kropotkin** Russian Fed
74E1 **Kruger Nat Pk** S Africa
74D2 **Krugersdorp** S Africa
56B4 **Krui** Indon
41D2 **Kruje** Alb
43F2 **Krupki** Belorussia
10F2 **Krusenstern,C** USA
41E2 **Kruzevac** Serbia, Yugos
32K7 **Krustpils** Latvia
10L4 **Kruzof I** USA
45E6 **Krym** *Pen* Ukraine
45F7 **Krymsk** Russian Fed
42D2 **Krzyz** Pol
71C1 **Ksar El Boukhari** Alg
71A2 **Ksar el Kebir** Mor
56A2 **Kuala** Indon
55C5 **Kuala Dungun** Malay
56F6 **Kuala Kangsar** Malay
56G7 **Kuala Kelawang** Malay
55C4 **Kuala Kerai** Malay
55C5 **Kuala Kubu Baharu** Malay
55C5 **Kuala Lipis** Malay
55C5 **Kuala Lumpur** Malay
56G7 **Kuala Pilah** Malay
56F7 **Kuala Selangor** Malay
56A2 **Kualasimpang** Indon
55C4 **Kuala Trengganu** Malay
56E1 **Kuamut** Malay
53A3 **Kuandian** China
55C5 **Kuantan** Malay
45H7 **Kuba** Azerbaijan
51H7 **Kubar** PNG
56D2 **Kuching** Malay
56E1 **Kudat** Malay
56D4 **Kudus** Indon
44J4 **Kudymkar** Russian Fed
42C3 **Kufstein** Austria
10M2 **Kugaluk** *R* Can
10M2 **Kugmallit B** Can
63E3 **Kuhak** Iran
63D2 **Kuh Duren** *Upland* Iran
63D3 **Kūh e Bazmān** *Mt* Iran
63C2 **Kūh-e Dinar** *Mt* Iran
63D1 **Kūh-e-Hazār Masjed** *Mts* Iran
63D3 **Kūh-e Jebāl Barez** *Mts* Iran
63C2 **Kūh-e Karkas** *Mts* Iran
63D3 **Kuh-e Laleh Zar** *Mt* Iran
63B1 **Kūh-e Sahand** *Mt* Iran
63E3 **Kuh e Taftān** *Mt* Iran
45H9 **Kūhhaye Alvand** *Mts* Iran
45H8 **Kūhhaye Sabalan** *Mts* Iran
63B2 **Kūhhā-ye Zāgros** *Mts* Iran
32K6 **Kuhmo** Fin
63C2 **Kūhpāyeh** Iran
63D2 **Kūhpāyeh** *Mt* Iran
63D3 **Kūh ye Bashākerd** *Mts* Iran
63B1 **Kūh ye Sabalan** *Mt* Iran
74B2 **Kuibis** Namibia
74B1 **Kuiseb** *R* Namibia
73B5 **Kuito** Angola
10M4 **Kuiu I** USA
54A3 **Kujang** N Korea
53E3 **Kuji** Japan
54B4 **Kuju-san** *Mt* Japan
10G4 **Kukaklek L** USA
41E2 **Kukës** Alb
10F2 **Kukpowruk** *R* USA
55C5 **Kukup** Malay
63D3 **Kūl** *R* Iran
41F3 **Kula** Turk
56G8 **Kulai** Malay
45K6 **Kulakshi** Kazakhstan
72D3 **Kulal,Mt** Kenya
41E2 **Kulata** Bulg
44C4 **Kuldīga** Latvia
56F6 **Kulim** Malay
44G2 **Kulov** *R* Russian Fed
71F3 **Kulpawn** *R* Ghana
45J6 **Kul'sary** Kazakhstan
60D2 **Kulu** India
64B2 **Kulu** Turk
66D4 **Kululli** Eth
48J4 **Kulunda** Russian Fed
75B2 **Kulwin** Aust
45H7 **Kuma** *R* Russian Fed
54C3 **Kumagaya** Japan
56D3 **Kumai** Indon
45L5 **Kumak** Russian Fed
53C5 **Kumamoto** Japan
54C4 **Kumano** Japan
41E2 **Kumanovo** Macedonia, Yugos
53B1 **Kumara** China
71F4 **Kumasi** Ghana
72A3 **Kumba** Cam
62B2 **Kumbakonam** India
71J4 **Kumbo** Cam
54A3 **Kūmch'ŏn** N Korea
67E2 **Kumdah** S Arabia
44K5 **Kumertau** Russian Fed
54A3 **Kumgang** N Korea
53B4 **Kūmhwa** S Korea
32H7 **Kumla** Sweden
54A4 **Kūmnyŏng** S Korea
54A4 **Kūmo-do** *I* S Korea
61E2 **Kumon Range** *Mts* Burma
62A2 **Kumta** India
59G1 **Kūmüx** China
60C2 **Kunar** *R* Afghan
53F3 **Kunashir, Ostrov** *I* Russian Fed
32K7 **Kunda** Estonia
60C4 **Kundla** India
60B1 **Kunduz** Afghan
68F9 **Kunene** *R* Angola
10M5 **Kunghit** *I* Can
32G7 **Kungsbacka** Sweden
44K4 **Kungur** Russian Fed
55B1 **Kunhing** Burma
59G2 **Kunlun Shan** *Mts* China
52A4 **Kunming** China
44M3 **Kunovat** *R* Russian Fed
53B4 **Kunsan** S Korea
32K6 **Kuopio** Fin
40D1 **Kupa** *R* Croatia/Bosnia & Herzegovina, Yugos
76B2 **Kupang** Indon
76D2 **Kupiano** PNG
10M4 **Kupreanof I** USA
10G4 **Kupreanof Pt** USA
45F6 **Kupyansk** Ukraine
59G1 **Kuqa** China
53C2 **Kur** *R* Russian Fed
45H8 **Kura** *R* Azerbaijan
54C3 **Kurabe** Japan
53C5 **Kurashiki** Japan
54B3 **Kurayoshi** Japan
63B1 **Kurdistan** Region, Iran
41F2 **Kŭrdzhali** Bulg
53C5 **Kure** Japan
44C4 **Kuressaare** Estonia
49L3 **Kureyka** *R* Russian Fed
48H4 **Kurgan** Russian Fed
Kuria Muria Is = Khūryan Mūryān
32J6 **Kurikka** Fin
Kuril Is = Kuril'skiye Ostrova
53F2 **Kuril'sk** Russian Fed
49Q5 **Kuril'skiye Ostrova** *Is* Russian Fed
xxviiiJ2 **Kuril Trench** Pacific O
45H8 **Kurinskaya Kosa** *Sand Spit* Azerbaijan
62B1 **Kurnool** India
54D2 **Kuroishi** Japan
54D3 **Kuroiso** Japan
78B2 **Kurow** NZ
75D2 **Kurri Kurri** Aust
45F5 **Kursk** Russian Fed
50B2 **Kuruktag** *R* China
74C2 **Kuruman** S Africa
74C2 **Kuruman** *R* S Africa
53C5 **Kurume** Japan
62C3 **Kurunegala** Sri Lanka
48K5 **Kuruktag** *R* China
44K3 **Kur'ya** Russian Fed
44K4 **Kusa** Russian Fed
41F3 **Kuşadasi Körfezi** *B* Turk
41F2 **Kus Golü** *L* Turk
53D5 **Kushimoto** Japan
53E3 **Kushiro** Japan
63E1 **Kushka** Afghan
61C3 **Kushtia** Bang
45J5 **Kushum** *R* Kazakhstan
44K4 **Kushva** Russian Fed
10F3 **Kuskokwim** *R* USA
10F4 **Kuskokwim B** USA
10G3 **Kuskokwim Mts** USA
61B2 **Kusma** Nepal
53E3 **Kussharo-ko** *L* Japan
48H4 **Kustanay** Kazakhstan
45D8 **Kütahya** Turk
56E3 **Kutai** *R* Indon
45G7 **Kutaisi** Georgia
54D2 **Kutchan** Japan
42D3 **Kutná Hora** Czech
43D2 **Kutno** Pol
72B4 **Kutu** Zaïre
61D3 **Kutubdia I** Bang
72C2 **Kutum** Sudan
7M4 **Kuujjuaq** Can
7L4 **Kuujjuarapik** Can
32K5 **Kuusamo** Fin
45K5 **Kuvandyk** Russian Fed
64E4 **Kuwait** Kuwait
58C3 **Kuwait** Sheikdom, S W Asia
54C3 **Kuwana** Japan
48J4 **Kuybyshev** Russian Fed
44H5 **Kuybyshevskoye Vodokhranilishche** *Res* Russian Fed
44E2 **Kuyto, Ozero** *L* Russian Fed
49M4 **Kuytun** Russian Fed
45F7 **Kuzey Anadolu Daglari** *Mts* Turk
44H5 **Kuznetsk** Russian Fed
44F2 **Kuzomen** Russian Fed
44C2 **Kvaenangen** *Sd* Nor
10G4 **Kvichak** USA
10G4 **Kvichak** *R* USA
10G4 **Kvichak B** USA
32G5 **Kvigtind** *Mt* Nor
44B2 **Kvikkjokk** Sweden
72D4 **Kwale** Kenya
71H4 **Kwale** Nig
53B4 **Kwangju** S Korea
72B4 **Kwango** *R* Zaïre
54A3 **Kwangyang** S Korea
54A2 **Kwanmo-bong** *Mt* N Korea
71H4 **Kwara** State, Nig
73C5 **Kwekwe** Zim
10F3 **Kwethluk** USA
10F3 **Kwethluk** *R* USA
43D2 **Kwidzyn** Pol
6B4 **Kwigillingok** USA
51G7 **Kwoka** *Mt* Indon
75C3 **Kyabram** Aust
55B2 **Kyaikkami** Burma
55B2 **Kyaikto** Burma
50D1 **Kyakhta** Russian Fed
75A2 **Kyancutta** Aust
55B1 **Kyaukme** Burma
55B1 **Kyauk-padaung** Burma
55A2 **Kyaukpyu** Burma

Limassol Lubefu

64B3 Limassol Cyprus
34B4 Limavady N Ire
28B3 Limay *R* Arg
28B3 Limay Mahuida Arg
73D5 Limbe Malawi
57B2 Limbotto Indon
42B2 Limburg W Gem
27J8 Limeira Brazil
33B3 Limerick Irish Rep
42B1 Limfjorden *L* Den
76C2 Limmen Bight *B* Aust
41F3 Límnos *I* Greece
27L5 Limoeiro Brazil
38C2 Limoges France
21D4 Limón Costa Rica
8C3 Limon USA
37B2 Limone Italy
38C2 Limousin Region, France
74E1 Limpopo *R* Mozam
22C1 Linares Mexico
57E8 Linapacan Str Phil
25B5 Linares Chile
8D4 Linares Mexico
39B2 Linares Spain
50C4 Lincang China
25D4 Lincoln Arg
17C1 Lincoln California, USA
35E5 Lincoln County, Eng
35E5 Lincoln Eng
12B2 Lincoln Illinois, USA
13F1 Lincoln Maine, USA
8D2 Lincoln Nebraska, USA
13E2 Lincoln New Hampshire, USA
78B2 Lincoln NZ
79A Lincoln *S* Greenland
18B2 Lincoln City USA
12C2 Lincoln Park USA
40B2 L'Incudina *Mt* Corse
42B3 Lindau Germany
27G2 Linden Guyana
32F7 Lindesnes *C* Nor
73D4 Lindi Tanz
72C3 Lindi *R* Zaïre
74D2 Lindley S Africa
41F3 Lindos Greece
4F5 Lindsay Can
20C2 Lindsay California, USA
11A2 Lindsay Montana, USA
xxixM4 Line Is Pacific O
52C2 Linfen China
55D2 Lingao China
57F7 Lingayen Phil
42B2 Lingen Germany
11B3 Lingle USA
52C4 Lingling China
52B5 Lingshan China
52C2 Lingshi China
70A3 Linguère Sen
53A1 Linhai Heilongjiang, China
52E4 Linhai Rhejiang, China
27L7 Linhares Brazil
52B1 Linhe China
53B3 Linjiang China
32H7 Linköping Sweden
53C2 Linkou China
52D2 Linqing China
29C3 Lins Brazil
52A2 Lintao China
37C1 Linthal Switz
11B2 Linton USA
50E2 Linxi China
52A2 Linxia China
42C3 Linz Austria
57F8 Lipa Phil
40C3 Lipari *I* Italy
45F5 Lipetsk Russian Fed
41E1 Lipova Rom
42B2 Lippe *R* Germany
36E1 Lippstadt Germany
72D3 Lira Uganda
72B4 Liranga Congo
72C3 Lisala Zaïre
39A2 Lisboa Port
Lisbon = Lisboa
11C2 Lisbon USA
35B4 Lisburn N Ire
10E2 Lisburne,C USA
52D4 Lishui China
52C4 Li Shui *R* China
45F6 Lisichansk Ukraine
38C2 Lisieux France
45F5 Liski Russian Fed
36B2 L'Isle-Adam France
37B1 L'Isle-sur-le-Doubs France
77E3 Lismore Aust
52B5 Litang China
65C2 Lītanī *R* Leb
27H3 Litani *R* Surinam
12B3 Litchfield Illinois, USA
11D2 Litchfield Minnesota, USA
76E4 Lithgow Aust
44C4 Lithuania *Republic* Europe
14B2 Lititz USA
53E1 Litke Russian Fed
53D2 Litovko Russian Fed
17C3 Little *R* USA
9F4 Little Abaco *I* Bahamas
66D4 Little Aden Yemen
62E2 Little Andaman *I* Andaman Is
78C1 Little Barrier I NZ
18D1 Little Belt Mts USA
65B3 Little Bitter L Egypt
3F3 Little Bow *R* Can
21D3 Little Cayman *I* Caribbean
4D3 Little Current Can
4E4 Little Current Can
14C3 Little Egg Harbor *B* USA
11D2 Little Falls Minnesota, USA
14C1 Little Falls New York, USA
16B3 Littlefield USA
11D2 Littlefork USA
11D2 Little Fork *R* USA
4B3 Little Grand Rapids Can
34E2 Little Halibut Bank *Sandbank* Scot
23C2 Little Inagua *I* Caribbean
74C3 Little Karroo *R* S Africa
10G4 Little Koniuji *I* USA
20D3 Little Lake USA
11B2 Little Missouri *R* USA
55A4 Little Nicobar *I* Nicobar Is
9D3 Little Rock USA
20D3 Littlerock USA
10B6 Little Sitkin *I* USA
3E3 Little Smoky Can
3E3 Little Smoky *R* Can
14B3 Littlestown USA
10C6 Little Tanaga *I* USA
16A2 Littleton Colorado, USA
13E2 Littleton New Hampshire, USA
53B3 Liuhe China
52B5 Liuzhou China
41E3 Livanátais Greece
43F1 Līvāni Latvia
36A2 Livarot France
10J2 Livengood USA
37E2 Livenza *R* Italy
15C2 Live Oak USA
19B3 Livermore USA
16B3 Livermore,Mt USA
7M5 Liverpool Can
35D5 Liverpool Eng
6E2 Liverpool B Can
35D5 Liverpool B Eng
7L2 Liverpool,C Can
75D2 Liverpool Range *Mts* Aust
8B2 Livingston Montana, USA
15B1 Livingston Tennessee, USA
17D3 Livingston Texas, USA
73C5 Livingstone Zambia
17C3 Livingston,L USA
40D2 Livno Bosnia & Herzegovina, Yugos
45F5 Livny Russian Fed
12C2 Livonia USA
40C2 Livorno Italy
29D1 Livramento do Brumado Brazil
73D4 Liwale Tanz
35C7 Lizard Pt Eng
40C1 Ljubljana Slovenia, Yugos
32G6 Ljungan *R* Sweden
32G7 Ljungby Sweden
32H6 Ljusdal Sweden
44B3 Ljusnan *R* Sweden
35D6 Llandeilo Wales
35D6 Llandovery Wales
35D5 Llandrindod Wells Wales
35D5 Llandudno Wales
35C6 Llanelli Wales
35D5 Llangollen Wales
16C3 Llano USA
16C3 Llano *R* USA
16C3 Llano Estacado *Plat* USA
Z4D2 Llanos Region, Colombia/Ven
26F7 Llanos de Chiquitos Region, Bol
Lleida = Lérida
22C1 Llera Mexico
39A2 Llerena Spain
35C5 Lleyn *Pen* Wales
68E7 Llorin Nigeria
3C2 Lloyd George,Mt Can
3G2 Lloyd L Can
6H4 Lloydminster Can
25C2 Llullaillaco *Mt* Chile/Arg
25C2 Loa *R* Chile
38C2 Loan France
72B4 Loange *R* Zaïre
74D2 Lobatse Botswana
72B3 Lobaye *R* CAR
28D3 Loberia Arg
73B5 Lobito Angola
28D3 Lobos Arg
37B2 Locano Italy
37C1 Locarno Switz
34C3 Loch Awe *L* Scot
34B3 Lochboisdale Scot
34B3 Loch Bracadale *Inlet* Scot
34C3 Loch Broom *Estuary* Scot
34C4 Loch Doon *L* Scot
34C3 Loch Earn *L* Scot
34C2 Loch Eriboll *Inlet* Scot
34C3 Loch Ericht *L* Scot
38C2 Loches France
34C3 Loch Etive *Inlet* Scot
34C3 Loch Ewe *Inlet* Scot
34C3 Loch Fyne *Inlet* Scot
34C3 Loch Hourn *Inlet* Scot
34B4 Loch Indaal *Inlet* Scot
34C2 Lochinver Scot
34C3 Loch Katrine *L* Scot
34D3 Loch Leven *L* Scot
34C3 Loch Linnhe *Inlet* Scot
34C3 Loch Lochy *L* Scot
34C3 Loch Lomond *L* Scot
34C3 Loch Long *Inlet* Scot
34B3 Lochmaddy Scot
34C3 Loch Maree *L* Scot
34C3 Loch Morar *L* Scot
34D3 Lochnagar *Mt* Scot
34C3 Loch Ness *L* Scot
34C3 Loch Rannoch *L* Scot
34B2 Loch Roag *Inlet* Scot
18C1 Lochsa *R* USA
34C3 Loch Sheil *L* Scot
34C2 Loch Shin *L* Scot
34B3 Loch Snizort *Inlet* Scot
34C3 Loch Sunart *Inlet* Scot
34C3 Loch Tay *L* Scot
34C3 Loch Torridon *Inlet* Scot
75A2 Lock Aust
5H5 Lockeport Can
34D4 Lockerbie Scot
13D2 Lock Haven USA
13D2 Lockport USA
55D3 Loc Ninh Viet
40D3 Locri Italy
65C3 Lod Israel
75B3 Loddon *R* Aust
44E3 Lodeynoye Pole Russian Fed
18E1 Lodge Grass USA
60C3 Lodhran Pak
40B1 Lodi Italy
19B3 Lodi USA
72C4 Lodja Zaïre
37B1 Lods France
72D3 Lodwar Kenya
43D2 Łódź Pol
74B3 Loeriesfontein S Africa
37E1 Lofer Austria
32G5 Lofoten *Is* Nor
16B2 Logan New Mexico, USA
8B2 Logan Utah, USA
6D3 Logan,Mt Can
10N3 Logan Mts Can
12B2 Logansport Indiana, USA
17D3 Logansport Louisiana, USA
14B2 Loganton USA
39B1 Logroño Spain
61B3 Lohārdaga India
32J6 Lohja Fin
36E2 Lohr Germany
55B2 Loikaw Burma
32J6 Loimaa Fin
36B2 Loing *R* France
38C2 Loir *R* France
36A3 Loir et Cher Department, France
38C2 Loire *R* France
36B3 Loiret Department, France
26C4 Loja Ecuador
39B2 Loja Spain
57C3 Loji Indon
32K5 Lokan Tekojärvi *Res* Fin
36B1 Lokeren Belg
72D3 Lokitaung Kenya
43F1 Loknya Russian Fed
71H4 Lokoja Nig
72C4 Lokolo *R* Zaïre
72C4 Lokoro *R* Zaïre
7M3 Loks Land *I* Can
42C2 Lolland *I* Den
57C2 Loloda Indon
18D1 Lolo P USA
41E2 Lom Bulg
71J4 Lom *R* Cam
73C4 Lomami *R* Zaïre
70A4 Loma Mts Sierra Leone/Guinea
57B2 Lombagin Indon
37C2 Lombardia Region, Italy
57B4 Lomblen *I* Indon
56E4 Lombok *I* Indon
71G4 Lomé Togo
72C4 Lomela Zaïre
72C4 Lomela *R* Zaïre
34G3 Lomond *Oilfield* N Sea
44D4 Lomonosov Russian Fed
37B1 Lomont Region, France
19B4 Lompoc USA
43E2 Łomza Pol
62A1 Lonāvale India
25B5 Loncoche Chile
7K5 London Can
35E6 London Eng
12C3 London USA
34B4 Londonderry County, N Ire
34B4 Londonderry N Ire
25B9 Londonderry *I* Chile
76B2 Londonderry,C Aust
25C3 Londres Arg
25F2 Londrina Brazil
20D1 Lone Mt USA
20C2 Lone Pine USA
9F4 Long *I* Bahamas
51H7 Long *I* PNG
56D2 Long Akah Malay
37E1 Longarone Italy
28A3 Longavi *Mt* Chile
23H2 Long B Jamaica
15D2 Long B USA
8B3 Long Beach California, USA
13E2 Long Beach New York, USA
13E2 Long Branch USA
52D5 Longchuan China
18C2 Long Creek USA
75E3 Longford Aust
35B5 Longford County, Irish Rep
35B5 Longford Irish Rep
34E3 Long Forties *Region* N Sea
52D1 Longhua China
7L4 Long I Can
76D1 Long I PNG
9F2 Long I USA
14D2 Long Island Sd USA
53A2 Longjiang China
4D4 Long L Can
11B2 Long L USA
7K5 Longlac Can
52B5 Longlin China
8C2 Longmont USA
56E2 Longnawan Indon
36C2 Longny France
11D2 Long Prairie USA
25B5 Longquimay Chile
5K4 Long Range Mts Can
76D3 Longreach Aust
52A2 Longshou Shan *Upland* China
16A1 Longs Peak *Mt* USA
34D4 Longtown Eng
13E1 Longueuil Can
28A3 Longuimay Chile
36C2 Longuyon France
9D3 Longview Texas, USA
8A2 Longview Washington, USA
38D2 Longwy France
52A3 Longxi China
55D3 Long Xuyen Viet
52D4 Longyan China
52B5 Longzhou China
37D2 Lonigo Italy
38D2 Lons-le-Saunier France
9F3 Lookout,C USA
72D4 Loolmalasin *Mt* Tanz
3E2 Loon *R* Can
55C3 Lop Buri Thai
72A4 Lopez *C* Gabon
50C2 Lop Nur *L* China
39A2 Lora del Rio Spain
9E2 Lorain USA
60B2 Loralai Pak
63C2 Lordegān Iran
77E4 Lord Howe *I* Aust
xxixK5 Lord Howe Rise Pacific O
7J3 Lord Mayor B Can
8C3 Lordsburg USA
29C3 Lorena Brazil
37E2 Loreo Italy
22B1 Loreto Mexico
38B2 Lorient France
75B3 Lorne Aust
42B3 Lörrach Germany
38D2 Lorraine *Region* France
8C3 Los Alamos USA
28A2 Los Andes Chile
25B5 Los Angeles Chile
8B3 Los Angeles USA
20C3 Los Angeles Aqueduct USA
19B3 Los Banos USA
28B2 Los Cerrillos Arg
22A1 Los Corchos Mexico
19B3 Los Gatos USA
40C2 Lozinj *I* Croatia, Yugos
28C1 Los Juries Arg
28A3 Los Lagos Chile
22C1 Los Laiaderoz Mexico
28A1 Los Loros Chile
16A3 Los Luncas USA
28B4 Los Menucos Arg
21B2 Los Mochis Mexico
20B3 Los Olivos USA
28A3 Los Sauces Chile
34D3 Lossiemouth Scot
28C1 Los Telares Arg
23E4 Los Testigos *Is* Ven
20C3 Lost Hills USA
18D1 Lost Trail P USA
25B4 Los Vilos Chile
38C3 Lot *R* France
28A3 Lota Chile
34D4 Lothian Region, Scot
72D3 Lotikipi Plain Sudan/Kenya
72C4 Loto Zaïre
74D1 Lotsane *R* Botswana
37B1 Lötschberg Tunnel Switz
32K5 Lotta *R* Fin/Russian Fed
38B2 Loudéac France
70A3 Louga Sen
33B3 Lough Allen *L* Irish Rep
35E5 Loughborough Eng
33B3 Lough Conn *L* Irish Rep
33B3 Lough Corrib *L* Irish Rep
33B3 Lough Derg *L* Irish Rep
6H2 Lougheed I Can
35B5 Lough Ennell *L* Irish Rep
33B3 Lough Erne *L* N Ire
33B2 Lough Foyle *Estuary* N Ire/Irish Rep
33B3 Lough Neagh *L* N Ire
33B3 Lough Ree *L* Irish Rep
35C4 Lough Strangford *L* Irish Rep
34B4 Lough Swilly *Estuary* Irish Rep
37A1 Louhans France
12C3 Louisa USA
56D1 Louisa Reef *I* S E Asia
10M5 Louise *I* Can
10J3 Louise,L USA
77E2 Louisiade Arch Solomon Is
9D3 Louisiana State, USA
74D1 Louis Trichardt S Africa
15C2 Louisville Georgia, USA
9E3 Louisville Kentucky, USA
15B2 Louisville Mississippi, USA
44E2 Loukhi Russian Fed
11D1 Lount L Can
37B3 Loup *R* France
16C1 Loup *R* USA
38B3 Lourdes France
75C2 Louth Aust
35B5 Louth County, Irish Rep
35E5 Louth Eng
Louvain = Leuven
38C2 Louviers France
44E4 Lovat *R* Russian Fed
41E2 Lovech Bulg
16A1 Loveland USA
16A2 Loveland P USA
18E2 Lovell USA
19C2 Lovelock USA
40C1 Lóvere Italy
16B3 Lovington USA
44F2 Lovozero Russian Fed
7K3 Low,C Can
9F2 Lowell Massachusetts, USA
18B2 Lowell Oregon, USA
14E1 Lowell USA
18C1 Lower Arrow L Can
78B2 Lower Hutt NZ
20A1 Lower Lake USA
10N4 Lower Post Can
11C2 Lower Red L USA
35F5 Lowestoft Eng
43D2 Łowicz Pol
75B2 Loxton Aust
74C3 Loxton S Africa
14B2 Loyalsock Creek *R* USA
41D2 Loznica Serbia, Yugos
22B2 loz Reyes Mexico
48H3 Lozva *R* Russian Fed
73C5 Luacano Angola
73C4 Luachimo Angola
72C4 Lualaba *R* Zaïre
73C5 Luampa Zambia
73C5 Luân Angola
52D3 Lu'an China
73B4 Luanda Angola
73B5 Luando *R* Angola
73C5 Luanginga *R* Angola
55C1 Luang Namtha Laos
55C2 Luang Prabang Laos
73B4 Luangue *R* Angola
73D5 Luangwa *R* Zambia
52D1 Luan He *R* China
52D1 Luanping China
73C5 Luanshya Zambia
73C5 Luapula *R* Zaïre
39A1 Luarca Spain
73B4 Lubalo Angola
43F2 L'uban Belorussia
57F8 Lubang Is Phil
73B5 Lubango Angola
8C3 Lubbock USA
42C2 Lübeck Germany
72C4 Lubefu Zaïre

Makurazaki

Maryborough

53C5 Makurazaki Japan
71H4 Makurdi Nig
10E5 Makushin V USA
57F9 Malabang Phil
62B2 Malabar Coast India
68E7 Malabo Bioko
28D1 Malabrigo Arg
55C5 Malacca,Str of S E Asia
18D2 Malad City USA
26D2 Málaga Colombia
39B2 Malaga Spain
16B3 Malaga USA
73E6 Malaimbandy Madag
77F1 Malaita *I* Solomon Is
72D3 Malakal Sudan
60C2 Malakand Pak
57B3 Malamala Indon
56D4 Malang Indon
73B4 Malange Angola
71G3 Malanville Benin
49S3 Mal Anyuy *R* Russian Fed
32H7 Mälaren *L* Sweden
28B3 Malargüe Arg
4F4 Malartic Can
10K4 Malaspina Gl USA
45F8 Malatya Turk
73D5 Malawi Republic, Africa
Malawi,L = Nyasa,L
53D2 Malaya Sidima Russian Fed
57G9 Malaybalay Phil
63B2 Malāyer Iran
51D6 Malaysia Federation, S E Asia
64D2 Malazgirt Turk
43D2 Malbork Pol
28C1 Malbrán Arg
42C2 Malchin Germany
17E2 Malden USA
59F5 Maldives Is Indian O
xxviiiE4 Maldives Ridge Indian O
36A1 Maldon Eng
25F4 Maldonado Urug
37D1 Male Italy
60C4 Malegaon India
42D3 Malé Karpaty *Upland* Czech
77F2 Malekula *I* Vanuatu
73D5 Malema Mozam
44F3 Malen'ga Russian Fed
36B2 Malesherbes France
60B2 Mälestän Afghan
32H5 Malgomaj *L* Sweden
72C2 Malha *Well* Sudan
18C2 Malheur L USA
70B3 Mali Republic, Africa
61E2 Mali Hka *R* Burma
57B3 Malili Indon
43F2 Malin Ukraine
56E2 Malinau Indon
72E4 Malindi Kenya
Malines = Mechelen
33B2 Malin Head *Pt* Irish Rep
61B3 Malkala Range *Mts* India
60D4 Malkāpur India
41F2 Malkara Turk
41F2 Malko Tŭrnovo Bulg
34C3 Mallaig Scot
69C2 Mallawi Egypt
37D1 Málles Venosta Italy
39C2 Mallorca *I* Spain
32G6 Malm Nor
32J5 Malmberget Sweden
36D1 Malmédy Germany
35D6 Malmesbury Eng
74B3 Malmesbury S Africa
32G7 Malmö Sweden
44J4 Malmyzh Russian Fed
57F8 Malolos Phil
13E2 Malone USA
74D2 Maloti Mts Lesotho
32F6 Måloy Nor
44J2 Malozemel'skaya Tundra *Plain* Russian Fed
22B1 Mal Paso Mexico
22D2 Malpaso Mexico
24B3 Malpelo *I* Colombia
28A2 Malpo *R* Chile
60D3 Mālpura India
18D2 Malta Idaho, USA
8C2 Malta Montana, USA
40C3 Malta *Chan* Malta/Italy
40C3 Malta *I* Medit S
74B1 Maltahöhe Namibia
35E4 Malton Eng
32G6 Malung Sweden
62A1 Mālvan India
17D3 Malvern USA
74E1 Malvérnia Mozam
60D4 Malwa Plat India
45G7 Malyy Kavkaz *Mts* Georgia/Azerbaijan
49Q2 Malyy Lyakhovskiy, Ostrov *I* Russian Fed
49M2 Malyy Taymyr, Ostrov *I* Russian Fed
45H6 Malyy Uzen' *R* Kazakhstan
49N4 Mama Russian Fed
44J4 Mamadysh Russian Fed
72C3 Mambasa Zaïre
76C1 Mamberamo *R* Aust
51G7 Mamberamo *R* Indon
72B3 Mambéré *R* CAR
57A3 Mamciju Indon
36A2 Mamers France
72A3 Mamfé Cam
19D4 Mammoth USA
12B3 Mammoth Cave Nat Pk USA
20C2 Mammoth Pool Res USA
26E6 Mamoré *R* Bol
70A3 Mamou Guinea
73E5 Mampikony Madag
71F4 Mampong Ghana
65C3 Mamshit *Hist Site* Israel
67G3 Ma'mūl Oman
74C1 Mamuno Botswana
70B4 Man Ivory Coast
20E5 Mana Hawaiian Is
73E6 Manabo Madag
26F4 Manacapuru Brazil
39C2 Manacor Spain
57B2 Manado Indon
26A1 Managua Nic
73E6 Manakara Madag
76D1 Manam *I* PNG
73E5 Mananara Madag
73E6 Mananjary Madag
78A3 Manapouri NZ
78A3 Manapouri,L NZ
61D2 Manas Bhutan
59G1 Manas China
48K5 Manas Hu *L* China
61B2 Manaslu *Mt* Nepal
14C2 Manasquan USA
27G4 Manaus Brazil
45E8 Manavgat Turk
64C2 Manbij Syria
71J4 Manbilla Plat Nig
35C4 Man,Calf of *I* Eng
12B2 Mancelona USA
62B1 Mancheral India
13E2 Manchester Connecticut, USA
35D5 Manchester Eng
12C3 Manchester Kentucky, USA
9F2 Manchester New Hampshire, USA
14B2 Manchester Pennsylvania, USA
15B1 Manchester Tennessee, USA
14D1 Manchester Vermont, USA
53B2 Manchuria Hist Region, China
63C3 Mand *R* Iran
73D5 Manda Tanz
29B3 Mandaguari Brazil
32F7 Mandal Nor
55B1 Mandalay Burma
50D2 Mandalgovĭ Mongolia
41F3 Mandalya Körfezi *B* Turk
8C2 Mandan USA
72E3 Mandera Eth
23B3 Mandeville Jamaica
73D5 Mandimba Mozam
57C3 Mandioli *I* Indon
61B3 Mandla India
73E5 Mandritsara Madag
60D4 Mandsaur India
41D2 Manduria Italy
60B4 Māndvi India
62B2 Mandya India
43F2 Manevichi Ukraine
66B1 Manfalût Egypt
35E5 Manfield Eng
40D2 Manfredonia Italy
29D1 Manga Brazil
71F3 Manga Burkina
72B2 Manga *Desert Region* Niger
78C1 Mangakino NZ
41F2 Mangalia Rom
72C2 Mangalmé Chad
62A2 Mangalore India
56C3 Manggar Indon
61E3 Mangin Range *Mts* Burma
50C3 Mangnia China
73D5 Mangoche Malawi
73E6 Mangoky *R* Madag
57C3 Mangole *I* Indon
60B4 Māngral India
29B4 Manguerinha Brazil
49O4 Mangui China
16C3 Mangum USA
45J7 Mangyshiak, Poluostrov *Pen* Kazakhstan
8D3 Manhattan USA
74E2 Manhica Mozam
27K8 Manhuacu Brazil
73E5 Mania *R* Madag
37E1 Maniago Italy
73D5 Manica Mozam
7M5 Manicouagan *R* Can
7M4 Manicouagan, Réservoir *Res* Can
67E1 Manifah S Arabia
57F8 Manila Phil
18E2 Manila USA
75D2 Manilla Aust
70B3 Maninian Ivory Coast
57C3 Manipa *I* Indon
61D3 Manipur State, India
61D3 Manipur *R* Burma
45D8 Manisa Turk
33C3 Man,Isle of Irish Sea
12B2 Manistee USA
12B2 Manistee *R* USA
12B1 Manistique USA
6J4 Manitoba Province, Can
6J4 Manitoba,L Can
3G3 Manito L Can
11C2 Manitou Can
11D1 Manitou Falls Can
12B1 Manitou Is USA
7K5 Manitoulin *I* Can
16B2 Manitou Springs USA
12C1 Manitowik L Can
12B2 Manitowoc USA
4F4 Maniwaki Can
26C2 Manizales Colombia
73E6 Manja Madag
76A4 Manjimup Aust
62B1 Mānjra *R* India
9D2 Mankato USA
70B4 Mankono Ivory Coast
10H3 Manley Hot Springs USA
78B1 Manly NZ
60C4 Manmād India
56B3 Manna Indon
75A2 Mannahill Aust
62B3 Mannar Sri Lanka
62B3 Mannār,G of India
62B2 Mannārgudi India
42B3 Mannheim Germany
3E2 Manning Can
15C2 Manning USA
75A2 Mannum Aust
70A4 Mano Sierra Leone
76C1 Manokwari Indon
73C4 Manono Zaïre
55B3 Manoron Burma
37A3 Manosque France
5G3 Manouane *R* Can
54C3 Mano-wan *B* Japan
53B3 Manp'o N Korea
60D2 Mānsa India
73C5 Mansa Zambia
7K3 Mansel I Can
17D2 Mansfield Arkansas, USA
75C3 Mansfield Aust
17D3 Mansfield Louisiana, USA
14E1 Mansfield Massachusetts, USA
9E2 Mansfield Ohio, USA
13D2 Mansfield Pennsylvania, USA
29B2 Manso *R* Brazil
51G5 Mansyu Deep Pacific O
57E9 Mantalingajan,Mt Phil
54A2 Mantap-san *Mt* N Korea
26C6 Mantaro *R* Peru
20B2 Manteca USA
15D1 Manteo USA
38C2 Mantes France
19D3 Manti USA
40C1 Mantova Italy
32J6 Mantta Fin
44G4 Manturovo Russian Fed
22C1 Manuel Mexico
16B4 Manuel Benavides Mexico
29B3 Manuel Ribas Brazil
57B3 Manui *I* Indon
57F9 Manukan Phil
77G4 Manukau NZ
51H7 Manus *I* Pacific O
39B2 Manzanares Spain
21E2 Manzanillo Cuba
21B3 Manzanillo Mexico
49N5 Manzhouli China
65D3 Manzil Jordan
73D6 Manzini Swaziland
72B2 Mao Chad
52A2 Maomao Shan *Mt* China
52C5 Maoming China
73D6 Mapai Mozam
61B1 Mapam Yumco *L* China
51G6 Mapia *Is* Pacific O
57E9 Mapin *I* Phil
6H5 Maple Creek Can
74E1 Mapulanguene Mozam
74E2 Maputo Mozam
74E2 Maputo *R* Mozam
Ma Qu = Huange He
52A3 Maqu China
61C2 Maquan He *R* China
72B4 Maquela do Zombo Angola
25C6 Maquinchao Arg
27J5 Marabá Brazil
26D1 Maracaibo Ven
29A3 Maracaju Brazil
29D1 Máracás Brazil
26E1 Maracay Ven
69A2 Marādah Libya
70C3 Maradi Niger
45H8 Marāgheh Iran
30E5 Marakech Mor
72D3 Maralal Kenya
77F1 Maramasike *I* Solomon Is
Maramba = Livingstone
56G7 Maran Malay
19D4 Marana USA
45H8 Marand Iran
29C1 Maranhão *R* Brazil
27J4 Maranhõa State, Brazil
75C1 Maranoa *R* Aust
26C4 Marañón *R* Peru
45F8 Maras Turk
7K5 Marathon Can
15E4 Marathon Florida, USA
14B1 Marathon New York, USA
16B3 Marathon Texas, USA
56E2 Maratua *I* Indon
29E1 Maraú Brazil
22B2 Maravatio Mexico
57F9 Marawi Phil
28B2 Marayes Arg
67F3 Mar'ayt Yemen
39B2 Marbella Spain
76A3 Marble Bar Aust
19D3 Marble Canyon USA
74D2 Marble Hall S Africa
14E1 Marblehead USA
42B2 Marburg Germany
28E1 Marcelino Ramos Brazil
42B2 Marche Belg
37E3 Marche Region, Italy
39A2 Marchean Spain
36C1 Marche-en-Famenne Belg
15E4 Marco USA
28C2 Marcos Juárez Arg
10J3 Marcus Baker,Mt USA
13E2 Marcy,Mt USA
45G8 Mar Dağlari *Mt* Turk
60C2 Mardan Pak
25E5 Mar del Plata Arg
45G8 Mardin Turk
77F3 Maré *I* Nouvelle Calédonie
72D2 Mareb *R* Eth
51H8 Mareeba Aust
72E3 Mareeq Somalia
16B3 Marfa USA
14C1 Margaretville USA
28C1 Margarita Arg
35F6 Margate Eng
41E1 Marghita Rom
75E3 Maria I Aust
xxviiiJ3 Mariana *Is* Pacific O
3F2 Mariana Lake Can
xxviiiJ4 Marianas Trench Pacific O
61D2 Mariāni India
17D3 Marianna Arkansas, USA
15B2 Marianna Florida, USA
77G4 Maria Van Diemen,C NZ
42D3 Mariazell Austria
67E3 Ma'rib Yemen
40D1 Maribor Slovenia, Yugos
74D1 Marico *R* Botswana/S Africa
20C3 Maricopa USA
72C3 Maridi Sudan
79F5 Marie Byrd Land Region, Ant
23E3 Marie Galante *I* Caribbean
32H6 Mariehamn Fin
36C1 Mariembourg Belg
27H2 Marienburg Surinam
74B1 Mariental Namibia
32G7 Mariestad Sweden
15C2 Marietta Georgia, USA
12C3 Marietta Ohio, USA
17C3 Marietta Oklahoma, USA
71H3 Mariga *R* Nig
23Q2 Marigot Dominica
25G2 Marilia Brazil
73B4 Marimba Angola
57F8 Marinduque *I* Phil
9E2 Marinette USA
25F2 Maringá Brazil
72C3 Maringa *R* Zaïre
17D2 Marion Arkansas, USA
12B3 Marion Illinois, USA
9E2 Marion Indiana, USA
9E2 Marion Ohio, USA
15D2 Marion S Carolina, USA
9E3 Marion,L USA
77E2 Marion Reef Aust
19C3 Mariposa USA
20B2 Mariposa *R* USA
20B2 Mariposa Res USA
57B2 Marisa Indon
45F6 Mariupol Ukraine
45D7 Marista *R* Bulg
44H4 Mariyskaya Respublika, Russian Fed
65C2 Marjayoun Leb
43F2 Marjina Gorki Belorussia
65C3 Marka Jordan
72E3 Marka Somalia
42C1 Markaryd Sweden
35D5 Market Drayton Eng
35E5 Market Harborough Eng
79E Markham,Mt Ant
20C1 Markleeville USA
49T3 Markovo Russian Fed
14E1 Marlboro Massachusetts, USA
14D1 Marlboro New Hampshire, USA
76D3 Marlborough Aust
36B2 Marle France
4E5 Marlette USA
17C3 Marlin USA
14D1 Marlow USA
38C3 Marmande France
41F2 Marmara Adi *I* Turk
64A1 Marmara,S of Turk
41F3 Marmaris Turk
11B2 Marmarth USA
12C3 Marmet USA
4C4 Marmion L Can
40C1 Marmolada *Mt* Italy
10H4 Marmot B USA
22D2 Mar Muerto *Lg* Mexico
37A1 Marnay France
36C2 Marne Department, France
36B2 Marne *R* France
72B3 Maro Chad
73E5 Maroantsetra Madag
73D5 Marondera Zim
27H3 Maroni *R* French Guiana
75D1 Maroochydore Aust
57A3 Maros Indon
72B2 Maroua Cam
73E5 Marovoay Madag
9E4 Marquesas Keys *Is* USA
9E2 Marquette USA
36A1 Marquise France
75C2 Marra *R* Aust
74E2 Marracuene Mozam
70B1 Marrakech Mor
76C3 Marree Aust
17D4 Marrero USA
73D5 Marromeu Mozam
73D5 Marrupa Mozam
66B1 Marsa Alam Egypt
72D3 Marsabit Kenya
40C3 Marsala Italy
36E1 Marsberg Germany
38D3 Marseille France
10F3 Marshall Alaska, USA
12B3 Marshall Illinois, USA
12C2 Marshall Michigan, USA
11C3 Marshall Minnesota, USA
17D2 Marshall Missouri, USA
9D3 Marshall Texas, USA
14B3 Marshall Virginia, USA
xxixK4 Marshall Is Pacific O
11D3 Marshalltown USA
17D2 Marshfield Missouri, USA
12A2 Marshfield Wisconsin, USA
23B1 Marsh Harbour Bahamas
17D4 Marsh I USA
10M3 Marsh L Can
26B4 Marta Ecuador
55B2 Martaban,G of Burma
56B3 Martapura Indon
56D3 Martapura Indon
13E2 Martha's Vineyard *I* USA
38D2 Martigny Switz
43D3 Martin Czech
11B3 Martin S Dakota, USA
15B1 Martin Tennessee, USA
78C2 Martinborough NZ
28B3 Martín de Loyola Arg
22C1 Martínez de la Torre Mexico
23E4 Martinique *I* Caribbean
15B2 Martin,L USA
10K1 Martin Pt USA
13D3 Martinsburg USA
12C2 Martins Ferry USA
13D3 Martinsville USA
xxxG5 Martin Vaz *I* Atlantic O
38D3 Martiques France
78C2 Marton NZ
39B2 Martos Spain
45G7 Martvili Georgia
56D2 Marudi Malay
60B2 Maruf Afghan
54B4 Marugame Japan
19D3 Marvine,Mt USA
60C3 Mārwār India
48H6 Mary Turkmenistan
77E3 Maryborough Queensland, Aust

Maryborough Metlakatla

75B3 **Maryborough** Victoria, Aust
6F4 **Mary Henry,Mt** Can
9F3 **Maryland** State, USA
34D4 **Maryport** Eng
5K3 **Mary's Harbour** Can
5K4 **Marystown** Can
19B3 **Marysville** California, USA
17C2 **Marysville** Kansas, USA
18B1 **Marysville** Washington, USA
17D1 **Maryville** Missouri, USA
15C1 **Maryville** Tennessee, USA
69A2 **Marzuq** Libya
65A3 **Masabb Dumyât** *C* Egypt
Masada = Mezada
65C2 **Mas'adah** Syria
72D4 **Masai Steppe** *Upland* Tanz
72D4 **Masaka** Uganda
64E2 **Masally** Azerbaijan
57B3 **Masamba** Indon
53B4 **Masan** S Korea
73D5 **Masasi** Tanz
21D3 **Masaya** Nic
57F8 **Masbate** Phil
57F8 **Masbate** *I* Phil
71C1 **Mascara** Alg
xxviiiD5 **Mascarene Ridge** Indian O
22B1 **Mascota** Mexico
29E2 **Mascote** Brazil
57C4 **Masela** *I* Indon
74D2 **Maseru** Lesotho
60B2 **Mashaki** Afghan
63D1 **Mashhad** Iran
63E3 **Mashkel** *R* Pak
72B4 **Masi-Manimba** Zaïre
72D3 **Masindi** Uganda
72C4 **Masisi** Zaïre
63B2 **Masjed Soleyman** Iran
73F5 **Masoala** *C* Madag
20C1 **Mason** Nevada, USA
16C3 **Mason** Texas, USA
9D2 **Mason City** USA
67G2 **Masqat** Oman
42B2 **Mass** *R* Neth
40C2 **Massa** Italy
9F2 **Massachusetts** State, USA
13E2 **Massachusetts B** USA
72B2 **Massakori** Chad
37D3 **Massa Marittima** Italy
73D6 **Massangena** Mozam
Massawa = Mits'iwa
66C3 **Massawa Chan** Eth
13E2 **Massena** USA
72B2 **Massénya** Chad
3B3 **Masset** Can
12C1 **Massey** Can
38C2 **Massif Central** *Mts* France
71C1 **Massif de l'Ouarsenis** *Mts* Alg
72B3 **Massif de l'Adamaoua** *Mts* Cam
23C3 **Massif de la Hotte** *Mts* Haiti
73E6 **Massif de l'Isalo** *Upland* Madag
72C3 **Massif des Bongo** *Upland* CAR
38D2 **Massif du Pelvoux** *Mts* France
73E5 **Massif du Tsaratanana** *Mt* Madag
12C2 **Massillon** USA
70B3 **Massina** Region, Mali
73D6 **Massinga** Mozam
74E1 **Massingir** Mozam
45J6 **Masteksay** Kazakhstan
77G5 **Masterton** NZ
53C5 **Masuda** Japan
72B4 **Masuku** Gabon
64C2 **Maşyâf** Syria
4E4 **Matachewan** Can
16A4 **Matachie** Mexico
72B4 **Matadi** Zaïre
26A1 **Matagalpa** Nic
7L5 **Matagami** Can
8D4 **Matagorda B** USA
17F4 **Matagorda I** USA
78C1 **Matakana I** NZ
73B5 **Matala** Angola
62C3 **Matale** Sri Lanka
70A3 **Matam** Sen
70C3 **Matameye** Niger
21C2 **Matamoros** Mexico
69B2 **Ma'tan as Sarra** *Well* Libya
7M5 **Matane** Can
21D2 **Matanzas** Cuba
13F1 **Matapédia** *R* Can
28A2 **Mataquito** *R* Chile
62C3 **Matara** Sri Lanka
76A1 **Mataram** Indon
26D7 **Matarani** Peru
29E1 **Mataripe** Brazil
39C1 **Mataró** Spain
74D3 **Matatiele** S Africa
78A3 **Mataura** NZ
21B2 **Matehuala** Mexico
37E3 **Matelica** Italy
23L1 **Matelot** Trinidad
40D2 **Matera** Italy
43E3 **Mátészalka** Hung
71D1 **Mateur** Tunisia
20C2 **Mather** USA
12C1 **Matheson** Can
17F4 **Mathis** USA
60D3 **Mathura** India
57G9 **Mati** Phil
22C2 **Matías Romero** Mexico
56E3 **Matisiri** *I* Indon
35E5 **Matlock** Eng
71D2 **Matmatma** Tunisia
27G6 **Mato Grosso** Brazil
27G6 **Mato Grosso** State, Brazil
27G7 **Mato Grosso do Sul** State, Brazil
74E2 **Matola** Mozam
67G2 **Matrah** Oman
37E1 **Matrel im Osttirol** Austria
64A3 **Matrûh** Egypt
53C4 **Matsue** Japan
53E3 **Matsumae** Japan
53D4 **Matsumoto** Japan
53D5 **Matsusaka** Japan
53C5 **Matsuyama** Japan
7K5 **Mattagami** *R* Can
4F4 **Mattawa** Can
5H4 **Mattawamkeag** USA
40B1 **Matterhorn** *Mt* Switz/Italy
18C2 **Matterhorn** *Mt* USA
23C2 **Matthew Town** Bahamas
4E4 **Mattice** Can
14D2 **Mattituck** USA
12B3 **Mattoon** USA
60B2 **Matun** Afghan
23L1 **Matura B** Trinidad
26F2 **Maturín** Ven
61B2 **Mau** India
73D5 **Maúa** Mozam
38C1 **Maubeuge** France
75B2 **Maude** Aust
xxxJ8 **Maud Seamount** Atlantic O
20E5 **Maui** *I* Hawaiian Is
28A3 **Maule** *R* Chile
12C2 **Maumee** USA
12C2 **Maumee** *R* USA
57B4 **Maumere** Indon
73C5 **Maun** Botswana
20E5 **Mauna Kea** *Mt* Hawaiian Is
20E5 **Mauna Loa** *Mt* Hawaiian Is
6F3 **Maunoir,L** Can
37B3 **Maures** *Mts* France
38C2 **Mauriac** France
70A2 **Mauritania** Republic, Africa
68K10 **Mauritius** *I* Indian O
12A2 **Mauston** USA
37E1 **Mauterndorf** Austria
73C5 **Mavinga** Angola
74E1 **Mavue** Mozam
61D3 **Mawlaik** Burma
79G10 **Mawson** *Base* Ant
11B2 **Max** USA
74E1 **Maxaila** Mozam
22C1 **Maxcaltzin** Mexico
56C3 **Maya** *I* Indon
49P4 **Maya** *R* Russian Fed
64D2 **Mayādīn** Syria
9F4 **Mayaguana** *I* Bahamas
23D3 **Mayagüez** Puerto Rico
70C3 **Mayahi** Niger
72B4 **Mayama** Congo
63D1 **Mayamey** Iran
57D4 **Mayanobab** Indon
34C4 **Maybole** Scot
9F3 **May,C** USA
75E3 **Maydena** Aust
36D1 **Mayen** Germany
38B2 **Mayenne** France
19D4 **Mayer** USA
3E3 **Mayerthorpe** Can
67E4 **Mayfa'ah** Yemen
12B3 **Mayfield** USA
16A3 **Mayhill** USA
45G7 **Maykop** Russian Fed
48H6 **Maymaneh** Afghan
55B1 **Maymyo** Burma
6E3 **Mayo** Can
14B3 **Mayo** USA
71J4 **Mayo Deo** *R* Cam
57F8 **Mayon** *Mt* Phil
39C2 **Mayor** *Mt* Spain
28C3 **Mayor Buratovich** Arg
78C1 **Mayor I** NZ
25D1 **Mayor P Lagerenza** Par
73E5 **Mayotte** *I* Indian O
23H2 **May Pen** Jamaica
14C3 **May Point,C** USA
37D1 **Mayrhofen** Austria
53B1 **Mayskiy** Russian Fed
14C3 **Mays Landing** USA
3G2 **Mayson L** Can
12C3 **Maysville** USA
72B4 **Mayumba** Gabon
11C2 **Mayville** USA
16B1 **Maywood** USA
73C5 **Mazabuka** Zambia
22B1 **Mazapil** Mexico
60D1 **Mazar** China
65C3 **Mazār** Jordan
40C3 **Mazara del Vallo** Italy
60B1 **Mazar-i-Sharif** Afghan
21B2 **Mazatlán** Mexico
44C4 **Mazeikiai** Lithuania
65C3 **Mazra** Jordan
73D6 **Mbabane** Swaziland
71J4 **Mbabo,Mt** Cam
72B3 **Mbaïki** CAR
73D4 **Mbala** Zambia
73C6 **Mbalabala** Zim
72D3 **Mbale** Uganda
72B3 **Mbalmayo** Cam
72B3 **Mbam** *R* Cam
73D5 **Mbamba Bay** Tanz
72B3 **Mbandaka** Zaïre
72B4 **Mbanza Congo** Angola
72B4 **Mbanza-Ngungu** Zaïre
72D4 **Mbarara** Uganda
71J4 **Mbé** Cam
71J4 **Mbengwi** Cam
72B3 **Mbènza** Congo
72B3 **Mbére** *R* Cam
73D4 **Mbeya** Tanz
72B4 **Mbinda** Congo
71J4 **Mbouda** Cam
70A3 **Mbout** Maur
72C4 **Mbuji-Mayi** Zaïre
71J3 **Mbuli** *R* Nig
72D4 **Mbulu** Tanz
28D1 **Mburucuyá** Arg
70B2 **Mcherrah** Region, Alg
73D5 **Mchinji** Malawi
4C2 **M'Clintock** Can
55D3 **Mdrak** Viet
16B2 **Meade** USA
10G1 **Meade** *R* USA
8B3 **Mead,L** USA
6H4 **Meadow Lake** Can
12C2 **Meadville** USA
54D2 **Me-akan dake** *Mt* Japan
7N4 **Mealy Mts** Can
75C1 **Meandarra** Aust
6G4 **Meander River** Can
35B5 **Meath** Irish Rep
38C2 **Meaux** France
66C2 **Mecca** S Arabia
19C4 **Mecca** USA
14D1 **Mechanicville** USA
48G2 **Mechdusharskiy, Ostrov** *I* Russian Fed
42A2 **Mechelen** Belg
71B2 **Mecheria** Alg
42C2 **Mecklenburger Bucht** *B* Germany
42C2 **Mecklenburg-Vorpommern** State, Germany
73D5 **Meconta** Mozam
73D5 **Mecuburi** Mozam
73E5 **Mecufi** Mozam
73D5 **Mecula** Mozam
56A2 **Medan** Indon
28C3 **Medanos** Arg
28D2 **Médanos** Arg
71C1 **Médéa** Alg
26C2 **Medellín** Colombia
71E2 **Medenine** Tunisia
8A2 **Medford** USA
41F2 **Medgidia** Rom
28B2 **Media Agua** Arg
41E1 **Mediaş** Rom
18C1 **Medical Lake** USA
11A3 **Medicine Bow** USA
16A1 **Medicine Bow Mts** USA
11A3 **Medicine Bow Peak** *Mt* USA
6G5 **Medicine Hat** Can
16C2 **Medicine Lodge** USA
29D2 **Medina** Brazil
11C2 **Medina** N Dakota, USA
14A1 **Medina** New York, USA
66C2 **Medina** S Arabia
39B1 **Medinaceli** Spain
39A1 **Medina del Campo** Spain
39A1 **Medina de Rio Seco** Spain
16C4 **Medina L** USA
61C3 **Medinīpur** India
68E4 **Mediterranean S** Europe
3F3 **Medley** Can
45K5 **Mednogorsk** Russian Fed
49S4 **Mednyy, Ostrov** *I* Russian Fed
61E2 **Mêdog** China
72B3 **Medouneu** Gabon
45G5 **Medvedista** *R* Russian Fed
49S2 **Medvezh'i Ova** *I* Russian Fed
44E3 **Medvezh'yegorsk** Russian Fed
76A3 **Meekatharra** Aust
16A1 **Meeker** USA
60D3 **Meerut** India
18E2 **Meeteetse** USA
72D3 **Mēga** Eth
41E3 **Megalópolis** Greece
41E3 **Mégara** Greece
61D2 **Meghālaya** State, India
61D3 **Meghna** *R* Bang
65C2 **Megido** *Hist Site* Israel
4F4 **Mégiscane** *R* Can
71C2 **Mehaïguene** *R* Alg
10E3 **Mehoryuk** USA
63C3 **Mehran** *R* Iran
63C2 **Mehriz** Iran
29C2 **Meia Ponte** *R* Brazil
72B3 **Meiganga** Cam
55B1 **Meiktila** Burma
37C1 **Meiringen** Switz
52A4 **Meishan** China
42C2 **Meissen** Germany
52D5 **Mei Xian** China
52D5 **Meizhou** China
26D8 **Mejillones** Chile
72B3 **Mekambo** Gabon
4E4 **Mekatina** Can
71C4 **Mek'elē** Eth
71A2 **Meknès** Mor
Mekong = Lancang
55D3 **Mekong, R** Camb
71G3 **Mekrou** *R* Benin
55C5 **Melaka** Malay
xxviiiJ5 **Melanesia** *Region* Pacific O
56D3 **Melawi** *R* Indon
76D4 **Melbourne** Aust
9E4 **Melbourne** USA
8C4 **Melchor Muźguiz** Mexico
44K5 **Meleuz** Russian Fed
72B2 **Melfi** Chad
6H4 **Melfort** Can
71B1 **Melilla** N W Africa
25B6 **Melimoyu** *Mt* Chile
28C2 **Melincué** Arg
28A2 **Melipilla** Chile
11B2 **Melita** Can
45F6 **Melitopol'** Ukraine
7M2 **Meliville Bugt** *B* Greenland
72D3 **Melka Guba** Eth
71D1 **Mellègue** *R* Tunisia
66D4 **Melli** *R* Eth
74E2 **Melmoth** S Africa
28C2 **Melo** Arg
25F4 **Melo** Urug
29A3 **Melo** *R* Brazil
20B2 **Melones Res** USA
10H2 **Melozitna** *R* USA
11D2 **Melrose** USA
37C1 **Mels** Switz
36E1 **Melsungen** Germany
56E1 **Melta,Mt** Malay
35E5 **Melton Mowbray** Eng
38C2 **Melun** France
6H4 **Melville** Can
23Q2 **Melville,C** Dominica
6F3 **Melville Hills** *Mts* Can
76C2 **Melville I** Aust
6G2 **Melville I** Can
7N4 **Melville,L** Can
7K3 **Melville Pen** Can
73E5 **Memba** Mozam
76A1 **Memboro** Indon
42C3 **Memmingen** Germany
56C2 **Mempawan** Indon
9E3 **Memphis** Tennessee, USA
16B3 **Memphis** Texas, USA
17D3 **Mena** USA
43G2 **Mena** Ukraine
35C5 **Menai Str** Wales
70C3 **Ménaka** Mali
12B2 **Menasha** USA
28B4 **Mencué** Arg
56D3 **Mendawai** *R* Indon
38C3 **Mende** France
72D3 **Mendebo** *Mts* Eth
10E4 **Mendenhall,C** USA
76D1 **Mendi** PNG
35D6 **Mendip Hills** *Upland* Eng
18B2 **Mendocino,C** USA
xxixM3 **Mendocino Seascarp** Pacific O
20B2 **Mendota** California, USA
12B2 **Mendota** Illinois, USA
25C4 **Mendoza** Arg
25C5 **Mendoza** State, Arg
41F3 **Menemen** Turk
36B1 **Menen** Belg
52D3 **Mengcheng** China
56C3 **Menggala** Indon
55B1 **Menghai** China
52A5 **Mengla** China
55B1 **Menglian** China
52A5 **Mengzi** China
5H3 **Menihek Lakes** Can
76D4 **Menindee** Aust
75B2 **Menindee L** Aust
75A3 **Meningie** Aust
12B1 **Menominee** USA
12B2 **Menomonee Falls** USA
12A2 **Menomonie** USA
73B5 **Menongue** Angola
39C1 **Menorca** *I* Spain
10K3 **Mentasta Mts** USA
16A2 **Mentmore** USA
56C3 **Mentok** Indon
37B3 **Menton** France
12C2 **Mentor** USA
36B2 **Ménu** France
52A2 **Menyuan** China
44J4 **Menzelinsk** Russian Fed
42B2 **Meppen** Germany
36A3 **Mer** France
56E2 **Merah** Indon
17D2 **Meramec** *R* USA
40C1 **Merano** Italy
76D1 **Merauke** Indon
8A3 **Merced** USA
20B2 **Merced** *R* USA
25B4 **Mercedario** *Mt* Chile
25C4 **Mercedes** Arg
25E4 **Mercedes** Buenos Aires, Arg
25E3 **Mercedes** Corrientes, Arg
25E4 **Mercedes** Urug
78C1 **Mercury B** NZ
78C1 **Mercury Is** NZ
6F2 **Mercy B** Can
7M3 **Mercy,C** Can
16B2 **Meredith,L** *L* USA
55B3 **Mergui** Burma
55B3 **Mergui Arch** Burma
21D2 **Mérida** Mexico
39A2 **Mérida** Spain
26D2 **Mérida** Ven
9E3 **Meridian** USA
75C3 **Merimbula** Aust
75B2 **Meringur** Aust
16B3 **Merkel** USA
72D2 **Merowe** Sudan
76A4 **Merredin** Aust
34C4 **Merrick** *Mt* Scot
12B1 **Merrill** USA
12B2 **Merrillville** USA
14E1 **Merrimack** *R* USA
11B3 **Merriman** USA
3D3 **Merritt** Can
15C3 **Merritt Island** USA
75D2 **Merriwa** Aust
66D4 **Mersa Fatma** Eth
39B2 **Mers el Kebir** Alg
35D5 **Mersey** *R* Eng
35D5 **Merseyside** County, Eng
45E8 **Mersin** Turk
55C5 **Mersing** Malay
60C3 **Merta** India
35D6 **Merthyr Tydfil** Wales
39A2 **Mertola** Port
72D4 **Meru** *Mt* Tanz
45F7 **Merzifon** Turk
36D2 **Merzig** Germany
8B3 **Mesa** USA
16A2 **Mesa Verde Nat Pk** USA
36E1 **Meschede** Germany
64D1 **Mescit Dağ** *Mt* Turk
10G4 **Meshik** USA
72C3 **Meshra'er Req** Sudan
37C1 **Mesocco** Switz
41E3 **Mesolóngion** Greece
19D3 **Mesquite** Nevada, USA
17C3 **Mesquite** Texas, USA
71C2 **Messaad** Alg
73D5 **Messalo** *R* Mozam
40D3 **Messina** Italy
74D1 **Messina** S Africa
41E3 **Messíni** Greece
41E3 **Messiniakós Kólpos** *G* Greece
Mesta = Néstos
41E2 **Mesta, R** Bulg
40C1 **Mestre** Italy
26D3 **Meta** *R* Colombia
44E4 **Meta** *R* Russian Fed
26E2 **Meta** *R* Ven
7L3 **Meta Incognita Pen** Can
17D4 **Metairie** USA
18C1 **Metaline Falls** USA
25D3 **Metán** Arg
73D5 **Metangula** Mozam
40D2 **Metaponto** Italy
37E3 **Metauro** *R* Italy
66C4 **Metemma** Eth
34D3 **Methil** Scot
14E1 **Methuen** USA
78B2 **Methven** NZ
10M4 **Metlakatla** USA

Metlaoui

Monett

71D2 **Metlaoui** Tunisia
12B3 **Metropolis** USA
62B2 **Mettūr** India
38D2 **Metz** France
36E2 **Metzingen** Germany
56A2 **Meulaboh** Indon
36A2 **Meulan** France
36A3 **Meung-sur-Loire** France
36D2 **Meurthe** *R* France
36D2 **Meurthe-et-Moselle** Department, France
36C2 **Meuse** Department, France
36C1 **Meuse** *R* Belg
38D2 **Meuse** *R* France
17C3 **Mexia** USA
21A1 **Mexicali** Mexico
19E3 **Mexican Hat** USA
21B2 **Mexico** Federal Republic, Central America
21C3 **México** Mexico
22B2 **México** State, Mexico
17D2 **Mexico** USA
21C2 **Mexico,G of** C America
37A2 **Meximieux** France
65C3 **Mezada** *Hist Site* Israel
22C2 **Mezcala** Mexico
22D2 **Mezcalapa** *R* Mexico
44G2 **Mezen'** Russian Fed
44H3 **Mezen'** *R* Russian Fed
43G1 **Mezha** *R* Russian Fed
44J1 **Mezhdusharskiy, Ostrov** *I* Russian Fed
22B1 **Mezquital** Mexico
22B1 **Mezquital** *R* Mexico
53E1 **Mgachi** Russian Fed
60D4 **Mhow** India
22C2 **Miahuatlán** Mexico
19D4 **Miami** Arizona, USA
9E4 **Miami** Florida, USA
17D2 **Miami** Oklahoma, USA
9E4 **Miami Beach** USA
45H8 **Miandowāb** Iran
73E5 **Miandrivazo** Madag
45H8 **Mīāneh** Iran
60C2 **Mianwali** Pak
52A3 **Mianyang** Sichuan, China
52C3 **Mianyang** Hubei, China
52A3 **Mianzhu** China
52E2 **Miaodao Qundao** *Arch* China
52B4 **Miao Ling** *Upland* China
44L5 **Miass** Russian Fed
43E3 **Michalovce** Czech
18D1 **Michel** Can
23D3 **Miches** Dom Rep
9E2 **Michigan** State, USA
12B2 **Michigan City** USA
9E2 **Michigan,L** USA
12C1 **Michipicoten** Can
7K5 **Michipicoten I** Can
22B2 **Michoacan** State, Mexico
41F2 **Michurin** Bulg
45G5 **Michurinsk** Russian Fed
xxviiiJ4 **Micronesia** *Region* Pacific O
56C2 **Midai** *I* Indon
xxxF4 **Mid Atlantic Ridge** Atlantic O
36B1 **Middelburg** Neth
18B2 **Middle Alkali L** USA
xxixO4 **Middle America Trench** Pacific O
62E2 **Middle Andaman** *I* Indian O
14E2 **Middleboro** USA
74C3 **Middleburg** Cape Province, S Africa
14B2 **Middleburg** Pennsylvania, USA
74D2 **Middleburg** Transvaal, S Africa
14B3 **Middleburg** Virginia, USA
14C1 **Middleburgh** USA
13E2 **Middlebury** USA
9E3 **Middlesboro** USA
35E4 **Middlesbrough** Eng
5H5 **Middleton** Can
14D2 **Middletown** Connecticut, USA
14C3 **Middletown** Delaware, USA
13E2 **Middletown** New York, USA
12C3 **Middletown** Ohio, USA
14B2 **Middletown** Pennsylvania, USA
14C1 **Middleville** USA
71B2 **Midelt** Mor
35D6 **Mid Glamorgan** County, Wales
66D3 **Midī** Yemen
xxviiiE5 **Mid Indian Basin** Indian O
xxviiiE5 **Mid Indian Ridge** Indian O
7L5 **Midland** Can
12C2 **Midland** Michigan, USA
8C3 **Midland** Texas, USA
73E6 **Midongy Atsimo** Madag
xxixK4 **Mid Pacific Mts** Pacific O
18C2 **Midvale** USA
xxixL3 **Midway Is** Pacific O
11A3 **Midwest** USA
17C2 **Midwest City** USA
64D2 **Midyat** Turk
41E2 **Midžor** *Mt* Serbia, Yugos
43E2 **Mielec** Pol
41F1 **Miercurea-Ciuc** Rom
39A1 **Mieres** Spain
14B2 **Mifflintown** USA
22B1 **Miguel Auza** Mexico
22C1 **Miguihuana** Mexico
54B4 **Mihara** Japan
52D1 **Mijun Shuiku** *Res* China
41E2 **Mikhaylovgrad** Bulg
45G5 **Mikhaylovka** Russian Fed
48J4 **Mikhaylovskiy** Russian Fed
65C4 **Mikhrot Timna** Israel
32K6 **Mikkeli** Fin
3F2 **Mikkwa** *R* Can
41F3 **Míkonos** *I* Greece
42D3 **Mikulov** Czech
73D4 **Mikumi** Tanz
44J3 **Mikun** Russian Fed
53D4 **Mikuni-sammyaku** *Mts* Japan
54C4 **Mikura-jima** *I* Japan
11D2 **Milaca** USA
26C4 **Milagro** Ecuador
Milan = Milano
15B1 **Milan** USA
39C2 **Milana** Alg
73D5 **Milange** Mozam
57B2 **Milango** *R* Indon
40B1 **Milano** Italy
45D8 **Milas** Turk
11C2 **Milbank** USA
76D4 **Mildura** Aust
52A5 **Mile** China
64D3 **Mileh Tharthār** *L* Iraq
76E3 **Miles** Aust
8C2 **Miles City** USA
14D2 **Milford** Connecticut, USA
13D3 **Milford** Delaware, USA
13E2 **Milford** Massachusetts, USA
17C1 **Milford** Nebraska, USA
14E1 **Milford** New Hampshire, USA
14C2 **Milford** Pennsylvania, USA
19D3 **Milford** Utah, USA
35C6 **Milford Haven** Wales
35C6 **Milford Haven** *Sd* Wales
17C2 **Milford L** USA
78A2 **Milford Sd** NZ
71C1 **Miliana** Alg
11A2 **Milk** *R* USA
49R4 **Mil'kovo** Russian Fed
3F4 **Milk River** Can
38C3 **Millau** France
14D2 **Millbrook** USA
15C2 **Milledgeville** USA
11D2 **Mille Lacs L** USA
11C3 **Miller** USA
10K3 **Miller,Mt** USA
45G6 **Millerovo** Russian Fed
14B2 **Millersburg** USA
75A1 **Millers Creek** Aust
14D1 **Millers Falls** USA
14D2 **Millerton** USA
20C2 **Millerton L** USA
75B3 **Millicent** Aust
15B1 **Millington** USA
13F1 **Millinocket** USA
75D1 **Millmerran** Aust
37E1 **Millstätter See** *L* Austria
13F1 **Milltown** Can
18D1 **Milltown** USA
20A2 **Mill Valley** USA
13E3 **Millville** USA
7Q2 **Milne Land** *I* Greenland
20E5 **Milolii** Hawaiian Is
41E3 **Milos** *I* Greece
76D3 **Milparinka** Aust
14B2 **Milroy** USA
15B2 **Milton** Florida, USA
78A3 **Milton** NZ
14B2 **Milton** Pennsylvania, USA
9E2 **Milwaukee** USA
4D3 **Miminiska L** Can
54D2 **Mimmaya** Japan
20C1 **Mina** USA
39C2 **Mina** *R* Alg
64E4 **Mīnā' al Ahmadī** Kuwait
63D3 **Mīnāb** Iran
57B2 **Minahassa Pen** Indon
4C4 **Minaki** Can
53C5 **Minamata** Japan
56B2 **Minas** Indon
25E4 **Minas** Urug
5J4 **Minas Basin** Can
5J4 **Minas Chan** Can
27J7 **Minas Gerais** State, Brazil
29D2 **Minas Novas** Brazil
21C3 **Minatitlan** Mexico
55A1 **Minbu** Burma
55A1 **Minbya** Burma
28A2 **Mincha** Chile
34B3 **Minch,Little** *Sd* Scot
34B2 **Minch,North** *Sd* Scot
33B2 **Minch,The** *Sd* Scot
10H3 **Minchumina,L** USA
37D2 **Mincio** *R* Italy
57F9 **Mindanao** *I* Phil
17D3 **Minden** Louisiana, USA
20C1 **Minden** Nevada, USA
42B2 **Minden** Germany
75B2 **Mindona L** Aust
57F8 **Mindoro** *I* Phil
57F8 **Mindoro Str** Phil
35D6 **Minehead** Eng
27H7 **Mineiros** Brazil
17C3 **Mineola** USA
22C1 **Mineral de Monte** Mexico
16C3 **Mineral Wells** USA
14B2 **Minersville** USA
5J3 **Mingan** Can
75B2 **Mingary** Aust
45H7 **Mingechaurskoye Vodokhranilische** *Res* Azerbaijan
53B2 **Mingshui** China
52A2 **Minhe** China
37D3 **Minialo** Italy
62A3 **Minicoy** *I* India
52D4 **Min Jiang** *R* Fujian, China
52A4 **Min Jiang** *R* Sichuan, China
20C2 **Minkler** USA
75A2 **Minlaton** Aust
52A2 **Minle** China
71H4 **Minna** Nig
9D2 **Minneapolis** USA
6J4 **Minnedosa** Can
9D2 **Minnesota** State, USA
11C3 **Minnesota** *R* USA
4C4 **Minnitaki L** Can
39A1 **Miño** *R* Spain
8C2 **Minot** USA
52A2 **Minqin** China
52A3 **Min Shan** *Upland* China
44D5 **Minsk** Belorussia
43E2 **Minsk Mazowiecki** Pol
10J3 **Minto** USA
6G2 **Minto Inlet** *B* Can
7L4 **Minto,L** Can
16A2 **Minturn** USA
50C1 **Minusinsk** Russian Fed
52A3 **Min Xian** China
65A3 **Minyael Qamn** Egypt
4F4 **Miquelon** Can
7N5 **Miquelon** *I* France
20D3 **Mirage L** USA
62A1 **Miraj** India
25E5 **Miramar** Arg
5J4 **Miramichi B** Can
60B2 **Miram Shah** Pak
29A2 **Miranda** *R* Brazil
39B1 **Miranda de Ebro** Spain
29A3 **Mirandia** Brazil
37D2 **Mirandola** Italy
60B2 **Mir Bachchen Kūt** Afghan
67F3 **Mirbāt** Oman
37A1 **Mirebeau** France
36C2 **Mirecourt** France
56D2 **Miri** Malay
63E3 **Miri** *Mt* Pak
70A3 **Mirik,C** Maur
28D1 **Mirinay** *R* Arg
63E3 **Mīrjāveh** Iran
37E2 **Mirna** *R* Croatia, Yugos
49K3 **Mirnoye** Russian Fed
49N3 **Mirnyy** Russian Fed
79G9 **Mirnyy** *Base* Ant
3H2 **Miron L** Can
43G3 **Mironovka** Ukraine
60C2 **Mirpur** Pak
60B3 **Mirpur Khas** Pak
41E3 **Mirtoan S** Greece
53B4 **Miryang** S Korea
61B2 **Mirzāpur** India
22C2 **Misantla** Mexico
5J4 **Miscou I** Can
60C1 **Misgar** Pak
53C2 **Mishan** China
12B2 **Mishawaka** USA
10F2 **Misheguk Mt** USA
54B4 **Mi-shima** *I* Japan
61E2 **Mishmi Hills** India
77E2 **Misima** *I* Solomon Is
25F3 **Misiones** State, Arg
43E3 **Miskolc** Hung
65D2 **Mismīyah** Syria
51G7 **Misoöl** *I* Indon
3H2 **Misow L** Can
69A1 **Misrātah** Libya
7K5 **Missinaibi** *R* Can
12C1 **Missinaibi L** Can
3H2 **Missinipe** Can
11B3 **Mission** S Dakota, USA
17F4 **Mission** Texas, USA
18B1 **Mission City** Can
13D2 **Mississauga** Can
9D3 **Mississippi** State, USA
9D3 **Mississippi** *R* USA
17E3 **Mississippi Delta** USA
8B2 **Missoula** USA
71B2 **Missour** Mor
9D3 **Missouri** State, USA
9D3 **Missouri** *R* USA
11C3 **Missouri Valley** USA
5G4 **Mistassini** Can
5G4 **Mistassini** *R* Can
5G3 **Mistassini Provincial Park** Can
5J2 **Mistastin L** Can
26D7 **Misti** *Mt* Peru
5J2 **Mistinibi L** Can
75C1 **Mitchell** Aust
8D2 **Mitchell** USA
76D2 **Mitchell** *R* Aust
9E3 **Mitchell,Mt** USA
51H8 **Mitchell River** Aust
65A3 **Mit el Nasâra** Egypt
65A3 **Mît Ghamr** Egypt
60B3 **Mithankot** Pak
41F3 **Mitilini** Greece
22C2 **Mitla** Mexico
65B3 **Mitla P** Egypt
77G2 **Mitre** *I* Solomon Is
10G4 **Mitrofania I** USA
72D2 **Mits'iwa** Eth
37E1 **Mittersill** Austria
26D3 **Mitu** Colombia
72C4 **Mitumbar** *Mts* Zaïre
73C4 **Mitwaba** Zaïre
72B3 **Mitzic** Gabon
54C3 **Miura** Japan
52C3 **Mi Xian** China
50G3 **Miyake** *I* Japan
54C4 **Miyake-jima** *I* Japan
50F4 **Miyako** *I* Japan
53C5 **Miyakonojō** Japan
53C5 **Miyazaki** Japan
54C3 **Miyazu** Japan
53C5 **Miyoshi** Japan
52D1 **Miyun** China
54D2 **Mi-zaki** *Pt* Japan
72D3 **Mīzan Teferī** Eth
69A1 **Mizdah** Libya
41F1 **Mizil** Rom
61D3 **Mizo Hills** India
61D3 **Mizoram** Union Territory, India
65C3 **Mizpe Ramon** Israel
79F11 **Mizuho** *Base* Ant
53E4 **Mizusawa** Japan
32H7 **Mjolby** Sweden
73C5 **Mkushi** Zambia
74E2 **Mkuzi** S Africa
42C2 **Mladá Boleslav** Czech
43E2 **Mława** Pol
41D2 **Mljet** *I* Croatia, Yugos
74D2 **Mmabatho** S Africa
60D2 **Mnadi** India
57C4 **Moa** *I* Indon
70A4 **Moa** *R* Sierra Leone
65C3 **Moab** Region, Jordan
8C3 **Moab** USA
74E2 **Moamba** Mozam
72B4 **Moanda** Congo
72B4 **Moanda** Gabon
73C4 **Moba** Zaïre
54D3 **Mobara** Japan
72C3 **Mobaye** CAR
72C3 **Mobayi** Zaire
9D3 **Moberly** USA
9E3 **Mobile** USA
9E3 **Mobile B** USA
15B2 **Mobile Pt** USA
8C2 **Mobridge** USA
73E5 **Moçambique** Mozam
Moçâmedes = Namibe
55C1 **Moc Chau** Viet
74D1 **Mochudi** Botswana
73E5 **Mocimboa da Praia** Mozam
26C3 **Mocoa** Colombia
29C3 **Mococa** Brazil
28D2 **Mocoreta** *R* Arg
22C1 **Moctezulma** *R* Mexico
22B1 **Moctezuma** Mexico
73D5 **Mocuba** Mozam
37B2 **Modane** France
74D2 **Modder** *R* S Africa
40C2 **Modena** Italy
36D2 **Moder** *R* France
8A3 **Modesto** USA
20B2 **Modesto Res** USA
40C3 **Modica** Italy
42D3 **Mödling** Austria
76D4 **Moe** Aust
37C1 **Moesa** *R* Switz
34D4 **Moffat** Scot
60D2 **Moga** India
68J7 **Mogadiscio** Somalia
61E2 **Mogaung** Burma
29C3 **Mogi das Cruzes** Brazil
43G2 **Mogilev** Belorussia
45D6 **Mogilev Podol'skiy** Ukraine
29C3 **Mogi-Mirim** Brazil
73E5 **Mogincual** Mozam
37E2 **Mogliano** Italy
28B2 **Mogna** Arg
50E1 **Mogocha** Russian Fed
48K4 **Mogochin** Russian Fed
61E3 **Mogok** Burma
74D1 **Mogol** *R* S Africa
39A2 **Moguer** Spain
78C1 **Mohaka** *R* NZ
74D3 **Mohale's Hoek** Lesotho
11B2 **Mohall** USA
71C1 **Mohammadia** Alg
71A2 **Mohammedia** Mor
61D3 **Mohanganj** Bang
19D3 **Mohave,L** USA
14C1 **Mohawk** USA
13E2 **Mohawk** *R* USA
73E5 **Mohéli,I** Comoros
10E3 **Mohican,C** USA
73D4 **Mohoro** Tanz
48J5 **Mointy** Kazakhstan
32G5 **Mo i Rana** Nor
5H3 **Moisie** *R* Can
38C3 **Moissac** France
19C3 **Mojave** USA
20D3 **Mojave** *R* USA
8B3 **Mojave Desert** USA
56D4 **Mojokerto** Indon
66C4 **Mokada** *Mt* Eth
61C2 **Mokama** India
78B1 **Mokau** *R* NZ
20B1 **Mokelumne Aqueduct** USA
20B1 **Mokelumne Hill** USA
20B1 **Mokelumne North Fork** *R* USA
74D2 **Mokhotlong** Lesotho
71E1 **Moknine** Tunisia
61D2 **Mokokchūng** India
72B2 **Mokolo** Cam
53B5 **Mokp'o** S Korea
44G5 **Moksha** *R* Russian Fed
22C1 **Molango** Mexico
41E3 **Moláoi** Greece
45D6 **Moldavia** *Republic* Europe
32F6 **Molde** Nor
41E1 **Moldoveanu** *Mt* Rom
71F4 **Mole Nat Pk** Ghana
74D1 **Molepolole** Botswana
36D2 **Molesheim** France
40D2 **Molfetta** Italy
28A3 **Molina** Chile
37E1 **Möll** *R* Austria
26D7 **Mollendo** Peru
44D5 **Molodechno** Belorussia
79G11 **Molodezhnaya** *Base* Ant
20E5 **Molokai** *I* Hawaiian Is
44H4 **Moloma** *R* Russian Fed
75C2 **Molong** Aust
74C2 **Molopo** *R* S Africa/ Botswana
72B3 **Molounddu** Cam
4B3 **Molson L** Can
76B1 **Molucca S** Indon
51F7 **Moluccas** *Is* Indon
73D5 **Moma** Mozam
27K5 **Mombaca** Brazil
72D4 **Mombasa** Kenya
54D2 **Mombetsu** Japan
72C3 **Mompono** Zaïre
42C2 **Mon** *I* Den
34B3 **Monach** *Is* Scot
38D3 **Monaco** Principality, Europe
34C3 **Monadhliath** *Mts* Scot
35B4 **Monaghan** County, Irish Rep
35B4 **Monaghan** Irish Rep
16B3 **Monahans** USA
23D3 **Mona Pass** Caribbean
3C3 **Monarch Mt** Can
16A2 **Monarch P** USA
6G4 **Monashee Mts** Can
33B3 **Monastereven** Irish Rep
54D2 **Monbetsu** Japan
37B2 **Moncalieri** Italy
27J4 **Monção** Brazil
32L5 **Monchegorsk** Russian Fed
42B2 **Mönchen-gladbach** Germany
21B2 **Monclova** Mexico
7M5 **Moncton** Can
39A1 **Mondego** *R* Port
40B2 **Mondovi** Italy
23H1 **Moneague** Jamaica
13D2 **Monessen** USA
4F4 **Monet** Can
17D2 **Monett** USA

Mudanjiang **Narovl'a**

53B3 **Mudanjiang** China
67F3 **Mudayy** Oman
11A3 **Muddy Gap P** USA
75C2 **Mudgee** Aust
20D2 **Mud L** USA
55B2 **Mudon** Burma
44F3 **Mud'yuga** Russian Fed
77F3 **Mue** Nouvelle Calédonie
73D5 **Mueda** Mozam
73C5 **Mufulira** Zambia
52C4 **Mufu Shan** *Hills* China
Mugadishu = Muqdisho
45K6 **Mugodzhary** *Mts* Kazakhstan
64C4 **Mughayra** S Arabia
64A2 **Muğla** Turk
45K6 **Mugodzhary** *Mts* Kazakhstan
61B2 **Mugu** Nepal
52A3 **Muguaping** China
66C2 **Muhammad Qol** Sudan
64D3 **Muhaywir** Iraq
36E2 **Mühlacker** Germany
42C3 **Mühldorf** Germany
42C2 **Muhlhausen** Germany
32K6 **Muhos** Fin
55C4 **Mui Bai Bung** *C* Camb
35B5 **Muine Bheag** Irish Rep
73C5 **Mujimbeji** Zambia
43E3 **Mukachevo** Ukraine
56D2 **Mukah** Malay
54D2 **Mukawa** Japan
50H4 **Muko-jima** *I* Japan
61B2 **Muktinath** Nepal
60B2 **Mukur** Afghan
53B2 **Mulan** China
17D2 **Mulberry** USA
10G3 **Mulchatna** *R* USA
28A3 **Mulchén** Chile
42C2 **Mulde** *R* Germany
11B3 **Mule Creek** USA
16B3 **Muleshoe** USA
51H8 **Mulgrave I** Aust
39B2 **Mulhacén** *Mt* Spain
36D1 **Mülheim** Germany
36D3 **Mulhouse** France
52A4 **Muli** China
53C3 **Muling** China
53C2 **Muling He** *R* China
34C3 **Mull** *I* Scot
62C3 **Mullaitvu** Sri Lanka
75C2 **Mullaley** Aust
76A3 **Mullewa** Aust
36D3 **Müllheim** Germany
14C3 **Mullica** *R* USA
35B5 **Mullingar** Irish Rep
34C4 **Mull of Kintyre** *Pt* Scot
34B4 **Mull of Oa** *C* Scot
75D1 **Mullumbimby** Aust
73C5 **Mulobezi** Zambia
60C2 **Multan** Pak
57C3 **Muluku** *Is* Indon
73C5 **Mumbwa** Zambia
45H6 **Mumra** Russian Fed
57B4 **Muna** *I* Indon
42C3 **München** Germany
3C2 **Muncho Lake** Can
54A3 **Munchŏn** N Korea
12B2 **Muncie** USA
75A1 **Munconnie,L** Aust
14B2 **Muncy** USA
42B2 **Münden** Germany
75D1 **Mundubbera** Aust
75C1 **Mungallala** Aust
75C1 **Mungallala** *R* Aust
72C3 **Mungbere** Zaïre
61B3 **Mungeli** India
61C2 **Munger** India
75C1 **Mungindi** Aust
Munich = München
12B1 **Munising** USA
25B8 **Muñoz Gomero,Pen** Chile
3J2 **Munroe L** Can
54A3 **Munsan** S Korea
36E2 **Münsingen** Germany
36D2 **Munster** France
37C1 **Münster** Switz
42B2 **Münster** Germany
36D1 **Münsterland** Region, Germany
41E1 **Muntii Apuseni** *Mts* Rom
41E1 **Muntii Călimanilor** *Mts* Rom
41E1 **Muntii Carpaţii Meridionali** *Mts* Rom
41E1 **Muntii Rodnei** *Mts* Rom
41E1 **Muntii Zarandului** *Mts* Rom
64C2 **Munzur Silsilesi** *Mts* Turk
48D3 **Muomio** Fin
55C1 **Muong Khoua** Laos
55D3 **Muong Man** Viet
55D2 **Muong Nong** Laos
55C1 **Muong Ou Neua** Laos
55C1 **Muong Sai** Laos
55C2 **Muong Sen** Viet
55C1 **Muong Sing** Laos
55C1 **Muong Son** Laos
32J5 **Muonio** Fin
32J5 **Muonio** *R* Sweden/Fin
66B3 **Muqaddam** *Watercourse* Sudan
72E3 **Muqdisho** Somalia
40C1 **Mur** *R* Austria
53D4 **Murakami** Japan
25B7 **Murallón** *Mt* Chile/Arg
44H4 **Murashi** Russian Fed
64D2 **Murat** *R* Turk
40B3 **Muravera** Sardegna
54D3 **Murayama** Japan
67F4 **Murcanyo** Somalia
63C2 **Murcheh Khvort** Iran
78B2 **Murchison** NZ
76A3 **Murchison** *R* Aust
39B2 **Murcia** Region, Spain
39B2 **Murcia** Spain
11B3 **Murdo** USA
41E1 **Mureş** *R* Rom
41E1 **Muresui** *R* Rom
15B1 **Murfreesboro** USA
15D1 **Murfreesboro** USA
36E2 **Murg** *R* Germany
48H6 **Murgab** *R* Turkmenistan
60B2 **Murgha Kibzai** Pak
75D1 **Murgon** Aust
61C3 **Muri** India
29D3 **Muriaé** Brazil
73C4 **Muriege** Angola
44E2 **Murmansk** Russian Fed
44G4 **Murom** Russian Fed
53E3 **Muroran** Japan
39A1 **Muros** Spain
53C5 **Muroto** Japan
54B4 **Muroto-zaki** *C* Japan
18C2 **Murphy** Idaho, USA
15C1 **Murphy** N Carolina, USA
20B1 **Murphys** USA
12B3 **Murray** Kentucky, USA
18D2 **Murray** Utah, USA
75B2 **Murray** *R* Aust
3D2 **Murray** *R* Can
75A3 **Murray Bridge** Aust
51H7 **Murray,L** PNG
15C2 **Murray,L** USA
74C3 **Murraysburg** S Africa
xxixM3 **Murray Seacarp** Pacific O
36E2 **Murrhardt** Germany
75B2 **Murrumbidgee** *R* Aust
75C2 **Murrumburrah** Aust
75D2 **Murrurundi** Aust
37B1 **Murten** Switz
75B3 **Murtoa** Aust
78C1 **Murupara** NZ
61B3 **Murwāra** India
75D1 **Murwillimbah** Aust
64D2 **Muş** Turk
41E2 **Musala** *Mt* Bulg
53B3 **Musan** N Korea
67G1 **Musandam** *Pen* Oman
Muscat = Masqat
67G2 **Muscat** *Region* Oman
11D3 **Muscatine** USA
76C3 **Musgrave Range** *Mts* Aust
72B4 **Mushie** Zaïre
14E2 **Muskeget Chan** USA
12B2 **Muskegon** USA
12B2 **Muskegon** *R* USA
17C2 **Muskogee** USA
66C3 **Musmar** Sudan
72D4 **Musoma** Tanz
76D1 **Mussau** *I* PNG
18E1 **Musselshell** *R* USA
73B5 **Mussende** Angola
38C2 **Mussidan** France
41F2 **Mustafa-Kemalpasa** Turk
61B2 **Mustang** Nepal
54A2 **Musu-dan** *C* N Korea
75D2 **Muswelibrook** Aust
69B2 **Mut** Egypt
73D5 **Mutarara** Mozam
73D5 **Mutare** Zim
57B4 **Mutis** *Mt* Indon
44K2 **Mutnyy Materik** Russian Fed
73D5 **Mutoko** Zim
73E5 **Mutsamudu** Comoros
73C5 **Mutshatsha** Zaïre
53E3 **Mutsu** Japan
53E3 **Mutsu-wan** *B* Japan
5K3 **Mutton Bay** Can
29C1 **Mutunópolis** Brazil
52B2 **Mu Us Shamo** *Desert* China
73B4 **Muxima** Angola
49N4 **Muya** Russian Fed
44E3 **Muyezerskiy** Russian Fed
72D4 **Muyinga** Burundi
73C4 **Muyumba** Zaïre
59E1 **Muyun Kum** *Desert* Kazakhstan
60C2 **Muzaffarābad** Pak
60C2 **Muzaffargarh** Pak
60D3 **Muzaffarnagar** India
61C2 **Muzaffarpur** India
48H3 **Muzhi** Russian Fed
59G2 **Muzlag** *Mt* China
3B3 **Muzon,C** USA
59F2 **Muztagala** *Mt* China
73D5 **Mvuma** Zim
72D4 **Mwanza** Tanz
73C4 **Mwanza** Zaïre
72C4 **Mweka** Zaïre
73C4 **Mwene Ditu** Zaïre
73D6 **Mwenezi** Zim
72C4 **Mwenga** Zaïre
73C4 **Mweru** *L* Zambia
73C5 **Mwinilunga** Zambia
61E4 **Myanaung** Burma
Myanma = Burma
61E3 **Myingyan** Burma
55B1 **Myingyao** Burma
55B3 **Myinmoletkat** *Mt* Burma
61E3 **Myinmu** Burma
61E2 **Myitkyina** Burma
55B3 **Myitta** Burma
61E3 **Myittha** Burma
61D3 **Mymensingh** Bang
50G3 **Myojin** *I* Japan
54A2 **Myongchon** N Korea
54A2 **Myonggan** N Korea
32F6 **Myrdal** Nor
32B2 **Myrdalsjökur** *Mts* Iceland
15D2 **Myrtle Beach** USA
18B2 **Myrtle Creek** USA
49U3 **Mys Chaplino** *C* Russian Fed
49M2 **Mys Chelyuskin** *C* Russian Fed
10D3 **Mys Chukotskiy** *Pt* Russian Fed
10E2 **Mys Dezhneva** *Pt* Russian Fed
32G7 **Mysen** Nor
42C2 **Mysiloborz** Pol
44G2 **Mys Kanin Nos** *C* Russian Fed
49S4 **Mys Kronotskiy** *C* Russian Fed
43D3 **Myślenice** Pol
49R4 **Mys Lopatka** *C* Russian Fed
49T3 **Mys Navarin** *C* Russian Fed
10D2 **Mys Nygchigen** *Pt* Russian Fed
49T4 **Mys Olyutorskiy** *C* Russian Fed
62B2 **Mysore** India
45E7 **Mys Sarych** *C* Ukraine
10D2 **Mys Serdtse Kamen** *Pt* Russian Fed
49T2 **Mys Shelagskiy** *C* Russian Fed
49U3 **Mys Shmidta** Russian Fed
49S4 **Mys Sivuchiy** *C* Kirgizia
44F2 **Mys Svyatoy Nos** *C* Russian Fed
14E2 **Mystic** USA
45J7 **Mys Tyub-Karagan** *Pt* Kazakhstan
49Q4 **Mys Yelizavety** *C* Russian Fed
48H2 **Mys Zhelaniya** *C* Russian Fed
55D3 **My Tho** Viet
18B2 **Mytle Point** USA
73D5 **Mzimba** Malawi
73D5 **Mzuzú** Malawi

N

20E5 **Naalehu** Hawaiian Is
32J6 **Naantali** Fin
35B5 **Naas** Irish Rep
54C4 **Nabari** Japan
44J4 **Naberezhnyye Chelny** Russian Fed
10K3 **Nabesna** *R* USA
71E1 **Nabeul** Tunisia
29A3 **Nabileque** *R* Brazil
65C2 **Nablus** Israel
73E5 **Nacala** Mozam
18B1 **Naches** USA
5H2 **Nachikapau L** Can
73D5 **Nachingwea** Tanz
20B3 **Nacimiento** *R* USA
20B3 **Nacimiento Res** USA
17D3 **Nacogdoches** USA
55A3 **Nacondam** *I* Indian O
21B1 **Nacozari** Mexico
36E1 **Nadel** *Mt* Germany
77G2 **Nadi** Fiji
60C4 **Nadiād** India
39B2 **Nador** Mor
63C2 **Nadūshan** Iran
44E3 **Nadvoitsy** Russian Fed
43E3 **Nadvornaya** Ukraine
42C1 **Naestved** Den
54B4 **Nagahama** Japan
61E2 **Naga Hills** Burma
54C3 **Nagai** Japan
10G5 **Nagal** *I* USA
61D2 **Nāgāland** State, India
53D4 **Nagano** Japan
53D4 **Nagaoka** Japan
62B2 **Nāgappattinam** India
60C4 **Nagar Parkar** Pak
53B5 **Nagasaki** Japan
54C4 **Nagashima** Japan
54B4 **Nagato** Japan
60C3 **Nāgaur** India
62B3 **Nāgercoil** India
60B3 **Nagha Kalat** Pak
60D3 **Nagīna** India
36E2 **Nagold** Germany
53D4 **Nagoya** Japan
60D4 **Nāgpur** India
59H2 **Nagqu** China
42D3 **Nagykanizsa** Hung
43D3 **Nagykörös** Hung
50F4 **Naha** Japan
60D2 **Nāhan** India
63E3 **Nahang** *R* Iran
6F3 **Nahanni Butte** Can
10N3 **Nahanni Nat Pk** Can
10O3 **Nahanni Range** *Mts* Can
65C2 **Nahariya** Israel
71C1 **Nahar Ouassel** *R* Alg
63B2 **Nahāvand** Iran
36D2 **Nahe** *R* Germany
52D2 **Nahpu** China
28B4 **Nahuel Niyeu** Arg
57B4 **Naikliu** Indon
52E1 **Naimen Qi** China
7M4 **Nain** Can
63C2 **Nā'īn** Iran
60D3 **Naini Tai** India
61B3 **Nainpur** India
34D3 **Nairn** Scot
72D4 **Nairobi** Kenya
63C2 **Najafābād** Iran
66D1 **Najd** Region, S Arabia
53C3 **Najin** N Korea
66D3 **Najrān** S Arabia
54A3 **Naju** S Korea
54A4 **Nakadori-jima** Japan
54B4 **Nakama** Japan
53E4 **Nakaminato** Japan
54B4 **Nakamura** Japan
54C3 **Nakano** Japan
54B3 **Nakano-shima** *I* Japan
53C5 **Nakatsu** Japan
54C3 **Nakatsu-gawa** Japan
66C3 **Nak'fa** Eth
45H8 **Nakhichevan** Azerbaijan
65B4 **Nakhl** Egypt
53C3 **Nakhodka** Russian Fed
55C3 **Nakhon Pathom** Thai
55C3 **Nakhon Ratchasima** Thai
55C4 **Nakhon Si Thammarat** Thai
3B2 **Nakina** British Columbia, Can
7K4 **Nakina** Ontario, Can
3B2 **Nakina** *R* Can
10G4 **Naknek** USA
10G4 **Naknek L** USA
32G7 **Nakskov** Den
54A3 **Naktong** *R* S Korea
72D4 **Nakuru** Kenya
3E3 **Nakusp** Can
45G7 **Nal'chik** Russian Fed
62B1 **Nalgonda** India
62B1 **Nallamala Range** *Mts* India
44C2 **Naltia** *Mt* Nor/Fin
69A1 **Nālūt** Libya
74E2 **Namaacha** Mozam
48G6 **Namak** *L* Iran
63D2 **Namakzar-e Shadad** *Salt Flat* Iran
48J5 **Namangan** Uzbekistan
73D5 **Namapa** Mozam
73B7 **Namaqualand** Region, S Africa
75D1 **Nambour** Aust
75D2 **Nambucca Heads** Aust
55D4 **Nam Can** Viet
59H2 **Nam Co** *L* China
55D1 **Nam Dinh** Viet
73D5 **Nametil** Mozam
3H3 **Namew L** Can
53B5 **Namhae-do** *I* S Korea
74A1 **Namib Desert** Namibia
73B5 **Namibe** Angola
73B6 **Namibia** Republic, Africa
57C3 **Namlea** Indon
61C2 **Namling** China
57B3 **Namo** Indon
75C2 **Namoi** *R* Aust
3E2 **Nampa** Can
18C2 **Nampa** USA
70B3 **Nampala** Mali
55C2 **Nam Phong** Thai
53B4 **Namp'o** N Korea
73D5 **Nampula** Mozam
32G6 **Namsos** Nor
55B1 **Namton** Burma
49O3 **Namtsy** Russian Fed
61E3 **Namtu** Burma
3C3 **Namu** Can
73D5 **Namuno** Mozam
36C1 **Namur** Belg
73B5 **Namutoni** Namibia
53B4 **Namwŏn** S Korea
3D4 **Nanaimo** Can
53B3 **Nanam** N Korea
75D1 **Nanango** Aust
53D4 **Nanao** Japan
54C3 **Nanatsu-jima** *I* Japan
52B3 **Nanbu** China
53B2 **Nancha** China
52D4 **Nanchang** China
52B3 **Nanchong** China
62E3 **Nancowry** *I* Indian O
38D2 **Nancy** France
61B1 **Nanda Devi** *Mt* India
62B1 **Nānded** India
75D2 **Nandewar Range** *Mts* Aust
60C4 **Nandurbar** India
62B1 **Nandyāl** India
72B3 **Nanga Eboko** Cam
57B4 **Nangahale** Indon
60C1 **Nanga Parbat** *Mt* Pak
56D3 **Nangapinoh** Indon
56D3 **Nangatayap** Indon
36B2 **Nangis** France
54A2 **Nangnim** N Korea
53B3 **Nangnim Sanmaek** *Mts* N Korea
61D2 **Nang Xian** China
62B2 **Nanjangūd** India
52D3 **Nanjing** China
Nanking = Nanjing
54B4 **Nankoku** Japan
52C4 **Nan Ling** Region, China
55D1 **Nanliu** *R* China
52B5 **Nanning** China
7O3 **Nanortalik** Greenland
52A5 **Nanpan Jiang** *R* China
61B2 **Nānpāra** India
52D4 **Nanping** China
7J1 **Nansen Sd** Can
72D4 **Nansio** Tanz
38B2 **Nantes** France
14C2 **Nanticoke** USA
3F3 **Nanton** Can
52E3 **Nantong** China
37A1 **Nantua** France
14E2 **Nantucket** USA
14E2 **Nantucket I** USA
14E2 **Nantucket Sd** USA
14A2 **Nanty Glo** USA
77G1 **Nanumanga** *I* Tuvalu
77G1 **Nanumea** *I* Tuvalu
29D2 **Nanuque** Brazil
52C3 **Nanyang** China
52D2 **Nanyang Hu** *L* China
72D3 **Nanyuki** Kenya
53D4 **Naoetsu** Japan
60B4 **Naokot** Pak
20A1 **Napa** USA
10F3 **Napaiskak** USA
13D2 **Napanee** Can
48K4 **Napas** Russian Fed
7N3 **Napassoq** Greenland
55D2 **Nape** Laos
78C1 **Napier** NZ
Naples = Napoli
15E4 **Naples** Florida, USA
14B1 **Naples** New York, USA
17D3 **Naples** Texas, USA
52B5 **Napo** China
26D4 **Napo** *R* Peru/Ecuador
11C2 **Napoleon** USA
40C2 **Napoli** Italy
63B1 **Naqadeh** Iran
65C3 **Naqb Ishtar** Jordan
54C4 **Nara** Japan
70B3 **Nara** Mali
76D4 **Naracoorte** Aust
22C1 **Naranjos** Mexico
62B1 **Narasarāopet** India
55C4 **Narathiwat** Thai
61D3 **Narayanganj** Bang
62B1 **Nārāyenpet** India
38C3 **Narbonne** France
60D2 **Narendranagar** India
7L2 **Nares Str** Can
43E2 **Narew** *R* Pol
54D3 **Narita** Japan
60C4 **Narmada** *R* India
60D3 **Nārnaul** India
44F4 **Naro Fominsk** Russian Fed
72D4 **Narok** Kenya
43F2 **Narovl'a** Belorussia

Narowal Nipomo

60C2 **Narowal** Pak
76D4 **Narrabri** Aust
75C1 **Narran** *L* Aust
75C1 **Narran** *R* Aust
75C2 **Narrandera** Aust
76A4 **Narrogin** Aust
75C2 **Narromine** Aust
12C3 **Narrows** USA
14C2 **Narrowsburg** USA
60D4 **Narsimhapur** India
62C1 **Narsīpatnam** India
7O3 **Narssalik** Greenland
7O3 **Narssaq** Greenland
7O3 **Narssarssuaq** Greenland
74B2 **Narubis** Namibia
54D3 **Narugo** Japan
54B4 **Naruto** Japan
44D4 **Narva** Russian Fed
32H5 **Narvik** Nor
60D3 **Narwāna** India
44J2 **Nar'yan Mar** Russian Fed
75B1 **Narylico** Aust
48J5 **Naryn** Kazakhstan
71H4 **Nasarawa** Nig
xxxD5 **Nasca Ridge** Pacific O
14E1 **Nashua** USA
17D3 **Nashville** Arkansas, USA
15B1 **Nashville** Tennessee, USA
41D1 **Našice** Croatia, Yugos
60C4 **Nāsik** India
72D3 **Nasir** Sudan
5J3 **Naskaupi** *R* Can
3C2 **Nass** *R* Can
23B1 **Nassau** Bahamas
14D1 **Nassau** USA
69C2 **Nasser,L** Egypt
71F4 **Nassian** Ivory Coast
32G7 **Nässjö** Sweden
7L4 **Nastapoka Is** Can
4F2 **Nastapoca** *R* Can
73C6 **Nata** Botswana
27L5 **Natal** Brazil
56A2 **Natal** Indon
74E2 **Natal** Province, S Africa
xxviiiC6 **Natal Basin** Indian O
63C2 **Natanz** Iran
7M4 **Natashquan** Can
7M4 **Natashquan** *R* Can
17D3 **Natchez** USA
17D3 **Natchitoches** USA
75C3 **Nathalia** Aust
7Q2 **Nathorsts Land** *Region* Greenland
3D2 **Nation** *R* Can
19C4 **National City** USA
National Republic of China = Taiwan
71G3 **Natitingou** Benin
54D3 **Natori** Japan
72D4 **Natron** *L* Tanz
76A4 **Naturaliste,C** Aust
4D4 **Naubinway** USA
37D1 **Nauders** Austria
42C2 **Nauen** Germany
14D2 **Naugatuck** USA
42C2 **Naumburg** Germany
65C3 **Naur** Jordan
77F1 **Nauru** *I* Pacific O
49M4 **Naushki** Russian Fed
74B2 **Naute Dam** *Res* Namibia
22C1 **Nautla** Mexico
63E2 **Nauzad** Afghan
8C3 **Navajo Res** USA
39A2 **Navalmoral de la Mata** Spain
25C9 **Navarino** *I* Chile
39B1 **Navarra** Province, Spain
28D3 **Navarro** Arg
17C3 **Navasota** USA
17C3 **Navasota** *R* USA
39A1 **Navia** *R* Spain
28A2 **Navidad** Chile
60C4 **Navlakhi** India
45E5 **Navlya** Russian Fed
21B2 **Navojoa** Mexico
41E3 **Návpaktos** Greece
41E3 **Návplion** Greece
71F3 **Navrongo** Ghana
60C4 **Navsāri** India
65D2 **Nawá** Syria
61C3 **Nawāda** India
60B2 **Nawah** Afghan
60B3 **Nawrabshah** Pak
52B4 **Naxi** China
41F3 **Náxos** *I* Greece
22B1 **Nayar** Mexico
22A1 **Nayarit** State, Mexico
63C3 **Nāy Band** Iran
63D2 **Nāy Band** Iran
53E3 **Nayoro** Japan
29E1 **Nazaré** Brazil
65C2 **Nazareth** Israel
38B2 **Nazay** France
26D6 **Nazca** Peru
64A2 **Nazilli** Turk
49L4 **Nazimovo** Russian Fed
3D3 **Nazko** *R* Can
58B5 **Nazrēt** Eth
67G2 **Nazwa** Oman
48J4 **Nazyvayevsk** Russian Fed
73B4 **Ndalatando** Angola
72C3 **Ndélé** CAR
72B4 **Ndendé** Gabon
77F2 **Ndende** *I* Solomon Is
72B2 **Ndjamena** Chad
72B4 **Ndjolé** Gabon
73C5 **Ndola** Zambia
71F4 **Ndouci** Ivory Coast
75C1 **Neabul** Aust
75A1 **Neales** *R* Aust
41E3 **Neápolis** Greece
10A6 **Near Is** USA
35D6 **Neath** Wales
75C1 **Nebine** *R* Aust
48G6 **Nebit Dag** Turkmenistan
8C2 **Nebraska** State, USA
17C1 **Nebraska City** USA
3D3 **Nechako** *R* Can
17C3 **Neches** *R* USA
36E2 **Neckar** *R* Germany
28D3 **Necochea** Arg
61D2 **Nêdong** China
19D4 **Needles** USA
12B2 **Neenah** USA
6J4 **Neepawa** Can
36C1 **Neerpelt** Belg
71D2 **Nefta** Tunisia
53E1 **Neftegorsk** Russian Fed
49M4 **Neftelensk** Russian Fed
72D3 **Negelli** Eth
65C3 **Negev** *Desert* Israel
29A3 **Negla** *R* Par
45C6 **Negolu** *Mt* Rom
62B3 **Negombo** Sri Lanka
55A2 **Negrais,C** Burma
26B4 **Negritos** Peru
26F4 **Negro** *R* Amazonas, Brazil
28C4 **Negro** *R* Arg
29A2 **Negro** *R* Mato Grosso de Sul, Brazil
29A3 **Negro** *R* Par
28D2 **Negro** *R* Urug
57F8 **Negros** *I* Phil
41F2 **Negru Voda** Rom
63E2 **Nehbāndan** Iran
53A2 **Nehe** China
52B4 **Neijiang** China
12A2 **Neillsville** USA
52B1 **Nei Monggol** Autonomous Region, China
26C3 **Neira** Colombia
72D3 **Nejo** Eth
72D3 **Nek'emte** Eth
44E4 **Nelidovo** Russian Fed
11C3 **Neligh** USA
62B2 **Nellore** India
53D2 **Nel'ma** Russian Fed
3E4 **Nelson** Can
78B2 **Nelson** NZ
6J4 **Nelson** *R* Can
75B3 **Nelson,C** Aust
10F3 **Nelson I** USA
74E2 **Nelspruit** S Africa
70B3 **Néma** Maur
52A1 **Nemagt Uul** *Mt* Mongolia
53D1 **Nemilen** *R* Russian Fed
41F1 **Nemira** *Mt* Rom
53B2 **Nemor He** *R* China
36B2 **Nemours** France
43E1 **Nemunas** *R* Lithuania
53F3 **Nemuro** Japan
49O5 **Nen** *R* China
33B3 **Nenagh** Irish Rep
10J3 **Nenana** USA
10J3 **Nenana** *R* USA
35E5 **Nene** *R* Eng
56F6 **Nenggiri** *R* Malay
53B2 **Nenjiang** China
17C2 **Neodesha** USA
17D2 **Neosho** USA
49M4 **Nepa** Russian Fed
59G3 **Nepal** Kingdom, Asia
61B2 **Nepalganj** Nepal
19D3 **Nephi** USA
65C3 **Neqarot** *R* Israel
28A3 **Nequén** State, Arg
50E1 **Nerchinsk** Russian Fed
41D2 **Neretva** *R* Bosnia & Herzegovina/Croatia, Yugos
51H5 **Nero Deep** Pacific O
44G2 **Nes'** Russian Fed
32C1 **Neskaupstaður** Iceland
36B2 **Nesle** France
16C2 **Ness City** USA
3B2 **Nesselrode,Mt** Can/USA
5G3 **Nestaocano** *R* Can
41E2 **Néstos** *R* Greece
65C2 **Netanya** Israel
14C2 **Netcong** USA
42B2 **Netherlands** Kingdom, Europe
2M7 **Netherlands Antilles** *Is* Caribbean
49N4 **Net Oktyobr'ya** Russian Fed
61D3 **Netrakona** Bang
7L3 **Nettilling L** Can
42C2 **Neubrandenburg** Germany
37B1 **Neuchâtel** Switz
36C2 **Neufchâteau** Belg
36C2 **Neufchâteau** France
38C2 **Neufchâtel** France
36A2 **Neufchâtel-en-Bray** France
42B2 **Neumünster** Germany
40D1 **Neunkirchen** Austria
36D2 **Neunkirchen** Germany
28B3 **Neuquén** Arg
25B6 **Neuquén** State, Arg
28B3 **Neuquén** *R* Arg
42C2 **Neuruppin** Germany
15D1 **Neuse** *R* USA
36D1 **Neuss** Germany
42C2 **Neustadt** Germany
36E2 **Neustadt an der Weinstrasse** Germany
36E3 **Neustadt im Schwarzwald** Germany
42C2 **Neustrelitz** Germany
36D1 **Neuwied** Germany
8B3 **Nevada** State, USA
17D2 **Nevada** USA
28A3 **Nevada de Chillán** *Mts* Chile/Arg
22B2 **Nevada de Collima** Mexico
22C2 **Nevada de Toluca** *Mt* Mexico
65C3 **Nevatim** Israel
44D4 **Nevel'** Russian Fed
53E2 **Nevel'sk** Russian Fed
53A1 **Never** Russian Fed
38C2 **Nevers** France
75C2 **Nevertire** Aust
64B2 **Nevşehir** Turk
44L4 **Nev'yansk** Russian Fed
12C3 **New** *R* USA
73D5 **Newala** Tanz
12B3 **New Albany** Indiana, USA
17E3 **New Albany** Mississippi, USA
27G2 **New Amsterdam** Guyana
75C1 **New Angledool** Aust
13D3 **Newark** Delaware, USA
9F2 **Newark** New Jersey, USA
14B1 **Newark** New York, USA
12C2 **Newark** Ohio, USA
35E5 **Newark-upon-Trent** Eng
13E2 **New Bedford** USA
3C3 **New Bella Bella** Can
18B1 **Newberg** USA
15D1 **New Bern** USA
15C2 **Newberry** USA
74C3 **New Bethesda** S Africa
23B2 **New Bight** Bahamas
12C3 **New Boston** USA
16C4 **New Braunfels** USA
14D2 **New Britain** USA
76E1 **New Britain** *I* PNG
76E1 **New Britain Trench** PNG
7M5 **New Brunswick** Province, Can
14C2 **New Brunswick** USA
14C2 **Newburgh** USA
35E6 **Newbury** Eng
14E1 **Newburyport** USA
14D2 **New Canaan** USA
75D2 **Newcastle** Aust
5H4 **Newcastle** Can
12B3 **New Castle** Indiana, USA
35C4 **Newcastle** N Ire
12C2 **New Castle** Pennsylvania, USA
74D2 **Newcastle** S Africa
11B3 **Newcastle** Wyoming, USA
34E4 **Newcastle upon Tyne** Eng
76C2 **Newcastle Waters** Aust
20C3 **New Cuyama** USA
60D3 **New Delhi** India
75D2 **New England Range** *Mts* Aust
10F4 **Newenham,C** USA
14A1 **Newfane** USA
35E6 **New Forest,The** Eng
7M4 **Newfoundland** Province, Can
7N5 **Newfoundland** *I* Can
xxxF2 **Newfoundland Basin** Atlantic O
17D2 **New Franklin** USA
34C4 **New Galloway** Scot
77E1 **New Georgia** *I* Solomon Is
7M5 **New Glasgow** Can
76D1 **New Guinea** *I* S E Asia
66C3 **New Haifa** Sudan
10H4 **Newhalen** USA
20C3 **Newhall** USA
9F2 **New Hampshire** State, USA
11D3 **New Hampton** USA
74E2 **New Hanover** S Africa
76E1 **New Hanover** *I* PNG
35F6 **Newhaven** Eng
13E2 **New Haven** USA
3C2 **New Hazelton** Can
77F3 **New Hebrides Trench** Pacific O
17D3 **New Iberia** USA
76E1 **New Ireland** *I* PNG
9F2 **New Jersey** State, USA
16B3 **Newkirk** USA
7L5 **New Liskeard** Can
14D2 **New London** USA
76A3 **Newman** Aust
20B2 **Newman** USA
35F5 **Newmarket** Eng
13D3 **New Market** USA
18C2 **New Meadows** USA
8C3 **New Mexico** State, USA
14D2 **New Milford** Connecticut, USA
14C2 **New Milford** Pennsylvania, USA
15C2 **Newnan** USA
75E3 **New Norfolk** Aust
9D3 **New Orleans** USA
14C2 **New Paltz** USA
12C2 **New Philadelphia** USA
78B1 **New Plymouth** NZ
17D2 **Newport** Arkansas, USA
35E6 **Newport** Eng
12C3 **Newport** Kentucky, USA
14D1 **Newport** New Hampshire, USA
18B2 **Newport** Oregon, USA
14B2 **Newport** Pennsylvania, USA
13E2 **Newport** Rhode Island, USA
13E2 **Newport** Vermont, USA
35D6 **Newport** Wales
18C1 **Newport** Washington, USA
20D4 **Newport Beach** USA
9F3 **Newport News** USA
23B1 **New Providence** *I* Caribbean
35C6 **Newquay** Eng
7L3 **New Quebec Crater** Can
35B5 **New Ross** Irish Rep
35B4 **Newry** N Ire
New Siberian Is = Novosibirskye Ostrova
15C3 **New Smyrna Beach** USA
76D4 **New South Wales** State, Aust
10G4 **New Stuyahok** USA
11D3 **Newton** Iowa, USA
17C2 **Newton** Kansas, USA
14E1 **Newton** Massachusetts, USA
17E3 **Newton** Mississippi, USA
14C2 **Newton** New Jersey, USA
35D6 **Newton Abbot** Eng
34B4 **Newton Stewart** N Ire
34C4 **Newton Stewart** Scot
11B2 **New Town** USA
35D5 **Newtown** Wales
35C4 **Newtownards** N Ire
11D3 **New Ulm** USA
14B2 **Newville** USA
5J4 **New Waterford** Can
6F5 **New Westminster** Can
9F2 **New York** State, USA
9F2 **New York** USA
77G5 **New Zealand** Dominion, SW Pacific O
xxixK7 **New Zealand Plat** Pacific O
44G4 **Neya** Russian Fed
63C3 **Neyrīz** Iran
63D1 **Neyshābūr** Iran
45E5 **Nezhin** Ukraine
72B4 **Ngabé** Congo
71J3 **Ngadda** Nig
73C6 **Ngami** *L* Botswana
71J4 **N'Gaoundéré** Cam
78C1 **Ngaruawahia** NZ
78C1 **Ngaruroro** *R* NZ
78C1 **Ngauruhoe,Mt** NZ
72B4 **Ngo** Congo
55D2 **Ngoc Linh** *Mt* Viet
72B3 **Ngoko** *R* Cam
50C3 **Ngoring Hu** *L* China
72D4 **Ngorongoro Crater** Tanz
72B4 **N'Gounié** *R* Gabon
72B2 **Nguigmi** Niger
51G6 **Ngulu** *I* Pacific O
71J3 **Nguru** Nig
55D3 **Nha Trang** Viet
29A2 **Nhecolandia** Brazil
75B3 **Nhill** Aust
74E2 **Nhlangano** Swaziland
55D2 **Nhommarath** Laos
76C2 **Nhulunbuy** Aust
70B3 **Niafounké** Mali
12B1 **Niagara** USA
13D2 **Niagara Falls** Can
13D2 **Niagara Falls** USA
56D2 **Niah** Malay
70B4 **Niakaramandougou** Ivory Coast
70C3 **Niamey** Niger
72C3 **Niangara** Zaïre
71F3 **Niangoloko** Burkina
72C3 **Nia Nia** Zaïre
53A2 **Nianzishan** China
56A2 **Nias** *I* Indon
21D3 **Nicaragua** Republic, C America
40D3 **Nicastro** Italy
38D3 **Nice** France
23B1 **Nicholl's Town** Bahamas
14C2 **Nicholson** USA
59H5 **Nicobar Is** Indian O
65B1 **Nicosia** Cyprus
21D3 **Nicoya,Pen de** Costa Rica
36E1 **Nidda** *R* Germany
43E2 **Nidzica** Pol
36D2 **Niederbronn** France
37E1 **Niedere Tauern** *Mts* Austria
42B2 **Niedersachsen** State, Germany
72C4 **Niemba** Zaïre
42B2 **Nienburg** Germany
36D1 **Niers** *R* Germany
70B4 **Niete,Mt** Lib
27G2 **Nieuw Amsterdam** Surinam
27G2 **Nieuw Nickeire** Surinam
74B3 **Nieuwoudtville** S Africa
36B1 **Nieuwpoort** Belg
22B1 **Nieves** Mexico
64B2 **Niğde** Turk
70C3 **Niger** Republic, Africa
71H4 **Niger** State, Nig
71H4 **Niger** *R* Nig
70C4 **Nigeria** Federal Republic, Africa
12C1 **Nighthawk L** Can
41E2 **Nigríta** Greece
54D3 **Nihommatsu** Japan
53D4 **Niigata** Japan
53C5 **Niihama** Japan
54C4 **Nii-jima** *I* Japan
54B4 **Niimi** Japan
53D4 **Niitsu** Japan
65C3 **Nijil** Jordan
42B2 **Nijmegen** Neth
44E2 **Nikel'** Russian Fed
71G3 **Nikki** Benin
53D4 **Nikko** Japan
45E6 **Nikolayev** Ukraine
45H6 **Nikolayevsk** Russian Fed
49Q4 **Nikolayevsk-na-Amure** Russian Fed
44H5 **Nikol'sk** Penza, Russian Fed
44H4 **Nikol'sk** Russian Fed
10E5 **Nikolski** USA
45E6 **Nikopol** Ukraine
64C1 **Niksar** Turk
63E3 **Nīkshahr** Iran
41D2 **Nikšić** Montenegro, Yugos
77G1 **Nikunau** *I* Kiribati
57C4 **Nila** *I* Indon
58B3 **Nile** *R* N E Africa
12B2 **Niles** USA
62B2 **Nilgiri Hills** India
22D2 **Niltepec** Mexico
60C4 **Nimach** India
38C3 **Nîmes** France
75C3 **Nimmitabel** Aust
72D3 **Nimule** Sudan
59F5 **Nine Degree Chan** Indian O
xxviiiF5 **Ninety-East Ridge** Indian O
75C3 **Ninety Mile Beach** Aust
53B3 **Ning'an** China
52D4 **Ningde** China
52D4 **Ningdu** China
50C3 **Ningjing Shan** *Mts* China
55D1 **Ningming** China
52A4 **Ningnan** China
52B2 **Ningxia** Province, China
52B2 **Ning Xian** China
52B5 **Ninh Binh** Vietnam
76D1 **Ninigo Is** PNG
10H3 **Ninilchik** USA
29A3 **Nioaque** Brazil
11B3 **Niobrara** *R* USA
72B4 **Nioki** Zaïre
70B3 **Nioro du Sahel** Mali
38B2 **Niort** France
6H4 **Nipawin** Can
7K5 **Nipigon** Can
4D4 **Nipigon B.** Can
7K5 **Nipigon,L** Can
7K5 **Nipissing,L** *R* Can
20B3 **Nipomo** USA

Nipton Oasis

19C3 **Nipton** USA
29C1 **Niquelândia** Brazil
62B1 **Nirmal** India
61C2 **Nirmāli** India
41E2 **Niẓ** Serbia, Yugos
67E4 **Nisāb** Yemen
53C5 **Nishinoomote** Japan
50G4 **Nishino-shima** *I* Japan
54B3 **Nishino-shima** *I* Japan
54A4 **Nishi-suidō** *Str* S Korea
54B4 **Nishiwaki** Japan
4D2 **Niskibi** *R* Can
10L3 **Nisling** *R* Can
77E1 **Nissan Is** PNG
10M3 **Nisutlin** *R* Can
7L4 **Nitchequon** Can
27K8 **Niterói** Brazil
34D4 **Nith** *R* Scot
57B4 **Nitibe** Indon
43D3 **Nitra** Czech
12C3 **Nitro** USA
77J2 **Niue** *I* Pacific O
77G2 **Niulakita** *I* Tuvalu
56D2 **Niut** *Mt* Malay
77G1 **Niutao** *I* Tuvalu
36C1 **Nivelles** Belg
38C2 **Nivernais** Region, France
32L5 **Nivskiy** Russian Fed
62B1 **Nizāmābād** India
65C3 **Nizana** *Hist Site* Israel
44J4 **Nizhnekamskoye Vodokhranilische** *Res* Russian Fed
50C1 **Nizhneudinsk** Russian Fed
44K4 **Nizhniye Sergi** Russian Fed
44G5 **Nizhniy Lomov** Russian Fed
44G4 **Nizhniy Novgorod** Russian Fed
44J3 **Nizhniy Odes** Russian Fed
44K4 **Nizhniy Tagil** Russian Fed
49L3 **Nizhnyaya Tunguska** *R* Russian Fed
44G2 **Nizhnyaya Zolotitsa** Russian Fed
64C2 **Nizip** Turk
73C5 **Njoko** *R* Zambia
73D4 **Njombe** Tanz
72B3 **Nkambé** Cam
71F4 **Nkawkaw** Ghana
73D5 **Nkhata Bay** Malawi
72B3 **Nkongsamba** Cam
70C3 **N'Konni** Niger
61D3 **Noakhali** Bang
10F2 **Noatak** USA
10G2 **Noatak** *R* USA
53C5 **Nobeoka** Japan
54D2 **Noboribetsu** Japan
29A1 **Nobres** Brazil
37D1 **Noce** *R* Italy
22B1 **Nochistlán** Mexico
22C2 **Nochixtlán** Mexico
17C3 **Nocona** USA
21A1 **Nogales** Sonora, Mexico
19D4 **Nogales** USA
22C2 **Nogales** Veracruz, Mexico
37D2 **Nogara** Italy
54B4 **Nogata** Japan
36C2 **Nogent-en-Bassigny** France
36A2 **Nogent-le-Rotrou** France
36B2 **Nogent-sur-Seine** France
44F4 **Noginsk** Russian Fed
53E1 **Nogliki** Russian Fed
28D2 **Nogoyá** Arg
28D2 **Nogoyá** *R* Arg
60C3 **Nohar** India
54D2 **Noheji** Japan
74C1 **Nojane** Botswana
54C4 **Nojima-zaki** *C* Japan
63E3 **Nok Kundi** Pak
3H2 **Nokomis L** Can
72B3 **Nola** CAR
44H4 **Nolinsk** Russian Fed
14E2 **Nomans Land** *I* USA
22B1 **Nombre de Dioz** Mexico
10E3 **Nome** USA
36D2 **Nomeny** France
52B1 **Nomgon** Mongolia
54A4 **Nomo-saki** *Pt* Japan
6H3 **Nonachol L** Can
53B3 **Nong'an** China
55C2 **Nong Khai** Thai
74E2 **Nongoma** S Africa
77G1 **Nonouti** *I* Kiribati
54A3 **Nonsan** S Korea
74B2 **Noordoewer** Namibia
10F2 **Noorvik** USA
3C4 **Nootka Sd** Can
22C2 **Nopala** Mexico
72B4 **Noqui** Angola
7L5 **Noranda** Can
36B1 **Nord** Department, France
48D2 **Nordaustlandet** *I* Barents S
3E3 **Nordegg** Can
32F6 **Nordfjord** *Inlet* Nor
32F8 **Nordfriesische** *Is* Germany
42C2 **Nordhausen** Germany
32J4 **Nordkapp** *C* Nor
7N3 **Nordre Strømfjord** Greenland
42B2 **Nordrhein Westfalen** State, Germany
32G5 **Nord Stronfjället** *Mt* Sweden
49N2 **Nordvik** Russian Fed
35B5 **Nore** *R* Irish Rep
35F5 **Norfolk** County, Eng
11C3 **Norfolk** Nebraska, USA
13D3 **Norfolk** Virginia, USA
77F3 **Norfolk I** Aust
17D2 **Norfolk L** USA
xxixK5 **Norfolk Ridge** Pacific O
49K3 **Noril'sk** Russian Fed
12B2 **Normal** USA
17C2 **Norman** USA
38B2 **Normandie** Region, France
15C1 **Norman,L** USA
76D2 **Normanton** Aust
10N2 **Norman Wells** Can
44B2 **Norra Storfjället** *Mt* Sweden
15C1 **Norris L** USA
13D2 **Norristown** USA
32H7 **Norrköping** Sweden
32H6 **Norrsundet** Sweden
32H7 **Norrtälje** Sweden
76B4 **Norseman** Aust
53C1 **Norsk** Russian Fed
29A1 **Nortelândia** Brazil
xxxJ2 **North** *S* N W Europe
35E4 **Northallerton** Eng
76A4 **Northam** Aust
74D2 **Northam** S Africa
xxxE3 **North American Basin** Atlantic O
76A3 **Northampton** Aust
35E5 **Northampton** County, Eng
35E5 **Northampton** Eng
13E2 **Northampton** USA
62E2 **North Andaman** *I* Indian O
6G3 **North Arm** *B* Can
15C2 **North Augusta** USA
7M4 **North Aulatsivik I** Can
3G3 **North Battleford** Can
7L5 **North Bay** Can
18B2 **North Bend** USA
34D3 **North Berwick** Scot
14E1 **North Berwick** USA
7M5 **North,C** Can
77G4 **North C** NZ
10D5 **North C** USA
16B2 **North Canadian** *R* USA
4C3 **North Caribou L** Can
9E3 **North Carolina** State, USA
18B1 **North Cascade Nat Pk** USA
4E4 **North Chan** Can
34C4 **North Chan** Ire/Scot
14A1 **North Collins** USA
8C2 **North Dakota** State, USA
35F6 **North Downs** Eng
36A1 **North Downs** *Upland* Eng
13D2 **North East** USA
xxxH1 **North East Atlantic Basin** Atlantic O
10E3 **Northeast C** USA
4B2 **Northern Indian L** Can
33B3 **Northern Ireland** UK
11D2 **Northern Light L** Can
23L1 **Northern Range** *Mts* Trinidad
76C2 **Northern Territory** Aust
34D3 **North Esk** *R* Scot
14D1 **Northfield** Massachusetts, USA
11D3 **Northfield** Minnesota, USA
35F6 **North Foreland** Eng
36A1 **North Foreland** *Pt* Eng
10H3 **North Fork** *R* USA
4E3 **North French** *R* Can
5K3 **North Head** *C* Can
78B1 **North I** NZ
4B2 **North Knife** *R* Can
53B4 **North Korea** Republic, S E Asia
North Land = Severnaya Zemlya
17D3 **North Little Rock** USA
11B3 **North Loup** *R* USA
79B4 **North Magnetic Pole** Can
15E4 **North Miami** USA
15E4 **North Miami Beach** USA
10O3 **North Nahanni** *R* Can
20C2 **North Palisade** *Mt* USA
16B1 **North Platte** USA
8C2 **North Platte** *R* USA
5J4 **North Pt** *C* Can
79A **North Pole** Arctic
23Q2 **North Pt** Barbados
12C1 **North Pt** USA
11D3 **North Raccoon** *R* USA
33B2 **North Rona** *I* Scot
34D2 **North Ronaldsay** *I* Scot
3G3 **North Saskatchewan** *R* Can
33D2 **North Sea** N W Europe
3H2 **North Seal** *R* Can
62E2 **North Sentinel** Andaman Is
10J2 **North Slope** USA
6D3 **North Slope** *Region* USA
75D1 **North Stradbroke** *I* Aust
14B1 **North Syracuse** USA
78B1 **North Taranaki Bight** *B* NZ
14A1 **North Tonawanda** USA
8C3 **North Truchas Peak** *Mt* USA
4F3 **North Twin I** Can
34B3 **North Uist** *I* Scot
34D4 **Northumberland** County, Eng
76E3 **Northumberland Is** Aust
7M5 **Northumberland Str** Can
18B1 **North Vancouver** Can
14C1 **Northville** USA
35F5 **North Walsham** Eng
10K3 **Northway** USA
76A3 **North West C** Aust
60C2 **North West Frontier** Province, Pak
7M4 **North West River** Can
6G3 **North West Territories** Can
11C2 **Northwood** USA
35E4 **North York Moors Nat Pk** Eng
16C2 **Norton** *R* USA
10F3 **Norton B** USA
10F3 **Norton Sd** USA
79F1 **Norvegia,C** Ant
14D2 **Norwalk** Connecticut, USA
12C2 **Norwalk** Ohio, USA
32F6 **Norway** Kingdom, Europe
6J4 **Norway House** Can
7J2 **Norwegian B** Can
xxxH1 **Norwegian Basin** Norewegian S
48B3 **Norwegian S** N W Europe
14D2 **Norwich** Connecticut, USA
35F5 **Norwich** Eng
14C1 **Norwich** New York, USA
14E1 **Norwood** Massachusetts, USA
12C3 **Norwood** Ohio, USA
41F2 **Nos Emine** *C* Bulg
53D3 **Noshiro** Japan
41F2 **Nos Kaliakra** *C* Bulg
44J2 **Nosovaya** Russian Fed
43G2 **Nosovka** Ukraine
34E1 **Noss** *I* Scot
74B1 **Nossob** *R* Namibia
63E3 **Nostrābād** Iran
73E5 **Nosy Barren** *I* Madag
73E5 **Nosy Bé** *I* Madag
73F5 **Nosy Boraha** *I* Madag
73E6 **Nosy Varika** Madag
42D2 **Notéc** *R* Pol
6G4 **Notikewin** Can
40D3 **Noto** Italy
32F7 **Notodden** Nor
54C3 **Noto-hantō** *Pen* Japan
7N5 **Notre Dame B** Can
4E5 **Nottawasaga B** Can
4F3 **Nottaway** *R* Can
35E5 **Nottingham** County, Eng
35E5 **Nottingham** Eng
7L3 **Nottingham I** Can
11A2 **Notukeu Creek** *R* Can
70A2 **Nouadhibou** Maur
70A3 **Nouakchott** Maur
77F3 **Nouméa** Nouvelle Calédonie
71F3 **Nouna** Burkina
74C3 **Noupoort** S Africa
77F3 **Nouvelle Calédonie** *I* S W Pacific O
29C2 **Nova América** Brazil
73B4 **Nova Caipemba** Angola
29B3 **Nova Esperança** Brazil
29D3 **Nova Friburgo** Brazil
73B5 **Nova Gaia** Angola
29C3 **Nova Granada** Brazil
29C3 **Nova Herizonte** Brazil
29D3 **Nova Lima** Brazil
Nova Lisboa = Huambo
29B3 **Nova Londrina** Brazil
73D6 **Nova Mambone** Mozam
37C2 **Novara** Italy
29C1 **Nova Roma** Brazil
57C4 **Nova Sagres** Indon
7M5 **Nova Scotia** Province, Can
20A1 **Novato** USA
29D2 **Nova Venécia** Brazil
45E6 **Novaya Kakhovka** Ukraine
49R2 **Novaya Sibir, Ostrov** *I* Russian Fed
48G2 **Novaya Zemlya** *I* Russian Fed
41F2 **Nova Zagora** Bulg
27K4 **Nove Russas** Brazil
41D1 **Nové Zámky** Czech
44E4 **Novgorod** Russian Fed
37E2 **Novigrad** Croatia, Yugos
53E2 **Novikovo** Russian Fed
37C2 **Novi Ligure** Italy
22A1 **Novillero** Mexico
41F2 **Novi Pazar** Bulg
41E2 **Novi Pazar** Serbia, Yugos
41D1 **Novi Sad** Serbia, Yugos
45K5 **Novoalekseyevka** Kazakhstan
45G5 **Novoanninskiy** Russian Fed
53C2 **Novobureyskiy** Russian Fed
45G6 **Novocherkassk** Russian Fed
44G3 **Novodvinsk** Russian Fed
45D5 **Novograd Volynskiy** Ukraine
43F2 **Novogrudok** Belorussia
28E1 **Novo Hamburgo** Brazil
48H5 **Novokazalinsk** Kazakhstan
48K4 **Novokuznetsk** Russian Fed
79F12 **Novolazarevskaya** *Base* Ant
40D1 **Novo Mesto** Slovenia, Yugos
43G3 **Novomirgorod** Ukraine
44F5 **Novomoskovsk** Russian Fed
Novo Redondo = Sumbe
45F7 **Novorossiysk** Russian Fed
49M2 **Novorybnoye** Russian Fed
48K4 **Novosibirsk** Russian Fed
49P2 **Novosibirskye Ostrova** *Is* Russian Fed
45K5 **Novotroitsk** Russian Fed
45H5 **Novo Uzensk** Russian Fed
43E2 **Novovolynsk** Ukraine
44H4 **Novo Vyatsk** Russian Fed
45E5 **Novozybkov** Russian Fed
48J3 **Novvy Port** Russian Fed
43E2 **Novy Dwór Mazowiecki** Pol
44L4 **Novyy Lyalya** Russian Fed
44N2 **Novyy Port** Russian Fed
45J7 **Novyy Uzen** Kazakhstan
42D2 **Nowa Sól** Pol
17C2 **Nowata** USA
61D2 **Nowgong** India
10H3 **Nowitna** *R* USA
75D2 **Nowra** Aust
63C1 **Now Shahr** Iran
60C2 **Nowshera** Pak
43E3 **Nowy SŞacz** Pol
10M4 **Noyes I** USA
36B2 **Noyon** France
71F4 **Nsawam** Ghana
71H4 **Nsukka** Nig
74E1 **Nuanetsi** Zim
74E1 **Nuanetsi** *R* Zim
71G4 **Nuatja** Togo
72D2 **Nuba** *Mts* Sudan
66B2 **Nubian Desert** Sudan
28A3 **Nuble** *R* Chile
8D4 **Nueces** *R* USA
6J3 **Nueltin L** Can
21B1 **Nueva Casas Grandes** Mexico
29A3 **Nueva Germania** Par
23A2 **Nueva Gerona** Cuba
28A3 **Nueva Imperial** Chile
28D2 **Nueva Palmira** Urug
21B2 **Nueva Rosita** Mexico
23B2 **Nuevitas** Cuba
22B1 **Nuevo** State, Mexico
21B1 **Nuevo Casas Grandes** Mexico
22A1 **Nuevo Ideal** Mexico
21C2 **Nuevo Laredo** Mexico
69D4 **Nugaal** Region, Somalia
7N2 **Nûgâtsiaq** Greenland
7N2 **Nûgussuaq** *Pen* Greenland
7N2 **Nûgussuaq** *I* Greenland
77G1 **Nui** *I* Tuvalu
52A5 **Nui Con Voi** *R* Vietnam
36C3 **Nuits** France
61E2 **Nu Jiang** *R* China
75A2 **Nukey Bluff** *Mt* Aust
64D3 **Nukhayb** Iraq
77G1 **Nukufetau** *I* Tuvalu
77G1 **Nukulaelae** *I* Tuvalu
77H1 **Nukunon** *I* Tokelau Is
48G5 **Nukus** Uzbekistan
10G3 **Nulato** USA
76B4 **Nullarbor Plain** Aust
71J4 **Numan** Nig
54C3 **Numata** Japan
72C3 **Numatinna** *R* Sudan
53D4 **Numazu** Japan
51G7 **Numfoor** *I* Indon
75C3 **Numurkah** Aust
10F3 **Nunapitchuk** USA
14A1 **Nunda** USA
10E3 **Nunivak I** USA
60D2 **Nunkun** *Mt* India
10C3 **Nunligran** Russian Fed
53A1 **Nuomin He** *R* China
40B2 **Nuoro** Sardegna
63C2 **Nurābād** Iran
37C2 **Nure** *R* Italy
75A2 **Nuriootpa** Aust
60C1 **Nuristan** *Upland* Afghan
44J5 **Nurlat** Russian Fed
32K6 **Nurmes** Fin
42C3 **Nürnberg** Germany
75C2 **Nurri,Mt** Aust
56E4 **Nusa Tenggara** *Is* Indon
57B4 **Nusa Tenggara Timor** Province, Indon
64D2 **Nusaybin** Turk
10G4 **Nushagak** *R* USA
10G4 **Nushagak B** USA
10G4 **Nushagak Pen** USA
60B3 **Nushki** Pak
7M4 **Nutak** Can
10K3 **Nutzotin Mts** USA
7L3 **Nuvukjuak** Can
61B2 **Nuwakot** Nepal
62C3 **Nuwara-Eliya** Sri Lanka
74C3 **Nuweveldreeks** *Mts* S Africa
45C3 **Nyac** USA
14D2 **Nyack** USA
72D3 **Nyahururu Falls** Kenya
75B3 **Nyah West** Aust
50C3 **Nyaingentanglha Shan** *Mts* China
72D4 **Nyakabindi** Tanz
44L3 **Nyaksimvol'** Russian Fed
72C2 **Nyala** Sudan
61C2 **Nyalam** China
72C3 **Nyamlell** Sudan
73D6 **Nyanda** Zim
44G3 **Nyandoma** Russian Fed
72B4 **Nyanga** *R* Gabon
61D2 **Nyang Qu** China
73D5 **Nyasa L** Malawi/Mozam
55B2 **Nyaunglebin** Burma
44K4 **Nyazepetrovsk** Russian Fed
32G7 **Nyborg** Den
32H7 **Nybro** Sweden
48J3 **Nyda** Russian Fed
7M1 **Nyeboes Land** *Region* Can
61D1 **Nyenchentanglha Range** *Mts* China
72D4 **Nyeri** Kenya
73D5 **Nyimba** Zambia
59H2 **Nyingchi** China
43E3 **Nyíregyháza** Hung
72D3 **Nyiru,Mt** Kenya
32J6 **Nykarleby** Fin
32F7 **Nykøbing** Den
32G8 **Nykøbing** Den
32H7 **Nyköping** Sweden
74D1 **Nyl** *R* S Africa
74D1 **Nylstroom** S Africa
75C2 **Nymagee** Aust
32H7 **Nynäshamn** Sweden
75C2 **Nyngan** Aust
37B1 **Nyon** Switz
72B3 **Nyong** *R* Cam
54A3 **Nyongwol** S Korea
54A3 **Nyongwon** N Korea
38D3 **Nyons** France
42D2 **Nysa** Pol
53E1 **Nysh** Russian Fed
18C2 **Nyssa** USA
44H3 **Nyukhcha** Russian Fed
50F1 **Nyukzha** *R* Russian Fed
49N3 **Nyurba** Russian Fed
72D4 **Nzega** Tanz
70B4 **Nzérékore** Guinea
73B4 **N'zeto** Angola
71F4 **Nzi** *R* Ivory Coast

O

11C3 **Oacoma** USA
11B3 **Oahe,L** *Res* USA
20E5 **Oahu,I** Hawaiian Is
75B2 **Oakbank** Aust
20B2 **Oakdale** USA
11C2 **Oakes** USA
75D1 **Oakey** Aust
19B3 **Oakland** California, USA
11C3 **Oakland** Nebraska, USA
18B2 **Oakland** Oregon, USA
12B3 **Oakland City** USA
12B2 **Oak Lawn** USA
20B2 **Oakley** California, USA
16B2 **Oakley** Kansas, USA
15C1 **Oak Ridge** USA
18B2 **Oakridge** USA
4F5 **Oakville** Can
78B3 **Oamaru** NZ
20D2 **Oasis** California, USA
18D2 **Oasis** Nevada, USA

Ossé Parkston

71H4 **Ossé** *R* Nig
12A2 **Osseo** USA
37E1 **Ossiacher See** *L* Austria
14D2 **Ossining** USA
5J3 **Ossokmanuan L** Can
49S4 **Ossora** Russian Fed
44E4 **Ostashkov** Russian Fed
Ostend = Oostende
32G6 **Østerdalen, V** Nor
32G6 **Östersund** Sweden
32H6 **Östhammär** Sweden
40C2 **Ostia** Italy
37D2 **Ostiglia** Italy
43D3 **Ostrava** Czech
43D2 **Ostróda** Pol
43E2 **Ostroleka** Pol
44D4 **Ostrov** Russian Fed
43D2 **Ostrów** Pol
43E2 **Ostrowiec** Pol
43E2 **Ostrów Mazowiecka** Pol
53C5 **Ōsumi-kaikyō** *Str* Japan
53C5 **Ōsumi-shotō** *Is* Japan
71G4 **Osun** *State* Nigeria
39A2 **Osuna** Spain
14B1 **Oswego** USA
14B1 **Oswego** *R* USA
35D5 **Oswestry** Eng
43D3 **OświŞecim** Pol
54C3 **Ota** Japan
78B3 **Otago Pen** NZ
78C2 **Otaki** NZ
53E3 **Otaru** Japan
26C3 **Otavalo** Ecuador
73B5 **Otavi** Namibia
54D3 **Otawara** Japan
14C1 **Otego** USA
18C1 **Othello** USA
3G2 **Otherside** *R* Can
41E3 **Óthris** *Mt* Greece
71G4 **Oti** *R* Ghana
71G4 **Otiki** *R* Nig
16B1 **Otis** Colorado, USA
14D1 **Otis** Massachusetts, USA
14C2 **Otisville** USA
74B1 **Otjimbingwe** Namibia
73B6 **Otjiwarongo** Namibia
52B2 **Otog Qi** China
54D2 **Otoineppu** Japan
78C1 **Otorohanga** NZ
41D2 **Otranto** Italy
41D2 **Otranto,Str of** *Chan* Italy/Alb
12B2 **Otsego** USA
14C1 **Otsego L** USA
4E5 **Otsego Lake** USA
54C3 **Otsu** Japan
32F6 **Otta** Nor
32F7 **Otta** *R* Nor
4F4 **Ottawa** Can
4F4 **Ottawa** *R* Can
12B2 **Ottawa** Illinois, USA
17C2 **Ottawa** Kansas, USA
7K4 **Ottawa Is** Can
7K4 **Otter Rapids** Can
7K1 **Otto Fjord** Can
74D2 **Ottosdal** S Africa
12A2 **Ottumwa** USA
36D2 **Ottweiler** Germany
71H4 **Otukpa** Nig
71H4 **Oturkpo** Nig
26C5 **Otusco** Peru
75B3 **Otway,C** Aust
43E2 **Otwock** Pol
37D1 **Ötz** Austria
37D1 **Otzal** *Mts* Austria
55C1 **Ou** *R* Laos
17D3 **Ouachita** *R* USA
17D3 **Ouachita,L** USA
17D3 **Ouachita Mts** USA
70A2 **Ouadane** Maur
72C3 **Ouadda** CAR
72C2 **Ouaddai** *Desert Region* Chad
71F3 **Ouagadougou** Burkina
71F3 **Ouahigouya** Burkina
72C3 **Ouaka** CAR
70C3 **Oualam** Niger
71G3 **Oualé** *R* Burkina
70C2 **Ouallen** Alg
72C3 **Ouanda Djallé** CAR
36B3 **Ouanne** *R* France
70A2 **Ouarane** Region, Maur
70C1 **Ouargla** Alg
72C3 **Ouarra** *R* CAR
70B1 **Ouarzazate** Mor
39C2 **Ouassel** *R* Alg
72B3 **Oubangui** *R* Congo
36B1 **Oudenaarde** Belg
74C3 **Oudtshoorn** S Africa
39B2 **Oued Tlělat** Alg
71A2 **Oued Zem** Mor
71F4 **Ouellé** Ivory Coast
72B3 **Ouesso** Congo
71A2 **Ouezzane** Mor
72B3 **Ouham** *R* Chad
71G4 **Ouidah** Benin
4D4 **Ouimet** Can
71B2 **Oujda** Mor
32J6 **Oulainen** Fin
32K5 **Oulu** Fin
32K6 **Oulu** *R* Fin
32K6 **Oulujärvi** *L* Fin
72C2 **Oum Chalouba** Chad
71D1 **Oum el Bouaghi** Alg
71A2 **Oumer Rbia** *R* Mor
72B2 **Oum Hadjer** Chad
72C2 **Oum Haouach** *Watercourse* Chad
32K5 **Ounas** *R* Fin
44C2 **Ounasjoki** *R* Fin
44C2 **Ounastunturi** *Mt* Fin
72C2 **Ounianga Kebir** Chad
36D1 **Our** *R* Germany
16A2 **Ouray** USA
36C2 **Ource** *R* France
Ourense = Orense Spain
36B2 **Ourcq** *R* France
27K5 **Ouricurí** Brazil
29C3 **Ourinhos** Brazil
29D3 **Ouro Prêto** Brazil
36C1 **Ourthe** *R* Belg
35E4 **Ouse** *R* Eng
35F5 **Ouse** *R* Eng
33B2 **Outer Hebrides** *Is* Scot
20C4 **Outer Santa Barbara** *Chan* USA
73B6 **Outjo** Namibia
3G3 **Outlook** Can
32K6 **Outokumpu** Fin
37A2 **Ouvèze** *R* France
75B3 **Ouyen** Aust
37C2 **Ovada** Italy
28A2 **Ovalle** Chile
73B5 **Ovamboland** Region, Namibia
19D3 **Overton** USA
32J5 **Övertorneå** Sweden
16B1 **Ovid** Colorado, USA
14B1 **Ovid** New York, USA
39A1 **Oviedo** Spain
45D5 **Ovruch** Ukraine
49O4 **Ovsyanka** Russian Fed
78A3 **Owaka** NZ
14B1 **Owasco L** USA
54C4 **Owase** Japan
11D3 **Owatonna** USA
14B1 **Owego** USA
20C2 **Owens** *R* USA
12B3 **Owensboro** USA
20D2 **Owens L** USA
4E5 **Owen Sound** Can
76D1 **Owen Stanley Range** *Mts* PNG
71H4 **Owerri** Nig
4C2 **Owl** *R* Can
18E2 **Owl Creek Mts** USA
71H4 **Owo** Nig
12C2 **Owosso** USA
18C2 **Owyhee** USA
18C2 **Owyhee** *R* USA
18C2 **Owyhee Mts** USA
26C6 **Oxampampa** Peru
3H4 **Oxbow** Can
32H7 **Oxelösund** Sweden
35E6 **Oxford** County, Eng
35E5 **Oxford** Eng
14E1 **Oxford** Massachusetts, USA
17E3 **Oxford** Mississippi, USA
14C1 **Oxford** New York, USA
20C3 **Oxnard** USA
53D4 **Oyama** Japan
3F3 **Oyen** Can
72B3 **Oyen** Gabon
34C3 **Oykel** *R* Scot
49Q3 **Oymyakon** Russian Fed
71G4 **Oyo** Nig
37A1 **Oyonnax** France
32F6 **Øyre** Nor
75E3 **Oyster B** Aust
57F9 **Ozamiz** Phil
43F2 **Ozarichi** Belorussia
15B2 **Ozark** USA
17D2 **Ozark Plat** USA
17D2 **Ozarks,L of the** USA
43E3 **Ózd** Hung
53E2 **Ozerskiy** Russian Fed
16B3 **Ozona** USA
22C1 **Ozuluama** Mexico

P

74B3 **Paarl** S Africa
34B3 **Pabbay** *I* Scot
43D2 **Pabianice** Pol
61C3 **Pabna** Bang
43F1 **Pabrade** Lithuania
26C5 **Pacasmayo** Peru
28E2 **Pacheca** Brazil
22B1 **Pacheco** Mexico
22C1 **Pachuca** Mexico
20B1 **Pacific** USA
xxixN7 **Pacific-Antarctic Ridge** Pacific O
20B2 **Pacific Grove** USA
xxixG8 **Pacific O**
56D4 **Pacitan** Indon
29D2 **Pacuí** *R* Brazil
56B3 **Padang** Indon
57B4 **Padang** Indon
56B3 **Padangpanjang** Indon
56A2 **Padangsidempuan** Indon
44E3 **Padany** Russian Fed
42B2 **Paderborn** Germany
6J3 **Padlei** Can
61D3 **Padma** *R* Bang
37D2 **Padova** Italy
8D4 **Padre I** USA
35C6 **Padstow** Eng
75B3 **Padthaway** Aust
Padua = Padova
12B3 **Paducah** Kentucky, USA
16B3 **Paducah** Texas, USA
32L5 **Padunskoye More** *L* Russian Fed
54A2 **Paegam** N Korea
53A4 **Paengnyŏng-do** *I* S Korea
78C1 **Paeroa** NZ
74E1 **Pafuri** Mozam
40C2 **Pag** *I* Croatia, Yugos
57F9 **Pagadian** Phil
56B3 **Pagai Seletan** *I* Indon
56B3 **Pagai Utara** *I* Indon
51H5 **Pagan** *I* Pacific O
56E3 **Pagatan** Indon
19D3 **Page** USA
51F8 **Pago Mission** Aust
41F3 **Pagondhas** Greece
16A2 **Pagosa Springs** USA
4C4 **Paguchi L** Can
4D3 **Pagwa River** Can
20E5 **Pahala** Hawaiian Is
78C2 **Pahiatua** NZ
20E5 **Pahoa** Hawaiian Is
15E4 **Pahokee** USA
71J4 **Pai** *R* Nig
32K6 **Päijänna** *L* Fin
28A4 **Paillaco** Chile
20E5 **Pailola Chan** Hawaiian Is
12C2 **Painesville** USA
19D3 **Painted Desert** USA
12C3 **Paintsville** USA
34C4 **Paisley** Scot
26B5 **Paita** Peru
32J5 **Pajala** Sweden
57B4 **Pajeti** Indon
58E3 **Pakistan** Republic, Asia
55C2 **Pak Lay** Laos
61E3 **Pakokku** Burma
3F4 **Pakowki L** Can
40D1 **Pakrac** Croatia, Yugos
41D1 **Paks** Hung
55C2 **Pak Sane** Laos
55D2 **Pakse** Laos
72D3 **Pakwach** Uganda
72B3 **Pala** Chad
40D2 **Palagruža** *I* Croatia, Yugos
36B2 **Palaiseau** France
74D1 **Palala** *R* S Africa
62E2 **Palalankwe** Andaman Is
49S4 **Palana** Russian Fed
56D3 **Palangkaraya** Indon
62B2 **Palani** India
60C4 **Palanpur** India
74D1 **Palapye** Botswana
15C3 **Palatka** USA
51G6 **Palau Is** Pacific O
55B3 **Palaw** Burma
57E9 **Palawan** *I* Phil
57E9 **Palawan Pass** Phil
62B3 **Palayankottai** India
32J7 **Paldiski** Estonia
57B2 **Paleleh** Indon
56B3 **Palembang** Indon
39B1 **Palencia** Spain
65B1 **Paleokhorio** Cyprus
40C3 **Palermo** Italy
65C3 **Palestine** Region, Israel
17C3 **Palestine** USA
61D3 **Paletwa** Burma
62B2 **Pālghāt** India
60C3 **Pāli** India
71G4 **Palimé** Togo
56E1 **Palin,Mt** Malay
16A2 **Palisade** USA
60C4 **Pālitāna** India
62B3 **Palk Str** India/Sri Lanka
45H5 **Pallasovka** Russian Fed
32J5 **Pallastunturi** *Mt* Fin
78B2 **Palliser B** NZ
78C2 **Palliser,C** NZ
73E5 **Palma** Mozam
39C2 **Palma de Mallorca** Spain
27L5 **Palmares** Brazil
28E2 **Palmares do Sul** Brazil
23A5 **Palmar Sur** Costa Rica
29B4 **Palmas** Brazil
70B4 **Palmas,C** Lib
29D1 **Palmas de Monte Alto** Brazil
23B2 **Palma Soriano** Cuba
15C3 **Palm Bay** USA
15E4 **Palm Beach** USA
20C3 **Palmdale** USA
29C4 **Palmeira** Brazil
27L5 **Palmeira dos Indos** Brazil
10J3 **Palmer** USA
79G3 **Palmer** *Base* Ant
79G3 **Palmer Arch** Ant
79F3 **Palmer Land** *Region* Ant
78B3 **Palmerston** NZ
78C2 **Palmerston North** NZ
14C2 **Palmerton** USA
15E4 **Palmetto** USA
40D3 **Palmi** Italy
28E1 **Palmiera das Missões** Brazil
22C1 **Palmillas** Mexico
26C3 **Palmira** Colombia
76D2 **Palm Is** Aust
4E5 **Palms** USA
19C4 **Palm Springs** USA
12A3 **Palmyra** Missouri, USA
14B1 **Palmyra** New York, USA
14B2 **Palmyra** Pennsylvania, USA
61C3 **Palmyras Pt** India
20A2 **Palo Alto** USA
56C2 **Paloh** Indon
72D2 **Paloích** Sudan
22C2 **Palomares** Mexico
19C4 **Palomar Mt** USA
57B3 **Palopo** Indon
57A3 **Palu** Indon
64C2 **Palu** Turk
60D3 **Palwal** India
10B2 **Palyavaam** *R* Russian Fed
71G3 **Pama** Burkina
56D4 **Pamekasan** Indon
56C4 **Pameungpeuk** Indon
38C3 **Pamiers** France
59F2 **Pamir** *Mts* China
48J6 **Pamir** *R* Russian Fed
15D1 **Pamlico** *R* USA
15D1 **Pamlico Sd** USA
16B2 **Pampa** USA
28B2 **Pampa de la Salinas** *Salt pan* Arg
28B3 **Pampa de la Varita** *Plain* Arg
57B3 **Pampanua** Indon
28D2 **Pampeiro** Brazil
26D2 **Pamplona** Colombia
39B1 **Pamplona** Spain
12B3 **Pana** USA
19D3 **Panaca** USA
41E2 **Panagyurishte** Bulg
62A1 **Panaji** India
26C2 **Panamá** Panama
26B2 **Panama** Republic, C America
23B5 **Panama Canal** Panama
15B2 **Panama City** USA
19C3 **Panamint Range** *Mts* USA
20D2 **Panamint V** USA
37D2 **Panaro** *R* Italy
57F8 **Panay** *I* Phil
41E2 **Pancevo** Serbia, Yugos
57F8 **Pandan** Phil
62B1 **Pandharpur** India
75A1 **Pandie Pandie** Aust
43E1 **Panevežys** Lithuania
48K5 **Panfilov** Kazakhstan
55B1 **Pang** *R* Burma
72D4 **Pangani** Tanz
72D4 **Pangani** *R* Tanz
72C4 **Pangi** Zaïre
57A3 **Pangkajene** Indon
56C3 **Pangkalpinang** Indon
7M3 **Pangnirtung** Can
55B1 **Pangtara** Burma
19D3 **Panguitch** USA
57F9 **Pangutaran Group** *Is* Phil
16B2 **Panhandle** USA
60D3 **Panipat** India
60B2 **Panjao** Afghan
63E3 **Panjgur** Pak
10F5 **Pankof,C** USA
71H4 **Pankshin** Nig
53B4 **P'anmunjŏm** N Korea
61B3 **Panna** India
29B3 **Panorama** Brazil
29A2 **Pantanal de São Lourenço** *Swamp* Brazil
29A2 **Pantanal do Rio Negro** *Swamp* Brazil
29A2 **Pantanal do Taquari** *Swamp* Brazil
57B4 **Pantar** *I* Indon
40C3 **Pantelleria** *I* Medit S
22C1 **Pantepec** Mexico
22C1 **Panuco** Mexico
22C1 **Pánuco** *R* Mexico
52A4 **Pan Xian** China
40D3 **Paola** Italy
17D2 **Paola** USA
12B3 **Paoli** USA
42D3 **Papa** Hung
20E5 **Papaikou** Hawaiian Is
78B1 **Papakura** NZ
22C2 **Papaloapan** *R* Mexico
22C1 **Papantla** Mexico
34E1 **Papa Stour** *I* Scot
78B1 **Papatoetoe** NZ
34D2 **Papa Westray** *I* Scot
65B1 **Paphos** Cyprus
76D1 **Papua,G of** PNG
76D1 **Papua New Guinea** Republic, S E Asia
28A2 **Papudo** Chile
55B2 **Papun** Burma
27H4 **Para** State, Brazil
27J4 **Pará** *R* Brazil
76A3 **Paraburdoo** Aust
26C6 **Paracas,Pen de** Peru
29C2 **Paracatu** Brazil
29C2 **Paracatu** *R* Brazil
55E2 **Paracel Is** S E Asia
75A2 **Parachilna** Aust
60C2 **Parachinar** Pak
41E2 **Paracin** Serbia, Yugos
29D2 **Pará de Minas** Brazil
19B3 **Paradise** California, USA
19D3 **Paradise** Nevada, USA
5K3 **Paradise** *R* Can
20D1 **Paradise Peak** *Mt* USA
17D2 **Paragould** USA
26F6 **Paraguá** *R* Bol
26F2 **Paragua** *R* Ven
29D1 **Paraguaçu** *R* Brazil
27G7 **Paraguai** *R* Brazil
29A4 **Paraguari** Par
25E2 **Paraguay** Republic, S America
25E2 **Paraguay** *R* Par
27L5 **Paraiba** State, Brazil
29D3 **Paraíba do Sul** *R* Brazil
22D2 **Paraiso** Mexico
71G4 **Parakou** Benin
75A2 **Parakylia** Aust
62B3 **Paramakkudi** India
27G2 **Paramaribo** Surinam
29D1 **Paramirim** Brazil
49R4 **Paramushir, Ostrov** *I* Russian Fed
29B4 **Paraná** Brazil
25F2 **Paraná** State, Brazil
28C2 **Paraná** Urug
25E4 **Paranã** *R* Arg
27J6 **Paranã** *R* Brazil
29C4 **Paranaguá** Brazil
29B2 **Paranaiba** Brazil
29B2 **Paranaiba** *R* Brazil
29B3 **Paranapanema** *R* Brazil
29B3 **Paranavai** Brazil
57F9 **Parang** Phil
29D2 **Paraope** *R* Brazil
78B2 **Paraparaumu** NZ
29D1 **Paratinga** Brazil
62B1 **Parbhani** India
71G3 **Parc National d'Arly** Burkina
71F4 **Parc National de la Komoé** Ivory Coast
71G3 **Parc National de la Pendjari** Benin
71G3 **Parcs Nationaux du W** Benin
65C2 **Pardes Hanna** Israel
28D3 **Pardo** Arg
29E2 **Pardo** *R* Bahia, Brazil
29B3 **Pardo** *R* Mato Grosso do Sul, Brazil
29C2 **Pardo** *R* Minas Gerais, Brazil
29C3 **Pardo** *R* Sao Paulo, Brazil
42D2 **Pardubice** Czech
50G4 **Parece Vela** *Reef* Pacific O
29A1 **Parecis** Brazil
4G4 **Parent** Can
57A3 **Parepare** Indon
28C3 **Parera** Arg
56B3 **Pariaman** Indon
26F1 **Paria,Pen de** Ven
57B3 **Parigi** Indon
38C2 **Paris** France
12C3 **Paris** Kentucky, USA
15B1 **Paris** Tennessee, USA
17C3 **Paris** Texas, USA
19D4 **Parker** USA
12C3 **Parkersburg** USA
75C2 **Parkes** Aust
14C3 **Parkesburg** USA
12A1 **Park Falls** USA
20B3 **Parkfield** USA
12B2 **Park Forest** USA
11C2 **Park Rapids** USA
11C3 **Parkston** USA

Rāvar Rolândia

63D2 Rāvar Iran
43E2 Rava Russkaya Ukraine
14D1 Ravena USA
37E2 Ravenna Italy
42B3 Ravensburg Germany
76D2 Ravenshoe Aust
35F4 Ravenspurn Oilfield N Sea
60C2 Ravi R Pak
60C2 Rawalpindi Pak
64D2 Rawāndiz Iraq
42D2 Rawicz Pol
76B4 Rawlinna Aust
8C2 Rawlins USA
25D6 Rawson Arg
61E2 Rawu China
56D3 Raya Mt Indon
62B2 Rāyadurg India
62C1 Rāyagada India
65D2 Rayak Leb
7N5 Ray,C Can
53B2 Raychikhinsk Russian Fed
66D3 Raydah Yemen
63D3 Rāyen Iran
20C2 Raymond California, USA
18D1 Raymond Can
14E1 Raymond New Hampshire, USA
18B1 Raymond Washington, USA
75D2 Raymond Terrace Aust
17F4 Raymondville USA
10H2 Ray Mts USA
22C1 Rayon Mexico
67F3 Raysūt Oman
63B1 Razan Iran
43G3 Razdel'naya Ukraine
53C3 Razdol'noye Russian Fed
41F2 Razgrad Bulg
41F2 Razim L Rom
35E6 Reading Eng
14C2 Reading USA
6G3 Read Island Can
14D1 Readsboro USA
28B2 Real de Padre Arg
28C3 Realicó Arg
69B2 Rebiana Well Libya
69B2 Rebiana Sand Sea Libya
32L6 Reboly Russian Fed
53E2 Rebun-tō I Japan
76B4 Recherche,Arch of the Is Aust
43G2 Rechitsa Belorussia
27M5 Recife Brazil
74D3 Recife,C S Africa
29E2 Recifes da Pedra Grande Arch Brazil
77F2 Récifs D'Entrecasteaux Nouvelle Calédonie
36D1 Recklinghausen Germany
28D1 Reconquista Arg
28C1 Recreo Arg
11C2 Red R Can/USA
17D3 Red R USA
55C4 Redang I Malay
14C2 Red Bank New Jersey, USA
15B1 Red Bank Tennessee, USA
5K3 Red Bay Can
3G3 Redberry L Can
19B2 Red Bluff USA
16B3 Red Bluff L USA
35E4 Redcar Eng
3F3 Redcliff Can
75D1 Redcliffe Aust
75B2 Red Cliffs Aust
16C1 Red Cloud USA
3F3 Red Deer Can
3F3 Red Deer R Can
3H3 Red Deer R Saskatchewan, Can
3H3 Red Deer L Can
18B2 Redding USA
11C3 Redfield USA
16C2 Red Hills USA
9D2 Red L USA
7J4 Red Lake Can
11C2 Red Lake R USA
20D3 Redlands USA
14B3 Red Lion USA
18E1 Red Lodge USA
18B2 Redmond USA
20D3 Red Mountain USA
17C1 Red Oak USA
38B2 Redon France
20C4 Redondo Beach USA
10H3 Redoubt V USA
52B5 Red River Delta Vietnam
58B3 Red Sea Africa/Arabian Pen
10N3 Redstone R Can
4C3 Red Sucker L Can
3F3 Redwater Can
3G4 Redwater R USA
11D3 Red Wing USA
20A2 Redwood City USA
11C3 Redwood Falls USA
12B2 Reed City USA
20C2 Reedley USA
18B2 Reedsport USA
13D3 Reedville USA
78B2 Reefton NZ
64C2 Refahiye Turk
17F4 Refugio USA
29E2 Regência Brazil
42C3 Regensburg Germany
70C2 Reggane Alg
40D3 Reggio di Calabria Italy
37D2 Reggio Nell'Emilia Italy
41E1 Reghin Rom
3H3 Regina Can
63E2 Registan Region, Afghan
22A1 Regocijo Mexico
74B1 Rehoboth Namibia
13D3 Rehoboth Beach USA
65C3 Rehovot Israel
26E1 Reicito Ven
15D1 Reidsville USA
35E6 Reigate Eng
36B2 Reims France
11D3 Reinbeck USA
3H2 Reindeer R Can
3H2 Reindeer L Can
39B1 Reinosa Spain
14B3 Reisterstown USA
74D2 Reitz S Africa
6H3 Reliance Can
18E2 Reliance USA
71C1 Relizane Alg
75A2 Remarkable,Mt Aust
56D4 Rembang Indon
63D3 Remeshk Iran
36D2 Remiremont France
36D1 Remscheid Germany
14C1 Remsen USA
37A2 Rémuzat France
12B3 Rend L USA
42B2 Rendsburg Germany
4F4 Renfrew Can
56B3 Rengat Indon
28A2 Rengo Chile
43F3 Reni Ukraine
72D2 Renk Sudan
7Q2 Renland Pen Greenland
75B2 Renmark Aust
77F2 Rennell I Solomon Is
38B2 Rennes France
19C3 Reno USA
37D2 Reno R Italy
14B2 Renovo USA
14D1 Rensselaer USA
18B1 Renton USA
57B4 Reo Indon
71F3 Réo Burkina
63E1 Repetek Turkmenistan
43G2 Repki Ukraine
29C3 Reprêsa de Furnas Dam Brazil
29C2 Reprêsa Três Marias Dam Brazil
18C1 Republic USA
16C1 Republican R USA
33B3 Republic of Ireland NW Europe
7K3 Repulse Bay Can
4F4 Réservoir Baskatong Res Can
13D1 Réservoir Cabonga Res Can
4F4 Réservoir Decelles Res Can
7L4 Réservoir de La Grande 2 Res Can
7L4 Réservoir de La Grande 3 Res Can
7L4 Réservoir de La Grande 4 Res Can
4F4 Réservoir Dozois Res Can
7L5 Réservoir Gouin Res Can
5G4 Réservoir Pipmouacane Res Can
63C1 Reshteh-ye Alborz Mts Iran
52A2 Reshui China
25E3 Resistencia Arg
41E1 Resita Rom
7J2 Resolute Can
78A3 Resolution I NZ
7M3 Resolution Island Can
74E2 Ressano Garcia Mozam
5H4 Restigouche R Can
28E1 Restinga Seca Brazil
28B2 Retamito Arg
36C2 Rethel France
41E3 Réthimnon Greece
xxviiiD6 Reunion I Indian O
39C1 Reus Spain
37C1 Reuss R Switz
36E2 Reutlingen Germany
37D1 Reutte Austria
44K4 Revda Russian Fed
3E3 Revelstoke Can
21A3 Revillagigedo Is Mexico
10M4 Revillagigedo I USA
36C2 Revin France
65C3 Revivim Israel
61B3 Rewa India
60D3 Rewari India
18D2 Rexburg USA
32A2 Reykjavik Iceland
14A2 Reynoldsville USA
21C2 Reynosa Mexico
38B2 Rezé France
43F1 Rezekne Latvia
44L4 Rezh Russian Fed
37C1 Rhätikon Mts Austria/Switz
65C1 Rhazīr Republic, Leb
36E1 Rheda Wiedenbrück Germany
42B2 Rhein R W Europe
42B2 Rheine Germany
37B1 Rheinfielden Switz
38D2 Rheinland Pfalz Region, Germany
37C1 Rheinwaldhorn Mt Switz
Rhine = Rhein
14D2 Rhinebeck USA
12B1 Rhinelander USA
37C2 Rho Italy
13E2 Rhode Island State, USA
14E2 Rhode Island Sd USA
Rhodes = Ródhos
74D1 Rhodes Drift Ford S Africa
18D1 Rhodes Peak Mt USA
38C3 Rhône R France
35D5 Rhyl Wales
27L6 Riachão do Jacuipe Brazil
39A1 Ria de Arosa B Spain
39A1 Ria de Betanzos B Spain
39A1 Ria de Corcubion B Spain
39A1 Ria de Lage B Spain
39A1 Ria de Sta Marta B Spain
39A1 Ria de Vigo B Spain
60C2 Riāsi Pak
39A1 Ribadeo Spain
29B3 Ribas do Rio Pardo Brazil
73D5 Ribauè Mozam
35D5 Ribble R Eng
29C3 Ribeira Brazil
29C3 Ribeirão Prêto Brazil
26E6 Riberala Bol
37E3 Riccione Italy
13D2 Rice L Can
12A1 Rice Lake USA
29D1 Richao de Santana Brazil
74E2 Richard's Bay S Africa
10L2 Richards I Can
17C3 Richardson USA
3F2 Richardson R Can
10L2 Richardson Mts Can
19D3 Richfield USA
14C1 Richfield Springs USA
20C3 Richgrove USA
5J4 Richibucto Can
18C1 Richland USA
12C3 Richlands USA
20A2 Richmond California, USA
74C3 Richmond Cape Province, S Africa
12C3 Richmond Kentucky, USA
74E2 Richmond Natal, S Africa
75D2 Richmond New South Wales, Aust
78B2 Richmond NZ
76D3 Richmond Queensland, Aust
13D3 Richmond Virginia, USA
78B2 Richmond Range Mts NZ
14C1 Richmondville USA
4F5 Rideau Lakes Can
15C2 Ridgeland USA
14A2 Ridgway USA
11B1 Riding Mountain Nat Pk Can
23D4 Riecito Ven
37D1 Rienza R Italy
42C2 Riesa Germany
25B8 Riesco I Chile
74C2 Riet R S Africa
40C2 Rieti Italy
37B3 Riez France
39B2 Rif Mts Mor
16A2 Rifle USA
43E1 Riga Latvia
44C4 Riga,G of Estonia/Latvia
63D3 Rigān Iran
18D2 Rigby USA
18C1 Riggins USA
7N4 Rigolet Can
32J6 Riihimaki Fin
40C1 Rijeka Croatia, Yugos
54D3 Rikuzen-Tanaka Japan
71H3 Rima R Nig
3F3 Rimbey Can
32H7 Rimbo Sweden
37E2 Rimini Italy
41E1 Rîmnicu Vîlcea Rom
5H4 Rimouski Can
22B1 Rincón de Romos Mexico
32F7 Ringkøbing Den
28A3 Riñihue Chile
57A4 Rinja I Indon
72A3 Rio Benito Eq Guinea
26E5 Rio Branco Brazil
28E2 Rio Branco Urug
29C4 Rio Branco do Sul Brazil
17F4 Rio Bravo Mexico
21B1 Rio Bravo del Norte R USA/Mexico
29B3 Rio Brilhante Brazil
28A4 Rio Bueno Chile
26D1 Riochacha Colombia
29C3 Rio Claro Brazil
23L1 Rio Claro Trinidad
28C3 Rio Colorado Arg
28C2 Rio Cuarto Arg
27L6 Rio de Jacuipe Brazil
29D3 Rio de Janeiro Brazil
29D3 Rio de Janeiro State, Brazil
28D2 Rio de la Plata Estuary Arg/Urug
25C8 Rio Gallegos Arg
25C8 Rio Grande Arg
28E2 Rio Grande Brazil
22B1 Rio Grande Mexico
23A4 Rio Grande Nic
21D3 Rio Grande R Nicaragua
21B2 Rio Grande R USA/Mexico
17F4 Rio Grande City USA
22B1 Rio Grande de Santiago Mexico
27L5 Rio Grande do Norte State, Brazil
28E1 Rio Grande do Sul State, Brazil
xxxG6 Rio Grande Rise Atlantic O
23C4 Riohacha Colombia
38C2 Riom France
26C4 Riombamba Ecuador
26E7 Rio Mulatos Bol
29C4 Rio Negro Brazil
28B4 Rio Negro State, Arg
25F3 Rio Pardo Brazil
28C2 Rio Tercero Arg
26F6 Rio Theodore Roosevelt R Brazil
25B8 Rio Turbio Arg
3G2 Riou L Can
29B2 Rio Verde Brazil
22B1 Rio Verde Mexico
29B2 Rio Verde de Mato Grosso Brazil
12C3 Ripley Ohio, USA
15B1 Ripley Tennessee, USA
12C3 Ripley West Virginia, USA
35E4 Ripon Eng
20B2 Ripon USA
53E2 Rishiri-tō I Japan
65C3 Rishon le Zion Israel
14B3 Rising Sun USA
36A2 Risle R France
32F7 Risør Nor
62E2 Ritchie's Arch Andaman Is
7N3 Ritenbenk Greenland
20C2 Ritter,Mt USA
18C1 Ritzville USA
28B2 Rivadavia Arg
28A1 Rivadavia Chile
28C3 Rivadavia Gonzalez Moreno Arg
37D2 Riva de Garda Italy
26A1 Rivas Nic
28C3 Rivera Arg
28D2 Rivera Urug
20B2 Riverbank USA
70B4 River Cess Lib
20C2 Riverdale USA
14D2 Riverhead USA
75B3 Riverina Aust
71H4 Rivers State, Nig
78A3 Riversdale NZ
74C3 Riversdale S Africa
20D4 Riverside USA
3C3 Rivers Inlet Can
4B3 Riverton Can
78A3 Riverton NZ
18E2 Riverton USA
37A2 Rives France
15E4 Riviera Beach USA
7L4 Rivière aux Feuilles R Can
5G2 Rivière aux Mélèzes R Can
5H3 Rivière aux Outardes R Can
7M4 Rivière de la Baleine R Can
5G4 Rivière du Lièvre R Can
5H4 Rivière-du-Loup Can
7M4 Rivière du Petit Mècatina R Can
5F2 Rivière Innuksuac R Can
5G1 Rivière Lepellé R Can
5H4 Rivière Pentecôte Can
5F1 Rivière Povungnituk R Can
5G1 Rivière Vachon R Can
36C2 Rivigny-sur-Ornain France
54A2 Riwon N Korea
67E2 Riyadh S Arabia
64D1 Rize Turk
52D2 Rizhao China
65C1 Rizokaipaso Cyprus
32F7 Rjukan Nor
7K2 Roanes Pen Can
38C2 Roanne France
15B2 Roanoke Alabama, USA
13D3 Roanoke Virginia, USA
13D3 Roanoke R USA
15D1 Roanoke Rapids USA
19D3 Roan Plat USA
18D2 Roberts USA
19C3 Roberts Creek Mt USA
32J6 Robertsforz Sweden
17D2 Robert S Kerr Res USA
74B3 Robertson S Africa
70A4 Robertsport Lib
7L5 Roberval Can
75B2 Robinvale Aust
3H3 Roblin Can
3E3 Robson,Mt Can
17F4 Robstown USA
21A3 Roca Partida I Mexico
xxxG5 Rocas I Atlantic O
27M4 Rocas I Brazil
37D2 Rocca San Casciano Italy
28E2 Rocha Urug
35D5 Rochdale Eng
29B2 Rochedo Brazil
38B2 Rochefort France
12B2 Rochelle USA
6G3 Rocher River Can
75B3 Rochester Aust
35F6 Rochester Eng
11D3 Rochester Minnesota, USA
14E1 Rochester New Hampshire, USA
14B1 Rochester New York, USA
3C1 Rock R Can
12B2 Rock R USA
12B2 Rockford USA
3G4 Rockglen Can
15C2 Rock Hill USA
15D2 Rockingham USA
12A2 Rock Island USA
5H5 Rockland Maine, USA
12B1 Rockland Michigan, USA
75B3 Rocklands Res Aust
15C3 Rockledge USA
17F4 Rockport USA
11C3 Rock Rapids USA
11A3 Rock River USA
11A2 Rock Springs Montana, USA
16B3 Rocksprings Texas, USA
18E2 Rock Springs Wyoming, USA
78B2 Rocks Pt NZ
75C3 Rock,The Aust
14D2 Rockville Connecticut, USA
12B3 Rockville Indiana, USA
14B3 Rockville Maryland, USA
13F1 Rockwood USA
16B2 Rocky Ford USA
4E4 Rocky Island L Can
15D1 Rocky Mount USA
3F3 Rocky Mountain House Can
16A1 Rocky Mountain Nat Pk USA
8B1 Rocky Mts Can/USA
10F3 Rocky Pt USA
42C2 Rødbyhavn Den
5K3 Roddickton Can
28B2 Rodeo Arg
38C3 Rodez France
41F3 Ródhos Greece
41F3 Ródhos I Greece
40D2 Rodi Garganico Italy
41E2 Rodopi Planina Mts Bulg
76A3 Roebourne Aust
74D1 Roedtan S Africa
36D1 Roer R Neth
36C1 Roermond Neth
36B1 Roeselare Belg
7K3 Roes Welcome Sd Can
43F2 Rogachev Belorussia
17D2 Rogers USA
12C1 Rogers City USA
20D3 Rogers L USA
12C3 Rogers,Mt USA
18D2 Rogerson USA
4F3 Roggan L Can
4F3 Roggan R Can
74B3 Roggeveldberge Mts S Africa
18B2 Rogue R USA
60B3 Rohn Pak
60D3 Rohtak India
43E1 Roja Latvia
29B3 Rolândia Brazil

Sharya Sirsi

44H4 **Sharya** Russian Fed
72D3 **Shashamenē** Eth
74D1 **Shashani** *R* Zim
74D1 **Shashe** *R* Botswana
52C3 **Shashi** China
18B2 **Shasta L** USA
18B2 **Shasta,Mt** USA
65D1 **Shathah at Tahtā** Syria
64E3 **Shaṭṭ al Gharrat** *R* Iraq
65C3 **Shaubak** Jordan
3G4 **Shaunavon** Can
20C2 **Shaver L** USA
14C2 **Shawangunk Mt** USA
12B2 **Shawano** USA
17C2 **Shawnee** Oklahoma, USA
11A3 **Shawnee** Wyoming, USA
5G4 **Shawinigan** Can
52D4 **Sha Xian** China
76B3 **Shay Gap** Aust
65D2 **Shaykh Miskīn** Syria
66D4 **Shaykh 'Uthmān** Yemen
44F5 **Shchekino** Russian Fed
45F5 **Shchigry** Russian Fed
45E5 **Shchors** Ukraine
48J4 **Shchuchinsk** Kazakhstan
12B2 **Sheboygan** USA
72E3 **Shebele** *R* Eth
72B3 **Shebshi** *Mts* Nig
53E2 **Shebunino** Russian Fed
5J4 **Shediac** Can
10K2 **Sheenjek** *R* USA
34B4 **Sheep Haven** *Estuary* Irish Rep
35F6 **Sheerness** Eng
5J5 **Sheet Harbour** Can
65C2 **Shefar'am** Israel
15B2 **Sheffield** Alabama, USA
35E5 **Sheffield** Eng
14A2 **Sheffield** Pennsylvania, USA
16B3 **Sheffield** Texas, USA
5K3 **Shekalika Bay** Can
60C2 **Shekhupura** Pak
3C2 **Shelagyote Peak** *Mt* Can
5H5 **Shelburne** Can
14D1 **Shelburne Falls** USA
12B2 **Shelby** Michigan, USA
18D1 **Shelby** Montana, USA
15C1 **Shelby** N Carolina, USA
12B3 **Shelbyville** Indiana, USA
15B1 **Shelbyville** Tennessee, USA
11C3 **Sheldon** USA
10M3 **Sheldon,Mt** Can
5J3 **Sheldrake** Can
10H4 **Shelikof Str** USA
3G3 **Shellbrook** Can
18D2 **Shelley** USA
75D2 **Shellharbour** Aust
78A3 **Shelter Pt** NZ
18B1 **Shelton** USA
64E1 **Shemakha** Azerbaijan
17C1 **Shenandoah** USA
13D3 **Shenandoah** *R* USA
14A3 **Shenandoah Mt** USA
13D3 **Shenandoah Nat Pk** USA
71H4 **Shendam** Nig
66B3 **Shendi** Sudan
44G3 **Shenkursk** Russian Fed
52C2 **Shenmu** China
52E1 **Shenyang** China
52C5 **Shenzhen** China
60D3 **Sheopur** India
43F2 **Shepetovka** Ukraine
14B3 **Shepherdstown** USA
75C3 **Shepparton** Aust
36A1 **Sheppey,I of** Eng
7K2 **Sherard,C** Can
35D6 **Sherborne** Eng
70A4 **Sherbro I** Sierra Leone
5G4 **Sherbrooke** Can
14C1 **Sherburne** USA
66B3 **Shereik** Sudan
60C3 **Shergarh** India
17D3 **Sheridan** Arkansas, USA
11A3 **Sheridan** Wyoming, USA
17C3 **Sherman** USA
3H2 **Sherridon** Can
42B2 **s-Hertogenbosh** Neth
10M4 **Sheslay** Can
3B2 **Sheslay** *R* Can
33C1 **Shetland** *Is* Scot
45J7 **Shevchenko** Kazakhstan
53C1 **Shevli** *R* Russian Fed
11C2 **Sheyenne** USA
11C2 **Sheyenne** *R* USA
63C3 **Sheyk Sho'eyb** *I* Iran
50J2 **Shiashkotan** *I* Russian Fed
60B1 **Shibarghan** Afghan
53D4 **Shibata** Japan
54D2 **Shibetsu** Japan
69C1 **Shibin el Kom** Egypt
65A3 **Shibin el Qanâtir** Egypt
4D3 **Shibogama L** Can
54C3 **Shibukawa** Japan
14B2 **Shickshinny** USA
52C2 **Shijiazhuang** China
60B3 **Shikarpur** Pak
47H4 **Shikoku,I** Japan
54B4 **Shikoku-sanchi** *Mts* Japan
54D2 **Shikotsu-ko** *L* Japan
44G3 **Shilega** Russian Fed
61C2 **Shiliguri** India
50E1 **Shilka** Russian Fed
50E1 **Shilka** *R* Russian Fed
14C2 **Shillington** USA
61D2 **Shillong** India
44G5 **Shilovo** Russian Fed
54B4 **Shimabara** Japan
54C4 **Shimada** Japan
53B1 **Shimanovsk** Russian Fed
53D4 **Shimizu** Japan
54C4 **Shimoda** Japan
62B2 **Shimoga** India
53C5 **Shimonoseki** Japan
54C3 **Shinano** *R* Japan
67G2 **Shināş** Oman
63E2 **Shindand** Afghan
14A2 **Shinglehouse** USA
4D4 **Shingleton** USA
53D5 **Shingū** Japan
54D3 **Shinjō** Japan
53D4 **Shinminato** Japan
65D1 **Shinshār** Syria
72D4 **Shinyanga** Tanz
53E4 **Shiogama** Japan
54C4 **Shiono-misaki** *C* Japan
52A5 **Shiping** China
5J4 **Shippegan** Can
14B2 **Shippensburg** USA
16A2 **Shiprock** USA
67E3 **Shiqāq al Ma'āṭif** Region, Yemen
52B3 **Shiquan** China
54D3 **Shirakawa** Japan
54C3 **Shirane-san** *Mt* Japan
54C3 **Shirani-san** *Mt* Japan
63C3 **Shīraz** Iran
65A3 **Shirbîn** Egypt
54D2 **Shiriya-saki** *C* Japan
63C2 **Shīr Kūh** Iran
54C3 **Shirotori** Japan
63D1 **Shirvān** Iran
10F5 **Shishaldin V** USA
10E2 **Shishmaref** USA
10E2 **Shishmaref Inlet** USA
52B2 **Shitanjing** China
12B3 **Shively** USA
60D3 **Shivpuri** India
65C3 **Shivta** *Hist Site* Israel
19D3 **Shivwits Plat** USA
73D5 **Shiwa Ngandu** Zambia
52C3 **Shiyan** China
52B2 **Shizuishan** China
54C3 **Shizuoka** Japan
41D2 **Shkodër** Alb
43G2 **Shkov** Belorussia
49L1 **Shmidta, Ostrov** *I* Russian Fed
75D2 **Shoalhaven** *R* Aust
54B4 **Shobara** Japan
62B2 **Shoranūr** India
62B1 **Shorāpur** India
19C3 **Shoshone** California, USA
18D2 **Shoshone** Idaho, USA
18E2 **Shoshone** *R* USA
18D2 **Shoshone L** USA
19C3 **Shoshone Mts** USA
18E2 **Shoshoni** USA
45E5 **Shostka** Ukraine
66C4 **Showak** Sudan
19D4 **Show Low** USA
17D3 **Shreveport** USA
35D5 **Shrewsbury** Eng
35D5 **Shropshire** County, Eng
53B2 **Shuangcheng** China
52E1 **Shuanglia** China
53C2 **Shuangyashan** China
45K6 **Shubar-Kuduk** Kazakhstan
5J4 **Shubenacadie** Can
10J2 **Shublik Mts** USA
44N2 **Shuga** Russian Fed
52D2 **Shu He** *R* China
52A4 **Shuicheng** China
60C3 **Shujaabad** Pak
60D4 **Shujālpur** India
53B3 **Shulan** China
50C2 **Shule He** China
10G5 **Shumagin Is** USA
41F2 **Shumen** Bulg
44H4 **Shumerlya** Russian Fed
52D4 **Shuncheng** China
10G2 **Shungnak** USA
52C2 **Shuo Xian** China
63D3 **Shūr Gaz** Iran
73C5 **Shurugwi** Zim
3E3 **Shuswap L** Can
44G4 **Shuya** Russian Fed
10H4 **Shuyak I** USA
61E3 **Shwebo** Burma
55B2 **Shwegyin** Burma
61E3 **Shweli** *R* Burma
63E3 **Siahan Range** *Mts* Pak
60A2 **Siah Koh** *Mts* Afghan
60C2 **Sialkot** Pak
Sian = Xi'an
57G9 **Siarao, I** Phil
57F9 **Siaton** Phil
57C2 **Siau** *I* Indon
43E1 **Şiauliai** Lithuania
44K5 **Sibay** Russian Fed
74E2 **Sibayi L** S Africa
40D2 **Şibenik** Croatia, Yugos
56A3 **Siberut** *I* Indon
60B3 **Sibi** Pak
53C3 **Sibirtsevo** Russian Fed
72B4 **Sibiti** Congo
72D4 **Sibiti** *R* Tanz
41E1 **Sibiu** Rom
11C3 **Sibley** USA
57A2 **Siboa** Indon
56A2 **Sibolga** Indon
61D2 **Sibsāgār** India
56D2 **Sibu** Malay
57F9 **Sibuguay B** Phil
72B3 **Sibut** CAR
56E1 **Sibutu Pass** Malay/Phil
57F8 **Sibuyan** *I* Phil
57F8 **Sibuyan S** Phil
52A3 **Sichuan** Province, China
40C3 **Sicilia** *I* Medit S
40C3 **Sicilian** *Chan* Italy/Tunisia
Sicily = Sicilia
26D6 **Sicuari** Peru
60C4 **Siddhapur** India
62B1 **Siddipet** India
61B3 **Sidhi** India
69B1 **Sidi Barrani** Egypt
71B1 **Sidi bel Abbès** Alg
71A2 **Sidi Kacem** Mor
34D3 **Sidlaw Hills** Scot
79F5 **Sidley,Mt** Ant
18B1 **Sidney** Can
11B2 **Sidney** Montana, USA
16B1 **Sidney** Nebraska, USA
14C1 **Sidney** New York, USA
12C2 **Sidney** Ohio, USA
15C2 **Sidney Lanier,L** USA
Sidon = Säida
29B3 **Sidrolândia** Brazil
43E2 **Siedlce** Pol
36D1 **Sieg** *R* Germany
36D1 **Siegburg** Germany
36D1 **Siegen** Germany
37A1 **Sielle** *R* France
55C3 **Siem Reap** Camb
40C2 **Siena** Italy
36C3 **Siene** *R* France
43D2 **Sierpc** Pol
22C2 **Sierra Andrés Tuxtla** Mexico
28B3 **Sierra Auca Mahuida** *Mts* Arg
16A3 **Sierra Blanca** USA
28B4 **Sierra Blanca** *Mts* Arg
28B4 **Sierra Colorada** Arg
39B1 **Sierra de Albarracin** *Mts* Spain
39B2 **Sierra de Alcaraz** *Mts* Spain
28B1 **Sierra de Ancasti** *Mts* Arg
28B2 **Sierra de Cordoba** *Mts* Arg
28B1 **Sierra de Famantina** *Mts* Arg
39A1 **Sierra de Gredos** *Mts* Spain
39A2 **Sierra de Guadalupe** *Mts* Spain
39B1 **Sierra de Guadarrama** *Mts* Spain
39B1 **Sierra de Guara** *Mts* Spain
39B1 **Sierra de Gudar** *Mts* Spain
22C2 **Sierra de Juárez** *Mts* Mexico
28C3 **Sierra de la Ventana** *Mts* Arg
39C1 **Sierra del Codi** *Mts* Spain
28D1 **Sierra del Imán** *Mts* Arg
28B2 **Sierra del Morro** *Mt* Arg
28B3 **Sierra del Nevado** *Mts* Arg
21B2 **Sierra de los Alamitos** *Mts* Mexico
39B2 **Sierra de los Filabres** *Mts* Spain
22B1 **Sierra de los Huicholes** *Mts* Mexico
22C2 **Sierra de Miahuatlán** *Mts* Mexico
22B1 **Sierra de Morones** *Mts* Mexico
39A2 **Sierra de Ronda** *Mts* Spain
28B2 **Sierra de San Luis** *Mts* Arg
39B2 **Sierra de Segura** *Mts* Spain
22C1 **Sierra de Tamaulipas** *Mts* Mexico
39B1 **Sierra de Urbion** *Mts* Spain
28B2 **Sierra de Uspallata** *Mts* Arg
28B1 **Sierra de Valasco** *Mts* Arg
28B2 **Sierra de Valle Fértil** *Mts* Arg
22B1 **Sierra de Zacatécas** *Mts* Mexico
22C2 **Sierra de Zongolica** *Mts* Mexico
28C2 **Sierra Grande** *Mts* Arg
70A4 **Sierra Leone** Republic, Africa
70A4 **Sierra Leone,C** Sierra Leone
57F7 **Sierra Madre** *Mts* Phil
22B2 **Sierra Madre del Sur** *Mts* Mexico
20B3 **Sierra Madre Mts** USA
21B2 **Sierra Madre Occidental** *Mts* Mexico
22B1 **Sierra Madre Oriental** *Mts* Mexico
28B2 **Sierra Malanzan** *Mts* Arg
8C4 **Sierra Mojada** Mexico
39A2 **Sierra Morena** *Mts* Spain
39B2 **Sierra Nevada** *Mts* Spain
19B3 **Sierra Nevada** *Mts* USA
26D1 **Sierra Nevada de santa Marta** *Mts* Colombia
28B2 **Sierra Pié de Palo** *Mts* Arg
19D4 **Sierra Vista** USA
37B1 **Sierre** Switz
29A3 **Siete Puntas** *R* Par
41E3 **Sifnos** *I* Greece
71B1 **Sig** Alg
44E2 **Sig** Russian Fed
56A3 **Sigep** Indon
43E3 **Sighetu Marmaţiei** Rom
41E1 **Sighişoara** Rom
56A1 **Sigli** Indon
32B1 **Siglufjörður** Iceland
36E2 **Sigmaringen** Germany
26A1 **Siguatepeque** Honduras
39B1 **Sigüenza** Spain
70B3 **Siguiri** Guinea
60D4 **Sihora** India
64D2 **Siirt** Turk
50C3 **Sikai Hu** *L* China
3D2 **Sikanni** *R* Can
60D3 **Sīkar** India
60B2 **Sikaram** *Mt* Afghan
70B3 **Sikasso** Mali
57B4 **Sikeli** Indon
17E2 **Sikeston** USA
41F3 **Síkinos** *I* Greece
41E3 **Sikionia** Greece
61C2 **Sikkim** State, India
49O3 **Siktyakh** Russian Fed
39A1 **Sil** *R* Spain
37D1 **Silandro** Italy
22B1 **Silao** Mexico
57F8 **Silay** Phil
61D3 **Silchar** India
4C2 **Silcox** Can
70C2 **Silet** Alg
61B2 **Silgarhi** Nepal
64B2 **Silifke** Turk
65D1 **Silinfah** Syria
59G2 **Siling Co** *L* China
41F2 **Silistra** Bulg
44A3 **Siljan** *L* Sweden
32F7 **Silkeborg** Den
37E1 **Sillian** Austria
17D2 **Siloam Springs** USA
17D3 **Silsbee** USA
72B2 **Siltou** *Well* Chad
43E1 **Şilute** Lithuania
64D2 **Silvan** Turk
29C2 **Silvania** Brazil
60C4 **Silvassa** India
11D2 **Silver Bay** USA
19C3 **Silver City** Nevada, USA
16A3 **Silver City** New Mexico, USA
18B2 **Silver Lake** USA
20D2 **Silver Peak Range** *Mts* USA
14B3 **Silver Spring** USA
3C3 **Silverthrone Mt** Can
75B2 **Silverton** Aust
16A2 **Silverton** USA
37D1 **Silvretta** *Mts* Austria/Switz
56D2 **Simanggang** Malay
55C1 **Simao** China
63B2 **Simareh** *R* Iran
41F3 **Simav** Turk
41F3 **Simav** *R* Turk
4F5 **Simcoe,L** Can
10G5 **Simeohof** *I* USA
56A2 **Simeulue** *I* Indon
45E7 **Simferopol'** Ukraine
41F3 **Sími** *I* Greece
61B2 **Simikot** Nepal
60D2 **Simla** India
16B2 **Simla** USA
36D1 **Simmern** Germany
20C3 **Simmler** USA
74B3 **Simonstown** S Africa
3C3 **Simoom Sound** Can
38D2 **Simplon** *Mt* Switz
37C1 **Simplon** *P* Switz
6C2 **Simpson,C** USA
76C3 **Simpson Desert** Aust
10N2 **Simpson L** Can
3B2 **Simpson Peak** *Mt* Can
7K3 **Simpson Pen** Can
32G7 **Simrishamn** Sweden
50J2 **Simushir** *I* Russian Fed
56A2 **Sinabang** Indon
72E3 **Sina Dhaqa** Somalia
64B4 **Sinai** *Pen* Egypt
22A1 **Sinaloa** State, Mexico
37D3 **Sinalunga** Italy
26C2 **Sincelejo** Colombia
15C2 **Sinclair,L** USA
60D3 **Sind** *R* India
60B3 **Sindh** *Region* Pak
41F3 **Sindirği** Turk
61C3 **Sindri** India
53E2 **Sinegorsk** Russian Fed
39A2 **Sines** Port
72D2 **Singa** Sudan
55C5 **Singapore** Republic, S E Asia
55C5 **Singapore,Str of** S E Asia
56E4 **Singaraja** Indon
36E3 **Singen** Germany
72D4 **Singida** Tanz
61E2 **Singkaling Hkamti** Burma
56C2 **Singkawang** Indon
75D2 **Singleton** Aust
56B3 **Singtep** *I* Indon
55B1 **Singu** Burma
74E1 **Singuédeze** *R* Mozam
54A3 **Sin'gye** N Korea
54A2 **Sinhŭng** N Korea
40B2 **Siniscola** Sardgena
57B4 **Sinjai** Indon
64D2 **Sinjár** Iraq
60B2 **Sinkai Hills** *Mts* Afghan
66C3 **Sinkat** Sudan
59G1 **Sinkiang** Autonomous Region, China
36E1 **Sinn** *R* Germany
27H2 **Sinnamary** French Guiana
54A3 **Sinnyong** S Korea
64C1 **Sinop** Turk
54A2 **Sinpa** N Korea
54A2 **Sinp'o** N Korea
54A3 **Sinp'yong** N Korea
41E1 **Sîntana** Rom
56D2 **Sintang** Indon
17F4 **Sinton** USA
39A2 **Sintra** Port
26C2 **Sinú** *R* Colombia
53A3 **Sinŭiju** N Korea
43D3 **Siofok** Hung
37B1 **Sion** Switz
11C3 **Sioux City** USA
11C3 **Sioux Falls** USA
4C3 **Sioux Lookout** Can
57F9 **Sipalay** Phil
23L1 **Siparia** Trinidad
53A3 **Siping** China
4B3 **Sipiwesk L** Can
79F3 **Siple** *Base* Ant
79F5 **Siple I** Ant
57F8 **Sipocot** Phil
56A3 **Sipora** Indon
15B2 **Sipsey** *R* USA
22A1 **Siqueros** Mexico
57F9 **Siquijor** *I* Phil
62B2 **Sira** India
40D3 **Siracusa** Italy
61C3 **Sirajganj** Bang
3D3 **Sir Alexander,Mt** Can
71G3 **Sirba** *R* Burkina
67F2 **Sīr Banī Yās** *I* UAE
76C2 **Sir Edward Pellew Group** *Is* Aust
41F1 **Siret** *R* Rom
10N3 **Sir James McBrien,Mt** Can
62B2 **Sir Kālahasti** India
3D3 **Sir Laurier,Mt** Can
64D2 **Şirnak** Turk
60C4 **Sirohi** India
62C1 **Sironcha** India
60D4 **Sironj** India
41E3 **Síros** *I* Greece
20C3 **Sirretta Peak,Mt** USA
63C3 **Sirri** *I* Iran
60C3 **Sirsa** India
3E3 **Sir Sandford,Mt** Can
62A2 **Sirsi** India

Villa Guillermina

Ware

28D1 **Villa Guillermina** Arg
29A4 **Villa Hayes** Par
21C3 **Villahermosa** Mexico
22B1 **Villa Hidalgo** Mexico
28C2 **Villa Huidobro** Arg
28C3 **Villa Iris** Arg
28C2 **Villa Maria** Arg
26F8 **Villa Montes** Bol
22B1 **Villa Neuva** Mexico
39A1 **Villa Nova de Gaia** Port
39A2 **Villanueva de la Serena** Spain
39C1 **Villanueva-y-Geltrú** Spain
28C1 **Villa Ojo de Agua** Arg
28B3 **Villa Regina** Arg
39B2 **Villarreal** Spain
28A3 **Villarrica** Chile
25E3 **Villarrica** Par
39B2 **Villarrobledo** Spain
28D2 **Villa San José** Arg
28C1 **Villa San Martin** Arg
28C2 **Villa Valeria** Arg
26D3 **Villavicencio** Colombia
38C2 **Villefranche** France
7L5 **Ville-Marie** Can
39B2 **Villena** Spain
36B2 **Villeneuve-St-Georges** France
38C3 **Villeneuve-sur-Lot** France
36B2 **Villeneuve-sur-Yonne** France
17D3 **Ville Platte** USA
36B2 **Villers-Cotterêts** France
38C2 **Villeurbanne** France
74D2 **Villiers** S Africa
36E2 **Villingen-Schwenningen** Germany
62B2 **Villupuram** India
43F2 **Vilnius** Lithuania
49N3 **Vilyuy** *R* Russian Fed
49O3 **Vilyuysk** Russian Fed
36A2 **Vimoutiers** France
71J4 **Vina** *R* Cam
28A2 **Viña del Mar** Chile
39C1 **Vinaroz** Spain
12B3 **Vincennes** USA
28B1 **Vinchina** Arg
32H5 **Vindel** *R* Sweden
60D4 **Vindhya Range** *Mts* India
14C3 **Vineland** USA
14E2 **Vineyard Haven** USA
55D2 **Vinh** Viet
55D3 **Vinh Cam Ranh** *B* Viet
55D4 **Vinh Loi** Viet
55D3 **Vinh Long** Viet
17C2 **Vinita** USA
41D1 **Vinkovci** Croatia, Yugos
43F3 **Vinnitsa** Ukraine
79F3 **Vinson Massif** *Upland* Ant
11D3 **Vinton** USA
74B2 **Vioolsdrift** S Africa
37D1 **Vipiteno** Italy
57C4 **Viqueque** Indon
57F8 **Virac** Phil
62B2 **Virddhāchalam** India
11B2 **Virden** Can
73B5 **Virei** Angola
29D2 **Virgem da Lapa** Brazil
19D3 **Virgin** *R* USA
74D2 **Virginia** S Africa
9F3 **Virginia** State, USA
11D2 **Virginia** USA
13D3 **Virginia Beach** USA
19C3 **Virginia City** USA
23E3 **Virgin Is** Caribbean
12A2 **Viroqua** USA
40D1 **Virovitica** Croatia, Yugos
36C2 **Virton** Belg
62B3 **Virudunagar** India
40D2 **Vis** *I* Croatia, Yugos
20C2 **Visalia** USA
57F8 **Visayan S** Phil
32H7 **Visby** Sweden
6H2 **Viscount Melville Sd** Can
41D2 **Vizegrad** Bosnia & Herzegovina, Yugos
39A1 **Viseu** Port
62C1 **Vishākhapatnam** India
44K3 **Vishera** *R* Russian Fed
37B1 **Visp** Switz
38C1 **Vissingen** Neth
19C4 **Vista** USA
Vistula = Wisla
42C3 **Vitavia, R** Czech
62A1 **Vite** India
43G1 **Vitebsk** Belorussia
40C2 **Viterbo** Italy
39A1 **Vitigudino** Spain
77G2 **Viti Levu** *I* Fiji
49N4 **Vitim** *R* Russian Fed
39B1 **Vitora** Spain
27L8 **Vitória** Brazil
27K6 **Vitória da Conquista** Brazil
38B2 **Vitré** France
36C2 **Vitry-le-Francois** France
32J5 **Vittangi** Sweden
36C2 **Vittel** France
40C3 **Vittoria** Italy
37E2 **Vittorio Veneto** Italy
50J2 **Vityaz Depth** Pacific O
Viveiro = Vivero
39A1 **Vivero** Spain
49L3 **Vivi** *R* Russian Fed
28D3 **Vivorata** Arg
49M4 **Vizhne-Angarsk** Russian Fed
62C1 **Vizianagaram** India
37A2 **Vizille** France
44J3 **Vizinga** Russian Fed
41E1 **Vládeasa** *Mt* Rom
45G7 **Vladikavkaz** Russian Fed
44G4 **Vladimir** Russian Fed
43E2 **Vladimir Volynskiy** Ukraine
53C3 **Vladivostok** Russian Fed
42A2 **Vlieland** *I* Neth
36B1 **Vlissingen** Neth
41D2 **Vlorë** Alb
42C3 **Vöcklabruck** Austria
37E2 **Vodnjan** Croatia, Yugos
55D3 **Voeune Sai** Camb
71J4 **Vogel Peak** *Mt* Nig
36E1 **Vogelsberg** Region, Germany
37C2 **Voghera** Italy
Vohémar = Vohimarina
73E5 **Vohibinany** Madag
73F5 **Vohimarina** Madag
72D4 **Voi** Kenya
70B4 **Voinjama** Lib
38D2 **Voiron** France
41D1 **Vojvodina** *Aut Republic* Serbia, Yugos
11A2 **Volborg** USA
23A5 **Volcán Baru** *Mt* Panama
22C2 **Volcán Citlaltepetl** *Mt* Mexico
26E8 **Volcán Lullaillaco** *Mt* Chile
28A3 **Volcáno Copahue** *Mt* Chile
28A3 **Volcáno Dumuyo** *Mt* Arg
Volcano Is = Kazan Retto
28A3 **Volcáno Lanin** *Mt* Arg
26E8 **Volcán Ollagüe** *Mt* Chile
28A3 **Volcáno Llaima** *Mt* Chile
28B2 **Volcáno Malpo** *Mt* Arg
28A3 **Volcáno Peteroa** *Mt* Chile
28B3 **Volcáno Tromen** *V* Arg
28A3 **Volcáno Villarrica** *Mt* Chile
22B2 **Volcán Paracutin** *Mt* Mexico
26C3 **Volcán Puraće** *Mt* Colombia
28A2 **Volcán Tinquiririca** *Mt* Chile/Arg
44K4 **Volchansk** Russian Fed
45H6 **Volga** *R* Russian Fed
45G6 **Volgodonsk** Russian Fed
45G6 **Volgograd** Russian Fed
45H5 **Volgogradskoye Vodokhranilishche** *Res* Russian Fed
44E4 **Volkhov** Russian Fed
44E4 **Volkhov** *R* Russian Fed
43E2 **Volkovysk** Belorussia
74D2 **Volksrust** S Africa
49L2 **Volochanka** Russian Fed
44G4 **Vologda** Russian Fed
38B2 **Volognes** France
41E3 **Vólos** Greece
45H5 **Vol'sk** Russian Fed
20B2 **Volta** USA
71G4 **Volta** *R* Ghana
71F3 **Volta Blanche** *R* Burkina
71F4 **Volta,L** Ghana
71F3 **Volta Noire** *R* Burkina
29D3 **Volta Redonda** Brazil
71F3 **Volta Rouge** *R* Burkina
37D3 **Volterra** Italy
37C2 **Voltri** Italy
45G6 **Volzhskiy** Russian Fed
10H3 **Von Frank Mt** USA
44F3 **Vonguda** Russian Fed
7R3 **Vopnafjörður** Iceland
37C1 **Voralberg** Province, Austria
37C1 **Vorder Rhein** *R* Switz
42C1 **Vordingborg** Den
45C8 **Voriái** *I* Greece
44L2 **Vorkuta** Russian Fed
32G6 **Vorma** *R* Nor
45F5 **Voronezh** Russian Fed
32M5 **Voron'ya** *R* Russian Fed
32K7 **Võru** Estonia
36D2 **Vosges** Department, France
38D2 **Vosges** *Mts* France
32F6 **Voss** Nor
53E2 **Vostchnyy** Russian Fed
53E1 **Vostochnyy** Russian Fed
49L4 **Vostochnyy Sayan** *Mts* Russian Fed
79F9 **Vostok** *Base* Ant
44J4 **Votkinsk** Russian Fed
36C2 **Vouziers** France
36A2 **Voves** France
11D2 **Voyageurs Nat Pk** USA
44K3 **Voy Vozh** Russian Fed
45E6 **Voznesensk** Ukraine
63E1 **Vozvyshennost' Karabil'** *Desert Region* Turkmenistan
49T2 **Vrangelya, Ostrov** *I* Russian Fed
41E2 **Vranje** Serbia, Yugos
41E2 **Vratsa** Bulg
41D1 **Vrbas** Serbia, Yugos
40D2 **Vrbas** *R* Serbia, Yugos
40C1 **Vrbovsko** Bosnia & Herzegovina, Yugos
74D2 **Vrede** S Africa
74B3 **Vredendal** S Africa
27G2 **Vreed en Hoop** Guyana
37F2 **Vrhnika** Slovenia, Yugos
41E1 **Vrzac** Serbia, Yugos
40D2 **Vrtoče** Bosnia & Herzegovina, Yugos
74C2 **Vryburg** S Africa
74E2 **Vryheid** S Africa
10E5 **Vsevidof,Mt** USA
41D1 **Vukovar** Croatia, Yugos
44K3 **Vuktyl'** Russian Fed
3F3 **Vulcan** Can
35G5 **Vulcan** *Oilfield* N Sea
40C3 **Vulcano** *I* Italy
55D3 **Vung Tau** Viet
32J5 **Vuollerim** Sweden
44E3 **Vyartsilya** Russian Fed
44J4 **Vyatka** *R* Russian Fed
53C2 **Vyazemskiy** Russian Fed
44E4 **Vyaz'ma** Russian Fed
44G4 **Vyazniki** Russian Fed
44D3 **Vyborg** Russian Fed
44F3 **Vygozero, Ozero** *L* Russian Fed
44J3 **Vym** *R* Russian Fed
35D5 **Vyrnwy** *R* Wales
44E4 **Vyshniy Volochek** Russian Fed
42D3 **Vyzkov** Czech
53D1 **Vysokogornyy** Russian Fed
44F3 **Vytegra** Russian Fed

W

71F3 **Wa** Ghana
36C1 **Waal** *R* Neth
3F2 **Wabasca** Can
6G4 **Wabasca** *R* Can
3F2 **Wabasca L** Can
12B2 **Wabash** USA
12B3 **Wabash** *R* USA
12C1 **Wabatongushi L** Can
6J4 **Wabowden** Can
7M4 **Wabush** Can
15C3 **Waccasassa B** USA
14E1 **Wachusett Res** USA
17C3 **Waco** USA
5H3 **Wacouno** *R* Can
60B3 **Wad** Pak
69A2 **Waddān** Libya
6F4 **Waddington,Mt** Can
3H3 **Wadena** Can
11C2 **Wadena** USA
65D3 **Wadi Abu 'Amūd** *V* Jordan
65B4 **Wadi Abu Tarfa** *V* Egypt
66D2 **Wadi ad Dawāsin** *Watercourse* S Arabia
67E3 **Wadi Adhanah** *Watercourse* Yemen
67F3 **Wadi al Amilhayt** *Watercourse* Oman
64E4 **Wadi al Bātin** *Watercourse* Iraq
64D3 **Wadi al Ghudāf** *Watercourse* Iraq
65D2 **Wadi al Harīr** *V* Syria
67F3 **Wadi al Masīlāh** *Watercourse* Yemen
64D3 **Wadi al Mirah** *Watercourse* S Arabia/Iraq
64D3 **Wadi al Ubayyid** *Watercourse* Iraq
67F3 **Wadi Aman** *Watercourse* Yemen
65C3 **Wadi 'Araba** *V* Israel
64D3 **Wadi Ar'ar** *Watercourse* S Arabia
67E2 **Wadi as Hsabā'** *Watercourse* S Arabia
64C3 **Wadi as Sirhān** *V* Jordan/S Arabia
45G8 **Wadi ath Thamhar** *R* Iraq
65D2 **Wadi az Zaydi** *V* Syria
66D2 **Wadi Bishah** *Watercourse* S Arabia
65D3 **Wadi edh Dhab'i** *V* Jordan
65C4 **Wadi el'Aqaba** *V* Egypt
65B3 **Wadi el 'Arish** *V* Egypt
65B3 **Wadi el Brûk** *V* Egypt
65A3 **Wadi el Gafa** *V* Egypt
65D3 **Wadi el Ghadaf** *V* Jordan
65C3 **Wadi el Hasa** *V* Jordan
65B3 **Wadi el Higayib** *V* Egypt
65D3 **Wadi el Janab** *V* Jordan
65C3 **Wadi el Jeib** *V* Israel/Jordan
65D4 **Wadi el Khush Shah** *V* Jordan
72C2 **Wadi el Milk** *Watercourse* Sudan
64A3 **Wadi el Natrun** *Watercourse* Egypt
65B4 **Wadi el Saheira** *V* Egypt
65B4 **Wadi el Sīq** Egypt
65C3 **Wadi es Sir** Jordan
65C3 **Wadi Fidan** *V* Jordan
66D3 **Wadi Habawnāh** *Watercourse* S Arabia
66B2 **Wadi Haifa** Sudan
65C3 **Wadi Hareidin** *V* Egypt
65B3 **Wadi Hasana** *V* Egypt
64D3 **Wadi Hawrān** *R* Iraq
72C2 **Wadi Howa** *Watercourse* Sudan
72C2 **Wadi Ibra** *Watercourse* Sudan
67E3 **Wadi Jawf** *Watercourse* Yemen
65D2 **Wadi Luhfi** *Watercourse* Jordan
67E3 **Wadi Makhay** *Watercourse* Yemen
66D3 **Wadi Mawr** *Watercourse* Yemen
67F3 **Wadi Mugshin** *Watercourse* Oman
65C3 **Wadi Mujib** *V* Jordan
65C3 **Wādi Mūsa** Jordan
66B1 **Wadi Ouena** *Watercourse* Egypt
65D4 **Wadi Qa'ash Shubyk** *V* Jordan
67F3 **Wadi Qināb** *Watercourse* Yemen
65C3 **Wadi Qītaiya** *V* Egypt
66D2 **Wadi Ranyah** *Watercourse* S Arabia
65D4 **Wadi Ratiyah** *V* Jordan
65D4 **Wadi Ruweila** *V* Jordan
66B2 **Wadi Sha'it** *Watercourse* Egypt
67F3 **Wadi Shihan** *Watercourse* Oman
66D2 **Wadi Tathlith** *Watercourse* S Arabia
66D2 **Wadi Turabah** *Watercourse* S Arabia
65C3 **Wadi Ugeiqa** *V* Jordan
72D2 **Wad Medani** Sudan
54A3 **Waegwan** S Korea
64E4 **Wafra** Kuwait
36C1 **Wageningen** Neth
7K3 **Wager B** Can
7J3 **Wager Bay** Can
75C3 **Wagga Wagga** Aust
76A4 **Wagin** Aust
11C3 **Wagner** USA
57C3 **Waha** Indon
20E5 **Wahaiwa** Hawaiian Is
17C1 **Wahoo** USA
11C2 **Wahpeton** USA
62A1 **Wai** India
20E5 **Waialua** Hawaiian Is
78B2 **Waiau** NZ
78A3 **Waiau** *R* NZ
78B2 **Waiau** *R* NZ
57C3 **Waigama** Indon
51G6 **Waigeo** *I* Indon
78C1 **Waihi** NZ
57A4 **Waikabubak** Indon
78C1 **Waikaremoana,L** NZ
78C1 **Waikato** *R* NZ
57A4 **Waikelo** Indon
75A2 **Waikerie** Aust
78B3 **Waikouaiti** NZ
20E5 **Wailuku** Hawaiian Is
78B2 **Waimakariri** *R* NZ
78B2 **Waimate** NZ
20E5 **Waimea** Hawaiian Is
76B1 **Waingapu** Indon
3F3 **Wainwright** Can
10F1 **Wainwright** USA
78B2 **Waipara** NZ
78C2 **Waipukurau** NZ
78C2 **Wairarapa,L** NZ
78B2 **Wairau** *R* NZ
78C1 **Wairoa** NZ
78C1 **Wairoa** *R* NZ
78B2 **Waitaki** *R* NZ
78B1 **Waitara** NZ
78C1 **Waitomo** NZ
78B1 **Waiuku** NZ
54C3 **Wajima** Japan
72E3 **Wajir** Kenya
54C3 **Wakasa-wan** *B* Japan
78A3 **Wakatipu,L** NZ
3G3 **Wakaw** Can
53D5 **Wakayama** Japan
16C2 **Wa Keeney** USA
35E5 **Wakefield** Eng
23H1 **Wakefield** Jamaica
12B1 **Wakefield** Michigan, USA
14E2 **Wakefield** Rhode Island, USA
55B2 **Wakema** Burma
53E2 **Wakkanai** Japan
75B3 **Wakool** *R* Aust
57D3 **Wakre** Indon
5H2 **Wakuach L** Can
42D2 **Walbrzych** Pol
75D2 **Walcha** Aust
42D2 **Walcz** Pol
36D1 **Waldbröl** Germany
14C2 **Walden** USA
36E3 **Waldshut** Germany
35D5 **Wales** Country, UK
10E2 **Wales** USA
7K3 **Wales I** Can
71F3 **Walewale** Ghana
75C2 **Walgett** Aust
79F4 **Walgreen Coast** Region, Ant
72C4 **Walikale** Zaïre
11D2 **Walker** USA
20C1 **Walker L** USA
20C3 **Walker Pass** USA
12C2 **Walkerton** Can
11B3 **Wall** USA
18C1 **Wallace** USA
75A2 **Wallaroo** Aust
75C3 **Walla Walla** Aust
18C1 **Walla Walla** USA
36E2 **Walldürn** Germany
14D2 **Wallingford** USA
xxixK5 **Wallis and Futuna** *Is* Pacific O
18C1 **Wallowa** USA
18C1 **Wallowa Mts** *Mts* USA
75C1 **Wallumbilla** Aust
17D2 **Walnut Ridge** USA
78C1 **Walouru** NZ
14D1 **Walpole** USA
35E5 **Walsall** Eng
16B2 **Walsenburg** USA
15C2 **Walterboro** USA
15B2 **Walter F George Res** USA
16C3 **Walters** USA
14E1 **Waltham** USA
14C1 **Walton** USA
68F9 **Walvis Bay** Namibia
74A1 **Walvis Bay** S Africa
xxxJ6 **Walvis Ridge** Atlantic O
71H4 **Wamba** Nig
72B4 **Wamba** *R* Zaïre
17C2 **Wamego** USA
57C3 **Wamsasi** Indon
18E2 **Wamsutter** USA
60B2 **Wana** Pak
75B1 **Wanaaring** Aust
78A2 **Wanaka** NZ
78A2 **Wanaka,L** NZ
4E4 **Wanapitei L** Can
53C2 **Wanda Shan** *Upland* China
54A4 **Wando** S Korea
75C1 **Wandoan** Aust
75B3 **Wanganella** Aust
78B2 **Wanganui** NZ
78C1 **Wanganui** *R* NZ
75C3 **Wangaratta** Aust
57B4 **Wangiwangi** *I* Indon
53B2 **Wangkui** China
71F4 **Wango Fitini** Ivory Coast
53B3 **Wangqing** China
68G9 **Wankie** Zim
72E3 **Wanlaweyne** Somalia
55E2 **Wanning** China
62B1 **Wanparti** India
52B3 **Wanxian** China
52B3 **Wanyuan** China
3H3 **Wapawekka L** Can
3D3 **Wapiti** *R* Can
17D2 **Wappapello,L** USA
14D2 **Wappingers Falls** USA
11D3 **Wapsipinicon** *R* USA
71J3 **Wara Nat Pk** Cam
62B1 **Warangal** India
75E3 **Waratah** Aust
75C3 **Waratah B** Aust
36E1 **Warburg** Germany
75C3 **Warburton** Aust
75A1 **Warburton** *R* Aust
75C1 **Ward** *R* Aust
74D2 **Warden** S Africa
72E3 **Warder** Eth
60D4 **Wardha** India
78A3 **Ward,Mt** NZ
3C2 **Ware** Can

Wind Yinchuan

18E2 **Wind** *R* USA
14A2 **Windber** USA
11B3 **Wind Cave Nat Pk** USA
35D4 **Windermere** Eng
74B1 **Windhoek** Namibia
11C3 **Windom** USA
76D3 **Windorah** Aust
18E2 **Wind River Range** *Mts* USA
75D2 **Windsor** Aust
14D2 **Windsor** Connecticut, USA
35E6 **Windsor** Eng
5K4 **Windsor** Newfoundland, Can
15D1 **Windsor** N Carolina, USA
7M5 **Windsor** Nova Scotia, Can
4E5 **Windsor** Ontario, Can
5G4 **Windsor** Quebec, Can
15C2 **Windsor Forest** USA
14D2 **Windsor Locks** USA
23E4 **Windward Is** Caribbean
23C3 **Windward Pass** Caribbean
3F2 **Winefred L** Can
15B2 **Winfield** Alabama, USA
17C2 **Winfield** Kansas, USA
75D2 **Wingham** Aust
4E5 **Wingham** Can
28C3 **Winifreda** Arg
4D2 **Winisk** Can
7K4 **Winisk** *R* Can
7K4 **Winisk L** Can
55B2 **Winkana** Burma
18B1 **Winlock** USA
71F4 **Winneba** Ghana
11D3 **Winnebago** USA
12B2 **Winnebago,L** USA
18C2 **Winnemucca** USA
11C3 **Winner** USA
17D3 **Winnfield** USA
11D2 **Winnibigoshish L** USA
6J4 **Winnipeg** Can
6J4 **Winnipeg,L** Can
4B3 **Winnipeg** *R* Can
6J4 **Winnipegosis** Can
4A3 **Winnipegosis,L** Can
13E2 **Winnipesaukee,L** USA
11D3 **Winona** Minnesota, USA
17E3 **Winona** Mississippi, USA
13E2 **Winooski** USA
19D4 **Winslow** USA
14D2 **Winsted** USA
15C1 **Winston-Salem** USA
36E1 **Winterberg** Germany
15C3 **Winter Garden** USA
15C3 **Winter Park** USA
20B1 **Winters** USA
36D1 **Winterswijk** Neth
37C1 **Winterthur** Switz
11D3 **Winthrop** USA
76D3 **Winton** Aust
78A3 **Winton** NZ
35F5 **Wisbech** Eng
9E2 **Wisconsin** State, USA
12A2 **Wisconsin** *R* USA
12B2 **Wisconsin Dells** USA
7K5 **Wisconsin Rapids** USA
10H2 **Wiseman** USA
43D2 **Wisla** *R* Pol
42C2 **Wismar** Germany
36D2 **Wissembourg** France
27G2 **Witagron** Surinam
74D2 **Witbank** S Africa
8D3 **Witchita Falls** USA
35E5 **Witham** *R* Eng
35F5 **Withernsea** Eng
35E6 **Witney** Eng
36D1 **Witten** Germany
42C2 **Wittenberg** Germany
76A3 **Wittenoom** Aust
36D1 **Wittlich** Germany
74B1 **Witvlei** Namibia
43D2 **Wladyslawowo** Pol
43D2 **Włocławek** Pol
43E2 **Włodawa** Pol
75C3 **Wodonga** Aust
37C1 **Wohlen** Switz
51G7 **Wokam** Indon
35E6 **Woking** Eng
14B1 **Wolcott** USA
51H6 **Woleai** *I* Pacific O
12B1 **Wolf** *R* USA
36E2 **Wolfach** Germany
18B2 **Wolf Creek** USA
16A2 **Wolf Creek P** USA
3B1 **Wolf L** Can
11A2 **Wolf Point** USA
42C3 **Wolfsberg** Austria
42C2 **Wolfsburg** Germany
3H2 **Wollaston L** Can
3H2 **Wollaston Lake** Can
6G3 **Wollaston Pen** Can
75D2 **Wollongong** Aust
74D2 **Wolmaransstad** S Africa
42D2 **Wolow** Pol
57B4 **Wolowaru** Indon
75B3 **Wolseley** Aust
35D5 **Wolverhampton** Eng
14B2 **Womelsdorf** USA
75D1 **Wondai** Aust
53B4 **Wŏnju** S Korea
75B2 **Wonominta** *R* Aust
3D2 **Wonowon** Can
53B4 **Wŏnsan** N Korea
75C3 **Wonthaggi** Aust
75A2 **Woocalla** Aust
14C3 **Woodbine** USA
13D3 **Woodbridge** USA
3F2 **Wood Buffalo Nat Pk** Can
75D1 **Woodburn** Aust
18B1 **Woodburn** USA
14C3 **Woodbury** USA
10K2 **Woodchopper** USA
20C1 **Woodfords** USA
3H2 **Wood L** Can
20C2 **Woodlake** USA
19B3 **Woodland** California, USA
20B1 **Woodland** USA
18B1 **Woodland** Washington, USA
77E1 **Woodlark** *I* PNG
76C4 **Woodmera** Aust
76C3 **Woodroffe,Mt** Aust
5H3 **Woods L** Can
12B2 **Woodstock** Illinois, USA
13F1 **Woodstock** New Brunswick, Can
4E5 **Woodstock** Ontario, Can
14A3 **Woodstock** Virginia, USA
14C3 **Woodstown** USA
78C2 **Woodville** NZ
17D3 **Woodville** USA
16C2 **Woodward** USA
75A2 **Woomera** Aust
13E2 **Woonsocket** USA
12C2 **Wooster** USA
35D5 **Worcester** Eng
74B3 **Worcester** S Africa
14E1 **Worcester** USA
37E1 **Wörgl** Austria
35D4 **Workington** Eng
18E2 **Worland** USA
36E2 **Worms** Germany
35C6 **Worms Head** *Pt* Wales
35E6 **Worthing** Eng
11C3 **Worthington** Minnesota, USA
12C2 **Worthington** Ohio, USA
11B3 **Wounded Knee** USA
57B3 **Wowoni** *I* Indon
10M4 **Wrangell** USA
10A5 **Wrangell,C** USA
10M4 **Wrangell I** USA
10K3 **Wrangell Mts** USA
33B2 **Wrath,C** Scot
16B1 **Wray** USA
35D5 **Wrexham** Wales
19D4 **Wrightson** USA
15C2 **Wrightsville** USA
20D3 **Wrightwood** USA
6F3 **Wrigley** Can
42D2 **Wrocław** Pol
43D2 **Wrzésnia** Pol
53B3 **Wuchang** China
55E1 **Wuchuan** China
52E2 **Wuda** China
67E3 **Wuday'ah** S Arabia
71H3 **Wudil** Nig
52C2 **Wuding He** *R* China
52A3 **Wudu** China
52C4 **Wugang** China
52B2 **Wuhai** China
52C3 **Wuhan** China
52D3 **Wuhu** China
52D5 **Wuhua** China
60D2 **Wūjang** China
52B1 **Wujia He** *R* China
52B4 **Wu Jiang** *R* China
71H4 **Wukari** Nig
57D4 **Wuliaru** *I* Indon
52B4 **Wuling Shan** *Mts* China
71J4 **Wum** Cam
52A4 **Wumeng Shan** *Upland* China
4D3 **Wunnummin L** Can
61E3 **Wuntho** Burma
36D1 **Wuppertal** Germany
52B2 **Wuqi** China
52D2 **Wuqing** China
42B3 **Würzburg** Germany
42C2 **Wurzen** Germany
53C2 **Wusuli Jiang** *R* China
52C2 **Wutai Shan** *Mt* China
51H7 **Wuvulu** *I* Pacific O
52A2 **Wuwei** China
52E3 **Wuxi** China
52E3 **Wuxing** China
52C2 **Wuyang** China
53B2 **Wuyiling** China
52D4 **Wuyi Shan** *Mts* China
52B1 **Wuyuan** China
53B2 **Wuyur He** *R* China
55D2 **Wuzhi Shan** *Mts* China
52B2 **Wuzhong** China
52C5 **Wuzhou** China
12C2 **Wyandotte** USA
75C1 **Wyandra** Aust
35D6 **Wye** *R* Eng
35D6 **Wylye** *R* Eng
35F5 **Wymondham** Eng
76B2 **Wyndham** Aust
17D2 **Wynne** USA
6G2 **Wynniatt B** Can
75E3 **Wynyard** Aust
3H3 **Wynyard** Can
8B2 **Wyoming** State, USA
12B2 **Wyoming** USA
18D2 **Wyoming Peak** *Mt* USA
18D2 **Wyoming Range** *Mts* USA
75D2 **Wyong** Aust
12C3 **Wytheville** USA

X

60D1 **Xaidulla** China
52D1 **Xai Moron He** *R* China
74E2 **Xai Xai** Mozam
22C2 **Xaltinguis** Mexico
73B5 **Xangongo** Angola
36D1 **Xanten** Germany
41E2 **Xánthi** Greece
74C1 **Xau,L** Botswana
12C3 **Xenia** USA
50C4 **Xiaguan** China
52A2 **Xiahe** China
52D5 **Xiamen** China
52B3 **Xi'an** China
52B4 **Xianfeng** China
52C3 **Xiangfan** China
52C4 **Xiang Jiang** *R* China
52C4 **Xiangtan** Province, China
52C4 **Xianning** China
52B3 **Xianyang** China
53A2 **Xiao'ergou** China
52C4 **Xiao Shui** *R* China
52D4 **Xiapu** China
52A4 **Xichang** China
22C1 **Xicoténcatl** Mexico
22C1 **Xicotepec** Mexico
55C2 **Xieng Khouang** Laos
52B4 **Xifeng** China
61C2 **Xigazê** China
52A1 **Xi He** *R* China
52B2 **Xiji** China
52C5 **Xi Jiang** *R* China
52E1 **Xiliao He** *R* China
52B5 **Xilin** China
22C1 **Xilitla** Mexico
52D4 **Xinfeng** China
52C1 **Xinghe** China
53C2 **Xingkai Hu** *L* China/ Russian Fed
52D5 **Xingning** China
52B4 **Xingren** China
52C2 **Xingtai** China
27H4 **Xingu** *R* Brazil
50C2 **Xingxingxia** China
52A4 **Xingyi** China
53B3 **Xinhan** China
52A2 **Xining** China
52E2 **Xinjin** Liaoning, China
52A3 **Xinjin** Sichuan, China
53A3 **Xinkai He** *R* China
52D2 **Xinwen** China
52C2 **Xin Xian** China
52C2 **Xinxiang** China
52C3 **Xinyang** China
52C5 **Xinyi** Guangdong, China
52D3 **Xinyi** Jiangsu, China
52D1 **Xi Ujimqin Qi** China
53A3 **Xiuyan** China
22C2 **Xochimilco** Mexico
52D3 **Xuancheng** China
52B3 **Xuanhan** China
52D1 **Xuanhua** China
52A4 **Xuanwei** China
52C3 **Xuchang** China
72E3 **Xuddur** Somalia
52A2 **Xunhua** China
52C5 **Xun Jiang** *R* China
53B2 **Xunke** China
52D5 **Xunwu** China
52C4 **Xupu** China
55E1 **Xuwen** China
52B4 **Xuyong** China
52D3 **Xuzhou** China

Y

52A4 **Ya'an** China
75B3 **Yaapeet** Aust
72B3 **Yabassi** Cam
53E2 **Yablochnyy** Russian Fed
50D1 **Yablonovyy Khrebet** *Mts* Russian Fed
65D2 **Yabrūd** Syria
18B2 **Yachats** USA
26F8 **Yacuiba** Bol
62B1 **Yādgīr** India
69A1 **Yafran** Libya
54D2 **Yagishiri-tō** *I* Japan
43G2 **Yagotin** Ukraine
28D2 **Yaguari** *R* Urug
28E2 **Yaguaron** *R* Urug
22B1 **Yahualica** Mexico
72C3 **Yahuma** Zaïre
54C3 **Yaita** Japan
54C4 **Yaizu** Japan
52A4 **Yajiang** China
18B1 **Yakima** USA
18B1 **Yakima** *R* USA
71F3 **Yako** Burkina
72C3 **Yakoma** Zaïre
53C5 **Yakujima-kaikyō** *Str* Japan
53E3 **Yakumo** Japan
53C5 **Yaku-shima** *I* Japan
10L4 **Yakutat** USA
10L4 **Yakutat B** USA
49O3 **Yakutsk** Russian Fed
49N3 **Yakutskaya** Respublika, Russian Fed
55C4 **Yala** Thai
22C2 **Yalalag** Mexico
18B1 **Yale** Can
72C3 **Yalinga** CAR
75C3 **Yallourn** Aust
50C3 **Yalong** *R* China
52A4 **Yalong Jiang** *R* China
41F2 **Yalova** Turk
45E7 **Yalta** Ukraine
53A2 **Yalu He** *R* China
53B3 **Yalu Jiang** *R* China
54D3 **Yamada** Japan
53D4 **Yamagata** Japan
53C5 **Yamaguchi** Japan
48J2 **Yamal, Poluostrov** *Pen* Russian Fed
50E1 **Yamarovka** Russian Fed
75D1 **Yamba** New S Wales, Aust
75B2 **Yamba** S Australia, Aust
72C3 **Yambio** Sudan
41F2 **Yambol** Bulg
57D4 **Yamdena** *I* Indon
61E3 **Yamethin** Burma
Yam Kinneret = Tiberias,L
75B1 **Yamma Yamma,L** Aust
16A1 **Yampa** *R* USA
49R4 **Yamsk** Russian Fed
60D3 **Yamuna** *R* India
61D2 **Yamzho Yumco** *L* China
49P3 **Yana** *R* Russian Fed
75B3 **Yanac** Aust
54B4 **Yanagawa** Japan
62C1 **Yanam** India
52B2 **Yan'an** China
66C2 **Yanbu'al Bahr** S Arabia
75B2 **Yancannia** Aust
52E3 **Yancheng** China
52B2 **Yanchi** China
75B1 **Yandama** *R* Aust
72C3 **Yangambi** Zaïre
50B2 **Yanggi** China
54A3 **Yanggu** S Korea
52C1 **Yang He** *R* China
52C5 **Yangjiang** China
Yangon = Rangoon
52C2 **Yangquan** China
54A3 **Yangsan** S Korea
52C5 **Yangshan** China
52C3 **Yangtze Gorges** China
52E3 **Yangtze,Mouths of the** China
54A3 **Yangyang** S Korea
52D3 **Yangzhou** China
52B4 **Yanhe** China
53B3 **Yanji** China
75C3 **Yanko** Aust
49P2 **Yanskiy Zaliv** *B* Russian Fed
11C3 **Yankton** USA
59G1 **Yanqqi** China
52D1 **Yan Shan** *Hills* China
75B1 **Yantabulla** Aust
52E2 **Yantai** China
52D2 **Yanzhou** China
72B3 **Yaoundé** Cam
51G7 **Yapen** *I* Indon
28D1 **Yapeyú** Arg
51G6 **Yap Is** Pacific O
21B2 **Yaqui** *R* Mexico
44H4 **Yaransk** Russian Fed
44H3 **Yarenga** Russian Fed
44H3 **Yarensk** Russian Fed
26D3 **Yari** *R* Colombia
53D4 **Yariga-dake** *Mt* Japan
59F2 **Yarkant He** *R* China
61D2 **Yarlung Zangbo Jiang** *R* China
66D4 **Yarmin** Yemen
7M5 **Yarmouth** Can
65C2 **Yarmūk** *R* Syria/Jordan
44F4 **Yaroslavl'** Russian Fed
65C2 **Yarqon,R** Israel
75C3 **Yarram** Aust
75D1 **Yarraman** Aust
75C3 **Yarrawonga** Aust
44N2 **Yar Sale** Russian Fed
44E4 **Yartsevo** Russian Fed
49L3 **Yartsevo** Russian Fed
26C2 **Yarumal** Colombia
77G2 **Yasawa Group** *Is* Fiji
71H3 **Yashi** Nig
71G4 **Yashikera** Nig
45G6 **Yashkul'** Russian Fed
60C1 **Yasin** Pak
43E3 **Yasinya** Ukraine
53B1 **Yasnyy** Russian Fed
75C2 **Yass** Aust
75C2 **Yass** *R* Aust
54B3 **Yasugi** Japan
17C2 **Yates Center** USA
6J3 **Yathkyed L** Can
72C3 **Yatolema** Zaïre
53C5 **Yatsushiro** Japan
65C3 **Yatta** Israel
26D4 **Yavari** Peru
60D4 **Yavatmāl** India
53C5 **Yawatahama** Japan
55D2 **Ya Xian** China
63C2 **Yazd** Iran
63C2 **Yazd-e Khvāst** Iran
17D3 **Yazoo** *R* USA
17D3 **Yazoo City** USA
55B2 **Ye** Burma
43F3 **Yedintsy** Moldavia
75A2 **Yeelanna** Aust
44F5 **Yefremov** Russian Fed
45G6 **Yegorlyk** *R* Russian Fed
72D3 **Yei** Sudan
71F4 **Yeji** Ghana
44L4 **Yekaterinburg** Russian Fed
53B1 **Yekaterinoslavka** Russian Fed
45F5 **Yelets** Russian Fed
33C1 **Yell** *I* Scot
62C1 **Yellandu** India
Yellow = Huang He
6G4 **Yellowhead P** Can
6G3 **Yellowknife** Can
75C2 **Yellow Mt** Aust
50F3 **Yellow Sea** China/Korea
8C2 **Yellowstone** *R* USA
18D2 **Yellowstone L** USA
18D2 **Yellowstone Nat Pk** USA
43G2 **Yel'nya** Russian Fed
43F2 **Yel'sk** Belorussia
7K1 **Yelverton B** Can
71G3 **Yelwa** Nig
58C4 **Yemen** Republic, Arabian Pen
55C1 **Yen Bai** Viet
71F4 **Yendi** Ghana
55B1 **Yengan** Burma
48K3 **Yenisey** *R* Russian Fed
49L4 **Yeniseysk** Russian Fed
49L3 **Yeniseyskiy Kryazh** *Ridge* Russian Fed
48J2 **Yeniseyskiy Zaliv** *B* Russian Fed
10H3 **Yentna** *R* USA
35D6 **Yeo** *R* Eng
75C2 **Yeoval** Aust
35D6 **Yeovil** Eng
49M3 **Yerbogachen** Russian Fed
45G7 **Yerevan** Armenia
19C3 **Yerington** USA
44J2 **Yermitsa** Russian Fed
19C4 **Yermo** USA
49O4 **Yerofey-Pavlovich** Russian Fed
65C3 **Yeroham** Israel
49S3 **Yeropol** Russian Fed
45H5 **Yershov** Russian Fed
Yerushalayim = Jerusalem
64C1 **Yeşil** *R* Turk
49M3 **Yessey** Russian Fed
65C2 **Yesud Hama'ala** Israel
75D1 **Yetman** Aust
70B2 **Yetti** Maur
61E3 **Yeu** Burma
45H7 **Yevlakh** Azerbaijan
45E6 **Yevpatoriya** Ukraine
52E2 **Ye Xian** China
45F6 **Yeysk** Russian Fed
28D2 **Yi** *R* Urug
65C1 **Yialousa** Cyprus
53B2 **Yi'an** China
41E2 **Yiannitsá** Greece
52A4 **Yibin** China
52C3 **Yichang** China
53B2 **Yichun** China
52B2 **Yijun** China
64C2 **Yıldızeli** Turk
53A1 **Yilehuli Shan** *Upland* China
52A5 **Yiliang** China
52B2 **Yinchuan** China

ASIA

48-49
50-51
53
54
54
65
64
63
58-59
52
66-67
60
61
57
55
62
56
57

AFRICA

70
71
69
72-73
71
74

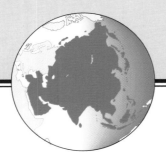

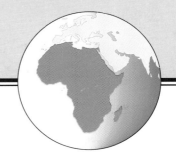

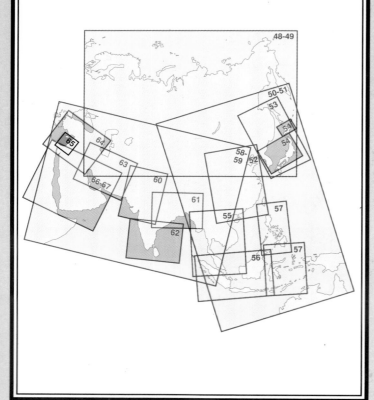

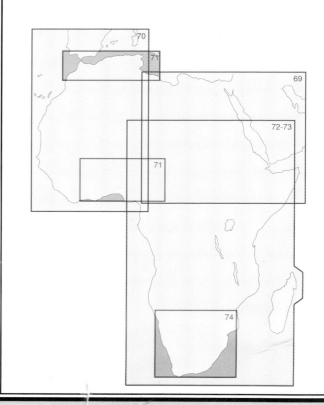